FOUNDATIONS OF ECONOMIC ANALYSIS OF LAW

FOUNDATIONS OF ECONOMIC ANALYSIS OF LAW

Steven Shavell

THE BELKNAP PRESS OF
HARVARD UNIVERSITY PRESS

Cambridge, Massachusetts
London, England
2004

Library of Congress Cataloging-in-Publication Data

Shavell, Steven, 1946–
    Foundations of economic analysis of law / Steven Shavell.
        p. cm.
    Includes bibliographical references and index.
    ISBN 0-674-01155-4 (alk. paper)
    1. Law—Economic aspects. I. Title.

K487.E3S53 2004
340'.1—dc21   2003056279

To my children, Amy and Robert

SUMMARY OF CONTENTS

CONTENTS

PREFACE

This book is intended to convey the basic ideas of what has come to be known as economic analysis of law. The subject areas of concern are central ones for any legal system, namely, the laws governing property, accidents, contracts, and crime, together with the litigation process. As will become evident to the reader, "economic" analysis of law is not restricted to conventionally understood economic factors but also includes all manner of noneconomic ones (such as altruistic motivations). Economic analysis of law is, however, characterized by the general social scientific point of view of the discipline of economics, under which actors are regarded as forward looking and rational, and the notions of the social good employed in evaluating policy are explicitly articulated.

Because my object is to present the principles of economic analysis of law in a way that is accessible both to individuals interested in law who do not have a background in the methods of economics and to the community of economists, I have avoided formal economic analysis (except in footnotes) as well as detailed discussion of legal doctrine.

In writing the book, I have benefited from the comments and advice of many individuals. I would especially like to thank Louis Kaplow and A. Mitchell Polinsky in this regard; other colleagues who furnished aid include Lucian Bebchuk, David Cope, Charles Donahue, Robert Ellickson, Daniel

Klerman, Douglas Lichtman, Thomas Miles, Eric Posner, Richard Posner, Mark Ramseyer, David Rosenberg, Kathryn Spier, and Cass Sunstein. I would also like to mention a number of students who have provided very able research assistance to me: Giorgio Afferni, Bert Huang, Sergey Lagodinsky, Lee Morlock, Dotan Oliar, Frederick Pollock, and Andrew Song. I wish as well to acknowledge research support from the John M. Olin Center for Law, Economics, and Business at Harvard Law School. Finally, I am grateful to Matthew Seccombe for outstanding editorial assistance, to Karl Coleman for help in the preparation of the manuscript, to Julie Carlson for copyediting the manuscript, and to Michael Aronson of the Harvard University Press for his stewardship of the publication process.

FOUNDATIONS OF ECONOMIC ANALYSIS OF LAW

1 ||| INTRODUCTION

Under the economic approach to the analysis of law, two basic types of questions about legal rules are addressed. The first type is *descriptive,* concerning the effects of legal rules. For example, what is the influence of our system of liability for automobile accidents on the number of these accidents, on the compensation of accident victims, and on litigation expenses? The other type of question is *normative,* pertaining to the social desirability of legal rules. Thus, it might be asked whether our system of liability for automobile accidents is socially good, given its various consequences.

In answering the two types of questions under the economic approach, theoretical attention is usually focused on stylized models of individual behavior and of the legal system. The advantage of studying models is that they allow descriptive and normative questions to be answered in an unambiguous way, and that they may clarify understanding of the actual influence of legal rules on behavior and help in the making of legal policy decisions.

Descriptive analysis. When considering the descriptive questions in the models, the view taken will generally be that actors are "rational." That is, they are forward looking and behave so as to maximize their expected utility. Given the characterization of individuals' behavior as rational, the influence of legal rules on behavior can be ascertained. This can be done with definitude in the world of the models, because all relevant assumptions about individuals' desires, their knowledge, their capabilities, and the environment will have been made explicit. For example, whether a person will drive carefully will be determinable, for it will have been stated how difficult it is for the person to exercise precaution, whether the person will himself be at risk of injury from an automobile accident, what the rule of liability is, what circumstances will give rise to suit, whether the person owns accident insurance and liability insurance, and so forth.

Normative analysis. The evaluation of social policies, and thus of legal rules, will be undertaken with reference to a stated measure of *social welfare.*[1] One legal rule will be said to be superior to a second if the first rule results in a higher level of the stated measure of social welfare.

It should therefore be noticed that normative analysis is *conditional* in nature, in that the legal rule that is best may depend on the social welfare criterion under consideration. If the social goal were simply to minimize the number of automobile accidents, the best rule might well involve severe punishment for causing an accident, whereas if the social goal were also to include the benefits people obtain from driving, the best rule would be unlikely to involve very rigorous punishment for causing an accident.

This raises the question of which measures of social welfare are considered in economic analysis of legal rules. Before discussing this question, let me comment briefly on the nature of the measures of social welfare.

According to the framework of welfare economics, social welfare is assumed to be a function of individuals' well-being, that is, of their utilities. An individual's utility, in turn, can depend on anything about which the individual cares: not only material wants, but also, for example, aesthetic tastes, altruistic feelings, or a desire for notions of fairness to be satisfied. Hence, social welfare can depend on any of these elements, and will depend on them to the extent that individuals' utilities do. It is thus a mistake to believe that, under the economic view, social welfare reflects only narrowly "economic" factors, namely, the amounts of goods and services produced and enjoyed.

Moreover, the measure of social welfare can embody the desirability of equality of utility among individuals. That is, the function that represents the measure of social welfare may be such that it is higher if individuals have similar utilities than if their utilities are dispersed (but have the same

---

1. The discussion of social welfare and normative analysis to follow is amplified in Chapters 26–28.

sum). Social welfare functions with the property that equality of utilities tends to raise social welfare are studied by economists in many domains, and notably in the area of income taxation.

Therefore, the conception of social welfare employed in welfare economics is quite general and plausibly can accommodate the views of the social good of most readers.

Nevertheless, it is standard for economic analysts to restrict attention to fairly simple measures of social welfare, and I will do that here. Two types of assumptions that I will tend to make should be noted at the outset. One is that the measure of social welfare will usually not accord importance to the distribution of utilities; thus, the effect of legal rules on the distribution of well-being will not be relevant to their evaluation under the measure of social welfare. This assumption is not made because of an opinion that the distribution of utilities is in fact unimportant. Rather, taking the effect of legal rules on distributional factors into account would complicate our analysis and yet would not in the end alter our conclusions. Why would taking into account distributional factors not alter our conclusions? The answer is that society has an income tax and transfer system that it can utilize to redistribute income. Thus, if I were to incorporate the income tax and transfer system into our analysis, a change in that system could offset any undesirable distributional consequence of a legal rule. If, for example, some legal rule turned out on balance to help the rich and hurt the poor, the rich could be taxed more heavily and the poor less, so that the use of the rule would not necessarily have any distributional effect after the optimal adjustment in the tax and transfer system were made. Hence, if one assumes that the income tax and transfer system will be used to bring about desirable changes in the distribution of income, the distributional effect of the choice of legal rules should not matter. Of course, one might not assume that the income tax and transfer system would always be used to redistribute wealth beneficially, in which case the choice of legal rules might be decided in part on the basis of their redistributive effects.

The other type of assumption concerns notions of fairness and morality. Consider, for example, the classical conception of corrective justice, demanding that a wrongdoer compensate his victim for harm sustained. It is clear, I think, that the idea of corrective justice has substantial importance to individuals, especially in the context of accidents, and thus might be thought to enter into measures of social welfare. I will usually exclude such notions of fairness, however, from the analysis proper for analytical convenience. I will, though, sometimes mention, after the analysis of a legal rule, how a relevant notion of fairness would affect my conclusions. (I will take up the general issue of the integration of morality and notions of fairness into normative analysis in Part Seven.)

What distinguishes economic analysis of law from other analysis of law? One might ask whether there is any qualitative difference between economic analysis of law, as defined here, and other approaches to its assessment. Is it not of interest to every legal analyst to determine how legal rules affect behavior and then to evaluate the rules with reference to some criterion of the social good? The answer would seem to be "yes," and thus in this general sense, one cannot distinguish economic analysis from other analysis of law.

What does seem to mark economic analysis are three characteristics. First, economic analysis emphasizes the use of stylized models and of statistical, empirical tests of theory, whereas other approaches usually do neither. Second, in describing behavior, economic analysis gives much greater weight than other approaches to the view that actors are rational, acting with a view toward the possible consequences of their choices. And third, in normative evaluation, economic analysis makes explicit the measure of social welfare considered, whereas other approaches often leave the criterion of the social good unclear or substantially implicit.

History of the economic approach. The economic view may be said to have originated mainly with writings on crime by Becarria (1767) and, especially, Bentham (1789). Bentham developed in significant detail the idea that legal sanctions may discourage bad conduct and that sanctions should be employed when they will effectively deter but not when they will fail to do so (as with the insane). Curiously, however, after Bentham, the economic approach to law lay largely dormant until the 1960s and 1970s. In that period, Coase (1960) wrote a provocative article on the incentives to reduce harms engendered by property rights assignments; Becker (1968) authored an influential article on crime, casting into modern terms and extending Bentham's earlier contributions; Calabresi (1970) published an extended treatment of liability rules and the accident problem; and Posner (1972a) wrote a comprehensive textbook and a number of articles, as well as established the *Journal of Legal Studies,* in which scholarship in economic analysis of law could be regularly published. Since that time, economic analysis of law has grown fairly rapidly.

Outline and goal of this book. This book is divided into a number of parts, the first of which are concerned with the basic areas of private law—property law, liability for accidents, and contract law—and with civil litigation. These areas of law are said to be private because they are enforced by the bringing of suits by private parties.

In the next part of the book, I deal with public law enforcement, in which the state uses enforcement agents, such as police, safety inspectors, and tax auditors, to detect violators and to sanction them. Crime and criminal law are discussed in this part. In a subsequent, brief part of the book, I examine general questions about the overall structure of the legal system, such as why some behavior is controlled through private law and other behavior through public law enforcement.

Then, in the final part, I consider the relationship between welfare economics and morality, issues relating to income distributional equity and the law, and commonly encountered questions about the economic approach to analysis of law.

The goal of the book is to set out the major elements of economic analysis of the central areas of law; the emphasis is on theory, but some statistical studies are noted. The analysis is presented in a way that should be accessible to a wide audience. Thus, although most sections of the book are organized around models of behavior and of the legal system, the analysis is not technical (all mathematics is contained in footnotes). Accordingly, legal readers without any formal background in economics should find the book easy to understand. At the same time, economists should find the subject matter to be of natural intellectual appeal, and they should not have any difficulty owing to their lack of legal background, for the law under discussion is for the most part common knowledge or nearly so.

PART I   PROPERTY LAW

This part deals with the basic elements of property law. I begin in Chapter 2 by examining the fundamental question of what justifies the social institution of property, that is, the rationale for the bundle of rights that constitute what we commonly call ownership. I also discuss examples of the emergence of property rights.

Then I consider a number of important issues about property rights. In Chapter 3, I inquire about the division of property rights (property rights may be divided contemporaneously, over time, and according to contingency). In Chapter 4, I study a variety of topics concerning the acquisition and transfer of property, including the discovery of unowned or lost property, registration systems for transfer of property, and the transfer of property at death. In Chapter 5, I investigate "externalities" and property—problems involving cooperation and conflict in the use of property, together with the resolution of such problems through bargaining and legal rules. In Chapter 6, I discuss public property; here I address the question of why the state should own property, and also the manner of state acquisition of property through purchase or by the exercise of powers of eminent domain.

Finally, in Chapter 7, I analyze the special topic of intellectual property.

2 | DEFINITION, JUSTIFICATION, AND EMERGENCE OF PROPERTY RIGHTS

In this chapter, I first define property rights, then address the question of their justification, that is, the advantages that might be thought to explain their existence, and last discuss several instances of their emergence.

1. PROPERTY RIGHTS DEFINED

I will use the term "property rights" to refer broadly to two subsidiary types of rights, possessory rights and rights of transfer.

1.1 Possessory rights. What are often called *possessory rights* allow individuals to use things and to prevent others from using them.[1] A particular possessory right is a right to commit a particular act or a right to prevent others from committing a particular act.[2]

---

1. Some writers define possessory rights to be only rights to use things, not also rights to prevent others from using things. The subject of the enforcement of these and other rights will be addressed generally in Part Five. Here I shall simply assume that property rights are upheld.

2. A completely specified act includes in its description the place, time, and contingency under which it is committed—for example, digging at a designated location, on Thursday at 4:00 P.M., if it is not raining (the contingency).

On reflection, it can be seen that common property arrangements entail considerable agglomerations of possessory rights, but with certain limitations. The basic notion of ownership embraces a large collection of possessory rights subject to exceptions. When we say that a person owns a parcel of land, we ordinarily mean that the person can do virtually as he pleases on the land (plant crops on it, build on it, leave it idle) over time and under most contingencies. Also included in the idea of ownership is the right of the owner to prevent others from using what he owns over time and in most contingencies. The owner's possessory rights are not absolute, however. If a use harms others (maintaining a compost heap that produces noxious odors), it may be proscribed; or, under certain conditions, an owner may be compelled to allow others to use his things (in an emergency, someone might be permitted to seek shelter on his land).

Likewise, under rental provisions, the renter of property generally enjoys a large swath of possessory rights, most of those associated with ownership. For example, someone who rents an apartment can use it more or less as he pleases and bar the entry of others, even generally the landlord. But there may be limitations on the renter's possessory rights that would not be faced by an owner-occupier; typically, a renter of an apartment is forbidden from making major modifications to it.

Another example worth noting is property arrangements within enterprises. When a person is working for an enterprise, he will often enjoy certain possessory rights. A person may be able to do a variety of things in the office to which he is assigned and exclude others from it under a fairly wide range of circumstances.

In strict logic, and for some purposes, it will be helpful to reduce such common property arrangements to their more basic elements, including the arrays of possessory rights that they encompass.

1.2 Rights of transfer. The other type of right associated with the notion of property rights is a *right to transfer a possessory right,* that is, the option of a person who holds a possessory right to give it to another person (usually, in exchange for something). Closely related, but distinct, is the right of the recipient subsequently to transfer his possessory right to another person (and for that person to do the same, and so forth). We will assume unless otherwise noted that rights to transfer possessory rights implicitly include these subsequent-order rights to transfer.

It is apparent that common property arrangements entail certain rights to transfer possessory rights. The concept of ownership incorporates not only possessory rights, but also rights to transfer these possessory rights; an owner is usually presumed to be able to sell or give away his property, in which case the acquirer obtains all the possessory rights held by the owner, as well as the rights to transfer these rights. Under rental arrangements, however, the renter of a thing may or may not enjoy the right to transfer his possessory rights to another. A person who rents an apartment may be allowed to rent to another (to "sublet"), or he may be prevented from doing this according to his rental agreement.

As a general matter, if we want to be precise about the meaning of property rights, we should describe an arrangement in terms of the entailed possessory rights and rights to transfer.

2. JUSTIFICATIONS FOR PROPERTY RIGHTS

2.1 The general question of justification.   A time-honored and fundamental question is why there should be any property rights in things. That is, in what respects does the protection of possessory interests in things and the ability to transfer them promote social welfare, broadly construed? I now consider a list of factors suggesting that the existence of property rights fosters social welfare.

2.2 Incentives to work.   It is often said that property rights provide individuals with incentives to work, and it is worth examining this argument in some detail. For this purpose, consider initially a stylized model in which individuals produce a good and in which the measure of social welfare is the utility from the good less the disutility of work. The determination of the socially optimal amount of work is plain in the model. It is best for an individual to work an additional hour if and only if the increment in utility from consuming what would be produced in that hour exceeds the disutility of work from the hour.

Example 1. Individuals can work either 0, 1, 2, or 3 hours, and each hour an individual works he produces one unit of output. The total utility he derives from output, the total disutility of work, and social welfare per

Table 2.1 Hours, output, and social welfare

Hours of work	Output	Utility from output	Disutility from work	Social welfare
0	0	0	0	0
1	1	10	6	4
2	2	18	13	5
3	3	24	22	2

individual (utility from output minus disutility from work) are as shown in Table 2.1.

Social welfare is maximized if each individual works two hours. Working the first hour is beneficial since it augments utility by 10 and involves disutility of only 6; working a second hour raises an individual's welfare further because it increases utility by 8 and increases disutility by only 7; but working a third hour would increase utility by only 6 and involve greater disutility of 9.

The socially optimal amount of work is not performed in the absence of property rights. If there are no property rights, individuals will tend not to work the socially optimal amount and social welfare will be less than optimal in the model just described because of problems with individuals' incentives to work. In a situation in which property rights do not exist, an individual will take into account that his output may be taken from him. In deciding whether to work an extra hour, an individual will compare the increment in utility from consuming the additional amount of his production that he will be able to keep—rather than the whole of the additional amount of his production—to the disutility of work from the hour. When the individual makes this determination, he may well decide to work less than optimally because he will enjoy less utility from the smaller amount of output that he will retain for his own use. Let me illustrate this point.

> *Example 2.* Modify Example 1 by assuming that each individual will lose half of what he produces to others who can take that amount. Then each individual will choose not to work at all, for the situation facing each individual will be as shown in Table 2.2.[3] Here an individual will not

3. The utilities for outputs of .5 and 1.5 are assumed to be as displayed and are consistent with the previous table.

Table 2.2 Hours and output in the absence of property rights

Hours of work	Retained output	Utility from output	Disutility from work	Individual welfare
0	0	0	0	0
1	0.5	5	6	−1
2	1.0	10	13	−3
3	1.5	14	22	−8

even work the first hour because he will be able to keep and consume only .5 units of output, and therefore enjoy utility of only 5, which is less than the disutility of work of 6, and so forth.

In this example, individuals decide not to work at all, so that social welfare is zero. If, however, the example is altered and individuals lose a smaller fraction of their output, they will work a positive amount. This also means that a positive amount would be taken from them, which raises two complications. First, whoever takes output will have it to consume—in other words, what is taken will still contribute to social welfare. Second, the incentives to work of whomever takes from others have to be reexamined. But neither of these complications changes the conclusion that the amount of work and the level of social welfare will generally deviate from the optimal.[4]

4. Suppose, for instance, that the individuals in the model are identical to one another and each has the opportunity not only to work and produce, but also to take freely a fraction of the output of another person. Then an individual's incentives to work will remain undesirable, for it will still be true that in deciding whether to work an extra hour, the individual will know that he will not be able to keep the full amount of what he produces in the hour. Formally, we can show that individuals will work too little under certain assumptions. Let α be the fraction of the output that is taken, w be hours of work and also output produced, $u(w)$ be utility from output consumed, where $u'(w) > 0$ and $u''(w) < 0$, and $d(w)$ be disutility of work, where $d'(w) > 0$ and $d''(w) > 0$. It is socially optimal for w to maximize $u(w) - d(w)$, implying that the optimal w satisfies $u'(w) = d'(w)$; let w^* be the optimal w. If a fraction α is taken from individuals, however, then if w^e is the work the identical individuals generally choose, each particular individual will be able to take αw^e from another. Hence, each individual will select his w to maximize $u(\alpha w^e + (1 - \alpha)w) - d(w)$, implying that $(1 - \alpha)u'(\alpha w^e + (1 - \alpha)w) = d'(w)$. But in equilibrium, $w = w^e$, so that we must have $(1 - \alpha)u'(w^e) = d'(w^e)$. This means that $w^e < w^*$ (implicit differentiation

In the absence of property rights it is also possible that individuals will choose to work more than the optimal number of hours, not less.[5] Suppose that having a certain minimum amount of output to consume is important for subsistence. Then, to guarantee that he will retain this amount after others have taken some output from him, an individual might well be inclined to work more than he otherwise would.[6] Although total output will be higher when individuals in the model work more than is optimal, social welfare will tend to be lower than optimal. This is for two reasons: The hours that individuals work in excess of the optimal number may be hours for which the disutility of work is high (the disutility of work may grow as the number of hours left in the day diminishes);[7] and the extra output

---

of $(1 - \alpha)u'(w^s) = d'(w^s)$ with respect to α shows that w^s is decreasing in α, and w^* corresponds to $\alpha = 0$).

5. This possibility, that individuals might work more in the absence of property rights than in their presence, is occasionally—and mistakenly—interpreted as an argument against property rights. As I am about to explain, when individuals do work more in the absence of property rights, social welfare still tends to be lower than in the presence of property rights. The issue in question is whether the absence of property rights affects work incentives in such a way as to reduce social welfare, not whether work effort and production themselves fall or rise.

6. Consider the following situation:

Hours of work	Output	Utility from output	Disutility from work	Social welfare
0	0	0	0	0
1	1	40	2	38
2	2	45	10	35

Notice here that an individual gains most of his utility from the first unit of output (interpreted as that necessary for subsistence) and that working one hour is socially optimal. But if individuals would lose half of what they produce, so that it would take two hours to obtain one unit of output, an individual would work two hours: His welfare would then be $40 - 10 = 30$, whereas if he would work one hour, his welfare would be only $20 - 2 = 18$ (assuming the utility from .5 unit of output is 20).

7. This is the case in the example of the previous note, where the second hour of work creates output that would be worth only 5 but involves extra disutility of 8.

may be unevenly distributed, contributing relatively little to an individual's utility if he already has substantial output.[8]

The socially optimal outcome is achievable under property rights: where each individual has rights in his own output. If each individual has possessory rights in the output he produces, he will work the socially optimal amount and social welfare will be maximized. This is one of the classic arguments for the desirability of property rights. In particular, an individual with possessory rights will know that he will be able to consume what he produces and thus he will compare the utility from the output he produces by working an extra hour to the disutility of work effort. In Example 1, individuals will choose to work two hours, the optimal amount. Another way of expressing why social optimality will result is that the goal of each individual will coincide with the social goal.

The socially optimal outcome is achievable under property rights: where a supervisory entity has rights in an individual's output. A different regime in which the socially optimal outcome may result involves an entity that enjoys possessory rights in individuals' output and that can supervise individuals' work. Such a supervisory entity might, for example, be a single-person owner of a farm. If a supervisory entity can monitor individuals' work,

8. To demonstrate the latter possibility, let us assume that individuals are identical and that there is a probability p that each person will lose a fraction α of his output and an equal probability of the independent event that he will obtain α of someone else's output. Then (using the notation from note 4) an individual's expected utility will be $p^2u((1 - \alpha)w + \alpha w^e) + (1 - p)pu(w + \alpha w^e) + p(1 - p)u((1 - \alpha)w) + (1 - p)^2u(w) - d(w)$; the terms correspond to the events that he loses α of his output and gains α of another person's, that he does not lose any of his but gains α of another person's, and so forth. Because he will select w to maximize his expected utility, and because $w = w^e$ in equilibrium, we obtain the equilibrium condition.

$$p^2(1 - \alpha)u'(w^e) + (1 - p)pu'((1 + \alpha)w^e) + (1 - \alpha)(1 - p)pu'((1 - \alpha)w^e)$$
$$+ (1 - p)^2u'(w^e) = d'(w^e).$$

Now the third term on the left side of this condition can be arbitrarily higher than $u'(w^e)$, for $(1 - \alpha)w^e < w^e$. Hence, the left side may exceed $d'(w^*)$, implying that $w^e > w^*$ is possible; that is, the equilibrium may be such that individuals work more and produce more than is optimal. They are also worse off than in the optimal situation. To see explicitly why this is so, note that, as is readily shown, if they work w^e and retain their entire output for sure, individuals are better off than in the risky situation; but we know that when they retain their output, they are better off working w^* than w^e.

then, through use of appropriate rewards or punishments, it may be able to ensure that they work the optimal amount. Whether a supervisory entity's incentives will lead it to choose the optimal outcome, and how a regime with supervisory entities compares to a regime with individuals as possessors of property rights in their output, are, of course, different questions. The point here is simply that it is possible for the optimal outcome to be achieved if a supervisor has information about individuals' work effort and possessory rights in output.

Comments. (a) The conclusions just discussed about property rights and incentives to work carry over to more general and realistic settings (as will the conclusions about the other advantages of property rights to be discussed). In particular, in an economy with many kinds of goods and money as a medium of exchange, an individual's incentive to work will not inhere in his being able to consume the literal product of his labor. Rather, his incentive to work will involve his being able to consume the various goods purchased with his money wages. But this difference does not alter the point that an individual's incentives to work will tend toward the desirable under property rights and will tend to be suboptimal in their absence.

(b) In modern industrialized countries, the majority of individuals are motivated to work not because they consume or sell the output they produce, but rather because of the incentives and salary structure established by supervisory entities where they are employed. The individuals who have property rights in their own output are restricted mainly to certain farmers, artisans, shopowners, and independent professionals.

(c) In extreme instances in which property rights break down, we observe that little productive work is done. During civil wars and other episodes of great upheaval, productive work generally ceases. (Instead, people devote themselves to protecting what they have, and some engage in looting.)

2.3 Incentives to maintain and improve things.   An essentially similar justification for property rights is that they are associated with incentives to maintain and improve things. If we reinterpret the model from the last section and assume that the result of work effort is the maintenance or improvement of durable things (as when individuals apply oil to machines or fertilize farmland), we may say that it is socially optimal for an individual to work an extra hour if the utility gained from maintenance and improvements exceeds the disutility of work. Further, this outcome will not occur in the absence of property rights; when durable things may be taken from individuals, they will not benefit from improving them (if a machine would be taken from an individual, he will not have an incentive to maintain it well). When, however, individuals hold possessory rights in durable things, they will have an optimal motive to improve the things because they will possess the things in the future and therefore be able to enjoy the gains from maintenance and improvements. Likewise, if there is a supervisory entity that can observe individual behavior, the supervisor can induce individuals to work optimally to maintain and improve things.

Comments. (a) Suppose that we take into account the possibility that durable things will be transferred in the future, for example, that farmland will change hands when the possessor becomes too old to continue to work. Then the socially optimal amount of effort to improve durable things will reflect the future use of things by new possessors as well as present ones; the socially desirable amount of fertilization of farmland will reflect the enhancement in its productivity for both current and future users. Moreover, the socially optimal improvement in durable things will be promoted not only by possessory rights, but also by rights to transfer things. Notably, possessors will often transfer things by selling them and sales prices will generally reflect improvements made in things. Because present owners will anticipate this, they will be led to make appropriate improvements for the advantage of future owners. The present owner of farmland will fertilize it for the benefit of future owners because that will allow him to sell the land to them at a higher price.

(b) Both forms of incentives to maintain and improve durable things, those deriving from ownership and those associated with a supervisory regime, seem important in reality. Individuals own many things, ranging from their clothing and other personal articles, to electronic equipment, automobiles, and real estate, and because they own such things, they are naturally led to take care of them. Where durable things are not owned but are rented (or are used by employees of enterprises), the present possessors need inducement to take into proper account the interests of future possessors. This is accomplished generally by use of maintenance requirements (to fertilize leased farmland), obligations to allow others to maintain things (to admit a landlord into an apartment to make repairs), and penalties for harm done (for damaging a rented vehicle).

(c) At the same time, we observe problems with the care of durable things when no one owns them or when there are substantial difficulties in monitoring the behavior of users of the things. For example, public parks often are treated irresponsibly (or are vandalized) because an individual will not generally be able to benefit personally in the future from any effort that he makes to maintain the park (if a person cleans a picnic table, he will probably not profit from that in the future because he will be unlikely to use that particular table again, or at least not before someone else does).

2.4 Incentives to transfer things.   An additional advantage of property rights is that they foster the beneficial transfer of things. Let us now consider a model in which there are several types of goods. Then there are both direct and indirect reasons why it will be socially desirable for goods to be transferred among people.

The direct advantage of transfer of goods, that is, of trade, is that it raises the utilities of those who engage in it. This may be because the preferences of individuals differ. If a person who possesses a parcel of land X and prefers parcel Y makes a trade with a person who possesses Y but prefers X, both will be made better off by the exchange. Trade may also raise the utility of individuals who have similar, or even identical, preferences, because they may wish to consume a mix of different types of goods but possess only one or only a few types of goods prior to trade. Suppose one person possesses two apples and no bananas, another possesses two bananas and no apples, and each would prefer to consume one piece of each fruit than two pieces of the same fruit. Then each person will be made better off by trading one piece of fruit for a piece of the other fruit.

In addition, the ability to trade enhances social welfare indirectly because it allows the use of efficient methods of production. Efficient methods of production take advantage of specialization and of agglomerations of individuals who devote themselves to making just one or several related goods. But this means that the allocation of goods immediately after they are produced is far from what is best for purposes of consumption; the individuals at a factory who produce thousands of units of some good cannot consume that good alone. The transfer and trade of produced goods enables each individual to consume many different types of goods.

It is clear that if only possessory rights exist, optimality will not be achieved because things that exist will not be traded. Individuals will produce solely for personal consumption rather than collectively organize and employ efficient production methods. If, however, individuals enjoy rights to transfer what they produce as well as possessory rights, then an optimal outcome is achievable. Mutually beneficial trades can in principle be consummated and, because this possibility will be anticipated, individuals will be willing to produce things that they would not want to consume but that they can trade to their advantage. Thus, efficient production will be promoted. Likewise, if supervisory entities have possessory as well as rights to transfer things, an optimal outcome is achievable. This presumes, however, that the supervisor has the necessary information, including in particular information about individuals' preferences.

Comments. (a) In the discussion of trade, mention has not been made of intermediate goods, that is, goods that are used in the production of other goods. The transferability of these intermediate goods is important to optimality. Were the transfer of intermediate goods hampered, enterprises would have to manufacture their own (automobile manufacturers would have to make their own computers, their own steel), which would be inefficient.

(b) We see in fact that both trade by individuals who enjoy rights of transfer and the command of supervisors help to achieve optimality. With regard to trade by individuals, the sale of personal property is obviously illustrative, as are transactions between enterprises in capitalist countries. With regard to the command of supervisors, transfers of equipment and also of output at different stages of production are typically governed by such a command within an enterprise. Another example is the transfer of goods between state enterprises in centrally planned economies.

(c) We also see that when the right to transfer does not exist, or is enjoyed by a supervisor who does not exercise it well, outcomes are not socially desirable. When rights to crop-growing land are governed by the classical usufruct—under which a person enjoys possessory rights in the land as long as he uses it but cannot sell it to another—it is often observed that the land is used too intensively because the possessor has no future interest in caring for it. When rights to apartments are determined by the assignment of a social authority, instances often arise in which some families would be happy to trade apartments with each other (because, for example, they would then each live nearer to where they work) but are not allowed to make an exchange. When the transfer of goods in an economy is carried out according to the dictates of central planners, inefficiencies abound, with many potentially mutually beneficial trades not being carried out.

2.5 Avoidance of dispute and of efforts to protect or to take things. Disputes, which may involve physical conflict, and efforts devoted to protecting things or to taking things from others, are socially undesirable in themselves because they may result in harm and because they do not result in the production of things, only in their possible reallocation. In the absence of property rights, individuals will often find it rational to devote effort and resources to taking things from others, leading to disputes, and individuals will also find it rational to devote time and resources protecting their things from being taken. These undesirable outcomes will be avoided if the state stands ready to prevent the taking of things; in the ideal, the guarantee of property rights by the state will remove the motive to take or to protect things, and also the occurrence of dispute.

Comments. (a) The problems that may arise when property rights are not well protected are rampant in certain parts of present-day Russia, South America, and Africa. Moreover, even in countries where the state makes a substantial effort to safeguard property, many individuals are engaged in the enterprise of theft, large sums are devoted to protecting property, and harm to individuals frequently comes about during robbery.

(b) There are two indirect but potentially important costs associated with lack of enforcement of property rights, in addition to the efforts expended to carry out theft and to preventing theft. First, things may be damaged when they are taken (when a radio is stolen from an automobile, the thief may break the automobile's window and damage the radio as well). Second, individuals may alter the types of things they use or produce in favor of what is most easily protected rather than what would best suit them (a farmer might grow crops rather than raise cattle, because the cattle could be stolen when grazing, even though the cattle would be more valuable to raise).

2.6 Protection against risk. Another advantage of property rights is that they provide individuals with protection against risk, which is socially valuable due to individuals' general risk aversion. The most obvious way that property rights afford such protection is by keeping individuals' holdings from being stolen by others. Moreover, the system of property rights allows for insurance and risk-sharing arrangements, and thus for protection against a whole range of risks, those due to the uncertainties of nature (crop loss due to pests, floods), technological uncertainty (malfunction of products), and market uncertainty.

2.7 Achievement of a desired distribution of wealth. Associated with any given measure of social welfare will be a socially optimal distribution of the available wealth, one that maximizes social welfare. In the absence of property rights, however, the distribution of wealth would be unlikely to tend toward the optimal, because it would be determined by the ability of individuals to take things from one another, to protect what they have, and by chance elements. By contrast, under a regime of property rights any desired distribution of wealth is achievable in principle, for the state may redistribute wealth and the new distribution will be maintained due to enforcement of property rights.[9]

Comments. (a) In fact, the problem of social welfare maximization involves not just the distribution of an available quantity of wealth, but also the production of wealth. And efforts to redistribute wealth in order to achieve a desired distribution generally influence incentives to produce wealth.[10] Notably, if the amount that an individual must surrender in taxes to the state rises with his wealth or income, his incentive to work will often be compromised. This problem generally renders achievement of the ideal distribution of wealth infeasible, but it is plain that there is great scope for improvement over the distribution that would result without a system of property rights.

(b) The advantage of property rights under discussion is obviously a potential one, because the actual distribution of wealth depends on the political system and may depart substantially from a notion of the ideal. The point here is simply that without property rights, the distribution of wealth is virtually certain to deviate greatly from the ideal (and the quantity of wealth available to be distributed will be small).

2.8 The foregoing are justifications for *some* form of property rights—not necessarily for private property. If the advantages of property rights are sufficiently great, they will warrant the existence of *some* form

---

9. This advantage of property rights is different from that concerning protection against risk, for individuals will be protected against risk under a regime of property rights regardless of the distribution of wealth.

10. This subject is discussed in section 2 of Chapter 28.

of the rights. But arguments have not been given that support any specific form of property rights, in particular, for a regime of *private property,* wherein things generally are owned (and can be sold) by private parties, as opposed to the state. The benefits of property rights may often be enjoyed under very different property rights regimes. Notably, in a socialist state, just as in a capitalist one, the protection of possessory rights results in avoidance of dispute and of effort to take or to safeguard things; further, incentives to work in a socialist enterprise, just as in a capitalist one, may be fostered through use of a salary structure that rewards good behavior, even though individuals do not own their output; and so forth. The question of the circumstances in which a private property regime versus a socialist or another property rights regime is best is obviously significantly more complex than that of the justification for property rights per se and is beyond our scope.[11]

Note on the literature.   The justification for property rights was of particular interest to seventeenth- and eighteenth-century political theorists, notably Hobbes, Locke, Hume, Blackstone, and Bentham (although the basis of property rights has been the object of scholarly inquiry from the earliest times).[12] These writers generally stress that in the absence of protection of possessory rights, individuals would take things from one another and disputes would arise, and the writers usually note that the motive to work would be compromised. They often mention also the advantages of trade in things, but they appear to see this more as a consequence of the existence of property rights than as an aspect of their justification.[13] Today,

11. There is, of course, a vast and now highly elaborated literature on the virtues of private property and the price system versus central planning and socialism. For accessible introductions to and commentaries on this literature, see, for example, Heilbroner 1987, Kowalik 1987, and Shleifer 1998.

12. There is a long history of writing on property rights, dating at least from Greek and Roman times. For example, Aristotle observes in his *Politics* that incentives may suffer when property is not private. For a critical chronology of the idea of property, see generally Schlatter 1951.

13. Hobbes ([1651] 1958) stressed that in the absence of a state to protect things, there would be perpetual violence and no industry because of uncertainty of return; see especially part 1, chap. 13. Locke ([1689] 1988) did not emphasize that property rights promote work effort. The core of his justification for property rights was that when a person devotes labor effort to produce something, it is only fair that he thereby acquires a property

most literature on property rights is concerned not with their basic justification, but rather with their most desirable character.[14]

3. THE EMERGENCE OF PROPERTY RIGHTS

3.1 In general.   We would expect property rights to emerge from a background of no rights, or poorly established rights, when the various advantages of property rights come to outweigh the costs of instituting and maintaining the rights. Property rights will be likely to arise in these circumstances because, if a substantial proportion of the population recognizes that it will be better off, or probably so, under a regime with property rights, individual or collective pressures will be brought to bear to develop them.[15]

3.2 Examples.   A number of examples of the establishment of property rights illustrate their advantages.

(a) *Rights in land during the California Gold Rush.* When gold was discovered in California in 1848, property rights in land and minerals were largely undetermined, because the territory was just being acquired from Mexico, the population of the region was low, and, in any case, there were virtually no authorities to enforce law. After a short time, however, the gold-bearing area of California found itself divided into districts. In each district, men had made an explicit agreement governing property rights.

---

right in it; see *Second Treatise,* chap. 5. Hume ([1739] 1992) discussed the state's establishment of property rights as necessary to prevent individuals from taking from one another, but was not explicit about incentives to produce; he did, though, mention the value of trade; see book 3, part 2, sections 2 and 4. Blackstone ([1765–1769] 1992) saw property rights protection as valuable because it averted disputes and furnished incentives to produce; he also noted the beneficial nature of trade; see book 2, chap. 1. Bentham ([1802] 1987) focused on the incentives created by property rights and mentioned as well the virtues of trade; see *Principles of the Civil Code,* part 1, chaps. 7, 8, and 10, and part 2, chap. 2.

14. Ellickson 1993, however, discusses the justification for property rights in land. Also, there are empirical studies of the general benefits of property rights; see the survey Besley 1998 and, for specific examples, Alston et al. 1996, Besley 1995, and Feder and Feeny 1991.

15. Literature on the emergence of property rights is reviewed in Libecap 1986; see also related work of Bailey 1998 and Rose 1998.

Their compacts typically stated in detail how land was to be assigned and how theft and other infractions of rules were to be sanctioned (often by the loss of the violator's land or gold).

Why did the gold-seekers enter into these bargains? To obtain gold, individuals had to expend effort and make investments of one type or another. For instance, excavations had to be undertaken and sluices had to be constructed in which to separate gold from dirt. These tasks would not have been performed, and relatively little gold would have been collected, if individuals could not be reasonably confident that their gold would not be stolen and that the land on which they dug a ditch or on which they had built a sluice would not subsequently be taken over and benefit others. Moreover, the agreements were designed to prevent violence (in fact, there was little) and to reduce the need for each person to spend valuable time protecting his land. These advantages of property rights were recognized as mutual by the men who made the compacts in this quite dramatic instance of the emergence of property rights.[16]

(b) *Rights in land on the Labrador Peninsula during the fur trade.* At the time of the development of the fur trade on the Labrador Peninsula in North America, certain Indian tribes established a system of property rights in land, where none previously existed. An owner's territory was often marked off by identifiable blazes on trees and proprietorship included retaliation against trespassers. The explanation that has been suggested for this system of rights is that without the rights, overly intensive hunting of fur-bearing animals (especially beaver) would have depleted the animal stock. With property rights, owners of land had incentives to husband their animal resources (for example, by sparing the young, and rotating the area of their land on which they trapped animals), because they would later be able to enjoy the benefits of having a larger stock. Before the advent of the fur trade, Indians had no reason to obtain furs in numbers beyond the small quantity required for their own use. Thus, there was no danger of depletion of the animal stock and, as a corollary, no need for property rights in land.[17]

16. The development of property rights during the California Gold Rush is well documented and is interpreted from the point of view of economics in Libecap 1989 and Umbeck 1981.

17. See Demsetz 1967.

(It is not clear, though, why the Indians did not make collective agreements to limit hunting rather than establish property rights.[18])

(c) *Rights to the resources of the sea: fisheries, oil, and minerals from the seabed.* For most of history, there were no property rights in the ocean's fisheries because fish were in inexhaustible supply for all practical purposes. Certain fisheries came under strain with the introduction of trawler fleets in the late nineteenth century, however, and fish populations are under significantly greater pressure today because of the increased scale of, and the modern methods employed in, fishing (factory fleets, miles-long nets, electronic detection of fish). In response to the need to preserve the fisheries, countries have developed, through a series of treaties, property rights in the fish found in their coastal waters; at present, a country enjoys such rights in an Exclusive Economic Zone (EEZ) extending two hundred miles from its coastline. This gives a country a natural incentive not to deplete its fisheries because it will then enjoy a greater catch in the future, provided that the fish in question do not tend to swim outside the EEZ.

Likewise there were no property rights established for oil and minerals from the seabed until it became apparent, around the end of the Second World War, that extraction might be commercially viable. Today, coastal countries have property rights to the resources of the seabed within the EEZ, which gives them (or, more precisely, companies granted licenses by them) a motive to explore, develop technology for extraction, and then to exploit oil and mineral resources (to date, principally manganese nodules). Outside the EEZ, property rights to the seabed will be partial, governed often by an international authority according to a complex provision of a treaty on the law of the sea.[19]

---

18. This advantage of property rights must have outweighed the costs of enforcing the rights. It is not evident what these costs were. It is unlikely that the Indians actively policed the borders of their lands, for that would have been inordinately expensive. Perhaps it was sufficient for a landowner to monitor the small area near his beaver lodges for strange traps and, if such traps were discovered, to lie in wait for interlopers.

19. For a brief description of the development of property rights in ocean resources, see Biblowit 1991, 79–81. See also Eckert 1979, Hannesson 1991, Scott 1988, and Sweeney, Tollison, and Willett 1974 for economically oriented analyses of the subject. On the law of the sea treaty, see Agreement Relating to the Implementation of Part 11 of the United Nations Convention on the Law of the Sea, with Annex, July 28, 1994.

(d) *Rights to the electromagnetic spectrum.* With the invention of the radio and other means of wireless communication, the electromagnetic spectrum—the medium through which electromagnetic signals travel—became valuable and property rights in it emerged. The main reason is that if two parties simultaneously attempt to transmit signals in the same area over the same frequency, their signals interfere with each other, resulting in garbled signals. In the early days of radio, this problem prompted the government to pass the 1927 Radio Act (and in 1934 to establish the Federal Communications Commission), under which it allocated exclusive rights to broadcast over particular ranges of the spectrum at particular times in particular areas. These property rights in the spectrum generally took the form of nontransferable licenses of limited duration that might be renewed. Inability to transfer licenses and the cost and other disadvantages of the licensing and renewal process has led over the years to dissatisfaction with the allocation of the spectrum. Recently, lotteries and auctions have begun to be employed to allocate rights to parts of the spectrum, where these rights have limited transferability.[20]

(e) *Rights to extraterrestrial bodies and outer space.* One can expect that as uses for extraterrestrial bodies and for outer space become apparent, property rights in them will be established. There is now a "Moon Treaty" that commits signatories to establish an international regime to govern the exploitation of the natural resources of the moon (but postpones allocation of property rights).[21] Also of note is discussion of (and some claims for) property rights to the geostationary orbit, the band of space 22,300 miles above the equator where satellites travel at the same speed as that at which the earth rotates and therefore maintain a fixed position relative to the earth. This is the most valuable orbit for communications satellites, yet the orbit is a scarce resource, principally because of electronic interference between satellites that are too close to one another.[22]

---

20. See Coase 1959, De Vany et al. 1969, and, more recently, Andrews 1995, McAfee and McMillan 1996, McMillan 1994, and Settanni 1994.

21. Agreement Governing the Activities of States on the Moon and Other Celestial Bodies, Dec. 18, 1979, art. 11(5), 18 *International Legal Materials* 1434–1441.

22. See Kosmo 1988, Roberts 2000, and Staple 1986.

3 ||| DIVISION OF PROPERTY RIGHTS

Having considered the general reasons for the existence of property rights, I now examine a number of topics about property rights, beginning with the advantages and disadvantages of their division.[1]

1. DIVISION OF RIGHTS DESCRIBED

The bundle of property rights in a thing may be partitioned in a variety of ways: into various rights that are enjoyed contemporaneously; into rights that are enjoyed only under certain contingencies; and into rights that are enjoyed only at certain times. Further, possessory rights and rights to transfer them may be separated from each other. Consider the following examples of division of property rights.

(a) An owner of land may not hold complete possessory rights, in that others may enjoy an easement, that is, the contemporaneous right of passage on his land, such as along a path or on a private road. Others may also have the right, known as a profit, to take something from the land, such as timber, oil, or minerals.

1. For an economically oriented survey of division of property rights, see Stake 2000.

(b) The provisions of a will may stipulate that the disposition of property will depend on various contingencies, such as whether grandchildren have been born, whether a child is still alive, or whether a person has obtained an education.

(c) The common rental arrangement constitutes a division of property rights over time, in which many of the rights are held by the renter during the rental period, but not before or after that period.

(d) The sale of property or its donation are occasions at which all rights associated with ownership pass to the buyer or recipient from that moment on.

(e) Under the trust relationship, the trustee holds title to property for the benefit of another. The beneficiary may enjoy the use of property but generally will not have the right to sell or transfer it, so that possessory rights and rights to transfer are divided. For instance, an orphaned child may live in a house but an adult trustee, such as a relative, may decide whether or not to sell it.

2. SOCIAL ADVANTAGES AND DISADVANTAGES OF DIVISION OF POSSESSORY RIGHTS

The division of possessory rights may be socially valuable when different parties derive different benefits from them because, other things being equal, gains can then be achieved if rights are allocated to those who obtain the most from them. This will be so, for instance, if the absentee owner of forest land gives hikers the right to pass through his property or if the owner of a home at a summer resort rents it to someone during the winter when the owner would not much want to use it.

There are several types of disadvantages of division of possessory rights, or of too fine a division of the rights. The first concerns the observation that certain minimal transportation and related costs must be borne in order to enjoy possessory rights in a thing. To benefit from use of land (to hike on it, to harvest timber from it), one must generally travel to the land and perhaps convey equipment to it. These costs are not worth bearing if the rights enjoyed are too limited (no one would make a long trip in order to hike along a mere fifty-foot path).

A second disadvantage of division of possessory rights is that division may lead to the chance of more than one individual wishing to exercise the same rights and thus of disputes. If many individuals have the right to use a person's backyard swimming pool at different times, the odds of different people wishing to use the pool simultaneously will increase. Although this difficulty should not arise if the division of property rights is unambiguous, as a practical matter that may not be so (watches may disagree).

A third disadvantage of division of possessory rights is that one person's use may conflict with another's, that is, give rise to a detrimental externality.[2] If a farmer gives an easement for right of passage on his land to someone, this person may, in exercising his right, trample the farmer's crops. These problems would not arise if possessory rights could be completely specified and enforced, for then the right to engage in the problematic behavior would not be granted: The farmer would not give the person with the easement the right to trample his crops. But to determine whether a person with an easement does or does not trample the crops might be difficult (perhaps he could claim that animals trampled the crops). Hence, in effect, giving a person an easement may mean that the person is obtaining also the right to trample crops.

A closely related disadvantage of division of possessory rights is that it may result in the failure to obtain benefits from the coordinated use of property; one person with rights may not do things that could aid another in his use of property because the first obtains no gain for himself from doing so. If a person has the right to use a farmer's land as pasture for his cattle, he could help the farmer by distributing manure so as to efficiently fertilize the farmer's land; but he might not do so because he may see no real gain in it. (By contrast, if the farmer grazes his own animals, he will naturally have the motive to use manure appropriately to fertilize his land.) As with the previously mentioned disadvantage of conflicting use, this disadvantage would not arise if possessory rights were completely specified and enforced, for then beneficial actions, like distributing manure, could be required.

Another disadvantage of division of rights arises when the division is long-lasting—as an easement allowing passage over land may be—and the property is sold. At that time, the cost of the transaction will rise somewhat,

2. On externalities, see generally Chapter 5.

because the buyer will need to understand the nature of the division of rights (or will wish to investigate the possibility that others have a right in the property of which he is not aware).

3. SOCIAL ADVANTAGES AND DISADVANTAGES OF SEPARATION OF POSSESSORY RIGHTS FROM TRANSFER RIGHTS

One would suppose that it is typically socially desirable for possessory rights and the rights to transfer them to be held by the same party, because the usual expectation is that the holder of possessory rights has both the knowledge and the motive to make good decisions about the transfer of the rights. The holder of possessory rights will typically have the requisite knowledge to decide about transfer because he will be familiar with the characteristics of the thing and will naturally know its value to himself. And he will generally have a socially desirable incentive to decide whether to transfer a possessory right because he will lose the benefit of his possessory right if and only if he decides to transfer it, and will gain from whatever is given in the transfer.

There are, however, circumstances in which separation of rights to transfer possessory rights from the possessory rights themselves is beneficial. One such circumstance arises when the holder of the possessory rights does not have the knowledge or the intellectual ability to decide about transfer, such as when a child owns property and an adult trustee has the right to decide whether to sell the property because he can make better decisions than the child could. Another major circumstance in which separation of possessory rights and rights of transfer may be beneficial occurs when the holder of possessory rights does not have a proper incentive to transfer them. For example, suppose that Alpha rents a room in Beta's house. Alpha would not have the motive to consider appropriately the character of another tenant (such as whether he would make noise), so that it may be best for Alpha not to have the right to sublet his room.[3]

3. This example may be expressed generally. Division of possessory rights may, as discussed earlier, be associated with problems of conflicting use and of coordination. If so, it may be beneficial not to allow a holder of some of the rights to transfer them to another because this may worsen the problems.

4. THE SOCIALLY OPTIMAL DIVISION OF PROPERTY RIGHTS, THEIR ACTUAL DIVISION, AND THE LAW

It will be socially desirable for property rights to be divided when, but only when, the accompanying advantages outweigh the disadvantages.

One would expect the actual division of property rights by private parties generally to reflect the socially optimal division. The fundamental reason is that when the transfer of certain rights would be socially desirable, there will typically exist a mutually beneficial private exchange involving the rights. If, for example, a landowner is not equipped to cut down his timber and someone else is, there will be a price at which the landowner will be willing to sell his timber rights and the other person will be willing to purchase them.

Furthermore, the law tends to aid the division of property rights that parties wish. Individuals are generally able to divide property rights as they please by means of contracts. Thus, the landowner might arrange for another party to enjoy timber rights during a specified period according to a contract. Also, individuals are often able to effect mutually desirable division of property rights, and over long periods, through recognized devices of property law, including, as mentioned, easements, profits, and trusts.

But the law places various limitations on division of property rights. The general forms of property rights that individuals are permitted to hold are restricted.[4] For instance, time shares in real estate were not an allowed form of property until relatively recently. Various commentators suggest that certain such limitations are socially desirable because they simplify sales transactions[5] or because they prevent excessive fragmentation of property

---

4. See Rudden 1987, who also emphasizes that restrictions on the form of property rights present a puzzle for economic thinking because they apparently hinder desirable division of rights.

5. Sales transactions might be eased by a limitation in property rights because, as noted in section 2, a buyer would then not have to interpret a new form of property right, or would not worry about or investigate the possibility of a hidden interest in the property that he is buying. Thus, if time shares are not allowed, a buyer of property need not concern himself with their meaning or ascertain whether some unknown person has a time share in his property. This view is discussed by Rudden 1987 and versions of it are developed and advanced by Merrill and Smith 2000 and by Hansmann and Kraakman 2002.

that would not be cured by private consolidation.[6] These views must be carefully interpreted.[7] In some cases, though, limitations on division of rights have a fairly clear justification. For example, consider zoning rules that prevent lot size from falling below a prescribed minimum. Small lots may be disliked by individuals in a neighborhood because they lead to congestion and reduce greenery for all to enjoy. If so, and if it would be difficult for the many individuals living in a neighborhood to contract with each other to keep lot sizes from being too small, regulation of lot size would be necessary to accomplish their common goal.

6. If too many time shares are sold and it would be more efficient for them to be consolidated, the argument is that consolidation might not come about through private purchase. Hence, the law might proscribe fragmentation in the first place. This possibility is also discussed by Rudden 1987 and is endorsed by Heller 1999.

7. Regarding the goal of simplifying sales transactions, two comments should be made. First, if division of property rights makes property harder to sell, an owner will have a natural reason to take into account the effect of division of rights on transactions costs. The argument has been made, however, that an owner does not have a reason to consider that transactions in property *other* than his could be impeded by general worry among buyers that their property might be burdened by hidden interests. This problem can be, and often is, alleviated by two types of legal rules: (a) A rule under which a division of property rights is not enforced unless the division is made explicit in the sales documents. In fact, division of property rights in this way is not legally limited because it is, by definition, accomplished by contracts between the immediately concerned parties. (What may be barred is a division of property rights that is enforced against a person who was not made aware of another person's property interest when he made a contract to acquire the property.) (b) A rule under which a division of property rights is not enforced unless the division has been entered into a registry, and possibly a fee has been paid for doing so (to induce those who obtain the rights to take into account the cost that others will bear in checking the registry). On these issues, see Hansmann and Kraakman 2002.

Regarding the inability of private parties to consolidate property if it is excessively fragmented, one wonders why consolidation by private parties would not usually occur (why, for example, a person would not ordinarily succeed in purchasing different individuals' time shares if an apartment is more valuable when lived in year-round by a single person). A satisfactory answer to this basic question has not been provided, even though it is possible that in some situations problems in bargaining might retard or prevent beneficial private consolidation.

4 ||| ACQUISITION AND TRANSFER OF PROPERTY

In this chapter, I consider the acquisition and transfer of property, an issue that is important because most property changes hands at least once (in a modern economy, it has to be sold by the producer to consumers). I begin with the acquisition of previously unowned property and with the related topic of the acquisition of lost or mislaid property. I next examine the more common ways of acquiring property, through its transfer by sale, by gift, or by bequest. Then I discuss state-imposed constraints on the sale of property, and last, involuntary transfer of property through so-called adverse possession.

1. ACQUISITION OF UNOWNED PROPERTY

1.1 Introduction. Here I inquire about the incentives of a single party, and then of multiple parties, to find previously unowned things, such as fish in the sea or wild animals, or oil or mineral deposits.[1] (Acquisition of things never previously owned is sometimes called *original acquisition.*)

---

1. Most of what is written in this section will apply also to abandoned property, on which see section 2.

The measure of social welfare will be the net expected value of things, that is, the probability of finding them multiplied by their value, minus the costs of search effort. I will first consider the simple situation of acquisition by a single individual and then the more complicated and realistic situation involving multiple parties.

1.2 Acquisition by a single individual.   Let me first describe socially optimal behavior. Consider a situation in which a single individual has the opportunity to invest effort or resources to discover a thing. It will be socially desirable for the individual to make an investment when the investment would increase the expected return by more than its cost. Thus, if an undersea mineral deposit is worth 1,000 and an exploration effort would increase the likelihood of finding it by 10 percent, the expected value of the effort would be 100, so the effort ought to be taken if and only if its cost is less than 100.

Finders-keepers rule leads to optimality. It is clear that an individual will invest socially optimally provided that he will obtain the full value of the thing if he discovers it. Consequently, the finders-keepers rule—under which the finder is deemed to be the owner of anything that he has found—will lead a finder to act desirably to locate things.[2] In contrast, a rule that accords a finder only part of the value of what he discovers leads to inadequate incentives to find things.

1.3 Acquisition by multiple individuals.   In this case, the description of socially optimal behavior involves a complication. When an individual searches for a thing, the increase in the probability that *the individual in particular* will find the thing typically exceeds the increase in the *total* probability of discovery—the probability that *some individual* will find the thing. The reason is that the person may search in places that others would have examined in any event, so that the increase in the particular person's likeli-

2. An exception to the point of this paragraph concerns unowned currency. The socially optimal effort to devote to finding it is zero, for there is no social value of currency: The state can print more currency at negligible cost. The value of currency to an individual is hardly zero, however; individuals will be willing to make substantial investments to obtain lost currency. Thus, perhaps, it would not be desirable to grant a person ownership of currency if, say, it was in the safe of a ship that was lost at sea and the person would mount an expensive effort to recover the currency.

hood of finding the thing will often come at the expense of others' likelihood of finding the thing. This factor needs to be taken into account in determining whether it is socially desirable for an individual to devote effort to search, for it is only the increase in the total probability of success that is relevant in deciding whether a given individual's effort is socially justified.

> *Example 1.* Suppose that if A alone searches for some thing, the odds of his discovering it will be 10 percent; and if B joins A, the odds of B finding it will be 4 percent and the odds of A finding it will fall to 7 percent because B will be looking in some of the places A would have. Thus, if B searches along with A, the overall probability of discovery will rise by only 1 percent—that is, by 4% + 7% − 10%—not by 4 percent.[3]
>
> Accordingly, the 1 percent increase in the total probability of discovery is what is relevant for calculating whether it is socially desirable for B to search. If the value of the thing sought is 1,000, the cost of search for A is 15 and the cost of search for B is 20, then A alone should search, for B's cost exceeds the increase of 10 (namely, 1% × 1,000) in the expected total return that he would bring about.[4]

As a general matter, it is socially worthwhile for an individual to search, or to make a greater effort to search, only if the cost of so doing is warranted by the expected increase in the total probability of finding the thing, which equals the increase in his probability of finding the thing minus the reduction in others' probability of doing the same.[5]

3. I assume that A and B do not simultaneously discover the thing; thus the probability that one of the two discovers the thing is simply the sum of 4 percent and 7 percent.

4. More precisely, if A alone searches, the net expected return is 10% × 1,000 − 15 = 85; if B alone searches (and finds the thing with probability 10%), the net expected return is 10% × 1,000 − 20 = 80; and if A and B search, the net expected return is 11% × 1,000 − 15 − 20 = 75; thus A alone ought to search.

5. To amplify, suppose that the per person cost of search is c, that x is the number of people who search, and that $p(x)$ is the probability each person has individually of finding a thing worth v. Note that the total probability that the thing will be found is $xp(x)$ (suppose that people will never find the thing simultaneously). Assume that $p'(x) < 0$ for the reasons discussed in text (notably, others will search where a given person might have) and that $p''(x) > 0$. The social objective is for x to maximize the social surplus, $xp(x)v − cx$, meaning that the optimal x (treated as continuously variable) satisfies $p(x)v + xp'(x)v = c$. That is, individuals should engage in search until the expected gain $p(x)v$ less the reduction in others' gain $xp'(x)v$ equals the cost c. Denote the optimal x by x^*.

Finders-keepers rule results in excessive search. If whoever discovers a thing will own it, then incentives to search will generally depart from the optimal and there will be a tendency toward socially excessive search activity. The reason is that a person's incentive to engage in search derives from the likelihood that he, specifically, will find the thing, whereas, as just mentioned, his search will tend to lower the chance that others will find the thing. Thus, the individual's personal return from search under the finders-keepers rule will exceed the social return, and because it is his personal return that will motivate him to engage in search, he will often search more than is socially desirable. In the preceding example, the rule giving ownership to a finder will result in B joining A in searching, even though this is not socially desirable: B will obtain an expected return of 40 as against his cost of 20, and B will not take into account that A's expected return will drop by 30 when B searches as well.[6]

Comments. (a) Qualifications: The point that search may be socially excessive bears several qualifications. First, it may be that different parties happen to search in different areas, so that their efforts are not competitive; if so, the private return and the social return will be the same, and search by each party will be optimal. Second, parties may sometimes cooperate and agree to divide their areas of search into mutually exclusive regions; in this case too, search by each party will be optimal. Third, if one person's search activity would convey information to others about the possible location of a thing, then search effort could be less than socially desirable: An individual might refrain from investing in search because he anticipates being joined by others, diluting his return, or he might limit his efforts in order to conceal them from others (work only at night in order to escape notice).

(b) Reality of the phenomenon of excessive search: Despite the foregoing qualifications, it seems clear that in a variety of instances too much effort is expended in trying to find things. A well-known case in point is

---

6. In the situation described in the previous note, it can be seen that too many individuals search. An individual will search as long as his expected return $p(x)v$ is at least c, so that the condition determining x is $p(x)v = c$; call the x so determined x^{**}. It is apparent that $x^{**} > x^*$, since x^* satisfies $p(x)v = c - xp'(x)v > c$. For a survey of the extensive economic literature on the possible inefficiencies under the finders-keepers rule, and its relation to law, see Lueck 1998.

fishing. It is a commonplace that the quantity of fish taken could be caught by a smaller fleet. Relatedly, investment in equipment for fishing (powerful engines for beating other vessels to a site, sonar for detecting fish) has arguably been excessive; cheaper methods would be sufficient to produce present yields.[7] Similarly, efforts to discover and extract oil have sometimes been unwarranted. For example, in the East Texas oil fields, over half of all the wells drilled as late as the 1930s were said to have been unnecessary.[8]

Possible remedies for the problem of excessive search. One response to the problem of excessive search activity under the finders-keepers rule is to reduce the return to discovery by granting only partial ownership to finders or by imposing taxes on what is found.[9]

Another remedy is for the state to control directly the volume of search activity (the number of fishermen, the length of the fishing season), their methods of search (allowable net sizes, types of vessels), or the quantity of their recoveries. The chief problem with this, as with any regulatory approach, concerns the quality of the state's information about proper regulation and the bluntness of its rules (regulating only the number of fishermen does not result in selection of those best able to fish).

An additional approach is for the state to sell or to grant some party an exclusive right to search. For example, the state could sell the right to search for oil in an offshore area. This would tend to cure problems of search incentives because the purchaser of the right would then be motivated to choose the optimal number of searchers and to coordinate their actions; the purchaser's motive would be to maximize the total expected return minus the total costs of all hired searchers.

It should be noted, though, that when search activity and discovery is not observed by the state, the situation is, de facto, identical to that when finders obtain ownership of what they discover, and no remedy is possible.

---

7. A dramatic example of this is that so much effort and equipment has been devoted to beating competitors to catch herring in Alaska that I was told on a visit that the season may last less than one hour. It would obviously be socially preferable for the herring to be caught more cheaply over a longer period of time. On the inefficiencies of investment and excessiveness of effort devoted to fishing, see, for example, Johnson and Libecap 1982.

8. See Ely 1938, 1233.

9. But this will lead to inadequate levels of search effort if searchers have cooperated and divided the territory into mutually exclusive regions.

1.4 The law.   The character of the law regarding the rights of finders of things depends importantly on what the things are—notably, whether they are fish, game, oil, or undersea mineral deposits.[10] To an important degree, finders are given title to what they discover, but they also are often restricted in various ways by the remedies just mentioned for the problem of excessive search effort.[11] Those who catch fish at sea and those who kill game in hunting areas usually are deemed to be proper owners, but limits on the quantity of fish and of game that may be taken, the times when they may be taken, and who may engage in search for them are commonly imposed.[12]

In the early days of oil exploration and recovery, those who obtained oil were given ownership of it, regardless of whose land the oil had lain under. Over time, however, various regulations curtailing quantities taken and methods of recovery emerged, and now in many jurisdictions the race to extract oil is prevented by unitization schemes, under which all owners of land over an oil reservoir are required to join into a single unit for the purpose of developing their oil.[13] Offshore oil exploration is governed differently. The state typically sells the right to search and produce oil in a given offshore area.[14]

The right to minerals on the ocean floor used to be enjoyed by whoever found them, but according to an international agreement, different areas of the ocean have been allocated across countries,[15] and the countries will presumably sell or grant the right to search for minerals to private parties.

2.   LOSS AND RECOVERY OF PROPERTY

2.1 Introduction.   The subject of the loss and the subsequent recovery of property involves the incentives of original owners to prevent loss

10. See generally Lueck 1998, 137–141, in addition to the references cited in notes 12–15.

11. The motive for using these remedies is not just to control excessive search effort. The remedies may also be employed to prevent the closely related problem of excessive depletion of stocks (in the case of fish and wildlife) or to raise revenue for the state.

12. See Brown 1975, 13–23, Bean 1983, and Lund 1980.

13. See, for example, Williams and Meyers 2001, chap. 9.

14. See, for example, Jones 1984 and Wiygul 1992.

15. See U.N. Convention on the Law of the Sea 1982.

of their property and then, if property is lost, the incentives of original owners or of others to recover the property. Both types of incentives are influenced by whether the law allows original owners to retain ownership in property that has been lost or instead accords ownership to finders.

2.2 Socially optimal effort to prevent loss of property and to recover lost property. Our social welfare criterion will continue to be the expected value of property minus the costs of effort, but now effort will include steps taken to prevent loss as well as the expected effort expended to recover lost property. It will be convenient to consider first socially optimal recovery effort and second, socially optimal effort to prevent loss.

Observe that once property is lost, the social welfare criterion reduces to just the expected value of property minus the cost of recovery effort, so that it is socially optimal to devote effort to recovery if and only if its cost is less than the expected return. Thus, the description of socially optimal recovery effort is identical to that of socially optimal search effort for un-owned property, as discussed in section 1.

Now consider socially optimal effort to prevent loss in the first place. This level of effort will reflect the point that, should a loss occur, there may be a subsequent recovery and hence no social loss ultimately suffered. Suppose that a stray cow worth 1,000 would, after recovery effort of 10, be found with probability 40 percent, and in that case no social loss would be suffered.[16] Then the expected social loss from the straying of a cow would equal only 60% $\times$ 1,000 or 600, not 1,000; and adding this to the cost 10 of recovery effort, we obtain 610 as the expected social costs associated with a stray. Thus, fencing in a cow to prevent it from straying will be socially desirable if and only if fencing costs less than 610. Fencing would not be worthwhile if it costs, say, 800, even though that is less than the 1,000 value of the cow; a cost of 800 would be worth bearing if a stray cow would definitely be lost, not if it would be found with probability 40 percent. As in this illustration, the socially relevant consequence of an initial loss of property is not the entire value of the property, but rather a smaller

16. I assume for simplicity that lost cattle would be worth the same amount to any person who finds them. In general, however, a lost thing might be worth a different amount (often a lesser amount) to a finder than to the original owner. The effects of this consideration will be obvious to the reader.

adjusted loss—equal to the probability of failure of someone to recover the property multiplied by its value, plus the cost of (optimal) recovery effort. Therefore, effort to prevent loss will be socially justified only to the extent that it reduces the chance of this adjusted loss, and thus will be desirable less often when there is a chance to recover lost property than when there is no such chance.[17]

2.3 Situations in which original owners have the opportunity to exercise recovery effort or to hire others for that purpose.

In many circumstances, original owners have at least as good an opportunity as others to find property that they have lost or to engage other individuals to do so, because they will be aware of when and approximately where they lost their property (such as where a ship went down, or approximately where a watch was mislaid). In such situations, let us consider the outcomes under the two legal regimes concerning ownership of recovered property.

Original ownership rule. It is evident that the outcome under the rule whereby original owners retain ownership in lost property will be socially desirable. Recovery effort will tend to be optimal because the original owner will retain ownership of what he finds. In particular, there will be no problem of excessive incentives to search, for no one will engage in search unless hired by the owner, and he will direct their efforts so that they are not working competitively and engaging in duplicative activities.

Also, effort to prevent loss from occurring will tend to be optimal; original owners will not invest excessively in preventing loss. Because original owners will anticipate that they will retain ownership rights if they recover their lost property, they will properly view a loss in adjusted terms

---

17. To express formally what has been written in this section, suppose that y is effort to prevent loss, $q(y)$ is the probability of loss, where $q'(y) < 0$ and $q''(y) > 0$, x is recovery effort, $p(x)$ is the probability of success in recovery, where $p'(x) > 0$ and $p''(x) < 0$, and v is the value of the property. The social object is to maximize the expected value of property minus expected effort, or equivalently, to minimize expected effort plus loss of value, namely, to minimize $y + q(y)[x + (1 - p(x))v]$. The optimal x clearly minimizes the term in brackets, so satisfies $p'(x)v = 1$, assuming as I shall that the optimal x, denoted x^*, is positive. The optimal y, denoted y^*, satisfies $-q'(y)[x^* + (1 - p(x^*)v] = 1$, the marginal reduction in the expected adjusted loss equals the marginal cost of prevention effort, 1. The optimal adjusted loss $x^* + (1 - p(x^*))v$ is less than v, for as x^* minimizes $x + (1 - p(x))v$ over x, we know that $x^* + (1 - p(x^*))v < 0 + (1 - p(0))v \leq v$.

and exercise the socially correct degree of effort to prevent loss. Because a cattle owner will know that he will retain property rights in found strays, he will treat straying as less serious than certain losses of cattle; accordingly, he will not invest socially excessively to prevent straying.[18]

Finders-keepers rule. By contrast, the outcome under the finders-keepers rule is socially less desirable. Under this rule, original owners and other parties might invest excessively in search effort to be the first to find lost property.

Furthermore, original owners will tend to exercise excessive effort to prevent loss because, if they lose their property and it is recovered by someone else, they will not retain ownership of it. That is, under the finders-keepers rule, the original owner will treat a recovery by another party as a full loss to himself, even though for society there will be no loss; he will thus see a loss as exceeding the socially relevant, lower, adjusted loss. If a stray would never be recovered by him but would be recovered by others with a probability of 40 percent, the owner will regard a stray as a certain loss. Hence, he will invest in fencing whenever the cost is less than 1,000, such as when its cost is 800, rather than only when the cost is less than 610.[19]

Comparison of rules. In the situations in which original owners have a good opportunity to engage in recovery effort, allowing original owners to retain ownership rights to property that they have lost is the better rule. Under the original ownership rule, there is no problem of a wasteful race to find property once it is lost, and there also is no problem of original owners investing excessively to prevent loss in the first place.

It should be observed that the possibility that original owners would be induced to take excessive care to prevent loss under the finders-keepers rule is of substantial importance in many settings, for the likelihood of recovery by others might be significant. The example of straying animals fits in this regard, for the odds of someone other than the owner finding a stray would often be high. Thus, were property rights not to remain with the owners of strays, owners might invest significantly in fencing where

18. In terms of the analysis in the preceding note, the original owner will himself seek to minimize $y + q(y)[x + (1 - p(x))v]$, so will choose x^* and y^*.

19. To amplify, assume for simplicity that the original owner will never be the one to recover his lost property. Then the owner will choose y to minimize $y + q(y)v$, so his choice of y will be determined by the condition $-q'(y)v = 1$; let this y be denoted y^{**}. Because $v > x^* + (1 - p(x^*))v$, as explained in note 18, we have $y^{**} > y^*$.

that would not be socially justified. Or, imagine that if a person leaves a personal article, such as a watch, someplace and another individual finds it, the finder automatically becomes the owner of it. Then people would arguably be led to take excessive care not to leave personal articles about, even temporarily.

2.4 Situations in which original owners do not have good opportunities to exercise recovery effort.   Let us now consider the many situations in which original owners do not have the best, or any practical, opportunity to exercise recovery effort. These include cases in which original owners have essentially no idea where they lost their property, so they would not know where to search for it. For expositional purposes, let us assume that the original owners have no opportunity to recover property themselves, and that others will have such opportunity.

Original ownership rule. Given our assumptions, the outcome under the original ownership rule leaves little incentive for other parties to recover lost property.[20] Thus, property that is lost often will not be recovered. Also, the owner's effort to prevent loss will be excessive because a loss for him will be a loss for sure.

Finders-keepers rule. If those who find lost property can keep it, then they will have an incentive to recover it; a single individual will have optimal incentives, and multiple parties will have excessive incentives. An owner's effort to prevent loss will be excessive because, for him, the chance of recovery will be zero.

Comparison of rules. The finders-keepers rule is superior. Under this rule, there is greater recovery of lost property than under the original ownership rule. Under both rules, original owners have excessive incentives to prevent loss. The main difference between the rules is that more lost property is recovered under the finders-keepers rule.

Although the finders-keepers rule is superior, it suffers from the problem that original owners have excessive incentives to prevent loss. A type

---

20. Some individuals may be altruistic, especially in a rescue situation, and make a recovery effort for that reason. Another reason that individuals might make a recovery effort in the presence of the original ownership rule is that there may be a chance that they will obtain ownership of what they find if the owners cannot be identified (see later) or if the things they find have been abandoned.

of rule that is superior to a finders-keepers rule and also to the original ownership rule is an original ownership rule combined with a *mandatory reward* paid by the owner to the finder. This hybrid rule has the attractive feature that it furnishes incentives to nonowners to recover lost property—because they receive rewards—and it also mitigates the problem of excessive loss prevention efforts by owners, because they retain ownership in lost property. The precise way in which such a rule would influence behavior would depend on the formula for the reward.[21]

2.5 Comments.   To round out our discussion, let us consider several other relevant issues.

(a) *Abandoned property.* The finders-keepers rule has appeal in regard to abandoned property, given the earlier analysis, assuming that abandonment tends to occur when original owners are not able to accomplish recovery (the situation in section 2.4). Moreover, abandonment may signal that the owner attaches relatively low value to the property, which also argues in favor of the finders-keepers rule.

(b) *Adventitiously discovered property.* Things that are found in the normal course of individuals' activities (such as a watch that a person finds lying on his seat on a bus) are things that would be found regardless of the legal rule concerning lost things. Thus, there is no need to create incentives to find such things (the watch is going to be found on the bus seat whatever the legal rule). Consequently, there is no need for the finders-keepers rule to be employed, and it is best for original owners to retain property rights in adventitiously found things, so that they will not invest excessively in prevention effort.

(c) *Identification of original owners of property.* It has been implicitly assumed that when the best rule favors original owners, they can be identified, but often, of course, they cannot. In this regard, a desirable rule is one that requires finders to make reasonable efforts to determine the identity of original owners (such as by reporting finds to the police) and that gives

---

21. If the reward is a simple fraction of the value of the recovered thing, the higher the reward fraction, the greater the incentive for recovery, which is desirable, but the more excessive is the incentive of original owners to prevent loss. If the reward depends on the optimal recovery effort, it can be shown to lead to optimal behavior for both types of party, and likewise if the reward is paid by the state to the finder.

title to finders if the owners cannot be located after a stipulated period. This rule also has the virtue that it stimulates original owners to mark their property as their own. Furthermore, it provides finders with some incentive to search for and/or bring into their possession things that it would be wasteful for no one to use.

(d) *Care of property.* Some types of lost property must be cared for in order to be preserved, a notable example being stray livestock. In such cases, it is desirable for finders who take possession of things to make reasonable efforts to maintain the things. Finders will be inclined to do this, or not disinclined, if they are compensated appropriately by the original owners if they are identified, so that a rule mandating such compensation is desirable.

(e) *Enforceability of original owners' rights.* Although it has been supposed that there is no difficulty in enforcing legal rules, there is obviously a problem in enforcing original owners' rights, for things will sometimes be found when no witnesses are present and can be used by finders without their being discovered. To the degree that this is so, the de facto rule is the finders-keepers rule.

2.6 Law concerning property rights in lost, mislaid, and abandoned property. As a general matter, owners of property retain rights in things that they have lost or mislaid.[22] Finders of such property are not usually entitled to a reward but are due reimbursement for reasonable expenses of securing and caring for found property.[23] Finders are entitled, however, to rewards based on value under maritime law, and often as well according to the codes in civil law countries.[24] When a finder does not know the identity of the original owner, many jurisdictions provide for finders to

22. See Brown 1975, sections 3.1, 3.4, and 3.5.

23. For example, those who find strays are allowed reimbursement for the expenses incurred in keeping them (if they can find the animals' owners); see St. Julian 1995, section 56. On the duty to reimburse finders for reasonable expenses of securing and keeping found property, see generally Brown 1975, section 3.5. It should be added that statutes sometimes provide for rewards also to be paid, as Brown notes.

24. Under maritime law, anyone who takes into his possession a ship lost at sea or its cargo is entitled to a reward that lies within the equitable powers of the courts, with the amount not exceeding the benefit to the owner; see generally Dietz 2000, sections 66–69. On rewards in civil law countries, see, for example, the description of the German situation in Dukeminier and Krier 1998, 115.

follow procedures allowing original owners to come forward to claim their property within a time limit, after which finders gain title to discovered property.[25] (Complications about who gains ownership may arise, though, where the thing is found on the property of a third party.[26]) Rights to *treasure trove,* that is, secreted money, gold, and silver whose owner is ancient or unknown, is ordinarily granted to the finder.[27]

Abandoned things generally become the property of finders (complications may arise, again, where abandoned things are found on the property of third parties).[28] This includes shipwrecks abandoned at sea; according to maritime law, they become the property of finders. But title to abandoned shipwrecks embedded in territorial waters sometimes goes to the state in which they are discovered.[29]

3. SALE OF PROPERTY—IN GENERAL

3.1 Reasons for sale.   Let us now turn to the most common way in which a party acquires title to property: through its sale. At various times, it will be desirable for property to be sold, for two basic reasons. First, efficient production requires that firms exchange intermediate products with each other and that final products be exchanged with ultimate consumers. Second,

25. See Brown 1975, section 3.5, and Dukeminier and Krier 1998, 116.

26. The owner of land on which a thing is found is often called the owner of the *locus in quo* or simply the locus owner. If the finder was trespassing, he is generally denied title as against the locus owner, but when the finder is an invitee or licensee of the locus owner, the authorities are divided as to who obtains title. Additionally, importance may be attached to the legal distinction between *lost* property—that which is inadvertently parted with, through negligence or oversight—and *mislaid* property—that which has been intentionally set aside or hidden, and then forgotten. When property is mislaid, rights to it are more often granted to the locus owner than when property is lost. See Brown 1975, sections 3.2 and 3.4. Also, when things found are embedded in or attached to the soil, title is generally given to the locus owner; see *Corpus Juris Secundum* 1961, 36A: 421–424.

27. The finder usually obtains title against the owner of the locus in quo (sometimes even if the finder was trespassing). Historically, however, treasure trove reverted to the Crown, and in most foreign countries, rights to treasure trove are divided between the finder and the locus owner. See Dukeminier and Krier 1998, 112–113, and Izuel 1991, 1665–1675.

28. The state also enjoys the power to claim apparently abandoned property under certain circumstances. On abandonment, see for example, Gabel 1994.

29. In the Abandoned Shipwreck Act of 1987, 43 *U.S. Code* secs. 2101–2106 (1988), the United States effectively grants title to a shipwreck to the state in whose waters the

changing needs for durable property, notably for land and equipment, leads to exchange of such property.

3.2 Problems surrounding sale: legitimacy of seller's claim of ownership; agreements concerning deferred exchange. A basic issue arising whenever property is sold concerns the legitimacy of the seller's claim of ownership, for the property might have been stolen, or improperly obtained, by the seller or by another party who held the property before the seller acquired it. This issue will be discussed in the next two sections of the chapter.

Another problem surrounding sale of property is that the parties may want to make advance agreements for their exchanges. Advance agreements are often desired by parties because, on one hand, it is inconvenient for them to make exchanges immediately, but, on the other, they want to be able to plan on the basis that exchanges will be made. For example, a person may be unable to move immediately into a home that he wants to purchase in a different city because he has to settle his affairs where he now lives and arrange for shipment of household goods, but at the same time wants to be able to plan on moving to the new home, to enroll children in school, purchase appropriate furniture, and so forth. The subject of ensuring that agreements for deferred exchange are honored when it is appropriate will be dealt with in the part of this book on contract.

4. SALE AND THEFT OF PROPERTY IN THE PRESENCE OF A REGISTRATION SYSTEM

4.1 Registration system defined. Let us now consider an important method for establishing the identity of property owners. Under a *registration system* a list is maintained of items of property, each uniquely identified and associated with the name of its owner. When there is a sale of registered property, the acquirer's name is recorded as the new owner. Under this system, if anyone desires to know the identity of the owner of a particular

---

shipwreck is located. Most states following the passage of the act claimed title to embedded shipwrecks but failed to develop adequate regulatory schemes, leading to incidents of vandalism and misuse. See Stevens 1992 and Foster 2000.

item of property in the registry, he need only check the registry, because the person whose name is in the registry is deemed to be the owner. Further, it is assumed that if an item of property listed in the registry is stolen from its owner and later discovered, it will be returned to the owner.

4.2 Costs and requirements of a registration system.   For a registration system to function, certain expenses must be incurred and requirements met. First, the registration system's records must be maintained. Second, individuals must communicate with the registry when they make a transaction. Third, each piece of property must be uniquely identified. Land is, of course, identified by its geographical boundaries. Moveables such as automobiles or aircraft are typically identified by their serial numbers as well as by their physical description (model and make), and animals, such as cattle and horses, may be identified by their brands and/or their physical description.

4.3 Principal virtues of a registration system: promotes sales transactions; discourages theft.   An advantage of registration systems is that they may ease sale and resale of things by assuring buyers of the validity of sellers' claims of ownership. In the absence of a registration system, uncertainty as to the validity of ownership might cause a wary buyer not to purchase. Alternatively, this uncertainty might cause the buyer to spend greater effort investigating the validity of ownership than would be necessary if there were a registry.

Furthermore, the existence of a registration system discourages theft in two major ways.[30] First, thieves face a higher risk of conviction if they steal registered property, for if discovered with such property, they cannot claim that they own it. If a thief is discovered in possession of an automobile that is registered in someone else's name, he cannot claim that it is his, whereas a thief found to have unregistered property, such as raw diamonds, might successfully deny that the diamonds are owned by someone else.

Second, the value of stolen property to a thief is lowered by the exis-

30. The reason that discouraging theft is socially advantageous is principally what was mentioned in section 2 of Chapter 2 as an advantage of protecting property rights: that the possibility of theft leads individuals to expend effort preventing theft and also induces some individuals to devote effort to carrying out theft; both types of effort are socially sterile.

tence of a registration system. If a thief plans to use stolen property himself, its value to him will be diminished by the chance that it will be discovered and taken away and that he will be punished. If a thief plans to sell stolen property, the existence of a registry may lower the price he will be able to obtain because the buyer can determine that the property is stolen by consulting the registry, because its value to the buyer may be diminished by the chance of its discovery, and because the buyer in turn may face difficulty in reselling the property.

4.4 Additional advantages of registration systems. Registration systems have several other advantages. First, because a registry allows owners to establish their ownership to lenders easily, their ability to use their property as collateral for loans is enhanced, as is their ability to insure it. Second, the state may use a registry to identify owners of valuable property for the purpose of imposing taxes. Third, the state may use a registry to identify owners of property (especially moving vehicles) in order to enforce safety regulations.

4.5 Social desirability of registration systems versus private incentives to establish and use them. Society will find use of a registration system advantageous if its costs are outweighed by its various benefits. Private incentives to establish and use registration systems, however, may deviate from social incentives to do so.

In particular, three of the social advantages of a registry will tend not to be counted as advantages by a private person contemplating incurring the expense of entering his item in a registry. A person will ordinarily not consider deterrence of theft as a benefit from placing his particular item of property in a registry: Deterrence will usually be affected by whether or not the mass of individuals use a registry, not by any one individual's decision about using it.[31] In consequence, an individual will be inclined to

---

31. This will be so if potential thieves have only statistical knowledge of owners' use of the registry, that is, if thieves do not know in advance of carrying out a theft whether a particular owner has had his property registered. While that would seem usually to be the case, it would not always be so. For example, if cattle thieves live nearby and know which ranchers brand their cattle and which do not, then a particular rancher's decision to brand his cattle would have a deterrent effect on theft from him, so he would take it into account in his calculus whether or not to brand.

obtain a free ride from the deterrence created by others who use a registry; he will not want to spend his own time and effort to register his property to promote deterrence. Also, an individual obviously will not credit an enhanced ability of the state to collect taxes or to enforce safety regulation as a benefit of his own use of a registry.

An individual may, though, want to use a registry for three reasons. The first two have been mentioned: He may anticipate reselling his property, which might be made easier by his having registered it, and he may want to be able to borrow against his property or to insure it. The third reason is that if a person's property is stolen, the probability of its recovery will be higher if it has been registered. If these private reasons to use a registry (the first two of which are also social reasons) are not enough to induce individuals to use a registry and the use of a registry is socially desirable, it will be best for the state to establish a registry and require or subsidize its use.[32]

4.6 Comments.   (a) *Property for which registries are likely to be socially desirable: durables of high value, especially real estate and vehicles.* Registries are more likely to be socially valuable for property of high value for two basic reasons. First, many of the benefits of registries increase with the value of property. This is true of the fostering of sales transactions (the higher the value of property, the higher the surplus from a transaction is likely to be for the buyer and for the seller), of deterrence of theft (the higher the value of property, the more parties will spend protecting it and trying to take it, so the greater the benefits from deterrence of theft), of the ability to borrow against and insure property, and of the ability of the state to raise tax revenues. Second, the costs associated with registries, being essentially bookkeeping costs, seem to be largely independent of the value of registered property. Thus, as a general matter, we would expect the benefits of registries to outweigh their costs more often for high-value property than for low.

32. One suspects that the social reasons for use of a registry generally outweigh the private ones. It is possible, however, that parties would use a registration system when that is socially undesirable. Suppose, for instance, that there is no social benefit from a registration system because it does not create deterrence (the expected ease of theft might outweigh expected sanctions despite the existence of the system) nor does it have other social benefits. Yet registration might still have private benefits because some stolen goods will be recovered if there is a registry. Thus, a registry might be set up even though it is not socially desirable. Such a case seems more theoretical than real.

Further, because durable property is often sold and resold, the benefit of promoting sales transactions is greater than for other property. Accordingly, we might well suppose that registries are often socially desirable for real estate and for certain other types of valuable durables. One category of valuable durable property that is often sold, and for which registries appear desirable, is patents and trademarks. Indeed, because this property is abstract rather than physical and cannot be possessed, registries have a special advantage.[33]

There are additional reasons why we might expect registries to be socially desirable for cars, boats, and aircraft. Namely, because these things are used for transportation and may cause accidents, the advantages to the state in terms of enforcing safety regulation may be substantial. Also, because these things are used for transportation, they are used in public areas—that is, in circumstances where the validity of ownership claims can readily be verified by law enforcement officers through a registration system. (The same is true about real estate, which by its nature cannot be concealed.)

(b) *Property for which registries are not likely to be socially desirable.* Contrast the situation with regard to the types of property just discussed to that with respect to radios, televisions, and similar items. As noted, the costs of registration systems will tend to be as high for property of low value as for property of significant value, but the benefits of registration systems will tend to be correlated with the value of the goods and thus to be less for lower value goods. Further, goods such as radios and televisions, although of some durability, are not as likely to be resold as are more valuable durable goods, reducing the transaction-related benefit of registries. Also, many of the lower-value goods under discussion are ordinarily used within domiciles; thus the likelihood that illegal possession of such goods would be detected were there a registry is smaller. Moreover, there is not a strong reason for the state to regulate safety in the use of these goods. Hence, the likelihood that registries for such goods would be socially desirable appears to be low relative to that for real estate and valuable durables.

Another category of goods for which registries are not likely to be desirable are those for which unique identification is difficult or costly relative to their value. Such goods include things whose appearance would be

---

33. The only obvious alternative to a registry would be a system in which a certificate is issued and the possessor of the certificate is deemed to be the holder of abstract property.

marred by the imprinting of a serial number or identifying mark, as well as many fungible goods, for instance, wheat and diamonds.

4.7 Actual use of registries. Ownership of land is recorded by the state in registries or similar systems, and although not necessarily required, recording is strongly encouraged.[34] Use of registries is mandatory for automobiles and motorcycles, aircraft, and boats over a certain size.[35] Additionally, cattle and other animals are frequently branded, with the brands being recorded in registries or generally understood; branding of animals is often mandatory but sometimes is voluntary.[36] Patents, copyrights, trademarks, and various security interests in property are also registered.[37] Fairly well-known works of art may often be viewed as implicitly registered because their true owners are commonly known. (If a person steals the *Mona Lisa* from the Louvre, he cannot resell it and hope that it will not be recognized as stolen.)[38] Use of registries for other types of property is infrequent.

34. In the United States, individuals generally enter real estate transactions into a *recording system;* a buyer is induced to record his transaction because, if he does not and the seller sells the same property to another party who does record his transaction, this second party will gain title (the first will only be able to sue the seller for money damages). Recording systems are not identical to the registration systems described in this section, for the party listed as title holder in the recording system may not in fact be the title holder, and the recording system does not reliably list all those who have interests in property. Eleven states do have registration systems, though their use is not required. See Stoebuck and Whitman 2000, 869–897, 923–930. In Europe, use of registration systems is more common; see McCormack 1992, 70. For economic analysis of recording systems versus registration systems, see Miceli 1998.

35. On registration of automobiles and motorcycles, see Bassano et al. 1997, section 55; on aircraft, see Philbin 1997, section 30; and on boats, see Zabolski 1997, sections 23–24.

36. More than thirty states have enacted some type of branding law, applying usually to cattle, horses, mules, and asses. In the West, branding is usually mandatory but elsewhere it may be optional. See Meyer 1990, and see also St. Julian 1995, sections 8–9. Use of brands is ancient (the Egyptians practiced branding); on the history of branding, see August 1993, 466–474.

37. On the registration of patents, copyrights, and trademarks, see, for example, Flinn 2001, 2-10, 2-23, 2-24, 2-42, 2-43, 2-44. On registration of security interests in property, see for example, Clark and Clark 2001, vol. 1, 1-13, 1-14, 2-118, 2-119, 2-120.

38. This undoubtedly reduces the problem of theft of well-known works. For art not widely known, however, the analogy does not hold; without there being a registry in art

5. SALE AND THEFT OF PROPERTY IN THE ABSENCE OF A REGISTRATION SYSTEM

5.1 Unregistered goods.   Let us assume now that there is no registry in which the lawful owners of property are recorded. This is the case with most goods; as just discussed, the actual use of registries is relatively limited. Unregistered goods may have no identifying marks or labels on them; this is typically true of common household goods, food, clothing, and jewelry, for instance. When such goods are in a person's possession or offered for sale, there will often be no easy way to determine whether the goods had previously been stolen or impermissibly obtained. It is also possible that unregistered goods do have an identifying label, notably, a manufacturer's serial number, as is the case with much electronic equipment. An owner of such goods could attempt to maintain proof of ownership, such as by recording the serial number of his property on a bill of sale.[39]

5.2 Two legal approaches concerning ownership: bona fide purchase rule; original ownership rule.   There are two basic approaches that the law may take in defining legal ownership when there is a sale in the absence of a registration system. One is to deem a purchaser to be the owner if, at the time of the exchange, he believed that the property was not previously wrongly acquired and he could not readily determine otherwise. This rule will be called the *bona fide purchase rule* because the purchaser believes the exchange to be bona fide. Under the other approach that the law may adopt, a purchaser must surrender a thing to a previous owner if the previous owner can establish that the thing was illegitimately taken from him. This rule will be called the *original ownership rule.*

5.3 Bona fide purchase rule fails to discourage theft and sale of stolen goods.   Under the bona fide purchase rule, an owner will be in the unfortunate position that, unless a thief is caught stealing, the owner

---

works, a person who steals, say, a statuette made by an undistinguished Renaissance sculptor might be able to sell it without much difficulty.

39. I am assuming that the manufacturer does not maintain (much less mandate) a list of current owners of its product. In fact, even original purchasers often do not register their property with the manufacturer. Otherwise, the situation might resemble that under a registration system.

will be unlikely to recover what has been taken from him. This is true, virtually by definition, of all goods for which owners do not have proof of ownership; if, after a thief steals my pen, I happen to see a person with what appears to be my pen (perhaps I recognize scratches on it), how do I establish this? Even if an owner does have proof of his ownership, it may well be difficult to prove that a person in possession was the thief or was not a bona fide purchaser. If I see a person riding my bicycle, for which I have a bill of sale recording the serial number, and I wish to reclaim it, I need to demonstrate either that that person stole it or that he purchased it from some other party knowing that it was stolen.

Next, consider the situation of a thief. As just discussed, thieves will know that if they are not caught in the actual act of theft, they will be relatively unlikely to be caught. Moreover, thieves will anticipate that if they attempt to sell what they have stolen—something they will want to do if they do not wish to use stolen items themselves—sales will often be relatively easy to make appear bona fide: Buyers will have little motive to discover whether they are making purchases from thieves; rather, buyers' self-interest is socially perverse, to overlook theft so that they can consummate purchases at advantageous prices and become the legal owners of goods. Further, a buyer's ability to determine whether a good was stolen by the seller will often be poor. If the thief claims the property is his, or if he produces a document that he says is a bill of sale, the buyer might not be able to check the veracity of the document very easily. Also, to impose a substantial burden on buyers to investigate the claims of sellers before sales are considered bona fide would disturb trade.

For these various reasons, it appears that the bona fide purchase rule dilutes deterrence of theft. Theft has to be discouraged primarily by the possibility of catching thieves in the act.[40]

5.4 Original ownership rule discourages theft and sale of stolen goods. The original ownership rule has contrasting effects on the sale of stolen goods and theft. First, an owner of a thing will have a positive incentive under this rule to obtain proof of ownership, for that will be of potential

---

40. This is not to deny that law enforcement agencies can succeed in such strategies as employing undercover agents to prove that certain buyers ("fences") knowingly buy stolen goods.

benefit to him after a theft: He will be able to recover his property if he can locate it even if it has been sold by the thief to an unknowing third party.

Further, because owners may possess proof of ownership and may be able to recover their stolen property, thieves will find stolen property less valuable and not be able to obtain as much for it in sales as they otherwise would. The reduction in sales price will reflect the likelihood that goods are stolen, and it will be in buyers' interests to determine whether goods are stolen.

5.5 Conclusion: Original ownership rule may be superior.   Because thieves will find stolen property less valuable, theft will be discouraged more under the original ownership rule than under the bona fide purchase rule. This suggests that the original ownership rule is the superior rule. But when one takes into account the transactions costs of exchange under the two rules—see paragraph (b) in the next section—it is conceivable that the bona fide purchase rule would turn out to be superior.

5.6 Comments.   (a) *Limited effect of the choice of rule on theft.* Although the original ownership rule should lead to greater deterrence of theft, its effect on theft appears to be limited by two considerations. First, original owners may not be led to obtain proof of ownership because of the certain costs of so doing and the uncertain nature of the benefits. This is especially true of goods that do not come with serial numbers. Second, even if original owners do have proof of ownership, it will frequently be difficult for them to locate stolen goods.

(b) *Argument that the original ownership rule undesirably encumbers trade.* It is sometimes thought that the original ownership rule might unduly curtail trade because buyers would be subject to uncertainty about sellers' ownership rights and thus of their own, or because buyers would have to expend great effort assuring themselves that sellers have good title. This view is oversimple, however. Buyers' risk will usually be modest or insignificant: The likelihood that goods were stolen will often be small and, as just discussed, if goods were stolen, original owners frequently will not have taken the trouble to maintain proof of ownership or will not know where to look for their property. For these reasons, buyers will not tend to expend much effort to verify sellers' title. Trade therefore will not be generally impeded under the original ownership rule. It will be impeded mainly when the fraction of stolen articles is great, which is also when it is probably socially desirable that trade be impeded.[41]

5.7 The law.   In the United States, the original ownership rule generally applies, although there are a variety of limitations to it under which a bona fide purchaser gains title over the original owner.[42] In Europe, the bona fide purchaser rule is more commonly employed, though with certain exceptions.[43] Historically, both types of rule have governed.[44]

6.   CONSTRAINTS ON THE SALE OF PROPERTY IMPOSED BY THE STATE

Having discussed the sale of property in the last two sections, let us now turn to consider briefly justifications for state intervention in sales.

6.1 Intervention to correct external effects.   One basic justification for the state to impose a constraint on the sale of property is that this may help to solve a problem of harmful external effects (on external effects, see generally Chapter 5). If the sale of property would result, directly or indirectly, in harm to people not involved in the transaction itself, then discouraging sales may be socially beneficial. Such state intervention may be helpful in solving problems with external effects because alternative methods, such as the use of liability, may not function perfectly or may be more difficult to employ. Let us consider several types of intervention.

(a) *Banning sales.* An extreme form of intervention is the outright ban of sales of particular types of property. For example, the sale of certain

41. Some buyers might expend effort to discern which goods are stolen, and this may only divert sellers to other buyers. To that extent, buyers' efforts to determine which goods are stolen might contribute little to deterrence and may constitute a social waste.

42. For example, if the original owner is induced by fraud to sell property to a person and this person sells to a bona fide purchaser, the purchaser will gain title as against the original owner. See generally Brown 1975, chap. 9, and Thomas 1994, section 13.

43. See Prott and O'Keefe 1995, 367–397.

44. See the economically oriented analysis of the two rules in Baird and Jackson 1984, Levmore 1987, and Weinberg 1980.

classes of firearms is proscribed, the justification being that the harmful external effect of their sale is that purchasers might use the weapons to hurt someone and/or to carry out crimes. A drawback of prohibiting sales is that there may be legitimate, non-harm-producing uses of the firearms. This disadvantage depends on the type of firearm; for hunting rifles it would be more significant than for, say, machine guns.

A type of good for which a ban on sales has, perhaps, the strongest justification is one that is used solely for circumventing the law, and thus one that contributes to the doing of harm and for which there is no social disadvantage to a ban. An example is the radar detector, which is used only for detecting the presence of police looking for speeders; if speeding is assumed to be socially undesirable, then radar detectors are disadvantageous because they reduce the likelihood of penalties for speeding.

In such cases where a ban on sales seems appealing, the justification for this categorical prohibition must rest on a comparison with other legal approaches to control of harmful external effects. For firearms and radar detectors, for example, it might be that a ban is superior to other methods of control, for once these goods have been sold, it is difficult for the state to monitor their use and the harm done with them.

(b) *Restrictions on the type of purchaser.* The state may intervene not by banning the sale of a product, but rather by restricting sales to certain classes of purchasers unlikely to use the property in the wrong way. Thus, the sale of firearms may be limited to private police, to shooting clubs, and so forth. The state may also intervene by restricting the type of purchase. For example, zoning laws may mandate minimum lot size, which implicitly alters the ambience of a neighborhood by increasing the amount of greenery, the wealth of residents, and the like.

(c) *Limitations on privately imposed constraints on sale.* Private parties may themselves wish to place constraints on the sale of property, and sometimes this will cause harmful external effects. For example, an individual might want to prevent the sale of land to persons of particular religions or races, and that might create social harm. If so, it could be desirable to prevent these constraints on sale.

6.2 Intervention to remedy problems of lack of information. A second general justification for state intervention in sales is to cure a problem of lack of information on the part of a participant in the sale, in order to effect a type of transaction more closely in line with what would have been consummated had parties been informed.

An example is that certain drugs cannot be sold except according to physician prescription. Without restrictions on sale, a person who does not understand which drugs to use might use the wrong one, a drug that the person would not have used if he or she had expert medical advice.

This line of reasoning overlooks two possibilities, however. First, a potential purchaser whose knowledge of a good is incomplete might well realize this deficiency and seek more information. A person who does not understand the properties of a drug might contact a physician or pharmacist to determine when it would be safe and helpful to take the drug. Second, the state might supply potential purchasers of goods with information. They might be informed of basic characteristics of goods on labels, for example, and be told to consult an expert if the characteristics are too complicated to state succinctly. If people are able to understand such information, its provision by the government would appear to be a superior solution to intervention against sale.

6.3 Intervention for paternalistic reasons.   Another justification often mentioned for intervention is paternalism, meaning that the state has a desire for individuals not to consume certain goods, at least under particular conditions. Sometimes paternalism reflects an external effect. For example, society's efforts to curb consumption of alcohol may be due to the fact that if people drink to excess, others can be harmed. It may also be the case that paternalism reflects a problem of lack of information. For instance, if minors are not allowed to purchase cigarettes, the justification may be that they are not old enough to evaluate properly the health risks of smoking. Paternalism is occasionally not readily viewed as reflecting externalities or lack of information, but rather as a desire of society to override the preferences of others for what society thinks is in their interests. For example, the view that adults who understand the risks of failure to wear seatbelts in cars should be required to do so may in part be a product of such paternalism.[45]

45. Still, in strict logic, it might often be said that a species of external effect is at issue when individuals in society want to override a person's preferences, such as a person's

7.   GIFTS

7.1 Gifts and their motivation.   Gifts are an important form of transfer of property, especially when one takes into account the size of bequests.[46] A major motivation for giving a gift is pure altruism: The donor cares about the well-being of the donee; that is, the donor obtains utility from the utility of the donee. This is frequently the case with gifts given to family members or to friends and may extend to the wider population and to organizations.

There are, however, a variety of reasons for gift-giving apart from altruism. One is that the act of giving itself may supply utility to the donor, independently of the degree of satisfaction it renders the donee.[47] Another is that a gift may produce expressions of appreciation or affection from the donee, or respect from those who learn of the gift (as might be true when the community is informed that a person has made a substantial gift to a symphony orchestra); thus, the gift is somewhat like a sale that is accompanied by receipt of a service (the expressions of appreciation). In addition, a gift may provide a signal about the donor that results in behavior that he considers valuable.[48]

7.2 Desirability of state encouragement of gifts.   A general reason exists for the state to support the giving of gifts and in principle to subsidize them: Because donors do not take the value of gifts to donees into full account, but that should be done from the perspective of promoting social welfare, donors may give too little, and the subsidy of gifts may therefore

---

preference for driving without a seatbelt: The externality is the disutility that individuals in society experience when some persons act on their preferences (drive without seatbelts).

46. For example, Gale and Scholz 1994, 152–154, estimate that intended giving amounts to 17 percent of individuals' net worth, and that annual bequests constitute almost 1 percent of net worth. Also, charitable giving accounts for slightly over 2 percent of household income; see *Statistical Abstract of the United States, 2001,* table 559, p. 360.

47. The utility from giving itself is sometimes described as a "warm glow"; see Andreoni 1990.

48. If I give a generous gift to my rather new employee, this may signal that I am pleased with his performance and am likely to continue to employ him, for why else would I have made the investment in the gift? This may inure to my benefit, for the employee will be more likely to work hard and less likely to search for another position.

be desirable. Consider the case where altruism is the motivation for gifts (the point largely applies as well with respect to the other motivations for gift-giving). Suppose that if A were to give a gift to B, A would obtain an altruistic benefit of 35, that B himself would obtain a benefit of 70 from the gift, but that the gift would cost A 40 owing to the consumption he would forgo. Individual A therefore would not give the gift: The altruistic benefit to him of 35 is outweighed by the cost to him of 40. But it is socially desirable for the gift to be given, assuming a sum-of-utilities measure of social welfare; for if the gift is given, the net change in welfare will be positive, $35 + 70 - 40 = 65$. A subsidy for gift-giving could induce A to give the gift, and therefore might be socially advantageous.[49]

There are also specific reasons for the state to support gifts to certain organizations. Notably, if an organization is furnishing a public good (see section 1 of Chapter 6), providing a benefit to society generally that cannot be provided by the private sector, then one way to finance it is by encouraging those who would give for whatever reason to give more, by subsidizing giving. Thus, a university, which provides public goods of a sort, could be financed in part by state encouragement of gifts.

8. TRANSFER OF PROPERTY AT DEATH: BEQUESTS

8.1 Transfer at death is an important event. A *bequest* is the transfer of property upon the death of an individual, the so-called *testator,* according to his wishes. Bequests are a significant form of transfer of property; at least

---

49. The argument of this paragraph is made by Kaplow 1995. To explain, let $u(y)$ be the utility of wealth y of the donor, $v(w)$ the utility of wealth w of the donee, and $\alpha v(w)$ the utility the donor derives from the donee's utility, where $\alpha > 0$ represents the strength of altruism and u and v are increasing and concave in wealth. The donor chooses a gift x to maximize $u(y - x) + \alpha v(w + x)$, so that he will give a positive gift if $u'(y) < \alpha v'(w)$, and if he gives a positive gift, it will be determined by $u'(y - x) = \alpha v'(w + x)$. Assuming that the measure of social welfare is the sum of the donor's and donee's utilities, x ought to maximize $u(y - x) + \alpha v(w + x) + v(w + x) = u(y - x) + (1 + \alpha)v(w + x)$, so that the socially optimal gift, if positive, is determined by $u'(y - x) = (1 + \alpha)v'(w + x)$, which implies that the socially optimal gift exceeds the size that the donor will give. Because a donor gives a smaller gift than is socially optimal, it can be shown that a subsidy raised by a lump-sum tax raises social welfare, where the state is unable to base the tax on who is a

30 percent of the total wealth of individuals in the United States is acquired through bequests.[50]

The principal aim in this section is to explain why bequests are made. In other words, why do individuals neither consume nor give away their entire wealth during their lives?[51] (Gifts made while a person is alive are known as *inter vivos* gifts because they are made between living persons.) As will be seen, the answer to this question is not self-evident. After exploring this question, I will comment on wills and on legal policy regarding bequests.

8.2 Altruism and uncertainty about donees. Altruism is a reason for a person to give property away, but it does not furnish an explanation for why a person should give his property away in a bequest rather than when he is alive. After all, if a person makes a gift when he is alive, the donee can make earlier use of it for some good purpose (for example, to obtain a college education) or at least plan his actions better knowing that he has the gift in hand. In either case, the advantage to the donee will indirectly benefit the donor because of his altruism (and perhaps this is why the dollar value of inter vivos gifts is estimated to exceed that of bequests).[52]

But uncertainty about donees can explain why altruists may defer gift giving, possibly until death. A donor may be uncertain about the needs of a potential donee (whether a relative will turn out to have a need for money may depend on his or her marriage, health, and employment) or about his or her character. The qualities and circumstances of people are revealed over time, so that a donor may not want to give a gift unless he has gathered as much evidence as possible about the need or the character of a potential donee. Closely related, a donor may not know to which person or organiza-

---

potential donor and who is a potential donee (this might be difficult for the state to determine and, if observable, would allow the state to achieve its object directly).

50. See Gale and Scholz 1994, 147.

51. For a useful and wide-ranging survey of the economic literature on bequests (dealing with accidental bequests, as described below, and with other issues in addition to altruism), see Kotlikoff 1988; see also Kotlikoff 2001. On gifts made during a person's life, and the choice between such gifts and bequests, issues to which somewhat less attention has been devoted, see, for example, Cox 1987, Gale and Scholz 1994, and Altonji, Hayashi, and Kotlikoff 1997.

52. See Cox 1987, 511.

tion he will want to give property. For example, a donor may imagine that some worthy cause may arise and reveal itself to him in the future (who could have imagined the AIDS epidemic before it materialized?). Thus, the donor may want to preserve his options in order to modify his plans about who should receive his property until he has died.

8.3 Uncertainty about length of life: accidental bequests. A second reason why property may be transferred only upon a person's death involves uncertainty over the length of one's life. If a person is uncertain how long he will live, he will want to keep enough wealth in his possession to support himself if he should be lucky enough to live longer than he expects. That, in turn, means that when he dies, he will die with property. Thus, bequests will result from the "accident" of death; this event will make a person's wealth available to be passed on to a donee.[53] Note that this reason for transmission of property at death applies even if a person does not have an altruistic motive.

The existence of a well-functioning annuities market, however, substantially qualifies the argument that individuals must hold property until death to assure themselves necessary support if they live unexpectedly long. Under an annuity contract, an individual pays a premium and in exchange receives a stream of income for as long as he lives, but for no longer.

A risk-averse person who is earning little or no income may find an annuity an attractive way to expend his wealth because it allows him to assure himself income for consumption no matter how long he lives. Indeed, if annuity contracts are actuarially fair, a risk-averse individual should want to invest much of his wealth in annuities, other things being equal.[54] And, by definition, the more an individual invests in annuities, the less wealth he will have in his possession when he dies; if he were to invest everything in annuities, he would die penniless and make no bequest. Hence, the significance of uncertainty over length of life as an explanation

53. On uncertainty about length of life as an explanation for bequests, see, for example, Abel 1985, Davies 1981, and Hurd 1989.

54. A risk-averse person would in principle want to invest *all* of his wealth in an annuity if it were actuarially fair, he did not have a bequest motive, and he were not subject to other uncertainties that will be mentioned in the text. On the theory of annuities and life insurance, see the early paper Yaari 1965, and for a relevant empirical study, see Bernheim 1991.

for the holding of wealth at the time of death, and thus for transmission of wealth at death, is reduced to the extent that individuals purchase annuities.

A person might not want to invest too heavily in annuities, though, even if he has no desire to make a bequest (obviously, if he does want to make a bequest, he will retain wealth for that purpose). This is because of uncertainty about his future needs and tastes. For example, he may not know how much he will want to spend if his health declines (will he want full-time nursing care?), or whether he will want to travel or buy a home at another location. If a person commits all of his funds to an annuity, he will have less freedom to increase his expenditures. To gain this freedom, he may rationally elect to retain a share of his wealth rather than devote it entirely toward annuities.[55]

8.4 Life insurance. Uncertainty about the length of one's lifetime can also lead a person to purchase life insurance, and therefore lead to his passing on wealth in the form of life insurance proceeds at the time of his death. In particular, a person who is earning a wage that he would spend in part on a donee for whom he has altruistic feelings may rationally purchase life insurance, if sold at approximately actuarially fair rates and the donee is risk averse.[56] The amount of coverage the donor purchases will reflect the income the donee would lose due to the donor's death. Note that this reason why a donee may obtain wealth when a donor dies applies even though the donor may be certain of the amount of wealth that he wants to give to the donee; the donor cannot give his future stream of earnings to the donee now, but he can purchase life insurance and name the donee as the beneficiary.

55. Several other reasons that a person may not want to invest in annuities should be mentioned. One is that annuity income is subject to income taxation at ordinary rates, whereas income from investments may be subject only to lower capital gains rates. Another is that annuity payments may not be actuarially fair due to administrative costs and adverse selection. (Adverse selection refers to the fact that purchase of annuities by the relatively healthy and long-lived reduces the annual annuity payment that companies can make. This renders annuity contracts actuarially unfair for the less healthy.) An additional reason is that a family's financial arrangements may mimic annuities. Notably, when husband and wife bequeath their assets to each other, the surviving spouse in effect obtains a kind of annuity. On the latter, see Kotlikoff and Spivak 1981.

56. On the theory of life insurance, see Yaari 1965.

8.5 Control over the behavior of children. Individuals often want children (or others) to give them care and attention, especially during their later years of life. It is occasionally argued that to foster this behavior, an individual can make a child's inheritance conditional on his providing a requisite degree of attention.[57] A parent might say, or might make it understood, that a child's inheritance depends on his being attentive, that otherwise he will be disinherited or his inheritance will be considerably reduced. A problem with this argument, however, is that if a parent desires attention, it is not obvious why the parent cannot "purchase" it through gifts during the parent's lifetime (such as through large holiday presents or loans for the education of grandchildren).[58] Thus, the desire of parents to influence the behavior of children does not by itself convincingly explain why parents would retain wealth until their deaths.

Nevertheless, the desire to affect the behavior of children reinforces other arguments that have been given for individuals to retain wealth until death. Notably, parents may want to retain wealth until their deaths because of continuing uncertainty about the needs of potential donees, and, independently, various uncertainties may lead parents to limit annuity purchases. As a by-product, they can obtain enhanced control over the provision of care and attention by their children.

8.6 Taxation. Tax considerations may favor giving property after death. For example, under the U.S. tax code, securities given after death have their "basis" increased, making them more valuable to donees than if the securities had been given as a gift before death.[59]

---

57. See Bernheim, Shleifer, and Summers 1985.

58. Indeed, if the desire for attention and his own personal consumption were all that a parent cared about and the parent's date of death were known in advance, the parent would have no reason not to expend his entire wealth on attention and on personal consumption; the parent would retain no wealth at death because this would represent a waste of assets.

59. See section 102(a) of the Internal Revenue Code, specifying that bequests are excluded from the income of the donee, and section 1014, stating that the tax basis of property acquired by inheritance becomes the market value of the property at the date of the testator's death. Section 1014 means that property that has appreciated in value over the testator's lifetime will be treated as having been acquired by the donee at its appreciated value at the time of the testator's death. Thus, if land purchased for $10,000 by the testator and worth $100,000 at his death is subsequently sold by the donee for $105,000, the latter will owe

8.7 The will: the legal instrument for effecting transfer of property at death.   General reasons have been offered earlier for why an individual may possess property at death and want to pass it on. The will is the instrument through which such an individual can direct the disposition of his property. A *will* is a document specifying the recipients of a person's property upon death.

Several characteristics of wills deserve comment. First, wills often contain conditional provisions. The reason is that certain contingencies (such as the needs of children) may affect the amount the writer of the will would like the donee to receive or the identity of preferred donees.

Second, and related, is that wills are often modified. Changes to wills are made because of the occurrence of contingencies that alter the writer's wishes. Yet one might ask why the occurrence of such contingencies should lead to modification of a will, for the writer could have obviated the need to modify his will by providing for the occurrence of the contingencies in the will. Sometimes, however, this is not feasible because the occurrence of the contingency cannot be verified by a court. For instance, the quality of an elderly parent's relationship with a child (revealed by such behavior as whether the child pays visits to the parent) may be difficult for courts to determine. If so, a provision in a will stating that the child's inheritance should be reduced if the child treats his or her parents poorly would be unworkable. Thus, the parent must change his will in order to alter the allocation to the child. A second reason why a person may modify a will is simply that the writer did not include a contingency in the will because, at the time the will was written, the contingency was unlikely or not even contemplated. (The rationality of not including certain provisions in contracts, of which a will is a special example, is taken up generally in section 4 of Chapter 13.)

Third, writers sometimes want to make wills irrevocable. One reason is that the donee can then rely on receipt of the gift, and therefore it will have greater value to him. For example, a child who expects an inheritance can invest his own funds in a promising business enterprise. The increased value of the gift bequest will inure to the benefit of the writer of the will

---

taxes only on $5,000—the difference between his sale price and his basis of $100,000—not on the gain of $105,000 − $10,000 = $95,000.

owing to his altruism.[60] A second reason for making a will irrevocable is that a writer may fear that he will later become incompetent (but not be so judged by a court) and act against his own best interests.

8.8 Policy in respect to inheritance.   Should society intervene in private decisions to bequeath property? In an important sense, bequeathing property is simply one way of using property. And therefore society should not interfere with bequests for the same general reasons that it is undesirable for society to constrain the use of property. Namely, this tends to reduce individuals' utility directly (a person will derive less utility from property if he wants to bequeath it but is prevented from doing so) and also lowers their incentives to work (a person will not work as hard to accumulate property if he cannot then bequeath it as he pleases).

It might be argued, however, that externalities (see Chapter 5) are relevant to inheritance. One might say that allowing families to retain large amounts of wealth detracts from social cohesion because it allows elites to sustain themselves. If so, the state might find some justification (apart from raising revenue) for imposing taxes on inheritance.[61]

Another externality of concern is that a spouse or dependent child who does not inherit wealth may receive public support (in the form of general welfare payments, education, or health care). A person might reduce or exclude his or her allocation to a spouse or children, depending on public support to take up the slack. This externality might justify a stipulation that some minimum fraction of property be given to spouses and children.

An additional factor that could justify a state-imposed guarantee of a minimum inheritance for spouses and children is that, had the family members made a contract, it would have specified such support. For example, a contract between a wife who does not work and a husband who does

60. See section 2 of Chapter 16 on donative contracts for further discussion.

61. To amplify, the rationale for such taxes cannot be solely to prevent a person from acquiring wealth. Were that the social goal, it would be best and most directly accomplished through a tax on wealth; there would be no need for an inheritance tax per se (and an inheritance tax would not prevent the living from accumulating excessive wealth); this type of argument is emphasized by Tullock 1971. The rationale for an inheritance tax must be that the retention of wealth by *particular* families across generations is deemed a social problem.

might have stated that half of the family's assets would be inherited by her if the husband predeceased her.[62]

The donor's inability to make a sound decision might also be suggested as a rationale for state control of bequests; in the late stages of life, an individual's judgment is often impaired.

It should be noted, however, that legal policies controlling inheritance can be partially circumvented by increases in inter vivos gifts. For example, were a law to require that half of a person's property pass to the person's spouse and children, the person could transfer much of his wealth to an alternative preferred donee during his life. The person would be unlikely to do this with all of his wealth, however: There must be some value to the person of retaining wealth until death, for he would otherwise already have given all of his wealth to the preferred donee.

8.9 The law.   Individuals generally have great freedom to designate to whom their property will pass at death, but most countries stipulate that a decedent's spouse (and sometimes his or her children) receive a minimum share,[63] and restrictions on inter vivos gifts are also frequently imposed to guarantee that these minimum shares will not have been diluted before testators die.[64] Wills may generally be altered whenever the writer desires, unless the writer is found to be incompetent, and the ability of a writer to make a will irrevocable is circumscribed or nonexistent.[65] Property given at death is generally taxed at high rates, but only if it surpasses a threshold level.[66]

---

62. Why a husband and a wife might not make a contract about the disposition of assets at death is another, somewhat problematic, question. It is sometimes suggested that doing so might be inconsistent with the trust and mutuality of confidence bound up in the marital relationship.

63. Almost every American jurisdiction allows the surviving spouse to claim a statutory portion (generally, from one-third to one-half) of the decedent's estate. In Germany and France, the law is similar; in Britain the spouse obtains maintenance and certain other benefits as decided by the court. See, for example, Glendon 1989, 238–251.

64. See, for example, Langbein and Waggoner 1987, 303–317.

65. See Waggoner et al. 1991, 531.

66. At present, the first $1,000,000 of a bequest is excluded from taxation (this amount will rise to $2,000,000 by 2006); *Internal Revenue Code* sec. 2010 (2002). The tax rate then applies, rising from 18 percent to 50 percent; see sec. 2001 (2002).

9. CONTROL OF PROPERTY LONG AFTER DEATH: THE "DEAD HAND"

9.1 Should the power of the "dead hand"—the power to control property for many years after a person's death—be constrained? The issue to be considered here is whether or not it is socially desirable for there to be limits on the power of individuals to exercise control over property for many years after their deaths.[67] For example, should a person be able to prescribe that his wealth accumulate for two centuries and then be given to his descendants, that his land be forever set aside as a memorial to his cat, or that his art collection be kept on permanent display at a named museum?[68]

9.2 Why individuals might or might not want to control property long after death. It should first be said that individuals often would rationally elect not to control property substantially after their deaths. An altruistic donor generally will be best off if he leaves a beneficiary free to use and to dispose of property as the beneficiary sees fit, for in that way the beneficiary can most raise his own welfare, which will inure to the donor's benefit. If I give wealth to a child and the child can use this wealth as the child desires as the future unfolds in its unpredictable ways, the child will be better off, and thus so will I be, anticipating this, given that I care about the child's well-being.

Nevertheless, a donor might want to control the use of property after his death for several major reasons. One is that, although the donor is altruistic, he does not believe that the donee will use property so as to raise his utility; an example is a donee who is too young to make wise decisions for

67. Although the power of a donor to control property after his demise is today often called the power of the dead hand, the term "dead hand" originally referred to the *donee*, notably, to a religious corporation that had been granted land. One speculation for this usage is that religious corporations that held land were early excused from the tenurial obligation to supply knight service, so it was as if there were only dead hands available to provide this form of military assistance. See Simes 1955, 2–3.

68. In these examples, and in general in this section, I will discuss the control of property substantially after a person's death, not merely in the period right after death that is necessary to settle and implement a will providing for the disposition of assets to parties— parties who are then free to use and to sell or transfer the property as they wish.

himself. A second reason is that future events might determine who the preferred donee will be. For instance, the donor might want to give wealth to
a child only if that child eventually has children. Another reason that a person
might wish to control property many years after his death is that he has a
direct desire to do this, that is, the donor derives utility from the knowledge
that the property will be used as he wishes, and not because that will serve
to advance the utility of some other persons who will be alive and about
whom the donor cares. The donor who specifies that land be set aside to
memorialize his cat might fit in this category, and possibly also the donor
who wishes paintings to be displayed in exactly the way he specifies (rather
than where and in the manner that future viewers would prefer).

9.3 General argument favoring dead hand control of property.
Just as it was observed in section 8.8 that bequeathing property is simply
one way of using property, so too is controlling property after one's death
merely a way of using property. And as such, a benchmark for thought is
that society should not interfere with parties' desires to control property
long after their deaths. Otherwise, individuals' utility from property will
be reduced and their incentives to work will be diminished.

9.4 Incorrect arguments against dead hand control of property.
One argument that is often offered in favor of interfering with dead hand
control of property seems problematic. Namely, because the dead cannot
enjoy utility, it would be socially wasteful, a folly, for the dead to control
property, interfere with its use, to the detriment of those who are living.[69]
This argument fails to reflect two points. First, individuals who desire dead
hand control will in fact suffer utility losses when they are alive, assuming
that they anticipate that property will not be used in the way they want
when they are dead. Thus a social policy of ignoring the wishes of the dead
will in fact hurt certain individuals when they are alive. Second, the detriment to the living due to dead hand control of property is not ignored by
a person who wants dead hand control, but rather is taken into at least
implicit account by such a person. For example, if a person sets aside land
as a memorial to his cat, he pays a price for the land (or gives up selling

69. See, for example, the summary of this point of view in Simes and Smith 1956,
10–11, and see also Stoebuck and Whitman 2000, 120.

the land if it already is in his possession), and this price embodies the value of the land to individuals in the future. (The price of any asset impounds all future values.) Thus, the decision of a person to control property after death involves a weighing of the utility of such control against the price, which represents its alternative value to others into the future. Accordingly, the decision of the person seems just as appropriate from a social standpoint as essentially any decision a person makes about consumption,[70] such as whether to purchase a tank of gasoline to run his automobile.[71]

Another argument against dead hand control that is sometimes encountered is that the benefits to the dead of controlling property decline with the passage of time and at some point are outweighed by the interests of the living.[72] This argument, however, is incomplete as stated, for it does not take into account that donors themselves are led to compare their benefits as a function of the period of time over which they exercise dead hand control with the corresponding costs to individuals who will be alive later. In particular, a person will in principle have to pay more for dead hand control the longer he wishes to exercise it. For instance, a person who wishes to rent land to memorialize his cat for only one year after his death will not have to pay much for this. But a person who wishes to rent land for ten years after his death will have to pay much more. Thus, a person will rent land to memorialize his cat for ten years rather than for one year only if the extra benefit he derives therefrom is worth the extra cost (this extra cost reflecting the value to others of the use of the land for the additional nine years). In other words, donors who wish to exercise dead hand control engage in the very type of weighing that the argument at issue suggests is

70. I am here referring to one of the basic conclusions of microeconomic theory, that consumption decisions based on price have a desirable social character, given the underlying distribution of wealth, if markets are competitive and complete. See, for example, Feldman 1987.

71. Indeed, when a person uses gasoline, he denies it to all future generations. Thus, using gasoline is very similar to tying up land forever. Hence, if one regards decisions to use gasoline based on its price to be socially reasonable and good (since people will then use gasoline when its value exceeds its social cost), so too should one regard decisions of persons to tie up land forever to be socially reasonable and good. (The main difference is that land, if tied up, can always be taken back by a future generation, but not so gasoline that is burned. This difference is inessential to the present point, but does have significance, as I will discuss in section 9.6.)

72. See, for example, Ellickson 1986.

socially desirable; hence, more must be said to justify interference with the
decisions that donors make about dead hand control.

9.5 Valid arguments against dead hand control of property.

Despite the foregoing, a number of justifications for interfering with dead
hand control of property can be identified.

One concerns the cost and impracticality of making highly refined arrangements for dead hand control of property, under which control would
be relaxed in various contingencies and at certain times. For example, a
person who stipulates that his paintings should always be shown in a particular way at a named museum might in fact prefer that his paintings be
shown at another museum if the named museum's patronage falls substantially (perhaps because of shifts in population over time) or if new ways of
displaying paintings come into existence that he had not contemplated during his lifetime. Or a person who apparently wants a named parcel of land
permanently set aside as a memorial to his cat might in fact prefer that the
memorial shift to another location if the land becomes very valuable at
some time after a century has passed or if a new and graphic way to memorialize the cat becomes possible (suppose DNA from the cat can be used to
clone it). For individuals to make highly detailed plans for the control of
property after death, however, would often be irrational, because the cost
of making a detailed provision is borne with certainty, whereas the benefit
is discounted by the often extremely small likelihood of the occurrence of
a contingency and perhaps by its remoteness in time. Moreover, many kinds
of future outcomes would not even be contemplated by a person when
making provisions for the control of property (the cat lover might have
made the provisions before DNA was discovered and the possibilities of
cloning were conceived). If, then, the plans that are made for the control
of property after death are not reflective of the true detailed plans that
would have been made if the individuals had the time and ability to consider all possibilities, the state's modification of their plans may sometimes
be justified as an attempt to carry out their true plans.[73]

73. There is, on reflection, no conflict between the point of this paragraph and the
general point, referred to in the previous section, that decisions based on market prices will
lead to socially desirable results. The reconciliation of the two points is that the optimality
of outcomes based on the market is premised on markets being complete. The interpretation

An observation that reinforces this argument for legal intervention in dead hand control is that, of course, the dead cannot be told of difficulties that arise and cannot give permission to alter the terms of their arrangements. Therefore, it is not inconsistent for society to modify or override dead hand arrangements to control use of property but not to intervene generally with use of property during a person's lifetime, when bargaining with a person is possible (if a person now alive is using land as a memorial to his dead cat and the land becomes very valuable, he can be asked and perhaps convinced to sell it).

An additional justification for staying dead hand control of property arises when the specified use of property causes harmful external effects. A classic example (see section 6.1) is a requirement that only individuals of a certain race or religion use property, such as land set aside as a park. The external effect here is that the restriction may increase feelings of separateness in the population at large and generally contribute to social friction. When dead hand control of property generates externalities, state intervention may be warranted.

A third possible justification for restricting the dead hand is inherent inequality in the wealth of the present generation versus that of future generations. By virtue of its priority in time, the present generation owns the whole of the earth and all the things on it. This means that the present generation has a greater ability to control property than is socially desirable, presuming that the measure of social welfare accords substantial weight to future generations.[74] Thus, in order to preserve intergenerational equity, limiting the ability of the present generation to control property after their death may be socially warranted.

---

of complete markets for land is separate markets for the use of land not only at each future time, but also under each future contingency. Were such markets to exist, the person who wants to control land for the use of his cat would make separate purchase decisions about land for the memorial to the cat for each future year and for each possible value the land might have. But such markets do not exist, for essentially the reasons discussed in the text.

74. For example, those alive today might care very little about the well-being of individuals ten generations in the future, but a social welfare measure might accord similar weight to the well-being of individuals ten generations in the future as it does to the well-being of the present generation.

9.6 Why we would *expect* the state to prevent dead hand control of property, independently of the social desirability of such policy.   Quite apart from whether or not there exists sound social justification for the state to prevent dead hand control of property, we would predict that the state will intervene for a simple reason: The generation that is alive always enjoys the power to use property that the dead would have wanted to control and certainly has an interest in doing so. This is especially true when the dead are at least a generation removed from the present generation, which is to say, when the present generation feels few personal bonds to them.

9.7 The law.   The law constrains the power of the dead to control property in a number of ways. First, courts can refuse to enforce conditions in bequests and trusts if they are deemed unreasonable or if they unduly constrain the ability of beneficiaries to sell property. Courts can, under the *cy pres* doctrine, refuse to enforce unreasonable or obsolescent conditions in charitable bequests or trusts, and hold that administrators substitute a related purpose for the original one. Also, courts can refuse to enforce certain types of restrictive covenants when they offend a public interest. Furthermore, according to the so-called rule against perpetuities, donors are barred from making bequests that will not necessarily vest in a donee until long into the future (for instance, a barred condition would be: to my first descendant who is elected to Congress). In effect, the rule against perpetuities prevents a certain kind of dead hand control of property for more than a limited time.[75]

10.   INVOLUNTARY TRANSFER OF PROPERTY: ADVERSE POSSESSION

10.1 Adverse possession defined.   Adverse possession occurs when a person who is not the owner of land takes possession of and uses land continuously, without permission, and openly, for at least a prescribed length of time, such as ten years. The rule of *adverse possession* gives legal title to the

75. On the law just described, see, for example, Stoebuck and Whitman 2000, 118–145, 471.

land to the adverse possessor (subject to certain additional conditions).[76] Thus, the rule effectively authorizes involuntary transfer of property.[77]

The rule will be considered in three contexts: when someone contemplates using land that he knows is not his; when a person contemplates using land that he is not sure is his because boundary lines are uncertain; and when a person is buying land and is not sure of the validity of the seller's title.[78]

10.2 Use of land that a person knows is not his.   In some situations, a person contemplates using land that he knows belongs to someone else. For example, a farmer might consider growing crops on vacant land owned by a large, abutting ranch or by a railroad. In such cases, the question arises whether the rule of adverse possession might be socially desirable because it functions to transfer land from an idle to a productive state.[79] The answer seems to be no. On one hand, idle land sometimes is really serving a useful purpose, as will be noted. On the other hand, a person wishing to use land can rent it or buy it, so that the rule of adverse possession is not necessary to achieve a change in its use. Furthermore, the rule can result in social waste.

To amplify, there are good reasons why an owner of land would want to keep it idle. A rancher may want to keep land in its natural state for animals to graze upon, a developer may wish to leave his land untouched because he is planning to build on it in the future, and an environmentalist owner may desire to maintain land in its pristine condition for the benefit of wildlife. Thus, the idle state of land may in fact be associated with a

76. For a description of the rule, see for example, Stoebuck and Whitman 2000, 853–860. A closely related rule of *prescription* states that a person will acquire not possession of land, but instead rights to use it in certain ways (such as to walk along a path) if the uses have occurred over a stipulated period and meet the other requirements of adverse possession; see, for example, Stoebuck and Whitman 2000, 451–457. Prescription will not be explicitly addressed in this section, but analogous points to those to be made here apply to it.

77. Whereas this rule allows involuntary transfer of land between individuals, another rule allows involuntary transfer of land to the state. This will be discussed in section 2 of Chapter 6.

78. For surveys of economic analysis of adverse possession, see Bouckaert and Depoorter 2000 and Netter 1998.

79. This possibility is frequently mentioned; see, for example, Ballantine 1918, 135, Stoebuck and Whitman 2000, 860, and Cooter and Ulen 2000, 143.

higher value than the state in which an adverse possessor would put the land.

Second, if the owner does not value his idle land as much as other parties do, he can lease the land or sell it. If the owner has not chosen to do this, the likelihood is that the value to him of keeping the land idle is greater than the alternative value of the land to others. Moreover, one assumes that the potential adverse possessor generally knows who the owner is—the adverse possessor usually knows the identity of his neighbors, and if land recording systems or registries exist, the adverse possessor can readily determine ownership—and can fairly easily locate him, so that the adverse possessor can bargain for lease or purchase of the land that he contemplates using. The farmer thinking about growing crops on railroad land can always contact the railroad and see if a mutually satisfactory deal can be made. Hence, it is hardly necessary for society to resort to the rule of adverse possession to foster the transfer of land to productive use; that can be done via the normal routes of lease or sale.

Third, the rule of adverse possession may lead to socially wasteful consequences. The rule may induce owners of land, such as the railroad, to fence their property and monitor it to prevent adverse possession. Also, the rule may induce adverse possessors to invest resources inappropriately (for instance, growing crops that have little economic value) in order to acquire land. This point aside, if adverse possessors proceed to use land and are subsequently discovered and forced to withdraw, their efforts may be largely wasted, and if they succeed, they may interfere with more valuable uses of the land.

Despite the foregoing, the requirements of the rule of adverse possession are such that it will normally be easy for an owner of land to detect incursions: The land must be used continuously for a period measured in years, and the use must be open, not surreptitious. In consequence, the ability of adverse possessors to succeed in taking someone else's land by using it is small and the waste of resources is ordinarily limited.

10.3 Use of land when boundaries are uncertain. A different circumstance in which the rule of adverse possession may apply arises because of uncertainty about boundaries.[80] For example, a person may not know

80. For economic analysis of this issue, see Miceli and Sirmans 1995.

whether the garage he is building will encroach on his neighbor's land because he is unsure of the boundary line. The rule of adverse possession is sometimes suggested to be socially beneficial in this context because it alleviates problems of mistake: A person who turns out to have built on another party's land will not have to alter his structure when that would be socially wasteful. If a person builds a garage that turns out to encroach by six inches on his neighbor's land, it would probably be wasteful for the person to incur a large expense to move the garage off of his neighbor's property. This argument favoring the rule of adverse possession, however, overlooks the possibility that bargaining would result in avoidance of undesirable outcomes. If the garage is more costly to move than the extra six inches of land is worth to the neighbor, the two individuals will often arrive at an agreement under which the garage will not be moved.[81]

Moreover, the argument favoring the rule of adverse possession fails to take into account possible disadvantages regarding investments in land, similar to those mentioned in the previous section. For instance, the rule might encourage individuals to invest wastefully (extend the garage when that serves no real purpose) in order to gain ownership of more land. Therefore, the argument favoring the rule of adverse possession does not have clear appeal.

10.4 Sale of land when seller's title is not clear.   Under the rule of adverse possession, sale of land is often said to be simplified because a buyer need only do the following to assure himself that the seller has good title to land: determine that the seller has himself lived continuously on the land for the period necessary to gain title through adverse possession.[82] If that is so, then even if there were another individual who previously had some claim to the land, that person would no longer have a valid claim; thus the seller would, by application of the rule of adverse possession, have the valid claim. By contrast, were there no rule of adverse possession, a

81. Of course, problems in bargaining might lead to impasse and to the garage being moved. To ameliorate this problem, it is not necessary to accord the encroaching party ownership in land, as under the rule of adverse possession, but rather only to grant the party the right of use for a limited time, such as the normal lifespan of a garage.

82. This point is emphasized by most commentators on adverse possession; see, for example, Ballantine 1918 and Netter 1998.

purchaser would in principle have to check into the infinite past to assure himself that no one other than the seller had good claims. This would be expensive and tend to impede the sale of land.

10.5 Historical origins of the rule of adverse possession. The rule of adverse possession apparently owes its origins to the advantage just discussed in section 10.4, namely, the motive to reduce transactions costs and to ease the settlement of disputes over land ownership.[83] The original act in England, from which the law of adverse possession in Anglo-American law derives, set a particular year (1189, the beginning of the reign of Richard I) as the point from which a person had to use land to obtain title through adverse possession. Eventually, the rule was changed so that a person had to use land for a certain number of years to obtain title through adverse possession. Today, it is doubtful that the rule of adverse possession lowers the costs of land sales because ownership of land is noted in recording systems or in registries.[84]

83. Ballantine 1918, 135, emphasizes that its central rationale is quieting title and correcting errors in conveyancing. The preamble to an early English statute allowing adverse possession is explicit about the statute's purpose, stating that to be "the avoiding of Suits" and the "quieting of Men's Estates." See 21 Jac. chap. 16 (1623). It is also suggested that the feature of Roman law that operated in ways similar to adverse possession, *usucapio,* was intended to cure defects in title and conveyancing; see, for example, Nicholas 1962, 122.

84. See Ballantine 1918 on the history of adverse possession and on the point that with registries and recording systems for land, the rule is not needed to facilitate transactions.

5 ||| CONFLICT AND COOPERATION IN THE USE OF PROPERTY: THE PROBLEM OF EXTERNALITIES

This chapter deals with various issues of conflict and cooperation in relation to the use of property. The plan of the chapter is first to describe how the behavior of a person in using property may influence the welfare of others, then to explain the ideal resolution of such effects, and subsequently to examine their resolution through bargaining and legal rules.

1. NOTION OF EXTERNAL EFFECTS IN THE USE OF PROPERTY

1.1 General definition. One party's action will be said to have an *external effect*—or to create an *externality*[1]—if it influences, or may influence with a probability, the well-being of another person, in comparison to some standard of reference.[2] When I write of external effects here, I shall

---

1. According to Coase 1988, 23, the term "externality" was apparently coined in Samuelson 1958.

2. It may be helpful to state the definition formally. Consider two parties, a potential *generator* G of an external effect, and a potential *recipient* R (victim or beneficiary) of the effect, and a *reference situation* described by a *reference act a* of G and possibly other factors pertaining to him and to R. In the reference situation, R will have a reference level of expected utility $ER(a)$. Another act a' of G is said to have an *external effect* on R, relative to the reference situation, if $ER(a')$ is unequal to $ER(a)$.

be referring in the main to those associated with property rights, that is, to external effects due to actions that are allowed given a person's property rights, where the effects are experienced by other individuals given their own property rights.[3]

Externalities vary along a variety of dimensions. They may be beneficial for, or detrimental to, the affected party. They may occur contemporaneously with actions taken or result in the future; and they may arise only under certain contingencies. Moreover, they may affect one, several, or many parties. Let us consider several classic examples of externalities.

(a) *Nuisance.* When a person disturbs his neighbors by making noise, producing foul odors, allowing a misbehaving pet to roam free, and the like, he is commonly said to be creating a nuisance. This species of external effect is detrimental, often contemporaneous (noise is immediately disturbing), and often affects a relatively small number of individuals.

(b) *Pollution.* When a firm discharges a substance into a body of water or into the air, it reduces the utility of others who use the water or breathe the air. This external effect is detrimental, may occur contemporaneously or in the future, and frequently involves many victims.

(c) *Dangerous, risk-creating behavior.* A party may act in a way that does not cause harm for sure but only in particular circumstances. Thus a firm may let sludge accumulate in a retaining area and there may be a chance—if there is an earthquake, for instance—that the material will burst forth and do harm to neighboring property. Dangerous, risk-producing behavior is behavior that causes damage under certain contingencies.

(d) *Use of a common resource.* Access to a resource such as pasture, a lake, or a reservoir of oil may sometimes be enjoyed by many individuals. In such cases, one person's use of the resource may harm others, usually by depleting or causing damage to the resource. This effect is detrimental to others, sometimes contemporaneous and sometimes not, and affects multiple parties.

(e) *Salutary behavior.* A person's actions may occasionally help not only him but others as well, as when an apiarist's bees help to pollinate a nearby

3. I shall exclude from consideration externalities associated with transactions in markets, for example, the harm a person causes other buyers of a commodity if he increases its price through his purchases. On the subject of such *pecuniary* externalities, see, for example, Laffont 1987a.

farmer's fruit trees, when one person's spraying to kill mosquitoes also rids his neighbors of the pests, or when a person beautifies his land to the advantage of others as well. These externalities are beneficial and may affect several or multiple parties.

(f) *Treatment of rental property.* When a person rents farmland, he may reduce its usefulness by abusing it, letting it erode, and so forth; he may also increase its future value by fertilization or by rotation of crops. When a person rents a dwelling or a movable good, such as an automobile, again he can affect the future utility of the property by the care that he exercises in using it and maintaining it. In these cases, the external effect is a future one, can be detrimental or beneficial, and usually affects one or a small number of parties.

1.2 Comments.   (a) For there to be an external effect when a person takes a particular action, it must be the case that a different party possesses relevant property rights so as to be affected. Thus, making noise late at night creates a nuisance only if there are other individuals who have rights in nearby land. If I mistreat an automobile that I will own until it is scrapped, there will be no external effect on future holders of rights to my automobile since there will be no future holders; all effects will be internal, on me.

(b) If the standard of reference mentioned in the definition of external effect changes, this may influence whether or not an act has an external effect and its description. For instance, if in the reference situation I am quiet, then my act of making noise would be said to create a detrimental external effect, whereas if in the reference situation I am noisy, then my being noisy would not be said to create an external effect, and if I keep quiet, this act would be described as having a beneficial external effect.

(c) Whether we tend to call an externality harmful or beneficial depends on what we are likely to assume, if only implicitly, about the standard of reference. We are inclined to say that building a compost heap that gives off foul odors is harmful because we are likely to assume that the standard of reference is that individuals do not engage in composting and that all enjoy clean air. And we are likely to say that a person's having bees is beneficial because the standard of reference is that people do not keep bees.

(d) An externality need not be associated with a physical effect. If, for instance, I erect an unsightly building, this may easily cause displeasure to neighbors despite the absence of any real change in their property. Indeed, it could be that even though others see no indication of it, their mere knowledge that I am doing something on my property (practicing a disfavored religion) will affect their well-being.

2. SOCIALLY OPTIMAL RESOLUTION OF EXTERNAL EFFECTS

2.1 In general. Behavior that maximizes social welfare will reflect possible external effects associated with the use of property. Specifically, it will be socially desirable for individuals to engage less often in acts that cause detrimental external effects than is in their immediate self-interest, and to engage more often in acts that engender beneficial external benefits than is in their self-interest.

2.2 Socially optimal resolution of externalities in a simple model. Consider a model in which the social goal is to maximize the sum of parties' utilities. Then it is optimal for an act to be committed if and only if its utility to the actor together with its external effect on the utility of others is, on net, positive.

In a simple version of this model, one party—the potential injurer— can prevent harm to a second party—the potential victim—if the former takes a precaution, which will involve a cost and therefore lower his utility. The precaution might be installing a smoke arrestor or putting a compost heap in a location where it will not create odors bothersome to others. In this model, it is desirable for the injurer to take the precaution if and only if its cost is less than the harm that would be prevented, for that will minimize losses to the two parties (or equivalently, maximize the sum of their utilities). Thus, if a smoke arrestor costs 30 to install and would prevent harm of 50, it would be optimal to install.

2.3 Comment on the reciprocal nature of external effects. As was mentioned in section 1.2(a), externalities are reciprocal in that a party must be present to be the victim (or the beneficiary) of an external effect; otherwise there will be no external effect.[4] This feature of external effects can readily be incorporated into the simple model just considered. For example, in the illustration of the smoke arrestor, suppose that the victim has the option to move to another location where he would be free from harm, but moving would involve a cost of 10. Then it would be optimal for the victim to move to this other location: Because there would then be no reason for the injurer to take the precaution to avoid causing harm, he could save 30, whereas the victim would bear a cost of only 10. This example should illustrate that the reciprocal nature of externalities can readily be analyzed and does not pose any conceptual difficulties.[5]

2.4 Comment on the conditional nature of the problem of the socially optimal resolution of external effects.   As it is usually expressed, the problem of optimally resolving externalities is not the same as the complete problem of maximization of social welfare, because the externality problem usually involves implicit assumptions about the assignment of property rights. In the externality problem involving pollution, for example, we took as given that the victim would suffer harm from smoke and asked whether installing the smoke arrestor would raise social welfare. But a complete solution to the social welfare maximization problem would not presume that the existing assignment of property rights is optimal. Instead, the complete solution would allow, among other elements, for a reassignment of property rights when that would be optimal. In the example just stated in section 2.3, this might involve the transfer of the victim to another location; as noted, that might lead to an increase in social welfare because it would mean that the injurer would not have to take a precaution. More generally, the positions of parties who are affected by external effects are determined by assumptions pertaining to a whole array of property rights; thus, the optimal resolution of externality problems, as usually phrased, must be regarded as a problem of partial social welfare maximization.

2.5 Examples of optimal resolution of externalities.   With the definition of optimality of section 2.2 in mind, let us consider the general

---

4. The reciprocal nature of externalities was emphasized by Coase 1960, 2, 12–13.

5. Nevertheless, it now seems to be part of legal academic folklore that the reciprocal aspect of externalities creates a fundamental theoretical challenge.

nature of socially optimal arrangements regarding externalities in the examples noted in section 1.1.

(a) *Nuisance, pollution, and dangerous behavior.* An action to ameliorate or eliminate a nuisance will be socially desirable when the cost of the action is less than the additional harm that would otherwise be caused. Thus, it will be socially advantageous for a factory to eliminate noxious odors if the cost of so doing—associated with a change in the production process or with the purchase of a device to remove the odors—is less than the harm to the people living nearby. And similarly with a pollutant, or with some dangerous act.

One aspect of optimal behavior may involve not the amelioration or elimination of the harm through the exercise of some precaution, but rather reduction or cessation of the activity that generates it. It may be optimal for a factory not to operate, for example, if it is very expensive to reduce the harm done and the benefit from its operations is small. Likewise, an aspect of optimal behavior may involve the potential victim of harm moving to another location, where he would not be exposed to harm. Similarly, optimal behavior may involve the victim taking steps to reduce harms, such as installing air filters or noise proofing.

(b) *Salutary behavior.* An act with beneficial consequences for another will be socially optimal when its cost, if any, is lower than its value to the person undertaking it and to others beneficially affected. Thus, spraying mosquitoes will be optimal when its cost is less than the sum of the benefits to the person spraying and to his neighbors.

(c) *Use of a common resource.* The use of a common resource by an individual will be socially desirable when and only when the benefits to him exceed the harm done to others. Thus, it will be socially desirable for a person to graze his animals in common areas when and only when the animals yield a benefit to him exceeding the harm they cause by denying other animals pasturage, by contributing to erosion, and so forth. Likewise, it will be socially desirable for a person to catch fish or to trap animals when and only when their value to him outweighs any reduction in the value of the future stock resulting from loss of fish or animals that would have reproduced—notably, if their numbers are too rapidly reduced, there will not be sufficient reproduction to maintain the population. Similarly, it will be optimal for a person to withdraw oil from a pool when and only when its value to him exceeds any increase in future costs of extraction.

(When oil is obtained, it may cause underlying gas and water pressure to fall, increasing the costs of future extraction because, for instance, water may have to be pumped underground to force up remaining oil.)[6]

(d) *Treatment of rental property.* Treatment of rental property will be optimal if and only if the treatment benefits the renter more than it harms the owner in the future. Thus, it will probably not be optimal for a renter to make major modifications in an apartment if they would impose a large cost on future users. Suppose, for instance, that the renter wants to remove an interior wall to make one large room from two smaller rooms, but that future users would be likely to want the two smaller rooms. It may be optimal for a person who is renting an apartment to modify it in minor ways, however, such as by hanging pictures on the walls, since these may benefit the renter by more than they will harm the owner in the future. (The owner will probably have to repaint in any case, and at that time it would be cheap for him to do any necessary replastering to repair damage from picture hanging.) It may also be optimal for certain things to be done during the rental period if they benefit the owner in the future more than they harm the renter. Many types of maintenance (fixing a slow leak that will cause damage only over time) have this character.

3. RESOLUTION OF EXTERNALITIES THROUGH FRICTIONLESS BARGAINING

In this section, I will briefly discuss the resolution of external effects through bargaining among the involved parties, assuming that bargaining is a cost-less and invariably successful process. In following sections, however, I will examine costs of bargaining and obstacles to it, and then the resolution of external effects through the use of legal rules.

3.1 The assumption of frictionless bargaining: that bargains are made whenever a mutually beneficial agreement exists. Our assumption here is that bargaining will take place and that a mutually beneficial

---

6. The point of this paragraph is closely related to that made in section 1.3 of Chapter 4 on the excessive incentives to search under the finders-keepers rule when there are multiple parties who might look for unowned property.

agreement about externalities will be concluded whenever such an agreement exists in principle. In the situation involving the smoke arrestor, the parties will each be better off if the injurer agrees to take the precaution at a cost of 30 in exchange for payment of, say, 35 by the victim; for then the injurer's utility will be augmented by 5 and the victim's utility will be raised by 15 because he will avoid harm of 50. Hence, our assumption is that such an agreement will be made. (Note also that if the victim's harm from the smoke would be only 25, there would be no mutually beneficial agreement possible and the injurer would not take the precaution.)[7]

The statement that a mutually beneficial agreement will be made whenever one exists—given the assumption that nothing will prevent parties from reaching this kind of agreement—is one version of the *Coase Theorem,* and is an immediate tautology.[8]

3.2 Mutually beneficial agreements exist whenever the sum of parties' utilities can be raised.   In the case of the smoke arrestor, a mutually beneficial agreement exists to install the arrestor whenever that change would raise the sum of the parties' utilities. That such mutually beneficial agreements generally exist between the generator of an externality and the affected party whenever the agreements would raise the sum of their utilities can be explained as follows. Figuratively, when a change raises the sum of the two parties' utilities, it raises the size of the pie available to be shared by them. And if the size of the pie can be increased, plainly there must exist some way of dividing it that will make each of the parties better off than he would have been with only his slice of the original, smaller pie.

---

7. To see that there is no mutually beneficial change possible in this case, observe that for the injurer to be willing to take the precaution, he must be paid at least 30 by the victim. But the victim would be willing to pay at most 25 to be free from harm.

8. This version of the theorem is sometimes expressed by saying that a mutually beneficial outcome will be achieved in the absence of *transaction costs,* where the latter are interpreted to be any hindrances to bargaining—whether literally costs of bargaining, or instead other obstacles, notably, asymmetries of information between bargaining parties (to be discussed later). The version of the Coase Theorem under discussion is sometimes called the *efficiency* version because it says that the outcome will be (Pareto) efficient, a synonym for mutually beneficial. Another version of the Coase Theorem, the *invariance* version, will be discussed later, in section 6. See Coase 1960 and De Meza 1998.

That is, there must exist some agreement between the generator of the externality and the affected party under which each is made better off.[9]

3.3 Social welfare maximization and frictionless bargaining.

It follows from the preceding discussion that the sum of utilities measure of social welfare will be maximized through frictionless bargaining despite the presence of externalities. Specifically, if the sum of their utilities is not maximized when parties act in their self-interest, then there exist mutually beneficial agreements calling for changes that maximize the sum of their utilities, and these agreements will be concluded through frictionless bargaining.

But a qualification should be made: Frictionless bargaining does not necessarily lead to maximization of social welfare if wealth is not distributed in a socially desirable way. Suppose, for example, that a party does not possess wealth sufficient to pay for a socially desirable change in another party's behavior. If the wealth of the victim of smoke is less than 30, he will not be able to pay the injurer enough to induce him to install the smoke arrestor even though this is socially desirable.[10] (Note here that the outcome in which the victim suffers from the smoke is not dominated by a mutually beneficial arrangement, for there is no feasible arrangement that is better in the eyes of both parties than the existing one; the victim's lack of wealth makes the outcome in which he pays the injurer enough to purchase the smoke arrestor infeasible.) Even if bargaining does not result in

---

9. The point can be expressed algebraically as follows. Let x_1 and y_1 be the levels of utility of the generator of the externality and the other party, respectively, in an initial situation and x_2 and y_2 be their levels of utility in a second situation with a higher sum of utilities, that is, $x_2 + y_2 > x_1 + y_1$. Assume, however, that the generator would be better off in the initial situation than in the second in the absence of an agreement, in other words, $x_1 > x_2$. (Otherwise, the first party would have made the change, whereas our supposition is that the change has not been made.) Then a mutually beneficial agreement can clearly be constructed: If the generator is compensated for making the change by at least $x_1 - x_2$ he will be willing to make an agreement. The other party gains $y_2 - y_1$ in the second situation, and this exceeds $x_1 - x_2$ (for $x_2 + y_2 > x_1 + y_1$); hence he will be willing to pay enough to the generator to induce him to agree to the change.

10. This point does not conflict with the demonstration of the previous note. It was shown there that the second party would be willing to make a payment sufficient to induce the first to alter the situation, but it was implicitly assumed that the second party had the wealth sufficient to do that.

the social welfare optimum, however, bargaining can only improve social welfare by raising the well-being of the parties involved in bargaining (assuming that all parties affected by the externality participate in the bargain and understand its nature).

3.4 Markets and the resolution of externalities.   We have been discussing so far how external effects may be mitigated through bargaining between a single generator of an external effect and potentially affected parties, such as neighbors. A related possibility is the resolution of external effects through the bargains that are effectively made between unrelated parties when a competitive market in an externality arises. For instance, instead of an apiarist bargaining with a particular neighboring farmer about whether he will release his bees into that farmer's orchard to foster pollination, we can envision the apiarist transacting in a market and transporting bees to any farmer who purchases bee services.

Where such a market exists, all mutually beneficial changes will automatically come about, owing to the standard argument concerning behavior in the presence of markets. To illustrate, suppose that the price for bee services is 5. Then any apiarist who can supply bee services at a cost less than 5 will do so, and any farmer who places a greater value than 5 on bee services will purchase them; this means that there is no unexhausted opportunity for mutually beneficial trade, namely, trade between an apiarist who can supply bee services at a cost of less than 5 and a farmer who values them more highly than 5.[11]

3.5 Actual resolution of externalities through bargaining.   It is a commonplace that parties often make bargains in order to resolve nuisances or other externalities. For example, a person might pay his neighbor to plant a screen of bushes around an unsightly garbage area so that the person can enjoy a better view (or he might simply ask his neighbor to do so, implicitly in return for his acting in similar ways vis-à-vis his neighbor in the future); a restaurant might pay nearby residents for the right to remain open late, when the residents have the right to insist that it be closed; a

---

11. On the general notion that the establishment of markets in certain goods or services, here bee services, can cure externality problems see, for example, Arrow 1969 and Laffont 1987a.

person might sell a part of his land with a restriction that prevents a harmful use (such as a business use); a group of individuals using a common resource (such as a grazing area) might agree to preserve it (not overgraze it).[12] Additionally, some experimental evidence suggests that, at least when the number of parties is small, individuals will often conclude mutually beneficial agreements to settle externality problems.[13] It is also evident that when parties are in an ongoing contractual relationship, they will frequently include terms in their contracts to resolve externalities. Thus, when a person rents land, real estate, or equipment, the contracts will generally specify that he cannot make major modifications to them or cause them to deteriorate (which would, as discussed, harm owners). Organized markets that resolve externalities are unusual (for reasons to be explained in section 4.5), but they do exist, and one well-known example concerns bees.[14]

4. WHY BARGAINING MAY NOT OCCUR AND, IF IT DOES, WHY IT MAY FAIL TO RESULT IN MUTUALLY BENEFICIAL AGREEMENTS

It is evident from experience that (a) bargaining does not always occur when a mutually beneficial agreement exists, and that (b) even when bargaining does occur, it may not be successful. Why this should be so is addressed in the present section.

4.1 Factors explaining why bargaining may not occur when mutually beneficial agreements exist.   At the most general level, the explanation for why bargaining may not occur (as opposed to occur but then not succeed) when mutually beneficial agreements exist is that the costs of bargaining—including the costs of coming together and the time and effort devoted to the bargaining process itself—outweigh the expected benefits.

---

12. On the general subject of arrangements to ameliorate externalities made by parties using a common resource, see Libecap 1989 and Ostrom 2000.

13. See, for example, Hoffman and Spitzer 1982, and Croson and Johnston 2000.

14. This highly developed market is characterized by farmers paying apiarists for rental of bees during the pollination season, and, after that season, by apiarists paying farmers for use of their land because bees' consumption of nectar raises honey production; see Cheung 1973. See also section 5.2 on the market in rights to pollute.

We can list particular factors bearing on the occurrence or lack of occurrence of bargaining.

(a) *Proximity of parties.* If the concerned parties are not physically proximate, bargaining may be difficult to arrange. For example, a person may be at the point of deciding whether to erect a fence, which his neighbor might find objectionable, but his neighbor may be away, making it impractical for him to discuss an alternative, possibly superior agreement (such as sharing the higher cost of planting a screen of trees instead of erecting a fence).

(b) *Number of parties.* If the number of involved parties is large, then their ability to all come together for the purpose of bargaining may be small, for difficulties of coordination tend to rise with the number of parties. In addition, the motivation of parties to bargain may diminish as their number increases. If, for example, each person in a neighborhood believes that he can depend on others to engage in bargaining for an agreement that will benefit him, such as for a factory to stop blowing its whistle early in the morning, then no one, or too few, will participate in bargaining with the factory to obtain an agreement. This problem of free-riding on others' efforts may be acute if the benefits that would be gained from bargaining are individually small.

(c) *Lack of knowledge of external effects.* Clearly, if a person who would suffer a loss or experience a benefit does not have prior knowledge of this, he will be unlikely to engage in bargaining. If I live near a factory and do not know that I am at risk of developing cancer from its discharges, then I will hardly bargain for a change in its behavior.

(d) *Probability of bargaining failure.* If a party believes that there is a substantial chance that bargaining will not lead to a successful outcome, then this will tend to dissuade him from engaging in bargaining at the outset. (As will be explained in the next section, if a party is imperfectly informed about the other side's costs or benefits, or if the other side has poor information about the first party's costs or benefits, the chances of failure to reach agreement in bargaining rise.)

4.2 Examples. Several contexts in which external effects exist may be reviewed in the light of the previously mentioned factors to see whether they help to explain why bargaining does or does not usually occur.

(a) *Accidents between strangers.* Bargaining is unlikely to help ameliorate the risk of the typical type of accident between strangers, such as that involving drivers of automobiles. Indeed, the very notion of bargaining between possible injurers and possible victims in such contexts seems fanciful, and on reflection it is evident why. The potentially involved parties, being strangers, are typically not in a sufficiently proximate relationship to bargain with each other about their behavior. Moreover, the benefit from bargaining between particular parties would be small, because of the remote likelihood that this or that pair of strangers would be involved in an accident.

(b) *Pollution caused by firms.* Here, we may imagine quite readily some situations in which bargaining would be likely to occur and others in which it would not be. Bargaining might well occur in situations where the number of people affected by pollution is small, the harm each sustains is substantial, and they are well aware of it. Bargaining would tend not to occur, however, if the pollution affects many individuals but each by only a small amount, or, apart from this, if the victims do not recognize the source of the pollution or even that they are suffering from it.

(c) *Nuisance between neighbors.* In this type of case bargaining would often occur. If my neighbor owns a dog that chews up my flower garden, then there will be no obstacle to bargaining posed by lack of proximity; I should not ordinarily find it difficult to get together with my neighbor. Also, we may well both know what the problem is. Hence, if a mutually beneficial agreement is feasible (because, for example, it is evident that my neighbor could fairly easily restrain his dog or teach it not to chew up my flowers), bargaining might occur (but setting aside the effect that an argument or emotionalism might have on the willingness of neighbors to negotiate about such a nuisance).

(d) *Rental agreement.* When parties have come together to bargain over rental, the marginal cost to them of bargaining over a potential externality problem will typically be small, so that, as remarked earlier, they will tend to include terms in rental agreements to resolve the problem. When a person rents a room in someone's home, for instance, we would often expect there to be bargaining about noise and other possible disturbances during the rental period and terms governing them in the rental contract.

4.3 Even if bargaining occurs and a mutually beneficial agreement exists, it may not be reached due to asymmetry of information. Suppose that bargaining does occur, that the bargaining process is not costly, and that a mutually beneficial agreement exists. Will such an agreement come to pass? We know that in fact success is not guaranteed, and as economists emphasize, the theoretical explanation involves asymmetric information between parties that leads to miscalculations in bargaining and failure to agree.

> *Example 1.* Let us return to the situation involving the smoke arrestor that would cost the injurer 30 but would eliminate smoke and thus harm of 50. Here, as discussed, a mutually beneficial agreement exists: If the victim pays the injurer any amount between 30 and 50 for him to install the arrestor, the victim and the injurer will each be made better off.
>
> Consider a simple bargaining process under which one of the parties, the victim for concreteness, makes a single, take-it-or-leave-it offer to the injurer. Assume first that the victim has perfect information about the cost to the injurer of the arrestor. Then the victim knows that if he offers any amount over 30, the injurer will accept this. Hence, there will definitely be an agreement; the victim will offer an amount just over 30 (such as 31) and the injurer will rationally accept. This illustrates that where one side's information about the other side is perfect, there will tend to be an agreement when a mutually beneficial agreement exists.
>
> Now assume instead that the victim does not know for sure the cost to the injurer of the smoke arrestor. Specifically, suppose that the victim thinks that there are two possibilities: The cost of the arrestor might be 20, with probability 80 percent, and it might be 30, with probability 20 percent. Then if the victim offers just over 20, he believes that his offer will be accepted with probability 80 percent and that his offer will be rejected with probability 20 percent—in which case he will suffer harm of 50. Hence, his expected losses will be approximately 80% × 20 + 20% × 50 or 26. If he offers just over 30, it is true that his offer will be accepted for sure, but his costs will be about 30, exceeding 26. His best offer is therefore just over 20, and there will be no bargain, because in fact we are supposing that the cost of the precaution to the injurer is 30.[15]

Thus, we see that, due to lack of precise knowledge of the other side's situation, a person in bargaining may rationally offer an amount that he

15. If there were a population of injurers, 80 percent of whom faced costs of 20 for smoke arrestors and 20 percent of whom faced costs of 30, then 20 percent of the time there would be no bargain, even though in all cases a mutually beneficial bargain exists.

is aware might be refused, in order to gain the best for himself in an expected sense.

Imperfection of information may concern not only costs of precautions, as in Example 1, but also the magnitude of externalities and the costs of bargaining itself. Such costs should not be overlooked as a source of bargaining failure. If, for instance, one side mistakenly thinks that the other side's cost of bargaining is low and that he will continue for another round, the first side may not make a sufficiently good offer before the second side withdraws. More generally, virtually any kind of asymmetry of information can produce a probability of failure to agree even when mutually beneficial agreements exist.

4.4 Evidence that parties who bargain may fail to reach mutually beneficial outcomes.   Ample evidence exists of the possibility that parties who bargain may not succeed in reaching a mutually beneficial agreement. There are many instances of nuisance where remedial action could have been taken at a lesser cost than the harm yet where the bargaining process broke down.[16] More broadly, the fact that parties often go to trial rather than settle, that employees strike rather than settle, that wars are fought after breakdowns in negotiations, all bespeak parties' failure to agree to mutually beneficial outcomes.[17]

4.5 Comment on the unlikelihood of markets for the resolution of externalities.   It was mentioned in section 3.4 that externalities might be resolved through market transactions rather than through bargaining between parties. Why in theory are market resolutions of externality problems unlikely? (They are unusual in fact, as I noted.)

A precondition for a market to exist is that each seller be able to transact with whichever buyer he chooses. That happens to be possible with respect to the pollination services of bees; a particular apiarist can provide his bees' services to the farmer he selects by transporting his bees to that farmer's land. For many external effects, however, a seller cannot transact with any buyer whom he chooses—he can transact only with a particular buyer—

16. For instance, W. Farnsworth 1999 finds no cases of bargaining in a study of nuisance disputes.

17. See the survey Kennan and Wilson 1993 and the references cited therein.

and a market therefore cannot occur. For example, if I landscape my yard, I will benefit only my close-by neighbors (and myself); I cannot transport the vision of my yard to any other buyer who desires beautified surroundings (in contrast to the apiarist who can transport his bees to any farmer who wants them). Likewise, if I make noise or if I maintain a compost heap, this will cause a nuisance only for my neighbors, not for a distant person who would wish to sell me the right to be the victim of a nuisance. In such cases, therefore, the only way that voluntary resolution of externalities can come about is through bargaining between just the two, or the small number of, parties who are effectively stuck with each other.[18]

Additionally, for some external effects there is another reason why a market may not be possible to establish. Notably, some externalities affect many parties simultaneously, as with general air pollution: When a factory spews smoke into the atmosphere, it harms the population in the area generally. Here there cannot be a market in which one individual victim sells rights to allow his property to be polluted and another individual does not. (Although there cannot be a market in which victims independently sell rights allowing themselves to be polluted, the state can decide to allow pollution and create a market in which polluters purchase rights to pollute. See section 5.2.)

5. RESOLUTION OF EXTERNAL EFFECTS THROUGH LEGAL RULES IN THE ABSENCE OF SUCCESSFUL BARGAINING

Assume for simplicity in this section that parties do not bargain, or do not bargain successfully, because of the various obstacles discussed earlier.

---

18. Even if the preconditions for a market to exist hold—individual generators of an externality can purchase rights to cause harm from individual victims (or sell their services to individual beneficiaries)—there may remain a problem with existence of competitive equilibrium. As Starrett 1972 emphasizes, if, for example, the price of the right to pollute is positive, a potential victim would have an incentive to sell an extraordinary, potentially infinite, number of these rights to polluters—for he can then always move away from his property and become rich through his sale of rights. This means that at any positive price, an infinite number of rights to pollute would be offered, preventing the market for rights from coming into equilibrium.

Instead, parties act in a self-interested way and, other things being equal, do not take into account how their actions influence others.[19] Legal rules, however, can alter their behavior in ways desirable to those affected.[20]

5.1 Types of legal rules for controlling externalities.   There are a variety of legal rules that can be used to control external effects, an important group of which are now described.

Under direct *regulation,* the state constrains the set of acts that would otherwise be permissible to commit given one's property rights, so as to optimally resolve an external effect. For instance, a factory may be required to use a smoke arrestor to prevent pollution, a fisherman may be required to limit his catch to alleviate depletion of the fishery, or a person may be prevented by a zoning ordinance from opening a business establishment in a residential area in order to preserve its ambience.

Closely related to regulation is the *assignment of property rights and their protection at the request of parties who hold the rights.* If a person possesses the right to clean air, for example, he can prevent a firm from continuing its polluting operations by asking the state to intervene.[21] Intervention is often accomplished through the complaining party's obtaining an *injunction* against the injurer; the police powers of the state then are brought to bear to enforce the injunction. Unlike the situation under regulation, where a polluter would be required not to pollute, under victims' property rights in clean air, it is up to the discretion of the potential victim of pollution whether to prevent the polluter from polluting (and the victim might allow the injurer to pollute if he were paid enough—but we are ignoring bargaining in this section).

Society can also make use of financial incentives to reduce harmful externalities. Under a *liability rule,* parties who suffer harm can bring suit against injurers and obtain compensation for their losses, motivating injurers to avoid causing harm. As I will discuss in Part Two, there are two

19. Here and later I will emphasize harmful external effects for simplicity; for the most part, the case of beneficial external effects is analogous.

20. I do not consider how informal social sanctions, such as reputational harm, may affect parties' behavior. For a notable treatment of this subject, see Ellickson 1991. See also the discussion of morality in Chapter 26.

21. Under a legal rule that we are not considering, the person can have the state prevent the pollution but would have to pay the firm for the decline in profits it thereby suffered.

major forms of liability: strict liability, under which the injurer must pay the victim even if the injurer was not at fault; and the negligence rule, under which the injurer is required to pay only if he was at fault. In terms of our simple model, an injurer is said to be at fault, to have acted undesirably, if the magnitude of the harm exceeds the benefit from the act or the cost of eliminating the harm.[22]

Another financial incentive to reduce harm is the *corrective tax*.[23] Under it, a party makes a payment to the state equal to the expected harm he causes, as when a firm pays for the expected harm due to its discharge of a pollutant into a lake. Because a corrective tax is envisioned to reflect anticipated harm (the harm the pollution is expected to do), it is different from strict liability, which is liability for harm actually done. Also, the corrective tax is paid to the state, whereas liability payments are made to victims.

An additional type of financial incentive is a *subsidy,* an amount paid by the state to a party equal to the reduction in expected harm from some benchmark level that the party accomplishes.

5.2 Comparison of rules.   Let me now sketch the comparison of the foregoing legal rules for controlling externalities, focusing on a list of factors of possible relevance.

(a) *Information of the state.* If the state has complete information about acts, that is, if it knows the injurer's benefit and the victim's harm, then each of the rules leads to optimality. To amplify in terms of the example of pollution, suppose that the state can ascertain whether the cost of the smoke arrestor is less than the harm from pollution and thus can determine whether it is best to prevent pollution. If the state decides that pollution should be prevented, the state can accomplish its purpose by regulation: It can forbid pollution. The state can also achieve optimality by giving the property right to clean air to the victim. The state can also employ strict

---

22. Corresponding to strict liability and the negligence rule are two types of *fines* paid to the state, a fine equal to harm paid whenever harm is done, or a fine equal to harm paid only when harm is done and the benefit was less than the harm. I omit consideration of such fines here.

23. Pigou 1912 first emphasized the utility of taxes for controlling external effects, and such taxes are sometimes called Pigouvian taxes.

liability. This will lead the injurer not to cause harm because he would have to pay for it, and by hypothesis the harm would exceed the prevention cost. Likewise, under the negligence rule, the injurer would have to pay for the harm and would thus not pollute. Similarly, under the corrective tax he would not pollute. Under a subsidy, the injurer would not pollute because he would receive a payment equal to the harm for refraining, and this exceeds the prevention cost.

If the state does not have complete information, however, it cannot determine with certainty whether or not an action such as polluting should take place. Hence, the state cannot necessarily achieve optimality through regulation, assignment of property rights, or the negligence rule—for under these approaches the state needs to know which action is optimal. For instance, under regulation, if the harm from pollution would be 100 and the state does not know whether the cost of an arrestor is 75 or 150, it does not know whether or not to require the arrestor.

Yet as long as the state has information about the magnitude of harm, it can still achieve optimality under strict liability, the corrective tax, and the subsidy. Because under strict liability or the tax it is the injurer who compares the cost of installing the arrestor to liability or to the tax for harm, and the injurer naturally knows the cost of the arrestor, then the injurer will cause pollution if and only if the cost of the arrestor exceeds the harm, which is optimal. The injurer for whom the cost of the arrestor is 75 will install it in order to avoid paying 100, and the injurer for whom the cost of the arrestor is 150 will not install it; in both cases the optimal result will occur. Essentially the same is true under the under the subsidy because the injurer will obtain a reward of 100 if he does not cause harm. The virtue of the strict liability, the corrective tax, and the subsidy is that they harness the information that potential injurers have about the costs of reducing harm, or the benefits they would obtain from acting, by making them compare these costs or benefits to the magnitude of harm.[24]

---

24. The argument given here assumed that the state knows the magnitude of the harm. It can be shown, however, that the argument also applies even if the state does not know the magnitude of harm: If the state bases liability, the corrective tax, or the subsidy on *expected* harm, then on average the outcome will be superior to that under the other rules, namely, regulation, assignment of property rights, or the negligence rule. See Kaplow and Shavell 1996b, 2002c.

Hence, we have explained why, when the state's information about the cost of reducing harm is imperfect, strict liability, corrective taxes, or subsidies have an advantage over regulation, property rights assignment, or the negligence rule.[25]

To illustrate this conclusion, let us consider why a scheme of *marketable pollution rights*[26] is inferior to corrective pollution taxes when the government's information about pollution control costs is imperfect. Under a marketable pollution rights regime, a firm must surrender a pollution right to the government for each unit of pollution it generates. The government initially issues rights to firms (perhaps on the basis of a firm's size). The total quantity of rights issued corresponds to the total amount of pollution the government decides is desirable, and a particular firm can either use the rights it is issued or sell rights to other firms in a market for the rights. There is an advantage of this scheme over conventional regulation of the amount of pollution each particular firm is permitted to generate: Firms that find it relatively cheap to prevent pollution tend to do so and thus have rights left over that they sell, whereas firms that find it expensive to prevent pollution need more rights than they are allocated and tend to purchase rights in order to pollute. As a result, the induced distribution of prevention effort and of pollution among firms tends to be socially desirable. But the total quantity of pollution is fixed by government, and in setting this quantity, the government must use its imperfect estimate of pollution control costs; in general, therefore, the total quantity of pollution

25. Although essentially this point is frequently mentioned by economists, especially in relation to regulation versus corrective taxes, it was apparently controverted in Weitzman 1974. Weitzman suggested that regulation, such as a required limit on the amount of pollution, might be superior to a corrective tax. His argument is essentially that expected harm might increase greatly if the quantity of pollution surpassed some threshold level. If a tax per unit were employed and the state chose the wrong rate, firms might generate enough pollution to exceed the threshold, whereas this danger can be averted by means of direct quantity regulation. Weitzman's argument, however, depends on the assumption that the corrective tax is a simple *constant* per unit tax. If the tax is equal to the expected harm, then the tax rate could increase with quantity if harm were thought to have that character. Consequently, it can readily be shown that the corrective tax is, as claimed in the previous note, superior to quantity regulation.

26. As will be explained, marketable pollution rights are a hybrid of regulation of the total quantity of pollution and of a pollution tax-like regime. See Dales 1968 for an early discussion of marketable pollution rights; for more recent discussions, see, for example, Cropper and Oates 1992, Hahn and Stavins 1991, and Tietenberg 1996.

will be socially inappropriate. By contrast, if the government employs pollution taxes, not only will the distribution of pollution among firms be socially desirable (firms that find it relatively easy to prevent pollution will be inclined to do so rather than pay the tax, and firms that find it relatively expensive will pay the tax and pollute), but also the total quantity of pollution will be socially desirable—since firms themselves will decide how much to pollute by comparing their pollution control costs (which they know) to the pollution tax, which is set equal to the expected harm from pollution.

(b) *Information of victims.* Information of victims is relevant to the functioning of those legal rules that require victims to play a role in enforcement. Namely, for victims to bring injunctions to prevent harmful acts and protect their property rights, they need to be aware of who might harm them, such as who might pollute, and of the harm if it occurs. If the pollution is difficult to detect (perhaps colorless and odorless), and does harm only over time, they might not observe it and thus would not have the knowledge to bring an injunction. Similarly, for liability rules to function, the victims must know who caused harm and that it did occur. For regulation or taxation or subsidies to function, victims do not need such information; the state imposes taxes or regulates harmful behavior regardless of whether victims understand who is causing them harm or its nature.

(c) *Information of injurers.* Injurers need to know certain things for the various rules to function appropriately, but it is not obvious that this consideration favors any type of rule over any other. It is tempting at first to believe that for liability rules to function well, injurers need to know more than they do under regulation and the other approaches, for under liability rules injurers must be able to predict their liability, they must have foreknowledge of it: whereas under the other approaches, they apparently need to know little. Under regulation, for instance, they must merely adhere to regulatory requirements. Yet if a regulatory requirement is easily understood, such as a requirement to install fire extinguishers, so should it be easy to understand that the courts will find a party negligent if he had not installed fire extinguishers.[27] Another appealing view is that the rules like strict liability that require injurers to calculate for themselves how to act

27. Conversely, if there are so many situations that could occur that one doubts the ability of a person to know or predict which situation will be found negligent, then if regulation were as detailed, it should be equally difficult to determine the actions that regulation requires.

impose a greater burden on injurers than regulation and the rules that stipulate their behavior. But this viewpoint is problematic, for if calculation were deemed to be difficult to carry out, the state could supply individuals with information about the correct choices to make (for example, a table showing whether or not to take a precaution, as a function of factors relating to harm, its likelihood, and the cost of taking precautions).

(d) *Administrative costs.* Administrative costs are the costs borne by the state and the parties in connection with the use of a legal rule (but of course excluding the costs of acting in conformity with the rule, such as the costs of installing a smoke arrestor). Liability rules possess a general administrative cost advantage over the other rules in that under liability rules the legal system becomes involved only if harm is done, whereas under the other approaches the legal system is involved whether or not harm occurs. This advantage may be significant, especially when the likelihood of harm is small. Nevertheless, administrative costs may sometimes be low under the nonliability approaches. For example, compliance with regulation may be easily determined in some circumstances (ascertaining whether factory smokestacks are sufficiently high would be easy) and may be accomplished through random monitoring, saving enforcement resources. Also, applying corrective taxes can be inexpensive if, for instance, it is done at the time of the purchase of a product (a firm could be made to pay the tax when it buys fuel that generates pollution).

Administrative costs also tend to be lower when the informational requirements of a rule are lower. This consideration favors strict liability and the corrective tax, rules that require the state to obtain information only about harm, compared to regulation and the other rules that require the state to obtain information about benefits as well (in order to determine proper behavior).

Against the background of these general factors bearing on administrative costs, one has to examine the particulars of the situation at hand to determine which type of rule is superior on grounds of administrative cost.

(e) *Level of activity.* A distinction that will be drawn in the discussion of accidents in Chapter 8 is between the precautions an injurer takes while engaging in a particular activity—does a firm use a smoke arrestor while producing, does a person keep his dog from barking at night?—and his level of activity—how many units of the good the firm produces, whether the person owns a dog. This distinction has relevance for the rules that control external effects because some of the rules do not lead injurers to curtail properly their level of activity.

Notably, regulation and the negligence rule are typically concerned with precautions taken but not with the level of activity. A factory may be required by regulation to install smoke arrestors or may be found negligent for failure to have installed them, but the factory's level of operations will not ordinarily be regulated or subject to the negligence rule. If so, the factory will have no motive to do anything more than comply with regulation or the negligence rule. Yet even if the factory does so, there may still be a residual harm caused by the factory's activity (for it will often not be optimal to take steps necessary to eliminate all chance of harm; this would be too expensive). In consequence, although increasing its level of activity increases harm, the factory will have no motive to take this into account.

By contrast, under legal rules that make parties *pay* for harm done, namely, under strict liability or the corrective tax, parties will moderate appropriately their level of activity. Thus, consideration of injurers' activity levels makes strict liability and the corrective tax appealing compared to regulation and the negligence rule.[28]

(f) *Ameliorative behavior of victims.* Victims can often take steps to reduce harm (purchasing dryers for their laundry rather than hanging it outdoors where it can be soiled by smoke), and it will thus be optimal for them to take these steps when they are sufficiently cheap and effective, taking into account injurers' opportunities to reduce harm. Under regulation, corrective taxation, and other approaches that do not compensate victims for their harm, victims have a natural incentive to take optimal precautions because they bear their losses; they will want to take any precaution whose cost is less than the reduction in harm it accomplishes.[29] Under strict liability, however, a victim would not have such an incentive because he will be compensated for any loss he suffers. But as will be discussed in

28. It should also be noted that under the subsidy approach, the problem of excessive levels of activity is exacerbated.

29. More precisely, victims have incentives to act optimally given the behavior of injurers. If, as under regulation, the state prescribes the behavior of injurers, it is important that the state take into account what victims can do to reduce risk and not, for example, insist that injurers take a step that is more expensive than an equally effective step that victims could take.

Chapter 8, strict liability with a defense of contributory negligence will provide victims with a motive to exercise proper precautions.

Another consequence of victims' opportunity to take ameliorative actions is that more information is required of the state to fashion optimal rules. Even to calculate corrective taxes—which as mentioned in subsection (a) required only that the state assess expected harm—may become difficult. For the state to determine the corrective tax, it needs to know the harm that the injurer's behavior would be expected to cause *assuming* that the victim is acting optimally, that is, taking ameliorative actions such as installing air conditioning (or even moving away). Thus, the state in effect needs to determine the optimal solution to the externality problem in order to formulate the optimal tax.[30]

(g) *Ability of injurers to pay.* For liability rules to induce potential injurers to behave appropriately, injurers must have assets sufficient to make the required payments; otherwise they will have inadequate incentives to reduce harm. As will be discussed in section 3 of Chapter 10, this is especially relevant when harm may be large and exceed the assets of a potential injurer (a fire could cause a large harm, exceeding the assets of the owner of property; an explosion at a factory or a leak of toxic material could cause much more harm than the company's assets). The problem of inability to pay is likely to be less serious for the corrective tax, for the tax equals the expected harm, an amount generally less than the actual harm. Also, the corrective tax is presumably paid as parties take harm-creating actions; thus, if the party could not pay the tax, he could be prevented from continuing (he would not be allowed to release a pollutant into the atmosphere if he could not pay the tax). Where inability to pay is a problem, regulation and the other approaches become more appealing (although they may need to be enforced through the threat of use of nonmonetary, criminal sanctions).

(h) *Conclusion.* This review of factors bearing on the effectiveness of the rules suggests that their relative strengths will depend very much on the context. Let me illustrate by considering the classic problem of pollution caused by burning a fuel at factories. Here, liability rules might not be expected to work well because of problems victims would have in detecting

---

30. This point can be exaggerated, however. While the tax in a literal sense cannot be chosen optimally without the state knowing the optimal behavior of the victim if there are interactions between victim behavior and injurer behavior, the tax may still be easy to approximate if the interactions are not very important.

harm and ascertaining who caused it, and the use of the injunction might not work well for similar reasons. Regulation of the quantity of fuel burned would be unappealing, because it would require the state to determine the optimal quantity, meaning that it would have to determine the value of production, or the cost of alternative fuels, and these would depend on many particular factors that would be expensive if not impractical to learn. Thus, the corrective tax, relying mainly on the state's knowing the harm that the pollution tends to cause, becomes appealing. Moreover, such taxes would often be inexpensive to administer, because they could be imposed when the fuel is purchased.

5.3 Actual use of legal rules to control external effects.   Regulation and the liability system are the preeminent tools that society employs to control externalities. The state uses a vast array of regulatory devices: safety regulations for food and drugs, consumer products, and the workplace; speed limits and other traffic safety rules; zoning ordinances governing the physical structure and use of buildings; and so forth.[31] Liability for harm is also omnipresent; individuals and firms are potentially liable for virtually all kinds of harm.[32] The injunction is somewhat limited in scope, applying only when a potential or actual victim establishes the existence of a fairly substantial and continuing danger.[33] Subsidies are utilized relatively infrequently, and corrective taxes are used rarely, although marketable pollution rights have been employed to control specific pollution problems.[34]

6. RESOLUTION OF EXTERNAL EFFECTS THROUGH LEGAL RULES GIVEN THE POSSIBILITY OF BARGAINING

Let us now briefly reconsider the resolution of external effects through the use of legal rules when, unlike in the last section, parties are assumed to

31. On regulation in general see, for example, Breyer 1982, Hahn 1990, Kahn 1988, and Viscusi, Vernon, and Harrington 2000.

32. See, for example, Dobbs 2000.

33. See, for example, *Federal Procedure* 2000, 19:526–527, and Thomas 1994, 8:122–124.

34. For descriptions of the use of subsidies, corrective taxes, and marketable pollution rights, see, for example, Hahn and Stavins 1991 and Menell and Stewart 1994, 69, 72, 377–384, 519–520.

be able to bargain with one another. This will be done supposing, first, that bargaining proceeds perfectly and without cost, second, that bargaining is a costly process, and third, that bargaining is subject to problems of imperfect information.

6.1 Frictionless bargaining and the irrelevance of legal rules: invariance version of the Coase Theorem. In this case the parties will always arrive costlessly at a mutually beneficial outcome and thus at the outcome that maximizes social welfare, assuming that social welfare equals the sum of utilities and that the simple model we have discussed earlier applies. In particular, the socially desirable outcome will be achieved whatever the starting point of the parties when they begin to bargain, whatever their property rights, or more generally, whatever the governing legal rule. That is, the legal rule will not matter to the outcome.

For example, in discussing the smoke arrestor in section 3, we saw that if the injurer enjoys the property right to generate smoke, bargaining would result in the victim avoiding harm of 50 by making a payment to the injurer of at least 30 to install a smoke arrestor. It is clear that if, instead, the victim possessed the right to prevent generation of smoke, he would do so, and the injurer would install the arrestor: The injurer would prefer to spend 30 to do this than to pay the victim at least 50 to obtain an agreement to suffer exposure to smoke. Hence, whether the injurer has the right to generate smoke or the victim has the right to enjoin this, the act chosen, after possible bargaining, will be the same.

Let us consider one more version of this example, and show that the outcome under the rule of strict liability where the harm is correctly estimated by courts will be the same as the outcome if the harm is incorrectly estimated (which may be considered to be another legal rule). If the harm is correctly evaluated by courts, then the injurer will of course be led to purchase the arrestor for 30 to avoid having to pay 50 in liability. What, however, if the harm is estimated to be only 25? In this event, in the absence of bargaining, the injurer will cause harm and pay damages of 25 rather than spend 30 on an arrestor. But the victim will be willing to pay the injurer sufficiently to induce him to purchase the arrestor: If the victim pays him 15 and the injurer purchases the arrestor for 30, his net expense will be 15 rather than 25, and the victim will lose 15 instead of 25 (if he were to suffer harm of 50 and collect a liability payment of 25).

Because, as in these examples, the outcome does not vary with the legal rule when bargaining occurs, the point under consideration is sometimes described as the invariance version of the Coase Theorem. It should be noted, however, that although the legal rule will be irrelevant to the outcome under present assumptions, the legal rule obviously does alter the utility positions of parties. The victim is worse off when the injurer is not liable, or when he, the victim, does not have the right to be free from smoke, because he then has to pay the injurer to install an arrestor.

6.2 Comments and limitations.   Although this invariance conclusion is correct in the simple model, as just illustrated by the examples, it is not necessarily valid more generally even though bargaining is frictionless, or apparently so.

(a) *Coase Theorem and wealth effects.* For reasons similar to those discussed in section 3.3, the effect of wealth on parties' behavior may make the outcome depend on the legal rule. To illustrate, if the victim does not have wealth of 30, the smoke arrestor will not be installed if the injurer has the legal right to generate smoke, whereas the injurer will install the arrestor if the victim has the right to be free from smoke.[35] Also, if the victim does have wealth of 30 but the marginal value of wealth to him is high because his level of wealth is low, the legal rule may affect the outcome and social welfare. The victim may not be willing to pay 30 for the injurer to install a smoke arrestor, so that no arrestor will be installed if the injurer has the right to generate smoke; yet the victim may insist on receiving more than 30 to be willing to be exposed to smoke, so that an arrestor will be installed if the victim has the right to be free from it.[36]

35. For the injurer would prefer to pay 30 for the arrestor than to pay the victim 50 to induce him to agree to exposure to the smoke.

36. Note that the amount that the victim would insist on being paid to accept exposure to smoke is the amount of wealth that would raise his utility by 50. This amount could easily exceed 30 units of wealth—even though losing 30 units of wealth might entail a loss of utility exceeding 50. The reason for these two possibilities—a loss of 30 units of wealth corresponds to a utility loss exceeding 50, and a gain of 30 units of wealth corresponds to a utility gain of less than 50—is that the marginal utility of wealth declines with its level. Formally, let h be the harm in utility the victim would sustain from a nonmonetary adverse event, let $v(\cdot)$ be his utility of wealth, where v is increasing but concave, let w be his initial wealth, and let c be the cost of the precaution that would prevent h. Then it is possible

As a general matter, then, because of the effects of the levels of wealth that parties happen to possess, the choice of legal rules may influence the ultimate outcome, even though there is no problem with bargaining between parties. Still, the invariance of outcome to the choice of legal rule is likely to hold, or at least approximately so, if the harm or cost of preventing it is not large in relation to the involved parties' assets.

(b) *Coase Theorem in an industry in the long run.* An issue that has received some attention is whether the invariance version of the Coase Theorem holds in the long run in an industry in which production causes externalities. It has been asserted that the theorem does not hold in this context because legal rules affect costs; thus, in the long run, when price and output adjust to costs, the legal rule that is adopted will influence the amount sold by an industry. Suppose, for example, that each firm in an industry is like the one we have discussed earlier and can suppress smoke with an arrestor that costs 30 and thereby prevent harm to victims of 50. It is true that, given frictionless bargaining between firms and potential victims, arrestors will be purchased whether or not the legal rule gives firms the right to pollute. But a firm's costs will depend on the rule; if firms have a right to pollute, their costs will be lower than if they do not have the right and must pay for the arrestors themselves. Hence, over time, when prices and output adjust, prices will be lower and the quantity produced and sold will be higher when firms have the right to pollute.[37]

As stated, this argument that the legal rule affects outcomes is correct,

---

that $v(w) - v(w - c) > h > v(w + c) - v(w)$, in which case the victim would not pay c to avoid h and yet would insist on more than c to accept h.

The literature concerning the point under discussion is often found under the heading of "offer versus asking price" (the offer price being what the victim would offer to pay for the smoke arrestor, the asking price being what he would want to be paid to accept exposure to smoke). Some writers explain a higher asking price than offer price not on the basis of wealth effects, but rather on the basis of an "endowment effect." The endowment effect refers to the tendency of an individual to attach an extra value to property if it comes into the individual's possession (if the person is "endowed" with the property). See, for example, Kahneman, Knetsch, and Thaler 1990, Korobkin 1994, Jolls, Sunstein, and Thaler 1998, 1497–1501, and Arlen, Spitzer, and Talley 2002.

37. Articles that assert that legal rules affect output, along the lines illustrated by the example just provided, include Carlton and Loury 1980.

and thus seems to invalidate the invariance version of the Coase Theorem. But the argument allowed only for bargaining between firms and the potential victims of pollution. If we permit victims to bargain with consumers of the product, then we can show that output will not be higher when firms have the right to pollute. (The reason is that victims will pay consumers to purchase less; victims will do this to save themselves from having to pay for as many smoke arrestors.[38]) Because the premise of the Coase Theorem is that there are no obstacles to bargaining, we should permit victims to enter into bargaining with consumers, so that we should conclude in strict logic that the theorem does hold in the present context. Yet because it is in fact implausible that victims would bargain with consumers,[39] one would predict that in reality the choice of legal rule would matter to output and sales.

(c) *Coase Theorem and corrective taxes.* The imposition of corrective taxes affects outcomes when parties bargain frictionlessly with each other, and so seemingly conflicts with the Coase Theorem. Specifically, in the presence of bargaining, corrective taxes generally result in suboptimal outcomes involving socially excessive effort to reduce harm.[40] To illustrate,

38. For instance, suppose that the cost and price of each unit is 10 when firms have the right to pollute, but that victims pay 5 per unit for smoke arrestors. Consider a consumer who places a value of 11 on having a unit of the good. He will buy it at a price of 10 in the absence of bargaining with victims. But a victim would be willing to pay a consumer up to 5 not to buy the unit—for 5 is the victim's savings for not having to support the purchase of smoke arrestors. Hence, the only consumers who would, after possible bargaining with victims, purchase the good are consumers who are willing to pay more than 15 for the good. But these are exactly the consumers who would purchase the good if firms had to spend 5 on smoke arrestors themselves and thus charged a price of 15 for units of the good.

It should be noted that the bargaining here between victims and consumers must be bargaining between all victims and all consumers. It is not enough for a single victim to bargain with a single consumer to refrain from consumption, for then another consumer could make a purchase from the factory near the victim and cause him to pay for a smoke arrestor. An agreement must be reached among all potential consumers to refrain from consumption.

The general point that, given sufficiently general bargaining, the invariance result will hold even in a long-run setting where output adjusts is made by Calabresi 1968, Frech 1973, and Hamilton, Sheshinski, and Slutsky 1989.

39. Especially because (see the previous note) victims would have to bargain with all consumers.

40. This observation was initially made in Buchanan and Stubblebine 1962.

suppose that a polluter could eliminate 100 of harm by spending 110 on a smoke arrestor, so that that expenditure would be undesirable. In the absence of a tax, say if the injurer had the right to generate smoke, the victim would not be willing to pay him enough to purchase the arrestor, so he would cause 100 of harm. In the presence of a tax for pollution harm, however, the injurer would purchase the arrestor, for by doing so he would avoid 100 in taxes and could collect more than 10 (in fact, up to 100) in addition from the victim for so doing.

Why do corrective taxes in the presence of bargaining lead to the wrong result, one different from the result that would obtain in the absence of taxes? The reason is that for the injurer and the victim considered jointly, harm has double the cost it should: not just the loss suffered by the victim but the tax as well. That the outcome under taxes is different from that in their absence does not contradict the invariance version of the Coase Theorem, however. The premise of the theorem is that all concerned parties bargain, meaning the government too. If the government were to bargain along with the injurer and victim, then it can readily be shown that the tax would not lead to an undesirable result.[41]

The points made here and in paragraph (b), that legal rules may have clear effects on outcomes, show that the invariance version of the Coase Theorem needs to be carefully interpreted, and is not necessarily a good guide for thinking, even when bargaining is apparently frictionless.

6.3 Bargaining is costly.   Suppose now that bargaining is a costly process. Hence, when the situation is not optimal and a mutually beneficial agreement exists in principle, one of two disadvantageous outcomes will occur. First, the parties may elect to bargain and incur bargaining costs in the process; this will be the result as long as bargaining costs are small enough. Second, the parties may decide not to bargain in order to avoid bargaining costs, and the suboptimal outcome will occur; this will be the

---

41. In the example with the smoke arrestor, suppose that, in the absence of government bargaining, the victim pays the injurer 20 for him to buy the arrestor. Hence, the government collects 0, the victim loses 20, and the injurer loses 90 (because he spends 110 on the arrestor). Now let the government bargain and offer to reduce the tax to only, say, 5 if harm occurs and the injurer pays the victim 82. Then all three parties will be better off: The government collects 5 rather than 0, the injurer loses 87 rather than 90, and the victim loses 18 rather than 20.

result if the costs of bargaining are sufficiently large. If the injurer has the right to generate smoke and the cost of bargaining is only 5 for each party, we would expect them to bargain and conclude an agreement. If the victim were to pay the injurer 38, say, to install an arrestor, the victim's total cost would be 43, making him better off than if he suffered harm of 50, and the injurer's net return after installing the arrestor at a cost of 30 would be 3, making him better off as well. But if the costs of bargaining for each party are larger than 10, the parties will not bargain and the injurer will not install the arrestor.[42]

It follows that the choice of legal rules will matter to social welfare; legal rules should be selected so that more costly bargaining is not needed to achieve the socially optimal outcome. Thus, if it is usually optimal for firms not to pollute, because the benefits they would obtain if they pollute are unlikely to exceed the harm caused, victims should enjoy the right to clean air. Or firms should be regulated, taxed, or held strictly liable for harm due to pollution, for under these legal policies, bargaining is not necessary when it is optimal for injurers not to pollute. By contrast, if firms have the right to pollute, bargaining will be required to achieve the optimal outcome whenever it is best for them not to pollute.

6.4 Bargaining is subject to problems of imperfect information. Just as the cost of bargaining may prevent formation of a mutually beneficial agreement, so may asymmetric information between the parties stymie such agreements, for the reasons discussed in section 4.3. Therefore, we have another basis for favoring legal rules (such as liability) that lead to optimal outcomes without parties having to bargain. For the state to know what legal rule to employ, however, requires that it has certain knowledge about parties (such as the harm from smoke). Yet our present assumption is that the parties themselves lack information about each other—this is why bargaining may not succeed. And, as a general matter, it would be unlikely for the state to possess more information about the parties than they have about each other. (If the injurer does not know the level of harm the victim would

---

42. When the cost of bargaining exceeds 10 for each party, the victim will not be willing to pay as much as 40 to avoid the harm of 50 (for 40 + 10 is 50). But the injurer will want at least 40 to be willing to purchase the arrestor since it costs 30 (for 30 + 10 is 40).

suffer from smoke, will the state?) Accordingly, the state may be unable to select a legal rule that leads to optimality without parties having to bargain, complicating the problem of the socially best choice of legal rule.

6.5 Conclusion about bargaining and legal rules for controlling externalities. We may summarize and conclude roughly as follows. When conditions are such that parties may bargain with one another, the choice of legal rules matters less to the optimal control of external effects than would otherwise be the case, because bargaining may lead to mutually and socially advantageous outcomes. Yet the choice of legal rules is important because it can produce such outcomes directly, reducing the need for parties to bargain and to incur associated transaction costs, and also avoiding suboptimality where bargaining would not succeed due to asymmetry of information between the parties.

Note on the literature.   The subject of externalities was adumbrated in Sidgwick (1901, 399–418) and may properly be said to have originated with Pigou (1912, 148–171; 1932, 172–203). Pigou first emphasized the generality of the problem of externalities and wrote of the solution as lying mainly in government intervention in the form of taxes, subsidies, and regulation. An extensive literature now exists on externalities.[43] Economists for the most part have emphasized corrective taxes and subsidies as the theoretically preferred solution to the externality problem (despite the infrequency of their use), though some have pointed to the difficulties in calculating appropriate taxes.[44] Economists have also considered regulation as a solution to externality problems and compared it to corrective taxes, finding it generally inferior because it requires the state to have more information.[45] Yet economists largely ignored liability and property law solutions to externality problems until the development of economic analysis of law, stimulated

43. See, for example, De Meza 1998, Bovenberg and Goulder 2002, Laffont 1987a, Ostrom 1990, 2000.

44. Difficulties in estimating harm necessary to impose proper taxes were early stressed by Davis and Whinston 1962, for example.

45. For a typical example, see the argument that taxes are superior to regulation in the introductory economics text of Mankiw 2001, 215–217. (Weitzman 1974 and others suggest that regulation may be superior to taxes, but this view is based on an assumption that seems unreasonable; see note 25.)

mainly by Coase (1960), Calabresi (1970), and Posner (1972a). Coase, whose work was particularly influential, stressed three points: (1) the reciprocal nature of the externality problem—the victim's ability to ameliorate harm or to alter his activity so as not to be exposed to it; (2) the possibility that externality problems would be cured by bargaining, and the consequent irrelevance of the law to substantive outcomes, when parties can bargain with little cost;[46] and (3) the problems of information that government faces in trying to correct externality problems, making its intervention problematic. Calabresi and Melamed (1972) contains a suggestive analysis of liability versus property rules as general solutions to externality problems,[47] and Landes and Posner (1987a) and Shavell (1987a) summarize economic analysis of the liability system. At present the comparative analysis of the various means of controlling externalities is relatively underdeveloped.[48]

46. Although Pigou is criticized by Coase for viewing government intervention as necessary to solve externality problems, Pigou himself emphasizes the possibility that externalities will be resolved through bargaining when parties are in a contractual relationship.

47. On property and liability rules generally, see also Ellickson 1973, Polinsky 1980b, and Kaplow and Shavell 1996b.

48. See Shavell 1993a for an attempt to compare systematically the major methods for controlling externalities. For examination of liability and regulation alone, see Wittman 1977, Shavell 1984b, 1984c, and Kolstad, Ulen, and Johnson 1990.

6 ||| PUBLIC PROPERTY

Much property in modern states is public, and I begin this chapter by inquiring about the justifications for the existence of public property. I then discuss acquisition of property by the state through purchase and through its unilateral power to take property.

1. JUSTIFICATIONS FOR PUBLIC PROPERTY

1.1 Definitions and general justifications. By *public property* I mean land, buildings, or moveable goods owned by the state. Public property is available for *free use* if a person can enter it and utilize it without real constraint. Clearly, much public property is available for free use: roads, sidewalks, parks, rivers and lakes, airspace, schools, and libraries are often open to all. Some public property, however, is only available *for use for a fee:* a person may be charged for driving on a turnpike, cutting timber from public lands, or entering a museum. Other public property is available *for use only by authorized parties*. Military bases and fire stations, for example, fall into this category.

I will attempt to explain in this section why it makes sense that property like that in these examples should be public, and why such property should or should not be available for free public use. The main justifications for public property are either that the private sector cannot profit sufficiently to be led to supply certain property when it would be socially desirable, or that a private supplier of property would charge too high a price for, and thus undesirably discourage, its use.

1.2 Provision and free use of certain property is socially desirable. Suppose that once the cost of developing or setting aside a piece of property for some purpose is incurred, there would be no added cost associated with an individual's use of the property. Suppose, for example, that once a road is constructed, its use by a person would not absorb additional resources.[1] Then *if* the property is developed, it will be socially desirable for it to be freely available for use. And because the property should be freely available for everyone to use if developed, it should be developed whenever the sum of its values to *all* individuals who would use it exceeds its development cost.[2]

1.3 Private provision of such property is unlikely to be adequate. Would the private sector be likely to supply property—for which a price would of course be imposed—that ought to be provided for free use? There are two reasons for thinking that private parties might not be able to profit sufficiently to provide such property.

First, to earn anything from the property, a private provider of it would plainly have to be able to prevent those who do not pay for use from using it. But this may be difficult or expensive; to exclude nonpayers from a road would require controlling access to it. The cost of excluding nonpayers

1. The assumption that there is no cost associated with an individual's use of property such as a road is closely related to the assumption of *nonrivalry* in the use of property— where one person's use of property does not detract from the ability of another person to use the property. The assumption of nonrivalry, or essentially equivalently, of no marginal cost of use, is of course an abstraction; use of a road in fact causes some wear and tear to the road and possible congestion. But such costs are often small, especially in relation to the cost of purchasing land and constructing a road. I will maintain the assumption until section 1.10, when I will consider explicitly the case where there is a positive marginal cost associated with a person's use of property.

2. In saying this, I am assuming for simplicity that the measure of social welfare is the sum of values individuals obtain from using things minus costs of production, and I will make this assumption in the chapter unless otherwise noted.

from property that ideally ought to be developed may mean that private providers would find it unprofitable to supply (or that the scale of its development would be suboptimal).

Second, and less obviously, even if a private provider can relatively cheaply exclude nonpayers and charge for use of property, the revenues the provider would be able to obtain would generally fall short of the total value people attach to its use. Suppose that the values that ten people place on use of property are 1, 2, and so on, up to 10, so that their total valuation is 55, and suppose that the price the provider would charge is 5. Then, because those individuals who value use at less than 5 would not use the property, the revenue the provider would receive from users would not reflect the sum of valuations of the individuals unwilling to pay 5 (namely, $1 + 2 + 3 + 4$, or 10). Moreover, the revenue received from those who do pay 5 would not fully reflect their valuations (these six people pay 30, but their total valuation is $5 + 6 + 7 + 8 + 9 + 10$, or 45). Because a private provider's revenues will tend to fall short of the total public valuation of property, the private provider might not earn enough to cover the cost of supplying it, even though the total valuation does exceed its cost.[3]

1.4 Even if property that is socially desirable to provide is supplied by private parties, two problems remain.   Suppose that, despite the factors just discussed, the private sector finds it worthwhile to develop property that is socially desirable to provide. Then two factors imply that there will still be disadvantages associated with private provision of the property. First, the expenses borne by private providers to exclude nonpaying parties from use represent a social waste. If a private company spends $2 million erecting gates and toll stations in order to collect revenue from use of a road, the $2 million constitutes a social waste: The barriers to entry on the road do not enhance the utility of the road and fulfill no direct social need; their sole purpose is to allow the owner to obtain revenues from the road.

Second, too few individuals will use the property because use is not

---

3. I am assuming in this paragraph that the provider is not able to identify each individual's valuation and charge him a separate price. If a provider is able to do this—to engage in perfect price discrimination—his revenue will equal total valuation, because he can charge each person a price fully equal to that person's valuation—the 1-valuation person will be charged 1, the 2-valuation person will be charged 2, and so on.

free. Individuals who place a value on use below the price charged will not use the property even though it would be desirable that they do. Individuals who place a positive value on use of a road that is below the price charged for access will not use it, even though all who place a value on it ought to be able to use it.

1.5 Public provision of property that ought to be provided for free use. The state does not face these problems associated with private provision of property that ought to be provided and be made available for free use. First, the state can, in principle, compare the cost of developing property, such as a road, to the total value placed on it, and supply it if the total value exceeds the cost. Unlike the private sector, the state does not have to incur costs to exclude nonpayers from property like a road for the simple reason that it does not need to finance property from revenues from use—the state can finance property from tax revenues (see the next section). Second, if the state does develop property that ought to be available for free use, it can simply allow the property to be freely used. Thus, the socially ideal outcome might be thought to occur if the state acts as the potential provider of this type of property.

1.6 Problems with public provision. There are, however, several possible problems with public provision of property for free use. One problem has to do with the state's need to raise revenues through taxation for development of property. The raising of revenues through taxation is not socially costless, but rather involves administrative expense and causes distortions of its own (notably, an income tax may depress work effort).[4] Thus, there is an implicit cost associated with public expenditures on development of property. It should be remarked, though, that this problem does not always arise because in some cases the state owns property from the outset (as with airspace and rivers).

A second possible problem with state provision of property concerns the state's ability to obtain information about the public value of property and also about the cost of its development. It was assumed earlier that the state is able to determine the total value that individuals would place on use of

---

4. Kaplow 1996, however, emphasizes that it is in principle possible to raise tax revenues for public property without distorting work effort.

property and the cost of developing it. In fact, the state may have difficulty obtaining such information (see the next section). Moreover, the state's decision may be influenced by a political process that leads to incorrect decisions.

1.7 Comment on elicitation of preferences.   How can the state obtain information about the value people place on property that it contemplates developing? One possibility is for it to make use of data on purchases relating to similar property or goods. Thus, if the state wants to determine whether to develop a park and there is a similar park for which individuals paid a fee for use, or which they had to spend time and money to reach, statistics on usage will provide information about valuation. Another possibility is to survey individuals, asking them for their valuations.[5] If, however, the question posed in a survey is simply what is a person's valuation, then he may have an incentive to distort his answer. Individuals who place a positive value on a park, say $100, may have a motive to exaggerate their valuation, reporting $1,000 or $10,000, since this may increase the chances that the park will be constructed.[6] Similarly, others may have an incentive to overstate their aversion to having the park developed. There are ways of designing questions that will tend to elicit the truth from individuals.[7]

5. Polling of individuals to determine their willingness to pay for things is called *contingent valuation* (the valuations that individuals report are contingent in the sense that they are hypothetical—what individuals say they would spend on things—not what they actually do spend). On contingent valuation, see, for example, Mitchell and Carson 1989 and, for a critical analysis, Hausman 1993.

6. To amplify, suppose that if the park is built, people know that each will have to pay $50 more in taxes, and that it will be built if the sum of reported values exceeds a threshold. Then anyone who values the park at more than $50 will have an incentive to exaggerate his value in order to increase the chance that the park will be built.

7. For example, suppose that a person is told that his reported valuation will be added to other reported valuations and that he will pay a tax only if his reported valuation is *pivotal*—only if his particular reported valuation turns out to make the sum of reported valuations exceed the cost of the park. Thus, if the sum of other reports is $2,000, his report is $200, and the cost of the park is $2,100, his reported valuation would be pivotal because it would make the reported sum rise from $2,000, which is below the cost of $2,100, to $2,200. If his reported valuation is pivotal, suppose that the tax he must pay equals the difference between the cost of the park and the sum of *others'* reported valuations. Thus, in the example just mentioned, he would pay a tax equal to $2,100 − $2,000 = $100 if his report is pivotal. Then it can be shown that the person will be motivated to report the truth about his own valuation. To illustrate, suppose that his true valuation is $200 and

But these techniques have problems of their own.[8] A distinct difficulty is that individuals may be unfamiliar with the type of good in question and therefore not really be capable of easily evaluating it.

1.8 When public provision is best. Public provision of property that ought to be developed and freely used is best, loosely speaking, when the disadvantages of private provision—the possible failure to supply the property, the cost of excluding nonpayers, and the underuse of privately supplied property due to the charging of a price for use—outweigh the disadvantages of public provision—the possible costs of raising funds through taxation, and the possibly problematic features of the process for deciding about development of property.

1.9 Examples. I consider here several examples of property that is usually publicly provided and discuss why their being so provided might make sense in light of the considerations just mentioned.

(a) *Roads.* It is self-evident that it is socially desirable for land to be set aside for the building of a network of roads; the need for people and goods to be able to move about on a road system in a modern economy

---

consider his situation if he reports a number, such as $300, that exceeds his true valuation. This will increase the probability that he is pivotal (make it more likely that his reported valuation will make the sum exceed $2,100—for this will be the case whenever others' reports sum to between $1,800 and $2,100, rather than only when they sum to between $1,900 and $2,100). But his incorrect report will have *no* effect on the tax he pays if he is pivotal, for that tax amount does not depend on the magnitude of his report (his tax equals $2,100, the cost of the park, less the sum of what others report). Further, the only new circumstances in which his higher than truthful reported value would result in his being pivotal are those in which he would be made *worse off* by having exaggerated his valuation: For instance, if other reports sum to $1,850, his tax would be $250, but since his valuation is $200, he is worse off by $50 relative to his situation if he reports $200, since then he would not be pivotal). A similar argument shows that he will not want to report a number less than his true valuation of $200. For further discussion of this and other mechanisms for eliciting the truth from individuals, see Atkinson and Stiglitz 1980, 513–516, and for a survey, see Laffont 1987b.

8. One problem is that individuals need to be rather sophisticated to understand that it is rational for them to report the truth; another is that the techniques are vulnerable to collusion among surveyed individuals. For further discussion, see the references in the previous note.

is obvious. It is clear as well that access to much of the road system should be essentially unrestricted (because wear and tear on the roads and congestion effects will often not be substantial).

It was suggested earlier that problems would arise if society were to rely on private provision of roads. To amplify, roads would then probably be far too few due to the cost and difficulty of restricting access in order for providers to charge for use; the expense of erecting fences and installing toll booths, together with the administrative costs associated with collecting payments, would be significant. Not only would the roads be too few, they would depart in character from what is desirable. It is beneficial for roads to allow people many points of entry and exit along the way, since places of origin and destinations are dispersed. But it would be too expensive for a private system to allow a real multiplicity of points of entry and exit, because the costs of control and collecting payments would become excessive. (Related to, and compounding, these difficulties is the factor of multiple private owners of roads; whenever a person passed from one owner's road to another's, a fee might have to be paid.) Of course, all the costs of controlling access and collecting fees would be a social waste because they do not produce anything of direct value to people. Further, many individuals would not use roads because they would be unwilling to pay the tolls, which would mean that a benefit that they could have enjoyed, at little or no social cost, would be forgone.

When roads are instead publicly provided, because access need not be limited, nothing is spent on controlling access and collection, roads may have many points of access and exit, and so forth. As a general matter, one suspects that these advantages of public provision of roads are so great as to outweigh the possible disadvantages of public provision associated with the need to raise money through taxation and with the political process. Were roads left for the private sector to supply, society would be much worse off.

This theoretical argument for the rationality of public provision of roads is borne out by fact: Road systems are predominantly public in all countries today, and the road system covers a substantial fraction (about a quarter) of land in developed urban areas.[9]

It should be stated, however, that with modern technology, it might

---

9. See, for example, Jacobs 1993, 6, who states that about 25 percent to 35 percent of developed land in cities in the United States is devoted to public rights of way, mostly

be possible in the future for private entrepreneurs to charge for use of roads without building expensive physical barriers to control access. If use of roads can be cheaply monitored by electronic means (each automobile might send out a distinct signal that is registered by receivers), making users pay might become relatively cheap. (Such electronic road pricing has actually been implemented in California, the northeastern United States, Hong Kong, and Singapore.[10]) If so, the disadvantages of private supply of roads would involve mainly the pricing of road use.[11]

(b) *Rivers.* As with roads, it is plain that it is socially desirable for many rivers to be freely available for transport. But a private owner of a river would not seem to face a significant expense for controlling access to it, or at least one comparable to that for roads. (People cannot move vessels on and off of rivers in the same way that they can drive cars on and off of roads; in part, this is because there is not a network of crisscrossing rivers similar to that of roads.) A potentially significant problem with private ownership of rivers, however, is that the prices charged might discourage their use. In fact, this problem emerged as a serious obstacle to trade in France and Germany in the Middle Ages, when territory was divided among many feudal lords who charged tolls individually for passage on sections of rivers that they controlled.[12] Indeed, it has been argued that one of the reasons for England's rise as an economic power at the time is that, owing to England's internal unification, transport on its rivers was not stifled by tolls.[13] Such problems with private ownership of rivers may justify their largely public ownership.

---

streets. Niedercorn and Hearle 1964, 6, estimate that about 26 percent of developed land in 48 large American cities is devoted to roads and highways.

10. In California, a private company has set up an electronic billing system for use of a toll road; see Ayres 1996. In the northeastern United States, the government has established the E-Z Pass electronic billing system for certain turnpikes, bridges, and tunnels; see *www.EZPass.com.* In Hong Kong and Singapore, the government has tested electronic billing systems; see McCarthy and Tay 1993, 297, and Hau 1990.

11. These disadvantages would be serious if there were not much competition among owners of alternative roads.

12. For example, in the late fifteenth century, half of the final selling price of grain shipped 200 miles down the Seine River was accounted for by tolls. See Postan and Miller 1987, 134–135.

13. See Heilbroner 1962, 51.

(c) *Airspace.* The case of airspace is similar to that of rivers. Airspace is useful for transportation and should be freely available for use (except for controlling congestion). Restricting access to airspace might or might not be difficult for a private provider (perhaps use of airspace could be monitored electronically). In any event, the expense involved in limiting access to airspace would be a waste, and the price charged would unnecessarily discourage use. Thus, as with rivers, the argument in favor of public ownership of airspace, which is what is observed, seems fairly strong.[14]

(d) *Recreational areas.* The social desirability of preserving certain areas for recreation and enjoyment of nature is apparent. The cost a private supplier would incur in controlling access to such areas would sometimes be relatively low. For example, control of entry into even a large park might be accomplished merely by collecting tolls along a single road entering the park; fencing in the park would not be necessary if the typical visitor would be traveling by automobile. Similarly, it might not be very expensive to erect a fence around a relatively small park in a city, and to collect for entry. Controlling access to miles of beachfront, however, or to a long hiking trail (such as the Appalachian Trail) would be so costly as to be impractical, so one could not easily imagine the private sector supplying such recreational areas. In any case, were a park or other recreational area to be provided by the private sector, the cost of controlling entry would be a social waste,[15] and the pricing policy that would be pursued would tend to discourage use relative to the optimal amount. Thus, there is a case for public ownership, although its strength depends on the cost of controlling entry and the degree to which use would be discouraged versus the disadvantages, discussed earlier, of public development.

In reality, parks—notably our municipal, state, and national parks—are often publicly owned. Also, much of the seashore is publicly held. There are, however, many private parks and camping grounds owned by profit-making entities.

(e) *Land and moveable things with unique characteristics.* Consider land

14. Ownership of airspace above five hundred feet is public in the United States; see, for example, Cahoon 1990.

15. If, however, it is optimal to control access to prevent congestion, then under public ownership, access would also be controlled. Thus, the cost of controlling access would not be a social waste; see the discussion in section 1.10.

of unique value (such as a natural wonder, or a historic battlefield) or moveable things of special significance to the public (such as paintings, documents of historical importance, and the like) and assume that it is socially desirable that the public be allowed free access to observe them (as long as congestion problems do not develop). Along with the two general problems with private provision of these goods, there is a special problem involving their enjoyment at a distance. It may be thought, for example, that an individual derives benefits from knowing that the Gettysburg battlefield, Yellowstone National Park, Declaration of Independence, and *Mona Lisa* are preserved, even if the individual never actually goes to see these things. That is, individuals may place a value on the *mere existence* of certain things.[16] A private owner, however, will not be able to capture much, or any, of this existence value, since the private owner will obtain revenue primarily from those who actually visit the land or the thing. Were a private company to own the Gettysburg battlefield, it might decide to sell the land to a real estate developer because the profits it makes from visitors are small, since the profits reflect only the valuations of those who go to Pennsylvania to visit the site; the profits would not reflect the amount that others in the population would pay, perhaps small on an individual basis but large when added, for the knowledge that the Gettysburg site is preserved. Hence, if existence value is significant, there is a special reason to expect an undersupply by the private sector. This might help to justify what we often observe: the public ownership of land and objects with unique character.

1.10 Public property that should only be available for use for a fee. The argument that certain property should be freely available was based on the assumption that one person's use did not absorb resources or detract from another's use. Let us now relax this assumption and take into account, for example, that wear on the roadbed and congestion (which slows traffic and increases accident risks) makes use of a road by an individ-

---

16. The notion of existence value was introduced by Krutilla 1967; it should be carefully distinguished from the value people place on their being able to see a thing in the future (or on their descendants being able to do so) or on their being able to see photographs or other images of a thing. The concept of existence value is felt to be overstated by some because, among other things, after proper account is taken of the values just noted, there may be little if any residual value—that is, little if any existence value. See, for instance, Milgrom 1993 for a skeptical discussion of existence value.

ual costly. This implies that, were it easy to impose fees on users of a road (or other property), it would be best that a public provider of the property impose a charge equal to the marginal cost of use. Then, as is socially desirable, a person would not use the property unless his valuation exceeded the marginal cost of his use. But because excluding nonpayers and imposing fees may be expensive, a public provider should make the expenditure in order to impose fees if and only if the expenditure is outweighed by the benefits from limiting use to those whose values exceed marginal cost. This might be the case, for instance, for a bridge or tunnel, since the cost of excluding nonpayers equals only that of controlling access at either end.

Note that when it would be desirable for a public provider of property to impose fees for use, one of the two advantages of public provision over private disappears—it is no longer true that only private providers bear costs of excluding nonpayers; now so does a public provider. But private providers would still generally tend to charge a price that is too high, one exceeding the marginal cost of use—consider the toll that might be charged for passage over a privately owned bridge—and thus undesirably discourage use.

1.11 Public property that is needed for the provision of public services.   There are a variety of *services* that are, or may well be, socially desirable for the public to provide, notably, national defense, certain educational and health-related services, and fire and police protection. For these services to be provided, the state needs to acquire certain property. The military needs bases for its troops and equipment; and schools, libraries, hospitals, and fire and police departments all need property to carry on their activities. In some cases, it would not be desirable for individuals to have access to the state's property. For example, there are obvious security reasons for limiting people's access to military bases and to police stations.

Two primary justifications exist for public provision of services. First, a service might not be privately provided because of the practical impossibility of a private seller preventing nonpayers from benefiting from the service. If nonpayers would automatically receive a service, no one but a public-spirited person would buy it, so that a private seller could not profit from offering it. A classic example is national defense. If a private company attempted to sell the service of national defense, which would be provided to the whole country, a self-interested person would rationally refuse to make a purchase, realizing that he would benefit from national defense even if he did not pay for it. A lighthouse, or more precisely, the navigational aid its lights furnish, is also a stock example of a service that must be publicly supplied. The argument is that it would be impossible for a private owner of a lighthouse to provide a light only to those ships that paid for it—all ships will see a light from a lighthouse, so none would voluntarily pay for what they will see in any event. Hence, the market would not be expected to supply lighthouses.[17]

The other justification for public provision of a service does not concern the difficulty of excluding nonpayers from receiving a service, but rather positive external effects associated with its purchase. Restricting use of libraries or schools to payers, or restricting immunizations to payers, would not be difficult, but if these services were privately provided, people would not be willing to offer as much for them as they are worth to society when they create beneficial external effects. For example, when a person receives an immunization against a communicable disease, he not only does himself good but he also does others good, because he will not spread the disease to them. What the person would be willing to pay for an immunization, however, will reflect only his personal benefit, and he might not purchase an immunization when, socially, it would be desirable that he do so. Similar arguments apply for education generally, including libraries, since there are various spillover benefits from receipt of an education; society profits from having an educated populace. When individuals value services at less than their social value, the privately sold quantity of the services will be undesirably low, and thus there is an argument for their public provision, or for subsidy of their purchase.

Both of these justifications are applicable with respect to some services. Consider, for example, fire protection. Although it would be possible for a fire protection company to limit its services to payers, a company might decide to put out a nonpayer's fire in order to prevent its spread to payers' property, and fear of public outrage for allowing a fire to burn might also lead a company to extinguish a nonpayer's fire. Thus, individuals might

---

17. A change in technology can alter this conclusion. Suppose that the warnings provided by electronic "lighthouses" could be furnished by devices that send out scrambled electronic warning signals that can be received aboard ship only by those who pay for unscramblers. Then a private supplier of warning signals might develop, because it could charge for its services.

rationally believe that they would benefit from fire protection services even if they do not pay for it. This point aside, the motive of a person to purchase fire protection services will only be to put out his own fires; he will not take into account the benefit he will provide to others by reducing the likelihood that he will have a fire that spreads. For these reasons, many might decide not to purchase fire protection service despite its social value, and this weakness in market demand may warrant its public supply. (These justifications are roughly consistent with the history of fire fighting in England, where private fire protection service was replaced by public service.)[18] Similar arguments can be made for the services of police. In particular, private police would have a reason to catch criminals who are about to victimize nonpayers, in order to prevent the criminals from later harming payers; and the motive of a person to purchase crime protection will not reflect the associated crime reduction benefits to others. In consequence, the private demand for police service might be weaker than is socially appropriate, justifying its public provision.[19]

A qualifying remark should be made about the arguments in this section rationalizing public provision of certain services (and therefore the public need for associated property). While the private market would not be expected to supply various services, or to supply them in adequate quantity, this does not imply that the public needs to provide them *directly*. The public can pay a private company to do that; for example, it can pay a private company to supply fire protection services. Such private provision of public services might be more efficient than direct public provision for various reasons, including the superior ability of private companies to dismiss employees for incompetence. (Note that this publicly financed private provision of services should not be confused with true private provision of services, that is, private provision financed by private sale in the market.)[20]

18. See Eyre and Hadfield 1945 and Evans 1987. In the United States, fire fighting was originally accomplished by volunteer organizations, and the history whereby fire fighting became public is different; see McChesney 1986.

19. The arguments concerning public versus private provision of police services involve a number of factors beyond those sketched here; for further discussion, see section 2.4 of Chapter 25.

20. An example of such confusion concerns lighthouses. Coase 1974 emphasized that lighthouses in England were generally provided by private parties in much of the eighteenth and nineteenth centuries. This has been interpreted by many as an example of direct private

1.12 Public property acquired by conquest or by purchase from other countries.   Another category of public property is undeveloped land obtained by conquest or by purchase from another state. There are arguments why such property originally should be owned by the state. In brief, this is to prevent a wasteful rush by private parties to acquire the land.[21] But public property acquired by the state through conquest or purchase should, over time, be sold or given over to private use, unless it has a valid public purpose as described earlier.

In some countries today, there is much public land that the state owns that falls into this category. Vast land areas in the western United States and most of Alaska are residues of conquest and purchase,[22] and the same is true in Brazil. Also, the point may be relevant for extraterrestrial bodies in the future.

Note on the literature.   The notion that the government ought to own certain property and supply certain services has been developed over the years, but was first given clear expression by Samuelson (1954) along the lines discussed here. For a history of the concept of public goods, see Musgrave (1985); for an accessible textbook exposition of the theory of public goods, see Stiglitz (1986), and for a survey of the theory, see Oakland (1987).

2. ACQUISITION OF PROPERTY BY THE STATE: BY PURCHASE AND BY POWER OF EMINENT DOMAIN

2.1 In general.   Acquisition of property by the state occurs because the state will sometimes need new property for the purposes discussed in

---

provision of lighthouses, but that is mistaken. The only reason that the lighthouses were provided by private parties is that the Crown forced ships that came into port to pay a fee to lighthouse owners. In other words, private providers were unable to charge fees for lighthouse services themselves and needed the power of the state to accomplish that crucial function. On this point, see Van Zandt 1993.

21. On this general subject, see for example Anderson and Hill 1990.

22. In 1999, 27.7 percent of land in the United States was owned by the federal government; 82.9 percent of land in Nevada, and 62.4 percent of land in Alaska was similarly held. See *Statistical Abstract of the United States, 2001,* 209.

the preceding sections. The state can either simply purchase property from private holders, or it can possess a legal right to take it—the power of *eminent domain*—and I will discuss when it is socially beneficial for the state to have that power. If the state has the power to take property, a subsidiary question then arises as to whether it should be required to pay compensation; I will also address this question.

2.2 The state will need to acquire property from time to time. As has been discussed, certain property ought to be public. Some of the property that ought to be public is known ab initio: The state knows from the start that rivers, airspace, natural wonders (the geysers at Yellowstone National Park) ought to be public; thus there is no need, or no recurring need, for the state to acquire additional property on this account. But the requirements of the state for roads, schools, libraries, and the like will vary and are in important respects unpredictable. For that reason, there will be a continuing need for the state to acquire property from private parties. Of necessity, therefore, the question arises as to how the state should acquire such property.

2.3 Acquisition of property by the state through purchase. When property is socially desirable for the state to acquire, one would usually expect the state to be able to purchase it. In some circumstances, however, problems in bargaining may stymie or at least delay purchase of property by the state when its acquisition is socially desirable. In particular, because the state generally will not know precisely how much a private owner values his property, it may offer him too little for the property; or because a private holder of property generally will not know exactly how much the state is willing to pay, he may hold out for more than the state is willing to pay. The possibility of such breakdowns in bargaining is not special to transactions involving the state, however—it is an aspect of virtually all trade—so this alone does not furnish a justification for the state to enjoy the power to take.

But the problem of an impasse in bargaining may become severe when there are many private owners who own parcels and when, if any one of them does not sell, the whole project would be seriously affected or halted. In the building of a road, for example, the ability of essentially any individual on its planned path to prevent the project from going forward could cause serious bargaining problems for a government agency that must acquire land through purchases.[23]

An additional problem that can prevent a bargain from being consummated when it is socially best for property to be acquired by the state is that no mutually agreeable price may exist. For example, a person might hold a sentimental attachment to his land, have sufficient wealth to meet his needs, and be unwilling to sell the land for any price that the state is willing to offer.[24]

Apart from these problems, two other factors must be assessed in considering the policy of state acquisition through purchases. One is transaction costs; these can be of substantial significance when there are many private owners with whom the state must deal. The other factor is that the state must raise funds for purchases through taxation, which involves administrative costs and distorts private behavior.

2.4 Acquisition of property through exercise of eminent domain power compared to acquisition by purchase.   What differences exist between a regime in which the state has power to take property and one in

---

23. In some cases, such problems could be alleviated by secret purchases by the government agency, in much the way that private parties manage to assemble large parcels (such as for a shopping center) through purchases made by agents who do not reveal the identity or purpose of the buyer of the parcels. But government is often unable to keep its plans quiet (indeed, the plans may have come about through a public decisionmaking process), and if so, the secret purchase option is not feasible.

24. To be specific, suppose that the utility of land to a person is v, and the utility he derives from wealth y is $u(y)$, where u is increasing in y but at a decreasing rate. Let w be the (for simplicity) monetary value of the person's land to the state (that is, w is the sum of values to individuals who will use the land, say for a library). If $w > v$, it is socially desirable (under a sum-of-utilities social welfare function) for the land to be used by the state. Because the landowner's utility from money u does not rise linearly with the amount of money, however, there may not exist a price the state is willing to pay sufficient to induce the owner to sell, that is, $u(y)$ may be bounded below v. (Indeed, because the expected utility theorem implies that utility must be bounded—see, for example, Arrow 1971—this is clearly possible.) The point, in essence, is that the increase in utility that receipt of money in payment for the property can bring is limited, and may be less than the utility of the property itself to the person. Hence, even though the value of the person's land to society may be large, exceeding its utility to the person, there is no price that can be offered that will induce him to sell his land.

which the state must purchase property that it desires? First, the problems in bargaining that can prevent or delay consummation of purchase of property are avoided when the state can appropriate property. If the state wants to assemble land to build a road, it can simply take the land; it need not bargain with the many owners to acquire the land and face delay or unwillingness to sell. This is a primary advantage of the use of eminent domain powers over acquisition by purchase.

Second, transaction costs may differ, but whether consideration of transaction costs favors eminent domain or acquisition by purchase is not clear. The cost of eminent domain proceedings could be imagined to exceed that of purchases, especially if the state is required to determine private values and to compensate property owners for takings. Yet the cost of takings could readily be lower than that of purchases. Suppose, for example, that an eminent domain proceeding that allows the state to lay a water pipe under peoples' land is quickly done and determines their compensation according to a simple formula (or that they do not even receive compensation). If the state had to purchase these rights to lay pipe, the transaction costs would be much larger, perhaps prohibitive.

Third, the state's costs of raising funds to acquire property may be relevant to a comparison of the two regimes. If the state must pay compensation when it takes property, then the implicit cost of raising funds through taxation will be borne under both regimes. If, though, the presumption is that the state will not compensate for takings, then eminent domain enjoys a cost advantage over acquisition by purchase.

Fourth, the possibility of undesirable state acquisition of property arises when it has eminent domain powers but not when it must acquire property through purchase. The state might underestimate the private value of property and take it when its true private value exceeds its value to the public.[25] This type of socially undesirable outcome could not occur if the state must acquire property by purchasing it, because a private owner will not accept an offer that is less than the value he places on the property.[26]

25. The state might also take property that it ought not because its incentives to take are socially undesirable; see section 2.8.

26. To amplify on the comparison between a regime of takings without compensation and a regime of purchase, taking into account the factors in the last two paragraphs, suppose that property owned by risk-neutral private parties sometimes has positive value to the state

2.5 Eminent domain power may be justified by the problems with state purchase. The rationale for eminent domain follows from the comparison just made. Eminent domain may be warranted by the advantage of avoiding the bargaining problems associated with purchase, and possibly by transaction cost savings. Such advantages must, however, outweigh the disadvantage that the state may mistakenly take property too often. Moreover, if the state is required to pay compensation when it exercises its power of eminent domain, then it will bear implicit costs of financing similar to those that it incurs when it must raise funds to purchase property. In any case, let us now assume that eminent domain power is warranted and consider whether the state should pay compensation for property that it takes.

2.6 Risk-averse individuals' desire for compensation for losses is *not* a reason for the state to pay compensation for the property that it takes. Does the risk aversion of individuals argue for government pay-

---

and that the state contemplates acquiring it. Let v be the value of a property to its owner, $f(v)$ be the density of v across the population of owners, where v is in $[0,m]$, and w be the value of the property to the state. Assume that the state does not know v in a particular case but does know the distribution f of v. Social welfare is the value of the property to whomever uses it, the state or the private party, less any costs of raising funds needed by the state to make payments; the costs of funds are assumed to be α per dollar, where $\alpha > 0$.

Under a regime of takings without compensation, the state will take a property if and only if $w > E(v)$, for that is when a taking would raise expected social welfare. (E is the expectation operator.)

Under a system of purchase, suppose for simplicity that the state makes a single offer x to a party, which he accepts or rejects. Social welfare as a function of x is $F(x)(w - \alpha x) + \int_x^m vf(v)dv$, for an offer is accepted when $v \leq x$. (F is the cumulative distribution of f.) The first-order condition determining the optimal x is $f(x)(w - \alpha x) - \alpha F(x) - xf(x) = 0$, or $x = w/(1 + \alpha) - \alpha F(x)/[f(x)(1 + \alpha)] < w$. Thus, were there no cost of funds, the optimal offer of the state would be w, since then all who valued the property less than the state would sell it; but since there is a cost of funds, the state shades down the offer.

Either takings without compensation or a regime of purchase could be superior to the other. For example, if the state is certain that w exceeds v for all possible v, it will take under a regime of takings and social welfare will be first best. But under a regime of purchase, its offer might be refused, and if accepted involves the social cost αx, so that social welfare will not be first best. If, though, w is less than many v, even though it exceeds $E(v)$, the government would take under a regime of takings and social welfare would be $w - E(v)$. Yet social welfare might be higher under a regime of purchase: As α tends to 0, the state's optimal bid tends to w, and social welfare tends to the first best level, $E(\max(w,v))$.

ment of compensation for takings? In a society like ours, with highly developed insurance markets, the desire of risk-averse individuals to have an arrangement under which they would be compensated for losses can be satisfied by their purchase of insurance coverage against takings by the state. There is no need for the state itself to insure individuals against takings by paying them compensation.

Indeed, one can see that, other things being equal, there is an equivalence between the state paying compensation in the event of takings and individuals purchasing insurance coverage against uncompensated takings. Suppose that individuals face a one-tenth of a percent risk of their property being taken by the state, and that the property that might be taken is worth $100,000. The fair premium for private insurance against a taking would then be $100. But if the state pays compensation for takings, it will have to impose higher taxes to finance its takings, and the increase in the tax burden necessary to do that will be the same as the insurance premium, $100. Hence, through payment of higher taxes to finance compensation for takings, individuals must implicitly pay exactly the premium they would be charged for private insurance coverage against takings. Thus, given the existence of well-functioning insurance markets, the social need for risk-averse individuals to be compensated against loss does not imply that the state should pay compensation if it takes property; a regime in which private parties purchase insurance coverage would be essentially the same as one of state payment of compensation.

Insurance markets may be subject to various problems, notably moral hazard (individuals insured against takings might have little reason to challenge them, raising the risk of excessive takings). But these problems do not seem to be substantially more serious with respect to the risk of takings than with respect to many other risks for which insurance is sold (for instance, that of fire). Further, even if the problems would reduce the amount of coverage sold in a private market, that would not justify provision of coverage by the state unless the state enjoyed an advantage over insurance companies in combatting the problems.[27]

---

27. For example, suppose the problem that insured individuals would not resist takings would so much raise their frequency that the insurance would not be sold, because premiums would be more expensive than is worthwhile. Then if the state were to pay compensation for takings, one would suppose that individuals would be equally lax about resisting takings,

2.7 Payment of compensation, administrative costs, and costs of raising funds. If the state pays compensation, two categories of cost are incurred: first, the administrative costs and distortions associated with taxation, and second, the administrative costs incurred in connection with the compensation process itself. In considering these latter costs, bear in mind that if the state does not compensate for takings and individuals purchase insurance, there will be administrative costs associated with the collection of insurance premiums, the settling of claims by insurers, and the state's determination of when a taking is appropriate. One suspects, however, that these insurance-related administrative costs would be lower than those of the state under a regime of compensation, for the process by which the state determines the amount of compensation is likely to be more cumbersome than insurers' procedures.

2.8 Payment of compensation and the state's incentives to take property. To this point it has been assumed that the state's motive to take property is socially correct, but in reality, of course, that may not be the case. In this regard, it is often asserted that if the state must pay for property that it takes, the frequency with which the state takes might be altered in a beneficial direction. Why might the state's motive to take property be socially inappropriate if it does not have to pay compensation for takings? Several answers are advanced: Those who are in control may wield their power to punish political opponents; individuals working for the state may benefit from taking property because their salary and status may increase as the scope of their activities broadens or because they enjoy the sheer exercise of authority; or individuals working for the state may be

---

so that the implicit insurance premium (in the form of taxes to finance takings) would be as high as the insurance premium would be. Hence, the lack of a market for insurance would imply that the state should not pay compensation for takings, rather than justify that. Blume and Rubinfeld 1984 suggest that problems with insurance markets might warrant payment of compensation as implicit insurance; but their argument is problematic, or at least incomplete, for essentially the reasons expressed in this note. Also, Michelman 1967, 1217, offers the argument that the risks associated with takings are systematic and would not be insured by private insurers, so that the government must compensate for them. This argument, however, is unpersuasive, at least because the reasons for takings seem many and varied, no more correlated with each other than many risks that are covered by the private market. For criticism of the notion that government is a superior insurer against the risk of takings, see generally Kaplow 1986a, 533–542.

bribed in some fashion by firms seeking profit from contracts to carry out public projects (such as road construction). If for such reasons the state's motive to take property would be excessive without a requirement to pay compensation, then a payment requirement might be thought to serve as a beneficial check on takings.

This argument, however, may be challenged on various grounds. First, perhaps the state's motive to take would not be excessive in the absence of a requirement to pay compensation. For example, individuals who work for the state might be overly cautious bureaucrats. If there is too little incentive for the state to exercise its powers of eminent domain even when it does not pay compensation, requiring the state to pay compensation would only exacerbate a problem of too little government activity. Second, supposing again that there would be a problem of excessive incentives to take in the absence of payment of compensation, one might question the degree to which payment would reduce takings: After all, the state may be able to raise taxes to finance takings, and in any case, the individuals who make decisions whether or not to take property may themselves not be much affected by the state's compensatory disbursements. Third, if compensation is paid for takings, then victims of takings will have less reason to resist them, so that a problem of excessive takings could arise *because* of the practice of paying compensation.

In a different vein, it is worth observing that the argument that compensation for takings is necessary to induce government to behave better is in some tension with our attitude toward government behavior outside of the domain of takings: We see no *general* call for government to pay for the negative consequences of its actions, even though enactment of virtually any regulation or law will disadvantage some persons. One presumes that the reason that there is no overall policy for government to compensate for the losses its regulations cause is that we believe that, on one hand, government's motives are in a rough but acceptable sense to advance social welfare and, on the other hand, that making government pay for negative consequences would not clearly cure incentive problems that exist. Thus, it needs to be explained why making government pay is of particular advantage in securing better government behavior in the context of its exercise of eminent domain powers.[28]

---

28. On the issue of how the compensation requirement may affect the incentives of the state to take, see, for example, Farber 1992, and see the general discussion and references cited in Kaplow 1986a, 566–575.

2.9 Payment of compensation and individuals' *excessive* incentives to invest in improvements of property. If the state pays compensation when it takes property, individuals may have a socially undesirable and excessive incentive to invest in improving their property. Suppose that there is a probability of 40 percent that a person's land will be taken for the purpose of building a road and that, if taken, anything built on the land would be destroyed. Then this probability ought to be accounted for in deciding whether to invest in improving the land: If the land is taken, the investment will turn out to be a social waste. For instance, suppose the person contemplates an investment, say adding a porch, that will increase the value of his home by $10,000. Then the expected social value of the investment in the porch is only $6,000 (because 60 percent is the probability that his land will not be taken), rather than $10,000, and it would be socially appropriate for him to build the porch only if the cost is less than $6,000. But if the person would be compensated for the value of his property in the event of a taking, he would decide whether to proceed with the investment in the porch without taking into account the probability of its being wasted. To him, the payoff to the investment would be certain—if his land is not taken, he benefits from the investment in the porch by $10,000, and if the land is taken, he benefits equally because of the $10,000 of additional compensation he will be paid by the state. Thus, he would be led to make the investment in the porch as long as his cost is less than $10,000. If the cost exceeded $6,000 but were less than $10,000, say if it were $8,000, he would make the investment even though, socially, that would be undesirable.[29]

29. Let z be the investment a risk-neutral party makes in property and $v(z)$ its value given z, where $v'(z) > 0$ and $v''(z) < 0$. Assume that with probability p, the property will have value w to the state, where $w > v(z)$ (for simplicity, whatever is z), so that it will be desirable for the state to take the property. The socially optimal investment z^* is the z that maximizes $(1 - p)v(z) + pw - z$ (note that the value of z is wasted with probability p); thus z^* is determined by $(1 - p)v'(z) = 1$. Now observe several points. (a) If there are takings without compensation, the party will maximize $(1 - p)v(z) - z$, so he will choose z^*. (Also, if parties are risk averse and insure, a person will choose z^*: The premium will be $pv(z)$, so he will maximize $v(z) - pv(z) - z$.) (b) If there are takings with compensation of $v(z)$, a party will maximize $v(z) - z$, because he will either obtain $v(z)$ if there is not a taking or will receive $v(z)$ as compensation if there is a taking. Hence, he will choose z determined by $v'(z) = 1$, so will choose $z^{**} > z^*$ (because $v''(z) < 0$). The reason that $z^{**} > z^*$ is, as emphasized in the text, that the party treats the investment in his property as one with a sure payoff even though, socially, its payoff is uncertain. (c) If there is acquisi-

This problem could be combatted by the state if it recognized that the person's investment was excessive under the circumstances. If the state knew that the value of the investment in the porch, discounted by the likelihood it would be a waste, did not justify its $8,000 cost, then the state could refuse to pay additional compensation for the porch. The state could adopt the policy of paying only for the unimproved value of property, and thus remove the incentive to improve property inappropriately. But the state would not always have the information needed to do this successfully.[30]

In the absence of payment of compensation by the state, there would be no problem with individuals' incentives to improve property (but see (b) in the next section). If individuals do not purchase takings insurance, this is obvious. A person would balance the cost of an improvement against the benefit, discounted by the probability that his property would be taken. Since he would suffer any loss due to a taking, he would properly take the likelihood of loss into account and not overinvest. On reflection, it can be seen that the same would be true if the person insured against a taking, for his insurance premium would rise if he improved his property and increased his coverage. In the example, if he improves his property by $10,000 and the likelihood of a taking is 40 percent, then his premium would rise by $4,000. Thus, he would obtain a net gain of $6,000 by making the investment, and he would thus make the investment only if the cost was less than $6,000, as is socially appropriate.

2.10 Comments on incentives to invest.   (a) *Limited practical importance of the excessive incentive to invest when government compensates for takings.* The importance of individuals' excessive incentives to invest in property due to payment of compensation for takings is often probably

---

tion by purchase, the outcome is similar to that when there is compensation of $v(z)$, for the state will have to pay at least $v(z)$ to induce the owner to sell. These points were first developed in Blume, Rubinfeld, and Shapiro 1984.

30. To be precise (and continuing from the previous note), assume that compensation equals a constant k, regardless of the actual $v(z)$. Then z will be chosen optimally: Parties will maximize $(1 - p)v(z) + pk - z$, so that the first-order condition determining z will be the optimal one. The constant k could in fact be set equal to $v(z^*)$—or an estimate of that. Thus, it is not payment of compensation for takings, but rather the linkage of compensation to the improved value of property, that creates excessive incentives to invest.

quite small, because the likelihood of takings is, for most property, insignificant and thus unlikely to figure in most investment decisions. One would imagine that, usually, property that is likely to be taken would be so identified only for a short period, during which few investments would be made.

(b) *Possibility of excessive incentives to invest when government does not compensate for takings.* A factor not yet considered is that a person might be able to prevent a taking by investing enough in property so as to raise its private value above the level of its public value if taken. This could lead a person to invest excessively if compensation is not paid for takings.[31] Such excessive investment, however, is unlikely when there is a large gap between the private value of an individual's property and the public value of property (as would typically be true if the relevant public value is that of an assemblage of many parcels) and when investment decisions in property are made facing uncertainty about government's need for takings.

(c) *The mistaken notion that compensation is needed to support investor expectations.* Some commentators and jurists find that fulfilling investors' expectations about their property interests is a justification for the state to pay compensation.[32] But, as has been explained, giving owners the expectation that their investments will pay off when there is a taking is socially disadvantageous because it creates socially perverse incentives (even if the incentives are small) to invest in property when such investments will

31. For instance, suppose that the public value of property if taken is $110,000, that the present private value of property is $100,000, and that a person can invest $30,000 in the property and raise its private value to $115,000, thereby preventing a taking (since $115,000 exceeds $110,000, a taking would not occur). The person would spend the $30,000 in order to avoid a loss from a taking of $100,000, but the expenditure would be socially undesirable as it would only raise the property value by $15,000. This possibility did not arise in note 29 because it was assumed there that the value of property to the state w exceeds the private value $v(z)$ regardless of investment z. If that assumption is relaxed and $v(z) > w$ is possible, individuals might choose an excessive z in the absence of compensation (as well as with compensation). This point is made by Blume, Rubinfeld, and Shapiro 1984.

32. See, for example, Jones 1995, 7–8, and Michelman 1967, 1208–1213, discussing this view. A number of commentators have criticized the argument about investor expectations on the ground of its circularity: There will be no expectation of investment returns if it is announced by the state that it will not compensate for takings; see, for example, Graetz 1985, 1823, Kaplow 1986a, 522–523, and Levmore 1993, 288.

be wasted. It is, in other words, socially *undesirable* to prop up these expectations.[33]

(d) *Qualification—when private investment is not rendered a waste by a taking.* The argument that payment of compensation leads to socially excessive investment depends on the assumption that, after a taking, investments made by private parties turn out to be a social waste, such as the addition of a porch on a home that will be leveled to make way for a road. But if the house would be used by the state for some purpose, then the porch would have social value after the taking. In that situation, payment of compensation might lead to proper investment, and failure to pay compensation would lead to underinvestment.

2.11 Compensation for takings; factors favoring and disfavoring summarized.   Our discussion concerning whether the state should be required to pay compensation for takings may be summarized as follows. First, favoring payment of compensation, is that payment may serve as a check on excessive takings. This point was significantly qualified, though, by questions concerning whether the actual incentives of the state to take are excessive and by related issues. Second, and working against payment of compensation, were higher administrative costs, the implicit costs of raising funds through taxation, and the potential for individuals to overinvest in their property.

2.12 Comment on actions by the state that affect property values even though they are not complete takings.   The state may sometimes act in ways that affect the value of property to an individual. For example, the state may build a school near a person's property and thereby lower its value to him, perhaps because of noise, or because there is interference with the view from the property. Or the state may pass regulations affecting the value of property, for example a regulation requiring expensive measures

---

33. The point reviewed here is that it is undesirable to compensate because this will lead to excessive investment *given* the probability of takings. A different point that could justify the compensation requirement is, of course, that the requirement would discourage a state with imperfect incentives from taking property when it ought not, as discussed in section 2.8.

to prevent soil erosion, lowering the value of land. (Such an outcome is sometimes referred to as a *regulatory taking.*)

In these cases, the state is not engaging in a complete taking, that is, it is not appropriating the entire bundle of property rights that a person has in a thing. The state is, however, taking particular property rights, and the analysis that has been presented may be applied to these particular property rights. Consider first the issue concerning whether the state needs to take property, rather than to acquire it through purchase. It was noted earlier that a primary advantage of allowing the state to take property was that this would prevent breakdowns in bargaining over purchase. Such breakdowns would seem likely to arise in certain contexts but not obviously in others. In the case of building a school, the number of individuals who would be affected in relevant ways (such as by noise) would typically be large. Accordingly, were the state to have to purchase the necessary property rights from all these individuals, the likelihood is substantial that some of them would refuse to sell and prevent the school from being built. In the case of a regulation requiring measures to prevent soil erosion, however, the situation seems different, because failure to conclude a bargain with an individual farmer would not imply that the whole prevention project would be compromised. The state could therefore be imagined to bargain with each individual farmer and purchase the rights to make him engage in practices to prevent soil erosion, rather than to mandate it by regulation.

Now consider the question of whether the state should pay compensation if it has the power to take certain property rights. It appears that the administrative costs of paying compensation would sometimes be relatively high in relation to the losses involved, due to the numbers of individuals who could claim some type of loss (some type of disturbance from the presence of the school) and the often modest nature of the loss. This problem might also sometimes be important in the regulatory context as well, if the cost of determining compensation would be high relative to the probable importance of the regulation.

In sum, it seems that in certain examples of government actions that may be regarded as implicit takings of property rights without compensation, the analysis of takings indicates that it is rational for the government to act in this manner (as with the building of the school). In other examples, it is not clear that present policy is desirable. In any case, the main point is that one can analyze the government's actions using the framework described.

2.13 The law.   The government enjoys a general right to take property in the United States when the taking is for a public use as long as it pays "just compensation," and the law is similar in other countries.[34] There is some uncertainty and debate, however, concerning the borderlines of this right and the obligation to pay compensation, notably, over what constitutes a public use. (If the government plans to sell the land it takes to a private corporation that will hire the unemployed, would that be a public use?) When government regulation and other government actions that are not complete takings (see the previous section) lower property value, they are deemed takings for which compensation is due only in limited circumstances.[35]

Note on the literature.   The major economic analyses of takings are Blume, Rubinfeld, and Shapiro (1984), focusing on the effects of compensation on incentives to improve property and first emphasizing that compensation may lead to overinvestment in property, and Kaplow (1986a), a synthetic, general article stressing not only that government compensation may lead to overinvestment, but also that the private market can supply insurance against government takings.[36]

---

34. On the law of takings in the United States, see generally Sackman 2000 and Nowak and Rotunda 2000, section 11.12; on the law in other countries, see, for example, Garner 1975 and Van der Walt 1999. On the history of takings, see, for example, Bosselman, Callies, and Banta 1973, chap. 6.

35. See, for example, Stoebuck and Whitman 2000, 524–545.

36. The economic literature is surveyed in Miceli and Segerson 2000. It includes Blume and Rubinfeld 1984, Epstein 1985, Farber 1992, Hermalin 1995, Knetsch and Borcherding 1979, Merrill 1986, Munch 1976, and Quinn and Trebilcock 1982; see also Fischel 1995, Miceli and Segerson 1996, 1998 on regulatory takings. Hermalin 1995 is of particular note because of its analysis of alternatives to takings with compensation, including a regime in which there are takings and individuals have the opportunity to buy back their property at a price government names. A number of earlier articles on takings that have significant economic and policy-analytic dimensions include Baxter and Altree 1972, Berger 1974, Michelman 1967 (which was especially influential), and Sax 1971.

7 ||| PROPERTY RIGHTS IN INFORMATION

In this chapter I will discuss the generation and the subsequent use of information, as well as the extent to which each is promoted in a socially desirable way by property rights in information. By property rights in information, I refer to patent, copyright, and trademark law, and I include also trade secret law and closely related aspects of contract law and tort law. For convenience, I will sometimes write of information in the abstract, but other times I will refer to embodiments of information in goods and services, and to particular forms of expression of information, notably, the spoken word, printed matter, and broadcasts and recordings in electronic media.

The chapter is divided into three major parts. The first part will examine information of *repetitive value:* information that is useful for producing multiple units of things. The words of a book, for example, are of repetitive value, because the book can be reprinted, and the design of a new device is of repetitive value, because multiple units of the device can be made with the design. Information of repetitive value is protected by patent, copyright, and trade secret law. The second part of the chapter will briefly consider various other types of information. For example, I will discuss information that can be used only once (such as information about the location of an oil deposit). The last part of the chapter will deal with information that possesses value as a *label* signifying characteristics of a good or service, such as logos, product packaging, and brand names. Labels are protected by trademark law.

1. PATENTS, COPYRIGHTS, AND TRADE SECRETS: PROPERTY RIGHTS IN INFORMATION OF REPETITIVE VALUE

1.1 In general. The social value of information of repetitive value often exceeds its cost of development, making it socially desirable to generate. If, however, information can be copied at low cost by those who come to possess it, the person who first develops information will not be able to sell it to very many buyers: Most buyers will be able to disseminate or resell the information themselves. As a consequence, the reward to a person who creates information will tend to be less, perhaps substantially less, than its social value. The development of information will therefore be undesirably retarded, other things being equal.

To spur the generation of information, the state can grant property rights in it. If the creator of information is granted an exclusive right to sell the goods embodying it, he may enjoy profits, and the prospect of such profits may encourage effort to produce information in the first place. Thus, property rights in information may be a socially valuable institution.

Yet the granting of property rights has a socially disadvantageous consequence: Too little of the goods embodying information will be produced, because those who hold property rights will be able to charge a price exceeding production cost of the goods. To ameliorate this problem (and others to be noted), property rights in information may be limited in various ways.

An alternative to property rights in information is a system of state rewards paid to the creators of information. The rewards provide a stimulus to creation of information. And because the creator of information does not gain property rights in information under the reward system, the goods embodying information will tend to sell at competitive prices and the level of production will thus be superior to that when creators possess property rights in information. Nevertheless, there are problematic features of reward systems.

Let me now amplify these points, beginning with a consideration of the socially desirable generation and use of information.

1.2 Socially ideal use of information that exists. How should information be used *once it has been developed?* Clearly, in the ideal, a good embodying information should be produced and obtained by a person whenever that would enhance social welfare, that is, whenever the value of the good to him exceeds its production cost.[1] Thus, a new device should be produced for any person who values it more highly than its cost of manufacture; a book should be printed for anyone who values it more highly than its printing cost; computer software should be made available to any individual who values it more highly than the cost of the disk on which the software is recorded (or the even lower cost—essentially zero—of downloading the software from the Internet).

1.3 Social value of information.   The social value of information is the amount by which it will raise social welfare for the entire group of individuals who obtain the good embodying the information. The *optimal* social value of information is its social value when the good is optimally produced, that is, produced for each and every individual who values it more highly than its production cost. For example, suppose that each of 1,000 people value a book at 10, and its printing cost is 4. Then the book should be produced for each of these people, and the optimal social value of the book is therefore 6,000.[2]

1.4 Socially ideal creation of information.   Given the optimal social value of information, it is evident how we should determine the socially ideal generation of information. Information should be created if and only if its development cost is lower than its optimal social value.[3] If the book

---

1. In this chapter I generally employ the usual criterion of social welfare: the sum of utilities obtained from goods minus costs associated with production, minus costs of developing information, and minus certain other costs, notably those of law enforcement.

2. In this example, the information allows production of a *new good,* namely, a new book. Another possibility is that the information constitutes a *process innovation,* that is, it allows an existing good to be more cheaply produced. Suppose in the numerical example that the process innovation lowers printing costs from 4 to 3 per book, saving 1 per book. Then the optimal social value of the information would be 1,000. More generally, the increase in social welfare associated with a process innovation equals the reduction in production cost per unit multiplied by the number of units presently produced, plus an amount reflecting the welfare gained by individuals for whom it is now optimal to produce because of the reduction in the production costs (there were no such individuals in the numerical example). For expositional simplicity, I will refer in the text mainly to information allowing production of new goods, not to process innovations.

3. For simplicity, assume the development cost is known in advance.

just mentioned can be written by the author at a cost of less than 6,000, then it is optimal for it to be written, but not otherwise.[4]

1.5 Use of created information in the absence of property rights: tends toward the optimal. In the absence of property rights in information, once information is released by a party who possesses it, goods embodying the information will tend to become available at their production cost, and thus the level of production of the goods will tend toward the socially optimal. If there were no property rights in books, then any printer could obtain a copy of a book and reproduce it. Assuming that there would be competition among book producers, the price of books would reflect production costs alone and thus the book would become available for purchase at this cost. Hence, anyone who valued the book above production cost would purchase it, so that the number of books printed would be optimal.

1.6 Creation of information in the absence of property rights: tends to be inadequate. In the absence of property rights in information, the reward to a creator of information will be lower than the social value of the information because goods embodying information will, as just discussed, tend to sell at prices reflecting their production cost alone. Indeed, if this is literally the case, a potential creator of information would not anticipate any profits and thus would have no incentive to develop information.

1.7 Qualification: it may be time-consuming or impossible to copy information. As a general matter, it will take time for competitors to copy the information and produce goods like that of the creator, and in the interim the creator can make profits. For a book, which is easily copied, the time during which the creator can obtain profits may be short, but for products that require engineering and a substantial manufacturing process to produce, the creator may enjoy a relative monopoly position for a significant period. In some cases the information necessary to reproduce a good may be so hard to deduce from the good itself that the creator will

4. If, however, the social value of the book would be less than optimal—because the production level of the book would be less than optimal—then it would be desirable for the book to be written only when the cost of so doing is less than this suboptimal value the book would have.

enjoy a monopoly position for an extended time. For instance, it may be very difficult to duplicate a food product (as is apparently the case with Coca Cola, which for more than one hundred years has not been copied even though there is no patent held in it).[5] Moreover, the creator of information will have an incentive to manufacture the good embodying it in such a way that it is difficult to copy.

1.8 Are property rights in information necessary to induce its creation?   For the reasons just given, creators of information can frequently look forward to positive profits even in the absence of a system of property rights, raising questions about the need for property rights in order to induce a tolerably good degree of development of information. Some commentators have argued that, even in the case of books, the returns to being first to publish might be sufficient to result in a satisfactory amount of writing and publication.[6] Although this belief about books is probably unduly sanguine, it is worth noting that in reality we could expect some substantial degree of creation of information in the absence of property rights protection. In this connection, it is relevant that, in historical terms, broad property rights protection in information is relatively recent (see section 1.15), and that some highly industrialized countries did not adopt patent law until the end of the nineteenth century.[7]

1.9 Property rights in information.   Property rights in information are rights of parties to use certain information to produce goods or services for sale and to prevent others from doing so. There are three

5. Pendergrast 1993, 11, 421. Coca Cola does, however, benefit from trade secret law, another form of property rights in information.

6. See, for example, Hurt and Schuchman 1966 and Breyer 1970. These writers also emphasized that authors are induced to write to win recognition and esteem. Such nonmonetary rewards, however, would not motivate editors and publishers. For other skeptical reactions to the view that copyright is not needed, see, for instance, the discussion following Hurt and Schuchman's article, 435–438, and also Tyerman 1971. It may also be mentioned that after the French Revolution, copyright was eliminated, the publishing industry was thrown into economic turmoil due to pirating of works, and as a consequence copyright was reinstated; see Hesse 1989.

7. This was true of the Netherlands and Switzerland; see section 1.21. Yet trade secret protection may have provided some intellectual property right protection in these countries; it should also be noted that they benefited from innovations developed abroad.

principal ways that the legal system accords parties property rights in information of repetitive value: through patent law, dealing with novel products and processes; through copyright law, concerning original written and certain other types of works that can be copied; and through trade secret and associated law, barring such behavior as an employee divulging a manufacturing process to his employer's competitor. Although it will be seen from their description (in sections 1.15–1.17) that these forms of property rights are incomplete in a variety of respects, in the next several sections I will assume for simplicity that property rights are complete.

1.10 Use of created information in the presence of property rights: tends to be inadequate.   When parties possess property rights in information, they will sell goods embodying the information at prices exceeding the cost of production, so that the level of purchases of the goods will be less than is socially desirable. If the holder of a copyright in a book that costs 4 to print charges 15 for it, then the number of copies printed will be socially inadequate, for individuals who would be willing to pay more than 4 for it, and thus should obtain it, will not purchase it if their valuation is below the sales price of 15. The importance of this point depends on the magnitude of the difference between price and the cost of production. The social loss will be great when the difference is substantial, as for instance is the case for patented pharmaceuticals selling at multiples of their cost of production,[8] and for copyrighted computer software for which prices are often $100 or more but for which the cost of copying the software on a storage medium is nominal.[9]

---

8. For example, Scherer 1980, 450, notes that during a period in which Pfizer Corporation held a patent in tetracycline, a powerful antibiotic, it sold 100-capsule bottles to druggists for about $30, whereas production cost ranged from $1.60 to $3.80. More generally, comparison of the prices of patented drugs to their prices when their patents expired and they became generic (and thus when their prices presumably approximated production cost) suggests that patent prices are often from 3 to 5 or more times production cost; see, for example, Berndt, Cockburn, and Griliches 1996 and Grabowski and Vernon 1992.

9. A qualification to the point of this paragraph arises in the case of process innovations. The holder of a patent in a process innovation may well not be charging a monopoly price, for his product might be sold on a competitive market. But there would still tend to be a

1.11 Creation of information given property rights: tends to exceed that in the absence of property rights. Because parties who possess property rights can sell the goods embodying the information at prices above marginal cost, they will obtain positive profits from generating information, in contrast to the situation in the absence of property rights where goods sell at cost due to competition. Further, where positive profits can be made in the absence of property rights, for the reasons discussed earlier (see section 1.7), one would still expect creators of information to obtain greater profits if they possess property rights (the time period during which the creator would enjoy monopoly power would be longer, and the creator would not have to take costly steps to keep his innovation secret).

It may be noted, however, that property rights do not engender socially perfect incentives to create information, for monopoly profits will generally fall short of the *full* social value of products; sellers will typically be unable to identify and to extract from each buyer an amount equal to his particular valuation. Thus, the incentive to generate information is not socially ideal under property rights, even though it exceeds that in the absence of property rights.

1.12 Sale of property rights. Allowing parties to sell property rights in information enables them to enhance their profits, especially because the creator of information may be poorly situated to produce the good embodying the information. The author of a book will generally not be in the printing and publishing business; the inventor will sometimes not be able to produce the machine he has designed. Thus, the ability of authors and inventors to sell and license their intellectual works may significantly raise the profitability of creation of information. For this reason, and because it tends to lower production costs, allowing the sale of property rights is

---

disadvantage due to the patent in the innovation because other producers would not be able to use the innovation to lower their production costs. (It is true that the patent holder might license his process innovation to them. But then the price charged in the industry would be likely to exceed the social cost of production because it would reflect the licensing fee.) It should be added that if the process innovation lowered production cost sufficiently, the patent holder would become a monopolist; this would be so when his monopoly price, given his low cost of production, would be lower than the price competitors could charge given their higher costs. Thus, the conclusion that there will be disadvantages associated with property rights in information holds in the case of process innovations, but differs in its details and reasoning from that in the cases of product innovations and copyrightable works.

socially desirable, on the assumption that property rights are socially desirable in the first place.

1.13 Are property rights in information socially desirable?
Whether property rights in information lead to a socially superior outcome depends on whether their advantage, inducing greater development of information, is more important than their disadvantage—curtailment of the production of goods embodying information due to the high prices charged by holders of property rights. In the simple situation in which a financially motivated creator of information would make virtually no profits because of the ease of reproducing the good embodying the information, the existence of property rights is unambiguously socially desirable: Property rights are necessary for there to be *any* incentive for information creation—and it is simply a moot point that, were information generated in the absence of property rights, the level of production of the associated goods would be higher.

Realistically, though, creators of information can often obtain positive profits in the absence of property rights, so that there will be a positive incentive to produce information in the absence of property rights, meaning that the answer to the question of the social desirability of property rights in information becomes ambiguous.[10] Nevertheless, and perhaps with justification, economists tend to assert that the added incentive to generate information under property rights outweighs their drawbacks, at least in a broad sense.[11]

1.14 Additional issues concerning property rights in information.
To round out our discussion, it is useful to consider a number of additional issues.

(a) *Wasteful effort to create information due to the race to be first.* Multiple parties who have the ability to generate information may each be induced to spend on development of the information in the hope of being the first

10. This ambiguity stands in contrast to the desirability of property rights in physical things (if we abstract from the cost of enforcing property rights). The reason for the difference is that allowing property rights in physical things does not lead in any automatic way to monopoly pricing of goods.

11. There are many features of property rights that seem undesirable, however; for a broad discussion and cataloguing of these, see Scotchmer 1998.

to succeed and thus of obtaining property rights. But this race to be first may well be socially wasteful, for it may involve duplication of efforts as well as expenditures to speed development when the social value of earlier generation of information is small.[12] Such problems can be mitigated if property rights are awarded early, notably, as soon as it is known that a party has worked out the essentials of an invention, without waiting for it to be refined; in this way, the period of the race and of duplicative effort can be truncated.[13] Further, the race can sometimes be avoided: If the parties contemplating developing information know each others' identities and successfully contract to conduct a joint venture, they would not be competing but rather cooperating and thus would not duplicate efforts or spend excessively to complete their research earlier.

It should be observed, however, that the problem of the race to be first is of no relevance for copyrightable works. Under copyright law, unlike under patent, intellectual property rights *are* given to innovators who are not first: As long as a person independently creates a work, he will obtain a copyright in it even if others already have done so.[14]

(b) *The duration of property rights.* The duration of property rights is of interest because the longer the life of a patent or of a copyright, the greater the profits and thus the incentive to create information, but the greater also is the disadvantage due to excessive prices. As a general matter, the optimal length of property rights for a class of possible inventions is the minimum period necessary to induce invention, that is, the minimum

12. Suppose that by spending an additional $10,000, a firm can develop an innovation a day earlier and therefore increase its likelihood of beating its competition and obtaining a patent worth $1,000,000 by 10 percent. The firm would definitely spend the $10,000, as the expected payoff from that would be $100,000, yet the social value of having the innovation made a day earlier might be negligible.

13. This point is a theme of Kitch 1977. It should be noted, though, that to some degree, the early award of property rights will not reduce the socially wasteful race so much as it will shift it forward in time.

14. See section 1.16. This aspect of copyright law, and the whole issue of the race to be first, would seem to be irrelevant in wide ranges of innovative activity, such as the writing of a book, for it is quite unlikely, if not impossible, that more than one individual would be attempting to author the very same book. As noted in section 1.16, however, it is possible that more than one individual would take the same photograph, or arrive at the same basic musical composition, so a race to be first would exist in these areas but for the doctrine of copyright law preventing that.

period necessary to generate monopoly profits usually sufficient to cover development costs. This suggests that the desirable length of property rights should be higher the greater the development costs, other things being equal. There is, however, no clear relationship between the social value of an innovation and the optimal length of property rights: More valuable innovations lead to higher monopoly profits per year, tending to reduce the period necessary to cover development costs, but more valuable innovations are also more desirable to stimulate (and may cost more to develop), tending to raise the desirable period of property rights protection.[15]

(c) *The scope of property rights.* Although I have written here of property rights simply as obtaining or as not obtaining, they may often better be viewed as applying to this or that degree, depending on what may be called their *scope.* Issues of the scope of protection are exemplified by whether a closely related improvement on a patented invention will be considered infringing (will a new tennis racket with a surface area of 145 square inches infringe on the patent of a racket with a surface area of 135 square inches?), by whether a patent holder will be forced to license his invention to others (and, if so, at what price), or by whether a copyright holder in a television broadcast will be allowed to prevent recording and later use of its broadcast.

---

15. It may be helpful to set out a simple model here. Suppose that possible inventions are described as follows: c is the cost of development; q is the likelihood of successful development if c is invested; b is the per period social benefit from an invention if there are no property rights given in it; $\pi < b$ is the per period profits given property rights in the invention; and $b - m$ is the per period social benefit if there are property rights, where m is the social loss due to monopoly pricing. Also, let r be the discount rate. Assume that the state can observe all the variables, c, q, π, b, and m and that an invention is socially worthwhile inducing. Then the optimal length of property rights is the minimum time T necessary to generate expected discounted profits of c for the innovator, that is, the optimal T is such that $\int_0^T q\pi e^{-rt}dt = c$. Note that, given this T, social welfare will be $\int_0^T q(b - m)e^{-rt}dt + \int_T^\infty qbe^{-rt}dt - c$. More generally, the state will not be able to observe the different variables but will have probability distributions over them. In that case, for any T, social welfare will equal the expected value (with respect to the probability distribution over the variables) of $\int_0^T q(b - m)e^{-rt}dt + \int_T^\infty qbe^{-rt}dt - c$ for all c for which invention is induced, that is, for which $c \leq \int_0^T q\pi e^{-rt}dt$. The optimal T will maximize this expected value over T.

The classic study of the optimal duration of patent protection is Nordhaus 1969; see also Scherer 1972. Scotchmer 1999 examines the policy whereby patent holders can lengthen their patents by renewing them if they pay a fee for renewal. Note as well the related discussion and references in the next subsection.

The larger the scope of property rights protection, the greater the profits to the property-right holder and the greater the incentive to create information, but the larger the scope, the greater also is the problem of excessive prices and inadequate use of information. Thus, the social tradeoff involved in increasing the scope of protection is of the same character as the one pertaining to duration of protection.

Two additional comments may be made about the scope of protection. First, the optimal scope of protection and its optimal duration are interrelated, because increasing the scope of protection and increasing the duration of protection are each means of enhancing profits and incentives to create information.[16]

Second, a given scope of protection can be achieved in many different ways, by the state's deeming some behaviors as infringing and not others. It is generally socially desirable for the state to treat as infringing those behaviors that produce profits for the property-right holder at relatively low social cost, and to treat as not infringing those behaviors that, were they infringing, would result in relatively high social costs per dollar of profits for the property-right holder. For example, it might be desirable to treat as infringing the recording and use by a sports bar of a televised sports event, but to treat as not infringing the recording and use of the same event by a person in his home. To treat home use of such television broadcasts as infringing might involve substantial social costs, especially due to high administrative and enforcement expenses per dollar of profits for the broadcast owner.[17]

16. When account is taken of the substitute nature of the scope and the duration of property rights as means of providing incentives to create information, the conclusions about their optimal nature can change. For example, under certain assumptions it is best for property rights to endure forever but for the monopoly pricing problem to be ameliorated by limiting the scope of property rights. On these issues, see Gilbert and Shapiro 1990 and Klemperer 1990.

17. The point of this paragraph may be expressed more formally as follows: Suppose that there are many different behaviors b_i that can be treated as infringing, and that if so treated, b_i would yield profit π_i to the property-right holder and involve social cost c_i due to reduced use of the goods embodying information and administrative and enforcement costs. A given *scope of protection* is a particular *selection* of the behaviors (such as b_2, b_5, b_8, and b_{10}). A selection is socially efficient if the total profit associated with it (such as $\pi_2 + \pi_5 + \pi_8 + \pi_{10}$) cannot be achieved at lower total social cost (lower than $c_2 + c_5 + c_8 + c_{10}$); that is, a selection is not socially efficient if there is another possible selection that

(d) *Dependence of present innovations on past innovations.*[18] Today's innovations stand on the shoulders of past innovations; the creation of knowledge and the development of products is a cumulative process. For example, James Watt's eighteenth-century invention of the separate condensor steam engine was improved on by Jonathan Hornblower and Richard Trevithick's high pressure engines; the latter could not have developed their engines had not Watt laid the groundwork with his. Similarly, the development of an efficient computer operating system like DOS enabled subsequent creation of computer software relying on it. How does the dependence of second innovations on first innovations affect the optimal breadth of protection accorded first innovations? The general answer is not in any clear direction, because of two competing factors. On one hand, the broader the protection granted first innovations, the greater the incentive to make such innovations. Indeed, for incentives to be ideal for first innovations, their creators should obtain the entire social benefits due to first innovations, meaning the direct benefits from the innovations *plus* those benefits due to dependent, second innovations, and patent holders in first innovations will be able to engross benefits from second innovations if their patent protection is broad enough to give them rights to these innovations. On the other hand, the broader the protection granted to first innovations, the lower the incentives of others to generate second innovations.[19] (In fact, Watt's refusal to license his steam engine retarded Hornblower and Trevithick's development of their engine; they had to wait until Watt's patent expired in 1800 to produce and sell theirs.[20])

---

would yield at least as much profit at lower social cost. If the π_i are individually small, then behaviors should be selected only if the *ratio* of profit π_i to social cost c_i is sufficiently high. This general theme is informally advanced in the area of patent in Kaplow 1984.

18. See generally Scotchmer 1991, and see also Chang 1995, Green and Scotchmer 1995, and Merges and Nelson 1990.

19. More precisely, consider the situation of a second innovator whose innovation infringes on the first innovation. The second innovator, having *already* expended resources on his innovation, may not succeed through bargaining with the first in obtaining enough profit to offset his expenses. (Furthermore, because inventive activity is inherently risky, he will need to obtain more than enough to cover his expenses on just those occasions when he is successful.) Anticipating the possibly inadequate profits they will be able to secure through bargaining with first innovators, potential second innovators may decide against investing effort to make their innovations.

20. See Singer et al. 1958, 188–197.

It should be observed, however, that if those who create initial innovations are likely themselves to be able to make subsequent innovations (which they would often be in a good position to do, given the knowledge they acquire from making first innovations), then broader protection should be given to first innovations: This will result in good incentives for initial innovations and not compromise incentives for second innovations. A similar conclusion holds when initial innovators, though not themselves well suited to make subsequent innovations, can form joint ventures with other parties.[21] Furthermore, giving broad protection to initial innovators can ameliorate the problem of a race among second innovators.

(e) *Effort to copy and to prevent copying of information.* An advantage of the system of property rights in information is that it reduces costly efforts of developers of information to protect their knowledge, and it likewise reduces the efforts of others to appropriate information through copying where possible, reverse engineering, and other "piracy" measures. For example, to the extent that property rights in computer software are enforced, a writer of software need not invest in a storage format that is hard to duplicate, and individuals are not led to try to deduce the source code of a program or to circumvent copy protection. Reduction of such socially wasteful efforts to protect information and to pry it out might constitute the major benefit of property rights in information in some contexts.

(f) *Disclosure of information and property rights.* Because society desires to eliminate the monopoly pricing problem when property rights in innovations expire, it will want patent holders to disclose information lying behind their innovations (obviously, there is no issue of disclosure for holders of copyrights in written material). Note, however, that this requirement can sometimes be avoided by not obtaining a patent, which is the course an innovator would take were he sufficiently confident that competitors could not duplicate his product through reverse engineering (see the discussion of trade secret law in section 1.17).

(g) *Enforcement costs of protecting property rights.* Of course, the advan-

---

21. If they can form joint ventures before undertaking effort to develop second innovations, then as long as the payoff to investment in a second innovation is outweighed by the benefits, there will exist in principle some agreement between the parties that they will each find acceptable. However, reaching an agreement may be problematic; on problems surrounding cooperation and patent, see, for example, Heller and Eisenberg 1998.

tages of property rights in information have to be compared to the costs of their enforcement. These costs include the expenses of detecting infractions of property rights in information and of imposing sanctions for violations. Detection of violations should often be easy, for when goods are offered for sale to the public by a party without property rights, this will usually quickly become known. If goods can be sold or exchanged secretly, detection may be problematic, but the necessity for secrecy will typically mean that the magnitude of the problem of violations will be small.[22] Detection of violations of process patents may be difficult, however, because it involves monitoring production activities that occur behind closed doors. Also, when information can be used in many indirect ways, or when it can be built on in combination with other information, the detection and policing of its use may be hard to accomplish (as is true of basic research; see section 1.22). In any case, another enforcement cost of a system of property rights is the cost of maintaining the administrative and legal apparatus for deciding who will obtain property rights and for settling disputes about property rights.

1.15 Patent law.   Patents are exclusive rights to use, make, and sell inventions for a specified period.[23] The first patent law generally granting rights to inventors was apparently that enacted by the city-state of Venice in the late fifteenth century (although patents had been given to innovators on an individual basis before). English patent law may be traced to a 1624 statute, and some of the American colonies adopted patent statutes not long afterward. The United States passed its first patent law in 1790, and most of the countries of Europe enacted patent legislation in the early 1800s (although—see section 1.21—some countries temporarily abolished patent law later in the century).[24]

The subject matter of patentable innovations encompasses products—

22. A possible exception concerns the private copying of computer software. One supposes that the magnitude of this violation of property rights is substantial and, perhaps, hard to defeat.

23. On patent law in the United States, on which I focus, see, for example, Chisum 1996, Chisum et al. 2001, Miller and Davis 2000, and Schlicher 2001. On patent law in other countries, see, for example, Dinwoodie, Hennessey, and Perlmutter 2001, and Metaxas-Meranghidis 1995.

24. See Machlup 1958, 2–4, and references cited therein.

machines, manufactures, and compositions of things (such as new chemicals)—processes (methods of making things), and several other categories, including plant forms, genetic information, ornamental designs for manufactured products, and certain computer programs.[25]

An innovation whose subject matter falls outside that stipulated in patent law cannot be patented (but might be protected by copyright or trade secret law). An important class of innovations that cannot be patented are abstract ideas. For example, Einstein's discovery of the law of nature $E = mc^2$ was not patentable, nor, probably, would be the idea of pouring boiling water on a tablecloth to remove wine stains. The sense behind barring patents in such discoveries is various: difficulty in enforcing property rights in abstract ideas (it is more difficult to police use of an idea than use and sale of products—how would one practically detect use of the idea of removing wine stains with boiling water?); the fact that some ideas are either fairly obvious (perhaps removing the wine stains), or, in any case, likely to be discovered in due course without substantial investment; the fact that individuals who discover significant new ideas often are rewarded, and thus motivated, in alternative ways (notably, by fame and professional advancement, or by receipt of grants and awards); and the great loss that society would suffer were very general and useful ideas to be restricted by giving a party a monopoly in them.[26] It should be emphasized, however, that ideas are patentable if they are not too abstract and are put in useful form. Process innovations typically fall in this category; for example, a specific method of packaging food. The resolution of the fact that process innovations are patentable but that abstract ideas generally are not may be found in part in the particularity of patentable process innovations and the ability to enforce property rights in them.[27]

To obtain a patent in a product or process, it must be shown to be

25. See, for example, Chisum 1996, vol. 1, chap. 1, Miller and Davis 2000, chap. 2, and Schlicher 2001, chap. 3.

26. On the inability to patent abstract ideas, see, for example, Chisum 1996, vol. 1, chap. 1, 84–85, and Schlicher 2001, section 3.032A.

27. Many if not most process innovations concern production of commercial products or services offered for sale, where the ability to determine whether there is infringement may well be tolerably good. For example, if a new method of cracking hydrocarbons for production of refined oil products is employed, this could perhaps be determined from observation of the design of the plant or from the character of the refined products.

novel, nonobvious, and useful.[28] To satisfy the novelty requirement, the invention must be shown to be new, meaning that it was not previously patented, sold, used, described in print, or anticipated (in the sense that enough was known to allow a person with expertise in the relevant field to make the product or determine the process).[29] An economic rationale for the novelty requirement is that products or processes that do not satisfy it are either ones that society already enjoys or will soon possess (that is, when already described in print or anticipated), so that society has no reason to suffer the losses associated with patent monopoly.

The second requirement goes beyond the novelty requirement in insisting that an invention not only be new, but also be nonobvious.[30] The meaning given to "nonobvious" is determined in a complicated manner, the thrust of which involves identifying those inventions that could not fairly readily have been generated by persons familiar with the relevant art. For example, an improvement to a machine that involves the straightforward application of engineering principles might well fail the nonobviousness test. A justification for the general nonobviousness requirement is similar to that for the novelty requirement: to ensure that society not bear the monopoly costs of patent if a product or process would probably have been created soon enough without the stimulus of patent, on account of its obviousness.[31]

The third requirement, of utility, is met by showing that the invention

28. The requirements for patents in plants and design are somewhat different; see Alces and See 1994, 55–56.

29. See, for example, Chisum 1996, vol. 1, chap. 3, Miller and Davis 2000, chap. 3, and Schlicher 2001, chap. 4.

30. See, for example, Chisum 1996, vol. 2, chap. 5, Miller and Davis 2000, chap. 5, and Schlicher 2001, chap. 5.

31. This is not to say, however, that the principles governing the nonobviousness requirement are always consistent with economic analysis. For instance, an invention that probably would not have occurred to a person familiar with the art because it had a surprising, nonobvious aspect would tend to pass the requirement. But such an invention might have been cheaply developed and have allowed its creator much greater profits than the development cost in the absence of a patent. Hence, economic analysis would suggest that no patent should be granted because the invention would have been made anyway. Conversely, imagine an invention that is obvious in the sense that those familiar with the art agree it can be developed. Such an invention would tend to fail to pass the nonobviousness requirement and thus not be patentable. But if the development cost is high and would clearly

passes some threshold of usefulness.[32] Thus, for example, a new drug that has no apparent function, or one whose value is too speculative, would not satisfy the requirement. It might seem that there is little affirmative need for the utility requirement, for why would a party bear patenting expenses for a useless drug that it is not anticipated will generate sales and profits? An answer that is often suggested is that useless patents can be indirectly profitable: A useless patent might block the patenting of a subsequent useful innovation and thus be employed to extract payments from the later innovator.[33] Although preventing such blocking patents might justify the utility requirement,[34] the requirement also has a drawback. Some innovations that appear to be useless to the patent office may in fact be valuable and be so judged by their creators. Thus, the hurdle of showing adequate utility to the patent office can discourage innovations recognized by their creators to be socially desirable. In sum, the case for the utility requirement is not as clear as that for the other two requirements.

To obtain a patent, it is not necessary that the innovation have been refined or made commercially viable. Indeed, studies show that for many important products (for instance, the automatic transmission, the ballpoint pen, and the safety razor), the period between the award of a patent and the sale of the product was more than five years.[35] The award of patents early in the stage of development meliorates the problems of patent races and duplicative effort, as noted earlier (see section 1.14).

The duration of patents is generally twenty years, although this may

---

not be covered by profits in the absence of patent protection, it would be a mistake, under economic analysis, not to award a patent.

32. On the utility requirement, see, for example, Chisum 1996, vol. 1, chap. 4, Miller and Davis 2000, chap. 4, and Schlicher 2001, sect. 3.02.

33. An additional argument for the utility requirement that is sometimes encountered is that it might reduce the costs of patent searches and also patent office administrative expenses, but this winnowing out function of the requirement could be achieved by imposing an appropriately high filing fee for patent applications.

34. I say "might" because (a) if a useless innovation is needed for a later useful innovation, then perhaps the "useless" innovation is socially desirable and should be encouraged; and, this point aside, (b) if the object is to prevent useless patents from being used to block later useful innovations, the courts could take the direct route of allowing patents to be obtained in the later useful innovations (in other words, of not finding them to be infringing on the useless patents).

35. See Kitch 1977, 272.

be extended for an additional period for drugs.[36] The patent length is apparently of historical origin (derived mainly from the period necessary to train two sets of apprentices).[37] Were the duration of patents decided with regard to the incentive benefits of patents and their social costs, patent length would depend on the class of innovations (for example, length might be shorter when profits that exceed development cost would be generated in just a few years). The uniform nature of the duration of patents stands in significant contrast to the highly elaborated legal consideration given to whether to award patents and to their proper scope.[38] One suspects, therefore, that the fixed twenty-year patent length could be improved.

During the life of a patent, a patent holder is for most purposes free to use or not to use it and free also to set prices.[39] In Europe, however, there are often requirements to use or "work" patents or else licensing of patents at court-determined prices is compelled.[40] Policies aimed at inducing working of patents prevent strategic patent shelving (obtaining a patent only to prevent a competitor from doing so and then competing with a company's existing product), but they may result in the use of patents before they have been adequately refined and developed by their holders.

Patent holders are also allowed to sell and license their patents, which, as remarked earlier, raises their value to society and to patent holders, thus increasing the incentive to innovate.

The scope of patent protection enjoyed by patent holders is determined by a complex of doctrines and principles.[41] In part, the tests of novelty, nonobviousness, and utility determine the scope of protection, because they affect whether other products can be patented. The scope of protection is

36. 35 *U.S. Code* sect. 154. On the possible extension of patent duration for drugs, see, for example, Chisum 1996, vol. 5, chap. 16, 210–214.

37. See White 1956.

38. Were the courts to employ the information that they use in these domains in relation to patent duration, they would presumably be able to improve on the present twenty-year duration.

39. Failure to use a patent may cause a patent holder to run afoul of antitrust law, however; see, for example, Miller and Davis 2000, sect. 8.4.

40. On working of patents and compulsory licensing in other countries, see, for example, Henry 1977 and Rüster 1991.

41. On the scope of protection and infringement, see, for example, Chisum 1996, vol. 5, chap. 16, Miller and Davis 2000, chap. 8, and Schlicher 2001, chap. 8.

also affected by determination of patent infringement, that is, by the products and practices of other parties that are deemed to interfere with the rights of a patent holder.

1.16 Copyright law.   Copyrights are similar to patents; they are essentially exclusive rights to reproduce writings and certain other intellectual products for a specified period.[42] In the Middle Ages, monasteries and other owners of manuscripts possessed the right to charge a fee for copying. With the invention of the printing press, exclusive privileges to print were granted. As with the award of privileges to manufacture new goods, the award of printing rights apparently occurred first in Venice, in 1469, and the practice quickly spread throughout Europe. In England, printing privileges were early awarded both individually and to the Stationers' Company, representing a guild of printers, which developed its own system of copyright. Copyright law in the United States began with a 1790 statute.[43] In most countries today, copyright is governed principally by general statutes that give exclusive rights to originators of works or to those to whom they assign their works.

Copyrightable material now includes not only compositions of words, but also maps, paintings and other works of art, photographs, motion pictures, musical compositions and musical recordings, computer programs, architectural plans, and semiconductor chip designs.[44] That there are so many types of copyrightable works raises the question of whether there is a general principle determining whether a work will be copyrightable as opposed to patentable. It seems from the list just given that copyrightable works have a self-revealing quality, making them easy to reproduce, whereas patentable works often cannot be duplicated without considerable reverse

42. On copyright law in the United States, see generally Goldstein 2001a, Nimmer and Nimmer 1995, Patry 1994, and Miller and Davis 2000. On copyright law in other countries, see, for example, Goldstein 2001b, Metaxas-Maranghidis 1995, Tritton et al. 2002, and Wineburg 1999.

43. For a summary of the general history of copyright, see Rose 1993, chap. 2; for the history in England, see Davenport 1993, 22–31 and Patterson 1968, chaps. 1–8, and for the history in the United States, see Goldstein 2001a, vol. 1, chap. 1, 32–40 and Patterson 1968, chaps. 9–11.

44. See Goldstein 2001a, vol. 1, chap. 2, Miller and Davis 2000, chap. 20, and Patry 1994, chap. 2.

engineering. This principle, however, does not fully account for the distinctions the law draws between copyrightable and patentable works and, in any event, it is not legally relevant.[45]

Two basic requirements must be met to obtain a copyright in a work (assuming that it falls into a copyrightable category). The first requirement is fixation, that a work must have been expressed in a tangible medium. For instance, for a speech to be copyrighted, it must have been written or recorded in some other way. Without this requirement of fixation, it would be difficult for courts to verify claims of copying, for there would be no tangible evidence of initial authorship.[46]

The other requirement for copyright is that of originality, meaning that a work must have originated with the claimant—he cannot have literally copied it— and often that it showed a modicum of creativity. Originality in this limited sense is, as previously remarked, usually also sufficient for copyright; it is not generally required that the work in question add substantially to the stock of similar works or be novel or nonobvious, unlike in the case of patent. For example, a photographer who takes a picture of the same sight as a previous photographer, say of Niagara Falls, can obtain a copyright in it, however close his image is to the earlier one.[47]

Why should originality generally be sufficient for the award of copyright but not for that of patent? Is this distinction socially rational? A speculative answer flows from the point that for much copyrightable material, the particulars of the expressive work explain its value more than the underlying ideas. The actual language employed by Shakespeare in *Romeo and*

45. The main problem with the distinction is that some patentable works are very easily copied, for example, the hula hoop. To an important degree, the courts do not use this distinction or other general principles to decide what is copyrightable—they instead refer to legislation that sets out in fairly specific terms what is copyrightable. But there are certain doctrines that are resorted to in problematic cases. Notably, "utilitarian" works, such as lamps, are not copyrightable; see Goldstein 2001a, vol. 1, chap. 2, 55–60, and Miller and Davis 2000, 300–301. (One may ask, however, why any book, especially a textbook, or a computer program is not utilitarian; they clearly provide utility. Yet they are copyrightable.) Finally, it should also be observed that the law sometimes allows a party to obtain both forms of protection for a work; see Goldstein 2001a, vol. 1, chap. 2, 57 and Miller and Davis 2000, 305.

46. See Lichtman 2003.

47. See Goldstein 2001a, vol. 1, chap. 2, 6–21.

Juliet is what makes it such a worthwhile contribution to literature (one can imagine that other plays built on essentially the same plot would be viewed quite differently). Thus, society should encourage creation of new written works, even if very similar to old works in underlying ideas, by giving copyright to most any expression of the ideas; in that way, a person whose expression of the ideas is highly valuable will be rewarded. By contrast, society does not want to encourage development of machines that are too similar to existing ones because the particulars of a machine are not what gives a machine its value; a new type of engine, like the steam engine, will be valued for its function, whether or not the size of its various components and other features are this or that.[48] A second justification for the sufficiency of originality for copyright concerns the difficulty a claimant would face in determining whether his work is close to another's. Because written works are not catalogued or registered in a way that lends itself to easy checking for similarity, it would be hard for a person to ascertain whether his work is close to any other existing work. Hence, were there a requirement of novelty, people would either bear the risk of infringement or be led to spend on verification for novelty. These social costs are avoided when originality guarantees copyright.[49]

The duration of copyright has changed over time and is presently equal to the author's lifetime plus seventy years (but somewhat different if the author is a company).[50] Why this should be, and why, for example, the duration of protection should be so much more generous than for patents, is not evident, and one surmises that it has no clear rationale.

Holders of copyrights are free to use or not to use their works, to set prices for use, and to sell their copyrights.

The scope of copyright protection depends in part on the factor of

48. Furthermore, and closely related, the granting of patents in a very similar steam engine would tend to reduce substantially revenues for the holder of the first patent. But the granting of a copyright in a book based on a very similar theme to that of another author might be thought not to reduce substantially the first author's revenues—because the differences in the books' expressions of the common theme will tend to make them more like independent products.

49. It is also true that checking whether one's innovation is similar to a patent is costly, but the organization of patents may make checking easier. This point is stressed by Landes and Posner 1989, 345.

50. 17 *U.S. Code* sect. 302.

similarity between works. The greater the similarity between a new work and a copyrighted one, the less likely a party is to obtain a copyright in the new work. Thus, a literary work that follows the plot of an existing one too closely, a musical composition that borrows too much from an existing one, a cartoon character that too much resembles in appearance and "personality" an established one (like Snoopy) may be judged infringing. (It appears, however, that a work must be subjectively very close to an existing one to be found infringing, which makes sense assuming that, as noted above, the particularity of the expression of underlying ideas is often what largely determines the value of a work.) Another factor that influences the scope of copyright protection is the access that a party had to a copyrighted work. The greater the opportunity that a party had to examine a copyrighted work, the greater the inference that his new work is not original and thus the less likely he is to obtain a copyright in his new work.

Also of importance to the scope of protection is the doctrine of *fair use,* which is a defense to a claim of infringement, and effectively sets out circumstances in which parties are allowed to use copyrighted works without paying copyright holders.[51] Examples of uses that have been treated as fair include: reproduction of short sections of copyrighted materials in class materials, the recording of a television program by an individual on a VCR for later viewing, and quotation from a copyrighted book in a book review or parody. The economic justification for permitting a use is that, on one hand, it may detract very little from the profit of the copyright holder (and thus not reduce by very much incentives to create), and on the other hand, it may add substantially to the utility of users.[52] To illustrate, permitting reproduction of several pages from a book for use in class materials might not much reduce sales of the book (students would have been unlikely to purchase the book to read just a few pages) and thus an author's incentive to write it, but their ability to read such selections may substantially enhance the educational value of their class materials.[53] Although uses that

51. On the law of fair use, see generally Patry 1995; this book also describes related doctrines in other countries, 589–599.

52. On the economics of fair use, see Fisher 1988, Gordon 1982, and Landes and Posner 1989, 357–361.

53. A potentially important qualification to the conjecture that the author of the book would not lose much profits should be mentioned: He might obtain profit not by selling extra copies of the book but by charging for reproduction of the pages. The transaction

are deemed fair seem in a rough and implicit way to reflect such economic reasoning, some of the legal tests used to decide fair use are inconsistent with the reasoning.[54]

Another significant aspect of the scope of copyright protection is that copyright holders enjoy rights to *derivative works,* such as translations, films based on books, clothing and other articles featuring copyrighted cartoon characters, and generally any form in which a work may be recast or transformed. This legal policy can be justified on the basis of the discussion of dependent innovations in section 1.14 (d). Namely, suppose that copyright holders often are well suited to develop derivative works themselves or can contract to have that done. Then the creation of derivative works will be encouraged (translations will be undertaken) and the possibility of duplicative effort to create derivative works (races to complete translations) will be avoided. Furthermore, the generation of original works will be enhanced since they might not be created if the only reward is from the original works themselves (a movie might not be produced if profits cannot be obtained from versions for foreign audiences). Where, however, the copyright holder would not be likely to develop or contract with a party to develop a derivative work, perhaps because it is not obvious, it is not clear that giving the holder the right to the derivative work is desirable.

1.17 Trade secret law.   Trade secret law is the name given to various doctrines of contract and tort law that serve to protect commercially valuable information such as designs, manufacturing processes, and customer lists.[55] In order to be protected, the information must not be known to the public and the holder of the information must take steps to prevent the information from becoming public. Trade secret law is governed by state law, as opposed to federal legislation that regulates patents and copyrights. Principal examples of trade secret law are the enforcement of employment

---

costs associated with securing permission and paying the author, however, might deter classroom use, meaning that the author would not be losing profits due to the fair use doctrine. On fair use and photocopying, see Goldstein 2001a, vol. 2, chap. 10, 7, 8, 36–39.

54. For an economically oriented, critical discussion of the rationality of the legal criteria used to determine whether a use is fair, see Fisher 1988, 1667–1695.

55. On trade secret law in the United States, see generally Milgrim 1995, Cohen and Gutterman 1998, and Pooley 2001, and on trade secret law in other countries, see, for example, Ladas 1964 and Dinwoodie, Hennessey, and Perlmutter 2001.

contracts stipulating that employees not use employer trade secrets to compete with their employer (typically after having left the employer); enforcement of similar contracts restricting the right of firms working for a given firm from using certain information to compete with it or from revealing it to a competitor; and allowing suit for tort damages to be brought for acquisition of valuable information by improper means, including not only illegal behavior, notably theft, but also such practices as flying a plane over a factory to take pictures to deduce its production process. The protection of property rights under trade secret law does not extend, however, to reverse engineering. A competitor is free to deduce trade secrets by, for example, examining a product and analyzing it or by identifying the customers of a competitor.

How does trade secret law relate to patent and copyright? It is of course similar in that it is a form of property right protection of information. Yet it is different in a number of respects. First, a party can obtain trade secret protection without incurring any real expense (but the party must have taken steps to guard its information) and without having to meet the tests necessary for patent or copyright protection. Second, trade secret protection is not limited in duration. Relatedly, trade secrets need not ever be disclosed. As mentioned earlier, Coca Cola's formula has been protected for over a century under trade secret law. Third, trade secret protection is in some respects weaker than patent protection. As noted, one such respect is that trade secret protection does not prevent reverse engineering. Another is that it may be difficult to sell a trade secret because the buyer often will not pay as much as the secret is worth unless he is first told what the secret is, but then he could refuse to purchase it and use it (a problem that does not afflict the sale of patent or copyright information).[56]

Trade secret protection is a supplement to patent and copyright because it can be obtained when parties are unable to secure patents or copyrights

---

56. See Arrow 1971, 152. To illustrate, consider the difficulty a party would face in attempting to sell a new marketing plan: Before seeing the actual plan in its details, the potential buyer would often have a difficult time evaluating it, so would not be willing to pay its full value. This problem does not always exist, however, for in some instances a buyer can evaluate the worth of a secret (and make the contract depend on this worth) without knowing the secret itself. For example, a buyer might be told by how much a secret production process will lower his production costs without being told what the secret process is.

or in addition to them. And trade secret protection is also an alternative to patent or copyright because a party is free to elect such protection instead of either of them.

An evaluation of trade secret law should include consideration of the following two points. First, because trade secret law furnishes the *only* form of property rights protection for some information, it would seem to be socially desirable on the general grounds that protection of property rights in information is thought to be socially desirable. This is especially likely to be true for information of relatively low value, and thus for which the expenditures that private parties and society make on the patent and copyright process would not be warranted. Second, giving individuals the option to choose between trade secret protection and patent or copyright (when they would qualify for these) has a desirable feature: If individuals have better information than the state about the relative benefits and costs of trade secret versus patent or copyright protection, they will make a better decision than the state about which form of protection provides them greater net benefits. But because net private benefits may be different from net social benefits, allowing parties to elect trade secret protection over patent or copyright might be disadvantageous. For example, if Coca Cola had obtained a patent for its formula, it would have enjoyed property right protection only for twenty years rather than for the much greater period that it has in fact kept its formula secret, and perhaps one substantially exceeding that usually necessary to induce development of such a formula.

1.18 Rewards for creating information: an alternative to property rights in information.   A system that provides a fundamental alternative to property rights in information is one in which the state pays rewards to creators of information and then places the information in the public domain, making it freely available to all—so that no property rights in the information exist. Thus, under the reward system, an author of a book would receive a reward from the state for writing the book (the reward might well be paid only over time—see later), but any firm that wanted to print the book and sell it could do so.

The reward system appears to have the virtue of the property rights system but not the drawback. Like the property rights system, the reward system encourages production of information because the creator of information obtains a financial benefit, namely the reward. But unlike the property rights system, the reward system appears to result in optimal dissemination of information because the information is in the public domain: Anyone can use it. Under the property rights system, a book would sell at a price exceeding cost because the copyright holder would be able to charge such a price, but under the reward system, the book would sell at a price reflecting only cost, because any firm could sell the book. In general, due to competition, goods embodying new information would tend to sell at prices resembling production cost, meaning that the quantity sold would tend toward the optimal. Hence, it seems that the reward system is superior to the property rights system because it provides incentives to innovate without causing prices to be high relative to cost, that is, without causing the use of information to be lower than socially desirable. We have not yet discussed, however, how the reward would be calculated.

1.19 Determination of the reward.   The reward system will generate incentives to create information in accordance with the magnitude of the reward the potential creators can expect. If the reward were to equal what the creators would obtain if they had property rights, then the reward system would lead to identical incentives to create information, and would therefore be superior to property rights, because the information created would be optimally disseminated. In the ideal, the reward system would result in a reward sufficiently high to induce creation of all socially worthwhile information; this could be accomplished by offering a reward reflecting the full social value of information.[57] To give rewards that reflect the social value of information, the state might base the reward on the volume of use of the information, such as the sales volume of a book, and on some measure of its utility as well. Presumably, the rewards would be paid over time, such as annually, as sales of the good embodying the information occur, and as information about its social value is developed. The difficulties that the state would face in deciding on rewards, however, might

---

57. The virtue of setting the reward equal to the social value of information is that then, other things being equal, a potential creator will make the socially correct decision whether to develop the information. Of course, if the state knows not only the social value of the information but also how much it would cost to develop it, the state can determine whether it is desirable to develop and can offer a reward just high enough to induce the information to be developed; such an award would generally be less than the social value of the information.

lead to outcomes inferior to those under property rights. For example, suppose that there is a book that an author knows he could sell at a high price because it will be very valuable to a small sector of the market, such as a specialty or technical book of great interest to several thousand individuals but not to others. Under the property rights system, the author might well write it because he knows that he would be able to sell it for a price sufficient to justify his efforts. By contrast, if under the reward system his payment would be based mainly on the volume of sales (because it might be hard for the state to measure the high value placed on the book), he might not receive enough to make it worth his while writing the book. Thus, it cannot be said that the reward system is unambiguously better than the property rights system. Still, one supposes that in many plausible situations, the reward system would be superior to the property rights system. In any case, it does not seem that there is a clear and appealing case for the property rights system over the reward system.[58]

1.20 Additional issues concerning the reward system. (a) *Duplicative effort and the race to be first.* It was observed that under the property rights system, there would often be duplicative effort to create information and a wasteful race to be first. The reward system would also suffer from these disadvantages, since only the first party to create information would receive the reward.

(b) *Dependence of present innovations on past innovations.* The reward system would enjoy an advantage over property rights systems with respect to the dependence of present innovations on past ones. Under the reward system, present innovators would, by definition of the system, be able to use freely all past innovations, whereas, as discussed before, under the patent

---

58. As will be noted later, the reward system was a subject of intense study by economists and of public debate in the nineteenth century. Today, however, it receives relatively little attention from economists; I am emphasizing it here because of its intellectual appeal and seeming potential. For discussion of the reward system versus patent, see Mill [1848] 1872, 563, Polanvyi 1944, and Scherer 1980, 458; and for theoretical analysis, see Wright 1983, Kremer 1998, and Shavell and van Ypersele 2001. In the latter article, it is demonstrated that despite the imperfect information faced by government, an optional reward scheme—under which innovators choose between intellectual property rights and a properly chosen reward—is unambiguously superior to the intellectual property rights system.

system, new innovation is sometimes retarded because it would be found to infringe on earlier innovation.

(c) *Social cost of protecting property rights; efforts to copy and to prevent copying.* Under the reward system, unlike under the property rights system, there would be no social effort expended protecting property rights, so there would be a savings on enforcement costs in that sense. Moreover, innovators would have no reason to prevent others from copying their work, and those who wanted to copy would not have to overcome obstacles to do so. But there would remain a cost of administering the reward system.

(d) *Financing the reward system.* The reward system would have to be financed by the state, which is to say, by taxes. Thus, an apparent disadvantage of the reward system is the social cost associated with income taxation.[59]

1.21 Actual use of the reward system and debate about it. A reward-like system is employed today in the United States for innovations of possible military use where granting patents might compromise our national security.[60] For example, the government might not want certain inventions in the area of atomic energy or germ warfare to be sold on the open market. A general system of rewards was used in the former Soviet Union and other socialist countries; for example, if a person devised a cost-saving innovation, he might obtain payment equal to a percentage of its value.[61] Of course, intellectual property rights could not have been employed in these countries, since parties were not free to produce, set prices, and sell goods in markets.

From the 1850s to the 1870s, the issue of how to promote inventive activity and creation of intellectual works was debated vigorously in Europe. The principal contest was between the patent system and the reward system. For a time, the reward system was believed to be the one that would be adopted, and it was championed by many economists. For example, in England a succession of parliamentary committees and royal commissions

---

59. As explained in section 4.6 of Chapter 28, however, to the extent that the social costs have to do with the distortion of work effort, these costs do not constitute an argument against a legal policy, such as a reward system, that is otherwise desirable. In any case, Lichtman 1997 suggests that a government subsidy of patented products may offer an advantage over rewards because the government will need less tax revenue to finance the subsidy.

60. See, for example, Payne 1996, section 78, Lee 1997, and Riesenfeld 1958.

61. See Sinnot 1988, 44, and Stepanov 1958.

were appointed to examine the patent system, and they proposed reforms or alternatives to it. In 1869, the *Economist* opined, "It is probable enough that the patent laws will be abolished ere long." Chancellor Bismarck announced his opposition to the principle of a patent system for Prussia in 1868, the Netherlands abolished its patent law in 1869, and Switzerland, which had never had a patent law, rejected several proposals for one. But for a variety of reasons, apparently more political than based on consensus about the intellectual appeal of the patent system, that system won out. Still, it was not until late in the nineteenth century and into the next that some European countries decided to adopt a patent law (Switzerland did so in 1887, the Netherlands in 1910).[62]

1.22 Practices similar to the reward system: state support of basic research; bestowal of prizes and honors.   The state carries out basic research through its own scientific agencies (such as the National Institutes of Health) and through the award of grants to private individuals and organizations. Those who carry out basic research usually do not obtain property rights in it and so do not profit thereby. Indeed, the notion of a system of property rights in basic research results seems largely unworkable. This is because, as a general matter, a basic research result is not useful in a particular embodied form, nor for producing any single named thing; rather, such a result is often used in combination with other knowledge to produce further knowledge or physical things. This makes the definition and enforcement of property rights in basic research results impractical. State support of basic research thus resembles a reward system in that payments to creators of information are made by the state and the creators do not usually obtain property rights in what they create.

It should also be observed that the bestowal of prizes and honors on creators of information and the social esteem that they may enjoy function as species of reward systems.

Note on the literature.   The extensive economic literature on property rights in information uniformly stresses the compromise that property rights strike between generating incentives to innovate and hindering the

---

62. See Machlup and Penrose 1950, 1–6; the quotation from the *Economist* is included in note 3 of their article.

sale of goods and services embodying the information. A review of the evolution of economic thinking about patent is contained in Machlup (1958). Summaries of the economics of property rights in information are found in chapter 17 of Scherer and Ross (1990) and in Menell (2000), and a concise, synthetic theoretical treatment of economic literature is contained in chapter 10 of Tirole (1988).[63] There is by comparison relatively little economically oriented writing analyzing the doctrines of intellectual property law; such literature includes Kitch (1977, 1998) on patent, Landes and Posner (1989) on copyright, Friedman, Landes, and Posner (1991) on trade secret protection, and the general work Landes and Posner (2003).[64] Empirical study of intellectual property rights is surveyed in Gallini (2002), Jaffe (2000), and Lanjouw and Lerner (1998).

2. PROPERTY RIGHTS IN OTHER TYPES OF INFORMATION

2.1 Variety of other types of information.   There are many diverse types of information different from that which is useful for producing multiple units of a good, and I mention several in illustration here. One is information that is useful only a single time, such as information about the location of oil under a particular parcel of land. Another is information that pertains to future market prices, for example, information about the production of commodities or about the earnings prospects of publicly traded companies. An additional type of information is personal information, from the mundane to the serious (such as about the commission of crimes).

2.2 Socially desirable generation and use of the foregoing types of information; property rights in such information.   With respect to information that can be used only a single time, there is sometimes no need for property rights protection. If the party who possesses the information can use it himself (perhaps the oil deposit about which he knows is located

63. See also Besen 1998, Besen and Raskind 1991, and Reinganum 1989.

64. See also Dam 1994 on patent law, Lemley 1997 and Gordon and Bone 2000 on copyright, and Cheung 1982 on trade secret protection.

under land that he owns), then once he does so, the issue of others learning it becomes moot—there will be no further value to the information. But to the degree that a person is unable to use the information himself (perhaps the oil is located on someone else's land and he cannot conveniently purchase drilling rights), his having property rights in the information might be valuable to him and might beneficially foster acquisition of information. Moreover, it should be emphasized that giving property rights in the information will not undesirably reduce the use of information when the optimal use of it is only once. In any case, the legal system usually does furnish property rights protection in such information as where oil is located, through trade secret law and the allied doctrines of tort and contract law.

Consider next information relevant to future market prices and observe that the private and the social value of gaining such information can diverge. For example, a person who first learns that a fungus has destroyed much of the cocoa crop and that cocoa prices are therefore going to rise can profit by buying cocoa futures; his profit measures the private value of his advance information. The social value of his information, however, inheres in any beneficial changes in nonfinancial behavior that it brings about. For example, an increase in cocoa futures prices might lead candy producers to reduce wastage of cocoa or to switch from chocolate candy production to production of another kind of candy. Now the profit that a person with advance information about future cocoa prices can make in the absence of property rights can easily be imagined to be either greater or less than the social value of this information.[65] Hence, it is not evident whether it is socially desirable to further encourage acquisition of such information about price movements by giving individuals property rights in the information, but the law does do so, again mainly through trade secret law.

65. For example, a single person with the information might not be able to capture much profit, because others might soon get wind of what he knows and quickly raise the price of cocoa futures. If so, his profit might be significantly less than the social value associated with a timely increase in cocoa futures prices. But another possibility is that the person will be able to purchase a substantial volume of cocoa futures before the price rises to reflect his information. Moreover, the social value of the information could be small—perhaps there is little that candy manufacturers could do to reduce cocoa wastage over the period in question. In this case, the private value of the information would exceed the social value. The general contrast between the private value of information about market prices and the social value of this information was first emphasized by Hirshleifer 1971.

Last, consider personal information. The costs of acquiring this information are the effort to snoop, although the information is sometimes adventitiously acquired and thus costless. The social value of the information involves various complexities, and I mention a few of the elements at issue. The release of information of a personal nature to the outside world generally causes disutility to those persons exposed and utility for others, the net effect of which is ambiguous. Further, the prospect of someone's obtaining personal information and then releasing it, or of his demanding payments not to reveal his information, can alter behavior of potential victims: They may be led not to engage in socially undesirable behavior (such as commission of crimes) or not to engage in socially desirable behavior that might be embarrassing if publicly revealed, and they may make costly efforts to conceal their behavior. Thus, there are reasons why acquisition and revelation of personal information may be socially desirable, and reasons as well why they might be socially undesirable.[66] Now although the law penalizes blackmail and in this way attempts to discourage profit from acquisition of personal information, it does extend limited property rights in personal information. For example, an individual who wants to sell personal information he has obtained to a publication can often make a contract to do that, which he may want to do when the information describes a public figure. This makes some sense in that a rough judgment might be that the social value of revelation of information about public figures outweighs the harm to them.

As this brief discussion illustrates, the factors bearing on the desirability of protecting property rights in information vary significantly according to the type of information, and the issue of the desirability of protection calls for analysis quite different from that concerning information of repetitive value that I considered earlier.

3. TRADEMARKS: PROPERTY RIGHTS IN LABELS

3.1 Goods and services whose quality is hard for consumers to ascertain directly. As will be explained, the social value of labels has to do with the many goods and services whose quality is hard for consumers

---

66. For consideration of these issues and the law of blackmail, see Lindgren 1984, Ginsburg and Shechtman 1993, Posner 1993, and Shavell 1993b.

to determine directly. For a consumer to be able to ascertain directly the quality of a hotel or of a breakfast cereal, for example, he would have to inspect the hotel room or sample the cereal. This would take time and would be impractical in many contexts (such as when making reservations at a hotel in another city). Furthermore, even if a person does examine a good, this would often reveal little, for in a modern economy products are often complicated in nature and their character is not clear from their outward appearance.

3.2 Social value of labels for goods and services whose quality is difficult to ascertain directly. By a label for a good or service is meant a word, phrase, or symbol that is uniquely associated with its particular seller. Labels have social value when consumers associate them with the true quality of labeled goods (or services) and when the quality of such goods would otherwise be hard to determine. The social value of labels inheres in two factors.

First, labels enable consumers to make purchase decisions on the basis of product quality or to do so without going to the expense of independently determining their quality (if this is even possible). A person who wants to stay at a high quality hotel in another city can choose such a hotel merely by its label, such as "Hilton Hotel"; the consumer need not visit the hotel. A person who wants assurance of the freshness and taste of a breakfast cereal, or who seeks a long-lasting consumer durable like a washing machine, will be able to find what he wants by reference to the brand name—he need not open the box of cereal or somehow test the washing machine. At the same time, someone who wants a medium-quality good or service, for instance, a Holiday Inn rather than a Hilton Hotel, will be able to identify and purchase that grade of good. That is, the existence of labels enables consumers to choose along a continuum of qualities when direct identification of qualities would otherwise involve cost or be practically impossible.

Second, and related, if labels can be established, sellers will have an incentive to produce goods and services of high quality, for a seller will know that the quality of his good or service will be recognized by consumers through its label and that the seller will therefore be able to charge a price reflecting true quality. If sellers did not have this incentive, high-quality goods would tend not to be sold when consumers could not readily independently ascertain quality.

3.3 Social value of property rights in labels. The existence of property rights in labels—that is, the power of holders of the rights to bar other sellers from using holders' labels—is necessary for the benefits of labels to be enjoyed. In the absence of property rights in labels, the label of a high-quality good or service would be adopted by a lower-quality competitor, who would be able to charge the same price but operate at lower cost. If any hotel could call itself a Hilton Hotel, it would be motivated to do so. In consequence, the term "Hilton Hotel" would lose meaning as hotel-goers discovered that Hilton Hotels are not necessarily of high quality. The informational content of labels would quickly erode, if it was ever established.

When property rights in labels exist, however, sellers will plainly have incentives to create effective labels in order that the labels come to be associated with the qualities of their products and services.[67] Specifically, these incentives will exist whenever sellers wish to make and sell products and services above the lowest quality.

3.4 Social costs of property rights in labels. Maintaining a system of property rights in labels involves certain administrative and enforcement costs, which most obviously concern preventing infringing uses of labels. Another cost of a system of labels is the advertising expenses borne promoting the labels. Closely related is that building up labels enables sellers to create or to preserve market power or to mislead customers about product quality. These problems, though, may be addressed directly through the antitrust statutes and truth-in-advertising laws, so that the degree to which they should be regarded as implicit costs of property rights in labels is attenuated.

There is also a latent cost of allowing property rights in labels: encumbering our use of language and symbols. Suppose that it were possible for a seller to obtain a property right in an ordinary descriptive phrase, such

---

67. The creation of labels per se can to some degree be counted as an independent benefit of property rights in them, for the labels add words (and symbols) to our vocabulary. For example, the words "aspirin" and "thermos" were originally trademarks and have now entered into our language. But because it seems that society can fairly easily invent new words as needed, I will not analyze the creation of new words as a benefit of property rights in labels in the text.

as "delicious soup" or "well-engineered automobile." Then sellers would generally face difficulty in describing their products; normal use of language would be problematic because it would expose sellers to the risk of liability for infringement of property rights in words, and they would thus be led to spend time and energy checking that their apparently innocuous descriptive language did not infringe on another's property rights. Such costs can be largely eliminated, however, by restricting property rights in labels to uncommon and distinctive usages. As will be discussed later, this is essentially what the law does, so that the potential cost in question should be considered negligible in reality.

3.5 Optimal duration and extent of property rights in labels.   It seems that the optimal duration of property rights in a label is potentially unlimited. A label might well best be continued as long as a seller is using it and society is therefore obtaining the benefits from consumer recognition of the associated product quality. Were property rights in a label discontinued after some stipulated number of years, the seller would have to invest, pointlessly, in a new label, and consumers would have to learn it, during which time they would not easily be able to recognize the quality of the seller's good.

There are, however, reasons apart from the mere passage of time for property rights in a label to be terminated. If a seller were to fail to employ his label, it might be desirable to withdraw the property right in the label, for the label might have some scarcity value. Also, were a seller to degrade the quality of his good in order to fool customers and enhance profits in the short run (perhaps because he is intending to go out of business), it might be desirable to cancel his property right in the label (and perhaps auction it off, so that it would be likely to be maintained).

What can be said about the desirable extent of property right protection in a label at any given time, that is, about such issues as the socially optimal geographic scope of protection or about protection against the use of similar but not identical labels? Evidently, the guiding principle should be that use of a label should not lead consumers to confuse different products, for the social desirability of labels rests on their furnishing consumers the ability to identify product quality. Suppose, for example, that a firm doing business in state A alone adopts the very same label for its product ("Party-time Pizza") as does another firm doing business in state B alone, and that consumers would thus not be likely to be confused about the meaning of the label in either state. Then it might well be desirable to allow the use of both labels even though they are identical. But suppose that a firm uses a label (such as the brand name "Liz Claborne") that is different from an established label (the brand name "Liz Claiborne"), but not so different as to be noticed by most consumers. Here it would seem that the new label should be barred even though the label is not identical to the first.

3.6 Property rights in labels contrasted with property rights in information of repetitive value. The chief difference between property rights in labels and property rights in information of repetitive value discussed earlier is that the granting of property rights in labels involves no significant social cost beyond that of enforcement. Society does not incur a cost when it gives the exclusive right to a label to a seller, whereas society does incur a cost—due to a suboptimal volume of sales—when it gives to a party the exclusive right to sell a book or a machine, for a monopoly price will be charged. Thus, unlike patents and copyrights, property rights in labels should be regarded as essentially socially unproblematic.

3.7 Trademark law. The area of law regarding what has been described here as labels is that of *trademarks*.[68] A trademark can be any word, name, symbol, device, or signifier used by a manufacturer to identify its goods. To obtain a property right in a trademark, it must be deemed distinctive. This requirement is automatically met by fanciful words, such as "Exxon" and "Sanka"; by words used in arbitrary combination, for example, "Apple Computer"; by words employed in suggestive ways, such as "Ivory Soap"; and even by words used in a straightforward descriptive sense if they have acquired special meaning (known as *secondary meaning*), for example, "Holiday Inn" or "Pizza Hut." The description of the distinctiveness requirement seems broadly consistent with the uses of trademarks discussed

---

68. I focus here on American and English trademark law, which is described in, for example, Kane 2001, McCarthy 1996, and Miller and Davis 2000. On trademark law in other countries (which resembles Anglo-American trademark law), see Jacobs 1987, Pinner 1978, and Rüster 1991. On the history of trademark law, see Schechter 1925 and McClure 1979.

earlier, especially in respect to the goal of minimizing interference with normal use of language.[69]

The legal treatment of symbols is similar to that of words. Symbols may be trademarks if they are specially conceived, like the three-spoked Mercedes symbol; common symbols (such as a circle) cannot receive trademark protection, nor can design characteristics that have functional significance (the feature of treads on a tire cannot be trademarked, but a logo on the tire wall can be).[70]

Trademarks can be acquired through use and through registration processes,[71] and they can be sold.

The duration of trademarks is indefinite; they can be held as long as they are employed. If abandoned, however, or if rapidly degraded, they can be lost. These aspects of trademark duration make economic sense, as explained in section 3.5.

If a trademarked word enters the language because it acquires generic meaning—as has happened, for example, with "aspirin," "thermos," and "yo-yo"—the trademark is lost. The social advantage of this doctrine is that it enables other sellers to describe their product without undue difficulty (how would a maker of yo-yos describe its product without using the word "yo-yo"?). A possible disadvantage of the doctrine is that holders of trademarks may be induced to spend to prevent the trademarks from becoming generic; such expenditures are a social waste and, if successful,

69. Clearly, the use of fanciful words and arbitrary combinations does not interfere with normal usage, nor, probably, do suggestive combinations of words. Additionally, the very definition of secondary meaning ensures that when words used in a normal descriptive sense are allowed to constitute a trademark they are so well associated with a particular seller that in fact other sellers would *not* be at risk of unknowingly using the words (no motel chain would unknowingly use the words "Holiday Inn" in describing its motels).

70. Note that, were a feature with functional significance like treads to constitute a trademark, the maker of treaded tires would effectively be given a monopoly in a product characteristic that directly benefits consumers. Thus, consumer welfare would fall; the manufacturer would charge a monopoly price for treads, resulting in a suboptimal volume of tires with treads.

71. In the United States, trademarks are governed by state common law and by federal trademark statutes, effectively establishing a federal registration system; see, for example, Hawes 1997 and McCarthy 1996.

imply that other sellers will have to establish a synonymous word for the product.[72]

The touchstone of trademark infringement doctrine is the likelihood of consumer misapprehension about the true seller of goods and services. Thus, as was suggested earlier (in section 3.5), to be socially desirable, infringement is more likely to be found the more the marks resemble each other, the more similar the marked goods, and the greater the geographic overlap in their markets.

Note on the literature.   Several articles adopt an economic orientation toward the analysis of trademark law, the most general of these being Landes and Posner (1987b).[73]

72. For literature on the genericness doctrine, see, for example, Palladino 2000 and Swann 1999.

73. See also Burgunder 1985, Economides 1988, 1998, Lemley 1999, and Mims 1984.

PART II ‖‖ ACCIDENT LAW

By accident law, I refer to the body of legal rules that govern the rights of victims of harm to sue and to collect payments from those who injured them. This area of law is part of what is known as tort law in Anglo-American legal systems. The analysis of accident law will begin in Chapters 8, 9, and 10, with a consideration of how legal rules of liability influence parties' incentives to reduce accident risks. Attention will be focused on the two major rules of liability, negligence and strict liability. Under the negligence rule, an injurer is liable to the victim only if the injurer was negligent, in the sense that his level of care was less than a minimum standard chosen by the courts. Under the rule of strict liability, an injurer is liable for having caused harm even if he was not negligent.

In Chapter 11 the consideration of accident law will be broadened to reflect the effect of liability rules on compensation of victims and the allocation of risk. In this chapter, a central issue will be the roles of victims' insurance and of liability insurance. Two points about insurance will be stressed: Victims' insurance diminishes the need for the liability system as a compensatory device; and liability insurance not only protects injurers from risk, but it also alters the incentives to reduce risk created by liability rules.

Last, in Chapter 12, the administrative costs of the liability system, namely, the private and public legal costs of litigation, will be examined. These costs are significant and thus bear importantly on whether use of accident law is socially desirable. It will be emphasized that social intervention—either to curtail use of the legal system or to encourage it—may well be needed because the private incentives to use the system are generally different from the socially desirable incentives to do so.

8 ||| LIABILITY AND DETERRENCE: BASIC THEORY

Here and throughout Part Two, we will consider a model of accidents involving two types of parties, injurers and victims. We might think, for example, of injurers as drivers of automobiles and of victims as bicyclists, or of injurers as parties conducting blasting operations and of victims as passersby.[1]

Injurers may face legal liability for accidents that they cause, and the effect of this possibility on their behavior, victims' behavior, and specified measures of social welfare will now be studied in several increasingly general versions of the model of accidents. The two major rules of accident liability, strict liability and negligence (and certain variations of them), will be the focus of our analysis.[2]

We will assume that accidents and consequent liability arise probabilistically. In order to analyze the effects of liability rules in an uncertain setting

1. Accidents involving parties of only one type—such as accidents involving just drivers of automobiles, or just hunters—are not in strict logic described by this model. But it will be evident to the reader that many of the conclusions that will be drawn would carry over to a model of these single-activity accidents.

2. This chapter is based on a more complete treatment of the subject in Shavell 1987a, which also presents proofs of claims that are made. In notes to this chapter, however, proofs of a number of the more important conclusions are given or sketched.

in the simplest way, we will often suppose that parties are *risk neutral*. A risk-neutral party makes decisions on the basis of probability-discounted, or expected, values. For example, a risk-neutral person who faces a liability of $100,000 with probability 10 percent will consider this uncertain payment to be equivalent to a certain payment of its expected value of $10,000.[3] An interpretation of the $10,000 expected liability amount is that it is the payment that the person would make on average were he repeatedly to face a 10 percent risk of having to make a $100,000 payment.

1. UNILATERAL ACCIDENTS AND LEVELS OF CARE

In the first version of the accident model, it will be supposed that accidents are *unilateral* in nature: Only injurers' exercise of care or precautions affects accident risks; victims' behavior does not. When an airplane crashes into a building, for example, or when a rupture in a water main causes a flood in a basement, the victims probably could not have done much to prevent harm. In these cases, the accidents may be seen as almost literally unilateral. Other types of accidents might be seen as approximately unilateral if the victims' role was slight; consider for example automobile-bicycle accidents in which bicyclists' actions are of minor importance in reducing risks.

The social goal here will be minimization of the sum of the costs of care and of expected accident losses. This sum will be called *total social costs*.

1.1 Social welfare optimum. Before determining how injurers will act under different liability rules, let us identify the level of care that minimizes total social costs. This socially optimal level of care will clearly reflect both the costs of exercising care and the reduction in accident risks that care would accomplish. Consider the following example.

---

3. If this assumption were not made, and account were taken of risk aversion, then a liability of $100,000 with 10 percent probability would deter more than a certain liability of $10,000. We will consider risk aversion in Chapter 11.

Table 8.1 Care of injurers and accident risk

Care level	Cost of care	Probability of accident	Expected accident losses	Total social costs
None	0	15%	15	15
Moderate	3	10%	10	13
High	6	8%	8	14

Example 1. Suppose that accidents that cause losses of 100 occur with a probability as described in Table 8.1. To understand why exercising moderate care minimizes total social costs, observe on one hand that raising the level of care from none to moderate reduces expected accident losses by 5, but involves costs of only 3; it thus lowers total social costs. On the other hand, raising care beyond the moderate level would further reduce expected accident losses by only 2, yet involve additional costs of 3; hence it would not be worthwhile.

Note that the example illustrates the obvious point that the optimal level of care may well not result in the lowest possible level of expected accident losses (for that would require the highest level of care).[4] Let us now examine how much care injurers will be led to exercise in the absence of liability and under various liability rules.

1.2 No liability.   If there is no liability for accidents, injurers will not exercise any care, for doing so would entail costs but not yield a benefit to them. Total social costs will therefore generally exceed the optimal level; in Example 1, for instance, total social costs will be 15 rather than 13.

1.3 Strict liability.   Under the rule of *strict liability,* injurers must, by definition, pay for all accident losses that they cause.[5] Hence, injurers' total costs will equal total social costs; and because injurers will seek to

4. The formal version of the model illustrated in the example is as follows. Let x be the level of care, $p(x)$ the probability of an accident (where p is decreasing in x), and h the harm that an accident would cause. The socially optimal x minimizes $x + p(x)h$ and is denoted by x^*. Unless indicated otherwise, I will assume that x^* is unique in these notes.

5. It is assumed for the most part in this and the next chapter that an injurer is able to pay for losses caused. The important possibility that injurers are unable to pay for losses caused is considered in section 3 of Chapter 10.

Table 8.2 Negligence rule

Care level	Cost of care	Liability	Expected liability	Injurer's total costs
None	0	Yes	15	15
Moderate (due care)	3	No	0	3
High	6	No	0	6

minimize their own total costs, injurers' goal will be identical to the social goal of minimizing total social costs. Consequently, strict liability induces injurers to choose the socially optimal level of care. In Example 1, strict liability leads injurers to exercise the optimal, moderate level of care.

1.4 Negligence rule. Under the *negligence rule,* an injurer is held liable for the accident losses he causes only if he was negligent, that is, only if his level of care was less than a level called *due care* that the courts specify. If the injurer exercised a level of care that equaled or exceeded due care, he will not be held liable. The negligence rule is sometimes said to be *fault-based* because liability is found only if the injurer was at fault in the sense of having been found negligent.

If the courts set the level of due care equal to the socially optimal level of care, then injurers will be led to exercise due care, and thus the outcome will be socially optimal. To see why, first reconsider Example 1. If courts define due care to be the socially optimal, moderate level, the expected liability for an injurer would equal total social costs when no care is taken and would be zero when moderate or high care is taken. When at least moderate care is taken, then, the injurer's total costs equal just the cost of care—see Table 8.2. Hence, injurers will indeed be best off exercising moderate care.

More generally, there are two reasons why injurers will necessarily be led to take due care if it is chosen by courts to equal the optimal level. First, injurers plainly would not take more than due care, because they will escape liability by taking merely due care. Taking greater care would therefore be to no advantage yet would involve additional costs.[6] Second, injurers

6. It is assumed here (and elsewhere in this chapter) that a court can determine a party's level of care with complete accuracy. Otherwise, it might well be worth a party's while to

would not wish to take less than due care if due care is set at the socially optimal level. If injurers took less than due care, they would be exposed to the risk of liability, so their expected costs would equal total social costs. Thus, injurers would want to choose their level of care so as to minimize total social costs. But this in turn means that they would wish to raise their level of care to the socially optimal point—which by hypothesis equals due care and therefore allows them to avoid liability entirely.[7]

1.5 Liability rules compared. Both forms of liability result in the same, socially optimal behavior, but they differ in terms of what courts need to know to apply them.[8] Under strict liability a court need only determine the magnitude of the loss that occurred, whereas under the negligence rule a court must in addition determine the level of care actually taken (a driver's speed) and calculate the socially optimal level of due care (the appropriately safe speed). To do the latter, in turn, a court needs to know the costs and the effectiveness of taking different levels of care in reducing accident risks.[9]

1.6 Several dimensions of care. Suppose, as would be usual, that there is more than one dimension of an injurer's behavior that affects accident risks (not only a driver's speed, but also the frequency with which he looks at the rearview mirror). In this situation, under strict liability an injurer would be led to choose optimal levels of *all* dimensions of care, because

---

take more than due care to reduce the likelihood of a court mistakenly finding him negligent. This and related issues are analyzed in section 1 of Chapter 10.

7. In terms of the model mentioned in note 4, the claim of this section is that if the due care level equals x^*, then injurers will be induced to choose x^*. To demonstrate this, observe that, as stated, an injurer will not choose $x > x^*$, for if he chooses x^*, he spends less and still bears no liability. Thus, $x \leq x^*$ must be true. If $x < x^*$, the injurer will be found negligent if he causes an accident, so that he will bear liability. Thus, given that $x < x^*$, the injurer will choose x to minimize $x + p(x)h$. But $x + p(x)h > x^* + p(x^*)h$ by definition of x^*, and because $x^* + p(x^*)h \geq x^*$, it follows that $x + p(x)h > x^*$; thus, the injurer will prefer to choose x^* than any x less than x^*.

8. The rules also differ in how they allocate risk, in the administrative costs that they generate, and in their distributional effects. These issues will be discussed in later chapters.

9. These disadvantages of the negligence rule (as well as the disadvantage to be noted in the next section) may become attenuated or may be reversed in the bilateral version of the model to be considered in section 2.

his goal would be to minimize his expected total costs. But under the negligence rule, an injurer would have a motive to choose optimal levels *only* of those dimensions of care that are incorporated in the due care standard. And in fact some dimensions of care will usually be omitted from the due care standard because of difficulties that courts would face in ascertaining them (how would a court obtain information about the number of times per minute a driver usually looks in his rearview mirror?) or in determining proper behavior in respect to them.

2. BILATERAL ACCIDENTS AND LEVELS OF CARE

Now let us consider a bilateral version of the model of accidents, where victims as well as injurers can take care and thereby lower accident risks. The social goal will continue to be minimization of total social costs, which here will be the sum of injurers' as well as victims' costs of care, plus expected accident losses.

2.1 Social welfare optimum.   The optimal levels of care of injurers and of victims will reflect their joint possibilities for reducing accident risks and their costs of care. Consider the following example.

> *Example 2.* The probability of an accident that would cause losses of 100 is related to the different possible combinations of injurers' and of victims' levels of care as shown in Table 8.3. In this example, it is assumed for simplicity that there is only one positive level of care for parties of each type.
>
> From the last column of the table, it is apparent that it is socially optimal for both injurers and victims to take care. To see why, observe, for instance, that if injurers alone take care, expected losses are 10, whereas if victims also take care, at a cost of 2, expected losses fall by 4; hence total social costs are reduced when victims also take care. Similar reasoning shows that the situation in which victims alone take care can be improved when injurers also take care.

Although in this example it is socially optimal for both injurers and victims to take care, other examples can obviously be constructed in which

Table 8.3 Care of injurers and of victims, and accident risk

Injurer care	Victim care	Injurer care cost	Victim care cost	Probability of accident	Expected losses	Total social costs
None	None	0	0	15%	15	15
None	Care	0	2	12%	12	14
Care	None	3	0	10%	10	13
Care	Care	3	2	6%	6	11

it is optimal only for injurers to take care or only for victims to take care (or for neither to do so). These possibilities are not the focus here (but see section 2.11) because in most real situations it would be best for both injurers and victims to take a positive degree of care, however small.[10]

2.2 Behavior in the bilateral model. In the bilateral context, the way in which one type of party behaves will often depend on how the other type of party behaves. For example, how watchful drivers are for bicyclists may depend on how cautious bicyclists tend to be (drivers might be very watchful if bicyclists are not very cautious), and how cautious bicyclists generally are may depend on the usual attentiveness of drivers.

The possible interdependence of parties' actions means that if we want to show that some pattern of behavior will hold true, we have to show that it will be an *equilibrium* pattern in the sense that neither type of party would want to change what he is doing given the behavior of the other type of party. Injurers' and victims' behavior in equilibrium will now be determined in various liability settings.

2.3 No liability. As before, injurers will not take care in the absence of liability, and the outcome will therefore generally depart from the optimal. Because victims bear their accident losses, however, they will have a reason to take care. In Example 2, although injurers will not take care,

10. The formal version of the bilateral model is the natural extension of that of the unilateral model (see note 4): Injurers choose a level of care x, victims choose a level of care y, the probability of an accident is $p(x, y)$, which is declining in both x and y, and the social goal is to minimize $x + y + p(x, y)h$. It will generally be assumed, as just noted in the text, that the optimal levels of care x^* and y^* are positive and also that they are unique.

victims will take care, because for a cost of 2 they will lower their expected accident losses from 15 to 12. Note that this outcome is an equilibrium. It is in victims' interest to take care, given that injurers do not take care; and it is in injurers' interest not to take care, given that victims take care (or, for that matter, if they do not). The reader will be able to verify similarly that other outcomes shown later are equilibria, even when this is not pointed out in the text.

2.4 Strict liability. Because injurers will be liable for the accident losses that they cause under strict liability, they will have a proper motive to take care. Because victims will be fully compensated by injurers for accident losses, however, victims will be indifferent to the occurrence of accidents. Therefore, victims will not take care,[11] and the outcome will not be optimal. In Example 2, injurers will take care because doing so will reduce their expected liability from 15 to 10 at a cost of only 3, but victims will not take care.

2.5 Strict liability with the defense of contributory negligence. Under this rule an injurer is liable for the accident losses he causes only if the victim's level of care was at least equal to the victim's due care level. If the victim's care level was less than due care for him, the victim is said to be *contributorily negligent* and must bear his losses. (Contributory negligence is a legal defense for the injurer; its successful assertion by the injurer relieves him of liability.)

If courts choose the level of due care for victims to equal the socially optimal level of care, then victims will prefer to exercise due care and injurers also will prefer to take the socially optimal level of care. Thus, the socially optimal outcome will occur. To establish that this is true, note, first, that injurers will exercise optimal care given that victims take due

---

11. But victims would obviously have an incentive to take care if they would not or could not be compensated fully for their accident losses, as where the losses involve serious personal injury or death (which will be considered in section 8 of Chapter 10 and section 6 of Chapter 11). Thus, here (and often later) the reader may find it useful to think about examples of accidents in which victims would suffer only property losses. Nevertheless, the example in which victims are bicyclists will continue to be discussed in the text for expositional convenience. One might imagine, for example, that bicycle accidents damage bicycles but do not injure riders.

care, because then injurers will be liable for accident losses. (If bicyclists take due care, then drivers will be liable for accident losses and will decide to take optimal care.) Second, observe that victims will take due care because they will wish to avoid being found contributorily negligent and thus having to bear their own losses. The specific reasoning is analogous to that in the explanation in section 1.4 of why injurers will take due care under the negligence rule.[12]

To verify the claim in Example 2, assume that due care for victims equals "care," because victims' exercise of care is socially optimal. Presuming that victims take care, injurers will be liable for accident losses that they cause. Therefore their expected liability will fall from 12 to 6 if they spend 3 to take care, and they will take care. Conversely, assuming that injurers take care, victims will be induced to take care; for if victims do not take care, they will bear their expected accident losses of 10, whereas if they take care at a cost of 2 they will not bear their losses.[13]

2.6 Negligence rule. As in the unilateral model, if the courts choose due care to equal the socially optimal level, then injurers will be led to take

---

12. This paragraph has explained only why both injurers and victims taking optimal care is an equilibrium. But the situation in which both take optimal care is in fact the only equilibrium that can exist. In other words, the only stable situation that can possibly exist under the rule of strict liability with the defense of contributory negligence (with due care for victims set at the optimal level) is that in which both injurers and victims take optimal care. That this equilibrium is unique follows from three observations: First, victims never have an incentive to take care y exceeding y^* (for once they take due care they will be compensated for their losses). Second, victims will not choose y less than y^*, for if they do so, they will bear their own losses, injurers will take no care, and victims thus will minimize $y + p(0, y)h$. But $y + p(0, y)h = 0 + y + p(0, y)h > x^* + y^* + p(x^*, y^*)h > y^*$, implying that victims must be better off choosing due care y^* than any $y < y^*$. And third, because in equilibrium victims thus take due care of y^*, injurers choose x to minimize $x + p(x, y^*)h$, which is minimized at x^*.

13. To see why the only equilibrium in this example is the situation in which both injurers and victims take care, consider the other possibilities. For injurers to take care and for victims not to take care cannot be an equilibrium, since victims will wish to take care if injurers take care (or, also, if they do not). Similarly, for injurers not to take care and for victims to take care cannot be an equilibrium, since injurers will wish to take care given that victims take care. Finally, for both injurers and victims not to take care cannot be an equilibrium, since victims will wish to take care to avoid liability (for if they take care, their costs will be 2, whereas if they do not take care, they will bear expected losses of 15).

due care. Victims too will be induced to take the optimal level of care because they will bear their losses if injurers take due care. (Drivers will be led to take due care; and knowing that they will bear their losses, bicyclists will decide to take appropriate care.)

To illustrate these conclusions, assume in Example 2 that due care for injurers equals "care." If injurers do not take care, their expected liability will be 12, presuming that victims take care; thus injurers will choose to avoid liability by spending 3 on care. Also, because victims will bear their losses when injurers take due care, victims will reduce their expected losses from 10 to 6 by taking care; as this will cost victims 2, they too will decide to take care.[14]

2.7 Negligence rule with the defense of contributory negligence. According to this rule, an injurer will only be liable for accident losses if he failed to take due care and the victim exercised due care himself. In other words, if the injurer was negligent, he still will escape liability if the victim was contributorily negligent.

An argument very close to that of the previous section shows that if courts choose injurers' and victims' levels of due care to equal the socially optimal levels, both injurers and victims will be led to take due care and the socially optimal result will be achieved. Injurers will wish to take due care to avoid liability, under the assumption that victims take due care and thus will not bear their accident losses on account of contributory negligence. Also, victims will want to take due care, presuming that injurers take due care; since victims will then bear their losses, they will be led to take the socially optimal level of care, which by assumption is due care. (This may be verified in Example 2 exactly as it was in the preceding section.)

Notice that the defense of contributory negligence is a superfluous addition to the negligence rule with respect to the objective of inducing victims to act optimally, for it was seen in the last section that victims take optimal care when the negligence rule is unaccompanied by the defense.

14. The equilibrium in which both injurers and victims take optimal care is the only equilibrium under the negligence rule (assuming that due care is optimal). The socially optimal outcome is also the unique equilibrium under the next rule that we consider.

Under the negligence rule without the defense of contributory negligence, injurers take due care to avoid liability. Consequently, victims bear their losses, and this by itself supplies them an incentive to take appropriate care. Accordingly, there is no need to provide victims another incentive to take care.[15]

2.8 Comparative negligence rule.   Under this rule, as under the last, an injurer will not be liable for accident losses he causes if he takes due care. But the comparative negligence rule differs from the previous rule in the situation in which *both* the injurer and the victim fail to take due care. In that case each party bears a fraction of the accident losses, where the fraction is determined by a comparison of the amounts by which the two parties' levels of care depart from the levels of due care. The fraction of losses a party bears will be higher the greater the difference between due care and his level of care.

If courts choose optimal levels of due care under the comparative negligence rule, then both injurers and victims will be led to take due care. The rationale for this conclusion is precisely that of the last section. (Injurers will take due care to avoid liability if victims take due care, and so on.)

The reason that there is no difference between the outcomes under the comparative negligence rule and under the negligence rule with (or without) the defense of contributory negligence is in essence this: Under both rules, if parties of one type take due care, then parties of the other type will reason that they alone will be found negligent if they fail to take due care. The allocation of accident losses when both injurers and victims are negligent—the distinguishing feature of the comparative negligence rule—therefore turns out to be irrelevant to the calculations of parties in equilibrium.[16]

15. The defense of contributory negligence may generate beneficial incentives, however, if some injurers act negligently. If some injurers act negligently and if there is no defense of contributory negligence, then a victim may decide not to take due care, since he may think he will be likely to obtain compensation for accident losses he suffers because they will be caused by a negligent injurer.

16. But the allocation of losses when both injurers and victims are negligent is relevant in situations in which there are reasons why some injurers and victims act negligently; on such reasons, see sections 1 and 3 of Chapter 10.

2.9 Liability rules compared. We have seen that in the bilateral version of the model, strict liability does not lead to the socially optimal outcome for the obvious reason that it fails to furnish victims a motive to take care. We have also seen that strict liability with the defense of contributory negligence and all forms of the negligence rule result in the socially optimal outcome. Under these rules, parties have one of two sufficient reasons to take optimal care: Either taking optimal care allows them to avoid entirely the bearing of accident losses (victims' situation under strict liability with the defense of contributory negligence, injurers' situation under the negligence rules), or else taking care reduces the level of (rather than the entirety of) expected losses that parties in fact bear (injurers' situation under strict liability with the defense of contributory negligence, victims' situation under the negligence rules).

To apply each of the rules leading to optimality, courts need to determine the magnitude of accident losses and the actual level of care and the optimal level of due care for injurers or victims. Moreover, to ascertain the optimal level of due care for just one party, a court must generally determine (if only implicitly) the optimal level of care for the other as well, because the optimal level of care for one party will in principle depend on the other's costs of, and possibilities for, reducing risk.[17] This latter point makes the comparison of liability rules with respect to their ease of application different from what it might at first seem to be.

Consider, for instance, the rule of strict liability with the defense of contributory negligence and the negligence rule with the same defense. It may seem initially that strict liability with the defense of contributory negligence is the easier rule to apply, because courts are not directly concerned with injurers' behavior under the rule, whereas courts must set due care for injurers under the negligence rule. But to apply the defense of contributory negligence, courts must determine optimal due care for victims, and, as

17. That courts must generally consider the entire tableau of costs and effectiveness of care for the two parties to determine optimal care for either should have been evident from Table 8.3 and section 2.1. But it should be mentioned that in some situations the optimal level of care for parties of one type may be determinable without precise knowledge of the other's optimal level of care. Suppose, for instance, that the use of lights by bicyclists when riding at night will dramatically reduce accident risks whatever the level of care taken by drivers. Then it would be optimal for bicyclists to use lights at night without determining what particular level of care is optimal for drivers.

just remarked, this effectively requires courts to determine the optimal level of care for injurers. Therefore, the main difference affecting the ease of application of the two rules is only that under the strict liability rule courts do not need to observe the actual level of care of injurers.

2.10 Liability rules compared when care has several dimensions. I noted in section 1.6 that there may be dimensions of injurers' care (such as the frequency with which drivers look in their rearview mirrors) that courts would not take into account in the determination of negligence because of difficulties in assessing them. Injurers may therefore not exercise care in an optimal way in every dimension under the negligence rule, but they will be led to do so under strict liability. It is clear that a similar point applies when there are dimensions of victims' care (such as the frequency with which bicyclists look for traffic behind them) that could not be included in their standard of due care. Specifically, victims will not take optimal care in these dimensions under strict liability with the defense of contributory negligence, but they will do so under the negligence rule (because they will bear their accident losses under that rule). In consequence, to know how the presence of multiple dimensions of care affects the comparison of liability rules, one must make a judgment about the relative importance of the dimensions of injurers' and of victims' behavior that would be excluded from their respective standards of due care.

2.11 The least-cost avoider. The notion of the *least-cost avoider* applies in situations in which the risk of accidents will be eliminated if *either* injurers or victims take care. In such situations it is clearly wasteful for *both* injurers and victims to take care; rather, it is optimal for the type of parties who can prevent accidents at least cost—the least-cost avoiders—alone to take care. Suppose, for example, that injurers can prevent accident losses of 100 by taking a precaution that costs 10, and that victims also can prevent the losses by taking a precaution that costs 20. In this case injurers alone ought to take precautions, because in that way the social goal of minimizing total social costs is achieved.

The model of the least-cost avoider may be misleading for thinking about the class of bilateral accidents examined in this book. In the situations examined here, there simply are no least-cost avoiders who alone ought to take care, for the usual assumption is that both injurers and victims generally ought to do something to avoid risk; the effect of liability rules is therefore different from that in the least-cost avoider model. If, say, injurers are the least-cost avoiders, an optimal outcome will be achieved under strict liability unaccompanied by the defense of contributory negligence. But in the bilateral model studied here, the defense of contributory negligence must accompany strict liability in order to induce victims as well as injurers to take appropriate care.

2.12 Liability rules in use.   The major rules of liability for accidents between strangers in the United States are the comparative negligence rule, the negligence rule with the defense of contributory negligence, and strict liability with that defense.[18] In England, France, and Germany, the usual forms of liability are the comparative negligence rule and strict liability with forms of the contributory negligence defense.[19]

2.13 The determination of due care and the *as if* interpretation.
Negligence in American law, according to the *Restatement (Second) of Torts*, is "conduct which falls below the standard [of due care] . . . for the protection of others against unreasonable risk of harm," and the concept of negligence is similar in other legal systems. Deciding on the standard of due care often requires some sort of weighing of the magnitude of risk against the disutility or cost of more careful conduct.[20]

As the reader has seen in the analysis here, the level of due care that minimizes total social costs implicitly involves just such a weighing of risk

18. See, for example, Keeton, Dobbs, et al. 1984, chaps. 5, 11, and 13; and Dobbs 2000, chaps. 6, 11, and 23.

19. See Tunc 1983 for a summary of and bibliography on tort law in the entire world; Fleming 1998, for a treatment of tort law focusing on England and Australia; Von Bar, 1998, vols. 1 and 2, for a description of tort law in Europe; Von Mehren and Gordley 1977, chaps. 8–10, for materials on tort law in France and Germany; and Zweigert and Kötz 1998, chaps. 40–43, for a description of tort law in England, France, and Germany.

20. See the *Restatement of the Law Second: Torts* 1965, sections 282, 291–293. The *Restatement* is a summary of and commentary on the doctrines of tort law produced by leading scholars under the aegis of the American Law Institute. For discussion of the determination of negligence in other legal systems see, for example, Limpens et al. 1983, sections 23–27; Markesinis 1994, 72–74; Von Bar 1998, 1:20–39, 2: part 2; and Zweigert and Kötz 1998, 599–600, 615–617.

against the cost of care. This suggests that due care is in fact found by a process that operates as if it were designed to identify behavior that minimizes total social costs, or at least approximately so (one does not know if the weighing is any more than qualitatively similar to that which minimizes total social costs).[21]

I use the words "as if" because the claim is hardly that individuals or courts *think* in terms of the mathematical goal of minimizing a sum. They obviously do not do anything so unnatural. Rather, they appear to gauge the appropriateness of behavior by a rough consideration of risk and the costs of reducing it, ordinarily on the basis of felt notions of fairness.[22] Likewise, the *as if* interpretation carries with it no specific implications about the degree to which individuals and courts concern themselves about goals of deterrence, although they sometimes appear to view deterrence as relevant.

With these caveats in mind, observe that the *as if* interpretation is borne out not only by the mere fact that there is a weighing involved in the negligence determination, but also by a consideration of the character of the weighing. First, the list of factors that courts take into account in setting due care—and the influence of those factors on the level of due care—are what we would expect if courts were aiming to minimize total social costs: The level of due care is generally higher the greater the likelihood of harm, the larger the probable extent of harm, the greater the number of individuals at risk, and the easier it is for injurers to alleviate risk.[23] Second, the choice of due care levels probably reflects the possibilities for

21. It will be clear to the reader that the "as if" interpretation can also be made about many other instances that will be mentioned in later chapters of this book of consistency between actual law and the law that is theoretically optimal (given the stated measure of social welfare).

22. An exception is Learned Hand's algebraic formula for determining the due care standard. In his judicial opinion in *United States v. Carroll Towing Co.,* 159 F.2d 169 (2d Cir. 1947), Hand said that a party is negligent if he failed to take a precaution when its cost, which he called its "burden," was less than its expected benefit; he denoted the burden by B, the probability of loss in the absence of precaution by P, the magnitude of loss by L, and said that negligence should be found if $B < PL$.

23. See Fleming 1998, chap. 7, section 2; Keeton, Dobbs, et al. 1984, sections 29, 31, 33; the *Restatement of the Law Second: Torts,* 1965, section 293. Note too that these effects on due care are consistent with Hand's formula.

both injurers and victims to reduce accident risks, as is consistent with the bilateral model of accidents. Consider, for instance, the risk of accidents in which bicyclists run into car doors as the doors are opened. My surmise is that most of us would say that bicyclists should not have to proceed so slowly that, were a car door to open suddenly, they could virtually always stop in time; rather, we would say that, before persons open their car doors, they should look around to see if anyone is approaching. I suggest too that in coming to this view, most of us would have at the back of our minds— if not in our conscious thoughts—such ideas as that it would be a burden for bicyclists to have to go so slowly that they could stop immediately before running into car doors, that it is relatively easy for persons leaving cars to look for danger, and that it is not necessary for bicyclists to go very slowly if persons are properly cautious when leaving their cars. In other words, when deciding on the care that parties of one type ought to exercise, we quite naturally factor into our thinking the ability of parties of the other type to take care, the burden of doing so, and what their taking care would accomplish.

Note on the literature.   The first writer to study in an analytical way the theory of the effect of liability rules on parties' behavior was Calabresi (1961, 1965, 1970). He examined the desirability of different rules, emphasizing the advantages of versions of strict liability, and assuming for the most part the goal of minimization of total social costs.[24] Posner (1972a, 1972b, 1973) later made significant contributions, especially in his analysis of the various principles and doctrines governing use of the negligence rule.[25] Although both these writers discussed suggestive numerical examples, neither recognized that liability rules would, as a general matter, lead calculating parties to choose levels of care such that total social costs are minimized. Brown (1973) put forward the first clear statement and formal proofs of this conclusion. He showed that the rules of strict liability with

24. Many previous writers had, of course, recognized that liability rules would have some effect on behavior, but usually only in passing. Calabresi differed from his predecessors in that he made the effect of liability on behavior the focus of his work and carried it out in a self-conscious, sustained, and careful way.

25. See also Landes and Posner 1981b, 892–903, discussing what is called here the "as if" interpretation of the negligence determination.

the defense of contributory negligence and the negligence rule (with or without the defense) induce injurers and victims to take optimal levels of care in equilibrium.[26]

3. UNILATERAL ACCIDENTS: LEVELS OF CARE AND LEVELS OF ACTIVITY

We will now consider an injurer's *level of activity*—that is, whether, or how much, he engages in a particular activity. The number of miles an individual drives, for instance, might be interpreted as his level of activity. An injurer's level of activity is to be distinguished from his level of care, which has to do with the precautions he takes *when* engaging in his activity (the precautions an individual takes when on the road, such as slowing for curves, as opposed to the number of miles he drives).

Our analysis will begin with the unilateral case, and we will assume for simplicity that an increase in an injurer's activity level will result in a proportionate increase in expected accident losses, given his level of care. Thus, a doubling in the number of miles that individuals drive will result in a doubling in the number of accidents they cause, given the care with which they drive; or a doubling in the number of times individuals walk their dogs will result in a doubling in the risk that their dogs will bite strangers, given the care (leashing the dogs) they take to prevent attacks. We will also assume that an increase in an injurer's level of activity will result in an increase in his utility (at least up to some point); the more individuals drive or the more they walk their dogs, the greater will be their utility (until their need to drive is met or until walking their dogs turns into a chore).

We will now assume the social goal to be maximization of the utility injurers derive from engaging in their activity less total social costs, that is, less the costs of care and expected accident losses. It makes sense, of course,

26. Soon afterward Diamond 1974a, 1974b also showed, in closely related models, that the negligence rule with the defense of contributory negligence induces parties to take levels of care that minimize total accident cost. See as well Green 1976, Shavell 1987a, 72–77, 86–91, Emons 1990, and Emons and Sobel 1991, who analyze liability when injurers and victims are heterogeneous; and see also the survey Schäfer 2000.

to introduce the utility that injurers derive from their activity into the measure of social welfare, because the level of their activity is now a subject of study.[27]

3.1 Social welfare optimum.   For social welfare to be maximized, an injurer must, as before, choose a level of care that is commensurate with the effect of care in reducing accident losses and with its costs. But now the injurer should also select his level of activity appropriately, which is to say, at the level that appropriately balances the utility he obtains against the additional risks he creates and the costs of care.

> *Example 3.* Let us build on Example 1 by assuming that it describes the situation each time injurers engage in their activity. Thus, injurers who behave optimally will take moderate care, at a cost of 3, and will reduce expected accident losses to 10. Consequently, if an injurer engages in his activity twice, taking optimal care each time, his total costs of care will be 6, and the expected accident losses he causes will be 20; if he engages in his activity three times, the figures will be 9 and 30, respectively; and so forth. These figures are shown in the third and fourth columns of Table 8.4. The second column in the table shows the total utility that injurers derive from engaging in the activity, from which the figures for social welfare in the last column—utility minus costs of care and accident losses—can be calculated.
>
> The optimal activity level is 2 because social welfare is highest at that level. One way of explaining why is as follows. Each time an injurer engages in the activity, he will increase total social costs by 3 + 10 = 13. Therefore, social welfare will be enhanced by his engaging in the activity another time if and only if the marginal utility he would gain exceeds 13. Because the utility he obtains from engaging the first time is 40, the marginal utility he obtains from the second time is 20 (that is, 60 − 40), and that from the third time is only 9 (that is, 69 − 60), it is best that he stop at the second time.[28]

27. The social goal considered earlier, minimizing total social costs, may be viewed as a special case of the present goal. If we imagine the level of activity, and hence the utility from the activity, to be held constant, as we implicitly assumed was the case earlier, then maximization of the utility derived from the activity less total social costs is obviously equivalent to minimization of total social costs.

28. Notice that utility actually falls beyond activity level 4. (The fifth time one walks one's dog, it is more a chore than a pleasure.)

Table 8.4 Activity level, accidents, and social welfare

Activity level	Total utility	Total costs of care	Total accident losses	Social welfare
0	0	0	0	0
1	40	3	10	27
2	60	6	20	34
3	69	9	30	30
4	71	12	40	19
5	70	15	50	5

The general point illustrated by this example is that the socially optimal behavior of injurers can be determined in two steps: first by finding (as in section 1.1) the level of care that minimizes total social costs incurred each time injurers engage in their activity, and then by raising the level of activity as long as the marginal utility that injurers derive exceeds the increase in total social costs.[29]

3.2 No liability. In the absence of liability, not only will injurers fail to take care; they also will engage in their activity to too great an extent. Indeed, they will continue to engage in it as long as they obtain any additional utility (individuals will go for a drive or walk their dogs on a mere whim) rather than, as would be socially desirable, only as long as they obtain additional utility exceeding the costs of optimal care plus the expected accident losses they cause. In Example 3 injurers will not take care and thus will choose activity level 4, the level at which they cease to gain utility from their activity, rather than the optimal activity level of 2.

29. The formal model illustrated in the example is as follows. Let z be the activity level, $b(z)$ be the utility or benefit from the activity, and assume the social object is to maximize $b(z) - z(x + p(x)h)$, where $x + p(x)h$ are social costs each time an injurer engages in his activity. Let z^* and x^* be optimal values of z and x. Note that x^* minimizes $x + p(x)h$, so x^* is as described above in section 1; x^* minimizes social costs whatever the level of activity. Therefore, z^* is determined by $b'(z) = x^* + p(x^*)h$, which is to say, the condition that the marginal benefit from the activity equals the marginal social cost, comprising the sum of the cost of optimal care and expected accident losses (given optimal care).

3.3 Strict liability. Under strict liability an injurer's utility, net of his expected costs, will be equal to the measure of social welfare, because he will pay for the accident losses he causes, will naturally enjoy the benefits of engaging in his activity, and will bear the costs of care. Accordingly, injurers will behave so as to maximize social welfare; they will thus choose both the optimal level of care and the optimal level of activity.

More directly, injurers will choose the optimal level of care because doing so will minimize the expected costs they bear each time they engage in their activity. And they will choose the optimal level of activity because they will wish to engage in the activity only when the extra utility they derive exceeds their costs of care plus their added expected liability payments for accident losses caused. (People will walk their dogs only when their utility gain outweighs the disutility of having to leash the dogs and the added liability risk due to dog bites.) In Example 3, we know (from section 1.3) that strictly liable injurers will take the moderate level of care. Hence, the last column in Table 8.4 will become injurers' utility, net of their expected liability costs, and they will therefore choose the optimal activity level of 2.

3.4 Negligence rule. As the reader recalls from previous analysis, injurers will be led to take optimal care under the negligence rule, assuming that courts choose the level of due care to equal the optimal level of care. Because they will take due care, however, injurers will escape liability for any accident losses they cause. They will therefore have no reason to consider the effect that engaging in their activity has on accident losses.

Consequently, injurers will be led to choose socially excessive activity levels. Specifically, they will engage in their activity whenever the utility they derive net of the cost of care is positive (whenever the pleasure from walking their dogs net of the disutility of leashing them is positive), rather than only when their net utility exceeds the additional expected accident losses they create.[30]

---

30. In terms of the model (see the previous note), the point is as follows. Because an injurer will escape liability by exercising care x^*, he will choose z to maximize $b(z) - zx^*$, so that z will satisfy $b'(z) = x^*$. But z^* is determined by $b'(z) = x^* + p(x^*)h$, so that z will be excessive under the negligence rule (assuming that $b(z)$ is a concave function).

Table 8.5 Negligence rule and activity level

Activity level	Total utility	Total costs of care	Total utility minus costs of care
0	0	0	0
1	40	3	37
2	60	6	54
3	69	9	60
4	71	12	59
5	70	15	55

This can be seen in Example 3, where we know that if due care is the optimal, moderate level, injurers will take due care. Because injurers take due care under the negligence rule, they will not be liable for accident losses and their situation will be that described in Table 8.5.

From the last column in the table it is evident that injurers will choose the activity level 3 rather than the optimal activity level 2: They will increase their activity level from 2 to 3 because this will raise their utility by 9 and their costs of care by only 3; they will not consider that increasing their activity level will also raise expected accident losses by 10 (as shown in Table 8.4), for they will not be liable for these additional social costs.

3.5 Liability rules compared. Under both strict liability and the negligence rule, injurers are led to take socially optimal levels of care, but under the negligence rule, they engage in their activity excessively because, unlike under strict liability, they do not pay for the accident losses that they cause.

The importance of this defect of the negligence rule will clearly depend on the expected magnitude of the losses caused by an activity. If an activity is by its nature very dangerous even when carried out with appropriate precautions, it will be significant that under the negligence rule the level of the activity would be socially excessive. For example, if the walking of dogs of a vicious breed or blasting creates high risks of harm despite the use of all reasonable (or due) care, it will be of real consequence that under the negligence rule people would walk their dogs excessively (rather than exercise them in a yard or rather than own dogs of another breed) or that firms would blast excessively (rather than employ other methods of demolition). If, however, an activity creates only a low risk of accidents when due care is taken, the importance of any excess in the level of activity under the negligence rule will be small. This is true, one suspects, of many, and perhaps most, of our everyday activities (mowing a lawn, playing catch, walking the friendly, domesticated dog).

3.6 The source of the defect of the negligence rule.   The failing of the negligence rule results from an implicit assumption that the standard of behavior for determining negligence is defined only in terms of the level of care,[31] an assumption that seems generally to be true in reality. Were the negligence standard defined so as to include the activity level, injurers would make sure not to engage in their activity to an excessive extent in order to avoid a finding of negligence.

This consideration, however, immediately raises the question why the courts do not usually include the activity level in the determination of negligence. A possible answer concerns the information that the courts would require. To formulate a standard for the level of activity, courts would need to ascertain the character of the benefits that parties derive from their activities. (Courts would have to inquire into the pleasure obtained from walking a dog or the importance of driving somewhere.) Because these benefits often seem practically unknowable, attempts by courts to determine appropriate levels of activity would probably land them in a speculative realm. Deciding on appropriate levels of care, although by no means an easy task, usually appears to be less problematic. (We can say with fair confidence that a dog that tends to snap at others should be leashed, or that a person should not drive at sixty miles per hour along a residential street.)

Aside from the difficulties that courts would face in formulating appropriate standards for parties' levels of activity, courts would have to verify what parties' levels of activity actually were. This additional burden might be a substantial one in some situations, especially because establishing an individual's level of activity would require knowledge of what he did in the past. (How many times did a person walk his dog before the last time,

---

31. Notice therefore that the defect is similar to that discussed in section 1.6 concerning dimensions of care omitted from the due care standard.

when it bit someone?) By contrast, assessing an individual's level of care often requires knowledge of his behavior only at the time of an accident.

Nevertheless, there may be situations in which a court would have sufficient information to incorporate the level of activity into the negligence determination. One notable example is when a party engages even once in an activity that is very dangerous despite the exercise of care, and the activity yields the party only an obviously small utility. In this case the party could be called negligent merely for having engaged in the activity.[32]

Note on the literature.   In Shavell (1980c) I introduced the distinction between the level of activity and the level of care and first developed the points about strict liability versus negligence and the activity level that are discussed here and in section 4.

4.   BILATERAL ACCIDENTS: LEVELS OF CARE AND LEVELS OF ACTIVITY

In this most general case victims as well as injurers will be assumed to choose levels of activity and levels of care. As with injurers' levels of activity, increases in victims' levels of activity will be assumed to raise their utility, at least up to some point, and will result in proportionate increases in expected accident losses. Thus, if a bicyclist rides an extra mile, he will enjoy extra utility and his chances of being involved in an accident will rise. The measure of social welfare will be taken to be the utility that victims and injurers derive from their activities less their costs of care and expected accident losses.

The analysis that follows will be brief because most conclusions can be explained by appeal to the previous cases.

32. In this regard, it is interesting to note the passage in the *Restatement of Law Second: Torts* 1965, section 297, which reads in part, "A negligent act may be one which involves an unreasonable risk of harm . . . although it is done with all possible care." By way of example, the *Restatement* comments that "there are many mountain roads which may properly be regarded as dangerous no matter how careful . . . the driver may be . . . there is an inescapable risk in driving down a narrow and ill-kept mountain road . . . particularly if . . . snow or ice has rendered the road slippery . . . mere use of such a route . . . may be negligent unless the utility of the route is very great."

4.1 Social welfare optimum.   Optimal behavior in the bilateral case
will reflect not only the cost of care and its effect on accident risks, but
also the utility that injurers and victims obtain from their activities.

> *Example 4.* Suppose for simplicity that victims either engage in their activ-
> ity or they do not, and suppose the same for injurers; in other words,
> for parties of each type, there is only one possible positive level of activity.
> Suppose also that if parties of one type engage in their activity and the
> others do not, no accidents can occur—it takes the presence of both
> injurers and victims for there to be accidents. Hence, if parties of only one
> type engage in their activity, it would be pointless and socially wasteful for
> them to take care. Finally, suppose that if both injurers and victims engage
> in their activities, the risk of accidents will be as described in Example
> 2. Thus in this case injurers ought to take care, which costs 3; victims
> also ought to take care, which costs 2; and expected accident losses will
> be 6. Therefore, total social costs will be 3 + 2 + 6 = 11 if both injurers
> and victims engage in their activities and take care.
>
> Given these assumptions, it is easy to determine when it is optimal
> both for injurers and for victims to engage in their activities, as a function
> of the utilities they would each derive from so doing. Were parties of
> only one type to engage in their activity, none of the accident costs of
> 11 would be borne (because no accidents could occur and no care would
> be taken). Therefore, it will maximize social welfare for both injurers and
> victims to engage in their activities only when each would obtain from
> their activity a utility exceeding 11. Otherwise, it will be best for the
> parties that would enjoy the greater utility to engage in their activity and
> for the other parties to refrain from engaging in their activity.
>
> To verify this claim, suppose for instance that injurers would obtain
> utility of 35 and victims 25 from engaging in their activities. If both
> injurers and victims engage in their activities, social welfare will be 35 +
> 25 − 11 = 49; if only injurers engage in their activity, social welfare
> will be 35; if only victims do so, social welfare will be 25; thus it will
> indeed be optimal for both injurers and victims to engage in their activi-
> ties. Next suppose that injurers would obtain 35 from engaging in their
> activity and victims would obtain only 8. Then if both injurers and vic-
> tims engage in their activities, social welfare will be 35 + 8 − 11 = 32;
> if injurers alone do so, social welfare will be 35; if victims alone do so,
> social welfare will be 8; and it will be best for injurers alone to engage

in their activity.[33] Similar calculations show that if injurers would obtain 8 and victims 25 from engaging in their activities, then it will be optimal for victims alone to engage in their activity.

The simplifying feature of this example, that parties either do not engage in their activity or engage in it at only one positive level, should not disturb the reader. The points to be illustrated later will carry over in obvious ways to the more realistic case in which there are many different positive levels of activity for each type of party.

4.2 Strict liability with the defense of contributory negligence.

As the reader knows from previous analysis, if courts select the optimal level of due care, then under strict liability with the defense of contributory negligence, both injurers and victims will be led to take optimal care when they engage in their activities. Furthermore, because victims will take due care, injurers will pay for the accident losses they cause and thus, as is explained in section 3.3, they will choose the correct level of their activity given victims' behavior.

Yet because victims will be compensated for their losses, victims may engage in their activity too often. A victim's only cost of engaging in his activity will be his cost of taking due care. Therefore, he will engage in his activity whenever his utility from so doing would exceed the cost of taking due care. But what would be desirable is that he engage in his activity only when his utility would exceed the cost of taking due care plus the expected accident losses that would result from his engaging in his activity. (A bicyclist will go for a ride whenever the pleasure he would gain from that ride exceeds the disutility from having to exercise appropriate care, rather than only when the pleasure exceeds the disutility of exercising such care plus the increment to expected accident losses.)

To illustrate this point, consider the case in Example 4 in which injurers would obtain utility of 35 and victims utility of only 8 from their activities, and thus in which it is not optimal for victims to engage in their activity.

---

33. It is not necessary that injurers enjoy utility greater than 11 for it to be optimal for them to engage in their activity. For instance, if injurers' utility were 10, it would still be optimal for them alone to engage in their activity, and social welfare would be 10.

Under strict liability with the defense of contributory negligence, victims need only take due care, at a cost of 2, to be assured of compensation for accident losses suffered. Hence, when they compare the utility of 8 that they would obtain from engaging in their activity to the cost of care of 2, victims will, undesirably, decide to engage in their activity (along with the injurers, who will compare their utility of 35 to their cost of care of 3 plus their expected liability of 6).

4.3 Negligence rule with or without the defense of contributory negligence.   Again, the reader knows from previous discussion that under the negligence rule, both injurers and victims will be induced to take optimal care when engaging in their activities if courts select optimal due care levels. And since injurers will escape liability by taking due care, it is evident from the argument of section 3.4 that injurers may engage in too high a level of their activity.

Victims, however, will choose the correct level of their activity given injurers' behavior. Because victims will bear their own losses, they will engage in their activity a further time only if the utility they would obtain (net of the costs of taking care) exceeds the addition to expected losses. Consider the situation in Example 4 in which injurers would obtain utility of 8 and victims utility of 25 from engaging in their activities. In this case it is optimal for victims alone to engage in their activity, and under the negligence rule they will do so (for they will compare 25 to 2 + 6), but so will injurers, undesirably (for they will compare 8 to 3).

4.4 Liability rules compared.   It should be evident from what has been said that strict liability with the defense of contributory negligence will result in higher social welfare if its disadvantage—that victims engage too often in their activity—is not as important as the disadvantage of the negligence rules—that injurers engage too often in their activity. That is, strict liability will result in greater social welfare if it is more important for society to control injurers' levels of activity than victims'.

Whether injurers' levels of activity are more important to control than victims' will depend on the context. As discussed before, when an activity of injurers (walking dogs of a vicious breed) creates substantial risks despite their exercise of due care, the activity will be desirable to control. This point is not fundamentally altered if account is taken of the activities of victims that expose them to risk. Especially if the victims' activities are just the activities of ordinary life (walking about, going to work), we would not want the activities constrained in favor of injurers' more dangerous activities. Conversely, when an activity of injurers (playing baseball) is not very dangerous if appropriate care is taken, the importance of controlling the activity will not be great; instead, we may see some advantage in reducing certain activities of victims that subject them to particular risks (such as pushing a baby in a stroller across a baseball field while a game is in progress).

4.5 Nonexistence of a liability rule leading to optimal levels of activity. Because neither of the liability rules, strict liability and negligence, induce both injurers and victims to choose optimal levels of their activities, one might ask whether there exists any conceivable liability rule that always results in optimal levels of activities. The answer is no. The reason, in essence, is that for injurers to choose the correct level of their activity they must bear accident losses, whereas for victims to choose the correct level of their activity they too must bear accident losses. Yet it is not possible for both injurers and victims to bear accident losses under a liability rule.[34]

Three comments should be made about this conclusion. First, the explanation just given for it directly suggests methods (different from liability rules) that in principle would lead to optimal behavior. For example, suppose that injurers pay fines to the state equal to harm done—or taxes equal to expected harm—and that victims bear their losses. Then the expected payments of injurers and of victims would each equal expected accident losses, and they would each choose optimal levels of their activity (as well as care). Second, the conclusion depends on the assumption that courts cannot incorporate parties' levels of activity into the negligence or the contributory negligence determination (an assumption that may be justified by what was written in section 3.6). If negligence and contributory negligence could be defined in terms of levels of activity as well as levels of care, then the usual liability rules would lead injurers and victims to choose

34. The specific conclusion described in this paragraph is as follows. Assume that a liability rule can depend only on the levels of care x and y of parties and harm h, but not on their levels of activity. Then the rule cannot in general induce both injurers and victims to choose optimal levels of activity; see Shavell 1980c.

optimal levels of both care and activity. Third, the conclusion should not be interpreted as an unduly negative one. As more factors are incorporated into a model, it naturally becomes less likely that a hypothetically ideal outcome can be achieved.

4.6 The reciprocal nature of harm.   It is a truism that harm has a reciprocal aspect in the sense that a victim must be present to suffer harm just as much as an injurer must be present to do harm. This observation has sometimes been taken to imply that injurers should not necessarily pay for harm done, that harm should not necessarily be "internalized" to injurers. That conclusion is supported by the analysis here, for as explained, either strict liability or negligence rules could turn out to be best.

The reciprocal nature of harm has also occasionally been suggested to mean that it is conceptually impossible to decide whether strict liability or the negligence rule should be applied, and even that the very notion of harm and its cause is rendered ambiguous.[35] This view is mistaken. There is no difficulty in principle in deciding whether strict liability or the negligence rule will be better in a given situation in a well-defined model (there was no difficulty in deciding the question with regard to Example 4, for instance),[36] and there is nothing problematic about the notion of harm.

4.7 Actual use of strict liability and negligence rules.   The choice between the two main forms of liability for accidents between strangers has been made in approximately the same manner in different legal systems.[37] Namely, negligence is the usual basis of liability; strict liability applies only in certain areas of accident. In Anglo-American law, liability for accident losses is "for most significant purposes governed by the concept of negligence"; use of strict liability is restricted to harms caused by wild animals, to certain types of harms due to fire, and to harms arising from "abnormally

35. See Donohue 1989, 1057.

36. That there are no difficulties in principle does not mean that there will be no difficulties in application. Suppose that, just as a woodsman cuts down a tree, a hiker happens to come along and is struck by the tree. Here we might feel that there is no appealing notion of who ought to have been present because it is hard to make a relative judgment about the benefits the hiker and the woodsman derived from their activities.

37. Liability for accidents involving firms and their customers will be discussed in the next chapter.

dangerous" or "ultrahazardous" activities, such as blasting, storage of flammable liquids, or transport of nuclear materials.[38] Most of the provisions of the German civil code impose liability only if the injuring party was at fault; strict liability is adopted in connection with harms due to animals other than domestic animals and, according to special legislation, in connection with harms arising from rail, road, and air traffic and from use of electricity, gas, and atomic energy.[39] The situation in France is similar.[40] Two important articles of the French civil code specify fault or negligence as the general principle of liability; strict liability applies to harms due to animals or to certain dangerous things (including automobiles and aircraft).

4.8 Strict liability and negligence rules in the light of the theory concerning levels of activity.
As stressed in the analysis, the use of strict liability rather than negligence rules in areas of behavior where activities create high risks, despite the exercise of reasonable care, has the advantage of tending to reduce in a desirable way participation in these activities.

This theoretical advantage seems consistent with reality in the sense that the impression given by the foregoing section is that the areas of activity covered by strict liability are *generally* more dangerous than those covered by negligence rules (certainly the reverse is not true). There are some exceptions to this pattern, however; the choices made between strict liability and negligence rules are not always easy to explain on the basis of differences in riskiness. (In the United States, is the danger due to the escape of wild animals from zoos, for which strict liability would probably apply, greater than that from automobile-pedestrian accidents, for which the negligence rule would govern?) Moreover, differences among countries in the areas of strict liability and of negligence are sometimes difficult to explain in terms of differences in dangerousness. (Why should the negligence rule govern liability for automobile-pedestrian accidents in the United States, while

38. See Dobbs 2000, chaps. 6, 23; Fleming 1998, chaps. 6, 15–18, quotation p. 97; and Keeton, Dobbs, et al. 1984, chaps. 5, 13.

39. See Limpens et al. 1983, sections 11–14; Markesinis 1994, 676–720; Opoku 1972, 230–243; Tunc 1983, sections 13, 79–85; Von Mehren and Gordley 1977, 557–566, 579–582; and Zweigert and Kötz 1998, chap. 42.

40. See Limpens et al. 1983, sections 5, 23; Tunc 1983, sections 12, 86–88; Von Mehren and Gordley 1977, 555–557, 579–582; and Zweigert and Kötz 1998, chap. 42.

strict liability applies in Germany and France?)[41] The conformity of the observed pattern of use of strict liability and negligence rules to what would be suggested by the theoretical considerations of this chapter is somewhat rough.

Putting aside questions concerning the actual dangerousness of the areas of strict liability versus those of negligence, I want to emphasize that one of the aims of the law is to impose strict liability on activities that are dangerous, or, more precisely, that are dangerous even if conducted with reasonable care. A particularly direct expression of this objective is provided by the *Restatement (Second) of Torts,* which states that, in deciding whether an activity should be subject to strict liability, one ought to take notice of possible "inability to eliminate the risk by the exercise of reasonable care." Further, the *Restatement* draws a contrast to most "ordinary activities" that can be made "safe by the taking of all reasonable precautions" and for which liability should be based on negligence.[42]

But it should be added that the deterrent effect of strict liability on the level of participation in activities is not mentioned in the *Restatement* and is only infrequently noted in other places. Evidently, the mere creation of an unusual risk is seen as a justification for imposition of strict liability.

Note on the empirical literature.   A somewhat limited amount of empirical work has been undertaken on the effect of liability on accidents. See Dewees et al. (1996) for a general survey and, among others, Devlin (1990), E. Landes (1982), Sloan et al. (1994), Sloan (1998), and Cummins et al. (2001) on automobile accidents.

41. On Germany, see Markesinis 1994, 710–720; and Opoku 1972, 240; on France, see Von Bar 1998, 2:410–411.

42. *Restatement of the Law Second: Torts* 1965, sect. 520.

9 ||| LIABILITY AND DETERRENCE: FIRMS

In this chapter I reconsider the basic theory of liability and deterrence under the assumption that injurers are firms.[1] The first part of the analysis addresses accidents in which the victims are strangers to firms, such as an accident in which a gasoline tanker truck crashes and explodes, harming other vehicles or homes near the roadside.

The second part of the analysis deals with accidents in which the victims are the customers of firms, for example, an accident in which a water heater that a person purchased ruptures and damages his property. The feature of chief interest about these situations is that customers' willingness to purchase products will be influenced by what they perceive to be the product risks. As a consequence, firms will be motivated to reduce product risks not only to avoid liability but also to sell products at a better price.

Firms will be presumed to maximize profits and to do business in a perfectly competitive environment. This means that the price of a product will equal the unit costs associated with production, including expected liability costs.[2]

1. The material here is based largely on chapter 3 of Shavell 1987a, which also contains proofs of conclusions.

2. Under perfect competition, a firm cannot maintain a product price exceeding total unit costs because competitors could then attract its customers by offering them the same

The measure of social welfare that will be studied is similar to that in Chapter 8: the utility customers derive from products (such as from gasoline or water heaters) and, where relevant, the utility that strangers obtain from their activities (such as driving, or locating their homes near roadsides), minus expected accident losses, the costs of care, and direct costs of production.[3]

1. VICTIMS ARE STRANGERS TO FIRMS

Although the conclusions to be drawn about liability rules will be essentially the same in this case as in the previous chapter, there are several differences in how the conclusions are demonstrated and interpreted that merit attention.

1.1 Levels of care. The arguments given in Chapter 8 with respect to parties' levels of care apply directly in the present case. Victims are in an identical situation whether injurers are firms or are other individuals; and, as before, injurers, who in this case are firms, want to minimize their costs of care plus expected liability expenses (by doing so, firms maximize their profits). Hence, both firms and victims will be led to take optimal levels of care under strict liability with the defense of contributory negligence and under the various negligence rules.

---

product at a lower, yet still profitable price. The assumption of perfect competition is made mainly for convenience—it means that the effect of changes in unit costs on price is simple to calculate. See section 2.9 for further discussion of this assumption.

3. This measure of social welfare should seem, on its face, a natural one to study, because it takes into account the obvious social benefits and costs associated with production of a risky product. Additionally, the measure is equivalent to the sum of the utilities of all relevant parties. In particular, the measure is the sum of the utilities of customers, owners of firms, and strangers in the case in which strangers are accident victims (the measure is the sum of the utilities of just the customers and the owners of firms in the case in which customers are accident victims). To verify this, observe that utility of customers = utility from product − price; utility of owners of firms is firms' profits, and firms' profits = price − direct production costs − costs of care − expected liability payments; utility of strangers = utility from their activity − costs of care − expected accident losses + expected liability payments. Adding these equalities and canceling offsetting terms, one obtains utility of customers + profits of owners of firms + utility of strangers = customers' utility from product − direct production costs − firms' cost of care + strangers' utility from their activity − strangers' costs of care − expected accident losses, which is as claimed.

Table 9.1 Care of firms and accidents

Care level	Cost of care	Probability of accident	Expected accident losses	Total social costs
None	0	9%	9	9
Care	2	3%	3	5

The type of liability rule employed will, however, affect product price, a factor that was not relevant in the previous chapter. In particular, the price will be higher under the strict liability rule than under the negligence rules. Under strict liability, the price will include expected accident losses, whereas under the negligence rules, it will not because, by taking due care, firms will avoid liability for accident losses.[4]

> *Example 1.* Firms' direct costs of production per unit are 10, and the risk of accidents that would cause losses of 100 depends on whether firms take care (for simplicity, we consider the case in which accidents are unilateral). The exercise of care reduces expected accident losses by 6 and raises costs by only 2, as shown in Table 9.1. Thus, it is socially desirable for firms to take care.
>
> Under the negligence rule, firms will have to take care to avoid liability. Firms therefore will take care, and their costs per unit will be 12— the direct production costs of 10 plus the costs of care. Accordingly, the product price will also be 12 (by assumption, competition will drive the price down to unit costs).
>
> Firms will take care under strict liability too, in order to minimize their unit costs. But these unit costs, and thus the price, will equal 15 because the unit costs will include expected liability expenses of 3.

1.2 Levels of activity. Assume, as is natural, that an increase in a firm's level of production will result in a proportional increase in expected accident losses, given the firm's level of care. The determination of the

---

4. As in Chapter 8, it is assumed here that the negligence rule works perfectly. If it does not and firms are sometimes found negligent, the price will include a component attributable to expected accident losses (but this component would be less than expected accident losses).

Table 9.2 Utility from the product

Customer	Utility from the product
A	40
B	20
C	17
D	13
E	11

socially optimal level of production of firms will then be virtually the same as the determination of the socially optimal level of injurers' activity discussed in the previous chapter. This is illustrated by elaborating the last example.

> *Example 2.* Because the social costs of production per unit, including expected accident losses, are 15 in Example 1, social welfare will be enhanced by production when and only when a customer obtains utility exceeding 15 from a unit. Suppose, for instance, that there are 5 customers who would derive the utilities shown in Table 9.2 from purchasing the product. (Or suppose that a single customer obtains increments to utility as shown in the table from purchasing successive units of the product.)
>
> Here, only customers A, B, and C, who derive utility greater than 15, should purchase the product; the optimal level of production (and of consumption) is thus 3.

The general point of this example is that it is socially optimal for production to proceed when, but only when, the utility customers derive from consuming additional units exceeds the sum of the direct production costs, the costs of care, and the expected accident losses associated with the additional units.

With this in mind, the analogues to the conclusions from the previous chapter about levels of activity can easily be seen to hold. Specifically, under the negligence rule the level of production will be higher than optimal (and thus too many accidents will occur): Because the price will not include expected accident losses, customers will make purchases when the utility they derive from the product is less than the social cost of production per unit. In Example 2, the price under the negligence rule will be 12. Therefore, not only A, B, and C, but also, undesirably, D will buy the product. (Because, under the negligence rule, the price of gasoline will not incorporate expected accident losses due to its transport, too much gasoline will be purchased.)

Under strict liability, however, the level of production will be optimal, because the price will equal the social costs of production per unit. In Example 2, the price will be 15, so only customers A, B, and C will purchase the product. (Because, under strict liability, the price of gasoline will include expected accident losses, the right amount of gasoline will be purchased.)

The conclusions about victims' levels of activity are also as before. Under the negligence rule, victims will choose their levels of activity optimally, for they will bear their accident losses. And under strict liability with the defense of contributory negligence, victims will engage in their activity to too great an extent, for they will be compensated for their accident losses as long as they take due care. Thus, again, the choice between strict liability and negligence rules will depend on whether it is more important to control injurers' levels of activity—here firms' levels of production—than victims' levels of activity.

1.3 Exclusion of the level of production from the determination of negligence. It was implicitly assumed earlier that the level of production is not taken into account in the determination of negligence. This assumption describes actual practice—firms, of course, are never found liable for having produced too much—and is justified by the fact that if courts were to decide on permitted levels of production, they would have to determine and balance costs of production against consumer valuations. The courts' problem, in other words, would be tantamount to that of devising production responsibilities in a centrally planned economy.

1.4 Actual liability of firms to strangers. The liability of firms for harm done to strangers is determined as described generally in Chapter 8. A distinction must be made, however, between accidents in which harm comes about in the course of productive activity (such as when gasoline explodes during transport) and accidents in which harm to strangers is caused by products after their sale (such as when a boiler is purchased and explodes, harming strangers). In accidents that occur after the sale, the finding of liability is complicated by certain doctrinal considerations and especially by the possibility that the purchasers of products may have played a contributory role.[5]

Note on the literature. Legal scholars and economists have virtually always mentioned that when strangers might be harmed by firms, imposing strict liability would raise prices and reduce purchases relative to not imposing liability. But a comparison with the situation under the negligence rule, in which prices do not reflect accident losses and are socially too low, has not usually been made. This comparison is first developed in Polinsky (1980c) and Shavell (1980c).

2. VICTIMS ARE CUSTOMERS OF FIRMS

As was indicated at the outset, firms' behavior in this case will be influenced not only by their potential liability, but also by customers' perceptions of product risks, for the latter will affect customers' willingness to make purchases.[6] More precisely, a customer will buy a product only if the utility of the product to him exceeds its perceived *full* price—the price actually charged in the market plus the perceived expected accident losses that liabil-

5. See Keeton, Dobbs, et al. 1984, sections 93, 95–98 on the United States; and Stone 1983, sections 260, 289–291, and Von Bar 1998, 2:297–311, 418–424, on European countries.

6. The analysis of liability when victims are the employees of firms would parallel the analysis of this part. In much the same way that customers, if informed, can decide not to purchase unsafe products or can insist on lower prices as compensation for bearing extra risk, employees, if informed, can decide not to work at firms with unsafe working conditions or can demand higher wages as compensation for bearing added risk. I do not examine the issue of firms' liability to employees in part because this would be similar to the present analysis and in part because, in fact, employers tend not to be liable to employees. Employees are generally barred from suing employers by workers' compensation legislation. (This legislation provides that employees may obtain compensation for accidents arising at the workplace and that employers must pay insurance premiums to support the compensation program.) See, for example, Dobbs 2000, 1097–1108; Keeton et al. 1983, chap. 19; and Larson 1994.

ity payments would not cover and thus that he would have to bear. The expected accident losses that a customer perceives that he would have to sustain will depend on his information about product risks. Alternative assumptions about customers' information are considered in the following two sections.

2.1 Customers' knowledge of risk is perfect. When customers' knowledge is perfect, firms will be led to take optimal care even in the absence of liability. To see exactly why, observe that in the absence of liability customers will bear their losses, and the full price will equal the market price plus expected accident losses. (The full price of a water heater will be seen as its price in the market plus the expected losses due to the possibility that it will rupture.) If a firm were to take less than optimal care, its potential customers would recognize this and factor into the full price the relatively high expected accident losses. Consequently, the firm's customers would go elsewhere; they would prefer to make their purchases from competitor firms exercising optimal care and offering the product at a lower full price, although at a higher market price. In other words, the force of competition will lead firms to take optimal care despite the absence of liability.

> *Example 3.* Suppose the situation is as in Example 1, except that the victims are customers; and assume that firms do not face liability for accident losses. A firm that does not take care may be able to set the market price of its product at the direct production cost of 10, but the full price will then be 19, for the firm's customers will add to the market price the expected accident losses of 9 that they will bear. The firm would thus lose its customers to firms that do take care. The price charged by firms that take care will be 12 (because the price will have to include the cost of care of 2), yet the full price will be just 15, because expected accident losses will amount to only 3. Hence, a firm that does not take care will not survive in competition against firms that do take care.

Firms will also be led to take optimal care under strict liability with the defense of contributory negligence and under the negligence rules. Similarly, customers will be led to take optimal care in their use of products under these liability rules,[7] as well as in the absence of liability.

Moreover, customers will buy the socially optimal amount of the product regardless of the absence or presence of the foregoing liability rules. This is true because the full price that customers will compare with their utility will not be affected by the absence or presence of such liability. In particular, the market price both in the absence of liability and under the negligence rule will equal the cost of optimal care plus direct production costs, because firms will be led to take optimal care in either case, and customers will add to this market price the expected accident losses in calculating the full price. Under strict liability with the defense of contributory negligence, the market price will simply equal this same full price. In Example 3, the market price will be 12 in the absence of liability and under the negligence rule, and the full price will be 15; under strict liability the market price and the full price will be 15. Thus in all cases only those customers for whom the utility of the product exceeds 15 will buy it, which is the socially desirable outcome.

2.2 Customers' knowledge of risk is imperfect.   Suppose now that customers do not have enough information to determine product risks at the level of individual firms. (Customers cannot ascertain the risk of rupture of a particular firm's water heaters.) Then firms will not take care in the absence of liability. No firm will wish to incur added expenses to make its product safer if customers will not recognize this to be true and reward the firm with their willingness to pay a higher price. Liability will thus be needed to induce firms to take optimal care.

Furthermore, the level of care taken by customers will not be optimal in the absence of liability. Customers will take too little care if they underestimate risks and too much care if they overestimate them. In the presence of liability, however, customers who possess accurate knowledge of the level of due care used to determine contributory negligence may be led to take due care despite their misperception of risk.

In addition, the quantity of customers' purchases will not be optimal

---

7. Under strict liability without the defense of contributory negligence, however, firms might take excessive care and customers might take inadequate care. For example, users of water heaters might not drain them or watch for signs of leakage even though this would

in the absence of liability or under the negligence rule. If customers over-estimate risks, they will overestimate the full price and might decide not to buy products when in fact the utility of the products exceeds the true full price. If customers underestimate risks, the opposite problem might occur; they might make purchases that are not in their interest. Under strict liability with the defense of contributory negligence, however, customers will make appropriate decisions whether to buy products regardless of their misperception of risk. It will not matter that customers incorrectly estimate risks since they will be fully compensated for their losses (because they will take due care); the market price will then reflect the true risk of accident losses, and it will be this market price alone on which customers base their decisions to make purchases.[8]

2.3 Actual customer knowledge of risk. Before I comment on the analysis of the last two sections, it will be helpful to consider briefly the likely character of customers' knowledge of risk.

One point to emphasize is that customers' knowledge of risk will vary with the type of product or service. Customers' knowledge of the risks attending use of a wide class of modern-day products (automobiles, drugs, machines) is, one assumes, limited in significant ways because of customers' quite natural inability to understand how the products function. And customers' knowledge of the quality of most professional services (medical, legal, architectural) is, one supposes, similarly limited. By contrast, customers' information about the risks of common items of fairly simple design (hammers, bicycles, can openers) is probably good on the whole, and the same is likely true of their knowledge of the risks of many of the services that they purchase in ordinary life (barbering, sports instruction).

Not only will customers' knowledge of risk vary with the type of product or service, it will vary also with the type of customer. Commercial

---

cost users little in time and effort. Manufacturers might therefore be led to produce heaters with safety features that are expensive relative to the cost of users' care.

8. This conclusion would usually be different, however, if losses include nonpecuniary elements for which liability awards would not or could not fully compensate. Suppose, for example, that product-related accidents could result in the death of a customer (as when an automobile's brakes fail). Then a customer would base his purchases in part on his estimate of the risk of death in an accident; if he incorrectly estimated this risk, his decision whether to purchase the product might be inappropriate.

customers will often have relatively accurate knowledge of risk because they tend to be repeat purchasers, buy in large quantity, and make decisions in a calculated way. The typical individual consumer may be in a quite different position; he buys many products (especially durables) only on an infrequent basis and may not have the ability or the motive to approach his purchase decision in the manner the commercial customer would.

When customers' knowledge of risk is imperfect, there does not seem to be an appealing general assumption to make about the direction of their errors. A customer's assessment of the risk of a particular product or service will tend to be based on his estimate of the average risk for the class of products or services that have the same outward appearance as the one in question. Because actual risks will deviate from average risks about as often from above as from below, the frequency with which customers underassess risks should approximate the frequency with which they overassess risks— assuming that they correctly perceive average risks. Of course, customers may not accurately perceive the average, but systematic mistakes in their assessment of risk for a class of products or services can be either positive or negative. Customers can readily be imagined to exaggerate certain kinds of risks, because, for instance, of their vivid aspect (dying in an airplane crash), and they can well be thought to underestimate other kinds of risk, because, say, of the innocuous appearance of the products creating the risks (could drinking hot liquids from styrofoam cups release a carcinogen resulting in stomach cancer?).[9]

That customers' information about risks may sometimes be imperfect seems inevitable. As was suggested earlier, customers' ability to ascertain risks directly is naturally limited by their incomplete knowledge of how products work and by their lay understanding of professional and many other services. Also, their ability to evaluate risks that are numerically small—as the risks of accidents often are—may be questioned. The problem that customers may be unable to learn directly about risks may be remedied if customers are apprised of risks by firms. But firms clearly lack

---

9. Eisner and Strotz 1961 discuss the overestimation of the risk due to airplane crashes. For a general discussion of pyschological factors affecting the assessment of risk, see Kahneman, Slovic, and Tversky 1982 and Tversky and Kahneman 1974; see also Jolls, Sunstein, and Thaler 1998 for a synthesis and review of literature. For empirical study of risk assessment, see, for example, Viscusi 1983, 1992, 1998.

appropriate incentives to provide information about the dangerousness of their products and services.[10] In addition, organizations specializing in the collection of information about risks may not be able to earn enough (through sale of publications like *Consumer Reports*) to finance their activities at a socially desirable scale, in part because individual buyers can pass on the information to others in various ways. Finally, the very capacity of customers to absorb and act on information about the risks they face seems restricted. Customers purchase a great variety of products and services, and the risks of even a single one may be complicated to describe because they depend on the manner and the circumstances in which the product is used or the service is performed. Customers could not realistically be expected to keep track of and to employ all this information even if it were freely available to them.

With these observations in mind, the reader should assume that there will sometimes be a useful role for liability to play in reducing risks and in influencing the volume of purchases.[11]

2.4 Problems in applying the negligence rule.   Information about firms' conduct and about their products and services may be particularly difficult for courts to obtain or evaluate as they arrive at a determination of negligence.[12] Such information may be of a complicated, technical nature (dealing, for example, with industrial engineering, or with the practice of medicine), or it may be special in character (concerning idiosyncratic features of the production process, or a particular patient's condition), or it may have to do with events that occurred relatively long ago (the production of an old machine, or the treatment of a patient many years earlier). Consider, by contrast, that information will be relatively easy to obtain or evaluate in the typical accident between strangers, as when a person fails to clear a sidewalk of ice and someone slips on it and breaks his leg.

Courts' difficulty in obtaining and evaluating information about firms'

10. This is not to deny that firms may have a legal duty to provide information about risk (liability for failure to warn of defects) or that they can secure marketing advantages or enhance their reputation by doing so. But such motives to provide information about risk arguably are imperfect.

11. This general view is a theme of Croley and Hanson 1993.

12. Much of what is written in this and the following sections applies equally in the context of accidents involving firms and strangers.

conduct leads to two problems. First, courts may be likely to make errors in determining optimal levels of due care. When firms are able to predict courts' incorrectly calculated levels of due care, firms will often be led to take these levels of due care and thus to take excessive or insufficient levels of care, as the case may be. And when firms are unable to predict levels of due care, or when there are other uncertainties surrounding the determination of negligence, firms may well be led to take excessive levels of care so as to avoid being found liable by mistake (a manufacturer may use an undesirably costly safety feature, or a physician may practice "defensive medicine").[13] The second problem is that courts may fail altogether to consider certain dimensions of firms' behavior in the negligence determination, either for want of any evidence or because evidence is scant. With respect to such dimensions of behavior, firms may do little or nothing to reduce risk.

These problems are avoided under the strict liability approach because firms will be motivated to take all justified steps to reduce risk, and only those steps, whether or not courts would be able to decide what steps could and should have been taken.

2.5 Problems in applying the negligence rule to research and development and product design decisions. An important illustration of the problems with the negligence rule concerns research and development with regard to product safety and design. To make a determination of negligence in this area, courts are faced with a complex task: They must decide whether, at the time that a firm had an opportunity to engage in an investigation, the then-relevant probability and value of success were sufficiently high to warrant the costs of the investigation. Because courts will be prone to make mistakes in determining the probability or value of success or the costs of investigation, firms may be led to make socially undesirable decisions. For instance, a firm that is highly uncertain whether a given degree of research or design effort will later be seen by courts as adequate may decide to engage in research to a socially excessive extent. Or a firm that believes that courts would never learn that it had a particular opportunity to reduce a risk (for example, that a pharmaceutical company

13. Why firms may be likely to take excessive care, even though mistakes in the negligence determination may favor them as well as disfavor them, is explained in section 1 of Chapter 10.

had a chance to develop a substitute drug without an adverse side effect) may decide not to pursue the opportunity. Indeed, the likelihood of this outcome is increased by the perversity that the initial pursuit of an avenue of investigation could provide the very evidence that would allow courts to conclude that a research opportunity had existed.

2.6 Problems in applying the defense of contributory negligence under strict liability.   Courts may experience difficulty in determining due care levels of customers and their actual care levels, as well as in incorporating various dimensions of their behavior into due care. It may be hard to determine what customers can and should do to reduce risk (whether users of lawn mowers should wear safety glasses in view of the danger that stones would be thrown up by the cutting blades), how customers actually use products (whether, when mowing, a person tries to steer clear of areas with stones), whether customers adequately maintain products, and the like. In addition, courts typically do not include the intensity of use of products (how often a lawn mower, a can opener, or a forklift is used) in determining customer negligence, because calculation of the appropriate intensity of use is a practical impossibility or because evidence on the actual intensity of use is difficult to obtain.

As with courts' difficulties in determining the negligence of firms, the courts' difficulties in determining the negligence of customers can lead to two types of problems. With respect to dimensions of behavior that are included in the determination of contributory negligence, customers may be led to do too little or too much to reduce risk, and with respect to dimensions of behavior that are left out of the determination, customers will do too little to lower risk. In any event, the problems would be lessened if, as under the negligence and no-liability regimes, customers expect to bear their losses.

2.7 Strict liability versus negligence reconsidered.   The discussion of the previous several sections should help to organize thinking about important factors bearing on the appeal of strict liability versus the negligence rules as means of providing incentives toward safety. To illustrate, suppose that individuals' knowledge of the health risks associated with use of microwave ovens is imperfect (there is a potential need for liability); that the harmful effects of microwave radiation might be of substantial importance (a liability-induced reduction in radiation might prevent significant injury); that the possibilities for changing the design of microwave ovens would be hard for courts to ascertain (a determination of negligence about oven design would be problematic); and that there is relatively little that users of microwave ovens can do to reduce risk (there is no real issue of contributory negligence).[14] In such a case, employment of the strict liability approach rather than the negligence rule would be desirable on grounds of creation of incentives toward safety in product design.

The situation might be different, however, with respect to use of commercial freezers and the risk that they would break down, causing frozen foods to thaw and spoil. Suppose that buyers of the freezers, being in business, know fairly well the risks that freezers would fail (the potential need for liability is small in the first place); that the scope for manufacturers of freezers to reduce risk of freezer failure is modest because the risk is already low (liability could not reduce risk substantially); that the adequacy of user maintenance of freezers—checking coolant levels—would be difficult for a court to determine in deciding contributory negligence; and that the intensity of use of freezers—the amount and value of frozen food kept in each freezer—would not be part of a contributory negligence determination (implying that users would be likely to overuse the freezers unless they bear the losses of freezer failure). Here the negligence rule would be the better form of liability on grounds of creation of incentives.

Note that in these two examples it was assumed that all the relevant factors worked in the same direction, in favor of either strict liability or the negligence rule; in reality, this will rarely be the case.

2.8 Product warranties.   An addition to the model so far considered would allow firms to offer product warranties, that is, an effective choice of liability rules.[15] The type of warranty that a firm would offer is the one that would minimize the full price of its product as perceived by customers. A firm not offering that warranty would lose its customers to competitors.

---

14. The doors of most microwave ovens must be closed for them to operate, so that users cannot "cook" themselves, but users could take care not to stand too close to such ovens when they are in operation.

15. On the economic theory of warranties, see Cooper and Ross 1985, Grossman 1981, Priest 1981, and Spence 1977; see also the survey of Wehrt 2000.

This means that if customers do not misperceive risks, the warranty that is sold will be the one that results in the lowest true full price and therefore is socially best. For example, if buyers of commercial freezers have good knowledge of the risks of breakdown, the character of the warranty on the freezers would reflect the optimal balancing of manufacturer and buyer incentives. A warranty that covered the freezer motor but not the coolant system might serve as an implicit inducement for manufacturers to improve the reliability of the motor and for buyers to maintain the coolant system properly. Such an arrangement would result in a lower full price of freezers than if the warranty covered the coolant system as well as the motor.

If customers misperceive risks, however, the warranty that is sold in the market may be socially undesirable. Notably, customers who mistakenly think that a risk is lower than it actually is will tend to buy warranties with terms limiting or disclaiming coverage of that risk. (If customers overestimate risk, they will buy warranties that are too inclusive.) To illustrate, consider the case where customers erroneously believe that a risk is nonexistent. Imagine, for instance, that they believe there is no chance that electric pencil sharpeners will throw off slivers of wood and cause injury when in fact there is this chance. Customers will therefore place no value on a warranty term giving coverage against injury due to such events, although offering the term would cost manufacturers a positive amount. Electric pencil sharpeners will therefore be sold without a warranty term covering injuries due to slivers, or with disclaimers of liability for these injuries. Consequently, manufacturers of electric pencil sharpeners will not have an incentive to reduce optimally the risk of sliver accidents. Moreover, because customers are unaware of this risk, they will buy too many electric pencil sharpeners (as opposed to safer hand-operated pencil sharpeners, or mechanical pencils).

It follows that where customers misperceive risks, it could be socially beneficial for courts to override certain terms of warranties, especially by broadening firms' responsibilities for injury. For courts to know when to override or to expand coverage terms in warranties, however, requires that they be able to distinguish between situations in which customers misperceive risk and situations in which they do not. Courts would have to be able to determine whether customers misperceive the risk that electric pencil sharpeners will cause injury from slivers, for if customers do understand this risk, they might still desire limitation of the warranty for such injuries (perhaps because they can reduce the risk of accident by discarding old pencils that are likely to break apart, or because they have health insurance that would cover losses due to such injuries).

2.9 Imperfect competition and market power.   It should also be noted how, if at all, the possibility that firms in a less than perfectly competitive market have the ability to set price above cost affects the conclusions of this chapter.[16] Firms that enjoy such market power will wish to minimize unit costs, as do firms in a perfectly competitive market, in order to maximize profits. Because the conclusions reached earlier about firms' exercise of care rested only on the assumption that firms seek to minimize unit costs, the statements made about liability and firms' levels of care will not be altered where firms possess market power.

The enjoyment of market power by firms will, however, make some difference with respect to the social desirability of the effect of liability on levels of production. Because firms with market power will set price higher than unit costs, customers will purchase less than they do in a perfectly competitive market setting. Therefore, under strict liability firms with market power will set price above the sum of their production cost, the cost of care, and accident costs per unit; and customers will tend to purchase too little, rather than the optimal amount, of the product due to the higher price. Under the negligence rule, because firms will set price above the sum of production cost and the cost of care per unit, customers' tendency to purchase too much if they underestimate risks will be counteracted, and so forth.

2.10 Actual liability of firms to customers.   In most jurisdictions in the United States today, firms are held strictly liable for accident losses caused by defects in their products, though an aspect of negligence is involved in the definition of product defect.[17] Customers need not prove negligence in the production process; they need only show that their losses were due to defects in products. Firms may sometimes avoid or reduce

16. On market power and the effect of liability rules, see Epple and Raviv 1978 and Polinsky and Rogerson 1983.

17. The description here is confined to liability of producing firms to customers; it does not include liability of dealers to customers. On product liability in the United States, see for example Dobbs 2000, chap. 24, Phillips 1998, Keeton, Dobbs, et al. 1984, chap. 17, and Shapo 1994.

their liability when accident losses were the result of product misuse or other contributory behavior of customers[18] or of dealers, and firms may challenge whether losses were in fact caused by their products. But there has been some narrowing of these defenses and thus an expansion of firms' liability; moreover, firms are increasingly prevented from escaping liability by having disclaimed it in warranties.[19]

In two important areas—product design and warning of risk—the negligence rule is employed. Specifically, a firm will be held liable for harms resulting from a dangerous characteristic in all units of its product if an alternative, safer design could have been used at reasonable cost. And a firm will be held liable for failure to warn of a product risk if the firm could have done so at a reasonable cost.

In England, France, and Germany, the trend in product liability has been in the direction of strict responsibility for defects, with this result often being reached by other legal doctrines (presumption of producer negligence where losses are caused by defects, contractual liability, or implied warranties). Yet the scope of product liability does not appear to be as great in these countries as in the United States.[20]

Note on the literature.   Oi (1973) and Hamada (1976) examine models of product liability in which victims are customers and possess perfect information about risk; Goldberg (1974) emphasizes that legal intervention must be premised on imperfect customer information. Spence (1977) analyzes strict liability in a unilateral model of accidents in which victims are customers who misperceive risk and firms offer warranties. In Shavell (1980c), I consider strict liability and negligence rules in a bilateral model of accidents along the lines presented here. For empirical work on product liability, see for example Higgins (1978), Priest (1988), and Viscusi (1991).[21]

18. Although the defense of contributory negligence is often not permitted, use of comparative negligence and doctrines relating to product misuse and to assumption of risk may allow courts the opportunity to take into account plaintiffs' behavior.

19. See, for example, Epstein 1980, Priest 1991, and G. Schwartz 1992 on the expansion of firms' liability.

20. See Fleming 1998, chap. 23, on product liability in England; Markesinis 1994, 79–95, on Germany; Zweigert and Kötz 1998, 676–678 on France and Germany; and Stone 1983, sects. 257–295, and Von Bar 1998, 2:418–424, on Europe.

21. See also Litan 1991 and the surveys of Dewees et al. 1996, chap. 4, and Geistfeld 2000.

10 ||| EXTENSIONS OF THE ANALYSIS OF DETERRENCE

In this chapter I consider a number of extensions of the basic theory of liability and deterrence. In the first four sections, I discuss various issues concerning the negligence determination, the judgment-proof problem, and vicarious liability; in the later sections, I examine a number of topics about damages, that is, about the magnitude of liability.[1]

1. PROBLEMS IN THE NEGLIGENCE DETERMINATION

Factors leading to uncertainty in the finding of negligence, and the consequences of such uncertainty, will be considered in the initial subsections here. Then the effect of systematic, anticipated error in the courts' determination of due care levels will be analyzed. At the end, the effect of misperception of due care levels will be discussed.

1.1 Uncertainty in the finding of negligence. One factor leading to uncertainty in the finding of negligence is that courts may err in assessing a party's true level of care. For example, a court might not accept a physi-

---

1. The material here draws on chapters 4, 6, and 7 of Shavell 1987a, which also contains proofs of conclusions.

cian's claim that he had performed a diagnostic test (that he listened carefully to a person's heartbeat after a series of exercises) when in fact he had done so. The possibility that a court would make an error of this type might lead a physician to administer a redundant but easily verifiable test (such as an electrocardiogram) that would reduce the chance of a court finding him negligent by mistake. Of course, the possibility that a court would make an opposite type of error may also exist. A court might decide that a physician had taken proper care when in truth he had not. For instance, a court might conclude from incomplete medical records that there was no need for a physician to refer his patient to a specialist when the patient should have seen one.

The significance of these two types of error, however, is not likely to be the same. The disadvantage to a party of being found negligent by mistake is that he will have to pay the victim's losses. This disadvantage will often be of greater importance than the savings that the party could obtain by reducing his level of care somewhat and hoping that he would erroneously escape liability if an accident occurred.

The reader should not be surprised, then, to learn that a fairly general consequence of uncertainty in the assessment of true levels of care is that parties will tend to take more than due care—and thus to take socially excessive levels of care (presuming that due care is set at socially optimal levels).[2] Consider the following example:

> *Example 1.* The probability of an accident that would cause a loss of 100 is related to the level of care as shown in Table 10.1. The socially optimal level of care, which is assumed to be due care, is moderate care. If there were no chance of mistake in courts' assessment of care, parties could avoid liability for sure by taking moderate care at a cost of 3; they would not take high care, since that would involve a greater cost of 5.
>
> Suppose, however, that there is a 33 percent chance that courts will misperceive care by one level and a 5 percent chance that courts will misperceive care by two levels. That is, there is a 33 percent chance that no care

2. I am not saying that uncertainty in the assessment of care will always lead to excessive care. Obviously, other things being equal, if there is a high enough chance of overassessment of care and a low enough chance of underassessment, parties will take less than due care. But in a wide class of situations (including ones in which the chance of overassessment of care exceeds by a significant amount the chance of underassessment), parties will take more than due care.

Table 10.1 Care level and accidents

Level of care	Cost of care	Accident probability	Expected losses	Total social costs
None	0	15%	15	15
Moderate	3	10%	10	13
High	5	9%	9	14

would be seen by courts as moderate care and a 5 percent chance that no care would be seen as a high level of care. Further, there is a 33 percent chance that moderate care would be seen by courts as none and a 33 percent chance that moderate care would be seen as high-level care. And there is a 33 percent chance that high-level care would be seen by courts as moderate care and a 5 percent chance that high-level care would be seen as none.

In this situation, parties will take a high level of care. If they take no care, their expected expenses will be $62\% \times 15\% \times 100 = 9.3$ (as they will mistakenly escape liability $33\% + 5\% = 38\%$ of the time). If they take moderate care, their expected expenses will be $3 + 33\% \times 10\% \times 100 = 6.3$ (for they will mistakenly be found liable 33 percent of the time). Yet if they take a high level of care, their expected expenses will be only $5 + 5\% \times 9\% \times 100 = 5.45$ (because they will mistakenly be found liable only 5 percent of the time).

As this example shows, if raising the level of care reduces the chance of being found negligent by mistake, parties may decide to take more than due care, even though the chances of courts' overestimating care are as large as the chances of their underestimating care.[3] The example illustrates also the point that despite parties' increasing their level of care, they may still

3. Actually, in the example, as long as the chance of overestimating care by one level is less than 58.66 percent—a chance substantially exceeding the 33 percent chance of underestimating care—parties will still take a high level of care. Assuming the chance of overestimating care by one level is 58.66 percent, parties who take no care will escape liability $58.66\% + 5\% = 63.66\%$ of the time, so their expected expenses will be $36.34\% \times 15\% \times 100 = 5.45$; parties who take moderate or high levels of care will expect to spend, as before, 6.33 and 5.45, respectively. Thus taking no care and taking a high level of care will result in equally low expected expenses. If the chance of overestimating care is lower than 58.66 percent, taking no care will result in higher expected expenses.

face a positive risk (5 percent in the example) of being found negligent if they cause accidents.

Much the same conclusions hold with respect to two other factors leading to uncertainty in the finding of negligence. One of these factors is that a party may be unable to control completely his *momentary level of care*. A driver may be unable to control completely his level of care at each instant (because of a lapse of attention, a sudden glare, a sneeze), or a physician may be unable to act with all the care he intends with each of his patients on each of their visits. But because it is the driver's care at the time of an accident and the physician's treatment of the particular patient on a particular visit that courts will ordinarily consider in determining negligence, the driver and the physician will generally bear some uncertainty regarding their being found negligent. A little reflection should convince the reader that such uncertainty will usually lead parties to try to take more than due care in order to reduce the likelihood that their momentary level of care will fall short of due care (in terms of their usual habits and attitudes—see the next section) and thus cause them to be found negligent. (The logic behind this assertion is essentially that of the previous paragraphs, that the disadvantage of being found negligent will outweigh the advantage of conserving on the cost of taking care.)

The other factor leading to uncertainty in the determination of negligence is the level of due care that will be applied by courts. It may be difficult for a party to predict how courts will assess the cost of care or its effectiveness in reducing risk, and thus what they will determine due care to be. There may be uncertainty, for instance, in how courts will evaluate the cost to a physician in time and effort of performing a diagnostic test or in how courts will assess the value of the test in providing information about a disease; in this case the physician will not know whether courts will see failure to perform the test as negligence. It should be clear to the reader that such uncertainty will tend to induce parties to take higher than desirable levels of care to guard against being found liable by mistake.[4]

---

4. The points made in this subsection were first studied by Diamond 1974a and further developed in Calfee and Craswell 1984, Craswell and Calfee 1986, and Shavell 1987a, chap. 4; qualifications to these points are pointed out in Grady 1983 and Kahan 1989, as observed in note 36. The notion of defensive medicine comports with the explanation for excessive care advanced here; for empirical evidence of defensive medicine, see, for example, Danzon 1985 and Kessler and McClellan 1996.

1.2 Remarks on uncertainty.   The relative importance of the three sources of uncertainty—courts' errors in assessing true levels of care, parties' inability to control their momentary level of care, and courts' errors in calculating levels of due care—will depend on the context.[5] For example, when there are few witnesses to, or little evidence concerning, a party's act, errors in assessing true levels of care may be important; when courts are not able to obtain or to evaluate reliably information about the costs and benefits of care, errors in the calculation of the level of due care may be important (a problem that may be of general significance for physicians and other professionals, or for firms using new technology).

With respect to parties' inability to control their momentary levels of care, three comments seem worth making. First, an individual's momentary level of care can be regarded as an imperfect indicator of his true, and inherently unobservable, level of care, namely, the degree to which he adopts a *prudential mental attitude.* Hence, in strict logic, the cause of uncertainty in the finding of negligence due to an individual's inability to control his momentary level of care may be viewed as courts' inability to assess an individual's true prudential mental attitude. Second, one wonders whether courts might sometimes lower the level of due care in implicit recognition of parties' problems in controlling their momentary level of care. (Might not courts allow for some irregularity in driving behavior, knowing that individuals cannot maintain full concentration at all times?) Third, there are two types of situations that appear to involve uncertainties similar to those regarding the momentary level of care: situations in which parties are responsible for the negligence of subordinates whose behavior they cannot control completely; and situations in which parties operate machines that occasionally function erratically.

Finally, it should be added that the more general interpretation of the fact that uncertainty in the level of due care may induce parties to take socially excessive care is that uncertainty about the law may lead parties to take socially undesirable steps in order to avoid liability.

1.3 Anticipated errors in the choice of due care.   Now suppose that parties know in advance that the level of due care set by courts will be different from the optimal level, and how so. (But, for simplicity, suppose

5. See Tunc 1983, sects. 141, 143–146, for a discussion of the importance of uncertainty in the negligence determination in different legal systems.

that the courts can correctly measure parties' true levels of care and that parties can control completely their levels of care.)

It might be that parties know that the due care level will be less than the optimal level. This would be true, for instance, when parties know that they will not be found negligent for failure to use a particular safety device despite its low cost and substantial effectiveness in reducing risk. In such a situation parties will obviously not choose to purchase the safety device; they will not take more than due care.

The other possibility is that the parties know that the level of due care will exceed the optimal level (that a safety device will be required despite its high cost and low effectiveness in reducing risk). In this situation parties will take due care unless its level is so high that they are better off acting negligently. In the latter case, parties will take optimal care since they will, in effect, be strictly liable.

1.4 Misperception of the level of due care.   Suppose, finally, that parties misperceive the level of due care that courts will apply. Then parties will take the level of care that they believe constitutes due care, unless it exceeds optimal care by so much that they are better off acting in a way they think is negligent, in which case they will take optimal care. Hence, parties who overestimate due care will either take more than due care or take optimal care; those who underestimate due care will take less than due care.

1.5 Comparison with strict liability.   The various reasons why uncertainty surrounding the negligence determination may lead to inappropriate levels of care constitute implicit advantages of strict liability. Because under strict liability there is no investigation of the adequacy of an injurer's care level, the problems that would occur in determining negligence are moot, and levels of care will tend to be optimal.

2.   WHY NEGLIGENCE IS FOUND AND IMPLICATIONS OF FINDINGS OF NEGLIGENCE

2.1 Reasons for findings of negligence.   What explains findings of negligence? This question arises because, as the reader will recall, according to the basic theory of liability presented in Chapter 8, parties were never found negligent: It was in an individual's interest to act with due care, and courts therefore always exonerated injurers.

It is evident from the discussion in the last section, however, that there are a variety of reasons why parties may face a risk of being found negligent, including errors in the courts' assessment of care actually taken or in ascertaining the proper standard of due care, inability of individuals to control their momentary behavior, and inability of firms to control the behavior of employees.

Another significant reason for findings of negligence is that parties may not find taking due care worthwhile, and thus will decide definitely to act in a negligent way. We saw that this might be so when parties anticipate an excessive standard of due care. Parties also might not find it in their interest to take due care because they do not have enough assets to pay a judgment or because they think they would escape suit (these possibilities will be discussed in sections 3 and 9).

2.2 Significance of findings of negligence. The occurrence of findings of negligence implies that there is an element of strict liability—of having to pay for harm done—associated with use of the negligence rule. Hence, many of the conclusions reached earlier about strict liability carry over to a degree to the negligence setting. For example, the point that under strict liability injurers will take into account the losses their activity creates has relevance under the negligence rule; injurers will take some account of the losses their activity creates because they will face some risk of being found negligent. In addition, the occurrence of findings of negligence will be referred to later, in Chapter 11, to explain why injurers should wish to purchase liability insurance against being found negligent.

3. INJURERS' INABILITY TO PAY FOR LOSSES: THE JUDGMENT-PROOF PROBLEM

3.1 Dilution of incentives to reduce risk. If injurers do not have assets sufficient to pay fully for the losses they cause—and may thus be *judgment-proof*—their incentives to reduce risk by taking care may be inadequate, because they will treat losses that they cause that exceed their assets as imposing liabilities only equal to their assets. For the same reason, injurers' activity levels will tend to be socially excessive and they will contribute too much to risk. These points are more important the lower are injurers' assets in relation to the harm they might cause (in the extreme, if injurers have no assets, they will have no liability-related incentive to reduce risk).[6]

3.2 Significance of dilution of incentives.   (a) There are many contexts in which inability to pay for losses plausibly may lead to dulling of incentives to reduce risk. This is so not only for parties with low or moderate assets, but also for parties with substantial assets whose activities pose special risks. (Consider, for instance, even large corporate enterprises and the chance of fires or explosions causing mass injuries, or the possibility that a widely distributed product has toxic or other dangerous properties.) Incentives are particularly likely to be diluted with respect to those actions that would serve primarily to lower the severity or likelihood of extremely large losses exceeding parties' assets, yet not of small or moderate losses. (Consider the motive of the owner of a nuclear power plant to spend on a safety measure, perhaps an extra concrete shell around the reactor core, that would limit harm only in a catastrophic accident involving rupture of the core and causing losses far greater than the owner's net worth.)

(b) Incentive problems are exacerbated if parties have the opportunity to shield assets, such as when an individual puts his property in a relative's name or when a firm transfers assets to a holding company.

(c) The problem of dilution of incentives is distinct from the problem that scholars and practitioners often identify with injurers' inability to pay fully for losses, namely, victims' inability to obtain complete compensation. This and related issues (concerning, chiefly, insurance) will be addressed in Chapter 11.

3.3 Solutions to the problem of dilution of incentives.   Several types of social responses to the problem of inadequate incentives to reduce risk are possible, depending on the circumstances.

One possibility is vicarious liability. If there is another party who has some control over the behavior of the party whose assets are limited, then

---

6. I analyze the nature of the dilution of incentives due to the judgment-proof problem in Shavell 1986; see also Pitchford 1998 and Ringleb and Wiggins 1990.

the former party can be held vicariously liable for the losses caused by the latter. This solution will be discussed in section 4.

A second possibility is minimum asset requirements. Parties with assets less than some specified amount could be prevented from engaging in an activity. This approach would ensure that parties who do engage in an activity have enough at stake to be led to take adequate care. The minimum asset requirement, however, is a blunt tool that could unduly discourage participation in an activity: Suppose that a person who could not meet the asset requirement would obtain a large benefit from the activity and would cause little expected harm, even though his incentives are diluted.

A third response is regulation of liability insurance coverage. This is a somewhat complicated topic, and discussion of it will be deferred until section 7 of Chapter 11.

A fourth approach is direct regulation of parties' risk-creating behavior.[7] Thus, for example, a regulatory authority might mandate that milk be pasteurized or that trucks carrying explosives not travel through tunnels. Such regulation could force parties to reduce risks in socially beneficial ways that would not be induced by the threat of liability, due to its dulled effect from the judgment-proof problem.[8] But a regulatory authority's ability to devise appropriate regulations is limited by its knowledge, as was discussed in section 5 of Chapter 5.

A final way of mitigating dilution of incentives is resort to criminal liability. A party who would not take care if only his assets were at stake might be induced to do so for fear of a criminal sanction; see Chapters 21 and 24.

4. VICARIOUS LIABILITY

4.1 Definition of vicarious liability. The concern here is with the imposition of liability on one party—the principal—for some or all of the losses caused by a second party—the agent. The principal is presumed to have a relationship with the agent that may allow him to observe the agent's

---

7. See, for example, Faure 2000, Kornhauser and Revesz 1998, and Menell 1998.

8. It should be noted that the judgment-proof problem also limits the ability of a regulatory authority to enforce regulations in some circumstances.

level of care and to control it or come to an agreement about it. The reader may wish to think of the principal and the agent as employer and employee, contractor and subcontractor, or parent and child.

4.2 Vicarious liability increases levels of care and reduces levels of activity if the agent is judgment proof. Suppose that the agent is judgment proof. Then, as discussed in section 3, the agent's incentives to take care will be inadequate if he alone is liable. Imposition of vicarious liability, however, alters the situation because it puts the principal's assets at stake.[9]

If the principal can observe and control the agent's level of care, then imposition of vicarious liability will induce the principal to compel the agent to exercise optimal care, because that will reduce the expected liability payments of the principal. (If the principal is in a contractual relationship with the agent, as would be true of an employer and employee, the principal might have to pay the agent to take added care, but the principal will still prefer to do that in order to reduce his liability payments if the level of care is optimal.)

If the vicariously liable principal cannot observe and directly control the agent's level of care, the principal will attempt to induce the agent to take care by instituting penalties for adverse outcomes, such as demotion, discharge, or suit in the case of employees. But since the agent's assets are less than the losses he might cause, the principal will not generally be able to induce the agent to choose the optimal level of care.

Whether or not the principal can observe and control the agent's level of care, imposition of vicarious liability will lead the principal to reduce the agent's participation in, and level of, risky activity, assuming that the principal can control the agent's level of activity.

---

9. Sykes 1984 contains a general analysis of vicarious liability stressing, in addition to some of the issues of incentives discussed here, the allocation of risk between agents and principals; see also Kornhauser 1982. For analysis of a particular form of vicarious liability, imposed on suppliers of services (such as lawyers, accountants, and lenders) to possibly judgment-proof parties, see Kraakman 1986 and Pitchford 1995. For analysis of another important form, imposed on owners of a firm, see Hansmann and Kraakman 1991 and Halpern 1998.

4.3 Factors bearing on the appeal of vicarious liability. (a) The advantage of vicarious liability in desirably affecting incentives to reduce risk will be greater the lower the agent's assets are, and the higher the principal's assets are, relative to the probable magnitude of harm the agent can cause. The advantage will also be greater the better able the principal is to control the agent's behavior.

To illustrate the relevance of these factors, consider the important example of the large firm and its employees.[10] It is apparent that the assets of employees are likely to be much lower than the losses they could cause, for the scope of a firm's activities is frequently such that a single employee's behavior may result in harm to many parties or otherwise lead to significant losses. Thus, were employees only individually liable, one suspects that their incentives to take care would often be seriously inadequate. One also supposes that imposition of vicarious liability on the firm helps to cure this problem because the firm's assets are usually much greater than those of any of its employees and because the firm typically has the ability to exert significant control over its employees' behavior.

In other contexts, and especially those in which a principal engages an agent on a one-time basis, vicarious liability is not necessarily as effective, because there is no natural presumption that can be made about the agent's assets relative to the principal's. Contrast the following two examples: (1) A homeowner (the principal) of average means pays a national pest-control firm (the agent) to carry out extermination services; here the principal's assets are much smaller than the agent's. (2) A large construction firm (the principal) subcontracts with a small, family-owned plumbing company (the agent) to help on a job; here the principal's assets are much greater than the agent's. These examples serve also to illustrate that the principal's ability to control effectively the agent's behavior may be adequate in one situation but poor in the next—whereas the construction firm should be able to watch over the plumbing subcontractor quite well, the likelihood that the homeowner can judge the performance of the exterminator is not great. Evidently, then, the attractiveness of vicarious liability will depend significantly on the features of the situation at hand.

10. The reader should be reminded that I am considering here only issues of incentives. In particular, I am not considering any advantages (or disadvantages) vicariously liable parties may have as risk bearers.

(b) The desirability of vicarious liability is enhanced by two additional factors. First, principals may have better knowledge than agents about the nature of risk or be able themselves to take actions that can reduce risk. Where this is so, imposition of vicarious liability will obviously lead principals not only to have agents take appropriate care, but also to take additional actions of their own to reduce risk. In the presence of vicarious liability, firms will be led to issue instructions, organize the conditions of the workplace, schedule operations, select employees, and so forth, in ways that better reduce risk. Second, principals may have more information than courts do about the appropriateness of agents' behavior. If that is the case, and if under vicarious liability principals frequently replace courts as the discipliners of agents, fewer mistakes will be made and better conduct will be promoted.

(c) There are, however, disadvantages of vicarious liability that should be kept in mind. Specifically, imposition of vicarious liability will increase the administrative cost of using the legal system, because it will raise the number of defendants named in actions brought by victims, otherwise complicate proceedings, and also engender claims by principals against agents.

4.4 Actual use of vicarious liability.   Vicarious liability is a significant feature of legal systems today.[11] Most important, firms are held responsible for the losses caused by their employees. Vicarious liability is in addition sometimes imposed on principals for losses caused by their agents (here I am using these terms in their legal sense), on automobile owners for accidents caused by those whom they allow to drive, on parents for harms resulting from their children's acts, on teachers for their students' negligence, and so forth. Although the pattern of use of vicarious liability is complicated and varies among legal systems, the general principles that are applied seem to be such that the greater the degree of one party's control and authority over a second party, and the more knowledge the first party

11. See Dobbs 2000, chap. 22, Fleming 1998, chap. 19, and Keeton, Dobbs, et al. 1984, chap. 12, on Anglo-American law; and Le Gall 1983, Eörsi 1983, and Von Bar 1998, 1:351–363, for comparative treatments.

has about the second party's behavior, the more likely the first party is to be held responsible for the losses caused by the second party.

5. DAMAGES AND THE LEVEL OF LOSSES

5.1 Damages equal to the level of losses. It was shown earlier, in Chapters 8 and 9, that the threat of liability generally leads parties to take optimal levels of care, and sometimes to choose optimal levels of activity. The arguments for these optimality conclusions were made using examples in which there is one possible level of harm that results if an accident occurs and in which the magnitude of liability—so-called *damages*—equals that level of harm. These optimality conclusions carry over to situations in which there are multiple possible levels of harm. Consider the following illustration, in which there are two possible levels of harm.

> *Example 2.* If injurers do not take care, the probability of an accident will be 10 percent. And if an accident occurs, there will be a loss of 100 with a probability of 80 percent and a loss of 500 with a probability of 20 percent. Expected losses if care is not taken will therefore be $10\% \times (80\% \times 100 + 20\% \times 500) = 18$. Hence, if exercising care eliminates the possibility of an accident and costs less than 18, it will be socially desirable to do so.
>
> Suppose that liable injurers must pay for the losses that occur, whether these are 100 or 500. Then under strict liability injurers will bear expected liability of 18 if they do not take care, and thus will be led to take care when they ought to. Injurers will behave in the same way under the negligence rule if the cost of taking care is less than 18 because they will be liable if they fail to take care.

This example illustrates why, in the general setting in which an accident can result in more than one level of harm, injurers will act optimally if damages equal actual harm. The reason is that if a liable party must pay for the actual harm he causes, whatever the level of harm happens to be, his expected damage payments will equal the expected harm he causes. And the condition that expected payments equal expected harm is exactly the assumption on which the arguments about optimality of parties' behavior under liability rules has been based in the previous discussion. If damages tend to fall short of harm, so that expected payments are below expected harm, incentives to reduce risk will be inadequate, and if damages exceed harm, so that expected damages exceed expected harm, incentives to reduce risk will be too high.[12]

5.2 Actual magnitude of damages.   The starting principle in most legal systems is that a liable party should pay for the actual level of losses caused, whether they be high or low. It is said, for instance, that an injurer takes his victim as he finds him, that the injurer should pay for harm caused if the victim turns out to be affected by a latent aggravating condition (a thin skull, hemophilia), and that the injurer should pay similarly if the property he damaged had some structural weakness or was unusually valuable. At the same time, a liable injurer is responsible only for small losses if only a small harm resulted from his act.[13] (Nevertheless, there are subsidiary principles, which will be noted in section 6, under which liable injurers do not pay damages equal to losses.)

6.   DAMAGES AND THE PROBABILITY OF LOSSES

6.1 Optimal damages are unaffected by the probability of losses. The conclusion from the last section that behavior will be optimal if the magnitude of liability equals the actual level of losses suggests that behavior will not be optimal if liability is adjusted on the basis of other factors— in particular, if damages are lowered because a loss was very unlikely, or if damages are raised because a loss was very likely. These two possibilities will now be considered.

6.2 Limitation of damages for unusual losses.   Suppose that damages are limited to an average or typical level when losses happen to be unusually high. Then expected liability payments will be less than expected

12. It should be noted, however, that if damages equal the expected harm regardless of the actual magnitude of harm, incentives to reduce risk will also be appropriate. This setting of damages, however, would usually not be desirable, for actual harm is generally easier to determine than expected harm (where that is not so, damages may be set equal to expected harm—see section 7). Moreover, it would mean in particular that damages would be less than actual harm when actual harm is higher than average, something that victims would view as problematic.

13. See for example Dobbs 2000, 464–465 and Fleming 1998, 234–237, on Anglo-American law, and Stoll 1983, sects. 26–28, and Von Bar 1998, 2:156–162, on law in other countries.

losses and the incentive to take care may be inadequate. In Example 2, if liability for the relatively unlikely losses of 500 is limited to 100, then an injurer's expected liability if he does not take care will be only 10% × 100 = 10, which is less than the expected losses of 18. An injurer will therefore take care only if the cost of doing so is less than 10, rather than whenever the cost is less than 18.

To better appreciate the conclusion that, under present assumptions, liability for unusual accidents should not be limited, observe that the contrary conclusion would lead to a reductio ad absurdum. Any accident, after all, can be seen as extremely unlikely if it is described in sufficient detail. For example, the initially likely sounding accident in which a person drives his automobile into his neighbor's picket fence becomes a very unlikely one when it is mentioned that the accident occurred on a Tuesday at 4:23 p.m., that the left side of the automobile's fender struck the fence, and that the eighteenth through twenty-seventh pickets were broken. Were one to contend that liability for unlikely accidents should be limited, one might thus be led to say that liability for any accident whatever should be limited.

Another way to understand this point is to recognize that the magnitude of expected losses reflects all manner of possible accidents (striking the neighbor's fence with the right side or the middle part of the fender if not with the left side, breaking the nineteenth through twenty-eighth pickets if not the eighteenth through twenty-seventh). Expected losses are a probability-weighted aggregation of losses that can arise in many individually unlikely ways. Were liability reduced because of the improbability of the particular accident, expected liability could not equal expected losses.

6.3 A qualification.   Nevertheless, it might be acceptable to limit liability for certain accidents: If the possibility of some type of accident is overlooked, then there would be no decrease in injurers' incentives caused by reducing liability for that type of accident. (Note that this argument is not an affirmative reason for reducing the magnitude of liability; it claims only that reducing liability may not have a detrimental effect on incentives.)

To decide which types of accident may be overlooked, consider that individuals cannot practically contemplate each and every one of the multitude of possible accidents that could follow from their actions. People must amalgamate potential accidents into a relatively small number of categories, assign probabilities to the categories, and make decisions with reference to them. In the process, the possibility arises that some accidents will not be taken into account because they do not fit into the list of categories used in decisionmaking. Such accidents might be described as freak.[14]

There are, however, several problematic aspects of a policy limiting liability for accidents whose possibility is overlooked. First, this policy invites parties to deceive courts about accidents that they had in fact contemplated; second, the policy reduces parties' incentives to consider the full range of consequences that could result from their actions; and third, it may increase the costs of adjudication.[15]

6.4 Actual damages for unlikely losses.   Although, as was stated in section 5.2, the starting principle in most legal systems is that liability equals losses caused, there are exceptions to the principle in Anglo-American law that fall under the rubric of unforeseeability.[16] According to this notion, liability should not extend to harms that the injurer could not reasonably foresee. It appears from examination of cases and legal commentary that the accidents that are held not to be reasonably foreseeable generally have a far-fetched, extraordinary character.

6.5 Damages for highly likely losses.   If liability for accidents that are very likely to occur exceeds the level of actual losses, then parties may have too great an incentive to reduce risk. Suppose that a construction firm

14. Consider what happened in the celebrated American case of *Palsgraf v. Long Island R.R.,* in which a package containing fireworks was dislodged from the arms of a man boarding a train and fell under the train's wheels, causing an explosion that knocked a scale onto, and injured a woman at, a platform some distance away.

15. Limiting the magnitude of liability will tend to increase the cost per case brought, but it may also reduce the number of cases that are brought and thus lower the costs of adjudication.

16. On unforeseeability, see Fleming 1998, 237–246, Keeton, Dobbs, et al. 1984, sect. 43, and the *Restatement of the Law Second: Torts* 1965, sect. 435. In other legal systems there are some parallels with unforeseeability (chiefly in the interpretation of the "adequacy" theory), but there does not seem to be an exactly corresponding notion; see the discussion in Honoré 1983, sects. 91–93, Markesinis 1994, 107–108, and Zweigert and Kötz 1998, 601–602, 621.

that blasts to excavate a large area will be virtually sure to cause some losses. If the firm has to pay for more than these losses because of their high likelihood, the firm may be led to take excessive precautions in blasting, or may decide to use alternative, more expensive means of excavation, even where blasting is socially best.

6.6 Actual liability for highly likely losses.   Again, because the starting principle is that liability should equal actual losses, the fact that the probability of losses might have been high does not ordinarily result in liability greater than the losses. A partial exception occurs when the injurer was reckless or knew harm would occur, especially when intended; see section 9.

7.   DAMAGES AND COURTS' UNCERTAINTY ABOUT THE LEVEL OF LOSSES

7.1 Damages equal to expected losses.   Suppose that courts are not able to assess accurately the level of losses that occur in individual accidents, but use estimates of losses that are correct on average. Then liable parties' expected damage payments will still equal the expected losses they cause, so they will still be led to act optimally under liability rules. In Example 2, for instance, suppose that courts are not able to assess whether losses are 100 or 500 but know that expected losses are 180 and impose damages of this amount. Then injurers will be led to behave optimally.[17]

7.2 Comments on courts' uncertainty.   Courts may be uncertain about the level of losses when the harm has already occurred, as when a house burns and the value of its contents is not easy to determine. Similarly, uncertainty may arise when some elements of the harm will occur in the future. A primary example of the latter is when an individual's subsequent earnings will be reduced due to an injury. The interpretation of the point

---

17. I am continuing to assume here, as in sections 5 and 6, that when the injurer chooses his level of care and activity level, he does not know what the magnitude of accident losses will be (100 or 500 in the example), he only knows the probability distribution of accident losses. Therefore, the injurer will have proper incentives to take care as long as his expected liability equals expected harm.

under discussion in this type of situation is that if courts' estimates of future losses are correct on average, injurers will have appropriate motives to reduce risk. There will be no need for courts to determine what victims' losses turn out to be.

It should also be noted that estimating uncertain elements of harm may be a difficult and much disputed process, raising the administrative costs of use of the legal system. Therefore, it may be socially desirable for courts to exclude uncertain components of losses from the computation of damages if the probable magnitude of these losses, and the consequent dilution of incentives to reduce risk, is not too large. An alternative and superior approach is for courts to approximate uncertain components by means of some easily applied formula, and not to allow dispute over this part of the damage calculation.

7.3 Actual determination of damages in the face of uncertainty over the level of losses.   When losses involve harm to property, courts ordinarily attempt to estimate uncertain components that are not too speculative; they follow the same course when property losses are associated with forgone profits, but their approach is conservative.[18]

With respect to accidents resulting in injuries to persons, courts can usually ascertain medical expenses borne and income lost up to the time of trial fairly reliably, but subsequent medical expenses and diminution in earning capacity may be highly uncertain. In many countries courts estimate these amounts as best they can, often using actuarial and statistical data to award a lump sum to injured parties or, in the case of fatal accidents, to their dependents for loss of support. In Germany, however, the preference is against lump-sum awards; instead, courts favor awards for reduced earnings to be paid on a periodic basis only as long as injured parties actually suffer them.[19]

18. The description here is based mainly on Fleming 1998, chap. 10, sections 1, 3, and on Stoll 1983, sections 12–48, a general comparative treatment of damages and other remedies.

19. See McGregor 1983, sections 49–52, and Von Bar 1998, 2:197–200.

8. DAMAGES AND PECUNIARY VERSUS NONPECUNIARY LOSSES

8.1 Definition of the two types of losses.   *Pecuniary* losses are those that either are monetary or are losses of goods that can be purchased in markets, in which case the measure of the losses comprises the replacement costs. *Nonpecuniary* losses correspond to the losses in utility suffered when irreplaceable things have been destroyed, such as family portraits or other unique objects, or, importantly, injuries involving individuals' health, physical integrity, or emotional well-being.[20]

8.2 Damages equal to the sum of pecuniary and nonpecuniary losses.   Because both pecuniary and nonpecuniary losses reduce social welfare, it is clear that parties will be led to act appropriately under liability rules only if damages equal the sum of pecuniary and nonpecuniary losses. If damages do not fully reflect nonpecuniary losses, parties' incentives to reduce risks may be inadequate.

8.3 Courts' ability to assess pecuniary and nonpecuniary losses. Because pecuniary losses are equal either to actual losses in wealth or to the cost of replacing goods, such losses are often easy for courts to determine. By contrast, because nonpecuniary losses cannot be observed directly, they are difficult for courts to estimate. Hence, it might be thought that courts ought not to attempt to estimate nonpecuniary losses if they are probably small: In this way administrative costs would be avoided, while incentives to reduce risk would be little affected, as was generally suggested in the case of courts' uncertainty about the level of losses. But, as was noted, in principle a better approach to adopt when nonpecuniary losses are likely to be small, and thus not worth the administrative costs of measuring, is to make use of simple tables or formulas. In any case, if nonpecuniary losses are likely to be large, it is important for courts to attempt to estimate them, and especially when pecuniary losses are small. Otherwise, incentives to

---

20. To be more precise about the definitions, consider a model in which there are two goods—a good that can be directly consumed and from which other goods can be produced, and an irreplaceable good, which cannot be produced. In this model, assume that the utility of an individual equals the number of units of the first good and its equivalent in produced goods, plus the utility to him of the irreplaceable good if he possesses it.

reduce risk may be seriously compromised. This may be the situation, for example, with respect to the death of young children.[21]

8.4 Actual liability for nonpecuniary losses. The categories of losses typically described as nonpecuniary include pain and suffering, emotional distress, and the like. Losses of money and of goods for which substitutes can be bought are regarded as pecuniary, with the prices of the substitutes measuring the losses.

The willingness of courts to increase awards on account of nonpecuniary losses varies considerably among legal systems. French law may be the most liberal in the types of nonpecuniary losses recognized. Anglo-American law is less liberal (though the size of awards, when given, seems highest, especially in the United States). German law is more restrictive than French or Anglo-American in the types of nonpecuniary losses for which damages are allowed.[22]

Moreover, treatment of nonpecuniary losses within legal systems may depend on the type of accident and other factors. Nonpecuniary losses are not usually compensated unless there is accompanying physical injury (but if the injury results in death, nonpecuniary losses suffered by the victim's family are not ordinarily compensated, at least in Anglo-American law). Additionally, nonpecuniary losses associated with losses of unique objects of property are rarely compensated.

9. DAMAGES GREATER THAN LOSSES: PUNITIVE DAMAGES

9.1 Note on use of terms. It is conventional to refer to damages that are greater than losses as *punitive,* and I shall sometimes use this terminology here. The explanation for the terminology is that damages exceeding losses are often imposed as a form of punishment (see section 9.7), even

21. As will be suggested later, the nonpecuniary component of awards for the death of children is low or nonexistent. The pecuniary awards are usually small as well, because they are based on the future loss of support—often zero—that parents will suffer in their later years. (For these reasons, one might wonder about the adequacy of the incentives of, say, toy manufacturers to reduce the risk of fatal accidents.) See McGregor 1983, sections 253–255, 273.

22. See Fleming 1998, 266–270, 285, for a description of Anglo-American law; Stoll 1983, sections 35–48, and Von Bar 1998, 2:69–88, 169–189, for a general comparative

though, as will be discussed, there are rationales for the imposition of damages exceeding losses that would not naturally be described as punitive.

9.2 Damages greater than losses generally create excessive incentives to reduce risk.   As was stated in section 5, if damages are set equal to losses, incentives to reduce risk will generally be desirable. If damages exceed losses, levels of care will tend to be excessive, and levels of activity will be too low (at least under strict liability). Nevertheless, there are several possible rationales for imposition of damages exceeding losses, including the following.[23]

9.3 Escape from suit.   Suppose that injurers who ought to be liable might escape suit. This could be so because it is difficult for victims to identify who injured them (as in the case of a driver who flees from the scene of an accident that he caused, or of a firm that discharges an untraceable but disease-causing pollutant into the air). In addition, suit might not be brought because of litigation costs.

If injurers who sometimes escape suit are made to pay only the usual level of damages on those occasions when they are sued, then their expected payments will be less than the expected losses they generate. Consequently, their incentives to reduce risk will be inadequate. For incentives to be restored appropriately, damages must be raised above the level of losses when they are found liable. Specifically, if damages equal losses multiplied by the inverse of the probability of suit, then expected damages will equal expected losses and incentives will be correct. If, for instance, the probability of suit is 50 percent and losses are $10,000, damages should be multiplied by $1/.5$ or 2, for then damages will be $20,000, so that expected damages will be $50\% \times \$20,000 = \$10,000$, the correct amount; and if the probability of suit is 33.33 percent, then damages should be multiplied by 3, making them $30,000 and expected damages will be $10,000; and so forth.[24]

---

survey; and McGregor 1983, sections 35–47, 146–172, 212–217, 264–273, for a comparative treatment of damages for personal injury and death.

23. On economic analysis of punitive damages, see generally Cooter 1989 and Polinsky and Shavell 1998b. For empirical work, see, for example, Eisenberg et al. 1997 and Karpoff and Lott 1999.

24. More precisely, if injurers are risk neutral and damages d equal h/p, where h is harm and p is the probability of suit, then expected damages will be $p(h/p) = h$, and incentives will

9.4 Illicit utility from causing harm.   Suppose here that an injurer will obtain utility from causing losses and that this utility is not credited in social welfare. When, for instance, a person breaks the windows of his neighbor's house because he positively enjoys the unhappiness his neighbor will experience, society may not want to count the person's utility as an addition to social welfare.[25] (Contrast this situation to one in which an individual playing catch throws a ball that breaks a window by accident; here his pleasure derives from playing catch, and breaking a window does not raise it.)

Given the assumption that the utility the injurer obtains from doing harm is not credited in social welfare, society wants to discourage the injurer's harmful act. To accomplish that, the damages that are imposed must exceed the utility that the injurer would obtain from his act. Therefore, damages may have to be higher than the losses caused. To discourage a person from spitefully breaking his neighbor's windows may require a penalty greater than the cost of replacing the windows because the person may derive substantial pleasure from committing this act.[26]

9.5 Encouraging market transactions.   In some circumstances it is possible for a party to communicate with a potential victim before causing harm, for example, when a firm contemplates infringing on another's copyright. When prior communication is possible, a potential injurer could negotiate in advance with the potential victim to purchase the right to engage

---

be correct. If injurers are risk averse, then damages need not be as high as h/p to give injurers adequate incentives to reduce risk.

25. I examine this assumption because it seems to be held by many individuals, and the view that different sources of utility might count differently in the social calculus has a distinguished pedigree—see for example Mill 1861, 56, and Harsanyi 1977, 62. I myself, however, do not find the trumping of malevolent (or other) preferences appealing, for reasons that are articulated in Kaplow and Shavell 2002b, section B.3, chap. 8. In brief, I see no principled basis for distinguishing among sources of utility to individuals, and any way of so doing leads to the possibility that all individuals would be made worse off.

26. A similar rationale concerns illicit disutility associated with the exercise of care. Suppose that some people claim that the exercise of care would cause them special and peculiar disutility that is not counted as a cost in the social welfare calculus. For instance, a driver might claim that to be attentive to the road is extraordinarily bothersome. If society does not credit this disutility, it will want to induce the person to be attentive to road conditions, and that may require a level of damages exceeding losses.

in the loss-creating conduct. The firm deliberating about the copyright violation could secure a license to use the copyrighted material.

In such circumstances, it may be socially desirable to induce a potential injurer to bargain and purchase the right to engage in harm-creating conduct; this can be accomplished by threatening to impose punitive damages on the potential injurer if he acts to cause harm.[27] Specifically, suppose that the usual level of damages would be an underestimate of harm for some reason (see section 7.2). A potential injurer then might cause harm when doing so is socially undesirable, because the benefit to the injurer might be greater than the low estimate of harm but less than the actual harm. There may be additional undesirable repercussions from an underestimate of harm. If injurers can take property from victims without having to pay its full value, injurers will devote effort to identifying and appropriating such property (copyright violators will seek out material to copy), and victims will expend effort to protect their property (copyright owners will invest resources in preventing duplication of their material). Such efforts are socially wasteful. The foregoing problems can be avoided if punitive damages are imposed for unilaterally causing harm, for that will induce bargaining and exchange only if the injurer's benefit exceeds the property owner's loss.[28]

Another possible reason to employ punitive damages to encourage bargaining and market transactions concerns administrative costs. If compensatory damages are used alone, harm and the taking of property might be more frequently mediated through the legal system by the bringing of law-

27. This point apparently originated with Calabresi and Melamed 1972 and was further developed by Biggar 1995, Haddock, McChesney, and Spiegel 1990, Kaplow and Shavell 1996b, and Landes and Posner 1981a.

28. An important qualification to the argument of this paragraph concerns the question of why the use of punitive damages should be expected to induce bargaining, for it might be expected to occur anyway. To illustrate, suppose that punitive damages are not employed and that the copyright holder is willing to pay more to prevent infringement than the potential infringer values infringement. One might expect the copyright holder to pay the potential infringer not to infringe. Thus, punitive damages would not be needed to induce bargaining—it would occur anyway. If there are multiple potential infringers, however, the copyright holder would be unwilling to bargain with each and every one, so punitive damages would be needed to induce bargaining and prevent infringement by an infringer unwilling to pay enough to satisfy the copyright holder. This point is emphasized in Kaplow and Shavell 1996b.

suits than if punitive damages are used as well; thus, if bargaining is less expensive than litigation, administrative costs will fall as a result of the use of punitive damages.

9.6 Punishment. A further rationale for punitive damages derives from a consideration that will be addressed later in this book (see section 3 of Chapter 23, on the retributive motive), namely, the objective of imposing proper punishment on a wrongdoer. Assume that, given the degree of a party's blameworthiness, individuals believe that there is a correct level of punishment, and that either higher or lower punishment detracts from the utility that individuals obtain from satisfaction of the punishment objective. (This utility is distinct from any utility that individuals obtain from deterrence of harm caused by imposition of penalties.) Acts that have certain outrageous qualities may call for levels of damages higher than losses to help satisfy the punishment objective and thus can justify punitive damages.

Two observations should be made about the punishment objective. First, the optimal level of damages will be an implicit compromise between this objective and deterrence, as discussed earlier. Second, in considering the punishment objective when the defendant is a firm, one presumes that the goal is to punish culpable individuals within the firm (not the firm as an abstract entity). This means that account needs to be taken of the degree to which blameworthy individuals within firms will be punished as a consequence of imposition of damages on the firm, and also of the degree to which those not considered responsible (employees generally, and perhaps stockholders) will be punished.

9.7 Actual award of punitive damages. Punitive damages are awarded in the United States in cases where parties acted with ill will, malice, or conscious disregard for others, or where their behavior was outrageous or provoked indignation for some other reason, although it is not very common in cases where harm has been done to property alone. In other countries, analogues to punitive damages are sometimes awarded, but are much less important than in the United States.[29]

29. See Dobbs 2000, Keeton, Dobbs, et al. 1984, section 2, and Fleming 1998, 2, 23, 27, 562–564, on Anglo-American law, and Stoll 1983, sections 103–125, and Von Bar 1998, 1:627–631, on law in other countries.

10. DAMAGES AND VICTIMS' OPPORTUNITIES TO MITIGATE LOSSES

10.1 Victim actions to mitigate losses.   In the event of an accident, the victim may be able to limit the harm by taking various actions. For instance, if workers from the telephone company accidentally cause a telephone pole to fall, and it breaks through the roof of a person's home, the homeowner may be able to keep his losses to a minimum by removing articles from his attic that could be damaged by rain and also by having his roof repaired promptly. (Such actions that victims can take to mitigate losses after accidents occur are, of course, to be distinguished from the precautions that victims can exercise before accidents occur in order to reduce the likelihood or severity of harm.)

10.2 Social welfare optimum.   Given the goal of minimizing total social costs associated with accidents, including here the costs of mitigation of losses, it will be socially desirable for a victim to act to mitigate losses if the cost of so doing is less than the reduction in losses thereby accomplished.

> *Example 3.* If a victim takes an action to mitigate losses due to an accident, the losses will equal 100; otherwise losses will equal 150. It will therefore be socially desirable for him to take the action if its cost is less than 50. If, for instance, the cost of the mitigation action is 10, the action should be taken.

Thus, in the case of the homeowner who can easily mitigate losses by removing articles from his attic, we might interpret 10 to be the cost of removing the articles, and 100 as the loss given that he does so.

If an accident occurs, total social costs due to it should be regarded as the optimally mitigated level of losses plus the costs of mitigation. In Example 3, therefore, the total social costs due to an accident are 110, for if an accident occurs, not only are 100 in direct losses suffered, but also costs of 10 are incurred in mitigating the losses (preventing them from rising to 150). Because total social costs due to an accident are 110, it is this figure that should determine the optimal level of care that injurers exercise to prevent accidents from happening.

10.3 Optimal damages.   The claim here is that the optimal level of damages is the level of losses that a victim would sustain had he optimally mitigated his losses—whether or not he actually did so—plus the costs of optimal mitigation actions. In the earlier example, therefore, the optimal level of damages is 110. If this is set as the level of damages, the assertion is that two things will be true: Victims will be led to mitigate optimally their losses, and injurers will be induced to choose the optimal level of care in order to prevent accidents.

To explain, consider the victim in Example 3. He knows that he will receive 110 in damages whether or not he mitigates losses, and in particular, he will not receive 150 if he fails to mitigate losses. Thus, the victim will decide to spend the 10 to mitigate his losses: If he does so, he will sustain true losses of 100 and mitigation costs of 10, so he will be fully compensated, whereas if he does not mitigate, he will lose 40 (that is, 150 in true losses less 110 in damages received). Because, then, victims are induced to mitigate losses optimally, the damages paid by injurers equal the social costs incurred, so that injurers will indeed be induced to take optimal precautions.[30]

10.4 Actual law regarding mitigation. In the Anglo-American and French legal systems, the size of awards is restricted to losses that an injured party could not reasonably have avoided plus expenses reasonably incurred in so limiting losses. Thus awards are based on the assumption that any reasonable repairs to damaged property have been made, that injured parties have obtained proper medical treatment to alleviate their condition (but not that they have submitted to dangerous procedures), and so forth. In the German legal system, as well as in some others, the problem of mitigation of losses is viewed as an aspect of the injured party's contributory fault. Since liability is normally reduced on account of contributory fault, the end result is apparently similar to that under Anglo-American and French law.[31]

11.   CAUSATION

11.1 Definition and introduction. The principal meaning of causation that will be employed here is the one used in ordinary language: we will say that a person's act caused harm if the harm would not have occurred

---

30. Wittman 1981 first suggested that both victims and injurers will act desirably if damages equal optimally mitigated losses plus optimal mitigation costs.

31. See Dobbs 2000, sections 203–205, Fleming 1998, 285–287, and McCormick 1935, chap. 5, on Anglo-American law, and Stoll 1983, section 155, and Von Bar 1998, 2:562–563, on law in other countries.

had the person not committed the act. For example, a person's speeding will be said to have caused an accident if the accident would not have occurred if he had not been speeding. This notion of causation is sometimes referred to as *causation in fact*, or as *but for causation* (as in "but for the speeding, the accident would not have occurred"), or as *necessary causation*, to distinguish it from other concepts of causation that fall under the heading of *proximate causation*.

A fundamental characteristic of liability law is that a party must have caused harm in order to be held liable for it.[32] The main question to be examined here is how this feature of law affects the functioning of the liability system under strict liability and the negligence rule. Then I will discuss proximate causation and uncertainty over causation.

11.2 Strict liability. As was elaborated in Chapter 8, if parties are held strictly liable for harm, they will generally be led to choose the socially desirable level of care and the socially desirable level of activity. The issue of causation, however, was not raised there, and once considered, it becomes evident that for parties to have socially correct incentives to take precautions and to engage in activities, they must escape liability for harms that they do not cause.

To illustrate that in order for the level of care to be optimal, parties must not be liable when they are not the causes of loss, suppose that a firm's production generates pollution, which can cause house paint to peel and will lead to aggregate repainting costs of $100,000. Suppose too that peeling may also come about from prolonged exposure to the sun and that the cost of repainting homes for this reason is $80,000. It is then socially desirable for the firm to invest in a device like a smoke scrubber to eliminate the pollution if and only if the device costs less than $100,000, for $100,000 is the increase in harm due to the pollution. Further, this is precisely how the firm will be motivated to act if it is liable for repainting homes if and only if its pollution is the cause of peeling house paint. In particular, if the firm is liable even when it is not the cause of losses, it will have an excessive incentive to spend on care. In that case, as its pollution-

32. See, for example, Dobbs 2000, chap. 9, on Anglo-American law, as well as Honoré 1983, sections 15, 106–118, and Zweigert and Kötz 1998, 601, 621, on the law in civil law countries.

associated liability would be $180,000, the firm would be willing to spend up to $180,000 on the smoke scrubber to eliminate pollution and avoid liability for the costs of repainting homes.

To illustrate that incentives to engage in activities may be inappropriate if parties are liable even when they are not the cause of losses, suppose that the firm in the example is unable to avert the pollution by taking care (perhaps smoke scrubbers are prohibitively expensive). In this case, the firm can discontinue the activity that generates pollution. Clearly, it should do so if and only if the benefit from the activity is less than $100,000; it is socially desirable for the firm to continue with its activity if the benefit from the activity exceeds $100,000. Again, this is what the firm will do if it is liable for repainting costs if and only if it is their cause. If by continuing its activity it becomes liable for all repainting—that is, for $180,000—the firm will be undesirably discouraged from continuing with its activity if the benefit from the activity is between $100,000 and $180,000.

The basic function of the causation requirement under strict liability, in other words, is that it furnishes socially appropriate incentives to reduce the risk of harm and to moderate the level of activity by imposing liability equal only to the *increase* in social costs due to a party's actions.[33]

11.3 Negligence rule.   Under the negligence rule, we know from Chapter 8 that parties will generally be led to exercise optimal care if due care is set at this level, but, again, the analysis did not take causation into explicit account. Is it necessary to allow parties to escape liability when they are not the cause of losses in order for their incentives to be correct (as it is under strict liability)? As will be discussed, the answer is that there is no need to allow parties to escape liability for negligence if they do not cause losses, but optimal incentives are maintained even if they do escape liability if they do not cause losses. In other words, basic incentives to take due care are correct whether or not there is a causation requirement.

To explain, let us reconsider the example of the polluting firm. Suppose

33. This tolling-of-social-costs function of the causal requirement was initially emphasized in an important article, Calabresi 1975, and was amplified in Shavell 1980a in a formal economic treatment of causation and liability.

that a smoke scrubber costs $30,000, an amount less than the $100,000 of additional harm the scrubber would avert, so that it would be negligent for the firm to fail to install it. Suppose too that if the firm negligently omits to install the scrubber, it will be held liable for harm even if it is not the cause of harm, that is, even if paint peels due to exposure to the sun rather than to pollution. This cannot induce the firm to take excessive precautions. All that it does is to increase the firm's incentive to take due care and install the scrubber, for the firm will be threatened with $180,000 of damages for failure to install the scrubber rather than with $100,000. A question arises, however: Could it be that allowing the firm to escape liability for negligence when it is not the cause of peeling paint dilutes unduly the firm's incentive to install the scrubber? The answer is no; the firm will be threatened with $100,000 of damages for the harm it does cause, so it will install the scrubber. Rational actors will always be led to act nonnegligently even if they would escape liability when they are not the cause of losses.[34]

Although allowing parties to escape liability if their negligence does not cause losses still leaves sufficient deterrence to induce proper care-taking, an affirmative reason for insisting on causation before imposing liability has not been supplied. One advantage of the causation requirement is that to the extent that there are errors in the negligence determination, the negligence system takes on aspects of strict liability, so that the problem of overdeterrence discussed in section 1.1 would be exacerbated were the scope of liability extended to losses not caused by negligence. A second advantage, probably more important, is that the administrative costs of the liability system are reduced because the volume of cases is lowered owing to the causation requirement.[35] These advantages of restricting liability under the

34. The general proof of this conclusion involves, among other elements, the point that the socially desirable level of care itself implicitly reflects causation; care is socially valuable only to the degree that it can reduce accident losses in circumstances in which losses would otherwise result. This was first demonstrated in Shavell 1980a; see also Shavell 1987a, 105–108, 118–121.

35. A qualification: Use of the causation requirement for liability means that, in cases that are brought, causation has to be determined (whether the pollution or exposure to sun caused paint to peel) with attendant costs. Consequently, it is possible that use of the causal requirement for liability increases rather than reduces administrative costs.

negligence rule to harm caused by the actor may justify the causation requirement.[36]

11.4 Proximate causation.   Even if a party is shown to be a cause of losses, he may still escape liability because he was said not to be the proximate cause of losses, where this term has two major meanings.[37] One connotation of proximate cause is that harm came about in a direct or expected way, rather than in an unusual, freakish manner. The legal policy of relieving a party of liability for unusual accidents was discussed in sections 6.2 and 6.3, where no clear justification was apparent.

A second notion of proximate causation concerns coincidence, and is illustrated by two cases. Suppose that a speeding bus happened to be at

36. An additional, somewhat subtle feature of the causation requirement under the negligence rule is worth mentioning. Under the negligence rule, a person's expected liability is often assumed to rise discontinuously with his level of care: Liability is zero if a person is not negligent, yet becomes distinctly positive as soon as his behavior crosses the negligence threshold. For example, if it is negligent to drive at speeds exceeding 50 mph, a person's liability will be zero if he drives at speeds up to 50 mph but suddenly will rise if he drives at 51 mph, for then he will be liable for all accidents that he causes. This jump in expected liability makes the incentive to be nonnegligent sharp, which has both socially advantageous and disadvantageous aspects. It may be socially advantageous because it means that parties will have incentives to be nonnegligent even if they cannot pay for the entire harm, or even if they will not always be sued for harm; see Cooter 1982 and Shavell 1986. And it may be socially disadvantageous because it means that parties may be led to take excessive care to reduce the risk of mistakenly being found negligent and bearing liability; if people drive at 45 mph they will lower the chance of erroneously being clocked at a speed of over 50 mph; see section 1.1. But, as originally noted by Grady 1983 and Kahan 1989, there may not be a sudden increment in expected liability—expected liability will rise continuously— if liability for negligence is properly limited by the causal requirement under discussion. If a person drives at 51 mph, it might be thought that he should be liable only for accidents that were caused by going the extra mile per hour beyond 50 mph; the driver should not be liable for accidents that would have occurred had he been traveling at 50 mph or less. But if the court is unable to tell whether or not an accident would have occurred had a person been driving more slowly (often a plausible assumption), the person driving 51 mph will be liable for any accident that his driving causes, and there thus would be a jump in his expected liability.

37. Other meanings will not be reviewed here. On proximate causation, see, for example, Dobbs 2000, chap. 10, Hart and Honoré 1985, and Keeton 1963 on Anglo-American law, and Honoré 1983, sects. 20, 80–90, and Zweigert and Kötz 1998, 601, 621, on the law in France and Germany.

just the "right" point on a road to be struck by a falling tree. Here, note that the excessive speed of the bus did cause the accident—had the bus not been speeding it would not have been struck—but the accident would also have been avoided if the bus had been going even faster. In the other case, a person negligently handed a loaded gun to a child to be used as a plaything and the child dropped the gun on his toe, suffering an injury. In such cases, liability is not found because of lack of proximate cause in the sense that the accidents are said to be coincidental to defendants' behavior, unrelated to the normal risk created by their behavior.

It can be demonstrated that allowing parties to escape liability for accidents like these does not lead to inadequate precautions. Holding a bus company liable when trees fall down on buses will not induce the company to have its buses go more slowly, for the probability of a bus being struck by a falling tree does not depend on the speed of the bus. Likewise, holding a person liable when an object he gives to a child drops on the child's toe will not induce people to remove bullets from guns, for the probability of a gun dropping on the child's toe will not be affected by its being loaded (setting aside the negligible weight of the bullets).[38]

An advantage of permitting defendants to escape liability when accidents are coincidentally caused is that this will lower administrative costs by reducing the scope of liability, unless the cost of deciding about the issue of coincidental causation exceeds the savings from the reduction in the scope of liability. A disadvantage of allowing defendants to escape liability for coincidental accidents is that this means that actors do not bear the full increase in social costs due to their activity (if people did not ride in buses, they might not be struck by falling trees), and the control of levels of activity is an object of, at least, strict liability.

11.5 Uncertainty over causation.   In many situations there is uncertainty about causation. For example, it may not be known which manufacturer out of many sold the product (a drug, lead paint) that caused the injury, or whether an injury was caused by the defendant or by background

---

38. See Calabresi 1975, Shavell 1980a, and Shavell 1987a, 110–115, 121–123; the latter references formalize the idea of coincidence as illustrated by the two cases mentioned in the text.

factors (was cancer caused by a firm's pollutant or by unknown environmental or genetic determinants?).

The law takes two approaches in such situations. The traditional approach is to hold a defendant liable if and only if the probability that the defendant was the cause of losses exceeds 50 percent.[39] This approach may lead either to inadequate or to excessive incentives to reduce risk. Suppose that a firm sells to only 20 percent of the market. Then the likelihood of the firm being the cause of losses from a product-related injury will lie below the 50 percent threshold and it will escape liability for any harm caused by its product. Consequently, the firm will have no liability-related incentive to take precautions. If, however, a firm's market share exceeds 50 percent, the firm will be liable for all harms due to the product it sells—and for all harms due to the products that others sell—for it will always be more likely than not the cause of harm. Thus, the firm's liability burden will be socially excessive. These potential problems of inadequate and of excessive incentives may arise under any liability criterion based on a threshold probability of causation; they are not unique to a 50 percent threshold.[40]

The second approach that the legal system has taken (though not often) is to hold defendants liable despite any uncertainty over causation, but to impose damages only in proportion to the likelihood of causation. Thus, liability has been imposed according to the share that firms have in the market for a product.[41] Under the proportional liability principle, it is readily shown that incentives to reduce risk are proper. If, for example, a firm has 20 percent of the market, it will pay 20 percent of harm in every case, so that its liability bill will be the same as if it pays for all the harm in the 20 percent of cases it truly causes—in which case we know that safety incentives will be socially appropriate. That the proportional liability principle engenders optimal incentives (without a need to establish causa-

39. See, for example, Dobbs 2000, 420–422; on civil law countries, see Honoré 1983, sections 201–203.

40. Essentially this point has been frequently mentioned (see, for example, Tribe 1971, and Landes and Posner 1983), and it is formally developed in Shavell 1985b.

41. This principle has been applied by some courts in cases involving the drug DES, which was made by many companies; the identity of the company that produced the drug that caused harm in particular instances often could not be determined. The proportional liability principle has so far not been widely used. See, for example, Dobbs 2000, 430–432.

tion in particular cases) is an advantage of the principle relative to the traditional threshold probability criterion.[42]

Yet a disadvantage of the proportional approach is that it could lead to a substantial increase in the volume, complexity, and cost of litigation, for under the proportional approach any party for whom the probability of having caused a loss is positive can be sued and may have to pay damages. Hence, the proportional approach should be employed only if the incentive advantage of so doing is sufficiently strong.

42. See Rosenberg 1984 and Shavell 1985b, 1987a, 115–118, 123–126. It should be noted that if products about which there is uncertainty as to causation differ in the risks they create, this must be recognized in the application of proportional liability. For example, if two products each command half of the market but the first creates twice the risk of the second, then the first product should bear two-thirds of damages, not one-half.

11 ||| LIABILITY, RISK-BEARING, AND INSURANCE

The accident problem involves not only the goal of appropriately reducing the risks of accidents, but also a second objective: allocating and spreading the risk of losses from accidents that do occur, so that those who are risk averse do not bear them, in whole or in part. Insurance—both accident insurance for victims and liability insurance for injurers—provides a method of allocating and spreading risks of loss.

Liability insurance is of particular interest for two reasons. First, it changes the way in which the liability system reduces accident risk, for to the degree that an injurer owns insurance coverage, he will not have to pay damages if found liable. The incentives to reduce risk thus have to do with the extent of insurance coverage and with other terms of liability insurance policies. Second, and related, the question arises whether, or in what sense, liability insurance is socially desirable if it might interfere with liability-related incentives to reduce risk, and thus whether liability insurance should be regulated. (As will be described below, serious doubts about the social wisdom of liability insurance have been raised, and its sale is subject to some restrictions today, although it is widely owned.)

I will begin by reconsidering the accident problem in the light of risk aversion. Specifically, I will discuss the socially ideal solution to the accident problem, what occurs in the absence of liability, what occurs in the presence of liability when insurance is not available, and finally what occurs in the presence of both liability and insurance. This step-by-step method of analysis will provide an understanding of the separate value of both liability and insurance in reducing accident risks and in allocating accident risks.

I will then address two important extensions to the foregoing analysis: nonpecuniary losses, and the judgment-proof problem.

1.   RISK AVERSION AND THE SOCIALLY IDEAL SOLUTION TO THE ACCIDENT PROBLEM

1.1 Risk aversion.   In this book *risk aversion* should be understood as a term of art, describing an attitude of dislike of pure financial risk. A risk-averse person would pay to avoid a risk, such as one involving a 50 percent chance of losing $1,000 and a 50 percent chance of winning $1,000.[1] A risk-averse person would also purchase insurance against risk if the insurance premium is actuarially fair.[2] A person will be risk averse if the marginal utility of money to him declines as his wealth increases; the reason is essentially that, for such a person, losing an amount of money will reduce his utility more than gaining the same amount of money will increase his utility.

Risk aversion is most relevant in situations in which losses would be large in relation to a person's assets and thus would impinge substantially on his utility. Individuals are typically viewed as risk-averse actors in relation to serious accidents, as these would be likely to cause losses that are significant in relation to their assets. If, however, losses would be modest relative to a person's assets, he would be likely to display a roughly risk-neutral attitude toward them. This would be the case for small accidents that individuals

---

1. This risky situation involves an expected return of zero: 50% × $1,000 − 50% × $1,000 = 0. But a risk-averse person would also pay to avoid a risky situation with a positive expected return, such as one in which there is a 51 percent chance of winning $1,000 and a 49 percent chance of losing that amount. At some probability of winning, however, even a risk-averse person would become just willing to participate in the risky situation. This probability reflects the individual's degree of risk aversion (the higher the probability needed to induce him to participate, the higher the degree of risk aversion).

2. An insurance premium is said to be actuarially fair if it equals the expected cost of coverage to the insurer. For instance, if a policy pays coverage of $1,000 with probability 10 percent, the fair premium is $100, for the expected cost of coverage is $100.

suffer. Also, firms might usually be considered as risk-neutral actors in relation to many accidents, for these would cause losses that are small in relation to their assets.[3] Moreover, firms are sometimes treated as risk neutral if they are owned by well-diversified shareholders, for being well diversified, the shareholders should not be concerned about the risk borne by a particular firm. To the degree that the managers of a firm are risk averse and have the freedom to make decisions, however, the behavior of the firm may reflect risk aversion.

1.2 Socially ideal solution.   Social welfare will be taken here to be a function of individuals' *expected utilities*.[4] Therefore, social welfare will depend not only on the factors emphasized in previous chapters—positively on the benefits parties obtain from their activities, and negatively on costs of care and on accident losses—but social welfare will depend as well on whether risk-averse parties bear risk. It follows that, under the socially ideal solution to the accident problem, two things will be true: Not only will parties make decisions about engaging in activities and about their exercise of care in the way that was described as optimal in Chapter 8, but also, risk-averse parties will not bear risks, which is to say, their risks will be perfectly spread through insurance arrangements or will be shifted to risk-neutral parties. It is important to emphasize that the risk-averse parties who ideally ought not to bear risk may be victims *or* injurers. Injurers will bear risk if they face the risk of liability; thus, ideally, risk-averse injurers should not bear this liability risk.

2.   THE ACCIDENT PROBLEM IN THE ABSENCE OF LIABILITY AND INSURANCE

Assume here that there is no liability system and also no insurance system. Then because injurers will not be liable for accident losses, they generally

---

3. If a firm faces the risk that it would cause harms that are small for each victim but the harms would simultaneously affect many victims (as might be true if there is a defect in the design or manufacture of a product), then the risk for the firm could be substantial, so that it might be appropriate to regard the firm as risk averse.

4. The expected utility of an individual is the sum over all possible outcomes of the probability of each outcome multiplied by its utility.

will not reduce risk appropriately. That is, they will tend to engage in risky activities to an excessive extent and will have no motive to take care. Still, injurers will bear no risk; this aspect of the outcome is socially desirable if injurers are risk averse.

Because victims will not be able to obtain judgments from injurers in the absence of liability, they will be left bearing risk. This bearing of risk is socially undesirable if victims are risk averse. Thus, the outcome is undesirable not only because risks are not reduced by injurers, but also because the risks that exist may be borne by uninsured risk-averse parties.

3. THE ACCIDENT PROBLEM GIVEN LIABILITY ALONE

Assume now that injurers are subject to liability, but that insurance is again unavailable; thus, injurers do not possess liability insurance coverage and victims do not hold accident coverage. In this situation, the outcome is, in essence, that injurers will be led to reduce risk due to the effect of liability, but the allocation of risk will depend on whether liability is strict or follows the negligence rule.

In particular, under strict liability injurers will have a motive to reduce risk and victims will, by definition, be compensated for any losses they sustain; it is injurers who will bear risk. If injurers are risk neutral, their bearing of risk will not matter, and the outcome will be socially ideal.

But if strictly liable injurers are risk averse, the outcome will not be socially ideal because injurers will bear risk. Moreover, they may be led to exercise excessive care to avoid liability (consider how cautiously risk-averse and uninsured individuals would drive if subject to strict liability). In addition, for these reasons injurers may be undesirably discouraged from engaging in an activity. One way of alleviating these problems of excessive care and too low a level of activity under strict liability is to reduce damages; indeed, it can be shown to be beneficial for damages to be less than harm for this reason. In other words, if injurers are risk averse, it is not socially desirable to "internalize" fully the harm they do.[5]

The situation is quite different under the negligence rule, because in-

---

5. See Proposition 2 in Shavell 1982a.

jurers will not bear risk provided that they take due care (and that the courts accurately assess their level of care), which they will decide to do. Hence there will be no particular problems respecting injurers when they are risk averse; they will not be led to take excessive care nor be undesirably discouraged from engaging in an activity. Victims, on the other hand, will bear their losses (presuming that injurers are not mistakenly found negligent). As a consequence, social welfare will be less than optimal if victims are risk averse and are not insured.

The foregoing points thus introduce a new element into the comparison of strict liability and the negligence rule. Under strict liability, risk will be borne by injurers, whereas under the negligence rule risk will be borne largely by victims. In the absence of insurance, therefore, the relative appeal of strict liability will be enhanced when injurers are risk neutral or, more generally, when they are less risk averse than victims, and the relative appeal of the negligence rule will be enhanced when victims are less risk averse than injurers.

4. THE ACCIDENT PROBLEM GIVEN LIABILITY AND INSURANCE

4.1 Insurance.   Now let us assume that insurance is available and sells at actuarially fair rates. One form of insurance is, as mentioned, accident insurance for victims. If victims are risk averse, they will buy complete coverage against any risk that they bear. Thus, for example, if injurers take due care under the negligence rule, so that victims bear the risk of accidents, victims will fully insure against these risks if they are risk averse.

The other form of insurance that we will consider is insurance for injurers against liability. If injurers are risk averse, they will wish to purchase such liability insurance. But the insurance purchase decision, and the nature of insurance policies, becomes somewhat complicated because ownership of insurance may itself change the incentives of injurers to prevent accidents, and thus the likelihood of liability. This will be discussed later.[6]

6. See Shavell 1987a, chaps. 8, 10, for a presentation of the elements of the theory of insurance that are relevant to this chapter.

4.2 Strict liability. As stated in section 3, when liability is strict, victims will be implicitly insured by the legal system, and so will not bear risk, but injurers will bear risk. Therefore, risk-averse injurers will wish to purchase liability insurance. In order to describe their insurance purchases, we will consider two standard cases about liability insurers: one in which the insurers can observe the level of care exercised by insureds and are able to link premiums to this factor, and another in which the insurers cannot observe the level of care and base premiums on it. In both cases, we will conclude that liability insurance is socially desirable.

Liability insurers can observe care. Suppose first that insurers can observe the level of care and thus can lower the premium to reflect the risk reduction that care engenders. An insurer might, for instance, inspect an insured injurer's building to see whether or not he purchased fire extinguishers to decrease the risk of liability for fires, and lower the premium if extinguishers were purchased. In such a setting, two points are true. First, insureds will purchase full coverage to protect themselves completely against risk. Second, insureds will be led by fair premium reductions to take optimal care. Suppose that an injurer purchases full coverage against a $1,000,000 liability for harm to others from fire and that extinguishers would lower fire risk from 5 percent to 1 percent, so would lower expected liability by $40,000. Then premiums for full coverage will be reduced by $40,000 if the extinguishers are purchased, implying that the insured will buy the extinguishers as long as their cost is less than $40,000; that is, the injurer's decision to take care will be optimal.

It should be noted as well that the outcome will be socially optimal. Risk-averse injurers will be fully protected against risk and will be induced by premium reductions to take optimal care. And victims will be protected against risk by definition of strict liability.

Because the outcome is socially optimal, liability insurance is socially desirable. To put the point differently, were liability insurance not present, or forbidden, injurers would be worse off because they would bear risk (and might take excessive care or engage too little in desirable activities), and victims would be just as well-off.

Liability insurers cannot observe care. Now suppose that insurers cannot observe the level of care and therefore do not charge a premium that depends directly on the level of care an injurer exercises. We might imagine, for instance, that in the example of fire risk, the level of care corresponds to the caution with which flammables are handled, something that an insurer would have a more difficult time checking than the presence or absence of fire extinguishers. In a case like this, injurers will usually purchase only partial coverage and the level of care will tend to be less than optimal.

To explain, observe first that because the assumption is that insurers cannot observe and thus cannot penalize injurers for not being careful with flammables, injurers will have no premium-related incentive to take extra precautions (like training workers in the handling of flammables). Consequently, if injurers have full coverage, the risk of a $1,000,000 fire liability would be 5 percent, and premiums would thus have to be $50,000. If, however, coverage is partial, then injurers will have some incentive to take care because they will suffer some uncompensated losses if held liable. For example, suppose that they have $600,000 of coverage, exposing them to a $400,000 risk. Therefore, a precaution that lowers risk from 5 percent to 1 percent would have value to them of at least 4% × $400,000 or $16,000. This factor in turn may lead injurers to prefer partial coverage. Suppose that the precaution costs $10,000. Then if coverage is $600,000, injurers will be led by their exposure to risk to take the precaution, for spending the $10,000 will save them $16,000 in expected losses that they will bear. And because the risk for injurers who buy partial coverage of $600,000 will thus be only 1 percent, the premium they will be charged will be $6,000.[7] Injurers might well prefer 60 percent coverage that costs them only $6,000 to full coverage that costs them so much more, $50,000. Such policies with less than complete coverage, however, do not expose injurers to enough risk to induce them always to take optimal precautions.

The outcome in the situation under consideration is thus not socially ideal for two reasons: Injurers tend to be only partly protected against risk, and their level of care tends to be less than optimal.[8] Victims, however, are protected against risk by definition of strict liability.

7. To amplify, insurers will charge $6,000 because injurers who purchase coverage of $600,000 will suffer losses and make claims with only a 1 percent probability. Insurers do not need to observe in a direct way that the injurers are led to take care; the insurers need only note the statistical fact that injurers who buy the $600,000 partial coverage policy make claims with a 1 percent probability.

8. In the example, care is discrete: care is either taken or not. Therefore, it turns out that if care is optimal to take, either there exists a partial coverage policy that insureds prefer that induces care to be exercised, or else there does not, in which case a full coverage policy

Nevertheless, liability insurance is socially desirable. (That the outcome is not socially ideal does not mean that liability insurance is undesirable.) One way of seeing that liability insurance is socially desirable is to notice that it obviously raises the well-being of injurers—after all, they choose to purchase liability insurance—and does not affect the well-being of victims—they are fully compensated for accidents whenever they occur. Thus, the presence of liability insurance raises social welfare.[9] Conversely, were liability insurance prohibited, injurers would be exposed to risk and made worse off (and perhaps would not engage in desirable activities and/or would take excessive care), whereas victims would not be helped.

4.3 Negligence rule.   Under this rule, I will argue that injurers will tend to take due care even though they can buy liability insurance, and that liability insurance will tend to be socially desirable. Because injurers tend to take due care, victims will bear the risk of losses and will purchase accident insurance if they are risk averse.

Consider initially a perfectly functioning negligence system. In such a regime, the basic logic from Chapter 8 about behavior under the negligence rule implies that injurers will be led to take due care, assuming that they are not insured. In our example, suppose that a $10,000 precaution reduces the $1,000,000 fire risk from 5 percent to 1 percent, so that the precaution is required to avoid negligence. An injurer will take the precaution, because that will free him of the liability he would otherwise bear, a 5 percent chance of a $1,000,000 liability. (More precisely, it is clear that the injurer will be led to take the precaution if he is risk neutral, and he will want to take it more strongly if he is risk averse, which is the assumption.)

Although an injurer will wish to take due care if he is *not* insured, might he want to purchase liability coverage in order to act negligently? The answer is no—because the insurance would cost him too much. If an

---

is purchased. In other words, either coverage is partial and care is optimal, or coverage is full and care is zero. But in a model with care continuously variable, it is usually true that coverage is partial and that the level of care is less than optimal.

9. This argument is not really a proof, because it presumes that the level of damages equals harm. In fact, that the level of damages equal harm can also be shown to be optimal; see Shavell 1982a.

injurer were to purchase an insurance policy that covered him for negligently caused harm, he would decide not to take the precaution, that is, to act negligently, and thus would cause harm of $1,000,000 with probability 5 percent. Hence, the premium for the insurance policy would have to be $50,000. Clearly, when faced with the choice of paying $50,000 for the insurance policy in question, or instead spending $10,000 on the precaution so as not to be negligent, the injurer would take the precaution.

In the basic model of a perfectly functioning negligence rule, therefore, the outcome is socially ideal. Injurers are led to take due care, and, being nonnegligent, do not bear risk. Victims purchase accident insurance if they are risk averse so they do not bear risk if they want to avoid it. Liability insurance is not undesirable, because it does not interfere with the deterrent of the negligence rule; indeed, liability insurance is essentially moot, because it is not purchased.

Next consider briefly the realistic situation in which the negligence rule does not function perfectly and there is a risk of findings of negligence due to errors in the negligence determination or to inability of injurers to control perfectly their levels of care (see section 1 of Chapter 10). In this case, the main difference to note is that injurers might be found negligent even if they try to take due care. Thus risk-averse injurers will decide to purchase liability insurance, and the type of policy that risk-averse injurers will purchase will protect them primarily against being found negligent through some type of error or lapse. The policy will not protect injurers so broadly as to induce them definitely to act negligently because, as explained earlier, a policy that induced injurers definitely and intentionally to act negligently would not be purchased because the premium would be too high. Therefore, the liability insurance coverage tends not to compromise deterrence, and is socially desirable because it protects injurers against risk. Moreover, its ownership reduces the problem of excessive care caused by uncertainty in the negligence determination (see again section 1 of Chapter 10).

4.4 Summary. Three points about liability and insurance summarize the analysis to this point. First, because liability insurers pay for some or all of the losses for which injurers are found liable, the manner in which liability rules alter injurers' behavior is to a significant degree indirect, being associated with the terms of their liability insurance policies (notably, the connection between premiums or the payment of claims and injurer behavior, and the level of coverage).[10]

Second, the availability of liability insurance is socially desirable. The particular arguments demonstrating this result depended on the form of liability and insurers' information about insureds' behavior. The arguments were, roughly, based on the following considerations. The availability of liability insurance increases the welfare of risk-averse injurers because it protects them from risk and ameliorates the problems that they would otherwise take excessive care or be discouraged from engaging in desirable activities. Moreover, the availability of liability insurance does not necessarily dilute injurers' incentives to reduce risk, and where it does do that, the dilution of incentives will be moderate, for policies that would substantially increase risks would be so expensive that they would not be attractive for purchase.

This conclusion about the social desirability of liability insurance is not to deny the possibility that liability insurance might be socially disadvantageous, and I will discuss later circumstances in which it should be regulated (see section 7). But the conclusion does mean that thinking about the social desirability of liability insurance should proceed from the understanding that, as in the basic model of liability studied here, the insurance is socially desirable.

Third, the availability of accident and liability insurance limits the importance of the allocation of risk as a factor to be considered in evaluating liability rules. For example, the fact that in some areas of accidents the typical injurers might be large, essentially risk-neutral firms and the victims risk-averse individuals will not constitute an argument in favor of imposing liability to the extent that the individuals are already insured against their losses.

4.5 Liability and insurance in reality.   The importance of insurance to the liability system is very great, so that the theory of this section, rather than that of section 3, is the most relevant for understanding the liability system. In particular, accident insurance is widely held.[11] Liability insurance

10. Other possible terms of coverage, though not discussed earlier, are the link between loss history and premiums or the future right to insure.

11. Notably, approximately 86 percent of the population possesses health insurance benefits; see U.S. Census Bureau 2001, 2. Also, approximately 85 percent of husband-wife families with children possess life insurance on at least one family member; see *ACLI Life Insurance Fact Book* 1999, 1. Additionally, in 2000 about 88 percent of the adult population

is also owned by many individuals, and an indication of its salience is that over 90 percent of all payments made to tort victims are paid by liability insurers.[12] Although commentators occasionally raise the issue that liability insurance might undermine deterrence, and there are some restrictions on its sale (see section 7), it is generally legal. Historically, however, the sale of liability insurance was resisted, and in some countries it was not permitted until the early twentieth century.[13] Perhaps the most notable instance of antagonism against liability insurance was the complete ban on its use in the former Soviet Union.[14]

Note on the literature. The functioning of the liability system together with insurance is first formally studied in Shavell (1982a, 1987a), where the social desirability of liability insurance is proved; this chapter largely follows my treatment there. But an early and insightful informal examination of the subject is contained in Calabresi (1970).

5. THE PURPOSE OF LIABILITY

5.1 Compensation of victims is the traditional conception of the purpose of accident liability.

The great majority of legal scholars, lawyers, and judges, and probably citizens, appears to assume that providing victims with fair compensation for harm is the primary purpose of accident liability. A representative statement is that of Prosser: "There remains a

---

was covered by the Social Security system; see *Statistical Abstract of the United States, 2001,* 13, 345. Moreover, over half of the workforce possesses some form of private disability coverage; see U.S Department of Labor 2001, 1.

12. See, for example, O'Connell et al. 1994, app. A, from which it is evident that total liability payments made in 1990 were $65.199 billion, of which $60.981 billion were made by liability insurers; thus about 93.5 percent of tort liability payments were made by liability insurers. See also Tillinghast-Towers Perrin 2002, app. 4, which reports that about 98 percent of personal tort costs were paid by liability insurers in the period 1973–2000.

13. As Tunc writes in his survey of tort law worldwide, "At the beginning of the nineteenth century, liability insurance would have been unthinkable. It would have been considered as immoral." He goes on to mention, among others, French and Scandinavian resistance to the sale of liability insurance. Tunc 1983, 50–51.

14. On the Soviet ban on coverage, see generally Rudden 1966; see also Tunc 1983, 51–52.

body of law which is directed toward the compensation of individuals. . . . This is the purpose of the law of torts."[15] That the object of accident law should be so viewed is not surprising, for the goal of the plaintiff in an action is generally to be compensated and that of the defendant is to avoid paying the plaintiff; the two do not usually consider deterrence to be nearly as important, if it is an issue. Moreover, the classical and intuitively appealing notion of corrective justice, that a wrongdoer should compensate his victim, comports with the view of compensation as the purpose of liability (at least under the negligence rule). This is not to say that deterrence is never seen as an additional purpose of accident law; one sometimes reads statements by commentators and judges to that effect. Rarely, however, does one encounter the belief that the main purpose of accident law is deterrence and not compensation.

5.2 Reduction of risk through deterrence of harm is the true purpose of liability today, but compensation and avoidance of strife were also important historically.   In contrast to the traditional view, and as the discussion of this chapter should make clear, compensation cannot be said to be a primary purpose of accident liability if, as is the case, accident insurance is largely available to victims (and could be provided to them through social insurance if need be). In other words, in the absence of the liability system, compensation of victims would probably be about as well accomplished through private and social accident insurance as it is today. The main difference that the liability system can make to outcomes is the creation of incentives toward safety. (Further, as explained in section 4, we know that the liability system can generate these incentives despite the existence of liability insurance.) Hence, if the liability system has a real purpose today, it must lie in the creation of incentives to reduce risk.[16]

It is worth noting, however, that the function of accident liability was

15. Keeton, Dobbs et al. 1984, 5. See also, for example, Fleming 1998, chap. 1. Fleming is quite direct in stating that deterrence is not a primary purpose of accident law; he writes on p. 10 that "in the core area of tort accidents . . . It is being increasingly realized that human failures in a machine age exact a large and fairly regular toll . . . which is not significantly reducible . . . through the operation of tort law."

16. To avoid confusion, let me note that I am assuming that the "purpose" of the liability system means the difference to outcomes that the liability system actually makes. This definition of the purpose of the liability system—as opposed to what people *say* its

different in the past. Before the development of insurance markets in the latter part of the nineteenth century, liability furnished victims a source of compensation that would not otherwise ordinarily have been forthcoming. Tort liability law thus served to an important degree the dual purposes of compensation and deterrence. Moreover, in early times before criminal law and tort law had emerged as separate branches of law, a significant additional purpose of the making of money payments for harm was the maintenance of social order. Without the system of money payments, private vengeance would often have followed the doing of harm.[17]

5.3 Is use of the liability system justified?   It has been explained that the main route through which the liability system benefits society is by reducing accident risks, so that this, if anything, should be the warrant for use of the liability system. But the deterrent benefit of the liability system is not necessarily sufficient to outweigh the costs of the system and thereby to justify its use. As I will discuss in the next chapter, the costs of the liability system are great. Moreover, safety regulation is available as an alternative means of reducing risk. Therefore, the question of the net social desirability of the liability system is a serious one.

6.   EXTENSION: NONPECUNIARY LOSSES

6.1 Nonpecuniary losses and insurance.   Let us consider the relationship between nonpecuniary losses and accident insurance before reexamining the functioning of the liability system.[18] To understand insurance for nonpecuniary losses, observe that suffering a nonpecuniary loss

---

purpose is—is both natural and a guide to policy, for policy must be based on the true effects of the liability system on outcomes, not the supposed effects.

17. On the point that the making of money payments for harm prevented feuds, when there was no criminal law, see, for example, Berman 1983, 55, and Pollock and Maitland 1911, vol. 2, chap. 8, section 1. When a criminal system exists, this system exacts punishment for many types of act that would give rise to feuds, so that tort and accident law are not as much needed to avert feuds.

18. Arrow 1974, Cook and Graham 1977, and Zeckhauser 1973 first developed the theory of insurance for nonpecuniary losses. For relevant empirical evidence, see Viscusi and Evans 1990.

often will not alter an individual's need for money or, more exactly, the utility he would derive from receiving additional money. If, for example, an irreplaceable family portrait with great sentimental value is destroyed, there is no obvious reason to believe that the owner's need for money will increase, however much he regrets the loss; the utility he would obtain from having more money to spend would be whatever it was beforehand. Similarly, if a person loses a small toe in an accident, then aside from requiring some money for medical treatment, he might well place the same value on having additional money as he had prior to losing his toe.

In some cases, though, events with adverse nonpecuniary consequences will result in a person attaching a higher value to money. An individual who is crippled by an accident may value money more, even after being compensated for medical expenses and forgone income, because of a need to obtain household help, special transportation services, and the like.

It is also possible that suffering a nonpecuniary loss will lower the utility of money to an individual. The individual who is crippled by an accident could turn out to value money less because venturing forth to spend is less pleasurable and more difficult. Perhaps the most important example of a nonpecuniary loss that results in a lower value of money involves death. The value of money in that contingency is, in effect, the value to a person of knowing that his survivors will receive a bequest, and this will often be less than the value to the person of having money while he is alive.

The amount of insurance coverage against nonpecuniary losses that an individual will in principle wish to purchase will depend on whether such losses will affect the utility he would derive from receiving additional money. The reason is that the purchase of insurance is in essence the giving up of money today for the receipt of money in a contingency, and this will make sense only if money is more valuable in that contingency.

Now if nonpecuniary losses will not result in a change in a person's valuation of money, then the best insurance policy for him, the policy under which his expected utility would be maximized, will not cover him for the nonpecuniary element of his losses. His coverage will be restricted to pecuniary losses, if any. Thus, a person might not insure against the loss of his family portrait and might limit coverage against loss of a toe to medical expenses. Notice that this implies that, under the optimal insurance policy, the coverage a person will receive will not make him whole in utility terms (even though this may be possible). In other words, the notion that optimal insurance for a loss will restore his utility to its level before the loss is incorrect.

If, however, nonpecuniary losses will raise the value of money to a person, then under the optimal insurance policy coverage will exceed his pecuniary loss. Thus a person might purchase greater coverage against the possibility of being crippled than an amount equal only to the costs of medical treatment and forgone earnings. It is unlikely, however, that he will purchase coverage sufficient to make him whole (if this is possible).

If the value a person will place on money will decrease as a result of a nonpecuniary loss, expected utility maximizing insurance coverage will be less than his pecuniary losses. A person who has little desire to leave a bequest will rationally purchase little or no life insurance, despite the possibility that the earnings forgone by his death will be large.

6.2 Actual insurance coverage against nonpecuniary losses. It seems that actual insurance coverage is intended mainly to remedy pecuniary needs created by losses, not to compensate for the disutility due to losses, suggesting that nonpecuniary losses tend not to raise the value of money to individuals or are small. In particular, insurance coverage against loss of property does not ordinarily seem to reflect its sentimental value, only its market value or replacement cost. Coverage against personal injury usually approximates only direct medical expenses and forgone earnings. Insurance against death is ordinarily bounded by lost earnings; if a person (such as an unmarried or elderly individual) has no dependents, he normally possesses little or no insurance coverage; parents do not often carry significant coverage on the lives of their children.

6.3 Nonpecuniary losses and the socially ideal solution to the accident problem. As just emphasized, the amount of insurance an individual would wish to purchase against nonpecuniary losses—and therefore the amount of money he will receive under the socially ideal solution to the accident problem—will be based on the value he will place on money if he suffers nonpecuniary losses; the amount he will receive will not generally make him whole. By contrast, and as was noted in section 8 of Chapter 10, the socially optimal level of care taken by injurers (and their level of activity) will fully reflect the nonpecuniary elements of accident losses as well as the pecuniary. Thus, for instance, it will be best that injurers take substantial care to reduce the risk of accidentally killing children even though their deaths may not impose an economic burden on their parents and consequently, in the ideal, may not call for the parents to receive significant amounts in compensation. It might be, say, that for injurers to be led to take appropriate care, they should pay $2,000,000 for the death of a child, but that the parents' optimal insurance coverage is only $10,000 for funeral expenses.

6.4 Socially ideal solution cannot be achieved under the liability system. Because injurers must exercise a degree of care reflecting both nonpecuniary and pecuniary components of victims' losses under the ideal solution to the accident problem, the magnitude of payments that injurers make under liability rules has to reflect both these components of losses for injurers to be led to take optimal care. But if injurers' damage payments are this high, then the amount victims receive will exceed optimal compensation, which may well usually approximate only pecuniary losses. If parents receive $2,000,000 for the wrongful death of a child, this will exceed the $10,000 optimal compensatory amount. Yet if injurers' damage payments equal only the $10,000 optimal compensatory amount, injurers' incentives to take care will be inadequate. Thus the socially ideal outcome cannot be achieved under the liability system.[19] The damage payments will inevitably result in a compromise between awarding victims correctly and creating appropriate incentives for injurers to reduce risk.[20]

6.5 The case for fines as a supplement to liability. An improvement over the situation with the liability system may be achieved by a

19. This statement is correct under strict liability, but under the negligence rule there is a qualification to it. Under a perfectly functioning negligence rule, the socially ideal outcome can be achieved, because under that rule injurers will always take due care and never be found negligent if damages are sufficiently high (that is, if they include nonpecuniary losses). Hence, victims will bear their losses and can and will optimally insure for amounts less than what injurers would have to pay were they liable. But if, as is realistic, findings of negligence occur, the optimal outcome cannot be achieved because victims will in fact sometimes receive awards.

20. This section is premised on the assumption that victims of harm are not buyers of a product sold by injurers. If victims are buyers, then an ideal outcome can clearly be

regime in which liability is supplemented by fines collected by the state.[21] With the use of fines, the total amount that injurers are made to pay can be raised to the point that their incentives to reduce risk are appropriate, while at the same time liability can be held to the lower level equal to optimal compensatory awards. Thus, in the example, under the contemplated regime injurers would pay fines of $1,990,000 reflecting non-pecuniary losses, whereas victims would receive in liability awards payments of $10,000 reflecting only their otherwise uncompensated pecuniary losses.

One way to understand why individuals may find a regime with supplemental fines advantageous is to recognize that their taxes can be lowered under it, because the state may use fine revenues to replace tax revenues. Specifically, individuals will find a regime with fines advantageous if they would prefer a savings in taxes to collecting higher liability judgments, or, equivalently, if they would not be willing to pay the insurance premium necessary to purchase coverage in the amount of the fine. Parents should thus find advantageous a regime with fines for the wrongful death of their children and with correspondingly lower taxes if the parents do not choose to insure their children's lives.[22]

Several comments should be added about supplemental fines. First, it would ordinarily be best for these fines to be insurable. The general argument made in section 4 that it is desirable to allow risk-averse injurers to

---

achieved, as long as liability does not exceed the optimal compensatory amount. On the latter issue, see, for example, Rubin 1993.

21. Spence 1977 first demonstrated the desirability of employing fines in addition to liability as a result of nonpecuniary losses.

22. To amplify, suppose that the likelihood of death of a child is .1 percent. Suppose too that a parent would not want to buy an insurance policy for $2,000,000 if a child died but rather would limit coverage to $10,000. Hence, the supposition is that the parent is worse off with coverage of $2,000,000 and a premium of $2,000 (that is, .1% × $2,000,000) than with $10,000 coverage and a premium of $10 (that is, .1% × $10,000). In other words, increasing coverage from $10,000 to $2,000,000 is not worth the $1,990 increase in premiums that would be required. But this statement implies that the parent is better off under a liability system that gives the parent $10,000 in damages and imposes a fine of $1,990,000 than under a liability system that gives the parent $2,000,000 in damages; for under the fine system, the state's expected revenues increase by $1,990, lowering the parent's taxes by that amount.

purchase coverage against liability can be employed to demonstrate this result.[23]

Second, to calculate the magnitude of supplemental fines for nonpecuniary losses, one can employ extrapolations from the amount individuals would be willing to pay for a small reduction in the probability of suffering nonpecuniary losses. Suppose, for instance, that an individual would be willing to pay $1,000 for a 1 percent reduction in the likelihood of losing his arm. Then the optimal fine for causing the loss of his arm would be approximately $100,000. Information about persons' willingness to pay for reductions in risk could in theory be obtained by survey or, in some cases, perhaps, by attributing wage differences to differences in risks of accidents.[24]

Third, the argument favoring supplemental fines applies more broadly than here, to any situation in which the amount that injurers should pay to be properly deterred exceeds the optimal compensatory amount for victims. Notably, it was emphasized that when liable injurers will not always be identified as responsible for harm done, the amount they pay if they are identified and sued must be raised so that their incentives to reduce risk will be maintained at the correct level. When, for instance, the likelihood is 50 percent that a liable injurer will be successfully sued, the amount he pays if sued must be on the order of twice the victim's losses. Optimal payments by injurers may therefore exceed optimal compensatory awards by a substantial factor, so fines would be desirable. Another reason why optimal payments by injurers may be greater than optimal awards concerns taxes that would have been paid on income forgone by accident victims. For injurers' incentives to reduce risk to be proper, they must pay an amount based on before-tax income forgone by victims. Yet the amount of money that victims will in fact lose, and thus the amount that will constitute the optimal compensatory award, is after-tax forgone income. An additional reason why optimal payments by injurers may exceed optimal compensatory awards is that victims may receive insurance benefits or gifts. In

23. It should be mentioned, however, that if fines are not employed, then in principle it could be advantageous to set liability at a level approximating optimal compensation and to limit purchase of liability insurance, so as to induce injurers to take more care.

24. On the latter, see Moore and Viscusi 1990 and Viscusi 1983. See also Danzon 1984, which discusses how such data can be used to calculate supplemental fines.

this case, optimal compensatory awards will equal only the shortfall between victims' receipts and their losses, but injurers must pay victims' entire losses to be adequately deterred.

7. EXTENSION: THE JUDGMENT-PROOF PROBLEM

7.1 The judgment-proof problem and insurance.   The possibility that injurers do not have sufficient assets to pay for harm has implications both for the purchase of accident insurance by victims and for the purchase of liability insurance by injurers.

First, the incentive of victims to purchase accident coverage is increased due to the judgment-proof problem, for it means that there is now a risk that a victim who ought to be able to collect from a liable injurer is unable to do so.

Second, the motive of injurers to purchase liability insurance is diminished because of the possibility that they would be judgment-proof.[25] The reason is that insuring against liability that one would not otherwise fully bear, because one's assets would be exhausted, is in a sense a waste for a party. An injurer with assets of $20,000 who faces a 10 percent risk of liability of $100,000 would have to spend $10,000 on premiums for full coverage, 80 percent of which would be attributable to coverage of the $80,000 that he could not pay in the absence of liability insurance coverage. Consequently, the individual might well decide against buying full liability insurance coverage even though he is risk averse. In general, a risk-averse party might rationally decide to purchase less than complete coverage, or no coverage at all; his purchase decision will depend on what his assets are in relation to the potential liabilities, their likelihood, and his degree of risk aversion.

7.2 Problems with the functioning of the liability and insurance system.   It was emphasized before, in section 3 of Chapter 10, that the judgment-proof problem dilutes injurers' incentives to reduce risk because

---

25. Calabresi 1970, 58, observed that the motive to purchase insurance will be diminished when parties' assets are less than the losses for which they may be held responsible; Keeton and Kwerel 1984 and Huberman, Mayers, and Smith 1983 first investigated the point formally.

they do not have the capacity to pay for the harm they might cause. The fundamental nature of this problem is not altered in the present context, but there are two differences in its character worth noting. First, to the extent that injurers are risk averse and do not own liability insurance coverage—a real possibility in view of their reduced incentives to purchase such coverage as just discussed—the problem of insurance-related dulling of incentives to lower risk will be less severe than before; moreover, a risk-averse injurer will tend to take more care to prevent liability than a risk-neutral injurer. Second, to the extent that injurers own liability insurance, the problem of the dulling of their incentives to reduce risk might be exacerbated. This could be so if liability insurers cannot observe injurers' levels of care and link premiums to those levels. If liability insurers can observe levels of care, however, the conclusion would be different.

The judgment-proof possibility not only lowers incentives to reduce risk; it also creates problems in respect to the bearing of risk. In particular, because injurers have a diminished motive to purchase liability insurance coverage, and may buy none at all, they are left bearing risk, which lowers social welfare. Victims, however, should not bear risk as a result of the judgment-proof problem because they will rationally purchase accident insurance coverage against not being compensated by liable injurers.

7.3 Regulation of liability insurance. The problems that the judgment-proof issue creates leads to the possibility that it would be desirable to regulate liability insurance in either of two contrasting ways— to require its purchase, or to forbid its purchase.[26] I will discuss the circumstances in which each type of regulation may be socially advantageous. It should be noted that the desirability of intervention in the purchase of liability insurance is different from the situation in the absence of the judgment-proof problem. As I emphasized in section 4, in the benchmark case without the judgment-proof problem, regulation of liability insurance coverage is not desirable.

---

26. The implications of the judgment-proof problem (and of escape from liability, see section 7.4) for the regulation of liability insurance were first addressed from an economic perspective in Shavell 1986 and Shavell 1987a. See also Jost 1996, Polborn 1998, Shavell 2000, and Skogh 2000.

Requirement to purchase coverage. Consider first a requirement to purchase complete liability insurance coverage. How will such a requirement affect incentives to reduce risk? If insurers can observe levels of care, a requirement to purchase coverage will lead to optimal incentives to reduce risk because premium reductions will reflect the full effect of care on expected harm. Suppose that an injurer with assets of only $100,000 who faces a $1,000,000 potential liability is required to buy complete liability insurance coverage and can reduce the risk of liability by 1 percent by spending $5,000. He would receive a premium reduction of $10,000 for taking the step, so would be properly led to do so, but he might well not do so if he did not own coverage and had only $100,000 at risk, for then the expected value of the reduction would be only $1,000 to him.

If liability insurers cannot observe levels of care, however, a requirement to purchase complete coverage will tend to reduce incentives to take care. If the injurer with assets of $100,000 is required to purchase full coverage against the $1,000,000 risk, and insurers cannot observe his level of care, he will have no incentive at all to take care. Yet if he had not purchased coverage (or his coverage was less than $100,000), he would have a positive incentive to take care, even though generally a suboptimal level of care. Thus, when insurers cannot observe levels of care, a requirement to purchase coverage tends to exacerbate the inadequacy of incentives due to the judgment-proof problem.[27]

In any case, a requirement to purchase coverage has the beneficial aspect that it improves the activity-level decision, because it confronts the injurer with the full social cost of his activity.[28] Otherwise, the activity level of injurers tends to be excessive, due to the judgment-proof problem.

A requirement to purchase coverage also has the advantage of pro-

---

27. A requirement to purchase coverage may increase the incentive problem for another reason: The payment of the premium for coverage itself reduces the assets that a person has at stake. For this reason, even a modified full coverage requirement—under which a person would be permitted to obtain partial coverage as long as his assets plus coverage are sufficient to pay for the harm—may also result in a worse incentive problem than would exist in the absence of any requirement.

28. This is clearly the case under strict liability. Under the negligence rule, there is a beneficial activity-level effect to the degree that injurers might be found negligent, as noted in section 2 of Chapter 10.

tecting injurers against risk. It should not, however, be considered to protect victims against risk, because our assumption is that victims can purchase accident insurance coverage against risk.

The conclusion is that a requirement to purchase full liability insurance coverage is desirable if liability insurers can observe injurers' levels of care, for in that case the requirement results in optimal levels of care, and has other benefits as well, concerning activity levels and risk-bearing. But the requirement may not be desirable when insurers cannot observe levels of care, for in that case there will be a perverse effect on incentives to reduce risk.

Prohibition against coverage. Now let us examine the opposite policy, of prohibiting the purchase of liability insurance. This may increase the level of care that injurers would take if injurers would otherwise have purchased some liability coverage. For if their entire assets are exposed to risk, injurers may well take more care than otherwise. The resulting level of care might be an improvement, but it might also be excessive.

A prohibition against coverage will also tend to reduce activity levels from their too high levels in the absence of regulation. As with the level of care, the reduction in activity levels might be an improvement, but it might also be excessive.

Also, a prohibition against coverage has the disadvantage that it subjects injurers to greater risk than they would bear if they had purchased any liability insurance coverage.

On balance, therefore, a prohibition against coverage might be beneficial (and superior to requiring coverage), but only if liability insurers are unable to observe levels of care. In that case, prohibiting coverage may increase levels of care and reduce activity levels. The potential social benefits of doing this might outweigh the disadvantages.

7.4 Comment on escape from liability and regulation of liability insurance. The arguments just discussed concerning regulation of liability insurance apply in part when injurers are not judgment-proof but nevertheless have inadequate incentives to take care because they escape liability with a probability (see the discussion in section 9 of Chapter 10). If this is the case, then regulation of coverage may help to increase an otherwise too low effort to reduce risk. In particular, prohibiting coverage may do that and thus might be beneficial. (Requiring full coverage would in principle be a moot form of regulation, because parties would not rationally under-insure due to the chance of escaping liability; they would only do that due to the judgment-proof problem.)

7.5 Regulation of liability insurance in reality.   Although, as stated in section 4.5, the sale of liability insurance is generally permitted, there are exceptions. Liability insurance is not allowed to be sold in some jurisdictions against punitive damages, against liability arising from certain willful acts, and against many criminal penalties.[29] The justification given is that this would tend to interfere with the public policy of deterring and punishing very undesirable behavior.[30] This justification comports with some of the points made in sections 7.3 and 7.4, in view of the possibility that deterrence may be inadequate because of the judgment-proof problem and the likelihood of escaping detection.[31] Liability insurance is also required in certain domains, notably for drivers of cars.[32] The chief justification given for such requirements is that they furnish implicit coverage to victims.[33] That seems a mistaken justification. The rationale ought to be, as argued here, that the requirement would improve incentives to reduce risk, moderate activity levels, and provide insurance for injurers.

29. See, for example, Jerry 1996, 471–477, Keeton 1971, 285–305, McNeely 1941, and Keeton, Dobbs, et al. 1984, 586.

30. See, for example, Keeton, Dobbs, et al. 1984, 586, and Jerry 1996, 400, 472.

31. This statement is speculative, in part because in some contexts it is not evident on a priori grounds why mandated liability coverage would not be a good way of increasing adherence to the law.

32. See, for example, Keeton, Dobbs, et al. 1984, 601–603, and Jerry 1996, 859–863.

33. See, for example, Keeton, Dobbs, et al. 1984, 600–603, and Jerry 1996, 860.

12 ||| LIABILITY AND ADMINISTRATIVE COSTS

In this chapter, I consider a third element, that of administrative costs, in evaluating the liability system. Administrative costs are the legal and other expenses borne by parties in resolving disputes that arise when harm occurs. I will first discuss the general nature and magnitude of administrative costs; as will be seen, they are of substantial importance. Then I will discuss the socially desirable use of the liability system given its administrative costs. Last, I will compare the private incentive to make use of the liability system to its socially desirable use.

1. NATURE AND IMPORTANCE OF ADMINISTRATIVE COSTS

1.1 Administrative costs described. As stated, administrative costs comprise the legal and other expenses that parties bear when accidents occur. These nonlegal expenses include the often significant time and effort of the involved parties as well as emotional costs and disutility. (There may also be utility enjoyed from the litigation process, especially by plaintiffs, and this must be set off against the costs of litigation.)

It is important to recognize that administrative costs are incurred not only with cases that go to trial, but also with cases that settle. Cases that settle involve substantial administrative costs because settlement may involve considerable time and negotiation, as well as the use of the legal system in motions and other actions that precede trial. Indeed, because more than 95 percent of cases settle,[1] accounting for settled cases is of major significance, and it would be a mistake to attribute administrative costs mainly to the costs of trials.

What is the magnitude of administrative costs? Existing data suggest that in the United States the administrative costs of the liability system are large. Many studies find that administrative costs, averaged over settled and litigated claims, approach or exceed the amounts received by victims.[2] That is, for every dollar received by a victim, a dollar or more is spent delivering the dollar to him. It is not clear, however, to what extent these administrative costs should be viewed as intrinsic to the liability system or as a feature of the particular system that has developed.[3]

1.2 Margin over administrative costs of insurance. For some important purposes, it is not the total administrative costs of the liability system, but only their margin over the administrative costs of the accident insurance system that matters. If the liability system did not exist in some

1. Recent data on state courts show that in fiscal year 1992, over 96 percent of civil cases were settled or otherwise disposed without trial; see Ostrom, Kauder, and LaFountain 2001a, 29. Similarly, statistics on civil cases in U.S. district courts during the 2001 fiscal year show that almost 98 percent of cases were resolved without trial; see U.S. Department of Justice 2001a, 154. Cane 1999, 213, cites various studies suggesting that perhaps 99 percent of claims are settled without trial in the United Kingdom.

2. Tillinghast-Towers Perrin 2002, 12, reports in a nationwide survey of the tort system that victims receive 42 percent of payments made by defendant parties; in an earlier version of the study, Tillinghast-Towers Perrin 1995, 8, the figure was 46 percent. Other studies include Danzon 1985, 187, who reports 60 percent as victims' share of medical malpractice liability insurance payments; Huber 1988, 151, who reports 40 percent as victims' share of medical malpractice liability insurance payments, 50 percent as victims' share of products liability insurance payments, and 50 percent as their share of motor-vehicle-accident liability insurance payments; Kakalik et al. 1983, who estimate 37 percent as victims' share of asbestos liability payments; Kakalik and Pace 1986, vii, who suggest from 45 percent to 47 percent as victims' share of tort payments; and Keeton et al. 1983, 891, who review studies implying 44 percent as victims' share of automobile accident liability insurance payments. For the United Kingdom, Cane 1999, 397, reports 15 percent as victims' share of tort compensation paid.

3. I can readily imagine much less complex systems (for example, employing tabular schedules to decide damages). Also, the costs of the liability systems in other countries, such as France and Germany, may be significantly lower than in the United States.

area of accident, those who would have received compensation under the liability system would often receive compensation through accident insurance. Therefore, the liability system increases administrative costs by the difference between its administrative costs and those of the insurance system.

The administrative costs associated with provision of accident insurance are much lower than those of the liability system, sometimes less than 10 percent of what victims receive.[4] The administrative costs of accident insurance are small by comparison because accident insurers have much less need than courts to inquire into the cause of losses or about injurers' behavior, because accident insurers have adopted comparatively simple procedures for verifying the magnitude of insureds' claims, and because accident insurers are not in an adversarial relationship with insureds.[5]

Because the accident insurance system is relatively inexpensive, the additional administrative costs of the liability system are quite high. Moreover, for victims who would not purchase accident insurance in the absence of liability (victims of low-magnitude harms, and large corporations), it is the total administrative cost of the liability system that should be considered to be its social cost, not its margin over insurance costs.

1.3 Strict liability versus negligence and administrative costs. The evaluation of strict liability and negligence rules depends on administrative costs as well as on incentives and risk allocation. As will be seen, however, it is not clear on a priori grounds whether administrative costs will be higher under one rule than under the other, because of two conflicting considerations.

---

4. For example, the cost of administering the federal Old Age and Survivors Insurance Program is one-half a percent of total expenditures and that of the Disability Insurance Program is 3 percent; see U.S. Social Security Administration 2000, 18. The sales and administrative costs of commercial lines of all property and casualty coverage is about 25 percent; see *Fact Book, 2001*, 24; but most of this is probably sales costs, not administrative. For instance, for automobile coverage, administrative costs are 5 percent and sales costs are 17 percent; see *Fact Book, 2001*, 50. And for homeowners' policies, administrative costs are 6 percent and sales costs are 22 percent; see *Fact Book, 2001*, 76.

5. While there may be disagreement between insureds and insurers, it is unlikely to be as serious as that between victims and injurers. In part this is because insurers have an interest in honoring their policies: Private insurers will want to maintain their reputations; social insurers are presumably strongly motivated to serve insureds in any event.

First, the total number of claims is likely to be larger under strict liability than under the negligence rule, suggesting that administrative costs tend to be higher under strict liability. Under strict liability, a victim will have an incentive to make a claim whenever his losses exceed the costs of making a claim (assuming that he can credibly establish that the injurer was the cause of harm and that he himself was not contributorily negligent). Under the negligence rule, a victim will not have an incentive to make a claim so often because he will also be concerned about establishing the injurer's negligence. If a victim and an injurer both believe that a court will find the injurer free of fault, the victim will be unlikely to make a claim under the negligence rule.

But second, the average administrative cost per claim should be higher under the negligence rule. Under the negligence rule, it is more probable that a claim will be litigated than under strict liability, for under the negligence rule there is an additional element of dispute—that of the injurer's negligence—and hence more room for disagreement leading to trial. Because the probability of trial should be greater under the negligence rule and because trials will usually be more costly than settlements, we have one reason for saying that average administrative costs per claim are likely to be larger under the negligence rule. A second reason is that the costs of trial itself are likely to be higher under the negligence rule than under strict liability because the issue of negligence must be adjudicated under the former rule.

In sum, then, the comparison of the size of administrative costs under the two forms of liability is ambiguous as a theoretical matter. One would predict that a greater number of claims will be made under strict liability, but one would expect the average cost of resolving claims to be higher under the negligence rule because of both a higher propensity to go to trial and a higher cost per trial.

2. SOCIALLY DESIRABLE USE OF THE LIABILITY SYSTEM GIVEN ADMINISTRATIVE COSTS

2.1 The question whether the liability system is socially worthwhile. Because of the administrative costs of the liability system, its use will be socially desirable if and only if its social benefits are sufficiently high.[6] In particular, these social benefits concern the reduction in accidents (net of the costs of preventing them) but not compensation of risk-averse victims, given the assumption that accident insurance would be likely to furnish victims with compensation in the absence of the liability system. Thus, the use of the liability system will be socially worthwhile if and only if the savings from accident reduction it brings about exceed its administrative costs.[7]

A general implication is that the liability system will not be socially worthwhile if it would produce a sufficiently small expected reduction in accident losses. We would expect that to be true when the magnitude of accident losses is low, and thus for a whole range of rather trivial harms, such as bumping into someone when boarding a bus or insulting someone in a minor way. The reduction in accident losses following from liability would also be small where, even if the magnitude of possible harms is not low, there is little that individuals would do to prevent losses on account of liability. For example, it might be that liability for automobile accidents does not much affect the incidence of these accidents, for drivers' precautions may be determined largely by their fear of injury to themselves in accidents and by criminal liability for traffic offenses and for drunk driving.[8]

When, however, the liability system creates substantial incentives toward safety that do exceed administrative costs, the liability system will be socially worthwhile. Other things being equal, that would be so when the magnitude of possible losses is high, and when there are steps that can be taken to reduce them or their likelihood substantially.

2.2 Optimal payments by liable injurers, given administrative costs.

If the liability system is worthwhile to employ, the presence of administrative costs affects the amount that liable injurers ought to pay, because these costs raise the social costs of accidents: When an accident occurs that results in a legal dispute, the true social costs of the accident are comprised of its

6. The subject of the socially desirable amount of litigation, and of the possible divergence between this and the privately determined amount of litigation (see the next section), will be considered in greater detail in section 2 of Chapter 17.

7. Of course, if the benefits of the liability system are properly conceived to be wider, this statement would be modified in a straightforward way.

8. For a particularly direct and sustained expression by a torts scholar of the general view that the costs of the liability system may outweigh its incentive-related benefits, see Sugarman 1985.

direct costs (harm to property and to person) plus administrative costs. The administrative costs are real social costs just as are the direct costs. For example, lawyers' services absorb valuable human resources, just as do physician services. Therefore, for injurers to have correct incentives to prevent harm, the amount that liable injurers ought to pay should equal the sum of the direct harm plus administrative costs. Now injurers naturally bear their own legal costs, time, and effort. Therefore, the optimal amount for injurers to pay equals the direct harm plus the legal and associated costs of victims and of the state. If the victim's harm is $100,000, his legal and other costs of handling the dispute are $30,000, and the court's costs are $5,000, the injurer's payment should be $135,000, not $100,000. For injurers' payments to be limited to $100,000 would lead to underdeterrence.

That injurers should pay for the direct harm plus the victim's and the state's costs does not imply that damages received by victims should equal this amount. The general argument made about victims' need for compensation and the optimality of fines (see section 6 of Chapter 11) suggests that damages should equal the direct (pecuniary) harm plus the victim's litigation costs, but that the state's costs should be collected from the injurer in the form of a fine.

In fact, damages are not generally raised according to the victim's or the state's litigation costs. Because the magnitude of victims' and the state's costs may average at least one-third of direct harm,[9] damages appear to be inadequate for purposes of deterrence by a significant amount—the situation is as if at least one-third of conventional damages are ignored by the legal system.

3.   PRIVATE VERSUS SOCIAL INCENTIVE TO USE THE LIABILITY SYSTEM GIVEN ADMINISTRATIVE COSTS

3.1 Private and social incentives may diverge.   When a victim is injured, he will make a decision whether to sue, that is, whether to make use of the liability system, based on a comparison of his private benefits, and notably the expected judgment, and his legal costs. How are such pri-

9. For example, in 1985 victims' legal payments as a fraction of harm was at least 33 percent; see Hensler et al. 1987, 29 (in which harm is estimated by subtracting defendants' legal fees from their total payments).

vate decisions concerning use of the liability system related to what is socially desirable, as discussed in section 2.1? The answer is that the private decision is quite different from the social one, and this leads to the possibility that the privately generated use of the system could be either too large or too small relative to what is socially desirable.

To illustrate the possibility that victims may bring a socially excessive number of claims, suppose that liability is strict, that there is absolutely nothing injurers can do to reduce risk, and that the social goal is to minimize the expected costs of accidents plus administrative costs. Clearly, in this example, it is socially undesirable for any claims to be made, for by assumption claims cannot result in any reduction in accident losses, yet claims do result in administrative costs for victims and injurers. Nevertheless, claims obviously will be made: Whenever a victim's loss exceeds his cost of making a claim, he will make a claim. The reason that claims are socially excessive here is evidently that victims' own financial return from making claims is often positive, even though the incentive thereby created is nil, a fact that is of no moment to a particular victim.

Let me now illustrate the converse possibility that there may be too few claims, that is, that victims might not make claims even though, were they to do so, social welfare would be improved. Suppose that victims do not make claims because the cost of doing so, say 200, would exceed their loss of 100, which they frequently suffer. Knowing that they would not be sued, injurers have no incentive to reduce the high risk of these losses. But suppose that injurers could very cheaply take a precaution that would reduce the chance of the losses to almost zero. Then it would be socially desirable for victims to bring suit, because that would serve to induce injurers to reduce risk, and thereby also reduce the number of claims and administrative costs. The reason that the making of claims is socially inadequate in this example is that a victim's personal return from suit is negative; that the social value of suit is positive, due to its deterrent effects, is not of consequence to a victim contemplating suit.

3.2 Divergence in incentives to bring suit may justify social intervention—to limit or to subsidize use of the legal system. Because the volume of use of the legal system that results from private decisions to bring suit may diverge from what is socially best, social intervention will sometimes be necessary and useful.

If the volume of litigation is too great because the administrative costs of suit outweigh the social benefits, reducing the use of the legal system will be worthwhile. For instance, it would be desirable to limit suits for automobile accidents if research showed that the deterrent effects of liability are modest (for the reasons noted above) in relation to the costs of the system. In such a case the state could contemplate such measures as imposing fees for bringing suit or banning suit altogether.

Conversely, if the volume of litigation is inadequate, then subsidy or some other means of fostering suit may be desirable. For example, some types of low-magnitude harms that would not be privately worthwhile to pursue in view of the cost might be socially worthwhile to promote due to the deterrent effect that the readiness of victims to sue would bring. To accomplish this, society could provide legal services for the bringing of the suits or otherwise support the process. Indeed, certain social efforts to promote access to the legal system, such as legal aid programs and small claims courts, might be rationalized in part along these lines.

The main point to stress is that the observed volume of litigation in any area of harm should not be viewed as approximately correct (in the way that the volume of some good sold in a normal market is so viewed). Because of the misalignment between social and private incentives to use the legal system, study of its benefits and costs is necessary to determine the direction and size of the divergence and the proper policy response to the divergence.

Note on the literature.   In Shavell (1982b) I first examined the contrast discussed here between the socially desirable and the privately motivated use of the legal system in view of its costs.[10]

---

10. See Menell 1983, Kaplow 1986b, Rose-Ackerman and Geistfeld 1987, and Shavell 1997, 1999, for further development of the social versus the private incentive to use the legal system.

PART III | CONTRACT LAW

In this part, I examine contracts—agreements between parties about certain of their future actions—and the law governing enforcement of these agreements. Chapter 13 presents an overview of the entire subject of contracts and provides the background for the remainder of the material. Chapter 14 is concerned with contract formation, that is, with the process through which parties find contracting partners, with aspects of contract negotiation, and with the rules governing when an arrangement between parties becomes legally recognized as a contract. Chapter 15 considers at length an important type of contract: the contract to produce something. Chapter 16 is concerned with two other types of contract: the contract for transfer of possession of something that already exists (such as land or a painting), and donative contracts.

13 ||| OVERVIEW OF CONTRACTS

This chapter presents an overview of contracts; it is concerned with the definition of contracts, the basic justifications for their existence, and important aspects of contractual practice and of the law of contracts. Subsequent chapters will deal in greater detail with certain aspects of contract law and with particular types of contracts.[1]

1. DEFINITIONS AND FRAMEWORK OF ANALYSIS

1.1 Basic definitions. By a *contract* I mean a specification of the *actions* that named parties are supposed to take at various times, generally as a function of the *conditions* that hold. The actions typically pertain to delivery of goods, performance of services, and payments of money, and the conditions include uncertain contingencies, past actions of parties, and messages sent by them. For example, a contract might state that a photographer should take pictures at a wedding on February 1, that the buyer should pay the photographer $1,000 within a week of the wedding, that the buyer

---

1. For general introductions to economic analysis of contract law, see, for example, Posner 1998, chap. 4, and Shavell 1998.

may cancel if he notifies the photographer by January 1st, and that the photographer may cancel if he becomes ill. It is apparent that because the notions of actions and of conditions are broad, the conception of a contract is very broad.

A contract will be said to be *completely specified* (or simply *complete*) if the list of conditions on which the actions are based is *explicitly exhaustive,* that is, if the contract provides literally for each and every possible condition in some relevant universe of conditions. In a contract for a photographer to take wedding photographs, suppose that the universe of conditions is everything that could happen to the photographer (becoming ill, receiving an offer to take photographs at another wedding the same day) and everything that could happen to the wedding couple (becoming ill themselves, breaking off their engagement). A completely specified contract would then have to include an explicit provision for each of these possible conditions pertaining to the photographer and to the wedding couple. Although, as we will discuss, contracts are far from completely specified in reality, the concept of a complete contract will be helpful for clarifying our thinking about contracts. Moreover, we will sometimes want to simplify by assuming that the universe of relevant conditions is small (we might suppose that it includes only the wedding photographer either becoming ill, or staying healthy), in which case we can well imagine a completely specified contract.

A contract will be said to be *incomplete* if it is not completely specified, which is to say, if the contract does not list explicitly all of the possible conditions under consideration. For example, a contract that reads "Photographer shall take wedding pictures on March 14," would obviously be incomplete because it does not list any conditions; so would a contract that says "Photographer shall take wedding pictures on March 14, unless the photographer develops appendicitis," because this contract mentions only the single condition of appendicitis in the universe of possible conditions. Note that although these two contracts are incomplete, they do *implicitly* provide complete instructions for what the parties are to do under all conditions. The contract that states simply that the photographer shall take wedding pictures on March 14 implies that he should take the pictures under all conditions. Thus, according to the definition we are employing, an incomplete contract may well provide a complete set of instructions by implication.[2]

2. The use of the term "incomplete contract" in the economics literature is consistent with the definition I have given in this paragraph. In the economics literature, a contract

An incomplete contract that does not provide a complete set of instructions explicitly *or* by implication is said to have *gaps.* For example, suppose that the wedding photography contract states that if the weather is sunny, the ceremony will be held in the backyard and a video camera should be used, and that if there is rain and the ceremony is held inside the house, only still photographs need to be taken. This contract does not state explicitly or imply what is to be done if the weather is cloudy; thus, it has a gap.

1.2 Mutually beneficial contracts. A contract is said to be *mutually beneficial* or, in the language of economics, *Pareto efficient,* if the contract cannot be modified so as to raise the well-being—the expected utility— of each of the parties to it. We would suppose that contracts would tend to be mutually beneficial: If a contract can be altered in a way that would raise the expected utility of each party, we would think that this would be done. For example, suppose that the wedding contract states that the photographer should appear at 10:00 in the morning, but that an alternative contract under which he would arrive at 9:00 and would be paid an additional $100 is preferred both by the wedding couple and by the photographer. Then the first contract would not be mutually beneficial, and we would expect the modification of the contract for earlier arrival of the photographer and higher payment to be made.

1.3 Enforcement of contracts. Contracts are assumed to be enforced by a court, which generally will be interpreted to be a state-authorized court. In many respects, however, an entity other than a state-authorized court—a decisionmaking body within a firm, a trade association or a religious group, or an arbitration organization—could serve as a tribunal and sometimes enforce contracts. Moreover, reputation and related factors may

---

is called incomplete if some variable on which the contract could depend (and typically would be valuable to include in the contract) is not included. For example, in the contract with the photographer, the contract could be imagined to depend on the photographer's effort (how well he circulated among guests), but if it did not depend on the photographer's effort, the contract would be considered incomplete. This contract would also be an incomplete contract according to my definition, for the photographer's effort level is a condition (a past action) on which the contract could in principle depend. Note too that in this example, as in many examples of incomplete contracts studied in the economics literature, an incomplete contract does provide, by implication, a complete set of instructions for the contracting parties.

also serve to some degree to enforce contracts. These extra-state means of enforcement will be discussed in section 10.

Contract enforcement involves the functions and actions of courts. Typically, courts act only when parties to contracts decide to come before them. Several general functions of courts should be mentioned.

A basic function of courts is to decide about *contract formation,* that is, when a valid contract has been made.

Given that a contract has been properly made and is deemed valid, courts must often engage in contract *interpretation,* notably, they must fill gaps in contracts and resolve ambiguities.

Another function of courts concerns *breach* of contract. Courts must decide when breach has occurred and impose sanctions or "remedies" for breach. Courts may impose two different types of sanctions for breach of a contract by a party to it: They may force a party in breach to pay money *damages* to the other, or they may insist that the contract be performed in a literal sense (for example, require land to be conveyed, as stipulated in the contract), that is, insist on *specific performance* of the contract.

Finally, courts may also decide to *override* a contract. That is, even though a contract was properly formed and is not invalid on that count, and has not been breached, the court may refuse to enforce it.[3]

1.4 Social welfare and the welfare of contracting parties.   It will generally be assumed that the goal of courts is to maximize social welfare. This will usually mean that courts act to further the welfare of the parties to the contract, for they will ordinarily be the only parties affected by the contract. If, however, other parties are affected by a contract, then the well-being of these parties outside the contract will also be assumed to be taken into account by the court.

2.   CONTRACT FORMATION

As mentioned, one of the basic functions of courts in relation to contracts is to decide when contracts are recognized as having been formed—that

---

3. From a formal point of view, all of these judicial tasks may be regarded as involving application of legal rules in a broad sense: Suppose that a legal rule is any function whose domain is the pair constituted of the contract of the parties (or, more exactly, various initial,

is, when they are deemed valid and will be enforced. Several aspects of the law of contract formation will illustrate its significance.

One dimension of the law of formation concerns the ease with which parties can determine whether contracts will be legally recognized. If legal recognition of contract formation is based on a clear sign of agreement from each party—such that each is easily able to know when there has been mutual assent and a contract has been formed—then two essential benefits will follow. First, because parties have the ability to make contracts and to know immediately that their contracts will be enforced, the parties will be able to benefit without any delay from undertaking value-enhancing activities (such as hiring workers and purchasing materials for construction). Second, because parties can avoid making contracts by not making the sign of agreement that would lead to recognition of a contract, they will not be afraid to engage in search for partners, to seek information about possible contracts, and to negotiate about them, for parties will not fear being said to be in a contract that they do not want.

Another aspect of rules regarding contract formation concerns whether one of the parties to a possible contract was under duress or in an emergency situation. If, despite otherwise proper signs of agreement to a contract, a contract is not recognized because of duress or emergency, two socially beneficial and one detrimental consequence follow. First, socially undesirable effort will not be spent in order to place certain parties in problematic situations in which, due to duress or emergency, they would be led to make contracts on terms very favorable to those that put them there. Second, parties will obtain a kind of implicit insurance against having to pay high prices if they find themselves in an emergency situation. But third, the incentives of potential contracting parties to help those in bad straits will be dulled.

An additional aspect of the law of contract formation involves the information that is divulged by potential parties to contracts. The more information that parties are required to reveal, the better the matching of partners to each other and the more efficient the actions of parties once they

---

observable statements they have made to each other) and certain subsequent events (observable actions of parties, messages, contingencies), and whose range is a set of actions of the court (such as declaring a contract to be formed, naming payments the parties must make, other actions of the parties, or revision of contract terms).

make contracts. But legal obligations to reveal information generally dilute incentives to acquire information, an outcome that can be socially undesirable.

These and other aspects of the law of contract formation will be considered in Chapter 14.

3. GENERAL JUSTIFICATIONS FOR CONTRACTS AND FOR THEIR ENFORCEMENT

3.1 Why contracts are made.   A basic question about contracts is why parties should want to make them, that is, why they should want to make plans with each other. Several important reasons may be offered.

An obvious warrant for contracts involves the future *provision of goods and services.* It is often the case that one party will want a good or service in the future, and that another party can supply the good or service, giving rise to the mutual desirability of a contract. It should be noted, however, that contracts will not be necessary for the future supply of goods or services if a well-organized market in them exists, for then a future need can be met on the spot. (If I will want food for dinner a month from now, I do not need to make a contract to get it, for I will be able to purchase the food at that time.) Thus, it is mainly for custom or specialized goods and services, not those readily available on markets, that production contracts may be beneficial.

Another reason for contracting is the mutually beneficial *reallocation* or *sharing of risks.* Insurance contracts, whereby risk-averse insureds pay premiums and are covered against risk by a risk-neutral insurer, are a primary example of agreements made for this reason, and other examples abound in which risk allocation is a primary feature, such as partnership agreements to divide total profits.

A third reason for contracts concerns *differences of opinion* about subsequent events. When transactions in securities or in durable assets occur, the explanation is often, at least in part, that the buyer and seller have different beliefs about their future prices; when bets occur, the explanation is typically that the two sides hold different beliefs about the likelihood of the bet event.

A fourth general reason for contracting involves altering the *timing of consumption.* When individuals borrow or lend, they are making mutually beneficial arrangements in which their temporal patterns of consumption are altered.

Of course, more than one of these reasons may apply in a given case. For instance, a cost-plus contract for the provision of a good may achieve not only provision of the good, but also beneficial risk-sharing (suppose the producer is averse to risk).[4]

3.2 Why enforcement is desired.   Given that there are reasons for parties to make contracts, to make plans for future actions with each other, why do parties want their contracts enforced by courts? That is, why might contracts be broken in the absence of enforcement by an outside party, and why, exactly, would such contract breach be undesirable for the parties?

There are three general answers to these questions. The first is that without enforcement, a party would be able to *appropriate funds* that had been paid before contract performance, generally rendering the contract unworkable. For example, because borrowers would be able to keep what they had been lent and would not be forced to repay loans, loans would become impossible without contract enforcement, and because insurers would be able to keep premiums and would not be made to cover losses, insurance would become impossible without enforcement. Thus, most financial contracts, bets, and risk-sharing arrangements would become unworkable. And any contract other than one in which there is a *simultaneous* exchange of money for goods or services would also become unworkable in the absence of contract enforcement.[5]

The second general reason for parties' desiring contract enforcement is that otherwise a party *might not deliver a promised good or perform a*

---

4. Although I believe that the reasons for contracts discussed in this section are the primary ones, others exist. For example, parties may want to warrant the quality of goods sold on spot markets and thus want contracts for that purpose, or parties may want to induce certain behavior on the part of the recipients of gifts and thus want to make donative contracts (on which, see section 2 of Chapter 16).

5. The enforcement of a contractual obligation to pay money, such as to repay a loan, might come, at least in part, under the head of tort law (to prevent "conversion" of assets) or criminal law, rather than contract law; but this is not of significance for our purposes, for what matters is that some form of legal enforcement of contractual obligations is needed.

promised service.[6] A party who has promised a good or a service may find that another, better opportunity has arisen, that costs of performance have increased more than expected, and the like. If so, and if negotiation with the other party to the contract would be inconvenient or unlikely to succeed smoothly, the promisor might decide not to perform. If there is failure to perform even though performance would be best because its value exceeds its true cost, then the value of the contractual arrangement is diminished for the parties. Such reductions in the value of contracts can be avoided if contracts are enforced.

The third reason for enforcement is that without enforcement, the *price cannot be fixed in advance,* which is to say, *price holdup* might occur—a party might *bargain opportunistically* about the price of a transaction— reducing the value of the contract or discouraging the making of it al- together. To illustrate, consider a buyer who wants a custom desk that would be worth $1,000 to him and would cost $700 for a seller to produce. In the absence of contract enforcement, the buyer and the seller cannot fix in advance the price that the buyer will pay for the desk at the time of delivery. (Note, the buyer will not pay the seller in advance, for the seller could then walk away with what he receives.) The buyer and the seller will agree on a price only *after* the seller makes the desk, and the buyer will at that time pay the seller in a simultaneous exchange of money for the desk. But at that point, the seller's production cost will be sunk and he will be vulnerable to holdup; the situation will be that he has a desk that, being custom-made, will have little or no alternative value.[7] The outcome of bargaining between him and the buyer might thus be a price lower than the seller's cost of $700; say, $500. If so, and the seller anticipates receiving only the $500 price, he will not produce the desk. This is true even though production and sale at a price between $700 and $1,000, such as $800, would be mutually beneficial for the seller and the buyer. More broadly,

6. Such failure might occur even though simultaneous exchange of money for the good or service is possible, so the present reason for enforcement is different from that of the last paragraph.

7. Similar forms of holdup would arise in the absence of contract enforcement where parties want to convey property that already exists, such as land; for instance, a seller might worry about being held up by the buyer if the seller waits and forgoes a present opportunity to sell his land to a new party who makes a bid for it.

the problem of holdup at the stage of negotiation for performance and for payment will result in all manner of underinvestment in the contractual enterprise.[8]

4. INCOMPLETENESS OF CONTRACTS

Having defined contracts and given general reasons why they are made and enforced, let me now examine the nature of contracts themselves. An aspect of contractual practice that will be seen to be of considerable importance is that contracts are significantly incomplete. Contracts typically omit all manner of variables and contingencies that are of potential relevance to contracting parties. A contract to take pictures at a wedding would be likely to fail to include many contingencies that might make it difficult or impossible for the photographer to perform, as well as many circumstances that would alter the couples' desire for photographs or for other types of records that they want to be made of their wedding.

There are several types of reasons for the incompleteness of contracts, that is, for why parties find it in their mutual interest to leave contracts incomplete. One category of reasons concerns the effort and cost of anticipating possible contingencies, bargaining about their resolution (given that they are anticipated), and then describing them adequately. In particular, parties will tend not to specify terms for low probability events, because the expected loss from this type of exclusion will be minimal, whereas the cost of including the terms would be borne with certainty. For example, it might take fifteen minutes to discuss and include a term about what to do if the photographer is involved in a car accident on the way to the wedding, but if such an event is very unlikely, it will not be worth

8. The idea of contract enforcement as a cure for holdup-related inadequacy of investment and effort in the contractual enterprise was initially stressed in the economics literature by Grout 1984, Klein, Crawford, and Alchian 1978, and Williamson 1975. But the general idea that contract enforcement is privately and socially desirable because it fosters production and trade is made (usually, with little articulation) by most writers on contract law and one supposes that it has always been appreciated. See, for example, E. A. Farnsworth 1999, 6–7, and Pound 1959, 133–134.

the parties' while to include a provision for such an outcome in the contract.[9]

A second general reason for incompleteness has nothing to do with the difficulty of including a term in a contract, but rather involves the subsequent cost of enforcing a contractual term. Notably, if the cost of providing evidence to the courts that a relevant contingency or condition has occurred is sufficiently large, then the term will not be worthwhile including.

A third important reason for incompleteness is that some contingencies (such as whether the seller has a stomachache) or some variables (such as the effort level of the seller, or technical production difficulties) cannot be verified by courts. If a contingency or the value of a variable cannot be verified by courts—if there is an asymmetry of information between the parties and the courts—then were the parties to include the contingency or variable in the contract, one of the parties would generally find it in his interest to make a claim about the contingency or the variable, causing problems. (For example, if the contract specifies that the seller need not perform if he has a stomachache, he would claim he had a stomachache if he later did not want to perform; or if the contract specifies that the buyer does not have to pay for a service if it is performed poorly and the quality of performance cannot be verified by the court, the buyer would always find it in his interest to claim that performance was subpar in order to escape having to pay.) It should be noted that even if the parties can themselves verify contingencies and named variables, contracts that include them will still be unworkable if the courts cannot verify them (even if the buyer knows the seller's effort level, a contract depending on effort level will be unworkable if the court cannot verify it, for both the buyer and the seller can make false claims about it). Of course, many variables that seem unverifiable can be made verifiable (perhaps the quality of service performance can be made verifiable through videotaping), but that would involve expense.

A fourth factor explaining incompleteness of contracts is that the expected consequences of incompleteness may not be very harmful to con-

---

9. More precisely, suppose that the cost of including a term for an (anticipated) contingency is c, that the likelihood of the contingency is p, and that the loss the parties would jointly suffer from failing to include a term for the contingency is l. Then the parties will tend to exclude the contingency if the associated expected loss of pl is less than the cost c of inclusion, that is, if p is less than c/l.

tracting parties.[10] To amplify, a court might interpret an incomplete contract in a desirable manner, as we are about to discuss. In addition, as we shall see, the prospect of having to pay damages for breach of contract may serve as an implicit substitute for more detailed terms because it may lead parties to act as they would have under more detailed terms. Furthermore, the opportunity to renegotiate a contract often furnishes a way for parties to alter terms in the light of circumstances for which contractual provisions had not been made, and will lead them to do what they would have provided for had they written a more detailed contract in the first place. Finally, incompleteness may not matter at all because it may concern contractually irrelevant events. There are a multitude of such irrelevant events—for example, whether it rains elsewhere in the world will be irrelevant to the parties to the wedding photography contract—and parties obviously will not specify terms for irrelevant events because of the positive cost of so doing.

5. INTERPRETATION OF CONTRACTS

Given that parties leave contracts incomplete, questions naturally arise about the interpretation of contracts by courts. As a general matter, parties will want incomplete contracts to be interpreted as if they had spent the time and effort to specify more detailed terms.[11] For example, suppose that a builder and a buyer do not include a term in their contract stating whether the builder is to perform if material prices rise steeply, but had they included the term, it would have relieved the builder of having to perform in that

10. In strict logic, this is not an independent reason for incompleteness but rather one that complements the previous reasons: The lower are the losses from incompleteness, the more likely it is that parties will find the costs of writing or enforcing terms not worthwhile bearing, and the more likely they will not find it worthwhile incurring the costs of rendering a variable verifiable to the court.

11. It should be noted that such interpretation can be carried out by courts only when the reason for incompleteness was the effort to anticipate or the expense for parties of specifying more terms. When the reason for incompleteness is that the court cannot verify a term (such as the wedding photographer's level of effort), then the courts by assumption cannot attempt to complete the contract (by taking into account the photographer's effort level).

circumstance. The parties would want the courts to interpret the incomplete contract in that way should prices rise steeply.[12]

The advantage to parties of correct interpretation of their intentions by courts is not only direct in this way, however. The advantage of correct interpretation is also indirect—that the parties can omit more explicit terms and thereby save drafting and negotiating costs. Indeed, the formal statement of how to evaluate a method of contract interpretation makes it clear that interpretation has both direct and indirect effects. The formal evaluation is as follows: Given a method M of contract interpretation, first determine what terms the parties to a contract would rationally choose to include, presuming that the parties know that M will be used to interpret their contracts (in other words, take into account the indirect effect of use of M);[13] and second, calculate social welfare having ascertained what terms the parties will include and how the courts will interpret incompleteness.[14]

---

12. To amplify why the parties would be made better off, suppose that the seller would insist on raising the contract price by $100 if he were obligated to perform when prices turned out to be very high—in order to cover his increase in expected costs—but that the buyer would only place an expected value of $50 on receiving performance in that circumstance. Then were the two parties to include an explicit term regarding high prices, the term would state that the seller not perform, for the buyer would not want to pay the extra $100 in the price for a $50 benefit. If the court interprets the contract in this way, the parties tend to be made better off. If the court, however, misinterprets the parties' intentions and they know this, then the cost of the contract to the buyer would rise by $100 for only a $50 benefit, making the contract less valuable for him. As a consequence of this and similar misinterpretation, the buyer's willingness to pay for the contract would fall, harming the seller as well. Conversely, correct interpretation tends to benefit both parties.

13. A sketch of how this could be done is as follows. Suppose that the parties contemplate including a term t in their contract. Each party can calculate his expected utility if t is not included, given that method M will be used to interpret the contract if a contingency relevant to t arises. (To calculate expected utility, some assumption about the determination of contract price must be made, such as that the price is such that one party obtains a fixed percentage of the surplus.) Each party can also calculate his expected utility if t is included; this calculation will take into account the cost of including t. It would be natural to assume that the contract excludes t if both parties are better off by so doing, and that it includes t if either party wants that.

14. The social welfare maximizing method of interpretation can be described loosely as that which minimizes the sum of writing costs (the cost of including terms) plus error costs of interpretation (the social welfare goal would be precisely this if social welfare equals

Several comments should be made about the courts' task of interpretation. Consider first the situation in which there is a literal gap in a contract, like the wedding photography contract that mentions sunny days, when videos should be taken of the ceremony, and rainy days, when only still pictures are to be taken of the ceremony, but fails to say what should be done on cloudy days. In such a case, courts know that they must fill the gap—if a cloudy day arose, the courts must say what should have been done, and the job of the courts is to determine from evidence what the parties would have wanted. Consider next an incomplete contract that does not have gaps, such as a contract that says the wedding photographer shall take videos of the ceremony unless there is rain, in which case stills are to be taken. By implication, this contract covers cloudy days—video pictures are to be taken of the ceremony on such days—but there are still possible ambiguities about the contract: Did the parties really mean for videos of the ceremony to be taken on cloudy days, or did they not mean that and leave out explicit mention of cloudy days because of the cost of so doing and, perhaps, knowledge of how the courts would interpret their contract if the weather were cloudy?[15] Incomplete contracts that do not contain literal gaps always involve such ambiguities about the parties' real desires, so that the need for judicial interpretation is not clear, and the possibility

---

the sum of parties' utilities and they are risk neutral). Therefore, a method M that tends to be an accurate reflection of parties' desires lowers error costs, and it also leads (as explained in the last footnote) to exclusion of terms and thus lower writing costs; thus, both the direct and indirect advantages of M enter into the formal calculus, as stated in the text. It should be observed that the optimal method of interpretation may involve some subtleties. For example, according to the optimal method, a term might not be interpreted in the way that is best in the majority of transactions. Suppose that term t_1 is best in the majority of transactions and that the parties to these transactions can include t_1 explicitly, at little cost on a per-contract basis, because they are repeat players. Suppose that term t_2 is best only in the minority of transactions, but that for the parties to these transactions to include t_2 explicitly will not be cheap on a per-contract basis because they are not repeat players. Then the optimal method of interpretation would make t_2 the default term in an incomplete contract even though it is best only in a minority of transactions.

15. The ambiguity that I am referring to here might arise when parties do not have a clear understanding of how the courts will interpret incompleteness; thus the situation may be more complicated than that described in the previous two notes, in which I assumed the parties know for sure the method M of interpretation.

that courts would err in determining what the parties want may increase as a consequence.[16]

6. DAMAGE MEASURES FOR BREACH OF CONTRACT

6.1 Damage measures defined.   As noted in section 1.3, when parties breach a contract, they often have to pay damages. The damage measure— that is, the rule or formula governing what a party in breach should pay— can be applied by the court or it can be stipulated in advance by the parties to the contract (in which case damages are sometimes referred to as *liquidated* damages because they are intended to liquidate, to terminate, the legal obligations of the party in breach).[17] One would expect parties to specify their own damage measure when it would better serve their purposes than the measure the court would employ, and otherwise to allow the court to select the damage measure. In either case, I now examine the functioning and utility of damage measures to contracting parties.

6.2 Damage measures and incentives to perform.   It is clear that damage measures provide parties incentives to perform, by threatening them with having to pay damages if they do not. Suppose that the buyer wants a custom desk built, and that the measure of damages for seller breach is $800. Then the seller would be induced to build the desk if he would

16. On various aspects of contract interpretation, see, for example, Ayres and Gertner 1989, Hadfield 1994, Katz 1990c, Katz 1998, and Schwartz 1992.

17. There is a possible ambiguity in the meaning of the word "breach." What is meant by breach in ordinary language is that a party does not do what the contract indicates he will do. For example, if the contract states that the seller shall deliver goods and the seller does not do that, he would usually be said to be in breach. Suppose, however, that the contract contains a liquidated damages provision stating that if the seller does not deliver goods, he should pay $100 in damages. Then if he does not deliver the goods and pays the $100, it might be said that he did not breach the contract because he did what was required in the contract, namely, pay the $100. In such cases where the contract names damage measures, however, we will still refer to an event in which a person does not do something specified in the contract and instead pays damages as being a breach. In any event, the issue under discussion is really semantic, because however we choose to describe parties' behavior, our analysis of behavior under different contracts, and under different legal rules, will be the same.

profit from so doing or if his losses would be less than $800, but the seller would commit breach if his losses from performing would be higher than $800. Thus, a particular damage measure provides a particular degree of incentive to perform, and in general, it is evident that the higher is the damage measure, the greater the incentive to perform.

Best measure of damages when contracts are completely specified. What measure of damages provides the best incentive for the parties to perform? That is, what damage measure would most raise their expected utilities from contracting? It might seem that a high damage measure, even a punitive measure, would be best, for that would give a strong motivation to obey a contract. This idea is correct if a contract is truly completely specified. In that case, a high damage measure—high enough that no party would ever breach the contract—would be in the parties' mutual interests because they would then be assured that exactly the contract they want would be obeyed.[18]

Let me illustrate with a contract for the building of the desk, and let us assume that the buyer places a value of $1,000 on having the desk. If such a contract were mutually beneficial and completely specified, then it can be shown to have the following simple character: The seller is to make the desk if the production cost would be less than $1,000; and the seller is excused from performance if the production cost would exceed $1,000. (In essence, the explanation is that the buyer would be willing to pay enough to the seller to induce him to accept terms specifying that the desk should be built if production cost is less than $1,000, but the buyer would not be willing to pay enough to the seller to induce him to include terms calling for performance when the production cost would be higher than $1,000.) Now note two points about the outcome if the damage measure for breach were high enough to guarantee performance of the terms in this contract: First, the seller would be led to construct the desk when the production cost would be less than $1,000, but second, the seller would *not* be led to construct the desk when the production cost would exceed

18. A slightly different way to express the point that the parties do not want breach is this: The hypothesis that the parties would want breach in some circumstance contradicts the assumption that the completely specified contract is mutually desirable in that circumstance (and could have been altered to allow for nonperformance in that circumstance, but was not).

$1,000, for the completely specified contract does not call for that, and thus no damages would be paid by the seller when he fails to construct the desk in such circumstances. Observe, moreover, that this statement is true no matter how high the damages for breach are. By contrast, under a damage measure that is not high enough always to induce performance of the contract, there will be, by hypothesis, some situations in which the construction cost is lower than $1,000 and the seller will decide to commit breach and pay damages. Thus, the actual outcomes under this contract will be different from what is intended by the parties, and it can be shown that the parties will generally be worse off under this lower measure than under a higher damage measure that always induces performance.

The general points illustrated by this example are that, under a damage measure that is sufficiently high so as necessarily to induce performance of a mutually beneficial completely specified contract, (a) performance is always guaranteed, yet (b) there is no risk of a party's having to perform when that would be onerous, and there is no risk of having to bear high damages for breach. The latter points are true because, whenever performance would be onerous, the contract, being completely specified and mutually beneficial, will not call for performance.

Best measure of damages when contracts are incomplete. When contracts are not completely specified, then damage measures that are high enough always to lead to performance of the incomplete contract, or to lead to too frequent performance of that contract, are often undesirable for the parties. Instead, only moderate damages are desirable, because they will result in breach when performance of the incomplete contract would be difficult.

Before amplifying this point, let us reconsider the earlier example. Suppose that the contract states simply that the seller shall make a desk for the buyer and the buyer shall pay for it at the outset. The contract does not have specific terms because, say, of the cost of taking the time to include them. Given this incomplete contract calling for performance under all circumstances, a high measure of damages would be needed to guarantee performance, to make it certain. For instance, suppose that production costs could range up to $5,000. Then the damage measure for breach would have to exceed $5,000 in order to guarantee performance; a lower measure, such as $3,000, would result in breach whenever production cost would exceed $3,000.

Now a damage measure that is so high as to result in performance of the incomplete contract all the time would result in outcomes very different from that under the mutually beneficial completely specified contract: Under the complete contract, the desk would be constructed *only* when its production cost is less than the buyer's valuation of $1,000, whereas under the incomplete contract with a high damage measure, the desk would be built even when the production cost exceeds $1,000. This suggests what will later be shown to be true, that the parties will be worse off with the high damage measure, due to the excessive performance it brings about. (The kernel of the explanation is that the seller will charge the buyer a higher price because of the costly performance he might be led to undertake, and the buyer by assumption would prefer not to have performance in these costly circumstances, in order to benefit from a lower contract price.)

A moderate damage measure, however, will not lead to the problem of excessive performance, for if damages are less than the high production cost levels, the seller will commit breach when production cost is high. Indeed, if the damage measure equals $1,000, the value of the desk to the buyer, the seller will be led to perform precisely when he would have performed in the mutually beneficial completely specified contract: For the seller will perform when production cost is less than $1,000, and he will breach the contract and pay damages when production cost would exceed $1,000. This damage measure, equal to the value of performance, is the *expectation measure,* the most commonly employed measure of damages, and as will be seen subsequently in Chapter 15, it leads under fairly general circumstances to performance when parties would wish that.

Because moderate damage measures allow breach of incomplete contracts when performance would be expensive and induce performance when it would not be expensive, moderate damage measures lead to performance in circumstances resembling those (and in the example, identical to those) under mutually beneficial completely specified contracts. This suggests what will be later shown, that moderate damage measures are preferred by *both* parties to other damage measures.[19]

Moderate damage measures serve as implicit substitutes for more complete contracts. One implication of the preference of both parties to a contract for moderate damage measures is that such damage measures function as

19. In particular, it will be shown in Chapter 15 that both parties would often elect to choose the expectation measure over other damage measures when writing the contract.

substitutes for detailed contracts. It has been seen that if a contract leaves out terms stating when contracts should be performed and when not, use of a properly chosen moderate damage measure will lead to performance in approximately the circumstances that the parties would have named in a more completely specified contract. That is, performance will be induced when it is not too burdensome to perform, and not otherwise. Therefore, the opportunity of the parties to employ moderate damage measures enables them to write contracts that lack great detail while still knowing that performance will occur roughly when they want.

The value of damage measures to parties as a substitute for more complete contracts depends on the transaction costs of the use of damage measures versus the costs of specifying contracts more fully in advance. It should also be observed that damage measures can serve implicitly to complete contracts when it would be impossible for parties to write them, due to the inability of courts to verify the occurrence of contingencies. Suppose that the production cost of making the desk in our example is something that is inherently unobservable by courts, because the production cost depends on idiosyncratic factors having to do with specialized carpentry, making it impractical for the builder to convince the court that the production cost would be high. Then a contract specifying that there should be no production when the production cost is high would not be workable. But a contract with a moderate damage measure of $1,000 for breach would be workable and would lead, as has been emphasized, to the result that the parties want, of no performance when production cost is high, and this would be so *without* the court's having to verify that the level of production cost would be high.

Qualification: When contractual duties are financial, damage measures cannot serve as substitutes for more completely specified contracts. If a contract is incomplete and a party's contractual duty is to pay an amount of money, then a damage measure cannot serve to induce performance when it would have occurred in a more complete contract. Consider a building construction contract and the obligation of the buyer to pay the seller $1,000,000 for the building when it is finished. Suppose that a complete contract would say that the buyer would only have to pay $700,000 if he suffers a significant financial reverse. If the contract is incomplete and does not have a provision for the financial reverse, the use of a damage measure cannot relieve the buyer's obligation in that circumstance. In particular, the damage measure must be $1,000,000 to induce the buyer to do what he promises (namely, pay $1,000,000) in ordinary circumstances; yet if that is so, the buyer has to do the same when he suffers a financial reverse.[20]

Thus, in general, when contractual obligations are financial, damage measures cannot serve to fill out incomplete contracts; they can only induce performance of the incomplete contract that is written. Hence, for parties to avoid the problems due to incompleteness, they must either rely on courts' interpretation of their contracts (perhaps the courts would lower the buyer's obligation to pay if he suffered a reverse) or they must simply take the trouble to write a more complete contract in the first place. This point, then, applies for the parties' obligations to pay in contracts to provide goods and services, and generally for purely financial contracts (loans, insurance, and the like).

6.3 Are breach and payment of damages immoral?   The discussion in section 6.2 sheds light on the often-debated question of whether a breach of contract is an immoral act, similar to the breaking of a promise.[21]

To understand and evaluate this assertion, let us assume in this section that the type of promise that ought to be kept is a completely specified promise that the parties could be imagined to make. This assumption is natural, for, by definition, it is only the completely specified promise that is explicit about the desires of the parties in each of the circumstances of possible relevance to them. It would not be natural to interpret an incompletely specified promise as embodying the desires of the parties in a particular circumstance if the parties would have stipulated something different from what the incomplete promise states for that circumstance, and if the reason that the parties did not provide for the circumstance was that it would have been inconvenient for them to take the time to do so.

Given, then, the assumption that the completely specified contract rep-

20. Note the difference when a party's obligation is to take an action other than pay money. If the action, such as building something, becomes difficult or expensive for the person, he can relieve his burden—benefit himself—by paying damages of a set amount. When his obligation is *itself* monetary, then paying damages equal to that amount cannot possibly help him.

21. In the philosophical literature, see, for example, Kant [1785] 1998, 15, 32, 38, Ross 1930, chap. 2, and Searle 1964; and in the legal literature, see, for example, Fried 1981, chaps. 1–2. These views are reviewed in Kaplow and Shavell 2002b, 157–165.

resents the promise of the parties that ought to be kept, and that incomplete contracts are not what ought to be kept, we can see that the view that it is immoral to breach contracts and pay damages is confused and may well represent the opposite of the truth. Consider the incomplete contract for the making of the desk that is worth $1,000 to the buyer, that names no contingencies concerning production cost, and for which the expectation measure would determine damages for breach. Under this measure, breach will occur whenever production cost exceeds $1,000. In such instances, nonperformance is exactly what would have been allowed in the completely specified contract that represents the real wishes of the parties and the promise that they would want met. Thus, the breach induced by the damage measure is seen to satisfy the true promise agreement of the parties, not to abrogate it; in this sense, the truth about breach and damage measures is the opposite of that suggested by the view that breach is immoral.[22] That view reflects a failure to recognize the possibility of—and the practical reality and reasons for—incomplete contracts.[23]

6.4 Incentives to rely. Another function of damage measures for breach is that, because they encourage contract performance, they provide contracting parties with incentives to take actions relying on performance. These actions can raise the value of contracts for parties, inuring to their benefit. For example, a restaurateur, expecting construction of a restaurant by his builder, could hire and train staff and advertise the opening of the restaurant, and thereby enhance the profitability of the contract. Such reliance actions are a byproduct of the confidence in performance that the use of damage measures produces. Although one might be inclined to think that the inducement of reliance is necessarily a good thing—there being too little reliance if there is no contract enforcement—it turns out that the use of damage measures also may actually lead to excessive reliance in a sense that will be made precise in Chapter 15.

22. This point was initially made in Shavell 1980b.

23. Lest I be misunderstood, what I have said implies that breach might be immoral if the damage measure is not sufficiently high to induce performance in a circumstance in which the completely specified contract would have called for performance. Thus, if the completely specified contract would have stipulated performance when the desk costs $500 to produce, and for some reason the seller is able to commit breach and pay only $100 in damages, breach might properly be considered immoral.

6.5 Risk-bearing. A third important function of damage measures concerns the allocation of risk. Notably, because the payment of damages compensates to one or another degree the victim of a breach, the measure might be mutually desirable as an implicit form of insurance if the victim is risk averse. For this reason, damage measures may gain additional appeal for the parties on risk-bearing grounds.

But the prospect of having to pay damages also constitutes a risk for a party who might be led to commit breach (such as a seller whose costs suddenly rise), and he might be risk averse. This consideration may lead parties to want to lower damages, or to avoid use of damages as an incentive device, by writing more detailed contracts. (For instance, the parties could go to the expense of specifying in the contract that a seller can be excused from performance when his costs are high.)

A full consideration of damage measures and efficient risk allocation would also take into account whether the risk that a party bears is detrimental or beneficial. For example, if a seller wants to breach, not because he has run into costly production difficulties, but rather because another party has bid more for what he has made, then risk-bearing considerations would not lead to lower damages for the seller. Another relevant consideration is whether a risk is monetary or nonmonetary. If, for instance, the victim's loss is nonmonetary, such as the loss due to the failure of a photographer to appear at a wedding, financial compensation in the form of damages may not constitute an optimal form of insurance.[24] An additional consideration is the availability of commercial insurance to the parties for the losses due to breach; if such insurance is available, then the need for damages to compensate the victim is negated, and damages have a role mainly as an incentive device.

Note on the literature. The point that a moderate damage measure, and in particular the expectation measure, is socially desirable because it induces performance if and only if the cost of performance is relatively low was originally stated, informally, in Posner (1972a),[25] but he did not ob-

---

24. Recall the discussion of insurance for nonmonetary losses in section 6, Chapter 11.

25. Two other writers, Birmingham 1970 and Barton 1972, adumbrate this point, although the meaning of their articles is at times obscure.

serve that the expectation measure is mutually desirable for the parties. In Shavell (1980b) I first stress the mutual desirability of moderate damage measures for the contracting parties themselves and the role of damage measures as implicit substitutes for more complete contracts, and I also first analyze damage measures and incentives to rely.[26]

7.   SPECIFIC PERFORMANCE AS THE REMEDY FOR BREACH OF CONTRACT

7.1 Specific performance defined.   As observed at the outset, an alternative to use of a damage measure for breach of contract is specific performance: requiring a party to satisfy his contractual obligation. The interpretation of specific performance depends on the nature of the contractual obligation. Usually, specific performance refers to obligations to deliver a good or to perform a service, in which case it means that exactly that must be done.[27] If the contractual obligation is to pay a given amount, such as for an insurance company to pay coverage to an insured, then the meaning of specific performance is the payment of money. Specific performance can be accomplished with a sufficiently high threat, or by exercise of the state's police powers, such as by a sheriff forcibly removing a person from the land that he promised to convey to another. Note too that if a monetary penalty can be employed to induce performance, then specific performance is equivalent to a damage measure with a high level of damages.

7.2 Incentives to perform and specific performance.   What I said earlier about damage measures bears on the desirability of specific performance.

Specific performance is desirable for completely specified contracts. If con-

26. On remedies for breach, see the surveys Edlin 1998, Shavell 1998, and the references cited in section 2 of Chapter 15.

27. Some economists, however, have employed "specific performance" in an unconventional sense: They would say that a contract to make something is specifically performed even if the seller breaches, provided that the contract names a liquidated damage amount that the seller pays (because then the seller is doing exactly what the contract requires).

tracts are completely specified, then parties want them adhered to, so that specific performance is a desirable remedy for breach, because it means that there will be no breach. In the example concerning the desk, the seller would be required, under specific performance, to make the desk whenever the production cost would be less than $1,000—but only then, as I emphasized. Specific performance would never constitute a burden for the performing party because any difficult contingency (such as production cost exceeding $1,000) would have been included in the contract and the provision for it would have allowed the party not to perform.

Specific performance is usually undesirable for incomplete contracts. If contracts are incomplete, then, for the reasons given favoring moderate damage measures, specific performance would not be desired by the parties. In the example of the desk, specific performance would lead the maker of the desk to construct it when the production cost exceeded $1,000, regardless of the magnitude of production cost. This would lower the value of the contract to the two parties. Thus, like very high damage measures, specific performance would not be what the parties would want as a remedy for breach.

Qualifications. Nevertheless, there are circumstances in which specific performance will be desirable for the parties, as will be explained in Chapters 15 and 16. One important situation concerns cases where courts would have difficulty in estimating the value of performance, meaning, among other things, that if a damage measure were employed, there would be a danger that breach would occur when performance would be in the mutual interests of the parties; use of specific performance would avoid this danger. Yet specific performance might result in the problem of excessive performance stressed above. That problem, though, will be mitigated in some circumstances, especially because of the possibility of renegotiation of contracts (see later). Thus, and as will be seen, the details of the argument suggesting that specific performance may be desirable as a means of inducing mutually desirable performance are somewhat subtle (see section 1 of Chapter 16).

7.3 Incentives to rely; risk-bearing. It is obvious that specific performance supplies parties strong incentives to rely on performance, so that this is generally a positive aspect of specific performance (again, though, see the discussion later for details).

With regard to risk-bearing, specific performance imposes large risks on sellers if, as is often the case, they might face very large costs of performance. When so, specific performance would frequently be mutually undesirable on grounds of risk-bearing; the parties would not choose it as the remedy for breach just on that ground, as the seller would charge more for bearing that risk than the buyer would be willing to pay. There are circumstances, however, in which the risk-bearing implications of specific performance are not onerous for the seller. Notably, and as mentioned in section 6.5, suppose that the seller might want to commit breach not because he faces high costs of performance, but rather because he encounters another party who would pay much more for his product or possession or for his service; then specific performance would not impose a cost on him, but merely deny him a positive opportunity.

7.4 Ability to enforce.   The ability of courts to enforce specific performance depends on the type of contractual obligation. If the obligation is to perform a service or make something, then enforcement means requiring a person to undertake particular actions, and thus may entail special difficulties, especially if the person is recalcitrant. If the obligation is to convey a material thing, such as a painting or land, then specific performance does not involve that difficulty, but does require that the thing be located (unless it is land) and for it to be taken from the holder and given to the buyer. Another point of note is that enforcement of specific performance does not require, as damage measures do, that the assets of the party in breach be found and that he be forced to pay, because the police powers of the state are used directly to force performance.[28]

8.   RENEGOTIATION OF CONTRACTS

8.1 Reasons why renegotiation may or may not occur.   Heretofore, the possibility that contracts might be renegotiated when difficulties occur has not been explicitly considered, but the possibility often arises. For example, if construction cost is high relative to the value of performance, and

---

28. For economic analysis of specific performance and its comparison to damage remedies, see Bishop 1985, Kronman 1978b, Schwartz 1979, Shavell 1984a, and Ulen 1984. (Specific performance is also examined in many of the articles cited in Chapter 15.)

the damage measure would induce seller performance, might not the seller renegotiate with the buyer and pay him to be allowed not to perform? There are appealing reasons to consider such renegotiation to be likely, the main ones being that, having made an initial contract, the parties know of each other's existence, will usually be aware of each other's locations, and will be cognizant of many particulars of the contractual situation that would make renegotiation mutually beneficial.[29]

Before discussing the implications of renegotiation, however, let me briefly note why renegotiation may not occur. One reason is simply that, when difficulties are experienced, one party might benefit from acting quickly but not be in contact with the other, and arranging immediate renegotiation might be costly. A producer might benefit from acting quickly because, for instance, a problem may occur during production and the producer may have to decide on the spot whether to abort the process or proceed at greater cost. Or a new bid may be heard and have to be immediately answered.

A second reason why renegotiation may not transpire, or more exactly, may not succeed, is that even if the parties are in contact with one another, asymmetric information between them may lead to breakdowns in bargaining.

Another reason why renegotiation may not occur is that it may be impossible to alter the outcome: Rather than a breach being the result of a party's decision that can be modified—such as whether the seller conveys a painting in his possession to the buyer—breach may be the result of a *past* decision of the party that cannot be undone—such as whether the seller took precautions to prevent one of his employees from selling the painting to another person.[30] If the breach event cannot be undone, then the issue of renegotiation of the contract is obviously rendered moot.

Despite these reasons why renegotiation may not result in a new contract, let us presume in the remainder of this section that when difficulties

29. For this reason, much of the economics literature on contracts assumes that renegotiation always occurs when outcomes that are not mutually beneficial would otherwise result; see, for example, Hart 1987, Hart and Holmström 1987, and Rogerson 1984.

30. Suppose the seller is a dealer and he failed to issue clear instructions to his personnel not to sell the painting. Thus, the breach may be said to occur as a probabilistic result of an action (issuing of inadequate instructions by the dealer). Such situations in which breach is a probabilistic result of actions are an important category of case.

arise and a mutually beneficial renegotiated contract exists in principle, it will be made.

8.2 Renegotiation and contractual performance. If contracts will be renegotiated when difficulties arise, then performance of contracts will occur whenever that would be mutually beneficial, despite the incompleteness of contracts.

Let me illustrate with the example of the production contract for the desk worth $1,000, and recall the statement that in a completely specified contract, the parties would have specified performance when production cost is less than $1,000 but not when it is more. Suppose, though, that the contract does not mention any contingencies and, initially, assume that the remedy for breach is specific performance. Then, in the absence of renegotiation, the seller would be led to make the desk when production cost exceeds $1,000 as well as when production cost is less than $1,000. But the contract would be renegotiated whenever the production cost exceeds $1,000. For instance, if the cost would be $1,500, the seller could pay the buyer $1,250 for an agreement to allow him not to perform; this would be mutually beneficial because $1,250 exceeds the $1,000 value of performance to the buyer, and $1,250 is less than the production cost of performance for the seller.[31] A similar argument shows that when a contract with damages for breach would result in outcomes that differ from those in the completely specified contract, renegotiation would occur. Specifically, if the seller would be induced by the threat of high damages to perform when the production cost exceeds the value of performance, an agreement will be made in which the seller pays the buyer an amount less than damages and does not perform. And if the seller would be led to commit breach, because damages are low, when production cost is less than the value of performance, then an agreement will be reached in which the buyer pays the seller to induce him to perform.[32]

In general, whatever the degree of incompleteness of the contract, and whatever the remedy for breach, renegotiation will lead to performance exactly when that would have been stipulated in a mutually desirable completely specified contract. Therefore, renegotiation reduces the need for

31. Any amount between $1,000 and $1,500 would be mutually agreeable.
32 Examples are given in section 4 of Chapter 15.

complete contracts and serves as an implicit substitute for them.[33] (In this sense, renegotiation serves a purpose that is similar to damage measures.)

Qualification for financial contracts. The argument that renegotiation may reduce the need for complete contracts assumes that when a mutually desirable provision for a contingency is left out of a contract and the contingency at issue arises, there will be, at that time, a mutually desirable alteration in the contract. Thus, when the production cost exceeds $1,000 and the contract calls for production, there is a mutually desirable change in which the seller does not produce. If purely financial contracts are incomplete, however, there generally is *not* a mutually desirable change when unprovided-for contingencies arise. For example, suppose that a contract between two companies stipulates that costs in a joint venture should always be shared equally, but the contract is incomplete in that it does not state that less than half of the costs should be paid by a company if it finds itself in very bad financial straits, a term that might be mutually desirable. If an event of financial stress for a company occurs, there is no mutually beneficial alteration in the contract terms that can then be arranged, for any reduction in the amount that one company pays hurts the other company. Thus, renegotiation cannot ameliorate the problem of contractual incompleteness for financial contracts.

8.3 Renegotiation and reliance. The prospect of renegotiation affects the incentives of parties to invest in the contractual relationship, and quite possibly it will result in inadequate investment because of the ability of one party to hold up another in renegotiating the contract. Suppose that a buyer who wants a building completed for his business invests in training workers and advertising and then finds that he must renegotiate with the seller for performance. At that point, the price that the seller would obtain would reflect the value that the buyer would receive from performance, having made his reliance investment. The knowledge that his profits from

---

33. Indeed, if the only issue of importance between the parties was when performance would occur, one might think that there would be no need for any specifications in contracts if renegotiation were costless and perfect. It should be noted, in reflecting on this point, that any losses faced by a party due to renegotiation can be adjusted for in the contract price, so that renegotiation does not lead to any disadvantage or advantage, all things considered, in the renegotiated contract, at least for risk-neutral parties (I will discuss risk aversion later).

reliance investments will be partially extracted from him through renegotiation might lead the buyer not to rely to a desirable extent in the first place, lowering the value of the contractual enterprise for the parties.

This general point, however, needs to be qualified because renegotiation is influenced by, among other elements, the damage measure that applies for breach. As will be seen in Chapter 15, the damage measure, together with renegotiation, sometimes may ameliorate or correct the problem of inadequate reliance, and also could lead to excessive reliance.

8.4 Renegotiation and risk-bearing.   Renegotiation of contracts has implications for risk-bearing. First, renegotiation tends to reduce risk for parties who make payments, for they would generally be worse off if they did not make these payments; if a seller who would otherwise face very high production costs pays to escape his production obligation, his risk is thereby reduced. But the uncertainty in the amounts that will be paid when contracts are renegotiated, because these amounts are not set in advance, implies that risk remains when contracts are renegotiated. To reduce the risk associated with contracts that will have to be renegotiated, parties can employ damage measures that lead to mutually beneficial behavior and/or more fully specify contractual terms.

8.5 Costliness of renegotiation.   Another point about renegotiation obviously is its cost, and several remarks about that are worth making. First, if one views writing an explicit term about a difficulty as an alternative to renegotiation over it, one is comparing the ex ante, sure cost of negotiating about the term to the ex post cost of renegotiating about it. Thus, if the negotiation and renegotiation costs are equal, the fact that the renegotiation cost is incurred only with a probability would make renegotiation preferable on grounds of expected cost (although the cost of renegotiation might not be equal—it could, for instance, be higher if the parties have to locate one another). Second, if one views a properly chosen damage measure as an alternative to renegotiation for the purpose of ensuring desirable performance, then the cost comparison between damage measures and renegotiation is one that arises only when a problematic contingency in question arises. It might be thought that damage measures involve less cost for parties than renegotiation, for if the damage measure is properly selected, it will automatically result in correct performance (either inducing performance, or leading to breach and payment of damages, usually after a settlement rather than litigation). But the damage measure that leads to proper performance (the expectation measure, as mentioned earlier, and as will be discussed in Chapter 15) may not be employed for one reason or another, in which case renegotiation will sometimes occur under the damage measure.

8.6 Desirability of enforcement of renegotiated contracts. One suspects that in most situations it is desirable for renegotiated contracts to be enforced. That is, prospectively, parties who make a contract will be made better off if they know that, should they renegotiate their contract, the modified contract will then be enforced. This is the case with our example of the contract for production of a desk worth $1,000 to the buyer and calling for specific performance; for if the parties know that the contract will be renegotiated when the production cost exceeds $1,000 and that the renegotiated contract will be enforced, then in effect performance will be exactly what the parties would want and arrange for in a completely specified contract. Yet they save the time and trouble of writing such a contract and can rely on renegotiation to cure problems if they arise. It is for such reasons that the enforcement of renegotiated arrangements is usually a good thing ex ante for contracting parties, and the law tends to enforce renegotiated contracts.[34]

For somewhat subtle reasons, however, it is not always true that the enforcement of renegotiated contracts will help the parties prospectively.[35]

34. Indeed, it is easily shown that enforcing renegotiated contracts must raise the expected utility of each contracting party to the original contract if the only effect of renegotiation in a contingency is to raise the expected utility of each party in *that* contingency: Formally, if $U(\theta)$ is the expected utility of a party under the initial contract given contingency θ, and allowing renegotiated contracts in a particular contingency θ' only has the effect of raising $U(\theta')$ but does not affect $U(\theta)$ for other θ, then allowing renegotiated contracts must raise $\int U(\theta)f(\theta)d\theta$, the expected utility of the party.

35. A case in point is provided by Fudenberg and Tirole 1990. They investigate a contract between a risk-averse agent and a risk-neutral principal, where the agent's effort is unobservable (so cannot be included in the contract) and output is a probabilistic function of agent effort. For example, the crop yield may be a function of the effort of a farmer (the agent) in planting and fertilizing and of weather (which is probabilistic). The original contract might specify that the farmer's pay depend substantially on the yield, in order to give him an incentive to devote effort to the crop. If the contract can be renegotiated, however, the two parties will have an incentive to do that *after* the farmer has sown the crops, for at that

This suggests that a desirable policy for courts to adopt is to enforce renegotiated contracts unless parties originally stated that the contract was not renegotiable. This policy would lead parties to specify as irrevocable contracts that they do not want renegotiated, but courts do not ordinarily allow that to be done.[36]

Note on the literature. The subject of renegotiation of contracts was analyzed initially by Rogerson (1984) and Shavell (1984a); and then, beginning with Hart (1987), Hart and Moore (1988), and Hart and Holmström (1987), it has been investigated in a more general setting that has led to substantial theoretical development.[37]

9. LEGAL OVERRIDING OF CONTRACTS

9.1 Harmful externalities. A basic rationale for legislative or judicial overriding of contracts is the existence of harmful externalities. Contracts that are likely to harm third parties are often not enforced, for example, agreements to commit crimes, price-fixing compacts, liability insurance policies against fines, and sales contracts for certain goods (such as for machine guns).

In such cases, the harm to third parties must tend to exceed the benefits of a contract to the parties themselves for it to be socially desirable not to enforce a contract. Thus, a contract between musical performers and a person who wants to have a party might cause some disturbance to neighbors who would prefer to enjoy a quiet evening, but if the disturbance is not great, the contract would on net be socially beneficial.[38]

---

juncture he can be protected against risk and his effort is determined. But anticipation of this renegotiation will undermine the farmer's initial incentives to devote effort to the crop. Hence, preventing renegotiation will be beneficial to these parties. Note that in this case, the crucial assumption of the previous footnote does not hold: By affecting effort, renegotiation affects the well-being of parties in *many* contingencies, not just in a particular contingency.

36. For an economic and legal analysis of the possible undesirability of enforcement of renegotiated agreements, see Jolls 1997 and the literature cited therein.

37. See in particular the references and discussion in section 4 of Chapter 15.

38. Moreover, virtually any contract may cause some external harm (denying other potential contracting parties the opportunity to contract with the parties to the contract in

9.2 Losses in welfare to the contracting parties.   Another general rationale for nonenforcement of contracts is to prevent a loss in welfare to one or both of the contracting parties. This concern may motivate nonenforcement when a party lacks relevant information, such as when a person buys food that is mislabeled or purchases a security that is not correctly described and as a result is made worse off by the transaction. Similarly, an incompetent person or a child might agree to a contract that makes him or her worse off, and transactions by such individuals are generally not enforceable.

The rationale for nonenforcement that parties would sometimes be made worse off by enforcement also may apply in the context of contract interpretation. As discussed in section 5, interpretation may amount to overriding terms of contracts (such as a term that simply says the contract should be performed), and still increase the welfare of both parties to the contract by making the contract more like a mutually beneficial completely specified contract.[39]

9.3 Inalienability; paternalism.   Two other rationales that are offered for not enforcing contracts may be noted. One is that contracts sometimes are not enforced because they involve the sale of things that are said to be inalienable, such as human organs, babies, and voting rights. It seems, however, that when the justification of inalienability is adduced, one or both of the previous two rationales, externality and losses in welfare to the parties themselves, usually apply (perhaps in subtle form).[40] For example, the sale of human organs might be thought undesirable because some individuals will sell their own organs (such as kidneys) without realizing the detrimental consequences to themselves (that is, the contracting parties will be made worse off due to a problem of lack of information); because some individuals will not receive the care they otherwise would and will die earlier than necessary in order for their organs to be harvested (the contracting

---

question), yet because the harm is generally less than the benefits to the parties, the contracts are desirable to enforce.

39. Additionally, at least in theory, nonenforcement of contracts might also be beneficial to parties where they would be led to include terms constituting wasteful signals of unobservable characteristics. See Aghion and Hermalin 1990.

40. See generally Rose-Ackerman 1985 and Trebilcock 1993.

parties will be made worse off on account of the contract-induced behavior of others); and because the very existence of the market will be understood by individuals as eroding norms of respect for human life (a species of harmful psychological externality), where these norms are themselves welfare-enhancing because they reduce violence and encourage beneficial behavior. When the inalienability justification is used, in other words, it is often really a stand-in for a set of such factors as these, either factors that lower the well-being of parties to the contracts or harmful externalities.

Similarly, contracts are sometimes not enforced because of paternalism, such as when a person is not allowed to purchase certain drugs or a child is not allowed to buy pornographic material. This rationale, like that of inalienability, seems usually to be reducible to the two previous rationales concerning externalities and harm to the contracting parties themselves. If a person is not allowed to purchase drugs, the justification may lie in the possibility that he or she does not understand the true properties of the drugs, or that using them (suppose they are addictive) may result in problems for third parties.

9.4 State's ability to prevent undesirable contracts.   The state often will not experience any difficulty in preventing the making of undesirable contracts, for all it need do is refuse to enforce them. Consider, for example, a socially undesirable contract between an insurer and an insured that covers fines of some type. For the insured to collect against an insurer who refuses to pay, he must bring a suit, and if the courts will not enforce the contract, then the insured will not be able to collect. Hence, the insured will never make the contract in the first place. Thus, as long as the courts are needed to enforce contracts, the contracts will not be made, and the state does not need to police the actual making of contracts and root out the undesirable ones.

10.   EXTRA-LEGAL MEANS OF CONTRACT ENFORCEMENT

Although I have assumed generally that state-authorized courts enforce contracts, other means of contract enforcement should be mentioned.

10.1 Private adjudication. Another avenue for enforcement of contracts is use of private adjudicators, such as are provided by arbitration organizations and some trade organizations.[41] Private adjudication can be superior for the parties because they can select adjudicators who have specific knowledge of the contractual context (often, industry-specific knowledge) and because they can choose the procedures to be followed (notably, they can simplify adjudication and save expense). Such opportunities are not open to those who go to the courts. For these reasons, it seems to be socially desirable for the courts generally to enforce the findings of private adjudicators, and this is in fact usually done.[42] (If private adjudication is employed where contracts would have harmful external effects, however, it would obviously not be desirable for courts to enforce the private adjudicative findings.)

10.2 Reputation. It is a commonplace that the fear of harm to reputation can induce parties to adhere to contracts. In principle, this reputational factor could lead to the same enforcement of contracts that we imagine to occur in courts. But that is unlikely for two reasons.

First, courts resolve disputes by taking into account much information about contractual situations, and probably more information than would tend to be reflected in parties' reputations. For example, if a person commits a breach, the court-awarded damages would often take into account all manner of factors relating to the victim's loss, whereas the effect of the breach on the person's reputation would be unlikely to be calibrated so well to the loss. Or, if a party wants his contract interpreted by the court in accordance with what would be provided in a completely specified contract, say such as to excuse him due to problems he is facing, the courts might do that knowing his true situation, but would his excuse be recognized generally, such that he would escape a reputational penalty?

Second, information aside, the reputational incentives of parties to adhere to their contracts may not be sufficient to induce that. Imagine a party who is not going to be transacting very often and whose transactions usually will be relatively modest in scope, but who is presently a party to a very

41. The subject of private adjudication is discussed more generally in section 1 of Chapter 19.

42. See Goldberg, Sander, and Rogers 1999, 235–236, 244–248.

large contract that it would benefit him greatly to breach. He may well rationally do so, paying little or nothing in damages, despite a loss to his reputation.

Thus, although reputation can help to enforce contracts, it will generally be an imperfect substitute for courts, both because it only crudely reflects reality and because its sanctions are less effective. Nevertheless, reputation is often a cheaper means of enforcement of contracts. Indeed, in many contexts, litigation costs are high enough to make court proceedings not worthwhile, so that only reputation can enforce contracts.[43]

43. See, for example, Bernstein 1992, 1998, Charny 1990, Greif 1998, and Klein and Leffler 1981.

14 ||| CONTRACT FORMATION

In this chapter I consider various issues concerning the formation of contracts.

1. SEARCH EFFORT

An important aspect of contract formation is the effort individuals devote to it—the time and resources they expend searching for and investigating contractual opportunities. I will begin our investigation of contract formation with a comparison of the socially ideal and the privately desired degree of search effort.

It is socially optimal for a person to search as long as the social benefit of search exceeds the cost to him. The social benefit of search over some time period by the person is the expected value of any contract made by that person and his contracting partner *minus* the expected value of any contract that was prevented because the person's contracting partner became unavailable for contracting with someone else (if A, who is searching, contracts with B, then B may be prevented from contracting with C).

The private incentive to search for a contract may diverge from the socially optimal incentive for two different, and countervailing, reasons. On one hand, a person who searches will be led to do so only by the return that he himself makes from concluding contracts; he will not count as a negative any benefit that society forgoes because he keeps certain others from making contracts. This suggests that too much effort is devoted by individuals to search for contracting partners. (Here finding a contracting partner is similar to catching a fish, which denies another fisherman the opportunity to catch the fish; see section 1.3 of Chapter 4.)

On the other hand (and putting to the side the possibility that when one contract is made another contract may be prevented), when a person makes a contract with someone, he usually obtains only a part of the surplus thereby created—it is divided between the two parties through the contract price. This means that the private return from making a contract is less than the social return. For instance, a contract that creates $100 of surplus would create only $50 of profit for each party if they split the surplus. As a consequence, the privately motivated degree of search could fall short of the socially optimal.

The conclusion, therefore, is that there may be, on net, either too much or too little search for contracts, depending on circumstances. If the first factor, that contract formation by one party tends to deny others from making contracts, is dominant, then search effort will tend to be socially excessive; if the second factor, that the return from making a contract is less than the surplus that that contract itself creates, is dominant, then search activity will tend to be socially inadequate.[1]

The nature of the comparison between the private and the socially

---

1. To illustrate, consider a simple situation in which a person decides on the amount of effort e to devote to search for a contract partner. There is one suitable partner, whom the person will discover with probability $p(e)$, where p is increasing in e. If the person discovers the partner, a contract will be made, resulting in surplus s, and the person will obtain a fraction α of this, so his net payoff from search will be $p(e)\alpha s - e$. If the person does not find the partner, the partner will make a contract with another party, and that will produce surplus t. The socially optimal amount of search is determined by maximizing the social payoff, $p(e)(s - t) - e$, since the social payoff to the person's finding the partner is $s - t$. Clearly, the person will search too much if $\alpha s > s - t$, and will search too little if $\alpha s < s - t$. Both of these possibilities arise in Diamond and Maskin 1979, who examine a specific model of search and contracting. Their model takes into account a complexity not mentioned in the text: that the contract price and net payoff from search will reflect to some degree the possibility of a party concluding a contract with other partners. For instance, if a seller knows that he might sell to a buyer other than the one with whom he decides to contract, he will tend to charge a higher price to that buyer. This effect lowers the buyer's anticipated return from

desirable degree of search effort raises questions about whether social authorities could obtain the information needed to formulate corrective policy. In any case, overt policies to alter search effort do not seem to exist.

2. FUNDAMENTAL RULE OF RECOGNITION OF CONTRACTS: MUTUAL ASSENT

The basic rule of legal recognition of contracts is that a contract is deemed valid if and only if both parties give a clear indication of assent, such as signing their names on a document.[2] This rule involving mutual assent has the two fundamental private and social virtues mentioned in section 2 of Chapter 13.

First, the fact that mutual assent is *sufficient* for a contract to be recognized, and that the two parties naturally have the power each to give assent, allows them to make enforceable contracts when they so desire. Further, their knowledge that they have in fact consummated a legally recognized contract allows parties to stop searching and immediately to engage in actions that will raise the value of the contract, such as hiring workers and buying materials for production.

Second, the fact that mutual assent is *required* for a contract to be recognized means that no party will become obligated unless he wishes that. This in turn is desirable for parties, and socially desirable, because it fosters search and negotiation for contracts. If a party were somehow to become legally obligated against his will, as a result of search and/or negotiation alone, then these activities would be curtailed, and the degree and quality of contracting would suffer.

It may be noted, however, that despite the usual requirement that mutual assent is necessary for contract formation, certain legal doctrines sometimes result in parties becoming contractually bound without having given their assent. This may occur when a party is led to make significant efforts or investments in anticipation of contract formation.[3] This legal policy not

---

search, and thus implicitly makes the buyer take into partial account the fact that when he makes a contract, he denies others the opportunity to do so.

2. See, for example, Calamari and Perillo 1998, 25, and E. Farnsworth 1999, 10–11.

3. See Bebchuk and Ben-Shahar 2001, 424, on the United States, and Wils 1993, 122–130, on civil-law countries.

only may result in a chilling of search effort, it may also induce wasteful early investment as a strategy to achieve contract formation.[4]

3. OFFER AND ACCEPTANCE

Mutual assent sometimes is not simultaneous; one party will make an offer and time will pass before the other agrees. This is of interest for several reasons, and I will discuss two prominent ones.

The first is that delay may occur between offer and acceptance because the offeree (the party to whom the offer is made) wants to investigate the offer. The information an offeree seeks might concern, for instance, the quality of the neighborhood in which a house offered for sale is located. The offeree's desire for information raises the issue of how long, and the circumstances under which, the offeror will want to be held to his offer, and whether he should be held to it. Suppose that an offeror is held to his terms, say that he offers to sell a house at the price of $100,000. Then an offeree will often be led to invest effort in investigating contractual opportunities, for he will know he can purchase the house at the named price. If, however, the price can be changed, the offeree might fear that if he comes back and expresses serious interest after investigation, the offeror will then raise the price, say to $125,000. The anticipation of such offeror advantage-taking would reduce offerees' incentives to engage in investigation and thus might undesirably diminish contract formation. Hence, it may often be both in offerors' and society's interests for offered terms to be enforced for some period of time. Yet offerors' circumstances may change, making it privately and socially advantageous for them to alter contract terms and thus, among other things, to hold open an offer only for a limited amount of time. In the light of these observations, it is not surprising that the law generally enforces the terms of offers that parties make, including the time during which an offer is intended to be effective.

4. It is true that early investment is sometimes efficient, and a number of articles find that some form of liability may be desirable to induce precontractual investment; see Bebchuk and Ben-Shahar 2001, Craswell 1996, and Wils 1993. A party who wants to make such early investment, however, could attempt to advance the time of contract formation or could make a preliminary contract that compensates him for his investment, whether or not a final contract is made.

A second reason for a delay between offer and acceptance is simply that the two parties are not physically proximate and therefore that it takes time for the offeror's message to be sent and for the offeree's response to be received. In this regard, two alternative legal rules generally govern contract formation: the so-called *mailbox rule,* under which an acceptance is legally recognized at the time that the offeree sends a message of acceptance (such as by putting it in the mailbox), and the *receipt rule,* under which an acceptance is recognized only at the time that the acceptance is received by the offeror, provided that he has not made another contract in the interim. Under the mailbox rule, early reliance by the offeree is promoted relative to reliance under the receipt rule, for the offeree is assured that there is a contract from the time that he sends an acceptance message. Further, the offeror is not encouraged to make alternative contracts until he hears from the offeree or sends him a message revoking his offer. Which rule will be the superior depends substantially on whether it is more valuable to promote early reliance by the offeree or freedom to make alternative contracts for the offeror. (For example, if the offeror is unlikely to be in contact with other potential contracting partners, but the offeree is likely to hear of many opportunities that he might have to act upon quickly, the mailbox rule would seem superior.) In any event, the adoption of a definite rule will prevent the taking of wasteful actions in a mistaken belief by either of the parties that a contract has or has not been made.[5]

4. FRAUD

A contract that is regarded as fraudulent generally will not be legally recognized even though it meets the usual requirements for validity.[6] Such a contract involves actions taken to deceive a party to the contract about information relevant to its value, notably, about the quality and character

---

5. For a summary of the law of offer and acceptance, see, for example, Calamari and Perillo 1998, 25–117, and E. Farnsworth 1999, 109–222. For economic analysis of offer and acceptance, emphasizing aspects of reliance, see Craswell 1996, Katz 1990b, 1996; see also Katz 1993.

6. See, for example, Calamari and Perillo 1998, 325–326, and E. Farnsworth 1999, 260–264.

of the contracted-for good or service or about the price. For example, the seller of a car may hide rust spots, the seller of a restaurant may doctor its sales records, or the buyer of a parcel of land may pay with securities that are worthless.

Fraud is socially undesirable for several obvious reasons.[7] First, efforts taken to carry it out are economically sterile. If the seller of a restaurant falsifies the records to show that it had more business than it actually did have, the resources devoted to this task are a waste, because they do not produce anything of direct value to anyone. Second, efforts made to detect fraud, such as by suspicious buyers of restaurants, also constitute a waste, and such efforts are made in a world with fraud, so are an indirect social cost of fraud. Third, to the extent that fraud is successful, it may result in inefficient actions (hiring more staff for the restaurant that will not in fact have many customers) and in poor matches between contracting partners.

By refusing to enforce contracts that were formed using fraudulent methods, the law discourages fraud. Thus, this aspect of the law of contract formation is socially desirable.

5. MISTAKE

A contract may involve a mistake in the sense that one side knows that the other side does not understand some relevant point about the contract. For example, a seller of a building that is not zoned for business might learn that the buyer believes it to be so zoned, or the buyer of furniture might realize that its price has been mismarked to a tenth of its normal level. (It is assumed here that the lack of information of the mistaken party comes about through his lack of precautions, not through the deceptive effort of the other party. That is what distinguishes fraud from mistake.)

In such situations, allowing the contracts that are made to be enforced has two social disadvantages compared to negating the contracts. First, the making of such mistaken contracts may result in socially inefficient use of resources, like the purchase of a building by someone who wants to use it for business purposes but who cannot really use it for that. (Note too that

---

7. The social welfare criterion that is implicitly under consideration here is the value of things to those who use them minus costs involved in transactions.

if the person purchases the building, learns that it cannot be used by him and resells it, transaction costs will have been needlessly incurred.) Second, the fear that one might lose by failing to notice one's mistake may lead to the taking of excessive precautions to reduce the likelihood of mistake. Rather than so inducing parties to reduce the likelihood of mistake, it may be preferable for society to harness the information that turns out to exist about the occurrence of mistake, by doing what the law does—refusing to enforce contracts that are mistakenly made.[8]

6.   INFORMATION DISCLOSURE

When contracts are formed, parties often possess private information that is relevant to the contract. For example, the seller of a house may know that the basement leaks when there is a heavy rain, the seller of a commodity may have information about the future course of commodity prices, and the buyer of a parcel of land may have information about its oil-bearing potential. The existence of such private information raises the question of whether parties should be obligated to disclose what they know when they make contracts.[9] In fact the law sometimes requires disclosure and sometimes does not.[10]

6.1 Effects of disclosure obligations.   Let us first discuss the effects of disclosure requirements. The direct effects of disclosure obligations are the transmission of information that otherwise would not have been forthcoming, and accompanying changes in prices. In the absence of a disclosure

8. This section discusses what is known as a unilateral mistake, because only one party has made a mistake; on the relevant law, see, for example, Calamari and Perillo 1998, 354–356, and E. Farnsworth 1999, 631–637. Not discussed is the subject of mutual mistake, such as where both parties believe that a cow that is sold is barren but in fact it is not. This subject raises different issues, including incentives to obtain information, and is beyond our scope. On economic analysis of mistake, see Rasmusen and Ayres 1993, and Smith and Smith 1990.

9. It may be noticed that in cases of fraud and (unilateral) mistake, just discussed, one side possesses private information, so the present case would seem to have a relationship to the previous cases. I will comment further on that in section 6.3.

10. See, for example, Calamari and Perillo 1998, 325–347.

requirement, sellers will tend not to disclose unfavorable information—such as that the basement of a home leaks—because this information would tend to lower the price; thus a disclosure requirement results in revelation of unfavorable information by sellers and lower prices.[11] Similarly, buyers will not disclose favorable information in the absence of disclosure requirements, for that would tend to raise the price that they would have to pay. For example, the buyer of a commodity that he knows is likely to go up in price would have to pay a higher price if he revealed that information, and a disclosure obligation would cause that to occur.

There is also an indirect effect of disclosure obligations: the dulling of incentives to acquire information before the making of contracts. If the buyer of the commodity has to disclose his information, he will have less incentive to invest in determining the likely future commodity price because he will have to pay a higher price if his information is positive; if a seller has to divulge the result of an appraisal, the value to him of an appraisal will fall, for he will have to accept a lower than usual price if the appraisal is below expectations.

It should be observed that this indirect effect is moot when information is naturally in the possession of a party. For example, we would expect a homeowner to know automatically whether his basement leaks; he will know this by virtue of living in the home. Likewise, if information comes to a party adventitiously, for free, there cannot be an effect of a disclosure obligation on the party's possession of the information.

6.2 Social desirability of disclosure obligations. The social desirability, or lack thereof, of disclosure obligations depends in a somewhat complex way on a number of factors. Three important ones will now be outlined.[12]

---

11. A complexity in determining the effect of a disclosure requirement is that, in the absence of a requirement, silence about something (such as whether there is a leaky basement) might lead to a rational negative inference (that there is a leaky basement). But rational inference from silence will generally leave parties with some uncertainty about the truth for a variety of reasons (for example, silence about whether there is a termite problem might mean only that the homeowner never tested for termites, not that he has something to hide). On inferences from silence, see, originally, Grossman 1981 and Milgrom 1981, and see also Gertner 1998, Fishman and Hagerty 1990, Okuno-Fujiwara, Postlewaite, and Suzumura 1990, and Shavell 1994.

12. The social welfare criterion employed here is the value of things to people, minus any costs involved in transactions, minus costs of acquiring information.

Whether the buyer or the seller possesses information. The appeal of requiring disclosure is stronger when sellers possess information than when buyers do, for the simple reason that it is buyers who typically can make socially valuable use of information. Thus, it is desirable that the seller of a house tell the buyer about the leaky basement so that the buyer will not store valuables there or can fix the problem. By contrast, it is not necessary for the buyer of land who has information about its mineral-bearing potential to divulge this to the seller for the information to be put to use, for the buyer of the land will be the party who extracts the minerals.[13]

Whether incentives to acquire information would be undesirably reduced. Because the incentives to acquire information are diluted by the obligation to disclose, disclosure obligations may sometimes be socially undesirable. If incentives of parties to appraise the mineral-bearing potential of land were negated by the obligation to disclose findings, such obligations would be undesirable. Indeed, this point was emphasized in a case in which a company undertook an aerial survey to determine the mineral-bearing potential of land and bought mineral rights to the land without divulging that information to the seller. It was suggested that the company would not have spent money on the aerial survey—and the minerals that were found would not have been discovered—had the company anticipated that it would have to report on its findings to sellers.[14]

But several important qualifying points should be made about this argument against disclosure obligations. One is that the incentives to invest in acquisition of information may be socially excessive if there is no obligation to disclose,[15] and certainly that will be the case if the information is not socially valuable in the first place (see later). A second factor is that the dulling of incentives tends to be less serious for sellers than for buyers, because sellers can obtain in bargaining some of the enhanced value from

13. This presumes that an agreement is made. If the buyer fails to conclude an agreement, and never divulges what he knows, then another buyer may be ignorant of the minerals on the land, whereas he would be informed if the seller were told, for the seller would then inform any other buyer in order to obtain a higher price for the land.

14. See Kronman 1978a, 20–21, and his discussion of a case involving the Texas Gulf Sulfur company.

15. It can be shown in a natural model of information acquisition that, in the absence of the requirement to divulge information, private incentives to obtain information will be excessive. But requiring that information be divulged may, as stressed in the text, result in insufficient incentives to invest in information.

information. A seller who learns that his land has valuable minerals can charge for the extra profit that can be made from the minerals; whereas if a potential buyer has to reveal this information, he cannot benefit from it assuming that, once the buyer has divulged it, the seller could refuse a deal and find another buyer who could extract the minerals.

Of course, there may be no effect on incentives to acquire information, as noted above. In the case of the leaky basement that would be true, so that a disclosure requirement about that information for the seller of the home would not detrimentally affect the acquisition of that information; he would have it regardless.

Whether information is socially valuable or merely has private value. Some information has social value in the sense that it can be used by someone to enhance the value of something. For instance, knowledge that the basement of a house is leaky has social value because, as stated, the person who comes to live in the house can take precautions not to store things in the basement or can have it repaired. Likewise, information about the mineral-bearing potential of land can be used to extract the minerals. Some information, though, has low or, in principle, no social value, even though it has definite private value. For example, advance information that the commodity price is going to rise due to a fungus that will reduce the supply of the commodity might have little social value if nothing productive can be done with that information, yet the information might have significant private value because of the profits from price changes that can be made from it. Where information has low social value, its costly acquisition should be discouraged, suggesting the desirability of requiring its disclosure. (Note that this is so even though there may be no intrinsic value in disclosure itself.)[16]

6.3 Comment on the relationship to fraud and mistake. Situations of fraud and mistake are similar to those considered here in that they also involve asymmetry of information. But here, unlike with fraud and mistake,

16. The general subject of the economic analysis of legal disclosure requirements relating to contracts is addressed in Kronman 1978a and Shavell 1994; for an empirical study, see Mathios 2000. Kronman originally emphasized the possibility that requirements might dull incentives to acquire information, but did not take into account the distinctions made in the text and in Shavell 1994 between buyers and sellers and between socially valuable and only privately valuable information.

it is sometimes desirable to allow a party to the contract not to disclose information. The main reason for the difference in conclusion is that in the context of this section, inducing acquisition of information may be socially desirable. In the context of fraud and mistake, however, allowing nondisclosure (that is, allowing fraud and allowing mistakes to go uncorrected) can only lead to socially undesirable effects, namely, to efforts to perpetrate fraud and to defensive efforts against fraud and mistake.

7. DURESS

It may happen in contractual situations that a party is in duress or finds himself in an emergency of some type. For example, a ship may be sinking and need to be saved and pulled to harbor by another vessel, or a person may be at the airport during a snowstorm and need a taxi to attend a very important business meeting. In such cases, the party under duress would be willing to make a contract under particularly disadvantageous terms. Let us evaluate the desirability of a legal rule that refuses to recognize certain contracts made under duress. In fact, the law generally refuses to enforce contracts made under duress.[17]

7.1 Induced duress.   Suppose first that situations of duress are engineered by other parties. For example, someone might direct an inexperienced sailor toward a dangerous area, and then, when he gets into trouble, come to his rescue, but only for a high price. It seems that in such situations of induced duress, it would be best not to enforce the contracts. If the contracts are not enforced, then the motive of parties to create situations of duress will be removed. Otherwise, social losses will arise: the effort made to engender the dangerous situations is a social waste, rescue effort is a social waste (since it would not be needed but for the induced occurrence of the dangerous situations), and, when rescue does not come about, serious harm can occur.

17. See, for example, Calamari and Perillo 1998, 308–321, and E. Farnsworth 1999, 264–276.

7.2 Naturally occurring duress. Now consider situations of duress that occur naturally, such as when ships get into trouble themselves and need rescue. Here there are still reasons for disallowing contracts in which rescuers, or more generally, contracting partners, obtain very high prices.

First, allowing exorbitant prices to be charged imposes risk on individuals, for they realize that should they find themselves in bad straits, they will have to pay a large amount to extricate themselves. Presuming that they are risk averse, they will be better off if the law provides them with an implicit insurance policy in the form of refusal to enforce contracts with onerous terms.

Second, risk aversion aside, allowing high prices for rescue might lead individuals to take excessive precautions in order to prevent the occurrence of situations in which they would need to be rescued. If it is in fact socially inexpensive to provide rescue to individuals in emergencies, then we would not want them taking extraordinary steps to prevent rescue situations from ever arising. Yet individuals would do that if they would have to pay extremely large amounts for rescue.[18]

An important qualification to these arguments is suggested by the example of rescue at sea, namely, that the likelihood of rescue may be affected by the contract amount; the higher the amount, the more vessels will be

---

18. To amplify, suppose that individuals who might be in duress and potential rescuers are risk neutral. Let x be an individual's effort to prevent a dangerous situation of duress from arising and $p(x)$ be the probability of such a situation, where $p'(x) < 0$ and $p''(x) > 0$. Suppose also that if duress arises, a potential rescuer's effort is y and $q(y)$ is the conditional probability of rescue, where $q'(y) > 0$ and $q''(y) < 0$. Let v be the individual's losses if rescue fails. The social object is to minimize expected effort plus losses: $x + p(x)[y + (1 - q(y))v]$. Let the optimal values of x and y be denoted x^* and y^*, and assume that they are positive. The optimal rescue effort clearly minimizes $[y + (1 - q(y))v]$, so satisfies $q'(y)v = 1$. The optimal effort to prevent duress thus satisfies $-p'(x)[y^* + (1 - q(y^*))v] = 1$. That is, the value of raising x is that it reduces the likelihood of *minimized* expected losses in the event of duress, which are less than v (because y^* minimizes $y + (1 - q(y))v$ over y, we know that $y^* + (1 - q(y^*))v < 0 + (1 - q(0))v \leq v$), and much less than v if the rescue likelihood $q(y^*)$ is high. Now suppose that an individual anticipates that if he is in duress, he will be led to agree to pay a high price to a potential rescuer, due to enforcement of contracts made at such times. In particular, suppose the rescue contract price is k, where $k > y^* + (1 - q(y^*))v$ (in fact, the individual in duress would be willing to pay as much as v). Since the individual will choose x to minimize $x + p(x)k$, where $k > y^* + (1 - q(y^*))v$, he will choose $x > x^*$.

willing to engage in rescue attempts and the greater the effort they will devote to an attempt.[19] This implies that in some cases it may be best for the law not to insist on low prices for enforcement of contracts, but to allow for premiums in prices to reflect the desirability of encouraging rescue.[20]

19. In the model of the previous note, it is assumed that rescue likelihood depends on rescue effort y. If the rescuer and the individual in duress cannot specify rescue effort in their contract, they will want payment to depend on the success of rescue effort, in which case, the higher the contract payment, the greater will be y. If the rescuer and the individual can contract on y, they will specify y^*. (This is consistent with the previous note, because the price k there can be interpreted as an expected contract price or a certain contract price.)

20. Two further points may be mentioned. One is that in many contexts, a modest payment will induce most of what can be done, and is optimal to do, to effect rescue. Thus, disallowing very high prices may have little effect on the rescue probability $q(y)$. Second, allowing high prices for rescue may lead to a socially excessive number of parties engaging in rescue activity (by the logic in section 1.3 of Chapter 4 leading to the conclusion that there is too much fishing activity). Both of these points suggest that the tradeoff between incentives to rescue and the disadvantages of high prices favors giving lesser weight to high prices. In any event, under admiralty and maritime law, contracts for salvage are enforced, but if the vessel was in an in extremis situation, courts often set aside the contracts if compensation is excessive; see, for example, Schoenbaum 2001, 846–847. On economic analysis of rescue and duress, see Landes and Posner 1978.

15 ||| PRODUCTION CONTRACTS

In this chapter, I will discuss a significant type of contract—that for production of a good (or for performance of a service).[1] The aim will be to develop a more detailed understanding of important themes emphasized in the overview of contracts in Chapter 13. In particular, I will consider here the nature of a completely specified contract, how damage measures serve as implicit substitutes for completely specified contracts, reliance activities, and renegotiation of contracts.[2]

1. COMPLETELY SPECIFIED CONTRACTS

1.1 Assumptions about the contractual situation. It will be supposed that there are two parties, a buyer and a seller, that the buyer places

---

1. For concreteness, I will usually refer to contracts for production of goods rather than for performance of services, even though the analysis of the two is the same.

2. In many respects, I will be using as a basis my articles Shavell 1980b, 1984a, but I will also be depending on numerous other articles, as I will note. See also the surveys Edlin 1998, Kaplow and Shavell 2002a, Mahoney 2000, Schwartz 1998, and Shavell 1998.

a value on having a customized good, and that the seller will need to produce the good.

In general, it will also be assumed that there are many sources of uncertainty that the two parties might face when they meet. The buyer might be uncertain about the value of the good to him (suppose it is a machine for production in his business, but the future demand he will face is uncertain). The seller might be uncertain about his production costs (material costs may rise unexpectedly, or unanticipated difficulties in the production process may arise), and the seller might be uncertain about whether another buyer will appear and bid more than the contract buyer for what he is producing. Mainly for expositional convenience, I will generally restrict attention to a situation with just one source of uncertainty—about the seller's production cost. But I will occasionally remark about conclusions under other sources of uncertainty.

The two parties will generally be assumed to be risk neutral; I will discuss the implications of their being risk averse in separate sections.

The contract price will be presumed to be paid at the time of performance. This assumption too is mainly one of convenience, and I will make occasional comments about the situation if payment is made at the outset or at different points of time.

1.2 Mutually beneficial completely specified contracts. A completely specified contract is a contract that contains a provision for each and every contingency. Under the simplifying assumption that there is only one source of uncertainty, a complete contract is a contract that provides explicitly for each possible level of production cost that the seller might encounter. Therefore, the contract states, for each possible production cost, whether or not the seller will perform.

A mutually beneficial contract, one may recall, is a contract that cannot be modified in a way that would make both parties better off. As was earlier noted, we would expect contracts to be mutually beneficial, because we would predict that if they could be modified so as to please both parties, that would happen. I now consider an example illustrating the fundamental point that *mutually beneficial completely specified contracts call for performance if and only if the value of performance exceeds its cost.*

Example 1. Suppose that the value of a machine to the buyer is 100 and that there are three possible costs of production, as shown below:

Production cost	Probability
20 (low)	30%
60 (moderate)	50%
200 (high)	20%

Assume that the parties contemplate a completely specified contract, naming whether there shall be performance in each of the three production-cost contingencies. If the contract does not specify production when the cost is 20 and 60 and no production when the cost is 200, then *both* parties would want to change the contract.

Suppose initially that the parties discuss a contract under which there is to be performance under all three contingencies and a price of, say, 80, to be paid at performance.[3] The value of the contract to the buyer would be $100 - 80 = 20$ since he is assured performance. The expected value of the contract to the seller would be $30\% \times (80 - 20) + 50\% \times (80 - 60) + 20\% \times (80 - 200) = 4$. Now suppose that the contract is altered, so that the seller has to perform only when the cost is 20 or 60. This is an advantage to the seller, for he will then not have to perform when it costs 200 and he would suffer a loss of 120 (which causes him an expected loss of $20\% \times 120$ or 24). Thus, the seller should be willing to accept a lower price in exchange for altering the terms of the contract. In particular, suppose that the price is lowered from 80 to 65. Then the seller's expected value will be $30\% \times (65 - 20) + 50\% \times (65 - 60) = 16$, so he will be better off under the altered contract (16 exceeds 4). Likewise, since the buyer will receive performance with probability 80 percent, his expected value will be $80\% \times (100 - 65) = 28$, so he too will be better off (28 exceeds 20) under the altered contract.

Next suppose that the parties initially discuss a contract calling for performance only when the production cost is 20 and a price of, say, 50. Under this contract, the buyer's expected value would be $30\% \times (100 - 50) = 15$ and the seller's expected value would be $30\% \times (50 - 20) = 9$. Now consider again a modified contract, calling for performance

---

3. Recall that I assume for concreteness that payment is to be made at the time of performance. The main conclusions would not be altered were payment to be made at the outset or partially at the outset and partially at performance, as I will comment on later.

whenever production cost is 20 or 60. This contract would be better for the buyer since he will receive performance more often, so he should be willing to pay a higher price. Let us suppose that he pays a price of 70. Then the buyer's expected value will be $80\% \times (100 - 70) = 24$, so he will be better off. The seller's expected value will be $30\% \times (70 - 20) + 50\% \times (70 - 60) = 20$, so he will also be better off.

This illustrates that the mutually optimal complete contract calls for production when the cost is 20 or 60; that contract is preferred by *both* parties either to a contract that calls for production all the time or to a contract that calls for production less often.

The point of the example, that the mutually optimal completely speci-fied contract is such that there is production when and only when the production cost is lower than the buyer's valuation, holds in general. The underlying reasons are twofold. On one hand, if a contract has a term resulting in performance when production cost exceeds the buyer's value, the seller will want the term changed and be willing to reduce the price for that by enough to make the buyer agree to it. On the other hand, if the contract has a term allowing the seller not to perform when production cost is lower than the buyer's value, the buyer will want that term changed and will be willing to alter the price by enough to make the seller agree.

1.3 Comments. (a) A mutually optimal completely specified contract is fully determined as to the conditions of performance, so that we can speak of "the" mutually optimal conditions under which there is perfor-mance. What is not determined is the contract price. In general, there will be a range of prices that one can imagine the two parties agreeing to, with the characteristic that, given the price, each of the parties will be better off than he would be if he made no contract. "Bargaining power," sophistica-tion, or other factors, not discussed at present, will determine the particular price that is agreed on.

(b) That the conditions under which there would be performance are entirely determined by mutual optimality is a powerful and strong theoreti-cal conclusion that merits reflection. It means that the two parties them-selves would be expected to draw up these contingencies as the ones calling for performance; for they would agree to alter any contract that called for performance under different conditions.

(c) One way of explaining why, under the mutually optimal contract, production occurs precisely when its value exceeds cost is that this means that the joint value of the contract is maximized—the figurative pie that the parties have to share is maximized. Both parties can always be made better off if the pie is made larger, for then each can be given a larger slice of it. The way that division of the pie is accomplished is through variation of the contract price (raising the price gives the seller a larger slice, lowering the price gives the buyer a larger slice).

1.4 Risk aversion.   If one or the other party to the contract is risk averse, how does that affect the mutually desirable completely specified contract that they would make? It would not alter the conditions of performance that they would specify: They would still decide that there should be performance if and only if the cost of performance is lower than the value of performance. The reasoning is essentially that already given (for instance, the variations in the contract terms and the price in Example 1 could be carried through, in modified form). Thus, the conditions of performance would be exactly the same as when parties were assumed to be risk neutral.

But there is a significant difference in the contracts the parties would want to make when one or both are risk averse: The parties would want to reallocate the risk in a contingency in accord with its size and their willingness and capacity to bear risk. Thus, for instance, if the buyer is risk neutral and the seller is risk averse, the buyer would act implicitly as an insurer for the seller, so that the buyer would pay the seller a fixed amount and absorb any variation in the seller's costs (as in a "cost-plus" contract). In general, the risk in the production cost would be allocated so as to reflect the degrees of risk aversion of the two parties, as described by the theory of optimal risk-sharing.

2.   REMEDIES FOR BREACH AND INCOMPLETE CONTRACTS

2.1 Damage measures given completely specified contracts.   As was emphasized in Chapter 13, the parties to a contract would want the terms of a mutually optimal completely specified contract enforced for sure; they would want *no* deviation from such contract terms. Thus, the parties would want a severe sanction—a very high damage measure (or specific performance)—to apply for any violation of terms. Because the terms in fact would not be violated, however, the severe sanctions would never be applied. The sanctions would serve only to obtain adherence to contract terms. Any problematic circumstances for the seller, such as high production costs, causing him not to want to perform, will already have been included in the terms of a contract—allowing him not to perform.

2.2 Assumption of incompleteness.   As was also stressed in Chapter 13, contracts are in fact incomplete, due to the cost of including provisions and to the difficulty courts would have in verifying contingencies, here production cost. In order to study the implications of incompleteness, it will be helpful to consider the assumption that the contract contains no specific terms at all; the contract merely states, "Seller shall make a good and deliver it to the buyer, who shall pay him price *P*."

2.3 Assumption about breach.   Let us also assume that there will be no renegotiation between the buyer and the seller when breach is contemplated. As discussed in Chapter 13, this assumption is often appropriate (and renegotiation will be considered later, in section 4). Thus, a party will be assumed to commit breach if his position after breach and payment of damages would be better than if he performed.

2.4 Behavior under damage measures.   A basic measure of damages for breach is the *expectation measure,* which is defined to be the amount that, if paid, will put the buyer (or, more generally, the party that is the victim of a breach) in the position he would have enjoyed had the contract been carried out.[4] For instance, suppose that there is a contract under which the buyer is to receive a machine worth 100 to him and for which he is to pay a price of 75 at the time of delivery. Then if the seller commits breach and does not produce and deliver the machine, the seller must pay 25 under the expectation measure: If there had been performance, the buy-

---

4. The term "expectation" is used because the buyer obtains an amount equivalent to what he expected; and this amount is sometimes called the *expectancy.* This is the usual measure of damages for breach of contract in major legal systems; see, for example, E. Farnsworth 1999, 784–791, on the United States, and Treitel 1988, 75–92, on other countries.

er's gain net of price would have been $100 - 75$, so the seller's paying him 25 in the event of breach puts him in the position he would have enjoyed had there been performance. I will now illustrate how the seller will behave under the expectation measure.

> *Example 2.* Suppose that the situation is as in Example 1, and that the contract sets a price to be paid at performance of 75. Then because the seller will have to pay 25 under the expectation measure if he breaches, he will clearly decide to perform if his production cost is 20 or 60, for in both cases he will make a profit. If, however, production cost is 200, the seller will breach, for were he to perform he would lose $200 - 75$ or 125, which is more expensive than paying only 25 in damages.

In this example, and in general, the expectation measure leads to performance if and only if the (gross) value of performance exceeds production cost—exactly when performance would occur under the terms of a mutually desirable completely specified contract. That the expectation measure leads to this precise result can, perhaps, be better understood by considering a modification of the example just considered in which production cost is imagined to be continuously variable. In this case, it can be seen that if the production cost is any amount below 100, the seller will perform; for then he will either make profits or, if his costs exceed the price of 75, his losses will be less than 25, so that he will be better off performing than breaching. If his production cost exceeds 100 by any amount, however, he will commit breach and pay 25, because his losses will then be greater than 25 if he produces the machine.[5]

Similar reasoning shows that damage measures exceeding the expectation measure, as well as specific performance, may lead to performance when its value exceeds production cost—more often than would occur under the terms of a completely specified contract. Suppose that damages are higher than expectation damages of 25, such as 50, and consider the

---

5. Algebraically, one can see this as follows. Let k be the contract price (75 in the example), c the cost of performance, and v the value of performance to the buyer. Then, if the seller performs, he makes profits of $k - c$ (which may be negative—that is, losses). If the seller commits breach, he pays damages equal to the buyer's expectancy of $v - k$, which is to say, the seller makes profits of $k - v$. Hence, the seller will perform if and only if $k - c > k - v$, or, equivalently, if and only if $v > c$.

situation in which production costs are continuously variable. Then the seller will perform as long as his losses would be less than 50, which is to say, as long as production costs are less than 125 (for at 125 his losses would be 125 − 75 = 50); thus he would be led to perform not only when production costs are less than 100, but also when production costs are between 100 and 125, exceeding the value of performance of 100.[6]

Conversely, damage measures that are less than the expectation measure may lead to breach even though the value of performance exceeds production cost—performance occurs less often than under a completely specified contract. We will consider later particular measures of damages that are less than the expectation measure.[7]

2.5 Mutually preferred remedy for breach: the expectation measure. It has been seen that under the expectation measure, but not under other remedies for breach, there will be performance in precisely the contingencies that would have been set out in a mutually optimal completely specified contract. Moreover, as was noted in comment (c) of section 1.3, the size of the pie to be shared by the parties is maximized under the mutually optimal completely specified contract. This suggests that the buyer and the seller would agree, ex ante, to employ the expectation measure rather than any other remedy for breach. And, in fact, this is true—the following proposition can be demonstrated: Given any proposed remedy for breach of contract other than the expectation measure, one can replace the proposed remedy with the expectation measure and adjust the contract price such that both the buyer and the seller would prefer the expectation measure and the modified price to the proposed remedy and the initial price.

---

6. In the version of the example with just three levels of production costs, damages of 50 would not lead to excessive performance, because the only level of costs exceeding 100 is very high, 200; damages would have to be higher than 125 to induce performance in this circumstance. Thus, if production costs are not continuously variable, damages exceeding expectation might not lead to excessive performance if they are not too much higher than the expectation measure.

7. It should be noted that the statements made in this section apply regardless of whether the seller is risk neutral or risk averse, for the seller makes the decision to commit breach after he knows what the production cost is, so that his decision at that point does not involve risk.

To illustrate the reasoning underlying this conclusion, let me show first that, given a contract and the remedy of specific performance, or a very high damage measure, both the buyer and the seller would prefer to use the expectation measure if the contract price is lowered appropriately.

Example 3. Assume that the situation is as described in Example 1 and consider a contract calling for specific performance and a price of, say, 80. The value of this contract to the buyer would be $100 - 80 = 20$, as he will obtain performance for sure. The value of the contract to the seller would be $30\% \times (80 - 20) + 50\% \times (80 - 60) + 20\% \times (80 - 200) = 4.$[8]

Now suppose that, instead, the parties consider a contract under which the expectation measure is employed. If the price is not changed from 80, we know that the buyer will be just as well off, for if he does not obtain performance, he will obtain its equivalent in damages. The seller, however, will be better off under the expectation measure, because he will have the opportunity, which he will take, to commit breach when the production cost is 200. More precisely, under the expectation measure, the seller will have to pay 20 if he commits breach (for if there were performance, the buyer would obtain $100 - 80 = 20$). The seller will be better off breaching and paying damages of 20 than sustaining a loss of 120 when production cost is 200 (note that 200–80 is 120). The seller, however, will be led to perform when production cost is 20 or 60. Hence, the seller's valuation of the contract will be $30\% \times (80 - 20) + 50\% \times (80 - 60) - 20\% \times 20 = 24$, so the seller will be better off by 20 under the expectation measure than he would be under specific performance.

Because the seller will be better off by 20 under the expectation measure and the buyer will be just as well off, it follows that if the price is lowered slightly from 80, the seller will still be better off and the buyer will now be strictly better off (rather than just as well off). Suppose, for instance, that the price is lowered to 75. The buyer's valuation will be $100 - 75 = 25$ (for he will obtain either performance or 25 in expectation damages), which exceeds the 20 he would have enjoyed under specific performance. The seller's valuation will be $30\% \times (75 - 30) +$

8. If the damage measure were very high, say 150, the seller would perform even if the production cost were 200, for then he would suffer losses of 120, which is better than paying damages of 150. Hence, because he would always perform, the situation would be equivalent to that under specific performance.

50% × (75 − 60) − 20% × 25 = 16, so the seller will be better off than he was under specific performance, when his return was 4.

The general logic employed in this example is worth restating. Under the expectation measure, the buyer is just as well off as he is under specific performance (or under a very high measure of damages): By definition of the expectation measure, the buyer receives the equivalent of performance if he does not obtain performance. But the seller is better off under the expectation measure than he is under specific performance because under the expectation measure he can commit breach when it would be very expensive for him to perform, whereas under specific performance he must perform. Because the seller is better off under the expectation measure, he will still be better off if he allows the price to be lowered somewhat, and this will make the buyer better off by agreeing to use the expectation measure.

Essentially the same logic can be applied to show that the two parties would prefer the expectation measure to any damage measure exceeding the expectation measure that would result in excessive performance.

Now let us review an example illustrating that the parties would prefer the expectation measure to a damage measure that is lower than the expectation measure and would result in excessive breach.

Example 4. Consider a contract under which the measure of damages for breach is 5 and the price is 50. Then the seller would perform if the production cost is 20, for he would make a profit of 30; he would commit breach if the cost is 60, for if he performed he would lose 10, and paying 5 in damages is better than that; and he would clearly commit breach if the cost is 200. Therefore the value of the contract to the buyer is 30% × (100 − 50) + 70% × 5 = 18.5. The value of the contract to the seller is 30% × (50 − 20) − 70% × 5 = 5.5.

Now suppose that the buyer proposes that the expectation measure be employed. If the price is not changed, the positions of the buyer and of the seller are as follows. The buyer's expected value is 100 − 50 = 50. Because the seller would be led to perform when the production cost is 20 or 60 and would pay damages of 50 otherwise, his expected profits would be 30% × (50 − 20) − 50% × (60 − 50) − 20% × 50 = −6, so he would sustain losses of 6.

Notice that the buyer's gain from switching to the expectation measure is 32.5 (namely, 50 − 18.5) and exceeds the decrease in the seller's position of 11.5 (namely, the difference between gains of 5.5 and losses of 6). This suggests that if the price is raised by enough to compensate the seller for switching to the expectation measure, the buyer can still be left better off than under the lower measure of damages. To verify this, suppose that the price is raised to 70. Then the buyer's expected value is $100 - 70 = 30$, so he is still better off than with the 18.5 under the original contract with low damages of 5. The seller, who would pay 30 if he breached, and would choose to commit breach only when his cost is 200, would value the contract as $30\% \times (70 - 20) + 50\% \times (70 - 60) - 20\% \times 30 = 14$, which exceeds 5.5. Hence, both the buyer and the seller would be better off under the contract with the expectation measure, and the altered price of 70, than under the contract with the low measure of damages of 5.

In this example, the reason that the buyer and the seller could each be made better off is that raising the measure of damages to the expectation measure induced the seller to perform in a contingency when the value of performance exceeded the cost. That in turn increased the value of the transaction to the buyer by more than it cost the seller. And this made it possible for the buyer to adjust the price by enough to make the seller willing to incorporate higher expectation damages into the contract.[9]

9. It may be helpful to sketch a proof of the general point that the parties would both prefer the expectation measure over any other measure of damages. This point was first emphasized in Shavell 1980b. Let v be the value of performance and c the uncertain production cost, where c is described by some probability distribution. Let k be the contract price, to be paid at performance. Let d be a damage measure: d determines how much the seller is to pay if he commits breach as a function of variables observable by the courts, say, c, v, and k. Given $d(c,v,k)$, a seller will breach if and only if $d(c,v,k) < c - k$ (for $c - k$ are his losses if he performs). Let $B_d(k)$ be the expected value of a contract to the buyer given a damage measure d and price k, and let $S_d(k)$ be the expected value to the seller. Let $T_d(k)$ be the total of their expected values.

Under the expectation measure E, the seller will pay $v - k$ if he commits breach, so he will perform when $v \geq c$ and breach when $c > v$. Hence, the total of the buyer's and seller's expected values $T_E(k)$ under the contract is the maximal possible value M (whatever is the contract price k): the sum of their values in any realization of c is either $v - c$, if there is performance, or 0 if not; thus, the sum is maximized given c if there is performance if and only if $v \geq c$, which is what occurs under the expectation measure; hence the expected sum is maximized under the expectation measure. Moreover, M can be divided between the parties in any way, by a suitable choice of the contract price k: It is clear that if k is

2.6 Generality of results about the expectation measure. The conclusion that the expectation measure is mutually preferred to other measures, and that it leads to the same behavior as would be observed in a mutually optimal completely specified contract, holds more generally than under the assumptions we investigated earlier. Let me mention three changes of assumption under which the conclusion continues to apply.

First, suppose that not only is the seller's cost uncertain, but also that the buyer's valuation is uncertain. In this context, a new factor is introduced: The buyer may be the party to commit breach. If his valuation falls below the seller's cost, it can be shown that the buyer will be led to breach and pay in damages the profits that the seller would have earned had he performed (which is the expectation measure for buyer breach). This behavior of the buyer is mutually optimal.

Second, suppose that payment is made at the outset instead of at the time of performance. This changes the amount that must be paid at breach under the expectation measure: If, for instance, the price is 70 and the value of performance is 100, a seller who breaches would have to pay the buyer 100 (not 30), for having already paid 70 at the outset, the buyer needs to receive 100 to be made whole. But behavior under the expectation measure is the same as was described above (the seller obviously will commit breach only if his production cost exceeds 100), and the expectation measure remains the mutually preferred damage measure.

Third, suppose that the losses due to breach can be mitigated by the victim; for example, the buyer might be able to find an alternative supplier of a good or service and thereby limit his losses from breach. In this case,

---

low enough, the seller's expected value $S_E(k)$ is 0; that $S_E(k)$ rises continuously with k; and that if k is high enough, $S_E(k) = M$.

Now consider a contract with price k and any damage measure d different from the expectation measure E. Because the damage measure is different from the expectation measure, behavior will in general be different under it—either there will be performance when $c > v$ or failure to perform when $c < v$, or both sometimes will occur. Hence, the expected sum of values $T_d(k)$ that the parties obtain under d is not maximized and is less than M, that obtained under the expectation measure. For this reason, and because we know that under the expectation measure M can be divided in any way by a suitable choice of the contract price, there must exist a price, say k', such that, under the expectation measure, $B_E(k') > B_d(k)$ and $S_E(k') > S_d(k)$, that is, such that both buyer and seller are better off under the expectation measure.

if the expectation measure is interpreted as the buyer's optimally mitigated level of losses, use of that measure will lead to desirable behavior in two regards: The seller will, as usual, perform if and only if the cost of so doing is less than the value of performance to the buyer; moreover, if there is a breach, the buyer will be led to take cost-justified steps to mitigate losses. For these reasons, the expectation measure can again be shown to be the mutually preferred damage measure.[10]

Fourth, suppose that breach is not an intentional act but a probabilistic phenomenon: Suppose that the seller invests in satisfactory performance, such as increasing his level of care to assure timely delivery, and that then performance either occurs or fails to occur due to chance elements. In this case as well, it can be shown that the expectation measure leads to mutually preferred behavior in the sense that the expectation measure induces the seller to exercise the level of care that would have been set forth in a completely specified contract,[11] and that the expectation measure is the mutually preferred damage measure.

The expectation measure, however, is not mutually preferred under all generalizations of our assumptions. As we will see shortly, when parties are

10. To amplify, let z be the mitigation expenditure of the buyer to raise his postbreach alternative value, say $w(z)$. It can readily be shown that it will be in the parties' joint interests for z to maximize $w(z) - z$; let z^* be this optimal value of z. If y is the gross value of seller performance to the buyer, then we can define v, the net value of performance, as $v = y - (w(z^*) - z^*)$. Thus, expectation damages should equal this v, not the gross value y, if z^* is in fact chosen by the buyer. And if damages equal v, the buyer will choose z^* if he is the victim of a breach, for the buyer's damage payment will be v independently of his choice of z, so he will choose z to maximize $v + w(z) - z$. On this issue of mitigation of the consequences of breach, see Wittman 1981.

11. In other words, the situation is like that discussed in Part Two of the book, on accidents, where here an accident is interpreted as a breach. Let x stand for the investment in care that the seller makes, $p(x)$ the likelihood of breach—failure of successful performance—and v the value of the contract. It is readily shown that if the parties made a completely specified contract and named x, they would choose the level of x that maximized the expected sum of values, namely, $(1 - p(x))v - x$, which is to say, they would choose the x that minimized $p(x)v + x$; call this x^*. Now if they make an incomplete contract not mentioning x, but stating that the seller should, under the expectation measure, pay the buyer $v - k$ in the event of breach, the seller will choose x to maximize $(1 - p(x))k - p(x)(v - k) - x = k - (p(x)v + x)$, so he will choose x^* as claimed. Probabilistic breach is discussed in Bebchuk and Png 1999, Cooter 1985, and Craswell 1988.

risk averse or when reliance decisions are at issue, the expectation measure may not be the mutually preferred remedy.

2.7 Risk aversion.   If parties are risk averse, then damage measures play a dual role. Not only do they induce parties to perform or allow them to commit breach, damages measures also allocate risk, and both elements have to be taken into account in determining how well a damage measure serves the parties' purposes.[12]

The expectation measure imposes risk on the seller, who might commit breach, and implicitly insures the buyer against nonperformance.[13] If the seller is risk neutral and the buyer is risk averse, that allocation of risk would be desirable, so that the expectation measure would be mutually desirable on grounds of both risk sharing and incentives to perform. Indeed, it would result in exactly the sharing of risk that would have been named in a completely specified contract between the parties (see section 1.4).

The expectation measure might also be mutually undesirable, however, because it may impose excessive risk on a risk-averse seller. Suppose, for instance, that the seller is a small company (say a several-person maker of machine tools) and the buyer is a large enterprise (a car manufacturer) that would face a substantial reduction in profits (the production line would have to stop) if the small company does not perform. In this case, the seller could easily be imagined to be unable or unwilling to bear the risk of paying the expectation damages, or else would charge a very high price to compensate it for bearing the risk. In a situation in which the expectation measure has such disadvantages on grounds of risk bearing, another damage measure, a lower one, may be mutually desirable even though it results in performance less often than is ideal.

An alternative approach that the parties may pursue when a damage measure, such as the expectation measure, results in excessive risk-bearing is to include more explicit provisions in their contract in order to achieve

12. On risk aversion and damage measures, see Polinsky 1983 and Shavell 1984a. On ways in which legal doctrines serve to allocate risk in the light of risk aversion, see, for example, Joskow 1977, Posner and Rosenfield 1977, and Sykes 1990.

13. I am here again assuming that the uncertainty in the contractual situation is only over production cost (not over buyer valuation), so that the party who might commit breach is the seller. The general points to be made will obviously carry over to the more general situation in which the buyer also might commit breach if his valuation falls.

performance when and only when it is mutually desirable. The contract could read that the seller will perform unless he runs into serious, named problems, and in that case he will be excused from his obligation to perform and need not pay damages. To write such a contract would take some time and would necessitate the buyer's later having to verify that the seller indeed encountered the stipulated problems when he claims that he did. But these difficulties and expenses may be worthwhile for the parties to incur in order to avoid the disadvantages attending the bearing of risk by the seller or the inefficiencies of employing a smaller measure of damages than the expectation measure.

With regard to specific performance as a remedy, a point worth stressing is that it imposes a heavy risk on the seller. Under specific performance, the seller will face a risk that is potentially unlimited, or as large as his cost of performance could be.

2.8 Liquidated damages versus court-determined damage measures. If the parties' mutually preferred measure of damages is one that the courts would apply, then the parties have no need to name damages in their contract and can save themselves the trouble of so doing (although this cost of naming damages would not seem to be great). In fact, the usual measure of court-determined damages is, as was noted, the expectation measure, so that if the parties do not name damages, the measure that would be employed will have attractive properties for them. But often the parties will not have confidence that the courts will employ the measure that they would desire. This is so even if they want the expectation measure, for the courts may not be able to determine the value of performance; notably, if the courts used too low a level, the parties would suffer from too little performance. Hence, parties will often want to name the measure of damages in a liquidated damages provision.[14]

Courts in fact generally enforce liquidated damages provisions, something that is socially desirable because it amounts to allowing parties to select the mutually preferred remedy for breach of contract. Often, how-

---

14. Yet that may not be an option for the parties: If the value of performance to the buyer v is uncertain, the parties cannot name it in advance; if the value of having a factory constructed on time will vary, due to market conditions for the product that the buyer is going to produce in the factory, then the parties cannot specify the damages to be paid in advance (although they might specify in advance a procedure to determine value).

ever, courts refuse to enforce damages that seem excessive (that constitute "penalties") in relation to the value of performance.[15] This tendency of courts is undesirable if the damages represent what the parties wish, because lower court awards will reduce the frequency of performance and the value of the contract. If the contract with high damages is not mutually desirable, however, but rather is the result of a party's failure to consider the contract carefully, then the courts' refusal to enforce it may be desirable, as an implicit form of insurance against mistaken behavior at the time of contracting.[16]

2.9 Asymmetric information and remedies for breach.   The buyer's value of performance may not be known to the seller at the time of contracting, and this may influence the remedy for breach that the courts will employ (if the parties do not specify a liquidated damages provision). In a famous English case, a factory owner wanted a broken mill shaft transported to a manufacturer for replacement, and the value of timely delivery was high because the factory was unable to operate without a replacement; but the shipper did not know that performance was so important.[17] In such situations, courts tend to employ the value of performance that the seller is likely to have believed when he made the contract—so that if a buyer's value was higher than usual, he will not receive a higher-than-usual level of damages. This legal rule regarding damages tends to induce buyers to reveal their high valuations at the time of contracting, for that will lead to more frequent performance, to their benefit, even though it will also result in their having to pay a higher price for their contracts. Thus, the rule under consideration appears to be socially desirable (but there are complicating issues).[18]

15. See, for example, E. Farnsworth 1999, 841–850, on the United States, and Treitel 1988, 223–228, on other countries. Hatzis 2002, however, suggests that in civil law countries high liquidated damage provisions usually are enforced.

16. For economic analysis of liquidated damage provisions, see, for example, Clarkson, Miller, and Muris 1978, Goetz and Scott 1977, and the surveys De Geest and Wuyts 2000 and Rea 1998.

17. The case is *Hadley v. Baxendale,* 9Ex. 341, 156 Eng. Rep. 145 (1854).

18. The principal complicating issues are first, that costs are involved in communicating values, and second, that sellers would have an incentive to ask buyers to state their valuations if the legal rule were that damages would equal buyers' actual valuations whether or not they revealed them. When these issues are taken into account, it turns out that, although the legal rule in question is socially desirable when it is socially best for there to be (costly) communica-

The seller's lack of knowledge of the buyer's valuation may also influence the choice of a liquidated damages measure. Because the price charged to the buyer may rise if he reveals his valuation or if he does not but asks for a high measure of damages, the buyer may purposely ask for damages in a liquidated damages provision that are lower, perhaps significantly lower, than his valuation. Although he sacrifices a gain in the frequency of performance, he may be better off because he avoids a larger increase in price paid.[19]

2.10 Contrast to views of legal scholars. The general views developed in this section stand in contrast to those emphasized in most legal scholarship about remedies for breach, and two related points are worth noting.[20] The first was mentioned in section 6.3 of Chapter 13, that most scholars view breach as in some sense a morally bad act, because it resembles a broken promise. Breach seems to be regarded by them as a practical necessity in some circumstances, but not intrinsically as a good thing. This view, as was stressed here and before, fails to take into account the difference between the notional, completely specified contract that truly represents the wishes of the parties, and the incomplete contract that the parties in fact make. Against that understanding, the function of damage measures can be seen to be, in substantial part, to induce performance when and only when the parties would have wanted it. In particular, this means that breach amounts to nonperformance when the parties would have allowed for nonperformance in a detailed contract, and breach is thus not an undesirable act but a desirable, good act from the standpoint of the parties and their true wishes.

The second contrast between legal scholars' orientation and that of the economic view concerns scholars' tendency to focus on the conflict of interest of the parties at the time of a possible breach. At that time, it is, of course, true that the more that a party has to pay if he commits breach, the worse

---

tion between parties, the rule may be undesirable when that is not true. For economic analysis of these issues, see Ayres and Gertner 1989 and Bebchuk and Shavell 1991.

19. In other words, although the joint value of the contract to the parties would be maximized if the buyer were to reveal his valuation and set damages for breach to reflect it, the distribution of the gains from contracting might move unfavorably against the buyer were he to set damages in that way. For further discussion of this and related issues, see Johnston 1990, Spier 1992b, and Stole 1992.

20. These points are emphasized in Shavell 1980b.

off he will be, and the better off the party expecting performance will be. This observation leads naturally to the view that the damage remedy is something that reflects a conflict of interest between the parties, and that the best remedy is that which resolves the conflict in a "fair" way. Such an orientation overlooks the desires of the parties at the time that they make contracts and the role of damage measures in furthering these wishes of the parties. In particular, and most significantly, the traditional scholars' view fails to acknowledge that a measure of damages may be mutually desired by the parties (the expectation measure given our assumptions and risk neutrality, or some other measure given other assumptions). That is, the view fails to recognize that there will be, in general, a measure that *both* parties would prefer to any other measure, so that naming a different measure, even if deemed fair at the time of breach, would make both parties worse off ex ante.

3. RELIANCE

3.1 Definition of reliance.   As was briefly discussed in Chapter 13, there are often actions that can be taken in advance of performance that will enhance its value to a party to a contract. A buyer expecting to receive a machine can train his employees to use it, move out an old machine, or do something else that will increase its value to him. Someone expecting a singer to appear at his nightclub can advertise the singer's appearance, thus increasing the number of people who will come to the club for the appearance. Such value-enhancing actions of parties to contracts will be called reliance actions, or simply *reliance,* because they are taken in reliance on performance.[21] I will assume for clarity that reliance actions must be undertaken before contractual uncertainty is resolved and thus before it is known whether there will be performance.[22]

---

21. Although I will generally interpret reliance to be an expenditure or effort that is made relying on performance, another meaning of the term reliance is an opportunity that is forgone on account of making a contract. For example, if the contract buyer forgoes making an alternative contract because he makes the one in question, then the expected value of the alternative contract might be considered his reliance. What I say below will, in some respects, apply to this alternative form of reliance.

22. Economic analysis of reliance is introduced in Shavell 1980b, which I largely follow here. The analysis in that article presumed, however, that parties do not renegotiate their contracts. On the important subject of renegotiation and reliance, see section 4.3.

3.2 Reliance as the measure of damages. When a party has relied on performance by making an expenditure and the other party commits breach, a possible measure of damages would compensate the victim of the breach for his reliance expenditure—so that the party is restored to the position he had before he made the contract; the amount that accomplishes this is the *reliance measure* of damages. The reliance measure of damages is ordinarily less than the expectation measure, and it will thus tend to result in more frequent breach than does the expectation measure. Therefore, both parties will prefer the expectation measure to the reliance measure of damages.[23] Consider the following illustration.

> *Example 5.* Suppose that in Example 1 the buyer must spend 5 in reliance on performance in order to obtain a benefit from it of 100. Consider a contract in which damages for breach are governed by the reliance measure, so that damages are 5; and assume also that the contract price is 50. Then the seller will commit breach when the production cost is 60, for he would prefer to spend 5 in damages rather than lose 10, and he will also commit breach when the production cost is 200. The value of the contract to the buyer will thus be $30\% \times (100 - 50) + 70\% \times 5 - 5 = 13.5$, and the value to the seller will be $30\% \times (50 - 20) - 70\% \times 5 = 5.5$.
>
> The parties will both be better off under the expectation measure, presuming that the price is raised suitably to compensate the seller for having to pay larger damages. Suppose that the price is 75 and that expectation damages of 25 are employed. Then the seller will perform when production cost is either 20 or 60. The buyer's value will be $100 - 75 - 5 = 20$, which exceeds 13.5, so he will be better off; even though the price is higher, the increased frequency of performance more than makes up for the price rise. The seller's value will be $30\% \times (75 - 20) + 50\% \times (75 - 60) - 20\% \times 25 = 19$, which exceeds 5.5, so he too is better off.

As is evident from this example, the reason that the reliance measure is inferior to the expectation measure is that reliance damages are only 5, and thus less than expectation damages. That reliance expenditures, 5 in the example, are less than the value of performance, 100 in the example, is a plausi-

---

23. This point, that parties prefer expectation damages to reliance, is also true under the interpretation of reliance that equates it with forgone opportunities.

ble general assumption because it would be irrational for a contracting party to plan to spend more on reliance than performance is worth; otherwise the contract would have negative worth to the party spending on reliance.[24]

3.3 Comment on views of legal scholars about the reliance measure. Some legal commentators favor the reliance measure over the expectation measure on grounds that we need not review here.[25] The point worth noting is that because they do not take into account the mutual interests of the contracting parties at the outset, they do not recognize that the expectation measure would be chosen by both parties over the reliance measure in important, general circumstances. Indeed, the contracting parties' preference would be quite strong for the expectation measure over the reliance measure if performance is very important and reliance by the buyer is small, so that under the reliance measure of damages there would be very little assurance of performance. That would reduce the value of the contract substantially, and make the buyer much less willing to pay the seller than otherwise.

3.4 Level of reliance; optimal reliance. A party to a contract often has a choice over whether, or how much, to rely on contract performance (for simplicity, the level of reliance was taken as fixed earlier). Reliance will be said to be optimal if it maximizes the expected joint value of a contract to the buyer and the seller, that is, if it maximizes the expected value of performance less production cost and less the costs of reliance. Let us consider an example before further discussion.

Example 6. Suppose that in the example we have been considering, the following is assumed about the level of reliance and the value of performance to the buyer. If reliance is 0, the value of performance is 50; if reliance is 5, the value of performance is 100; and if reliance is 50, the

24. If the buyer's valuation were uncertain, however, it could turn out that his valuation happens to fall below the level of reliance. This would result in too little breach under the reliance measure. Whether the reliance measure is below the expecation measure or above, the expectation measure will be preferred by both parties given the general assumptions now under consideration.

25. In a much-cited article, Fuller and Perdue 1936 favor the reliance measure over the expectation measure as a matter of theory, although they often find the expectation measure attractive, mainly for reasons of administrability.

value of performance is 150. (The costs of performance are as has been assumed—20 with probability 30 percent, 60 with probability 50 percent, and 200 with probability 20 percent.)

What level of reliance is optimal—will lead to the highest expected value of performance net of production cost and of the cost of reliance? If reliance is 0, then because the value of performance will only be 50, it will be optimal for production to occur only when the production cost is 20, so the joint value of the contract will be 30% × (50 − 20) = 9. If reliance is 5, the value of performance will be 100, so production will be optimal when its cost is 20 or 60, so the joint value of the contract will be 30% × (100 − 20) + 50% × (100 − 60) − 5 = 39. If reliance is 50, the value of performance will be 150, so production will again be optimal when its cost is 20 or 60, so the joint value of the contract will be 30% × (150 − 20) + 50% × (150 − 60) − 50 = 34. Thus, reliance of 5 is optimal.

It should be noted that increasing reliance from 5 to 50 involves an extra cost of 45 and results in an enhancement of 50 in the value of performance, from 100 to 150. Why then is 50 not the optimal level of reliance? The answer is that the extra 45 cost of reliance is incurred with *certainty*, whereas the benefit from performance comes only with a *probability*, of 80 percent, so that the expected value of the enhancement in the value of performance is only 80 percent of 50, or 40, which is lower than 45.

This example illustrates that an expenditure on reliance is optimal only if its *expected* benefits exceed the expenditure; if performance is not optimal, then reliance will have been a waste.

If parties make a mutually optimal completely specified contract and it stipulates the level of reliance, that level will be the optimal level of reliance; for as explained earlier (see section 1.3(c)), the parties will want to arrange the contract to maximize its joint expected value.[26]

---

26. To be precise about the notion of optimal reliance, let r be the buyer's reliance investment and $v(r)$ be the value of performance given r, where v is increasing in r. The buyer chooses r before the seller learns the production cost c and decides about producing. The optimal decision of the seller is to produce if and only if $c < v(r)$, and the joint value maximizing decision of the buyer is therefore to choose r to maximize

$$\int_0^{v(r)} (v(r) - c) g(c) dc - r,$$

where g is the probability density of c. Thus, the optimal r, denoted r^*, is determined by

3.5 Remedies for breach and the level of reliance.   Consider now incomplete contracts and the question of how remedies for breach affect decisions about reliance.

Under the expectation measure, there will be a tendency toward excessive reliance: Because the buyer is implicitly insured by receipt of damages against losses from breach, he will view his investment in reliance as one with a certain payoff. Yet, as just emphasized in section 3.4, reliance has in fact only a probabilistic payoff because performance may not occur, and that needs to be taken into account in determining optimal reliance. The next example shows that under the expectation measure, the buyer will tend to choose more than the optimal level of reliance.

> *Example 7.* Suppose that, in the circumstances of the previous example, the contract price is 70 and the buyer is deciding whether to choose 5 or 50 as his level of reliance.[27] If he selects 5, then because 100 would be the value of performance, the buyer will either obtain performance, and enjoy a net value of 30, or receive 30 in damages; hence the buyer's valuation would be $100 - 70 - 5$ or 25. If he chooses 50 as reliance, 150 would be the value of performance, and his valuation would by similar logic be $150 - 70 - 50 = 30$. Thus, he would choose 50 as his level of reliance. When the buyer increases his level of reliance to 50, he benefits for sure because he effectively receives 150 either in performance or its equivalent in the form of expectation damages.

As this example illustrates, the reason that the expectation measure leads to too much reliance is that the buyer knows that if he increases reliance, not only will he obtain more if there is performance, but he will also obtain more if there is a breach, because the damages put him in the position he would have enjoyed had there been performance.[28]

$v'(r) G(v(r)) = 1$, where G is the cumulative distribution of c. Note here that the marginal return to reliance investment is only a contingent return, for the investment pays off only with probability $G(v(r))$, that is, when $c < v(r)$ (when production turns out to be efficient).

27. For simplicity, I will not consider whether he would want to choose 0 as the level of reliance; it is easy to show that he would not.

28. Specifically, if the expectation measure is employed, the buyer will always receive $v(r) - k$ (either he obtains performance, worth $v(r)$, and pays the contract price k, or he receives damages of $v(r) - k$). Hence, he will choose r to maximize $v(r) - k - r$. Consequently, r will be determined by $v'(r) = 1$ rather than by $v'(r) G(v(r)) = 1$ (see note 26), so the buyer will select an inefficiently high r; the problem is that the buyer does not take

The conclusion under the expectation measure exemplifies a more general point about the receipt of damages: Because damages dull the effects of breach, they tend to lead to excessive reliance, for optimal reliance requires a party to take into account that breach means that reliance involves waste.

Under the reliance measures of damages, there is excessive reliance not only for the general reason just given, but also for another reason: Because reliance damages are less than the expectation damages, the buyer will be made worse off if there is a breach. Hence, the buyer will want to reduce the likelihood of breach, and this in turn he can accomplish by increasing reliance—for the higher is reliance, the more the seller will have to pay in damages if he breaches, and thus the less often he will commit breach. For this reason, it can be shown that the level of reliance undertaken under the reliance measure of damages tends to be even more excessive than under the expectation measure.

The fact that the expectation measure and other damage measures often result in improper reliance complicates the determination of the mutually desirable damage measure. The best measure will represent an implicit compromise between providing proper incentives to rely and proper incentives to perform. There does not exist any damage measure that provides optimal incentives both to perform and to rely: only the expectation measure provides optimal incentives to perform, yet it does not provide proper incentives to rely.[29]

3.6 Further on reliance and remedies for breach. Let me make several additional remarks about the theory of reliance and about the interpretation of what has been discussed.

(a) *Sophisticated damage measures.* On reflection, it can be seen that the tendency toward excessive reliance caused by receipt of expectation damages can be combatted if the level of damages is not automatically increased to reflect the actual value of performance. If the expectation measure of dam-

---

into account that investment does not have any value when performance does not occur. This point was first made in Shavell 1980b.

29. More precisely, this statement that there does not exist any damage measure that leads to optimal performance and optimal reliance assumes that a damage measure d is a function only of the variables v, r, c, and k—the value of performance, reliance, production cost, and the contract price. In particular, d may not depend on more information, such as about the function $v(r)$ or the density $g(r)$. See Shavell 1980b.

ages is sophisticated in the sense that damages are set equal to the level reflecting *optimal* reliance, there will be no incentive to rely excessively, for increasing reliance will not raise damages received in the event of breach. (This will be true in Example 7, for instance, if expectation damages are set presuming that reliance is 5.)[30] Indeed, in general this sophisticated expectation measure leads to both optimal reliance and to optimal performance.[31] Use of such a sophisticated version of the expectation measure, however, requires that the court knows much more than the actual level of reliance and the actual value of performance; it must know the functional relationship between reliance and the value of performance and the entire probability distribution of production costs—everything about the contractual situation—in order to calculate optimal reliance. The parties themselves, though, would often be presumed to have approximately enough information to determine optimal reliance (or much more than the court), and so could name the expectation measure given optimal reliance in a liquidated damages provision.

(b) *More general forms of reliance.* In the earlier discussion, we considered reliance by the buyer that raised the value of performance. More generally, however, the seller can also take actions that will alter the value of the contract, perhaps that will lower his expected production cost or the quality and value of performance for the buyer. These issues introduce new considerations into the analysis of damage measures and reliance.[32] For example, to the extent that seller reliance augments the buyer's value of performance, it may well be jointly beneficial for the seller to undertake that reliance,

30. If 5 is reliance, the value of performance will be 100, so the expectation measure will be $100 - 70 = 30$. As a consequence, the seller will perform when the cost is 20 or 60. Hence, the buyer will reason as follows. If he chooses reliance of 0, the value of the contract to him will be $80\% \times (50 - 70) + 20\% \times 30 = -10$. If he chooses reliance of 5, the value of the contract will be $80\% \times (100 - 70) + 20\% \times 30 - 5 = 25$. If he chooses reliance of 50, the value of the contract will be $80\% \times (150 - 70) + 20\% \times 30 - 50 = 20$. Hence, he will choose reliance of 5, the optimal level, as claimed.

31. Recall from note 26 that r^* denotes optimal reliance. If $d = v(r^*) - k$, the seller will perform when $c < v(r^*)$, so the buyer will maximize his expected return, $(v(r) - k) G(v(r^*)) - (v(r^*) - k)(1 - G(v(r^*))) - r$. Accordingly, r will be determined by $v'(r) G(v(r^*)) = 1$, and this condition is clearly satisfied at r^*. The explanation is that the buyer's choice of r affects his return only when he obtains performance. Hence, r^* will be chosen and performance will also be optimal. This point was first made by Cooter 1985.

32. See Che and Chung 1999 and Che and Hausch 1999.

but he will hardly have an incentive to do so if this were to increase the damages he would have to pay under the expectation measure.

(c) *Damage measures still needed to induce reliance.* Although damage measures may be imperfect and may often lead to reliance exceeding the optimal level, one should not lose sight of the fact that the use of damage measures does generally induce parties to invest in reliance by giving them reason to believe that performance is likely to occur. Were there no contract enforcement, there would be too little reliance.

4.   RENEGOTIATION

4.1 Introduction.   To this point in the present chapter, the possibility of renegotiation of contracts has not been considered. As discussed in Chapter 13, however, renegotiation of contracts sometimes may take place and lead to mutually desirable performance if that would not otherwise occur. Here we will assume that renegotiation of contracts in such circumstances will take place costlessly, unless otherwise mentioned, and we will briefly consider the effect of renegotiation on performance, reliance, and risk aversion.

4.2 Performance.   Given the assumption that renegotiation will take place whenever the mutually desirable outcome as to performance would not otherwise occur, it is essentially a tautology that performance will always be mutually desirable. Thus, regardless of the remedy for breach, performance will be mutually optimal and identical to what would be provided for in the mutually desirable completely specified contract. That is, performance will occur if and only if its value exceeds the cost of performance.[33]

> *Example 8.* In the example that we have been considering, suppose that the contract price is 50 and that the measure of damages for breach is 5. Then the seller would decide to commit breach when production cost is 60 or 200, but when the production cost is 60 there would be an incentive for renegotiation. In particular, if the seller breaches, his losses are the damages of 5, whereas if he performs he spends 60 and receives 50, so loses 10. Hence, if the buyer increases the price he pays sufficiently above

33. In this section, I largely follow Shavell 1984a.

50, say to 65, the seller will agree to perform; if the price is 65, the seller will make a profit of 5. The buyer himself will be better off paying 65 and obtaining performance worth 100 than receiving damages of 5. Such mutually desirable renegotiation for performance is always possible when the cost of performance is less than its value and the seller would otherwise be led not to perform.[34]

If the measure of damages is the expectation measure, namely 50, then we know that the seller will decide to commit breach only when the production cost is 200, which is what is mutually desirable. Hence, there will never be renegotiation of the contract.

If the damage measure is high enough to induce performance when production cost is 200, however, there will be renegotiation, in which the seller pays the buyer in order not to have to perform. Assume for instance that damages for breach are 175. Then if production cost is 200, the seller will lose less, namely 150, if he performs than if he commits breach, so he will perform in the absence of renegotiation. But there is an incentive for the parties to renegotiate. Suppose that the seller pays the buyer 70 in exchange for not performing. The buyer will be better off than if there is performance, in which case he would obtain a net value of 50. The seller will also be better off because he pays 70 rather than losing 150 from performing. Such mutually desirable renegotiation is always possible when the cost of performance exceeds its value and the seller would otherwise be led to perform.[35]

Because performance will occur exactly when it is mutually desirable—when cost is less than its value—under any remedy for breach, it follows that all remedies for breach will be equivalent ex ante in the eyes of the contracting parties. Specifically, it can be shown that, given any damage

---

34. To see why algebraically, note that our hypothesis is that the cost of performance c is less than its value v, and that the loss from performance $c - k$ exceeds damages d—for that is why the seller would commit breach. We want to show that there is an increase t in the price that will lead the seller to perform and also leave the buyer better off. Thus, t must satisfy two conditions: $c - (k + t) < d$ and $v - (k + t) > d$. Now if $t = c - k - d + .5(v - c)$, both conditions will be satisfied, since $v - c > 0$.

35. In the present situation, our hypothesis is that $v < c$, so that performance is not mutually desirable, and yet that $c - k < d$, so that the seller would perform. We want to show that there exists a payment t that the seller could make to the buyer for not performing that each would prefer to the alternative. Thus, for the seller to be better off, we want $t < c - k$, and for the buyer to be better off, we want $t > v - k$. Let $t = v - k + .5(c - v)$.

measure and price for a contract, a change to any other damage measure will leave both parties exactly as well off if the price is changed appropriately; moreover, no damage measure will be mutually preferable to any other damage measure.[36] In sum, because damage measures serve no role in inducing mutually desirable performance when renegotiation is a costless and smooth process, damage measures offer no advantage to the contracting parties if performance is the only relevant factor in a contractual situation.

4.3 Reliance.   Renegotiation will generally affect the choice of the level of reliance by a buyer, for the terms of the renegotiation will tend to be influenced by the value of performance, which reliance affects. The particular way in which renegotiation affects reliance will depend on the measure of damages, so that the remedy for breach does affect the degree of reliance.

To illustrate, consider initially the case if damages for breach are zero—so that the seller will want to commit breach whenever the production cost exceeds the contract price that he would receive if he performed. Then the buyer will have to pay the seller to perform when production cost exceeds the price, and the payment he will make will have an effect on his reliance.

> *Example 9.* Suppose that, given some contemplated level of reliance by the buyer, the value of performance would be 100, that the contract price is 50, and that there are no damages for breach. Then the seller will commit breach whenever production cost exceeds 50, so he will want to

36. The argument that parties will be just as well off under a change in damage measures if the price is adjusted can be outlined as follows. From the previous two notes, we know that under any damage measure d, renegotiation will, if necessary, always lead to performance if and only if $c < v$. This implies that the sum of parties' values under d, denoted $T_d(k)$ (see note 9) will be maximal, M, regardless of d and of the contract price k. Moreover, for any measure d, M can be divided between the parties in any way through the choice of k. Now let d be a damage measure and k, the price, so that the buyer obtains $B_d(k)$ and the seller $M - B_d(k)$. Change the damage measure to any other measure d' and set the price equal to k' such that $B_{d'}(k') = B_d(k)$. Because $T_{d'}(k) = M$ for any k, we know that the seller's value under k' must be $M - B_{d'}(k') = M - B_d(k)$, so he is also just as well off as under d and k.

That both parties cannot be better off is clear. Were both parties better off under a change of damage measures, the sum of values would have to exceed M, but that cannot be because M is the maximal sum of values.

commit breach when production cost is 60 in the absence of renegotiation. There will, however, be renegotiation in which the buyer pays the
seller to perform. If the seller is paid at least 60, he will perform when
production cost is 60. Suppose that renegotiation leads to a price of 80—
the nature of renegotiation is that the two parties split equally the surplus
(of $100 - 60 = 40$) that they would gain from renegotiation (how they
split it will not matter to the point to be made, as long as the seller obtains
some fraction of it).

Now suppose that the buyer thinks about investing in another,
higher, level of reliance, which would lead to a value of performance of
120 instead of 100. Then, if production cost is 60, there will be renegotiation and the buyer will pay a price of 90—for this will split the higher
surplus of 60 (that is, $120 - 60$). Thus, the buyer's net value in the event
of renegotiation rises from $100 - 80 = 20$ to $120 - 90 = 30$, which
is to say, by 10, when the value of performance goes up by 20, from 100
to 120. The reason is that in the process of renegotiation the seller is
extracting half of the reliance-created increase in the value of performance.

As a consequence of this extraction of the value of reliance, the buyer
may decide not to increase his reliance even though that would increase
the joint value of the contract. For example, suppose that by increasing
reliance expenditures by 15, the value of performance would be increased
by 20. This would be mutually desirable, but the buyer would not do it.[37]

As this example shows, when the buyer has to renegotiate and bargain
for performance, some of the value of reliance to him is extracted in the
process, and anticipating this, he will tend to rely too little.

If, however, the remedy for breach is such that the seller has to renegotiate and pay so that he will not have to perform, the buyer will be led to
rely too much. The reason is, in essence, that when he increases his level
of reliance and thus the value of performance, he will be able to obtain a
higher payment from the seller in renegotiation. Because this motive to
rely has to do with increasing the payment made to the buyer rather than

37. Because performance will occur when production cost is 20 or 60, and thus with
probability 80 percent, the expected value of the increase in the value of performance is
$80\% \times 20 = 16$, which exceeds the cost of 15, so that the increase in reliance expenditures
does increase the expected net value of the contract. The buyer will obtain a benefit of $30\%
\times 20 + 50\% \times 10 = 11$, for when he renegotiates his benefit is only 10. Thus, he will
not spend 15 to achieve a personal benefit of only 11.

with increasing realized value from performance, it leads to excessive reliance.

It should also be stated that, under the expectation measure, the incentive to rely is excessive, just as it was before when renegotiation was not at issue. The reason is that, because there is no renegotiation under the expectation measure, its possibility is essentially irrelevant.

In general, then, because damage measures provide the backdrop against which renegotiation occurs, the choice of damage measures affects reliance decisions. Which damage measure results in the best level of reliance for the parties is a complicated subject and depends on, among other factors, whether both parties have opportunities to rely and the nature of their reliance.[38]

4.4 Risk aversion. As was discussed in sections 1.4 and 2.7, when parties are risk averse, the allocation of risk enters into the determination of the mutually beneficial contractual arrangement, and renegotiation affects this point to some degree.[39] In general, renegotiation would seem to reduce risk-bearing that is due to otherwise inappropriate performance decisions. Notably, the seller may bear a large risk in the absence of renegotiation if damages exceed the expectation measure or if specific performance is the remedy, for if the seller's production costs are high, he will have to

---

38. There is a large and growing literature in economics on this subject. Rogerson 1984 first analyzed reliance decisions in the presence of damage measures for breach, assuming costless and perfect renegotiation and that only one party relies. Beginning with Hart and Moore 1988, economists have focused on a more general situation in which both the buyer and the seller rely. This literature furthermore usually supposes that none of the variables (costs, values of performance, reliance investments) are verifiable by courts. Thus, a contract can depend only on what is recorded in it, certain subsequent communications between the parties, whether there has been performance, and, if not, who committed breach. Of note are a number of results establishing the existence of contracts that will produce optimal outcomes, that is, in both parties choosing optimal levels of reliance investment (performance will always be optimal). Aghion, Dewatripont, and Rey 1994 and Chung 1991 demonstrate that reliance will be optimal using a contract in which one party is effectively given the right to make a single take-it-or-leave-it offer to the other in renegotiation. Edlin and Reichelstein 1996, Nöldeke and Schmidt 1995, and Rogerson 1992 establish closely related optimality results. These optimality results fail to hold, however, if reliance by one party affects the return of the other; see Che and Chung 1999 and Che and Hausch 1999.

39. The points of this section are discussed in Shavell 1984a.

incur them in order to perform. The seller's ability to renegotiate the contract in such circumstances will lower the risk for him.

Renegotiation cannot alter risk in a substantial way, however; only ex ante provisions in contracts can do that, as was indicated in Chapter 13. If the seller bears a large risk due to damages being high or the use of specific performance, this risk is moderated but not eliminated by renegotiation. The only way to substantially alter the risk to the seller is for the seller to adopt a different damage measure, such as expectation, or else to write a more complete contract governing when performance shall occur and allocating risk independently.

4.5 Summary of conclusions about renegotiation and remedies for breach. Although renegotiation leads to performance when that is mutually desirable regardless of the remedy for breach, remedies for breach exert an important influence on reliance and also on the allocation of risk. Thus, even if renegotiation is costless and operates successfully, remedies for breach remain relevant. In fact, of course, renegotiation is a costly process and may not be successful, so that the role of remedies for breach in promoting mutually desirable performance retains significance.

16 ||| OTHER TYPES OF CONTRACT

Here I will discuss two additional types of contract: contracts for the transfer of possession of things that already exist, and donative contracts. These two types of contracts are of substantial importance and present us with features different from those of production contracts.[1]

1. CONTRACTS FOR TRANSFER OF POSSESSION

1.1 Introduction and description. By contracts for transfer of possession, I refer to contracts for delivery or conveyance of things that already exist rather than things that need to be produced. Examples are contracts for transfer of ownership of real estate, paintings and other art objects, used consumer durables, and goods held in inventory.

The type of uncertainty that we will consider in examining such contracts concerns outside-the-contract bids for the contract good that is supposed to be transferred between the contract seller and the contract

---

1. There are, of course, a variety of other types of contracts of significant interest (such as principal and agent contracts), but they will not be treated here.

buyer.[2] For example, if a house is supposed to be transferred, the uncertainty will concern what an outside party might bid for the house before it is supposed to be conveyed to the contract buyer.[3]

We will distinguish for analytical purposes three categories of situations involving bids of outside parties: (a) when outside parties make bids only to the contract seller, (b) when outside parties make bids only to the contract buyer, and (c) when outside parties can make bids to either the contract buyer or the contract seller. Consider, for example, a contract for the sale of a painting by an art dealer to an individual. One would expect outside bids for the painting to be made primarily to the dealer, because of his business enterprise, rather than to the individual (unless he were a well-known collector). If, however, we consider a contract for the sale of a house, then we might expect that outside bids would be made either to the contract seller or to the contract buyer.

Another point: We will sometimes consider the possibility that there would be two transactions, one in which the outside party buys from the contract seller, and then a second in which the contract buyer purchases from the outside party.[4]

1.2 Completely specified contracts.   Let us now consider the nature of mutually beneficial completely specified contracts, that is, contracts that state whether the good will be transferred to the contract buyer as a function of the bid made by outside parties. As with production contracts, we will subsequently examine what remedies for breach will lead to outcomes most

2. For simplicity, the bids will be assumed to be exogenously determined, even though in reality they will depend, among other factors, on how much the seller would have to pay for breach. This issue is noted in section 1.5.

3. There cannot be uncertainty over production cost, of course, because the good is presumed already to exist, so that the issues discussed in the last chapter surrounding production cost uncertainty are not directly relevant. But, as will be seen, many of the points made there have analogues here. Moreover, much of what is written here will have application in the production contract context, because in that context it is quite possible that outside parties would make bids for the goods that are supposed to be produced.

4. Reliance will not be considered because the issue of interest concerning contracts for transfer of possession involves outside bids, and consideration of reliance would be a distraction. See, however, note 12 on reliance.

closely resembling what the parties would have described in a completely specified contract.

Bids made only to the contract seller. Consider initially the situation in which outside parties make bids only to the contract seller, who for concreteness we can think of as a dealer. In this situation, the mutually desirable completely specified contract would call for performance if and only if the buyer's valuation exceeds the outside bid. This is illustrated in the following example.

> *Example 1.* Suppose that the value of the good to the buyer is 100 and that there are three possible outside party bids, as shown below:

Outside bid	Probability
50	50%
90	10%
150	40%

Suppose that the parties contemplate a completely specified contract—one that states whether there shall be performance in each of the three contingencies. Let us show that if the contract does not specify performance when and only when the bids are 50 and 90—that is, less than the buyer's valuation of 100—then both parties would want to change the contract.

Suppose initially that the parties discuss a contract under which there is to be performance under all three contingencies and a price of, say, 80, to be paid at performance.[5] The value of the contract to the buyer will be $100 - 80 = 20$ since he is assured performance. The value to the seller will be 80. Now suppose that the contract is altered, so that the seller has to perform only when the outside bid is 50 or 90. This is an advantage to the seller, for he will then be able to sell for a high price of 150, rather than at 80, with a probability of 40 percent; indeed, the advantage of receiving an extra 70 is worth $40\% \times 70$ or 28 to the seller. Thus, the seller should be willing to accept a lower price in exchange for being allowed not to perform when the outside bid is high. In particular, suppose that the price is lowered from 80 to 55. Then the seller's expected value will

---

5. As in the previous chapter, I will assume for concreteness that payment is to be made at the time of performance. Again, the main conclusions would not be altered if payment were to be made at the outset.

be 60% × 55 + 40% × 150 = 93, so he will be better off under the altered contract (93 exceeds 80). Likewise, the buyer's expected value will be 60% × (100 − 55) = 27, so he too will be better off (27 exceeds 20).

Next suppose that the parties initially discuss a contract calling for performance only when the outside bid is 50 and a price of, say, 60. Under this contract, the buyer's expected value will be 50% × (100 − 60) = 20 and the seller's expected value will be 50% × 60 + 10% × 90 + 40% × 150 = 99. Now consider an altered contract calling for performance whenever the outside bid is 50 or 90. This contract will be better for the buyer since he will receive performance more often, so he should be willing to pay a higher price. Let us suppose that he pays a price of 66. Then the buyer's expected value will be 60% × (100 − 66) = 20.4, so he will be better off. The seller's expected value will be 60% × 66 + 40% × 150 = 99.6, so he will also be better off.

Thus, the mutually optimal contract calls for performance whenever the outside bid is 50 or 90; this contract is preferred by both parties either to a contract that calls for performance all the time, or for performance less often than whenever the outside bid is 50 or 90.

The underlying reasons for the result just illustrated are twofold. On one hand, if the contract calls for a sale to the contract buyer even though the outside bid is 150, the parties would be wasting the joint opportunity to sell at a higher price than the value that the buyer places on the good. On the other hand, the parties obviously do not want to sell the good to the outsider if his bid is less than the buyer's valuation. In other words, the joint value or pie that the contracting parties have to split will be maximized provided that performance occurs when but only when the outside bid is less than the buyer's valuation.

It should be noted that this conclusion does not change if we consider the possibility that, were the good sold to the outside party when the bid is less than the contract buyer's value, the buyer could then repurchase it from him. Suppose for instance that the contract price is 60 and that, when the outsider bids 90, the seller sells to him, but then the buyer repurchases it from the outsider at a price of, say, 95.[6] This means that, although the

---

6. That is, I am as usual presuming that the surplus from a transaction is divided between the parties to it. Because the hypothesis is that the outsider bid 90 for the good, he must attach a value of at least 90 to it, so that any transaction that occurs between the outsider and the buyer must be at a price over 90 and not more than 100. (If it so happens

buyer does obtain the good, he pays more for it than the seller receives—
he pays 95 whereas the seller receives 90. Thus, the two parties to the
contract jointly surrender 5 to the outside party in the process of effecting
a transfer of the good to the contract buyer—there is in effect a *leakage of
funds* to the outsider that lowers joint value to the contracting parties. For
that reason, it is readily demonstrated, along the lines of the logic of the
earlier example, that the buyer and seller would not make a contract under
which the outsider would purchase the good for 90; they would continue
to find mutually desirable the contract in which there is performance
whenever the outside bid is lower than the buyer's valuation. Moreover, this
conclusion is reinforced by the fact that an additional transaction, involving
extra cost, would be involved were the contract buyer to purchase from an
outsider.

Bids made only to the contract buyer. Next consider the situation in
which outside parties make bids only to the contract buyer, who we can
now think of as a dealer. In this situation, the mutually desirable completely
specified contract would call for performance under all circumstances. Let
me illustrate with the previous example under the present assumption about
outside bids.

> *Example 2.* In the previous example, but where the outside bids are now
> made only to the contract buyer, suppose the parties contemplate a con-
> tract in which the good is not always sold to the buyer. For example,
> suppose that they contemplate a contract with a price of 60 and in which
> the good is sold to the buyer when the outside bid is 50 or 90, but not
> when it is 150. The value of this contract to the buyer is 60% × (100
> − 60) = 24. The value to the seller is 60% × 60 + 40% × 10 = 40,
> where 10, say, is the value of the good to the seller for his own use.[7] (The
> seller cannot sell the good to the outside party when he does not convey
> it to the buyer, for the assumption is that outside bids are made only to
> the buyer.)

---

that the outsider's valuation exceeds 100, there would be no transaction with the contract
buyer, which only strengthens the argument made in the text.).

7. The argument to be given can be shown not to depend on precisely what this value
is, only that it is lower than the buyer's valuation—which must be true because the seller
is willing to sell to the buyer.

Now consider as an alternative a contract in which the good is also sold to the buyer when the bid is 150. The buyer will be willing to pay more for such a contract, because he will then be able to, and will, sell the good to the outsider for 150, rather than keep it and enjoy a value of only 100. Suppose then that this contract is made and that the price is raised to 70. The buyer's value will be $60\% \times (100 - 70) + 40\% \times (150 - 70) = 50$, so he is better off, and the seller obtains 70, so he too is better off.

The reason that the parties want performance all the time is that this means that the two guarantee that they will obtain the highest value from the good: The contract buyer will keep the good for himself if his valuation exceeds the outside bid, and the buyer will sell to the outsider when the outside bid exceeds his valuation. Because the hypothesis is that it is the contract buyer who faces the outside bid, the good must be transferred to the buyer for the good to be sold to the outsider when the bid is higher than the buyer's valuation. (Note that the contract seller too wants this to happen because that enables the buyer to pay him more in the contract price.) The conclusion here can be understood as again reflecting the point that the parties want a contract that leads to the maximization of the joint value that they have to share.

Bids made either to the contract buyer or the contract seller. In this situation, the conclusion is that the mutually desirable completely specified contract is not unique: The contract is mutually desirable as long as it calls for performance at least whenever the buyer's valuation exceeds the outside bid—and in particular if it calls for performance under all circumstances. The logic behind this conclusion can be understood by reference to the arguments of the previous two cases.

Let me first explain why the completely specified contract would require performance when the buyer's valuation exceeds the outside bid, that is, when the outside bid is 50 or 90 in the example. If there were no performance in such a case and the seller sold the good to the outsider, there would be a decrease in joint value, for the buyer values the good at 100. Moreover, even if the buyer can repurchase from the outsider, the joint value will not be maximized because of leakage of funds to the outsider, as described earlier.

Let me now explain why does it not matter what the contract specifies when the outside bid exceeds the buyer's valuation, that is, when the bid is 150 in the example. In that case, whoever has the good, the contract buyer or the contract seller, will sell to the outsider for 150, for the assumption is that either party has the opportunity to do so. Thus the opportunity to sell to the outsider when his value exceeds the buyer's will not be lost, and it does not matter to the joint maximization of value who has the opportunity to sell to the outsider. (Who has the opportunity will affect the contract price, of course; if the buyer obtains performance all the time, he will tend to pay more to the seller than if the seller does not have to perform when the outside bid is 150 and thus can sell for the high bid price.)

1.3 Comments. (a) *Mutual desirability and social desirability.* As we have seen, completely specified contracts are mutually desirable for the contract buyer and seller to ensure that there is performance whenever the buyer's valuation exceeds the outside bid—even if the buyer could, in a second transaction, repurchase the good from the outsider. The reason that the two contracting parties do not want the buyer to obtain the good through repurchase from the outsider is that it would result in a leakage of funds to the outsider. Yet that is not a *social* reason for there to be performance; it is only a reason applying to the two contracting parties who want to preserve value for themselves. But the additional transaction costs associated with resale to the contract buyer would constitute a social reason for there to be performance whenever the buyer's valuation exceeds the outside bid.

(b) *Risk aversion.* The influence of risk aversion on the mutually desirable completely specified contract was not discussed earlier. Risk aversion does not affect the conclusions about when performance would be mutually desirable. As was the case with production contracts, risk aversion affects only the allocation of risk that the parties would want to effect through their payment arrangements. For example, suppose that outside bids are made only to the contract seller and that he is risk averse and the buyer is risk neutral. Being risk averse, the seller would prefer to have a certain sum than a probability of selling for a high outside bid, such as 150. Thus, under a mutually desirable risk-sharing agreement, the seller would receive a guaranteed price from the contract buyer and give the proceeds from any sale to a high outside bidder to the contract buyer.

Note, however, that the risk at issue in the context of uncertainty about outside bids is a *beneficial* risk—the opportunity to sell to a high outside bidder. Thus, risk aversion does not seem to be nearly as important a consideration as in the production contract context, where the risk is detrimental, notably, that the production cost might be high.

1.4 Remedies for breach. Let us now inquire about the mutual desirability of different remedies for breach, assuming that the contract is not completely specified, and for simplicity that it merely says that the good is to be conveyed to the buyer. Which remedies will be best for the parties will follow in a fairly straightforward manner from the description of completely specified contracts. Let me again discuss the different types of contractual situation separately in order to maintain clarity, and then take stock of the conclusions reached.

Bids made only to the contract seller. In this case, the expectation measure leads to the same outcome as in the mutually desirable completely specified contract, and the expectation measure is the mutually preferred remedy for breach. Let me first illustrate this conclusion.

> *Example 3.* Assume in the example that the contract price is 70. Then under the expectation measure, the seller has to pay the buyer 30 in damages, for that would have been his net benefit from performance, namely, $100 - 30$. Under this measure, the seller obviously will not commit breach when the outside bid is 50, for that is less than the price from the buyer, and he would not breach when the outside bid is 90, for this would give him only 20 more than the buyer would pay but he would have to pay damages of 30. The seller will commit breach only when the outside bid is 150, which is the outcome under the mutually desirable complete contract, as discussed in Example 1.
>
> That the expectation measure is mutually preferred to other measures can be shown by the usual kind of reasoning. Suppose, for instance, that the damage measure is only 10 and the contract price 70, so that the seller would breach when the outside bid is 90. In this case, the value of the contract to the buyer is $50\% \times (100 - 70) + 50\% \times 10 = 20$ and the value to the seller is $50\% \times 70 + 10\% \times (90 - 10) + 40\% \times (150 - 10) = 99$. If the parties change to the expectation measure and the price is raised to 79.5, both will be better off: The value to the buyer will be 20.5, and that to the seller will be $60\% \times 79.5 + 40\% \times (150$

$- 20.5) = 99.5.$[8] (It is also straightforward to demonstrate that if damages are high enough to result in performance all of the time, the parties will both prefer to use the expectation measure.)

The explanation for the result just illustrated is along lines that are familiar from Chapter 15 on production contracts. Under the expectation measure, the seller is induced to perform whenever the outside bid is less than the buyer's valuation (just as the seller was induced to perform whenever the production cost was less than the buyer's valuation in the production contract context). Because this outcome is what would have occurred under the mutually desirable completely specified contract, and maximizes the joint value the parties have to share, the expectation measure turns out to be preferred by the parties to other, lesser damage measures, or to higher ones, or to specific performance.

Bids made only to the contract buyer. In this case, specific performance leads to the same outcome as in the mutually desirable completely specified contract and is the mutually preferred remedy for breach. The explanation is immediate from what was discussed about the completely specified contract. Because it is the contract buyer who has the opportunity to sell to the outside bidder, it is best for the parties to give that opportunity to him, which is what specific performance accomplishes.

Bids made either to the contract buyer or the contract seller. Here, the expectation measure or higher measures—as well as specific performance—lead to the same outcomes as in mutually desirable completely specified contracts and are equivalent, mutually preferred, remedies for breach. Because the expectation measure or higher measures result in performance at least as often as whenever the outside bid is less than the buyer's valuation, they result in the behavior called for in completely specified contracts. Therefore, these remedies for breach lead to maximized joint value and are

8. The example can be modified to take into account the possibility of repurchase by the contract buyer from the outsider. If damages are 10, the seller breaches and sells to the outsider when his bid is 90, and the contract buyer then buys back from him at a price of 95, again both parties can be made better off. In particular, the value of the contract to the buyer would be $50\% \times (100 - 70) + 10\% \times (10 + (100 - 95)) + 40\% \times 10 = 20.5$, and the value to the seller would be as before, 99. If the parties change to the expectation measure and the price is raised to 79.4, both will be better off: The value to the buyer will be 20.6, and that to the seller will be $60\% \times 79.4 + 40\% \times (150 - 20.6) = 99.4$.

equivalent for the parties.[9] A damage measure that is less than the expectation measure would be undesirable for the parties, however, because it might lead to an outcome in which the seller sells to an outsider when his bid is less than the buyer's valuation, resulting in a loss in total value to the two contracting parties. For this reason, such a damage measure is inferior to the others.

The last point, that a damage measure less than the expectation measure is not desirable for the parties, has an important implication: *Specific performance is mutually preferred to the expectation measure if courts might underestimate the value of performance.* The reason is that, if the expectation were to be underestimated, then the seller might breach when the outside bid is less than the buyer's true valuation. In the example, if the court thought the value of the good to the buyer were 80 (instead of 100), then it would compute expectation damages to be only 10 (instead of 30) when the contract price is 70, so that the seller would commit breach when the outside bid is 90 (instead of performing). Such outcomes reduce joint value to the contracting parties.[10] They can be avoided for sure under specific performance. To put the point differently, under specific performance, it is always the buyer who decides whether to sell to an outside bidder, and thus he will do so naturally if and only if the outside bid exceeds his valuation. Under the expectation measure, in contrast, the seller decides whether to sell to an outside bidder, and will do so on the basis of a possibly too-low court estimate of the buyer's valuation.

1.5 Comment.   It has been assumed throughout this section that the magnitudes of outside bids are given, but it may be that these bids are influenced by the remedy for breach. Notably, other things being equal, one might expect the price that the seller could obtain through bargaining with an outsider to be higher the more the seller would have to pay in

9. By equivalent is meant that for any contract of one type, there is a contract of the other type that is equivalent for both parties (given a suitable change in the contract price).

10. Note that the possibility of overestimation of the value of performance by courts does not affect the argument under discussion. If overestimation occurs, it only means that the contract buyer will receive the good and then sell to the outside bidder, rather than the seller selling to the outside bidder when the outside bid exceeds the buyer's value but is less than the court's overestimate of the buyer's value. This does not alter the joint value of the contract to the contracting parties.

damages for breach. This gives the parties to the contract an incentive to employ higher damages for breach than they otherwise would.[11]

1.6 Interpretation of the discussion of this section: the appeal of specific performance. An interpretation of our discussion of remedies for breach is that the parties will find specific performance appealing. The virtue of specific performance is that it guarantees that the good will never be sold to outsider bidders at a price less than the buyer's valuation. As has been emphasized, to the extent that that occurs, it reduces the joint value of the contract to the contracting parties (even if the buyer re-purchases from the outsider). Moreover, such value-reducing sales to outside bidders are a danger under the expectation measure if there is a risk of underestimation of the value of performance. Therefore, if the buyer and seller have equal access to outside bids, or if the buyer alone has access to outside bids, the parties to the contract will prefer specific performance to the expectation measure, and the more so the greater the likelihood of underestimation of the true value to the buyer.[12] Only if the seller has better access to outside bids would the parties prefer the expectation measure.

1.7 Contract law. In Anglo-American law, the usual remedy for breach of contract is, as was stated earlier, the expectation measure. Specific performance is sometimes employed, however, mainly for certain types of contracts for transfer of possession: for land contracts and for things whose value is idiosyncratic and hard to assess, such as paintings.[13] Under French law, specific performance is the standard remedy for all contracts for transfer of things, while damages are the remedy for breach of contracts to make things or to perform services.[14] Under German law, the remedy for all con-

11. This point was originally made by Diamond and Maskin 1979 and has been developed by, among others, Aghion and Bolton 1987, Chung 1992, and Spier and Whinston 1995.

12. Another reason the parties would prefer specific performance concerns reliance: under specific performance, the buyer's degree of reliance would be optimal, whereas under the expectation measure such reliance tends to be excessive for the reasons given in section 3 of Chapter 15.

13. See, for example, Calamari and Perillo 1998, 614–617, and E. Farnsworth 1999, 773–777.

14. See, for example, Treitel 1988, 55–63, and Zweigert and Kötz 1998, 475–479.

tracts is nominally specific performance.[15] Thus, in important legal systems, specific performance plays a major role as a remedy for breach of contracts for transfer of possession, in contrast to the dominating role of damage measures for contracts to produce things. The mutual appeal of specific performance for contracts for transfer of possession, as I have explained in this section, may help to describe the pattern of its use in legal systems.

1.8 Contrast with production contracts. Recall from Chapter 15 that in the case of production contracts, specific performance is undesirable because of its effect on performance: It may lead to inefficient production when production cost exceeds the value of performance. Here, by contrast, specific performance has a beneficial effect on performance: Its use means that the jointly undesirable outcome of sale to outsiders when bids are less than the buyer's valuation will be avoided (presuming that outside bids are available to the contract buyer). Also, in the case of production contracts, the use of specific performance imposes great detrimental risk on sellers. But here specific performance imposes no risk of loss, only a transfer of the opportunity to avail oneself of the benefit to sell to a high outside bidder. Thus, the mutual desirability of the two types of remedy is quite different in the two contexts.[16]

Note on the literature. Most legal writing on the use of specific performance has focused on the inability of courts to estimate the value of performance and has justified specific performance on that ground. Thus, the notion has been that the purpose of remedies is to guarantee that the victim be made whole, and the insufficiency of expectation damages has therefore led to the conclusion that specific performance would be needed to accomplish this purpose.[17] This view, note, makes no reference to the mutuality of interests of the contracting parties, to the fact that the potential

15. See, for example, Treitel 1988, 51–55, and Zweigert and Kötz 1998, 472–474.

16. The possibility of outside bids is also present in the production context; a good that has to be produced is also one for which an outsider might make a bid. Therefore, what was noted here about outside bids also has implications for production contracts. The main implication is that, after a good is produced but before it is delivered, specific performance would seem to have some advantages.

17. See, for example, E. Farnsworth 1999, 773–777, and references cited therein.

victim of a breach may not be risk averse, nor to the fact that, in contracts for production, the expectation measure may also be difficult to estimate yet is employed. The explanation for the use of specific performance given in this section, concerning the mutual interests of the parties to the contract and avoiding sale to outside bidders at a price less than the buyer's valuation, is developed in Shavell (1984a).[18] Kronman (1978b) also considers an explanation for use of specific performance based on its mutual desirability. He suggests that sellers tend to believe that high outside bids are unlikely, whereas buyers believe that high outside bids are likely; hence, buyers will value specific performance substantially and sellers will view it as costing them little. But the basis for Kronman's assumption of asymmetric beliefs about outside bids between sellers and buyers is unclear.[19]

2. DONATIVE CONTRACTS

2.1 Definition and questions to be addressed. A donative contract is an agreement under which one person, the *donor,* binds himself to give a gift to another party, the *donee,* but in which the donee does not agree to do anything directly in return for the donor. For example, a person may contract to give a gift to a relative or to a charitable or educational institution without such a donee promising anything in return. We will be concerned with three questions in analyzing donative contracts. The first is why gift-giving occurs at all. The second is why donors who want to give gifts may wish to defer them rather than give them immediately. The third is why donors who wish to defer gifts would want to obligate themselves contractually, that is, why they do not merely wait to give gifts without obligating themselves to do so.

2.2 Why gifts are given: altruism. Perhaps the most prominent motive for the giving of gifts is altruism, by which I mean that the donor derives utility from increasing the well-being of the donee. An altruistic donor will want to give a gift if the altruistic utility he derives from doing so exceeds the utility he would have obtained from using his gift for his own purposes.

---

18. This analysis is amplified in Bishop 1985.

19. See also Schwartz 1979 and Ulen 1984 on economic analysis of specific performance.

2.3 Why altruistic donors may defer giving gifts.   One reason why a donor may wait before making a gift is simply that his assets may not be liquid. Another reason for deferral is that the donor may earn a higher rate of return on funds than the donee during the period before the donee actually needs to use the funds. A third reason for deferral concerns uncertainty. The donor may be uncertain about his financial situation; he may worry that he will suffer a financial reversal or find that his needs for funds are unexpectedly high. If so, he might turn out not to want to give a gift. Likewise, the donor may be uncertain about the donee. The donee's needs or his financial position may change, or he may reveal characteristics that alter the donor's altruistic feelings about him. By deferring their gifts, donors preserve their options and need not give gifts, or can limit their size, according to the resolution of uncertain factors.[20]

2.4 Why altruistic donors may—or may not—want to make contracts to give gifts.   Why would a donor who wishes to defer a gift want to bind himself contractually to give it? Why not merely wait and give the gift?

An apparent answer concerns reliance by the donee. If a donee relies on receiving a gift, the value of the gift to the donee will often be enhanced, and this will inure to the benefit of the altruistic donor. If a nephew expects to receive a gift financing his college education, he may be led to study harder now and thereby gain admission to a better college or otherwise increase the value of the gift to himself; if a symphony orchestra relies on receiving a gift, it may decide to hire talented new members who are now available and thereby raise the value of the gift to itself.[21] Thus, if a contract

---

20. The reasons given in this paragraph also help to explain why donors whose motivations are different from altruism (see section 2.6) may defer gifts.

21. It may be clarifying to express the underlying idea of this paragraph formally; for details, see Shavell 1991a. Suppose that $v(x, r)$ is the value to the donee of a gift of magnitude x, given that the donee has engaged in the level of reliance r, so that the donee's net utility is $v(x, r) - r$. Let the donor's utility be given by $u(w - x) + \alpha[v(x, r) - r]$, where w is the donor's wealth, u is his utility from his own use of his wealth, and $\alpha > 0$ measures the strength of his altruistically derived benefit from the donee's net utility. Thus, it is apparent that if raising r increases the donee's net utility $v(x, r) - r$, it will also raise the donor's utility.

is necessary to induce value-enhancing reliance by the donee, the donor might want to make a contract to give a gift.

But a contract may not be needed in order to induce donee reliance. Consider the situation of a donor who does not make a contract to give a gift but announces his intentions to do so and whose financial situation and altruistic feelings are known to the donee. The donee may well then find it rational to rely, for he will know that it will probably be rational for the donor to follow through with the gift. If the nephew knows his uncle's altruistic feelings, the nephew knows that it will likely be rational for his uncle to give him the gift; thus the nephew may well have an incentive to study for college. Indeed, it can even be shown that, in the absence of a contract, a donee who understands the altruistic tastes of the donor will have an incentive to rely excessively, in order to induce an even larger gift from the donor.[22]

It follows that for a donor to want to make a contract to make a gift in order to induce reliance, the situation must be that the donee is unsure of the donor's financial situation or unsure of his motivations, perhaps suspecting him of masquerading as an altruist for some other reason, such as to enhance his reputation. Thus, if a person who is not well known to

---

22. The reason for this is that, on one hand, the donee knows that the higher his level of reliance, the greater the gift that the donor will be induced to give due to his altruism; and, on the other hand, the donee does not count as a cost to himself (whereas the donor does) the gift itself. In particular, and using the notation of the previous note, observe the following about the situation in which no contract is made, and the donee has knowledge of the donor's utility function and strength of altruism α: (a) If the donee selects r, then the donor will choose his gift x to maximize $u(w - x) + \alpha[v(x,r) - r]$. Call the donor's choice $x(r)$, which can be shown to be increasing in r (presuming that w is above a threshold). (b) The donee will select r to maximize $v(x(r), r) - r$, because the donee knows the function $x(r)$. The donee's choice, denoted r^*, must obey $v_x(x(r), r)x'(r) + v_r(x(r), r) - 1 = 0$. (c) The donor would like the donee to choose r to maximize the donor's utility, namely, $u(w - x(r)) + \alpha[v(x(r),r) - r]$, which for simplicity we will assume is concave in r. The donor's preferred choice, denoted r^{**}, must satisfy $-u'(w - x(r))x'(r) + \alpha[v_x(x(r),r)x'(r) + v_r(x(r),r) - 1] = 0$. (d) It is apparent that $r^{**} < r^*$; the donor's preferred level of reliance is less than what the donee will actually choose. Specifically, from the first-order condition in (b), we know that the left-hand side of the condition in (c) reduces to $-u'(w - x(r^*))x'(r^*)$ when evaluated at r^*. But $-u'(w - x(r^*))x'(r^*) < 0$. Hence, given the assumption of concavity, r must be lower than r^* to satisfy the condition in (c); thus, $r^{**} < r^*$.

the nephew (an elderly, distant cousin) announces his intention to finance his college education, the nephew might be much less sure that the gift will be forthcoming and not have the same incentive to study for college that he would if the uncle who is known to be fond of him had made the same statement. As a consequence, the distant cousin might have to make a contract to give the gift in order to induce the nephew to study for college.

The conclusion is that there is not always a need for altruistic donors to make a contract to induce reliance; they will need to do that only if the donees are not aware of the donors' financial situation or their altruistic feelings. Moreover, even if donors would need to make a contract to induce beneficial reliance by donees, there is an important reason why a donor will not want to make a contract to give a gift. As discussed earlier, uncertain events, such as an unanticipated loss of the donor's wealth, might lead him not to want to make a gift after all, so he would not want to be bound to do so. Hence, donors may or may not want to make contracts to give gifts even if that is necessary to induce the best level of reliance.

2.5 Implications for contract law.   (a) The possibility that donors may want to make contracts to give gifts in order to induce reliance by donees implies that the law ought to allow contracts to give gifts. For then donors will more often make gifts, raising both their overall utility and that of donees.

(b) But the point that altruists' announcements of their intentions to give gifts are often sufficient to induce reliance, together with the point that donors may not want to be bound due to various uncertainties, suggests that it may well be desirable for the law to allow donors to state their intentions to give gifts without binding them to do so. Accordingly, a two-tier system of informal nonbinding announcements of intention, coupled with a formal binding gift contract, may actually be best (see section 2.7).

2.6 Nonaltruistic motivations for gift-giving.   Let us now consider two motivations for gift-giving other than altruism and consider their implications for contracts.

(a) *Paternalism.* A paternalistic donor may be defined as one who, like the altruistic donor, wants to enhance the well-being of the donee but, unlike the altruistic donor, has a view of the donee's well-being that is different from the donee's own view of his well-being. Thus, an altruistic donor may well desire that the donee engage in a pattern of consumption or of behavior that departs from what the donee would choose for himself. For example, a paternalistic donor may want a donee to take music lessons because the donor believes this will benefit the donee, even though the donee does not want the lessons.[23] It seems that paternalistic donors often have a stronger reason than do altruistic donors to make contracts to give gifts in order to induce behavior that they desire. To induce a donee who does not wish to take music lessons to take the lessons, the paternalistic donor will have to make a contract to give the gift and tie the gift to the taking of music lessons: Without the contract, the donee will not take the lessons because, by hypothesis, he does not want to, whereas with the contract, he may well be led to do so. In contrast, the nephew of the altruistic uncle often does not need a contract to induce him to study; his expectation of a gift combined with his desire to go to a good college and further himself may lead to his doing so.

(b) *Enjoyment of gratitude and reputational enhancement.* Another motive for giving gifts is enjoying gratitude from others or securing an enhanced reputation. When a person gives a gift to a relative, for example, an important reason may be to benefit from the gratitude expressed by the recipient and other family members; when a donor makes a gift to a university, it may be that what he wants is to be honored by the university community and the general public. If, however, the donor has to defer the gift (perhaps because of liquidity problems), he faces a difficulty: He would like to benefit from the appreciation of others during the period before he actually makes the gift, but in the absence of making a contract to give the gift, the donee may not believe that he will receive the gift and therefore not express gratitude for it. For example, someone who claims that he will give a large sum to endow a university professorship in ten years might not be believed by the university and thus not be honored during the ten-year period. Such donors may find it advantageous to make contracts to give gifts in the future so that they can enjoy donee gratitude before they complete their gifts.[24]

23. In some cases what is described as paternalistic might be interpreted as due to the donee's failure to understand what is in his true interests. For our purposes, however, it will not matter whether this is what underlies paternalism.

24. This argument for why donors may want to contract to make gifts must be qualified to the degree that a person who made an unenforceable promise to give a gift would be induced

2.7 The law. In the United States, promises to give gifts are not legally enforceable in many jurisdictions (those that have abolished the seal). Promises to give gifts that are reasonably relied upon by donees usually are enforceable, however, and promises to give gifts to charitable institutions are generally enforceable as well.[25] These exceptions suggest that the law does provide donors the opportunity to make binding gifts when they would want to. Note especially that, as explained, the principal reasons that donors would want to obligate themselves are to enjoy gratitude and to induce reliance, and when reliance is induced, they do become bound (presuming the reliance they want is reasonable). At the same time, it is unlikely that a person would become bound against his will, for he could state his intent but not promise to give a gift, and thus not be bound even if there were reliance. In France, Germany, and most civil law jurisdictions, a donor obligates himself if and only if he makes a sufficiently formal written promise, typically before a notary; so the donor has effective control over the enforceability of donative promises.[26]

Note on the literature. Posner (1977) and Goetz and Scott (1980) analyze donative contracts from an economic orientation, the latter emphasizing that such contracts may induce donee reliance, to the donor's benefit. Shavell (1991a) asks why gifts are often deferred, and for deferred gifts compares donative contracts with mere statements of intention as ways of inducing donee reliance.[27]

---

to carry through with it due to a desire to maintain his reputation. But this factor is limited by, among other elements, the possibility that a donor could claim that changes in circumstance forced him not to make the gift. Also, many gifts are made at or near the end of a person's life, and at that point, the importance of the reputational element may be attenuated.

25. On the enforceability of donative promises, see, for example, Calamari and Perillo, 1998, 166–171, 175–180, 247–267, Eisenberg 1979, and E. Farnsworth 1999, 50–52, 85–87, 91–101.

26. See, for example, Zweigert and Kötz 1998, 389–390.

27. Other economically oriented analyses of donative contracts include Posner 1997; see also Kull 1998.

PART IV | LITIGATION AND THE LEGAL PROCESS

Here I investigate what has so far largely been taken for granted, namely, that when a party has a legal right to collect from an injurer, he can do so. In fact, a party must expend effort and funds to obtain a settlement or a judgment from trial. Indeed, as will be indicated, litigation to achieve settlements or judgments is so costly that its expense appears on average to outweigh the amounts received by victims of harm. Moreover, the costs of litigation mean that it may not occur, with significant consequences for the effectiveness of the legal system.

In Chapter 17, I consider the basic theory of litigation, where I describe the three phases of litigation: its initiation through suit, the determination of whether the parties will settle their case or proceed to trial, and, if trial results, the trial expenditures. I also analyze the social desirability of parties' decisions, a major theme being that the private incentives to litigate may diverge from what is socially desirable. In Chapter 18, I extend the basic theory of litigation, examining among other issues the bringing of negative value suits, the shifting of legal fees to losers at trial, lawyer-client fee arrangements, and the influence of insurers on litigation.

Then, in Chapter 19, I discuss several general aspects of the legal process not considered in the basic theory and its extensions, including private systems of adjudication, the value of accuracy in adjudication, the appeals process, and the function of legal advice.

17 ||| BASIC THEORY OF LITIGATION

In this chapter, I take up the basic theory of litigation. Three stages will be considered. In the first, the party who has suffered a loss decides whether to bring a suit. A party who brings a suit is the *plaintiff,* and the party who is sued is the *defendant.* In the second stage, the plaintiff and the defendant decide whether or not they will settle the case—in the event of a settlement, the plaintiff agrees to drop the suit, usually in exchange for a payment from the defendant. If a settlement is not reached, the third stage, that of trial, occurs.

In each stage, I discuss how the parties behave and then how this compares to what is socially desirable. I emphasize that the private incentives of parties in litigation may diverge significantly from socially appropriate incentives, given that litigation is costly.

1. BRINGING OF SUIT

1.1 Definition of suit. By a suit, I mean the taking of a costly initial step that is a prerequisite to further legal proceedings and trial. One may interpret suit as a formal legal action, such as the filing of a complaint, or as an action short of that, notably, the hiring of a lawyer. Bringing a suit involves costs; the plaintiff will expend time and energy and possibly incur a bill for legal services and filing fees.

1.2 Private incentive to sue. The plaintiff will sue when his cost of suit is less than his expected benefits from suit.[1] The plaintiff's expected benefits from suit involve possible settlement payments or gains from trial. For the purposes of this and the next section on suit, it will be sufficient to assume simply that there is an expected benefit from suit, without inquiring into its determination.

From the simple description of suit, note that suit is more likely the lower the cost of suit, the greater the likelihood of winning at trial, and the greater the plaintiff's award conditional on winning. Suit is also more likely the less averse to risk the plaintiff is and the more averse the defendant is.

1.3 Volume of suit and its costs. About 2.3 million noncriminal cases were filed in federal courts in 2000, and approximately 20.1 million noncriminal cases were filed in state courts.[2] These figures are probably underestimates, because many individuals who threaten suit settle without ever having filed suit in a formal sense and many disputes are arbitrated.

The total costs of litigation, including those of suit, are great, as is indicated by the facts that legal services absorb approximately 1 percent of the labor force and 1.3 percent of gross domestic production.[3] The costs of suit, that is, of initiating legal action, are difficult to estimate, but a simple calculation is suggestive. If the hourly rate of a lawyer is, say, $250 and suit would require only twenty hours of the lawyer's time, the cost would be $5,000, excluding the consideration of the plaintiff's time, which could well be significant.[4] Thus, even if individuals are certain to prevail in trials, they will not bring suit unless their losses surpass a fairly significant threshold.[5]

---

1. In this chapter it will be assumed that parties are risk neutral unless otherwise noted.

2. See Ostrom, Kauder, and LaFountain 2001a, 13. The number of cases stated in the text for state courts excludes not only criminal cases, but also juvenile cases and traffic cases.

3. See *Statistical Abstract of the United States, 2001*, tables 596, 641, pp. 384, 418.

4. The average hourly rate of a partner in a law firm as of January 1, 2001, was $246; see *2001 Survey of Law Firm Economics*, 11–39.

5. This statement applies as well if the lawyer is bearing his own costs, under a contingency fee (see section 7 of Chapter 18).

2. FUNDAMENTAL DIVERGENCE BETWEEN THE PRIVATE AND THE SOCIALLY DESIRABLE LEVEL OF SUIT

2.1 In general.   I now take up the question of how the number of suits that parties are motivated to bring compares to the socially optimal level of suit. The main point that will be made is that the private incentive to bring suit is fundamentally misaligned with the socially optimal incentive to do so, and the deviation between them could be in either direction. The reasons for this conclusion may be understood as follows.

On one hand, there is a divergence between the social and the private costs of suit that can lead to a socially excessive level of suit. Specifically, when a plaintiff contemplates bringing suit, he bears only his own costs; he does not take into account the defendant's costs or the state's costs that his suit will engender. Hence, the plaintiff might be led to bring suit when the total costs associated with suit would make that undesirable.

On the other hand, there is a difference between the social and private benefits of suit that may lead to a socially inadequate level of suit or may reinforce the cost-related tendency toward excessive suit. In particular, the plaintiff would not usually be expected to treat as a benefit to himself the social benefits flowing from suit, notably, its deterrent effect on the behavior of injurers (and more generally, other effects as well).[6] What the plaintiff does consider as the benefit from suit is the gain he personally would obtain from prevailing. This private gain is not the same as the social benefit from suit—the private gain is a transfer from the defendant and, as will be seen, could be either larger or smaller than the social benefit from suit.

2.2 The divergence in a simple model.   To clarify these points, let us consider for concreteness the model studied in Part Two of the book, on accidents, in which injurers can exercise care to lower the risk of accidents, and the social welfare goal is minimization of total social costs, comprised of the costs of precautions, those of accidents that occur, and also

---

6. One way of expressing this point about deterrence is to observe that by bringing suit, plaintiffs contribute to potential injurers' general impression that they will be sued if they cause harm. Were the law only on the books, but never to result actually in suit, potential injurers would have nothing to fear.

the costs of litigation. Thus, the socially optimal amount of suit is that which minimizes total social costs. We want to show that the amount of suit that private parties find it in their interest to bring could be greater or less than the socially optimal amount. Let us assume that liability is strict (I will comment on the negligence rule below), and consider two examples.

> *Example 1.* To illustrate the possibility of socially excessive suit, suppose that the losses a victim would suffer in an accident are $10,000, that a victim's cost of bringing suit is $3,000 and an injurer's cost of defending is $2,000, that the probability of accidents is 10 percent, and that there is no precaution that injurers can take to lower the accident risk.
>
> Victims will then bring suits whenever accidents occur, for suing will cost a victim only $3,000 and yield him $10,000. From the social perspective, this outcome is undesirable. Suit creates no beneficial deterrent, because injurers by assumption cannot do anything to lower risk. Yet suit does generate legal costs: Expected legal costs are 10% × ($3,000 + $2,000) = $500. The bringing of suits is not socially desirable in this example because there are no incentives toward safety created by the suits. This fact is of no moment to victims, nor are other parties' litigation costs. Victims bring suits for their private gain of $10,000.

Although in this example there was no deterrent benefit whatever from the bringing of suits, it should be obvious that the point of the example would hold if the deterrent benefit were positive and not too large.

Let us now illustrate the opposite possibility, that suits might not be brought even though it would be best that they are brought.

> *Example 2.* Suppose here that the losses victims suffer in accidents are $1,000 and that an expenditure of $10 by injurers will reduce the probability of accidents from 10 percent to 1 percent. The costs of suit and of defending against suits are as in the previous example.
>
> In this case victims will not bring suits, because doing so would cost a victim $3,000 but yield him only $1,000. Because injurers will not be sued, they will have no reason to take care to reduce risk, and total social costs will therefore be 10% × $1,000 = $100.
>
> It would be socially desirable for victims to bring suit, however. If they were to do so, injurers would be led to spend $10 to lower risk from 10 percent to 1 percent, and total social costs would thus be $10 +

1% × ($1,000 + $3,000 + $2,000) = $70. The bringing of suits is socially worthwhile here ($70 being less than $100), because of the significant reduction in accident losses that would result. (And observe that this is true even though the total legal costs of $5,000 exceed the victim's losses of $1,000.) But victims do not take the deterrence-related benefits of suit into account. Each victim looks only to his own gain from suit, which is negative.

As emphasized, a victim does not bring suit in this example because his private gain, the harm he has sustained, is not sufficient to outweigh his legal costs, even though the general deterrent that would be engendered by the bringing of suits would so reduce accident losses that the bringing of suits would be socially worthwhile.[7]

2.3 The divergence continued; its importance and interpretation. There are a number of issues that bear on the foregoing and its interpretation.

(a) *Negligence rule and the divergence between the private and the socially optimal level of suit.* Under the negligence rule, there is some reason to believe that the possible problem of excessive suit is less serious than under

---

. 7. A formal explanation of the points made in this section is as follows. Suppose that liability is strict. Victims will sue if and only if $c_P < h$, where c_P is the victim's (plaintiff's) cost of suit and h is the harm suffered and what he will collect if he sues. Let q be the probability of harm h if suit is not brought, let q' be the probability of harm if suit is brought, and let x be the precaution expenditures that injurers will be induced to make if there is suit. (Thus, q' will be less than q if x is positive.) If suit is not brought, total social costs will simply be qh. If suit is brought, social costs will be $q'h + x + q'(c_P + c_D + c_S)$, where c_D is the injurer's (defendant's) litigation cost and c_S is the state's cost. Hence, the bringing of suit will lower total costs, be socially worthwhile, if and only if $q'(c_P + c_D + c_S) < (q - q')h - x$. In other words, suit is socially worthwhile if the expected litigation costs are less than the net deterrence benefits of suit. It is clear that this social condition for when suits should be brought, and the private condition for when they will be brought, namely, $c_P < h$, are very different. Whether victims will sue does not depend on the costs c_D and c_S. Moreover, the private benefit of suit is h, the amount of harm (conditional on harm occurring), because this is what the victim will receive as a damages award; in contrast, the social benefit depends on the harm weighted by the reduction in the accident probability, $q - q'$, net of the cost of precautions x. Therefore it is evident (as the examples illustrate) that victims might sue when suit is not socially optimal, and that victims might not sue even when suit would be socially optimal.

strict liability. The main reason is that, under the negligence rule, a harmful outcome is less likely to produce a suit than under strict liability because negligence must be shown in order to prevail. Indeed, in a hypothetical, perfectly working negligence system, a harmful outcome that is not the result of negligence would never result in suit, and this turns out to imply that there will never be a problem of excessive suit, and indeed that it would be desirable for the state to subsidize suits.[8] Of course, the negligence system does not operate perfectly in practice; victims sometimes bring suit against nonnegligent injurers and injurers sometimes act negligently. Therefore, problems of socially excessive suit may well exist under the negligence rule, but it is plausible that they would be worse under strict liability.

(b) *Generality of the divergence between the socially optimal and the privately induced amount of suit.* It should be clear from the discussion in section 2.1 that the point that the private and the social incentives to bring suit may diverge is quite robust. On one hand, it will always be the case that the private cost of use of the system will be less than the social cost. And, on the other hand, the private benefits from suit will be what the plaintiff will win from suit, usually money, whereas the social benefits from suit will ordinarily be different: They will always include deterrence benefits and may also include compensation of victims (if insurance is unavailable) and the setting of precedent. Potential plaintiffs will not tend to take all of these social benefits into account.

The private and social incentives to bring suit may, however, roughly coincide in contract disputes. In such cases, the interested parties (with the exception of the state) are present at the bargaining table and actively design their contracts before disputes arise. Hence, we would expect contracting parties to set the terms of their agreements to minimize their expected losses *plus* their joint litigation costs. For example, to avoid litigation costs, contracting parties might stipulate that certain problems will not be deemed breaches of contract, or they might require that disputes will be inexpensively arbitrated. Nevertheless, many contracts will not be suffi-

---

8. If the state's policy is to subsidize suit such that victims would always be willing to bring suit for negligently caused harm, injurers would be led by the threat of suit to take due care. Hence, no suits would actually result, and no litigation costs would in fact be incurred by society.

ciently detailed to include such remedies for problems of inappropriate suit, so that an attenuated private-social divergence to sue may still exist.

(c) *Practical importance of the divergence.* The difference in the private and the social costs of suit is often large, at least in percentage terms. As emphasized, the private cost divergence is that victims do not take into account injurers' and the state's litigation costs. Thus, it is not unreasonable to expect that victims may fail to take into account around half of total litigation costs.[9]

The difference between the private and the social benefits of suit can also be substantial. First, many harms are serious and give the victim significant incentives to sue, yet deterrence effects may be relatively small for a variety of reasons. To illustrate, let us consider two important areas of litigation: automobile accident litigation and product liability litigation.

With regard to automobile accidents, we know that harms are sufficient to generate a tremendous volume of suit: It is estimated that automobile accident disputes make up at least half of all tort litigation.[10] But intuition suggests that liability-related deterrence of these accidents may be modest. Individuals have good reasons not to cause automobile accidents apart from wanting to avoid liability: They may be injured themselves, and they face fines for traffic violations and also serious criminal penalties for grossly irresponsible behavior (drunkenness, excessive speed). Given the existence of these incentives toward accident avoidance, and given that the deterrent due to liability is dulled by ownership of liability insurance, one wonders how much the threat of tort liability adds to deterrence.[11]

In the area of product liability, it also appears plausible that the incentives created by the prospect of liability are not substantial in relation to litigation costs. Whether or not they will be held liable, firms do not want their products to harm their customers because, if this occurs, firms will

9. For example, in 2000, victims' fraction of total litigation expenditures by victims and defendants in tort cases was approximately 52 percent; see Tillinghast-Towers Perrin 2002. Also, in 1986, victims' fraction of total litigation expenses in automobile litigation was about 54 percent, and their fraction of total litigation expenses in nonautomobile tort litigation was about 42 percent; see Hensler et al. 1987.

10. See Kakalik and Pace 1986, x, and Ostrom, Kauder, and LaFountain 2001b, 28.

11. Dewees, Duff, and Trebilcock 1996, 15–26, and Sloan 1998 survey empirical studies of the effects of liability on automobile accidents; as they discuss, the evidence is mixed and in some respects contradictory.

tend to lose business and/or have to lower their prices as a consequence. It is true, admittedly, that this inducement toward safety relies on the assumption that consumers will learn about the risks of different product defects, whereas consumer information is almost never perfect. But it may well be that consumer information is often tolerably good and that, on net, the marginal deterrence engendered by the threat of product liability is not great. Although study of the effect of product liability on accidents is, as with automobile accidents, somewhat sparse, it is not inconsistent with the hypothesis of low deterrence.[12] The litigation costs of product liability, however, are high. Therefore, it again appears conceivable that the private incentive to sue has resulted in an excessive volume of suit.[13]

The opposite possibility, that the volume of suit is socially inadequate, also seems to be of practical significance. Recall Example 2 in which an individual's losses were relatively low, so that suit would not be brought, but in which the frequency of harmful events could be fairly cheaply reduced. This example seems to be of real relevance. One can readily imagine situations in which firms know that the harms that they cause will not be great enough to be worthwhile for a typical victim to pursue, even though the incidence of the harms could be decreased substantially by modest expenditures. (Consider low-level pollution damage, such as more frequent peeling of paint in a neighborhood near a factory, that the factory could eliminate by installing inexpensive smoke scrubbers.) One can also envision situations in which, even though the magnitude of harm might be high, the expected value of suit is still low because of difficulty in proving causation. (Suppose the pollution from the factory can produce cancer but its etiology

---

12. For example, in one of the few empirical studies on product liability and deterrence, Priest 1988 examined aggregate statistics on accident and fatality rates; he found no evidence that the amount of litigation activity influenced injury or death rates. Also, Dewees, Duff, and Trebilcock 1996, 205, conclude their survey of empirical literature on product liability by stating that there is little evidence that strict product liability has brought socially desirable safety gains.

13. Note that the argument of this paragraph does not apply with regard to product liability provisions that the parties write into their contracts, but only to court-mandated product liability. Note also that the argument obviously does not apply to harms to parties who are not injuring firms' customers (such as people who live near a factory and are harmed by an explosion), for in the absence of liability, firms will have no financial incentive to avoid causing them loss.

is hard to demonstrate.) If, once causation were established, many other suits could easily be brought, then it might be socially valuable for suit to be filed in the case at hand even though that would not be advantageous to the individual plaintiff.

(d) *Cost of suit leads to inadequacy of precautions.* An issue that we have not adequately discussed concerns the effect of the costs of suit on the level of precautions that injurers are led to take. As a general matter, the costliness of suit means that injurers' incentives to take precautions will be too low, for two reasons. First, and obviously, injurers might not be sued due to litigation costs faced by victims, and thus injurers' expected liability will tend to be too low; this is especially likely if the level of harm they are likely to cause is lower than victims' costs of suit. Second, even if injurers expect to be sued when they cause harm for which they should be liable, their level of precautions will still be too low: The damages that injurers have to pay equal the direct harm they cause for their victims, but the full social costs include also the litigation costs associated with suit—the full costs that society incurs when harm leads to suit is not only the direct harm, but also the resources absorbed in the litigation process. Thus, for injurers' incentives to be correct, injurers should bear, in addition to the direct harm caused to victims, the litigation costs borne by victims and by the state (injurers bear their own litigation costs already). If, for example, the harm is $10,000 and litigation costs of the plaintiff are $3,000 and those of the state $1,000, the injurer should pay $14,000, not $10,000.[14] This point is significant because the litigation costs of plaintiffs are substantial; to ignore these costs is to omit perhaps a third of the damages that are needed to provide injurers with proper incentives to reduce harm.[15]

---

14. It should be observed that the conclusion of this paragraph applies whether or not the volume of suit is optimal. Even if suit is brought when it should not be, causing harm still leads society to incur litigation costs. Thus, the level of precautions should still reflect the harm plus total litigation costs, so that the injurer should still pay for the defendant's and the state's litigation costs.

15. As previously mentioned with respect to tort litigation (section 1.1 of Chapter 12), total litigation costs appear to be about equal to amounts received by plaintiffs. Also, litigation costs may be borne roughly equally by plaintiffs and defendants (note 9). Hence, for every dollar that defendants pay to plaintiffs, plaintiffs may spend 50 cents in litigation costs, and defendants need to pay this (and the state's costs) as well in order for their incentives to take precautions to be appropriate.

2.4 Corrective policy. It should be straightforward in principle for the state to remedy an imbalance between the privately determined and the socially best level of litigation. If there is excessive litigation, the state can discourage it by imposing a properly chosen fee for bringing suit or by some other device to make suit more expensive; the state could also refuse to allow unwanted categories of suit to be brought. Conversely, if there is an inadequate level of suit, the state can subsidize or otherwise encourage suit.

But the state requires a great deal of information to be able to assess the socially correct volume of suit. To determine whether suit is socially desirable, the state must ascertain not only the costs of litigation for both sides, but also the deterrent effect of suit. This means that the state needs to deduce the cost of precautions and their effectiveness.

It should be noted that, by contrast, for the state to ameliorate the problem of inadequate precautions due to the cost of suit, as just discussed in section 2.3(d), a corrective policy that will be helpful is easily identified and should not be difficult to implement. Namely, when suit is brought, liable defendants should have to pay more than the harm done; they should also have to pay victims' litigation costs and the states' costs, for only then will they be bearing the full social costs associated with harm.[16]

2.5 Comments on the foregoing. Let me now make a number of remarks about the divergence between the actual and the socially desirable amount of suit and about corrective policy.

(a) *Policies wrongly thought generally to improve the volume of suit: making plaintiffs pay the state's litigation costs, and loser-pays fee-shifting.* It follows from what has just been said that two policies that are popularly suggested as cures for an improper volume of suit cannot be taken to be so in any general sense. The first policy is making those who sue pay for the state's litigation costs, on the ground that it is economically rational for a party to have to purchase the services that he uses.[17] It is true, of course, that

---

16. If it is desirable to increase victims' incentives to sue, then the augmented damages could be paid to them; if it is best to discourage suit, certainly it would not be good to allow victims to collect more, and the extra payments of defendants should thus be made to the state.

17. For discussion of this argument, see, for example, Lee 1985 and Posner 1985b, 136.

society would usually want a person to pay for the cost of provision of any service that he enjoys. If a farmer uses the services of a government veterinarian, we would want him to pay for the veterinarian's time, for then the farmer will use veterinary services when and only when he places a value on them exceeding their cost. This is desirable because we ordinarily assume the farmer's benefit to be coincident with the social benefit, so when he decides that his benefit exceeds the veterinarian's cost, that is true for society as well. But when a person brings suit, his benefit is, as stressed, generally different from the social benefit. Hence, it is not clear that making him pay the full social costs of suit will lead to a better decision from society's perspective. (More to the point, perhaps, we know that the policy of making plaintiffs pay for the state's costs cannot be desirable in all cases, because we know that it might discourage suit when suit would be socially beneficial.)

The second policy that many find appealing is fee-shifting, under which the losing party pays the fees of the winning party. This policy is sometimes advanced on the theory that it is just or fair that someone who has been shown wrong in court should pay the other side's legal expenses.[18] The question for us to consider, however, is whether loser-pays fee-shifting will have a beneficial effect on the volume of suit.[19] In the examples and analysis that I presented above, fee-shifting would simply encourage litigation because victims—whom we have assumed to have good cases—would always be able to pass on their litigation costs to injurers. Thus, fee-shifting would tend to worsen any problem of excessive suit. Moreover, in situations where those who bring suit do not win with certainty, it can also be demonstrated that there is no general basis for a policy of loser-pays fee-shifting. This is not to deny that fee-shifting can have socially desirable effects in particular circumstances. For instance, in the example in which it was desirable for the state to subsidize suit, fee-shifting would equally induce suit; and in contexts in which some individuals would bring unmeritorious suits to extract settlements, fee-shifting might be desirable because it would discourage suits that are unlikely to succeed. But we are here examining the issue of whether there is a systematic advantage of fee-shifting in regard to controlling the volume of litigation, and there is not.

---

18. For discussion of this fairness rationale, see, for example, Rowe 1982, 653–657.

19. The proper consideration of notions of fairness from the perspective of welfare economics is discussed in Chapters 26 and 27; the relevant issue here is the effect of fee-shifting on social welfare through its influence on litigation costs and the volume of suit.

The two policies just considered thus cannot serve as general correctives for problems with the volume of suit. Furthermore, a little reflection reveals that there does not exist any simple policy tool, any "magic bullet" for achieving that purpose, because appropriate social policy depends inherently on assessment of the deterrent effect of suit, and this is intrinsically complicated.

(b) *Practical use of corrective policy.* Policies to correct the volume of suit in broad categories of cases may be desirable and feasible. If, for example, serious study of automobile accidents and/or product accidents suggests that suit is excessive—see section 2.3(c)—one could imagine imposition of fees on plaintiffs for bringing suit, or even a ban on suit, for these accidents. Similarly, if it were concluded that we ought to encourage suit for certain types of low-magnitude harms—see again section 2.3(c)—one could envision the adoption of subsidies or loser-pays fee-shifting to stimulate legal action. Such policy responses are fairly easily envisaged because they would not be difficult to implement and because we have observed their use before. On one hand, worker's compensation legislation[20] and automobile no-fault statutes have removed important categories of accident from the domain of tort law,[21] New Zealand has barred suit for all cases of personal injury,[22] and certain jurisdictions have shifted legal fees to losing plaintiffs to discourage litigation. On the other hand, legal aid programs have been employed to subsidize litigation, statutes have authorized the award of multiplied damages to spur certain types of litigation, and legal fee-shifting has been permitted in some areas for the same reason.[23]

Whether judges could reasonably decide to discourage or encourage suit in individual cases is another matter. To do this, judges would need to obtain information about, or gain a fairly good intuitive understanding of, the deterrent effect of bringing a specific type of case. One suspects that judges would not usually be able to evaluate deterrence on such a refined

20. See, for example, Dewees, Duff, and Trebilcock 1996, 387–394.

21. See, for example, Joost 1992 and Carroll et al. 1991.

22. See, for example, Palmer 1994.

23. This is not to say that these policies have been adopted on the basis that I have discussed. For example, it seems that worker's compensation legislation was enacted primarily because workers were not able to obtain compensation under the tort system, rather than because the litigation costs of the tort system were felt to outweigh its deterrence benefits.

level. Unless they could do so, the most likely type of policy that could justifiably be employed to correct the volume of suit would be legislative actions applying to whole categories of cases.

Note on the literature.   The subject of the private versus the social incentive to bring suit was first developed in Shavell (1982b).[24]

3.   SETTLEMENT VERSUS TRIAL

Assuming that suit has been brought, I now take up the question of whether parties will reach a settlement or instead go to trial. A settlement is a legally enforceable agreement, usually involving a payment from the defendant to the plaintiff, in which the plaintiff agrees not to pursue his claim further. If the parties do not reach a settlement, we will assume that they go to trial, that is, that the court will determine the outcome of their case.[25] I discuss here two different models describing whether settlement occurs and then consider the socially optimal versus the private decision of whether to settle.

3.1 Simple model.   Let us suppose for simplicity that the plaintiff and the defendant each has somehow formed beliefs—which may differ—about the trial outcome. Then we can discuss settlement possibilities in terms of two quantities. Consider first the minimum amount that the plaintiff would accept in settlement. Assuming that the plaintiff is risk neutral, this minimum acceptable amount equals his expected gain from trial less the cost of going to trial. For instance, if the plaintiff believes he will prevail with probability 70 percent, would obtain $100,000 upon prevailing, and the trial would involve expenses to him of $20,000, the minimum amount he

24. See also extensions and further developments in Kaplow 1986b, Menell 1983, Rose-Ackerman and Geistfeld 1987, and Shavell 1997, 1999; and see Ordover 1978 for related analysis.

25. The underlying assumption that there is either a settlement or a trial is to a degree an abstraction, because there can be both: A trial can proceed and before it ends, the parties can settle. Taking this possibility into account would not alter the qualitative nature of the conclusions to be reached, because it would remain true that settlement saves litigation costs and occurs before the full judicial conclusion is reached.

would accept in settlement is 70% × $100,000 − $20,000 = $70,000 − $20,000 = $50,000; if he were offered anything less than this amount, he would be better off going to trial. The other quantity is the maximum amount that the defendant would be willing to pay in settlement; this is his expected loss from trial plus his expense of going to trial. If the defendant believes the odds of the plaintiff's winning are, say, only 50 percent, and the defendant's trial costs would be $25,000, then he would pay at most 50% × $100,000 + $25,000 = $50,000 + $25,000 = $75,000 in settlement.

It is evident that *if the plaintiff's minimum acceptable amount is less than the defendant's maximum acceptable amount, a mutually beneficial settlement is possible*—a settlement equal to any amount in between these two figures would be preferable to a trial for each party. Thus, if the plaintiff's minimum is $50,000 and defendant's maximum is $75,000, any amount in between, such as $60,000, would be preferred by each to going to trial. But if the plaintiff's minimum exceeds the most that the defendant will pay, settlement cannot occur. If, for instance, the defendant thought the plaintiff's chances of winning were only 20 percent, the defendant's maximum amount would be $20,000 + $25,000 = $45,000, so the most he would pay is less than the minimum $50,000 that the plaintiff would be willing to accept, and settlement could not occur.

Can more be said about when a mutually beneficial settlement will exist? That is, under what conditions will the plaintiff's minimum acceptable demand be less than the defendant's maximum acceptable payment? It is clear that if the plaintiff and the defendant have the same beliefs about the trial outcome, then there should always exist mutually beneficial settlements, because they can each escape trial costs by settling. Suppose that they both believe that $50,000 is the expected judgment the defendant will have to pay if there is a trial. Then the trial costs that the plaintiff would bear would lead to his willingness to accept a lower figure than $50,000; if his trial costs would be $10,000, he would accept $40,000, and so forth. Conversely, any trial costs that the defendant would have to bear would increase above $50,000 what he would be willing to pay; if his trial costs would be $10,000, he would be willing to pay $60,000. Thus, the settlement range would be from $40,000 to $60,000. For settlement possibilities to be eliminated, the plaintiff's minimum amount must rise far enough from $40,000 and/or the defendant's fall far enough from $60,000 such that the plaintiff's minimum turns out to exceed the defendant's maximum. That can occur only if they have different beliefs about the trial outcome. This line of thought suggests the following conclusion: A mutually beneficial settlement amount exists as long as the plaintiff's and defendant's estimates of the expected judgment do not diverge too much. Indeed, it can be shown that *a mutually beneficial settlement exists as long as the plaintiff's estimate of the expected judgment does not exceed the defendant's estimate by more than the sum of their costs of trial.*[26] Let me illustrate.

> *Example 3.* Consider the situation mentioned earlier in which the plaintiff's expected gain from suit is 70% × $100,000 = $70,000, his costs of trial are $20,000, the defendant's expected loss is 50% × $100,000 = $50,000, and his costs of trial are $25,000. Here, we observed that mutually beneficial settlements exist, for the plaintiff would accept as little as $50,000 and the defendant would pay as much as $75,000. Notice that it is also true that the difference between the plaintiff's estimate of the expected judgment and defendant's is $70,000 − $50,000 = $20,000, and that that is less than the sum of their costs of trial, $20,000 + $25,000 = $45,000. This is consistent with the italicized statement just made. Moreover, we observed that if the defendant's estimate of the expected judgment is $20,000, he would pay only $45,000, so that no settlement exists. In this case, notice that the difference in the plaintiff's and the defendant's estimates is $70,000 − $20,000 = $50,000, which exceeds the $45,000 sum of litigation costs.

3.2 Interpretation of the model.   A number of comments may help us to interpret and understand the foregoing model.

(a) *Does the existence of a mutually beneficial settlement amount imply that settlement will occur?* Although we know that there cannot be a settlement when a mutually beneficial settlement amount does *not* exist, what can be said about the outcome when a mutually beneficial settlement

---

26. To be explicit, let p_P be the plaintiff's estimate of the probability of winning w at trial and p_D be the defendant's probability estimate that the plaintiff will prevail; and let c_P and c_D be their respective trial costs. Then the plaintiff's minimum settlement amount is $p_P w - c_P$, and the defendant's maximum settlement amount is $p_D w + c_D$. Hence, a settlement is possible if and only if $p_P w - c_P \leq p_D w + c_D$, which is to say, if and only if $p_P w - p_D w \leq c_P + c_D$.

amount does exist? The answer is that there may or may not be a settlement, depending on the nature of bargaining between the parties and the information they have about each other. This issue will be discussed in greater detail in sections 3.3 and 3.4.

(b) *Parties' beliefs.* The effect of parties' beliefs on the existence of mutually beneficial settlement amounts, and thus on the tendency toward settlement, can be easily understood from the italicized conditions stated in the preceding section. Specifically, the greater the amount by which the plaintiff's estimate of the likelihood of winning exceeds the defendant's, the smaller the tendency toward settlement, because it is the excess of the plaintiff's expected judgment over the defendant's expected payment that leads to trial. It is important to emphasize that what leads to trial is not that a plaintiff is confident of winning, but rather that he is *more* confident than the defendant thinks he has a right to be. A plaintiff's belief that he is very likely to win does not itself suggest that trial will occur, as might naively be thought. If the plaintiff is likely to win, it is true that he will ask for more in settlement from the defendant than otherwise, but it is also true that if the defendant agrees that the plaintiff is likely to win, the defendant will be willing to pay more in settlement. What makes for trial is a refusal of the defendant to pay what the plaintiff demands, and this will be the case when the defendant does not believe the plaintiff's demand is warranted, which is to say, when the defendant holds different beliefs about the expected trial outcome.

Of course, if the plaintiff assesses his chances of winning as lower than the defendant assesses the plaintiff's chances, there will be a range of mutually beneficial settlements. If, for example, the plaintiff thinks his chances of winning are 30 percent and the defendant thinks the plaintiff's chances are 50 percent, then, given the figures mentioned above, the plaintiff would accept any amount over $50,000, and the defendant would pay any amount up to $80,000. (Note also that in such cases, the italicized condition automatically holds, because the difference in the plaintiff's expected gain and defendant's expected loss is negative and therefore definitely is less than the sum of trial costs.)

What would we expect the parties' beliefs about the likelihood of trial outcomes to be? The parties may, and often will, be in possession of different information about a case when it begins. For instance, the defendant may know more about whether he would be found liable than the plaintiff knows. Also, the two sides may initially have in mind different legal arguments that they can make. But the parties may elect to share information or may be forced to do so (on which see sections 2 and 3 of Chapter 18), and parties often can independently acquire information that the other side possesses (for instance, the plaintiff could interview witnesses to an accident and learn more about the defendant's behavior). To the degree that the parties do come to similar beliefs, settlement becomes more likely.

We would not predict, though, that beliefs will always converge. For example, the parties might not want to share certain legal arguments with each other, believing that if a trial comes about, they would lose the advantage of surprise; yet in light of these arguments, each party might believe it is more likely to win than the other. Another factor standing in the way of convergence of beliefs is the element of natural optimism about one's chances.[27] Additionally, a divergence of interests between the lawyer and the client (see section 7 of Chapter 18) may lead the lawyer to tell the client less than the whole truth.

But, by and large, especially because parties have legal counsel who are likely to be familiar with the same body of law and because of opportunities for acquisition of information about facts material to disputes, we would expect beliefs about trial outcomes to be relatively close by the time of a trial, leading toward settlement.

(c) *Judgment amount.* If the size of the judgment rises, then the likelihood of trial rises, other things being constant. This is because the effect of a divergence in the assessments of the likelihood of winning is magnified if the judgment that would be awarded becomes larger. If there is, for instance, a 20 percent difference in beliefs and the judgment award would be $10,000, the difference in expected judgments would be only $2,000, perhaps not enough to exceed the sum of legal costs of trial and thus not enough to cause trial. But if the judgment would be $1,000,000, the 20 percent difference in trial outcomes would signify a $200,000 difference in expected awards, and thus be more likely to exceed the sum of trial costs, leading to trial.[28]

---

27. Loewenstein et al. 1993 and Mnookin 1993 suggest that overoptimism is plausible.

28. The condition for trial was seen to be that $p_P w - p_D w > c_P + c_D$. This is equivalent to $(p_P - p_D)w > c_P + c_D$, from which it is apparent that if w rises, trial is more likely.

Another point about the judgment amount is that, although we have assumed for simplicity that the parties agree on what the judgment amount would be, that might not be so. Differences in the parties' beliefs about the amount that would be won affect their expected judgments and thus the existence of mutually beneficial settlements, according to the italicized condition. If the plaintiff thinks he would win a larger amount than the defendant thinks, then again this would lead toward trial. Suppose, for instance, that although the plaintiff and the defendant agree that the plaintiff has a 60 percent chance of winning at trial, the plaintiff thinks the amount he would win would be $200,000 and the defendant thinks the amount would be only $100,000. Then the plaintiff's expected judgment is 60% × $200,000 = $120,000 and the defendant's expected payment is 60% × $100,000 = $60,000, a difference of $60,000. Thus, the italicized condition indicates that unless the sum of their legal costs exceeds $60,000, there exists no mutually beneficial settlement. This can be directly illustrated; if the plaintiff's trial costs are $30,000 and the defendant's are $20,000, the sum would be less than $60,000, and the minimum acceptable settlement of the plaintiff would be $90,000 and the maximum the defendant would pay would be $80,000, thus leaving no room for settlement.[29]

(d) *Legal expenses.* The larger are the legal expenses of either party, the greater are the chances of settlement, clearly, since the sum of legal costs will rise, and thus the greater will be the likelihood that the sum of legal costs will exceed any excess of the plaintiff's expectation over the defendant's expectation. One would expect legal expenses to rise with the size of the potential judgment. This factor tends to increase the chances of settlement for large stakes cases, and thus works opposite to the tendency just discussed in (c) toward litigation.

(e) *Risk aversion.* When we introduce risk aversion into the basic model, we see that it leads to a greater likelihood of settlement. The reason is simply that a trial is a risky venture because its outcome is unknown. To a risk-averse party, settlement is more attractive than it is to a risk-neutral party. Further, as the degree of risk aversion of either party increases, or

29. If we let w_P and w_D denote the amount that the plaintiff and the defendant respectively believe that they would win at trial, then the condition for trial becomes $p_P w_P - p_D w_D > c_P + c_D$, from which the statements in the text follow.

as the amount at stake increases—the size of the judgment or the size of legal fees—settlement becomes more likely, other things being equal.

3.3 Models with explicit bargaining and a locus of information.
The model so far discussed is simple in two important respects, among others. First, the bargaining process is not explicit; the range of possible settlements is determined, but whether a bargain in the range will be reached, and where so, is not predicted within the model. Second, the origin of the differences in beliefs is not explained by the model; it was merely assumed that the parties somehow come to their beliefs. More sophisticated models of settlement versus trial attempt to remedy these gaps and thus to provide additional insight into the settlement process (but, as will be re-marked, they achieve less success than might at first appear).

The most basic version of such models is that in which bargaining consists of a single offer, and the party who makes the offer lacks knowledge about the opposing side. For concreteness, assume that the plaintiff makes a single offer to the defendant, and the plaintiff does not know the probability of defendant liability, whereas the defendant does know this (be-cause, say, he has information about his own level of care). In this situation, we can determine the rational settlement offer for the plaintiff to make, and then whether or not it will be accepted. Consider the following illustration.

> *Example 4.* If the plaintiff prevails, he will obtain a judgment of $100,000. The cost of trial for the plaintiff would be $10,000. There are three types of defendants, whom the plaintiff cannot tell apart: a minority group of 10 percent, who would lose for sure; a large group of 60 percent, who would lose with probability 50 percent; and a remaining 30 percent group, who would lose only with probability 20 percent. Thus, the expected gain from trial for a plaintiff depends on which type of defendant the plaintiff in fact faces: If success against a defendant is certain, the plaintiff's gross gain from trial would be $100,000; if the likelihood of success is 50 percent, the expected gain would be $50,000; and if the likelihood of success is 20 percent, the expected gain would be $20,000. If the legal costs for a defendant would be $10,000, the plaintiff could demand and obtain as much as $110,000 from the first kind of defendant, $60,000 from the second type, and $30,000 from the third. If the plaintiff demands only $30,000, this will be accepted by all three types of defen-

dants, so the plaintiff would obtain $30,000. If the plaintiff demands
$60,000, this will be accepted by the first two types of defendants but
rejected by the third, so that the plaintiff's expected gain would be 70%
× $60,000 + 30% × ($20,000 − $10,000) = $45,000. If the plaintiff
demands $110,000, this will be accepted only by the first type of de-
fendant, so the plaintiff's expected gain would be 10% × $110,000 +
60% × ($50,000 − $10,000) + 30% × ($20,000 − $10,000) = $38,000.
Hence, the plaintiff will demand $60,000 in settlement. A consequence
of $60,000 being the rational demand for the plaintiff to make is that
in the 30 percent of cases where the defendant would lose only with a
20 percent chance, the defendant will spurn the offer and there will be
a trial.

Note that in this example, and in general, the rational settlement demand for the plaintiff may create a chance of trial. In essence, the rational
demand for the plaintiff to make may not be so low as to produce a yes
answer from any and all possible types of defendants; to ask for so little is
usually not in the expected interest of the plaintiff.[30] This feature of the
outcome, that trial may result, may be considered to be due to asymmetry
of information. For if the plaintiff knew the type of defendant he faced,
he would ask for a different amount for each type, namely, the maximum
amount that that type of defendant would be willing to pay rather than
go to trial. It is therefore the asymmetry of information that leads the ratio-

30. The model under discussion and illustrated in the example is developed in Bebchuk
1984. Its formal nature is roughly as follows. The plaintiff makes a single settlement demand
x, knowing only the probability distribution over the probability p that he will prevail over
a particular defendant, who does know his p. Thus, if $pw + c_D < x$, the defendant will
reject the demand and the plaintiff will therefore obtain only $pw − c_P$; but if $pw + c_D \geq$
x, the defendant will accept the demand and pay x. Let $z(x) = (x − c_D)/w$, the p at which
defendants will just accept the offer x rather than go to trial. Therefore, the plaintiff's
expected payoff as a function of x is

$$\int_{a}^{z(x)} (pw − c_P)f(p)dp + (1 − F(z(x)))x,$$

where a is some minimum probability of plaintiff victory (it is assumed that $aw − c_P >$
0, so the plaintiff will always want to go to trial), f is the density of p, and F is the cumulative distribution of p. The plaintiff chooses x to maximize this expression.

nal plaintiff to ask for more than some defendants are willing to pay, and thus to the possibility of trial.

3.4 Comments on and interpretation of the foregoing models. (a) *Variation of assumptions about the bargaining process.* If the bargaining process is different from that in the model just discussed, complications may arise, but the fundamental conclusion that trial may result, and that it is due to asymmetry of information, is not altered. Important changes in assumptions that have been studied involve the making of offers by parties who possess private information (in the model just discussed, the party who did not possess private information made the offer), sequences of offers and counteroffers, and possession of private information by both the defendant and the plaintiff. In these more complex models, the main conclusion about trial does not change because, as in the model sketched in the previous section, a rational bargainer chooses his offer or demand to obtain the highest expected payoff, meaning that he may have the bad luck to be facing an opponent who will reject his offer. A new element that arises in the more complicated models, however, is that parties may learn something about their opponents' information from their bargaining behavior.

(b) *Nature of private information.* Any kind of information that one side does not observe that could affect the other side's willingness to pay has the same general significance as private information about the trial outcome, and in particular, can lead to trial. The information might be about a party's costs of trial, his willingness to bear risk, or his need for funds. If, for instance, the plaintiff does not know what the defendant's trial costs will be and thinks they are probably high, when in fact they are low, the plaintiff may ask for too much and a trial might result.

(c) *Relationship to the simple model.* The simple model of section 3.1 is roughly consistent with the explicit models of bargaining and asymmetric information now under discussion. In the simple model, trial resulted if parties' beliefs were sufficiently different, and in the explicit models of bargaining here, trial also results from differences in beliefs, where the differences are due to asymmetry of information. Moreover, the influence of trial costs and of other factors on trial outcomes is similar in both models.[31]

31. See Bebchuk 1984.

The main difference between the models is, as emphasized, that an explicit account of bargaining—and thus of the magnitude of settlements and their probabilities—and of the source of differences in beliefs is given in the explicit models. But the definiteness of the account of settlement versus litigation in these explicit models is to some extent misleading. First, the models make use of essentially arbitrary assumptions about whether it is the informed or the uninformed party who makes the offer and about the number of rounds of bargaining; these assumptions substantially influence the probability of settlement and the settlement offers.[32] Second, the reasons for the differences in information between the parties are largely unexplained in the models, even though parties often have strong motives to share information (in order to reach settlement) and may be forced to do so (see sections 2 and 3 of Chapter 18).

3.5 Actual amount of trial versus settlement.   In fact, the vast majority of cases settle. Data on state courts show that over 96 percent of civil cases do not go to trial.[33] Similarly, recent data on federal courts demonstrate that, for fiscal year 2001, almost 98 percent of federal civil cases were resolved without trial.[34] These figures, however, may either overstate or understate the true rate: Because cases that are not tried may have been dismissed by a court, 96 percent or 98 percent is the settlement rate plus the dismissal rate, not the settlement rate; but because many disputes are settled before any complaint is filed, 96 percent or 98 percent may understate the settlement rate. In any event, it is evident that the vast majority of cases settle.

Note on the literature.   The simple model used to explain settlement and trial, based on the minimum amount the plaintiff would accept and the maximum that the defendant would pay, was first put forward in Friedman (1969), Landes (1971), and Gould (1973), and further articulated in Posner (1972a) and Shavell (1982c).[35] The explicit models of bargaining and asym-

32. Daughety and Reinganum 1993 attempt to explain what the nature of the bargaining process governing settlement negotiation will be.

33. See Ostrom, Kauder, and LaFountain 2001a, 29.

34. See U.S. Department of Justice 2001a, 154, table C-4.

35. For general surveys of the literature on settlement, see Cooter and Rubinfeld 1989, Daughety 2000, and Hay and Spier 1998.

metric information were strongly influenced by Bebchuk (1984), and have been developed by, among others, Reinganum and Wilde (1986), Schweizer (1989), and Spier (1992a).[36]

4. DIVERGENCE BETWEEN THE PRIVATE AND THE SOCIALLY DESIRABLE LEVEL OF SETTLEMENT

4.1 In general. The private and the social incentive to settle may diverge for a number of reasons that are related to those explaining the difference between the private and the social incentive to sue (see section 2).[37]

First, the litigants may have a socially insufficient motive to settle because they do not take all of society's trial costs into account. In particular, the parties involved in litigation do not bear the salaries of judges and of ancillary personnel, the value of jurors' time, the implicit rent on court buildings, and the like; the parties thus save less by settling than society does. For this reason, they may proceed to trial more often than would be socially desirable.

A second reason that the private incentive to settle may be socially inadequate concerns asymmetric information. As discussed in sections 3.3 and 3.4, asymmetric information leads parties to fail to settle because they may misgauge each others' situations. But that a party may incorrectly estimate the other's situation does not imply that social resources should be expended on trial.

A third factor suggesting that private incentives to settle may diverge from social incentives is that settlement affects deterrence. The parties

36. See also Hay 1995. See as well Farmer and Pecorino 1996 for a survey of asymmetric information models of litigation, and Kennan and Wilson 1993 for a general survey of asymmetric information models of bargaining. See Farber and White 1991, Osborne 1999, and Sieg 2000 for empirical investigations of litigation emphasizing asymmetric information, and see also Ramseyer and Nakazato 1989, and Viscusi 1986a.

37. The subject of the social desirability of settlement as opposed to trial, and of possible divergence between private and social incentives to settle, has received very little attention (as opposed to the description of the private incentives to settle, the subject of section 3). A mainly informal discussion of the topic, however, is contained in Shavell 1997, and some formal analysis is undertaken in Polinsky and Rubinfeld 1988, Shavell 1999, and Spier 1997.

themselves would usually not be thought to consider deterrence as an important factor in deciding between settlement and trial; for them, the event giving rise to a legal action has occurred and it might seem irrational to them to give deterrence of others any weight. (In the standard models, they would give it no weight.) Thus, if settlement were to reduce deterrence, and that were thought undesirable, we would conclude that there is a reason for parties to settle too much.

But does settlement reduce deterrence? One would suppose that settlement exerts a diluting effect on deterrence because defendants want settlement. Yet the prospect of settlement is also an advantage to potential plaintiffs (because it means that they do not bear litigation costs or risk) and may, at least in principle, result in suits that would not otherwise occur; thus it seems possible that settlement might increase deterrence.

A further complication is that even if we know in what direction settlement will affect deterrence, that does not tell us if the effect is socially desirable, for, as explained in section 1, the private incentive to bring suit could be socially excessive or socially inadequate. Still another complication is that the information brought out at trial may improve incentives as well as affect the expected judgment, and in different ways.[38] In the end, therefore, we can say that the effect of settlement on deterrence may result in a divergence between the private and the social motive to settle, but for a variety of reasons we cannot generalize about the nature of the divergence.

Thus, the conclusion to this point is that two underlying factors suggest that parties have an inadequate incentive to settle—they do not consider the full social costs of trial, and they may misgauge each other's situation. There is also an underlying factor of unclear consequence—that settlement affects deterrence.

4.2 The divergence between private and social incentives to settle continued.   Let me review several other factors bearing on the comparison between private and socially desirable settlement incentives that go somewhat outside the type of model that we have been implicitly considering.

One factor is settlement as a means of securing privacy. When parties settle, information that would have emerged at trial may not come to the attention of the public. The privacy that can be achieved by settlement

---

38. I discuss aspects of this point in section 5.3 and in section 2 of Chapter 19.

often constitutes an advantage to the settling parties and may help to explain why they settle. For example, a defendant firm whose product was defective may not want this information to come to light and thus may be willing to pay an extra amount to achieve settlement (the victim may not much care whether the information is revealed). A victim may be embarrassed by the facts of a dispute (suppose the suit is for sexual harassment) or not want to acquire a reputation as a troublemaker, and so wish to settle for that reason. In some cases, the parties' desire for privacy may be socially beneficial, but many times it seems that society would benefit from the information that would be revealed through trial. This would be the situation with regard to the firm that wants to keep its product defect secret; if the public learns about the defect, perhaps people can take precautions to reduce harm, and further, the firm will suffer adverse consequences, leading to improved deterrence. In circumstances like this, then, the private motive to settle may be excessive.

Another factor is that valuable interpretations of the law may be made and new precedents established through trial. Yet many trials do not make new law: Trials are often the result of disagreements about facts, not about law, and where trial is the product of disagreement about law, published opinions that create new law are not automatic. Furthermore, a natural conjecture is that the number of cases the courts need to hear in order to modify the law is trivial in relation to the total volume of cases that do go to trial.[39] Therefore, it would seem that in the great majority of cases, the issue of the elaboration of the law will not be of real importance to the social versus the private incentive to go to trial.

A similar factor is that social norms may be validated through trial, in the sense that they may be publicly invoked to justify legal outcomes. Thus, the importance of the norms may be reinforced by the trial process. Because this factor is not one that individuals would tend to count as a private benefit of trial, it suggests a tendency toward insufficient trial. In assessing the relevance of the factor, however, one must consider not only the limited value of trials (as opposed to parents, schools, religious institutions) in

39. Moreover, there are arguments for not viewing trial as necessary for the development of the law: Courts could issue advisory opinions interpreting the law in the absence of particular disputes; in principle, there is no reason why courts require the occasion of a legal dispute in order to interpret the law.

teaching morality, but also that, as with the development of law, the number of trials necessary to meet this goal is probably not large.[40]

Finally, it is often said that trial is socially desirable because it helps to keep peace in society and promotes solidarity by allowing individuals to air grievances and express their views. But this social benefit of trial appears often to be in alignment with the private benefit (when the social peace would be compromised if a person did not air his grievance, he might well want to do so). Nevertheless, the social benefit under discussion is not coincident with the private benefit (social peace benefits more than just the aggrieved party), and suggests that the social incentive to have a trial may sometimes exceed the private incentive.

4.3 Legal policy bearing on settlement versus trial. The legal policies that we observe bearing on settlement versus trial predominantly foster settlement. This is accomplished by allowing parties to engage in discovery, sometimes requiring them to participate in nonbinding arbitration prior to trial, holding settlement conferences, and so forth. These devices work principally by increasing the information that parties have about each other and thus tend to reduce the possibility of bargaining impasses. In addition, the law promotes settlement negotiations by prohibiting settlement offers from being introduced as evidence at trial, and by the basic policy of making settlement agreements binding on the parties (otherwise the meaningfulness and value of settlements would be compromised). Further, courts often use their powers of suasion to encourage settlement.

The justification that one usually sees offered for the general promotion of settlement is that it clears dockets and saves public and private expense. This justification comports with economic analysis in the obvious sense that the parties do not consider the court's time and other public costs associated with trial as a saving from settlement. The policy of fostering settlement is also justified by a factor that is not usually mentioned by commentators, that parties may want go to trial for reasons that often are not socially relevant, notably, because of disagreement about the likely trial outcome.

---

40. It seems that the potential for teaching morality lessons from trials can be well achieved through adjudication of a small, select group of cases.

Yet the possibility that trial ought to be held despite the parties' wishes to settle receives relatively little attention. One wonders, for example, about the wisdom of promoting settlement, let alone allowing it, in situations in which deterrence is likely to be compromised by the fact that in a settlement the identity of defendants, the fact of harm, and/or important aspects of the defendants' conduct do not become public knowledge.

4.4 A chief social purpose of the institution of trial is paradoxical— to foster settlement.   A final comment about the social purposes of maintaining our system of trial adjudication should be made. It seems that the socially desirable fraction of trials relative to settlements is small, given the high costs of trials and the often limited and unclear benefits of trials over settlements. That the actual fraction of settlements is about 98 percent is consistent with this view. At the same time, there would be no settlements, and the great social benefits derived from them (notably, deterrence of unwanted behavior and compensation of victims), would not be achieved in the absence of the ability of parties to go to trial (as was discussed at length in section 3). Hence, it may be said that *an important justification for society's having established the legal apparatus for the holding of trials is, paradoxically, not actually to have trials occur. Rather, it is to provide victims with the threat necessary to induce settlements.*

5.   TRIAL AND LITIGATION EXPENDITURE

5.1 Private incentives to spend on litigation.   For a variety of reasons, expenditures will tend to increase a litigant's chances of prevailing at trial or will influence beneficially the magnitude or character of the judgment. A party will generally make a litigation expenditure as long as it costs less than the expected benefit it yields. To assess the expected benefit due to a particular legal step, a party will often have to consider not only the court's reaction to it, but also the reaction of the other litigant to it.[41]

41. For analysis of expenditures of the two sides during litigation, see Braeutigam, Owen, and Panzar 1984, Katz 1988, and Posner 1972a; these writings are mainly descriptive in character.

5.2 Actual litigation expenditures.   Amounts spent on litigation are substantial, as indicated by the statistic that about 1.25 percent of our gross domestic product is spent on legal services.[42] Much of these expenditures are made before trial, however, in anticipation of possible trial (it is for expositional convenience that I often refer to them as trial expenditures).

5.3 Social versus private incentives to spend on litigation.   There are several sources of divergence between social and private incentives to spend during litigation. First, litigants may well be spending in ways that offset each other, and thus that have little or no social value. A classic instance is when both parties devote effort to legal arguments of roughly equivalent weight but supporting opposite claims, or when both hire experts who produce equally convincing reports favoring opposite assertions.

Second, expenditures that are not offsetting may mislead the court rather than enhance the accuracy of outcomes. For example, a guilty defendant may be able to escape liability for harm for which he was responsible, and this possibility dilutes deterrence. Legal expenditures resulting in such outcomes have a negative social value even though they have positive private value.

Third, expenditures that are not offsetting and that do not mislead courts may not be socially optimal in magnitude. By analogy to what was stressed in section 1 about the bringing of suits, the parties decide on their level of expenditures based on how the expenditures will influence the litigation outcome, without regard to the effect (if any) on incentives to reduce harm. This could lead to expenditures that are too great or that are too small, relative to what is socially desirable. Consider a victim's decision to hire an expert to produce a report on his behalf. The victim will not consider the cost that his expert's report imposes on the injurer: The injurer may need to hire an expert of his own to limit the influence of the victim's expert. Nor will the victim consider the cost due to the increased time the court will devote to listening to his expert and the injurer's expert should there be a trial. The victim will also fail to consider the effect of his expert's report on deterrence. Victims' ignoring the costs they impose on others may lead them to spend socially excessively on experts, while their not considering the deterrence produced by their experts' reports could result in their not spending enough on experts. Similar observations apply to

42. See *Statistical Abstract of the United States, 2001,* 418.

virtually any type of legal expenditure, whether made by victims or by in-jurers. Thus, although nonoffsetting expenditures do by definition help the parties who make them, we cannot say in theory whether or not they are socially excessive or inadequate; which is so depends on the particulars.

An important instance of the possibility that expenditures could be socially excessive concerns the assessment of damages.[43] Suppose that the presently estimated harm deviates from the truth by $100. Then one of the litigants will be willing to spend up to $100 to prove the correct amount (the defendant will do so if the estimate exceeds the correct level, and the plaintiff will do so if the estimate is too low). It can be shown that the social value of the more accurate estimate tends, however, to be lower than $100, because the social value of accuracy is based on its effects on incen-tives. Indeed, there will sometimes be no beneficial incentive effect from more accurate assessment of harm, such as when errors are unbiased and not predictable ex ante by potential injurers. Consider, for example, the precise extent of harm the victim suffered in an automobile accident. Much may be spent establishing the magnitude of harm by presenting evidence on medical bills, the time lost from work, and the victim's wages. But these expenditures will not improve the incentives of drivers to prevent accidents, presuming that they do not know ahead of time the magnitude of harm that will result in the event that they cause an accident (that is, if all that they know is the probability distribution of possible harms, depending on who is in the car they strike, the nature of the impact, and so forth). If this is the case, injurers' incentives to prevent accidents will be essentially identical to what they are now if instead there is no real inquiry into the scale of harm, and damages are simply set equal to the average harm that victims sustain in that kind of automobile accident.[44]

43. This point is developed in Kaplow and Shavell 1996a.

44. For example, suppose that all that injurers know when deciding on a precaution is that if an accident occurs, it will result in harm of $1,000, $2,000, or $3,000, each with equal probability—injurers thus do not know the particular magnitude of the harm that would occur. If damages are set equal to actual harm (after a perhaps costly legal determina-tion), injurers obviously will not know ex ante what their liability will be if an accident occurs; they will know only that their expected liability given an accident will be $2,000 (that is, $(1/3) \times \$1,000 + (1/3) \times \$2,000 + (1/3) \times \$3,000$). If instead damages are simply set equal to the average harm of $2,000, injurers' expected liability given an accident will be the same. Therefore, injurers will behave identically.

5.4 Legal policy bearing on litigation expenditure. There are several means of influencing litigation expenditures that exist, given the basic form of legal rules and legal procedure. Expenditures can be encouraged through subsidy and discouraged through monetary disincentives such as fees or taxes, and they can also be regulated through constraints on the time parties are given to prepare for trial, restrictions on discovery, limits on the length of permitted submissions and the number of testifying experts, and so forth. In fact, controls on expenditures seem to be made largely through such forms of regulation of the pretrial and trial process rather than through financial inducements.

In addition, litigation expenditures could be controlled through changes in substantive legal rules. A notable example of such a change is one under which damages would be based on a table rather than on an elaborate presentation of evidence. As was suggested earlier, it may well be that incentives toward desirable behavior would not be much affected were damages based on tables of expected values rather than on individual assessment of harm, so that this rule change could substantially reduce the private expenditures on litigation with little change in deterrence.

Finally, litigation expenditures can be modified through revision of legal procedure. A possibility that would be desirable in some circumstances is for certain types of evidence to be produced not by the parties but by court-appointed experts. Especially where private knowledge of the parties is not needed in order to develop evidence, court direction of the acquisition of information might be more beneficial than the parties', which might both mislead courts and result in duplication of efforts.

18 ||| EXTENSIONS OF THE BASIC THEORY

I discuss here various extensions of the basic theory discussed in Chapter 17. In particular, I investigate negative value suits, voluntary and required disclosure of information prior to trial, shifting of legal fees depending on the outcome at trial, inference from trial outcomes, elements of trial outcomes apart from the judgment, and the roles of lawyers and insurers in litigation. Consideration of these topics should help to round out our understanding of litigation.[1]

1. NEGATIVE VALUE SUITS

1.1 Definition and a puzzling aspect of negative value suits. It is often noted that plaintiffs sometimes bring suits that they would not in fact be willing to proceed to litigate. These suits are called *negative value*

---

1. There are obviously many other topics not discussed here that are of interest in respect to litigation; for example, class actions, and sequential versus joint adjudication of the issues in a case. My object is not to be comprehensive but rather to illustrate how the basic analysis of the previous chapter can be elaborated to take into account additional factors of relevance and to treat some of the more important factors.

suits because, for the plaintiffs who bring them, the expected benefits of litigation would be outweighed by the costs. The reason that the suits are said to be brought nevertheless is that plaintiffs may be able to extract positive settlements from defendants. This claim about settlements arising from negative value suits raises an immediate question: Why would a defendant be willing to pay a positive amount in settlement to a plaintiff who would not actually go through with trial? That is, if the plaintiff does not have a credible threat to proceed to trial, why would a defendant rationally pay a settlement—and if the defendant would not be willing to pay, why would the plaintiff bring suit in the first place? Two basic answers to this question, resting on different assumptions, may be offered.[2]

1.2 Explanations for negative value suits.   The first answer concerns the possibility that defendants do not know whether a plaintiff would or would not be willing to go to trial. If a defendant lacks this information, then it may be rational for him to settle with a plaintiff because of the possibility that the plaintiff might be one who would be willing to go to trial. The defendant will be willing to pay a positive settlement if the proportion of plaintiffs who would be willing to go to trial (because they would obtain a positive expected return from trial) is sufficiently high relative to those plaintiffs who are masqueraders. In other words, the masqueraders ride on the coattails of those plaintiffs who are willing to go to trial. Let me illustrate.

Example 1. There are two groups of plaintiffs: a minority of 10 percent for whom losses are low, say 20, and the other 90 percent for whom losses are 100. Plaintiffs will collect their losses in judgments if they go to trial. The cost of trial is 30 for all plaintiffs. Thus, the low-loss plaintiffs are not willing to go to trial, for the cost of 30 outweighs their judgment of 20. The other plaintiffs, who would net 70 from trial, will be willing to go to trial.

Defendants are assumed to be unable to tell whether a plaintiff is a low-loss plaintiff or a high-loss one—and thus whether a plaintiff would be willing in fact to go to trial. Let us show that a defendant would rationally offer 70 in settlement in order to achieve settlements with the

2. For a survey of literature on negative expected value suits, see Bebchuk 1998.

high-loss plaintiffs. Assume that the defendants' trial costs would be 25. If a defendant offers 70, he knows that all plaintiffs will settle, so his cost will be 70. A defendant will not offer a positive settlement amount less than 70, for any positive amount less than 70 will be refused by the high-loss plaintiffs, so would only benefit the low-loss plaintiffs, who would not have gone to trial. If the defendant offers nothing, then all high-loss plaintiffs will go to trial, so his expected cost will be 90% × 125 = 112.5, which exceeds 70. Hence, it is better for the defendant to offer 70, meaning that he pays the 10 percent of low-loss plaintiffs 70 even though they would not go to trial, in order to achieve settlement savings from the 90 percent of plaintiffs who would go to trial.

If, however, the fraction of low-loss plaintiffs who are masquerading as high-loss plaintiffs is sufficiently large (greater than 44 percent), defendants will not make a positive settlement offer.[3]

More generally, the presence of masqueraders will tend to lower the settlement offers that defendants make, and this means that there will be more trials than otherwise, because more plaintiffs who would be willing to go to trial will refuse the lower settlement offer and go to trial.[4]

A second explanation for negative value suits arises when the plaintiff would be able to win a judgment if the defendant does not spend an amount on defense (for instance, to develop evidence to defeat a groundless claim)—even though the plaintiff would lose if the defendant does spend this amount (because the claim is groundless). In such a situation, the defendant will rationally pay a positive amount in settlement in order to avoid having to bear the defense cost. Thus, even though the plaintiff would not bring the suit if there were no chance of extracting a settlement, the plaintiff will bring the suit. An example will clarify this point.[5]

3. At 44 percent, the expected cost to a defendant who offers nothing is 56% × 125 = 70, just equal to his cost if he offers 70.

4. In our example, this phenomenon did not occur because there was only one group of plaintiffs who would be willing to go to trial. But if there had been more than one group, or a continuum, then the presence of plaintiffs who are unwilling to go to trial can be shown generally to reduce the magnitude of any positive offer the defendant would otherwise make. This is shown in Bebchuk 1988, who first developed the point under discussion; see also Katz 1990a.

5. The point under discussion, as illustrated in the example, is developed in Rosenberg and Shavell 1985.

Example 2. A plaintiff can bring suit at a cost of 10. If the plaintiff does bring suit, he will obtain a judgment of 100 if the defendant does not defend himself. If the defendant does defend himself, at a cost of 30, the defendant will prevail and the plaintiff will obtain nothing. Note, therefore, that if there were no settlement negotiations, the plaintiff would not bring suit, for if he did so, he would spend 10, then the defendant would rationally defend, and the plaintiff would definitely lose.

Once the plaintiff brings suit, however, he will be able to extract as much as 30 from the defendant in a settlement. The defendant would, for example, pay 25 in order for the plaintiff to drop the case, for otherwise the defendant would have to spend 30 to avoid paying the plaintiff 100. Knowing that he can extract a positive settlement from the defendant, the plaintiff may bring suit, and he will do so as long as the settlement he can extract exceeds the cost of bringing suit of 10.[6]

The key assumptions here that allow the plaintiff to extract a settlement, even though he would lose if the defendant spent on defense, are two: first, that it is cheap for the plaintiff to bring suit and thereby create the threat to win, and second, that it is relatively expensive for the defendant to defend himself. This is the situation in a significant number of contexts, but is not the situation in many others, where the plaintiff would not win easily just because he brought suit and would have to go to considerable additional expense to prevail at trial.[7]

1.3 Are negative value suits socially undesirable?   Although negative value suits often are socially undesirable, it cannot be said that they are necessarily socially undesirable.

---

6. In strict logic, the plaintiff might be able to extract a settlement from the defendant without bearing the cost of 10 to bring suit: he can threaten to bring suit and thus be able to extract a settlement, and a rational defendant may settle immediately (for up to 20— his defense costs of 30 minus the plaintiff's cost of suit of 10).

7. Although the two explanations given in this section are the major ones for negative value suits, there are others. Bebchuk 1996 shows that the fact that legal expenses are made in stages over time may lead to negative value suits. In particular, if a plaintiff brings suit and spends funds prior to trial, then just before trial, having already spent some funds, the *remaining* trial cost may be less than the expected judgment. Hence, at the point just before trial, he may have a credible threat to sue. This implies that, at the beginning, he may have a credible threat to sue and be able to extract a settlement even though, were he to go to

Consider first a suit that is without merit in the sense that the plaintiff definitely would not prevail if the facts were known. For example, imagine that the plaintiff did not really suffer injury. If such a plaintiff brings a negative value suit (as he might for either of the reasons discussed above), this is socially undesirable. Notably, it tends to distort incentives; for example, it makes parties who might face negative value suits take excessive precautions or discourages them from engaging in activities for which the benefits exceed the true social costs. Such suits also generate litigation costs, and impose risk, to no social purpose.

Next consider suits that have possible merit, and perhaps suits that the plaintiff is certain to win, but which are nevertheless negative value suits because the trial costs exceed the expected judgment. These suits may or may not be socially undesirable. As was discussed in section 2 of Chapter 17, the private incentive to bring suit may diverge from the social, and it is possible that suits that victims would not be inclined to bring, because their harm and thus their awards would be less than their trial costs, would be socially good for them to bring because of the beneficial incentives that they would create. If it so happens that such victims find that they can in fact bring suits because, say, they can pretend to be high-loss victims and obtain positive settlements, this may be socially desirable because it compensates implicitly for the underdeterrence of low harms that would ordinarily occur due to litigation costs. This illustrates that negative value suits might be socially desirable, even though the usual expectation is that they would not be.[8]

2. SHARING OF INFORMATION PRIOR TO TRIAL

2.1 Motive to share information. In the discussion of settlement versus trial in Chapter 17, I assumed that the information of parties was somehow exogenously determined: Either information was in the background and influenced parties' perhaps disparate beliefs, or information

---

trial, his total cost would exceed his expected judgment (the logic is similar to that in the preceding note).

8. For examination of how negative value suits might be discouraged, see Katz 1990a and Polinsky and Rubinfeld 1993, 1996.

was explicitly presumed to be asymmetric. In general, however, litigants have strong motives to share information with each other prior to trial, in order to foster settlement and to improve its terms.[9] A plaintiff, for example, would want to show the defendant information establishing that his losses were in fact higher than the defendant believes, so as to secure a settlement and a higher one than he could otherwise obtain. If a defendant thinks that a plaintiff who does not reveal information about his losses probably suffered losses in the neighborhood of $10,000, but the plaintiff really experienced losses of $20,000, the plaintiff will want to establish to the defendant that his losses are $20,000 in order to induce the defendant to pay more in settlement and perhaps avoid an impasse leading to trial. (An essentially equivalent way of expressing this point is to observe that the plaintiff will want to reveal that his losses are $20,000 in order to avoid a negative inference that the defendant would make from his failure to disclose information that his losses were relatively high.)[10] Likewise, a defendant would want to show the plaintiff evidence pointing toward the defendant's lack of legal responsibility in an accident, in order to convince the plaintiff to accept a lower settlement offer.

The incentives that parties have to reveal information to one another tend to produce significant voluntary disclosure of information. Indeed, it can be shown that, due to rational voluntary disclosure of information, there will *always* be settlement in a benchmark model of litigation in which there is one-sided private information that that side can choose to disclose.[11] In other words, the fact that there is initial asymmetry of information will not lead to trial when the party with private information is able to share

9. The motive to share information prior to trial was analyzed in Shavell 1989, which this section largely summarizes.

10. The revelation of information to avoid a negative inference from silence is sometimes referred to as the unraveling phenomenon. On this, see the survey in Gertner 1998.

11. Suppose for concreteness that plaintiffs have private information about the magnitude of their losses. In the model, the assumptions are as follows. The plaintiff first decides whether or not to reveal his losses to the defendant. The defendant then makes a settlement offer. The plaintiff either accepts the offer or goes to trial. Of course, each side acts rationally in his self-interest. One aspect of rationality is that when the defendant decides how much to offer to a silent plaintiff, the defendant takes into account the probability distribution of losses among silent plaintiffs (which is to say, makes a negative inference about their true losses—why else did they remain silent?).

it.[12] Thus the explanation for the occurrence of trial must rest on a deeper understanding of the litigants' situation.

2.2 Why some information is not shared and trial may result.   In spite of the incentives to share information, some information will not be shared, and this may lead to trial.[13] There are two principal reasons why information might not be shared. The first is simply that information may be difficult to share in a credible way, even though a party wants to do that. For instance, a plaintiff might know that his losses are $20,000, but not be able to demonstrate this during settlement negotiations (because, say, experts will have to be hired by the time of trial to demonstrate the losses). Hence, trial could result because the defendant might make an offer based on his belief that the plaintiff's losses are only $10,000.

A somewhat subtle coattails effect follows when some parties are unable to share information credibly: Certain parties who are able to reveal their information will decide to remain silent, so that they can be mistaken for

12. This is true even though, in general, the sharing of information is *not* complete. Consider the following example. Plaintiffs' losses are distributed between $10,000 and $50,000, plaintiffs' trial costs are $3,000, and defendant's trial costs are $5,000. Now it is true that a situation in which too large a range of plaintiffs are silent cannot occur, because the putatively silent plaintiffs with relatively high losses would choose to disclose their losses in order to obtain a higher amount. For instance, suppose that all plaintiffs with losses between $10,000 and $30,000 are silent and that silent plaintiffs receive an offer of $18,000 (the defendant will choose his offer knowing the probability distribution of losses of silent plaintiffs). Then plaintiffs at the high end, such as those whose losses are $30,000, would choose to reveal their losses, for if such a plaintiff revealed his losses, he could obtain at least $30,000 − $3,000 (his litigation costs) or $27,000 from the defendant. This "unraveling" effect, however, will not result in the topmost silent plaintiffs revealing their losses if the silent group is sufficiently small. For instance, suppose that the silent group is plaintiffs between $10,000 and $15,000 and that the defendant offers silent plaintiffs $12,000. Then the topmost plaintiff whose losses are $15,000 would not benefit by revealing his losses— for he would then receive an offer of $15,000 − $3,000, or $12,000. Moreover, it can be shown that the defendant might well not want to reduce his offer below $12,000, because even though this would save him money from the majority of silent plaintiffs, he would lose more on account of the minority who would reject and go to trial, because he would then have to pay his own litigation costs.

13. The reasons to be given here for why parties do not reveal information are distinct from that discussed in the previous note, which was a reason for failure to disclose, but not one that leads to trial.

those who are unable to reveal their information. For example, if the group of plaintiffs who are unable to demonstrate their information credibly have losses that average $20,000, then a plaintiff whose losses are only $5,000 and who is able to reveal them might well choose to remain silent, so that he will be treated more like the plaintiffs with losses that average $20,000 and thus will be offered more in settlement than he would obtain if he revealed his low losses. Therefore, as a general matter, when some parties are unable to reveal information, it will become advantageous for other parties who could reveal their information to remain silent.[14]

The second major reason why information might not be revealed is that revelation of information may reduce its value to a party because the opposing party may be able to counter it at trial once that party has fore-knowledge of it. For example, the plaintiff might not reveal information showing that his losses are $20,000 because the defendant will then have the time to find an expert who can cast doubt on the plaintiff's evidence so as to reduce what he can collect at trial to $15,000. The plaintiff's with-holding of this information could lead to trial.[15]

3.   FORCED DISCLOSURE OF INFORMATION PRIOR TO TRIAL: DISCOVERY

The courts may require that a litigant disclose certain information to the other side; that is, one litigant may enjoy the legal right of *discovery* of information held by the other side.

3.1 Effect of discovery is only *in addition* to that flowing from voluntary disclosure.   It is commonly believed that the right of discovery significantly increases the likelihood of settlement because it reduces differ-

---

14. This in turn can increase the likelihood of trial. In the example of the low-loss plaintiffs who decide to remain silent and join the group who are unable to reveal their information, the rational offer that defendants make will be lower than otherwise (since defendants will know that some silent plaintiffs are silent just because their losses are low). And this reduced settlement offer will be rejected by more of the silent plaintiffs who cannot reveal their losses, so the likelihood of trial will rise.

15. Note in particular that if the plaintiff reveals the information, his threat becomes one of winning only $15,000 at trial, so the defendant could offer him as little as $12,000

ences in parties' information. But, as just emphasized in section 2, there may well be substantial voluntary sharing of information, so that the influence on settlement of compulsory disclosure through discovery will not necessarily be significant. Indeed, the effect of discovery on settlement is nonexistent in the benchmark model in which the party with private information is able to disclose it, for in that situation settlement always occurs due to voluntary disclosure.[16]

To understand how discovery affects outcomes, consider the reasons why information might not be voluntarily shared. The first reason that I noted, in section 2.2, was that a party might be unable to demonstrate his information credibly, such as a plaintiff who is unable to establish his losses until an expert is hired. Discovery cannot have an effect on this type of plaintiff because, by hypothesis, he is unable to establish his losses (since he does not yet possess an expert's report). But I also noted the coattails effect—that some parties who are able to disclose information would choose not to do so (such as low-loss plaintiffs who could reveal their losses). These parties would be forced by discovery to reveal their information. Moreover, just because these parties would reveal their information, there would be an indirect, complex effect on settlement offers that would tend to raise the settlement rate.[17]

Next consider the more direct effect of discovery on parties who are able to disclose information but do not do so because it could be countered at trial. These parties will be forced to reveal their information by discovery, and that will clearly lead to more settlement.

(that is, $15,000 less his $3,000 of litigation costs). If the plaintiff is silent and goes to trial, he is better off because his net gain is $17,000.

16. The first model of discovery was Sobel 1989, but his analysis does not determine behavior of parties who voluntarily disclose information, so the effect of discovery against the background of voluntary disclosure is not ascertained. Shavell 1989, however, determines the difference that discovery makes, given that there will be voluntary disclosure of information without discovery; the main points of this article are noted here. See also the subsequent related work of Cooter and Rubinfeld 1994, Hay 1994, Mnookin and Wilson 1998, Schrag 1999, and Shepherd 1999, as well as the survey Rubinfeld 1998.

17. Because low-loss plaintiffs who can reveal their losses would be forced to do so, defendants would raise their settlement offers to plaintiffs who cannot supply information about their losses. That will raise the settlement rate because more of the plaintiffs who are unable to disclose their losses will accept the settlement offer rather than go to trial.

3.2 Discovery as a costly threat.   Wholly apart from its effects on information transmission, obeying discovery requests is often expensive because significant time and resources may be needed to produce the desired information. This raises questions about the use of discovery requests as a threat, for the costs of compliance with discovery requests are, under our current system, generally borne by the side asked to comply.

3.3 Discovery and social optimality.   The question of the social optimality of discovery involves a number of issues. As just noted, to the extent that the side requesting discovery does not bear its costs, there is reason to believe that the private incentive to engage in discovery may be socially excessive. Also, the social benefits of discovery involve, among other elements, the promotion of deterrence through development of better information (which will affect both settlements and trial outcomes), and more effective trials, owing to the parties' having relevant information in advance of trials. Because these social benefits generally diverge from the private benefits, the suspicion is that the private incentives to engage in discovery may often be socially undesirable, either excessive or insufficient, depending on the particulars of the situation.[18]

4.   SHIFTING OF LEGAL FEES TO THE LOSER AT TRIAL

Thus far we have assumed that parties bear their own legal fees, which is often referred to as the American rule for the allocation of legal fees. By contrast, the bearing of legal fees can be made to depend on the outcome of trial.[19] A major form of such fee-shifting is the so-called English rule, under which the loser at trial bears his opponent's legal fees as well as his own. I will restrict our attention here to this form of fee-shifting.[20]

18. One occasionally encounters the view that discovery is socially undesirable if its costs exceed the benefit to the party who obtains discovery. This is not a correct view, for the private benefits to the party seeking discovery, an improvement in settlement terms or the trial outcome, have only a weak connection to the social benefits of discovery.

19. For a survey of economic literature on fee-shifting, see Hughes and Snyder 1998. For empirical study of fee-shifting, see, for example, Hughes and Snyder 1995, Kritzer 1984, and Snyder and Hughes 1990.

20. There are other forms of fee-shifting, and the analysis of them would in many respects follow in a straightforward way from what will be said here about the English rule.

4.1 Effects of fee-shifting on the bringing of suit. Fee-shifting has implications for the incentive to sue. Fee-shifting leads to more suit in situations in which plaintiffs are likely to win, for this means that plaintiffs are unlikely to have to pay their legal expenses. Suppose that the probability of plaintiff victory is 70 percent, that the judgment amount would be $100,000, and that the plaintiff's trial costs and the defendant's would each be $80,000. Then under the American rule, the plaintiff would not bring suit because his costs of $80,000 exceed his expected gain of $70,000. Under the English rule, however, he would bring suit because his expected costs would be only 30% × $160,000 or $48,000.

Conversely, fee-shifting leads to less suit in situations in which plaintiffs are unlikely to win. Suppose that the plaintiff's probability of victory is now only 30 percent, that the judgment amount would be $100,000, that the plaintiff's legal costs would be $10,000, and that the defendant's legal costs would be $80,000. Under the American rule, the plaintiff would sue, $10,000 being less than the $30,000 expected gain, but under the English rule the plaintiff would not sue because his expected expenses would be 70% × $90,000 = $62,000.

As a general matter, the range of high probabilities of prevailing for which fee-shifting increases suit (and the complementary range of low probabilities for which fee-shifting reduces suit) depends on the legal costs that the parties would bear at trial. If they would each bear equal trial costs, then 50 percent is the threshold probability: Suit is more likely under the English rule when the likelihood of victory exceeds 50 percent. And if the plaintiff's costs are less than the defendant's, the threshold probability is higher.[21]

Under plaintiff-favoring fee-shifting, the defendant has to pay the plaintiff's fees if the plaintiff prevails, but the plaintiff does not have to pay the defendant's fees if the defendant wins. Under defendant-favoring fee-shifting, the converse is true. Fees may also be shifted in a more complicated way, depending on whether the amount of the award at trial exceeded or fell below a settlement offer; for economic analysis of such "offer-of-settlement" rules, see Bebchuk and Chang 1999, Miller 1986, and Spier 1994a. For a general description of the actual use of fee-shifting, see Derfner and Wolf 1995.

21. To amplify, let p be the probability of plaintiff victory, x the judgment amount, and c_P and c_D the plaintiff's and the defendant's trial costs respectively (and let us abstract from issues relating to settlement). Under the American system, the plaintiff will sue if $c_P < px$ or, equivalently, if $x > c_P/p$. Under the English rule, the plaintiff will sue if $(1 - p)$

The foregoing analysis presumes that plaintiffs are risk neutral. If plaintiffs are risk averse, then superimposed on the effects just mentioned is a disinclination to bring suit, because the risk of trial is increased by the fact that the sum of the legal fees depends on the trial outcome. If the judgment amount is $100,000 and the legal fees of each side are $80,000, the plaintiff obtains $100,000 if he wins and loses $160,000 otherwise—meaning a difference of $260,000 in result under the English system. Under the American system, the difference in result is only $100,000, a significantly smaller risk. Another factor (to be discussed later) is that the English system may turn out to increase legal fees, and this in turn also works to reduce the frequency of suit.

4.2 Effects on settlement versus trial. Given that suit has been brought, fee-shifting has an underlying tendency to increase the likelihood of trial. The reason, in essence, is that fee-shifting magnifies the effects of differences of opinion about the trial outcome. If a plaintiff is more optimistic about the chances of winning than the defendant thinks is correct, then fee-shifting will raise the plaintiff's demand relative to the defendant's offer because a plaintiff victory will now mean not only a judgment for him, but also escaping legal fees.

> *Example 3.* Suppose that the plaintiff thinks his chances of winning $100,000 are 80 percent, that his trial expenses would be $50,000, that the defendant thinks the plaintiff's chances of prevailing are only 30 percent, and that his trial expenses would be $40,000. Then under the American rule, there would be room for settlement: The plaintiff's minimum acceptable amount is $80,000 − $50,000 = $30,000, which is less than the defendant's maximum acceptable amount of $30,000 + $40,000 = $70,000. Under the English rule, however, there would be a trial, for the plaintiff's minimum acceptable amount is $80,000 − 20% × $90,000 = $62,000 (note that $90,000 is the sum of the parties' legal costs),

---

$(c_P + c_D) < px$, or equivalently, if $x > (1 - p)(c_P + c_D)/p$. Hence, there will be more suit (a greater range of x will result in suit) under the English rule if and only if $(1 - p)(c_P + c_D)/p < c_P/p$, which is to say, if and only if $p > c_D/(c_P + c_D)$. In particular, if $c_P = c_D$, there will be more suit under the English rule if $p > .5$. The effects of fee-shifting on the incentives to bring suit are examined in Shavell 1982c.

whereas the defendant's maximum acceptable amount is $30,000 + 30% × $90,000 = $57,000.

This example illustrates that when the plaintiff's estimate of the probability of winning is higher than the defendant's estimate, fee-shifting means that each side believes it is relatively likely to lay off its legal expenses on the other side, which widens the difference between them and may lead to trial.[22]

But the factor of risk aversion counters the tendency toward trial. Because fee-shifting makes trial a more risky proposition, fee-shifting tends to promote settlement. Also, the likelihood that fee-shifting leads to larger legal fees also makes settlement more likely. Therefore, the effect of fee-shifting in the end might not be to increase trial, even though that is its influence on risk-neutral parties.

4.3 Effects on trial expenditures.   Fee-shifting will generally lead parties to spend more on legal fees than they otherwise would, for two reasons. First, fee-shifting means that a party will not necessarily have to pay the bill for legal services that he orders, making legal services effectively cheaper. If the plaintiff has a lawyer spend $1,000 more of time and expects to win with a probability of about 70 percent, the odds that he will have to pay for the extra $1,000 of services are only 30 percent, so their effective cost to him is only $300. Hence, if the expected payoff from the services

---

22. To show this result in the simple model of settlement versus litigation, let p_P be the plaintiff's estimate of the probability of winning w at trial and p_D the defendant's probability estimate, and c_P and c_D their respective trial costs. Under the American system, the plaintiff's minimum settlement amount is $p_P w - c_P$, and the defendant's maximum amount is $p_D w + c_D$. Hence, a trial occurs if $p_P w - c_P > p_D w + c_D$, which is to say, if $p_P w - p_D w > c_P + c_D$. Under the English system, the plaintiff's minimum settlement amount is $p_P w - (1 - p_P)(c_P + c_D)$ and the defendant's maximum is $p_D w + p_D(c_P + c_D)$, so that trial occurs if $p_P w - p_D w > (1 - p_P)(c_P + c_D) + p_D(c_P + c_D)$. We want to show that trial occurs more often under the English rule. Hence, assume that trial occurs under the American rule. Then it must be that $p_P > p_D$, which implies that $c_P + c_D > (1 - p_P)(c_P + c_D) + p_D(c_P + c_D)$, from which the conclusion follows. This conclusion was demonstrated by Posner 1972a and Shavell 1982c. The same conclusion holds in the asymmetric information bargaining model for closely related reasons; see Bebchuk 1984. Similar conclusions hold for fee-shifting favoring defendants and fee-shifting favoring plaintiffs, as shown in Shavell 1982c.

is $500, he would spend the $1,000 under fee-shifting, but he would not have done so in its absence.

The second reason that fee-shifting leads to greater expenditures is that fee-shifting increases the payoff from winning, because the fees themselves are at stake in the trial outcome. This can be a significant factor when the fees are substantial in relation to the judgment. Recall the example where the judgment amount is $100,000 and the legal fees of each side are $80,000. Here, because the plaintiff obtains $100,000 if he wins and loses $160,000 otherwise, there is a $260,000 difference between winning and losing under the English system, as opposed to only a $100,000 difference under the American system. Hence, the value of an expenditure to increase the chance of winning is 2.6 higher than its value under the American system, reinforcing the other effect that leads to higher spending under the English system.[23]

4.4 Social desirability of fee-shifting. It is not possible to draw general conclusions about the social desirability of fee-shifting, although statements can be made in particular circumstances. In section 2.5(a) of Chapter 17, we discussed an example in which fee-shifting had a socially beneficial effect on the bringing of suit, and also an example in which it had a socially undesirable effect on the bringing of suits.[24] Additionally, it is apparent that the influence of fee-shifting on settlement might be socially beneficial or detrimental (in part because fee-shifting can either promote trial or settlement) and that the effect of fee-shifting on trial expenditures could be similarly ambiguous from a social standpoint.

5. DIFFICULTY OF STATISTICAL INFERENCE FROM TRIAL OUTCOMES

A question of interest is whether cases that go to trial are representative of the underlying population of cases, and notably, whether the likelihood of plaintiff victory at trial or the amounts won are similar to those that characterize the cases that settled. This question is important because, often, the

23. The effects of fee-shifting on expenditures at trial are discussed in Braeutigam, Owen, and Panzar 1984, Hause 1989, and Katz 1987.

24. This point is emphasized by Gravelle 1993.

most readily available data is on cases that go to trial, whereas the great majority of cases settle. Unfortunately, as I am about to explain, the cases that go to trial may be very different from the population of cases that settle, so that generalizing from trial cases is difficult and may be misleading.

Consider two examples. First, suppose that 99 percent of defendants are guilty of negligently causing $100,000 of harm, and that 1 percent are not and have exonerating evidence, but the plaintiffs cannot tell who is guilty and who is not. Then in settlement negotiations, plaintiffs' settlement demands would reflect their correct belief that virtually all defendants would be liable, and let us say their demands would approximate the $100,000 judgments that the 99 percent of liable defendants would have to pay. Thus, we would expect that essentially all of the 1 percent of defendants who would not be found liable would go to trial rather than accept the $100,000 demands of plaintiffs, whereas essentially all of the 99 percent of defendants who would be found liable would accept plaintiffs' settlement demands to avoid litigation costs. In this situation, then, only 1 percent of cases go to trial, and all of them are won by defendants. Obviously, it would be a gross mistake to extrapolate from the uniformity of trial results in favor of defendants to conclude that, in the entire population of cases, defendants are usually not negligent, for the truth is that 99 percent of them are negligent.

Second, suppose that all defendants are liable, that 99 percent of plaintiffs suffered losses of $100,000, and that 1 percent of plaintiffs suffered losses of $200,000, but defendants cannot tell them apart at the time of settlement negotiations. Then, by logic similar to that of the previous paragraph, we might expect defendants to offer around $100,000 as a settlement, that the 99 percent of plaintiffs with $100,000 losses will settle, but that the other plaintiffs will reject the settlement offer, go to trial, and obtain judgments of $200,000. In this situation, it would again be a mistake to infer from the $200,000 judgments made in all of the trials that this amount is the typical loss of plaintiffs, when the truth is that $100,000 is the typical loss.

These examples illustrate how dramatically trial outcomes can diverge from the actual statistics characterizing the population of all cases, in terms of both who wins and the amounts awarded. The differences between trial outcomes and the population of cases have to do with the fact that the cases that go to trial are not a random sample from the population of cases, but rather are those cases in which there was a reason—something not anticipated by one of the sides to the litigation, and thus something atypical—that led to a bargaining impasse.[25]

6. ELEMENTS OF TRIAL OUTCOMES APART FROM THE JUDGMENT

We have assumed that the only outcome of a trial is a judgment paid by the defendant and received by the plaintiff, but there are other possibilities that affect litigation. First, a trial outcome may have implications for a litigant beyond the immediate judgment. For example, a firm may believe that a loss at trial would invite a string of future lawsuits; thus, a loss would be more costly for it than the judgment.[26] This would tend to make settlement more likely than otherwise, because it would raise the amount the defendant firm would be willing to pay in settlement. Another possibility is that a trial might prevent future lawsuits, by revealing the defendant to be tough-minded. This would make trial more likely than we had suggested.

Second, a litigant may care whether a trial is held per se: A plaintiff might, say, wish the defendant to be exposed to public scrutiny. This would make both suit and trial rather than settlement more likely. Or a party might want to avoid a trial because it would result in the airing of embarrassing facts or the disclosure of valuable business information, which would tend to make trial less likely. In all, it is apparent that the consequences of trial apart from the literal judgment may affect the tendency to sue and the decision over settlement versus litigation.

25. The general point that cases that go to trial are not representative of the underlying population of cases was first emphasized by Priest and Klein 1984. (They also suggested that cases that go to trial would be won by plaintiffs approximately 50 percent of the time, regardless of the underlying population of cases. This somewhat surprising conclusion of theirs is correct given their assumptions; but it is not borne out in fact, and, as illustrated in the text, it does not hold under general assumptions about the population of cases and bargaining over settlement and trial.) See also Eisenberg 1990, Eisenberg and Farber 1997, Hylton 1993, Shavell 1996, Waldfogel 1995, and Wittman 1985. For a survey of the literature, see Waldfogel 1998.

26. See Che and Yi 1993.

7.   ROLE OF LAWYERS

Although we have so far spoken of "the" plaintiff and "the" defendant, each litigant is typically represented by a lawyer, and the lawyer and his client are distinct individuals. Let me briefly indicate how recognition of the lawyer as distinct from the client affects the prior analysis of the bringing of suits, of settlement versus trial, and of trial effort. I will assume that the lawyer has superior information about the law and about the likely outcome of a case to that of the client, and, to begin with, that parties are risk neutral. Two basic payment arrangements will be considered: hourly fees for services, and an outcome-based or *contingency fee* arrangement, under which the plaintiff's lawyer's fee equals a percentage of the judgment or settlement amount (and the lawyer receives no fee for time worked).

7.1 Description of lawyers' decisions.   Regarding the incentive to sue, it is clear that under an hourly fee arrangement, lawyers will have incentives to accept cases in which the expected gains are less than the legal costs, for lawyers will be paid regardless of the outcome. Under contingency fees, this effect will be dulled because, if a case is not promising, the lawyer will not want to spend his time on it for a low expected fee. The lawyer might also be unwilling to take a case for which the expected gain exceeds the legal costs, because the lawyer obtains only a fraction of the gains but bears the full costs. In summary, relative to the benchmark of maximizing the expected gain minus legal costs, the incentive to take cases under the hourly fee is excessive, and the incentive to take cases under the contingency, outcome-based arrangement is inadequate.

Next, consider settlement negotiations. In this context, the lawyer who obtains hourly fees will have an incentive to go to trial if the lawyer wants more work, so that he will be inclined to go to trial more often than he would were the goal to maximize expected gains minus legal costs. (If trial work is less attractive than other available work, however, perhaps because of the intensity of a trial, then the incentive would be in the opposite direction and the lawyer would push the client to settle.) Under contingency fee arrangements, the lawyer's incentives are different, leading the lawyer to press for settlement more often than when the settlement offer exceeds the expected judgment net of litigation costs, because the lawyer bears all the litigation costs but obtains only a percentage of the settlement.

Thus, relative to the benchmark of maximizing the expected gain minus legal costs, the incentive to go to trial under the hourly fee is excessive, and the incentive to go to trial under the contingency fee contract is too low.

For similar reasons, if a case has gone to trial, then under the hourly fee arrangement, the lawyer will want to work more than may be worthwhile in terms of the expected judgment. And under the contingency fee arrangement, this is not likely; the lawyer will tend to work less than would be worthwhile in terms of the expected judgment, for again, the lawyer obtains only a fraction of that for himself but bears the entire litigation costs.

7.2 Mutually beneficial lawyer-client arrangements. What can be said from the foregoing description about mutually beneficial contracts between lawyers and clients? We would expect contracts to gravitate toward those that result in maximization of the expected gains less litigation costs, for that is the pie that lawyers and clients have available to share. From this perspective, it appears that either hourly fee or outcome-based contingency arrangements could be superior to the other, because either could lead to a higher expected gain minus litigation costs. In particular, the hourly fee arrangement would be superior if the excess incentives associated with it—to take cases, and then to go to trial and work more during trial—are not as important a drawback as the inadequacy of incentives under contingency fees.

The incentive problems facing clients, however, are reduced by their ability to obtain information about lawyer behavior. Clients can seek second opinions, and sometimes lawyer behavior will become apparent and harm a lawyer's reputation or even result in suit for malpractice. These factors mitigate the incentive problems under different fee arrangements.

When risk-bearing is taken into account, additional considerations become relevant. Under hourly fees, lawyers bear little risk relative to what they bear under outcome-based contingency fees. Hence, if lawyers are more risk averse than clients, the mutual appeal of hourly fees will be increased, whereas if lawyers are less risk averse than their clients, the mutual appeal of contingency fee arrangements will rise. It is often emphasized that, when clients' assets are limited, having to bear legal fees (or the inability to pay them) would discourage suits under an hourly fee arrangement, and only under contingency fee arrangements will they be brought.

In any event, hourly fee arrangements seem to be the dominant form of compensation, and contingency fees seem to be limited mainly to tort actions. Moreover, contingency fee arrangements are regulated and seem to be frowned upon.[27] Thus, the relative absence of contingency fees, based on trial outcomes, may not really reflect the desires of lawyers and clients.[28]

7.3 Socially desirable arrangements.   We can also inquire about the social welfare implications of lawyer-client arrangements. Of course, the general argument that contracts raise the well-being of the contracting parties suggests that it is socially desirable to allow lawyers and clients to make the fee arrangements that they wish. As we also know, however, it may be socially desirable to limit private contracting when contracts have external effects (see section 9 of Chapter 13).[29] Hence, if lawyer-client fee arrangements have external effects, it might be advantageous to regulate them. Suppose that contingency fee arrangements lead to more suit because they enable risk-averse clients to bring cases that they would not otherwise have brought, and suppose also that the level of suit is felt to be excessive. Under these assumptions, it might be thought desirable to regulate contingency fee arrangements. Yet such a conclusion overlooks the possibility of using other policy tools to cure externality problems. If the volume of suit is excessive, that can be corrected by imposing fees for bringing suit. This kind of approach, being tailored to a specific externality problem, may often be superior to intervention in contractual relations, for that is likely to deny parties benefits of a broader nature (contingent fee arrangements will help parties for many types of suit, not just those that are excessive).

8.   ROLE OF INSURERS

Insurers tend to have interests in the outcome of litigation. First, plaintiffs may be insured against the losses for which they are suing, and their insur-

27. See, for example, Brickman, Horowitz, and O'Connell 1994, Rubinfeld and Scotchmer 1998, 415–416, and Wolfram 1986, 526–542.

28. Literature on the effects and the mutual desirability of lawyer-client fee arrangements includes Dana and Spier 1993, Danzon 1983, Emons 2000, Hay 1996, Miller 1987, Rubinfeld and Scotchmer 1993, and is generally described in the survey by Rubinfeld and Scotchmer 1998.

29. Another major reason for intervention in private contracting is lack of information by contracting parties. This applies only if disclosure requirements and/or public provision of information about fee arrangements do not function well.

ance policies often have clauses allowing the insurers to be reimbursed from payments made by defendants. For example, a plaintiff who sustains losses of $100,000 due to a negligently caused fire may have a fire insurance policy providing $60,000 of coverage and thus will be able to collect this amount immediately from his insurer. But the policy may also stipulate that if the plaintiff wins a judgment or obtains a settlement, the insurer will have the right to as much as $60,000 of that amount (this feature of fire insurance policies would lower insurer costs and thus premiums). Accordingly, the insurer may have an interest in the plaintiff's suit. Second, defendants frequently own liability insurance policies, and defendants' insurers therefore obviously have an incentive to defeat plaintiffs in litigation or to pay them less rather than more in settlements.

8.1 Description of effects. In discussing the effects of insurance, let us consider the example just mentioned, of a plaintiff's policy giving him $60,000 of coverage against his $100,000 loss, and allowing the insurer to collect up to $60,000 from suit or settlement. We also will assume for concreteness that the defendant's liability insurance coverage is $70,000. Further, we will suppose that the insurers will bear all legal costs and make litigation decisions. Examination of this example will reveal important aspects of the effects of insurance, and I will offer some comments later about how the conclusions would be altered were one to relax various assumptions of the example. Note that in this example the insurance coverage is not full.[30] This case is significant because, as will be evident, it means that the interests of the insurer and of the insured are each positive and generally different.

Consider first the effects of plaintiffs' insurance on incentives to sue. If the plaintiff's losses are $100,000 and he collects $60,000 from his insurer, his gain from suit will only be $40,000, not $100,000. Likewise, his insurer's gain from suit will be only $60,000. Thus, the gain of the plaintiff and of his insurer from suit is, for each separately, only partial when the insurance coverage is less than the plaintiff's losses. Because of the assumption that the insurer bears all the litigation costs, the insurer will have a reduced incentive to bring suit, relative to the standard case of a single

30. As I discussed in Chapter 11, coverage is often partial, due to moral hazard, the judgment-proof possibility, and administrative costs of insurance.

plaintiff who would gain $100,000 from suit. The plaintiff would very much want to bring the suit to win the extra $40,000, however, for he does not have to bear any of the costs of suit. This creates a conflict between the plaintiff and the insurer.[31] In any event, the incentive to bring the suit is dulled relative to the standard case because the assumption is that the insurer decides whether the suit goes forward.

There is also an important, and opposite, effect of defendants' liability insurance on the plaintiff's incentive to sue: The existence of liability insurance is a spur to suit, for otherwise many defendants would be unable to pay judgments and thus not be sued—plaintiffs and their insurers will not bring suit if they know that defendants do not have the assets or liability insurance to pay the judgments that they seek.

With regard to the decision about settlement versus trial once a suit has been brought, the situation is complicated, as the following illustration shows.

> *Example 4.* Assume that litigation costs for the plaintiff's side would be $15,000, that he and his insurer believe the chance of victory is 50 percent, that his insurer would bear litigation costs, and that the insurer would receive the first $60,000 of any settlement or judgment and the plaintiff the remainder. What would be the plaintiff's minimum acceptable settlement? If there is a trial, the plaintiff's expected return would be 50% × $40,000 = $20,000, because he does not bear legal costs. Thus, the settlement would have to be at least $80,000 to satisfy him (because the insurer would obtain the first $60,000 of a settlement). Now consider the insurer's minimum acceptable settlement offer. The insurer would net 50% × $60,000 − $15,000 = $15,000 from trial, so it would be willing to accept any amount over $15,000 in settlement. Hence, the insurer would accept a lower settlement than the plaintiff, owing to its bearing the legal expenses and also to its obtaining only the first $60,000 of any settlement. Note also that, were the plaintiff a single uninsured

---

31. Such conflict can sometimes be resolved through bargaining between insurer and insured. For example, if the insurer does not want to press a suit and the plaintiff does, it may be that if the plaintiff makes a contribution toward the cost of suit, then the insurer would agree to go forward with it. Of course, bargaining costs and asymmetry of information may hinder such renegotiation, so that conflicts often remain even where mutually beneficial changes exist. (Comments similar to this one will apply to most of what is written later about differences between insureds and their insurers.)

party, the plaintiff's minimum settlement offer would be 50% ×
$100,000 − $15,000 = $35,000, which is between the insured plaintiff's
and the insurer's minimum acceptable settlement offers.

Now consider the defendant's side. Because the defendant's liability
insurance coverage is for $70,000, his exposure is for $30,000. Assume
that the defendant's legal expenses would be $10,000 and would be paid
by the liability insurer, and also that the first $70,000 of any settlement
or judgment is to be paid by the insurer. The defendant's expected loss
from trial would thus be 50% × $30,000 = $15,000. Therefore, the
defendant would agree to any settlement amount up to $85,000 (recall
that the liability insurer pays the first $70,000 of any settlement). The
liability insurer would lose 50% × $70,000 + $10,000 = $45,000 at
trial, so would pay up to $45,000 in settlement. Thus, the liability insurer
would be less willing to settle than the defendant. If there were a single
uninsured defendant, that defendant would pay up to 50% × $100,000
+ $10,000 or $60,000 in settlement, which also exceeds what the liability
insurer would be willing to pay.

We have seen that each litigant and his insurer have disparate interests
in this example. The plaintiff's insurer is more likely to want to settle than
the plaintiff, and the defendant's insurer is less likely to want to settle than
the defendant—the plaintiff's insurer will demand less than the plaintiff
would, and the defendant's insurer will pay less than the defendant would.[32]
The same relationship holds between the insurer's demands and offers and
those in the standard case of plaintiffs and defendants who do not possess
insurance. Thus, it is not evident, in the circumstances of the example,
whether settlement will be more likely or less likely than in the standard
case.

Insurance generally reduces incentives to spend at trial, for the simple
reason that the insurers have less at stake than the full $100,000, yet bear
the entire legal costs. Of course, the plaintiff and the defendant would each
like their insurers to spend more than the insurers wish, because the plaintiff
and defendant each have some stake in the outcome.

32. In our example, it so happens that there will be settlement, for the plaintiff's insurer
will accept any amount over $15,000, and the defendant's insurer will pay up to $45,000.
Of course, if beliefs were different, or if information were asymmetric, settlement might
not occur.

To summarize, we can see that, given our assumption that insurers bear legal expenses and make litigation decisions, insurance coverage leads to conflicts between insurers and insureds, a reduced incentive to sue, and a lower incentive to spend at trial. The specific conclusions about the direction of effects may well be altered if we were to consider different assumptions about the nature of the insurance contract, especially about who bears legal costs and about who makes litigation decisions or about whether agreement about litigation decisions between insurer and insured is necessary.[33]

An important assumption that we implicitly made is that insurers and insureds do not renegotiate during litigation. This assumption might be justified when the costs of renegotiation are significant, or when asymmetry of information between insured and insurer (especially about the likelihood of the trial outcome) would often result in failure to come to an agreement. In any event, if the parties are able to renegotiate and come to an agreement, they would tend to act approximately in the same way that a single litigant would, so that the conclusions of the standard case would be maintained. For instance, it was stated earlier that the plaintiff's insurer has a lower incentive to sue than in the standard case because the insurer will gain only $60,000 of the $100,000 judgment, whereas the insurer bears all the legal costs. If, though, the plaintiff cooperates and contributes toward legal costs, his interest in obtaining $40,000 will make their joint willingness to bring suit similar to that in the standard case.[34]

8.2 Mutually desirable insurance contract terms regarding litigation. The parties will tend to elect a type of insurance contract that, in its terms regarding litigation, is jointly beneficial to them. Such contracts

33. For example, if the legal fees are divided pro rata between insurer and insured and they make a joint decision on litigation, their incentive to bring suit would be the same as in the standard case. A systematic account of the conclusions as a function of the type of insurance policy is, however, beyond our scope, and has not been undertaken in the literature to my knowledge. Only a few papers examine litigation-related conflicts of interest between insureds and insurers from an economic perspective; see, for example, Meurer 1992 and Sykes 1994. These papers are suggestive, but are limited in nature, focusing on aspects of liability insurer incentives to settle.

34. It might not be identical to that in the standard case because the plaintiff is risk averse and thus would be less likely to want to engage in the risky venture of suit than the risk-neutral party of the standard case.

will reflect several factors. One is that it is often efficient to have a single party control the litigation and bear the litigation costs, for that reduces the need for costly negotiation and coordination during litigation. An additional factor is that the insured will, being risk averse, want coverage not only against loss and liability, but also against legal expenses; this favors insurers bearing legal expenses and controlling litigation. Another factor is that the party with the most experience with litigation is the natural one to assume the responsibility of decisionmaking about litigation and thus to bear litigation costs; this party is generally the insurer, not the insured. These factors all suggest the mutual desirability of insurer control and expenditure on litigation. A factor working in a different direction is that it tends to be jointly beneficial for the litigation decisions to maximize joint expected returns for the plaintiff and his insurer, or to minimize joint payments for the defendant and his insurer. If, however, the insurer is in control of the litigation and bears all the litigation costs, then, as was seen in the previous section, the incentives of the insurer generally diverge from those of the standard case in which joint net returns are maximized for plaintiffs or joint costs are minimized for defendants. The character of the mutually desirable terms of the insurance contract thus reflects concerns that are competing in some respects.

8.3 Social desirability of the foregoing contractual terms. The main point to be made about the social desirability of the contractual terms that insurers and insureds select is the analogue of that of section 7.3: Because contractual terms of insurance policies raise the well-being of insureds and insurers, these terms are socially desirable unless they have unwanted external effects (such as on the volume of suit) that cannot be alleviated through some other policy (typically they can be).[35]

It is sometimes suggested that the fact that insurers often display different interests from their insureds is socially undesirable and calls for legal intervention. Consider the situation in which a plaintiff would like the insurer to sue for $100,000, but the insurer hesitates to do so because it

---

35. Again, lack of information by contracting parties, here by insureds about the nature of insurance contracts, may also justify intervention in contracts. That may be so if requirements to disclose clearly the nature of terms in contracts and publicly provided information do not perform well.

would gain only $60,000 and would pay the entire legal fees. The reluctance of the insurer to sue when the insured wants suit, and when the expected total gain exceeds the cost of suit, might be seen as justifying a legal response to force the insurer to do what the insured wants.[36] Such a view overlooks the point that the insurance contract is elected by the insured and the insurer, and that the conflict of interests at the time of possible suit is a by-product of their contractual terms, which were chosen for their beneficial joint purposes. In the example in question, the terms that give the insurer control over litigation decisions may be warranted because the insurer is best suited to control legal expenditures efficiently (given the scale of its business), and the terms that limit coverage of the insured to $60,000 (which is what gives rise to the conflict) may be best because they combat moral hazard and fraud. For the courts to intervene, such as to prevent the insurer from maintaining control over litigation, is effectively to hurt the insured ex ante by preventing him from obtaining certain types of contractual terms, which would tend to raise insurance prices and lower insureds' expected utility.

36. Indeed, in many jurisdictions, liability insurers have a duty in settlement negotiations to act beyond their own interests—effectively to act as if they were covering the entire liability, not just an amount up to the coverage limit of the policy. See Sykes 1994.

19 ||| GENERAL TOPICS ON THE LEGAL PROCESS

By the *legal process,* I refer to the set of rules governing the actual exercise of legal rights of parties and the manner in which opposing parties defend themselves. Thus, the legal process comprehends the rules of procedure, evidence, lawyer conduct, and other factors bearing on the application and adjudication of legal rights. The legal process is often contrasted to the *substantive law* that lays out the underlying legal rights of parties (such as a rule of tort liability giving a victim of harm the right to collect from an injurer) but that does not state how these rights are to be exercised.[1] In this chapter, I will address several important general issues concerning the legal process and certain related aspects of the substantive law.

---

1. The definition of the substantive law, as opposed to the legal process, is not always clear. For example, would we say that joint and several liability—allowing a plaintiff to collect from any of the defendants when more than one injured him—is an element of the substantive law or of the legal process? The question of rigorous definition of the two notions need not detain us, however, for what is of interest is the analysis of the rules of the legal system, not the headings under which its rules are placed.

1. PUBLIC VERSUS PRIVATE LEGAL SYSTEMS

1.1 Introduction.   A basic question about the design of the legal system is whether the state-authorized legal system should be the sole system of substantive law and of the legal process or whether, and in what circumstances, private legal systems should be allowed a role.[2] In fact, we observe that the public legal system provides the default system of substantive rules and adjudication but that private systems, notably arbitration and trade association regimes, have substantial importance.

1.2 Socially optimal legal system.   To analyze the desirable relationship between public and private legal systems, it will be helpful to have in mind the socially optimal legal system, that is, the system with the socially optimal substantive legal rules and also the socially optimal system of adjudication. The socially optimal legal system will also have to be enforced to be effective, of course, and that may require use of state power to collect funds, to transfer property, and the like.

Of importance for us is that this optimal system—both the substantive legal rules and the method of adjudication—will vary with the characteristics of the involved parties. For example, the best set of legal rules and adjudication for breach of contract may be different for businesses in some industry from what they are for other types of parties.

1.3 Assumptions about public and private legal systems.   Let us make the following simplifying assumptions about the public and private legal systems. First, the state's goal, as reflected in the public legal system, is to maximize social welfare. Second, the state can employ its various powers to enforce the law. Third, however, the state may suffer from lack of information about the best legal system, either about the best rules or the best method of adjudication, for certain groups of parties. Fourth, private parties themselves will have at least as good—and sometimes better—infor-

---

2. One of the first economically oriented articles on this subject is Landes and Posner 1975. This section builds on their article and on Shavell 1995a, which emphasizes the distinction that will be made here between ex ante and ex post choice of private judicial systems. For economic literature focusing on private arbitration (but not on it as an alternative to public adjudication), see, for example, Ashenfelter 1998, Ashenfelter and Bloom 1984, and Benson 2000.

mation about what legal system is best for them than the state will have. And fifth, private legal systems will typically have less power to enforce their decisions than the state enjoys, because they lack the power to appropriate funds and to imprison, but they may still sometimes possess methods of enforcement, such as expulsion from a group.

1.4 Public legal system as the sole system. If the public system is the sole legal system, the outcome will deviate from the optimal because of the state's lack of information about what is best for certain groups of parties. Such deviations from what is best suggest that if the state can harness parties' superior knowledge about the best legal system for them and allow the public system to be appropriately modified, the altered system will be superior to the public system alone. We now consider the conditions under which the public system would and would not be expected to be changed in a beneficial way.

1.5. Choice of private system by a single party is undesirable. We can first dispense with the possibility that unilateral choice of a private legal system by a party to a dispute would tend to be socially desirable. It would not, for the party would select a system that favored him, reducing or eliminating the capacity of the law to channel behavior or to remedy loss desirably. For example, a rule of tort law requiring injurers to pay for harm, which could be beneficial due to the incentives it provides to take care, would be robbed of force if defendants could select their own legal system. They would choose a different rule that allowed them to escape responsibility, or if they were permitted only to elect the method of adjudication, they would select a tribunal that watered down the ability of plaintiffs to collect. Converse problems, involving excessive liability, would arise if plaintiffs could unilaterally choose liability rules or methods of adjudication. It is plain, therefore, that permitting unilateral modification of the public system of law is socially undesirable.

1.6 Choice of private system by affected parties is desirable if made ex ante. By contrast, it will be socially desirable to allow modification of the public legal system in many circumstances where the decision is made by the parties who are affected by the legal system. An important example is where the parties to a contract stipulate that they want a private system to govern contractual problems that may arise. The reasons that allowing them to choose a private system is socially desirable are twofold. First, if each of the contracting parties agrees to the private system, it must make each of them better off. Second, no one else will be made worse off, presuming that the parties to the contract are the only people affected by it.

This argument applies more generally than just to contracts—it applies whenever all the parties who are affected by some type of behavior make an ex ante agreement about a private legal system. Suppose that the trucks owned by a company present the risk of accidents to citizens of a community, and the company and the community agree to their own legal system to govern accidents. Perhaps they choose strict liability with agreed-on formulas for damages, rather than the negligence rule and the complicated and costly methods of adjudication that we generally employ, in order to give truckers good incentives to take care and also to streamline dispute resolution. Here, as in the contracting context, the use of the private legal system will be socially beneficial. For if the parties agree to a private system as an alternative to the public system, they must be made better off, and others are not made worse off, because by hypothesis the group in question includes all potentially affected parties.

Two comments should be made about the foregoing: First, the private system that the parties elect may differ from the public system in its substantive legal rules (such as employing strict liability rather than negligence for truck accidents) or in its methods of dispute resolution (such as in the manner of determining damages). Second, the private system will often use the public system of enforcement. Private parties will not usually have a good way to enforce the decisions of a private system, such as of arbitrators, and will wish to rely on the state to accomplish this. Thus, it will be desirable for the state to lend its enforcement apparatus to the private system; otherwise the private system would be rendered ineffective.

1.7 Choice of private system by affected parties may or may not be desirable if made ex post. The parties to a dispute may mutually desire to choose a private system of adjudication over the public system. Notably, they may want to do this to lower the costs of dispute resolution and to reduce risk. Allowing them to choose a private system, however,

[handwritten margin note: looking backward]

does not necessarily raise social welfare.[3] Consider an accident between an individual and a firm. They may decide that it is in their joint interests to elect arbitration for its simplicity and speed, but that may mean that the firm escapes with inadequate liability or that the firm's fault is never properly investigated and made known to the public. And if firms anticipate often being able to reach such agreements to arbitrate, they may not be properly deterred. In other words, because the ex post incentives of parties to use private adjudication are naturally divorced from considerations of deterrence, their use of private systems may be undesirable.[4] By contrast, when parties make agreements ex ante, and all potentially affected parties are involved in the agreements, deterrence is not overlooked; in the case of truck accidents in a community, if the citizens make an agreement to

3. The argument to be made is in some respects similar to the point made in section 4.1 of Chapter 17 about the possibility that settlement may be socially undesirable; here the decision to use a private legal system (often because it is less costly than the public one) is analogous to the decision to settle.

4. An example may clarify this point. Suppose that if firms exercise care at a cost of $10, accidents causing harm of $15 will be prevented, so that the exercise of care is desirable. Suppose too that liability is strict, that the probability that a firm will be sued is only 50 percent—there is difficulty in proving causation—and that the costs of use of the public legal system would be $6 each for the plaintiff and the defendant, and only $2 each for use of a streamlined private arbitration system. Then, if an accident occurs for which causation is clear (and for which there is thus a threat of suit under the public legal system), the parties would elect the private system, in order to save $4 each in adjudication costs. This, however, means that the expected liability of the firm if it does not take care will be 50% × ($15 + $2) = $8.50, so it will not be led to spend $10 on care. But if the public system were employed, the firm's expected liability if it does not take care would be 50% × $21 = $10.50, so it would be led to take care (in which case, note, there would never be any litigation expenses, because no accidents would occur). Thus, social welfare, and the well-being of the victims of accidents, are lowered because of the ability of the victims and the firms to make ex post agreements that reduce firms' incentives to take care.

The reader might wonder whether the point of the example depends on the fact that not all of the affected parties participate in the decision to employ the private system of adjudication—for the 50 percent of victims who are not able to prove causation are left out of negotiations. This feature of the example, however, is not intrinsic to it. For instance, one could alter the example by assuming that all individuals sue but that a fraction of losses cannot be proved due to difficulties in establishing causation, and the same point could be made even though all victims would be participating in the decision to use a private legal system.

use a private legal system, it can only be because the system does not result in too much dilution of deterrence.

Of course, ex post agreements to use private legal systems may also be socially desirable, because their potentially undesirable effect on deterrence is outweighed by their value in reducing the costs of dispute resolution and perhaps in increasing its accuracy. Therefore, it is possible, if not plausible, that ex post agreements to employ private legal systems are often socially desirable.

An observation that should be made about ex post agreements to use private legal systems is that such agreements will generally be limited to the method of dispute resolution and will not alter the basic thrust of the legal rules of the state, for that would be against the interests of one or the other of the parties. For example, if the substantive legal rule is the negligence rule, then a nonnegligent injurer would be unlikely to agree to a private system in which liability would be strict. Were victims and injurers to choose a private system ex ante, however, they might opt for strict liability.

1.8 The notion that selection of legal rules and adjudication are natural functions of the state. The foregoing analysis helps to answer the question of whether the choice of substantive legal rules and the system of adjudication are natural functions of the state, as some seem to think is so.[5] The answer, we have seen, depends importantly on whether the parties that are affected by some type of behavior are likely to bargain with one another ex ante about the choice of a private legal regime. When they are likely to do so, and when they have superior information to the state about the legal rules or manner of adjudication that best serves their purposes, it is best for them to select it. In this circumstance, the idea that the state is naturally the entity that should choose the legal system is incorrect (although the state may still play a role in enforcement).

When affected parties cannot bargain with each other ex ante, which is the case when they are strangers to one another, the state will play a natural role in the selection of substantive legal rules. Thus, in the usual tort context, for instance, the state must make the substantive legal rules in order for there to be any rules that will influence parties' behavior. But

5. See, for example, Couture 1999.

there still may be scope for private parties to beneficially elect a private system of adjudication after harm is done, as discussed in section 1.7.

1.9 Actual practice in the light of the theory. Actual practice conforms broadly to what has been described as socially desirable. In particular, we observe that private parties often opt out of the state-authorized legal system, as noted at the outset. There is significant use of arbitration and of other private means of adjudication, such as those of trade associations, employers, and religious organizations.[6] Also, as stated earlier, the private systems that are chosen ex ante often involve procedural and substantive legal rules that depart significantly from those of the public system.[7] But there does not appear to be a tendency in practice to distinguish between ex ante agreements to use private systems and ex post agreements, even though the case in theory for respecting agreements made ex post is less strong.

At least in the United States today, there is a tendency of commentators, and of the state itself, to encourage use of alternatives to the public system of adjudication, and even to subsidize it or require private parties to employ it. The only apparent justification for encouragement or subsidy of private alternatives to the public system is that parties do not pay legal fees that cover the actual costs of use of public courts, so that the public system may appear cheaper than it should relative to private systems; fostering the use of private systems might correct this distortion.[8]

2. ACCURACY OF THE LEGAL PROCESS

2.1 Introduction. By the accuracy of the legal process is meant the absence of error. Error may arise in the determination of whether or not a person is liable—an innocent person may mistakenly be found liable or

---

6. See, for example, Benson 2000, 159–162, Bernstein 1998, Cooley and Lubet 1997, 20–23, and Goldberg, Sander, and Rogers 1999, 10–11.

7. See, for example, Bernstein 1998, Goldberg, Sander, and Rogers 1999, 233–234, and Ware 2001, 21, 80–86, and for case studies, Bernstein 1992, 2001.

8. A better answer to this distortion in relative prices would seem to be to price the public system appropriately, not to subsidize the private system, for that may lead to excessive litigation. Yet this whole issue is complicated by the concern, discussed at length in

a guilty person not found liable—or in the determination of the level of sanctions to be imposed on a liable person.

The accuracy of the legal process is influenced by its design; indeed, all of the rules of legal procedure and evidence bear on the incidence of error. And the accuracy of the legal process is also affected by the actions of litigants; their gathering of information, selection of evidence, and use of legal procedure influence the likelihood of error.

Here I will discuss first the social value of accuracy of the legal process: the increase in social welfare that greater accuracy brings about. The social value of accuracy inheres in its effects on outcomes, and notably in its effects on the behavior of parties who anticipate greater accuracy of the legal process; accuracy is not valued in itself. As will become evident, the social value of accuracy depends in significant ways on context.

Given the social value of accuracy, the socially optimal level of accuracy can be determined. As a general matter, increasing accuracy is socially costly, because it requires a lengthier and higher-quality legal process. Therefore, the level of accuracy that maximizes social welfare will reflect a compromise between the value of increasing accuracy and the cost of achieving it.

I will then examine the private value of accuracy; for example, the value to a plaintiff of establishing that the defendant is the party who harmed him. It will be seen that the private value of accuracy generally diverges from the social value, calling in principle for the legal process to include features that remedy the divergence.[9]

2.2 Social value of accuracy. The social value of accuracy can usefully be divided into three components.

(a) *Improved control of behavior.* It is intuitively clear that greater accuracy of the legal process should tend to bring about improved control of behavior, but why exactly should this be true?

Consider, first, accuracy in the determination of liability. Greater accuracy in imposition of liability on truly guilty parties clearly leads to an

---

Chapter 17, that the private incentive to use the legal system differs from the social, so that pricing legal services at cost is not generally optimal in the first place.

9. This section is largely a synthesis of Kaplow and Shavell 1994a, 1996a, and Kaplow 1994.

enhanced incentive to obey the law, for it means that the expected sanction for violations is higher. Not so obvious, however, is that greater accuracy in respect to exonerating innocent parties enhances deterrence. The reason is that the incentive to obey the law is not simply equal to the expected sanction if one violates the law, but rather to the *difference* between the expected sanction if one violates the law and the expected sanction if one does not. If the expected sanction suffered by the innocent, due to error, is 20, and the expected sanction experienced by the guilty is 60, then the effective sanction for a violation is 40, not 60, for 40 is the added sanction brought about by a violation. Hence, the incentive to obey the law is enhanced by reducing errors that penalize the innocent (if, for instance, the expected sanction suffered by the innocent fell from 20 to 10, the effective sanction for violations would rise from 40 to 50).[10]

An additional social benefit from increased accuracy in the determination of liability is improved decisions about whether to engage in an activity (such as to operate a motor vehicle). Greater accuracy implies that fewer parties will be undesirably discouraged from engaging in such an activity because of mistakenly imposed liability on the innocent. It also means that fewer parties will be undesirably encouraged to engage in the activity because of the guilty mistakenly escaping liability.

Another, more particular social benefit from increased accuracy applies when liability is based on whether or not a party's level of care falls below a fault standard. In these situations, as was discussed in section 1.1 of Chapter 10, error in the assessment of care may lead to the exercise of excessive care (such as defensive medical practices) to reduce the chance of mistakenly being found liable. Here greater accuracy in the assessment of care will lead to less excess in precautions.[11]

too much

10. The point under discussion may be stated algebraically. Let s_I be the expected sanction if a person is innocent, obeys the law, and let s_G be the expected sanction if a person is guilty and violates the law. Then if b is the benefit from violating the law, a person will violate the law if $b - s_G > -s_I$, that is, if $b > s_G - s_I$, so that the incentive to obey the law is the difference between the expected sanctions. This point was initially emphasized in Png 1986.

11. There is no conflict between this point and the point that greater accuracy increases deterrence, for the presumed contexts are different. It was assumed earlier that a party chooses between two actions, obeying the law or not, whereas here the assumption is that

Next, consider accuracy in the assessment of damages. In this regard accuracy tends to improve behavior because if an actor knows that the harm he might cause will be accurately assessed, he will tend to take steps to prevent harm commensurate with its magnitude; he will appropriately do more to prevent harm the larger its magnitude. It is important to note, however, that the actor can only take these harm-appropriate steps if he knows what the harm will be at the time he decides on precautions. In many contexts, actors will have relatively little such knowledge. For instance, a driver will typically have relatively little knowledge of the harm he would cause in a collision (the harm would depend on the speed of the other vehicle, where it was struck, the number of occupants in it, and so forth). This possibility reduces the social value of accuracy in the assessment of damages.[12]

(b) *Reduced social costs from litigation and from imposition of sanctions.* Another social advantage of accuracy is a higher frequency of settlement, and thus of savings in litigation costs. Specifically, if greater accuracy of the legal process means that litigants are more likely to agree on their estimates of trial outcomes, settlement will be promoted. Additionally, accuracy may reduce the need to impose sanctions and thus the costs of so doing.[13] Specifically, greater accuracy leads to reduced imposition of sanctions when the accuracy results in better identification of the innocent. But greater accuracy in identification of the guilty results in more frequent imposition of sanctions, and thus greater costs from imposing sanctions.

(c) *Lowered costs of risk-bearing.* Greater accuracy tends to lower risk, for it means that outcomes as to whether parties are liable and the amount

---

a party chooses a level of care that is continuously variable (or has many levels), and it is possible for the party to choose a higher level than is called for and thereby to lower the chance of erroneous imposition of liability.

12. See Kaplow and Shavell 1996a, but see also Spier 1994b for a qualification to this point: that there is social value in accuracy in assessing damages even when an actor does not know the magnitude of harm in advance, if the level of his precautions lowers the probability distribution of harm given that an accident occurs.

13. These costs are the various administrative costs associated with settlements and judgments, which were noted to be large (see section 1.3 of Chapter 17). In the criminal context, which will be considered later in the book, the costs of imposing sanctions also include the expenses of incarceration.

that liable parties pay are more predictable. The reduced risk is socially valuable in itself, to the extent that parties are risk averse and uninsured against the risks in question. *disliking*

2.3 Socially optimal degree of accuracy.   As indicated, the socially optimal level of accuracy will depend on a tradeoff between its social value and its cost. For example, where potential injurers have relatively little knowledge of the precise magnitude of harm when they choose their levels of care (plausibly the case with drivers, as suggested earlier), the social value of accuracy in assessing harm will be low. Thus, the best policy might call for little to be spent on accuracy, meaning that *simply* streamlined methods (such as simple tables) to ascertain damages might be best. The optimal degree of accuracy will depend generally on the context, because the social value and the costs of accuracy will depend on the particulars of the area of behavior at issue.

2.4 Traditional view of accuracy versus the economic view.   The *against* traditional view of legal scholars about accuracy has several features. One is that accuracy is of intrinsic value; this is inconsistent with the economic view. A second strand of traditional thinking is that accuracy is necessary in order to maintain the legitimacy of the legal process. The economic view is not inconsistent with this point, for if individuals respect the legal system and cooperate in its application, it will work more effectively to further social ends. A third element of traditional writing on accuracy is that accuracy serves instrumental purposes. This, of course, is entirely consistent with the economic view, but the instrumental purposes of accuracy are rarely analyzed in a sustained way by traditional scholars, whereas these purposes are the focus of economic analysis.

2.5 Private versus social value of accuracy, and implications.   Let us now turn to the value of accuracy to private parties themselves, as opposed to its social value.

Perhaps the first point to note is simply that accuracy may not be desired—it may have negative value—to a private party. A plaintiff may want to conceal facts in order to prevail against a defendant who is in fact innocent or may want to exaggerate his losses; a defendant may have similarly perverse incentives to prevent the truth from becoming known.

Of course, private parties may also have incentives to prove the truth. A plaintiff will want to show that he is really the victim of harm and that the named defendant is the liable party, or a defendant will want to establish that the plaintiff was truly contributorily negligent, and the like. The incentives of private parties to establish the truth, however, will tend to diverge from the socially optimal, and in either direction. The private reason to spend in order to establish a fact is, for the plaintiff, to increase his expected judgment, and for the defendant, to reduce it. From the social perspective, however, the justification for expenditures lies in improved control of behavior and the other factors mentioned in section 2.3; these social benefits may be quite different from the private ones. For example, it may be that increased accuracy in determining liability would be socially very valuable in deterring negligent behavior, but that the private value of establishing negligence is too low to induce a plaintiff to do so.[14] Or it might be that increased accuracy in ascertaining liability has small social value, because there is little that potential injurers can do to reduce risk, yet the private value of establishing liability may be quite high, because of the damages that the plaintiff can collect, so that more would be spent establishing accuracy than is socially desirable.[15] In general, the reasons for the private-social divergence in the value of accuracy are analogous to those discussed in Chapter 17 on the private-social divergence in the value of bringing suit.

14. Suppose that defendants can reduce the risk of harm of $1,000 from 100 percent to 1 percent by exercising a precaution at a cost of $100, and that proving negligence—that the precaution was not taken—would cost a plaintiff $2,000. Then a harmed plaintiff would not spend the $2,000 to prove negligence, and since defendants would anticipate this, they would not take the $100 precaution; thus, social costs would be $1,000. But it would be socially desirable that plaintiffs spend $2,000 to prove negligence whenever accidents occur, for then defendants would expect that negligence would be found out and would be led to spend the $100. As a consequence, if, say, plaintiffs were given free legal services costing $2,000 to investigate possible defendant negligence, social costs would be only $100 + 1% × $2,000 = $120 (and thus lower than $1,000).

15. Suppose that liability is strict, that losses of $1,000 occur with probability 10 percent, that nothing at all can be done to prevent the losses, and that plaintiffs must spend $100 to prove causation, and thus to establish liability accurately, if a loss occurs. Clearly plaintiffs will do that, because $100 is less than the $1,000 they will collect; yet socially that is undesirable because social costs would be only 10% × $1,000 = $100 if suit is not brought, but social costs are 10% × $1,100 = $110 if suits are brought (actually, they would be higher if we take into account the defendant's and state's litigation costs).

Indeed, a factor stressed there, that each side generally fails to take into account the litigation costs that it induces the other side to incur, is also relevant in the present context.

An additional point relating to the private incentive to establish the magnitude of harm should be recalled (see section 5.3 of Chapter 17). Namely, there is a systematic tendency for private parties to value accuracy in determining the magnitude of harm above its social value. This is suggested by the observation that a plaintiff will be willing to spend as much as $100 to prove that his losses are in fact $100 higher (or a defendant to spend as much as $100 to prove that the losses he caused are in fact $100 lower), but the social value of establishing that losses are $100 higher is generally less than $100.

What are the implications of the divergences between the social and the private values of accuracy? When private parties have incentives to withhold information, the state should attempt to prevent that if the social value of the information outweighs its cost. Of course, much of the law of procedure is designed to address this problem. When private parties have incentives to supply information rather than to conceal it, the state should encourage its provision if parties' incentives are inadequate, but limit its provision if parties' incentives are excessive. The limiting may be accomplished through the use of procedural rules that, for instance, restrict the number of witnesses or that simplify the calculation of damages. A conjecture is that the problem of excessive private incentives to establish facts is considerable— especially in respect to the proof of the magnitude of damages—and that it is not properly appreciated.

3. APPEALS AND THE LEGAL SYSTEM

3.1 Introduction. An important feature of our legal system is the inclusion of an appeals process, whereby a disappointed litigant can make a request for reconsideration of the initial trial result.[16] It should be emphasized, however, that a legal system might not include an appeals process— whether it does so is an element of the design of the system—and in some

---

16. That all developed legal systems generally recognize some form of appeal process is discussed, for example, in Herzog and Karlen 1982, chap. 8, and Platto 1992.

contexts there is no appeals process.[17] Notably, when parties elect binding arbitration, they are usually choosing to forgo an appeals process.[18]

Why may the appeals process be socially desirable? In answering the question, one must explain, among other things, why society (or an organization) may find the appeals process superior to the alternative of enhancing the quality of the trial process. Society enjoys the option, after all, of investing in more skilled trial court judges, of lengthening trial proceedings to allow for more evidence and argument to be considered, and the like. Moreover, one must address why, if society does decide to employ a tribunal that supersedes the trial courts, it should wish to grant disappointed litigants the right to instigate action by the higher tribunal—rather than, say, permit the higher tribunal to reconsider trial outcomes on its own initiative.

The theme to be advanced here is that the appeals process may correct errors in an economic way (other functions of appeals will be noted in sections 3.3 and 3.4). If litigants tend to possess information about the occurrence of error and appeals courts can frequently verify it, then litigants may tend to bring appeals when errors are likely to have been made but not otherwise. Under these circumstances, not only may the appeals process result in error correction; it may also do so cheaply, for the legal system will be burdened with reconsidering only the subset of cases in which errors were more probably made. This may render society's investment in the appeals process economical in comparison to an investment in improving the accuracy of the trial process—an approach that, by its nature, would require extra expenditure in *every* case rather than only in a subset of cases. The appeals process, in other words, may allow society to harness information that litigants have about erroneous decisions and thereby to reduce the incidence of mistake at relatively low cost.[19]

17. A number of legal systems, for example, those of France and Italy, do not allow appeal of cases for which the amount at stake is below a threshold; see Byrd and Barbier 1992, 160, and Beltramo 1995, 470.

18. Decisions of arbitrators generally may not be appealed to the legal system; see, for example, Goldberg, Sander, and Rogers 1999, 235, and Ware 2001, 21. Moreover, the arbitration process itself ordinarily does not allow for appeal to other arbitrators; see, for example, the website of the American Arbitration Association at *www.adr.org*.

19. The analysis that follows is based on Shavell 1995b. For studies of the appeal process emphasizing factors other than error correction, see Daughety and Reinganum 2000 and Spitzer and Talley 2000.

3.2 Basic model: the appeals process and error correction.   Suppose in this section that litigants are able to recognize when error occurs at trial, that the state chooses whether or not to establish an appeals court, and that the state can increase the accuracy of adjudication at both the trial court level and the appeals court level by making appropriate expenditures. If there is an appeals court, then, it is assumed that a disappointed litigant may bring an appeal if he chooses. To bring an appeal, the litigant must pay his private legal costs. In addition, the litigant may have to pay a fee, or possibly will receive a subsidy. Thus, the total cost to a litigant for bringing an appeal is his private cost plus a potential fee or minus a possible subsidy.

The state's objective is assumed to be minimization of total social costs: the sum of the social costs of adjudication—the costs of trial together with the expected costs of appeal, if there is an appeals process—plus the social harm from erroneous decisions.

Consider first the best that the state can do if it does not allow appeals. In this situation, the state's problem is simply to select the level of trial court accuracy so as to minimize trial costs plus expected harm from trial court error. The optimal level of accuracy will be dictated by the effectiveness of legal resources in promoting accuracy and by the magnitude of harm from error.[20]

Now suppose that the state establishes an appeals court and, provisionally, takes its accuracy as given, but assume that it is minimally accurate in the sense that it is more likely to reverse trial court errors than to reverse correct decisions. Hence, a disappointed litigant's expected gross return from an appeal, via a reversal, will be higher if an error occurred than if it did not. For example, if the reversal probability following a mistake is 80 percent but is only 30 percent following a correct decision, then if a litigant's gain from reversal would be $100,000, the expected gross return from an appeal would be $80,000 after a mistake but only $30,000 after a correct adverse decision.

20. Let x be the investment in trial court accuracy, $p(x)$ the probability of trial court error, where p is decreasing and convex in x, and h the social cost of error. Then, in the absence of an appeals process, the state should choose x to minimize $x + p(x)h$; let the optimal x be x^*. (This notation will be used in later notes without further comment.) Observe that, in a formal sense, the state's problem is identical to that of choosing the optimal level of precautions in the model of accidents considered in Chapter 8; the level

Accordingly, there may be *separation* of disappointed litigants, wherein those who are the victims of error find it worthwhile to bring appeals and those who are not victims of error do not find it worthwhile to bring appeals. There will be such separation of disappointed litigants if the private cost of an appeal is less than the expected return given mistakes but exceeds the expected return given correct decisions. In the example just mentioned, there will be separation if the cost of an appeal is, say, $50,000; $50,000 is less than $80,000, meaning that there will be appeals after mistakes, but $50,000 exceeds $30,000, meaning that there will not be appeals after correct adverse decisions.

If separation of disappointed litigants would not occur naturally, due to whatever happens to be the private costs of appeal, the state can ensure that separation occurs by selecting the right fee or subsidy. If appeals would be made even after correct decisions, because the private cost of an appeal is lower than the expected return, the state can impose a fee in order to achieve separation.[21] Conversely, if appeals would not be made even after mistakes, because the private cost of an appeal is higher than the expected return from appeal, the state can grant a subsidy to induce separation.[22]

Moreover, it is clear that the state would want to achieve separation of disappointed litigants when it has an appeals process. On one hand, if litigants never bring appeals, the appeals process can hardly achieve good.

---

of precautions to prevent accidents in that model corresponds here to the level of investment in the accuracy of trial courts to prevent errors.

21. Appeals would be made in the example even after correct decisions if the private cost of an appeal were $10,000, for this is less than the $30,000 expected return from an appeal. Hence, if a fee of, for instance, $40,000 were imposed, the total cost of making an appeal would become $50,000, and appeals after correct decisions would be discouraged (but appeals after mistakes would still be brought, because the return from them is $80,000).

22. In the example, appeals would not be made after mistakes if the private cost of an appeal were $100,000 because this exceeds $80,000. If, however, a subsidy of, say, $50,000 were employed, appeals would be made after mistakes (but not after correct decisions).

More generally, to show that separation of disappointed litigants is always possible, let g be the gain to a litigant from winning an appeal, a be the litigant's private cost of making an appeal, and b be the fee (a positive b) or subsidy (a negative b). Also, let q be the probability of reversal of an error and r the probability of reversal of a correct decision, and assume that $q > r$. Then there will be separation of disappointed litigants if $rg < a + b < qg$. It is clearly always possible to find a b satisfying that inequality because $q > r$.

On the other, if litigants bring appeals even when correct decisions are made, society incurs needless costs in the appeals process and also, to its detriment, finds that a certain number of these correct decisions are reversed.

Knowing that separation of disappointed litigants is socially desirable and that the state can, if need be, accomplish separation through an appropriate fee or subsidy scheme, we can easily determine whether the appeals process will be socially helpful. If the appeals process is not used, then when an error is made, the associated social harm will definitely be suffered. But if the appeals process is utilized, an error will result in an appeal, so that the social costs incurred will instead be those of the appeal and the expected harm due only to the possible failure to reverse error. It follows that *the appeals process will be socially desirable to establish if and only if the social harm from certain error exceeds the social cost of an appeal plus the expected harm from failure to reverse error,* the latter being the probability of failing to reverse error multiplied by the harm from error.[23] If the social harm from error is $500,000, the social costs of an appeal are $150,000, and the probability of reversal of error is 80 percent, then the appeals process will be advantageous because it will reduce the certain harm from error of $500,000 to $150,000 + 20% × $500,000 or $250,000. In general, therefore, the appeals process is more likely to be socially desirable the lower the cost of the appeals process, the greater the chance of reversing error, and the greater the social harm from error. In particular, and other things being equal, the appeals process will be desirable if the social harm exceeds a certain threshold and will not be desirable if the harm lies below this threshold.

To this point, we have taken the cost and accuracy of the appeals process as given, as well as those of the trial process, but as the reader knows, these are variable. What can be said about their optimal choice? With regard to the appeals process, it is socially desirable to invest in accuracy as long

23. To amplify, given that the state can ensure that disappointed litigants sue if and only if an error was made, social costs under an appeals process will be $x + p(x)[y + (1 - q(y))h]$, where y is the state's expenditure on the appeals process. If there is no appeals process, social costs will be $x + p(x)h$. Hence, it will be desirable to append an appeals process to a trial process if and only if $y + (1 - q(y))h < h$, which corresponds to the italicized statement in the text.

as the increase in costs is outweighed by the increase in the expected gain, that is, the increase in the probability of reversal of error multiplied by the social harm from error.

With regard to the trial process, it is socially advantageous to invest in accuracy as long as the increase in costs is outweighed by the increase in the expected gain from a lower probability of error. But the social harm from error at trial, it should be emphasized, is *less* than the harm flowing from a sure error. The social harm from error at trial is instead measured by what follows trial court error, namely, the cost of the appeals process plus the expected harm from failure to reverse error; this amount is lower than the sure harm from error (in the example of the appeals process above, the cost of that process plus the expected harm from failure to reverse was $250,000, much less than the $500,000 harm from error in the absence of the appeals process). Hence, *the optimal investment in, and accuracy of, the trial process is less than it would be if there were no appeals process and no opportunity to correct errors.*[24]

3.3 Qualifications and extensions to the basic error correction model. Let me briefly consider a number of qualifications to, and modifications of, the foregoing model.

(a) *Factors limiting error correction under the appeals process.* Two important factors reduce the ability of the appeals process to correct errors as described in the model. One is that the separation of disappointed litigants may not occur naturally and the state may not employ fees or subsidies to accomplish separation. Another limiting factor is that litigants may not be able to tell when errors were made at trial, so that the likelihood that errors result in appeals is lowered, and the likelihood that correct decisions are appealed is raised.

(b) *Multiple levels of appeal.* The basic model can be extended in a

---

24. To demonstrate this, denote the x that minimizes $x + p(x)z$ by $x^*(z)$ and observe that $x^*(z)$ is increasing in z (this is readily shown to follow, given convexity of p). Let y^* be the optimal investment in the appeals process, so that social costs under the appeals process are $x + p(x)[y^* + (1 - q(y^*))h]$. Hence, the optimal x given that there is an appeals process, denoted by x^{**}, must equal $x^*(y^* + (1 - q(y^*))h)$. But the optimal x without the appeals process, x^*, equals $x^*(h)$ (see note 20). And because $x^*(z)$ is increasing in z, and $y^* + (1 - q(^*y))h < h$ (this must be true, given note 23, for the appeals process to be desirable to employ), it follows that $x^{**} < x^*$.

straightforward manner, whereby the state chooses the number of levels of appeal and the resources and accuracy of the process at each level. The conclusions about this extended model are natural generalizations of those for the basic model. In particular, given any number of levels of appeal, an additional level of appeal will be desirable if, for some investment in the accuracy of the next level, the cost of that level of appeal plus the expected harm from failure to reverse error at that level is less than the certain harm that would be incurred if that level of appeal were not allowed. Additionally, under certain conditions, the optimal level of investment in, and the accuracy of, appeals courts increases with their level. This reflects the point that the higher the level of appeal, the fewer the number of opportunities that remain to correct error, so the more valuable is accuracy.

(c) *Judges' incentives to avoid reversal.* In the basic model, the appeals process increased accuracy through correcting errors in trial court decisions, but the appeals process may also increase the accuracy of trial courts by influencing the behavior of judges who dislike being reversed (because reversal may harm their reputation, lower their salaries, and the like). In particular, judges who fear reversal will have a greater incentive to avoid error the more likely erroneous decisions are to be appealed and reversed, than are correct decisions. (Note, therefore, that if the errors were no more likely to be reversed than correct decisions, judges would have no incentive, on these grounds, to decide cases accurately; hence improving judges' incentives cannot alone justify the appeals process but is instead a by-product of the error correction function of the appeals process.)

(d) *Inference from the fact that an appeal is brought.* In the basic model, because litigants bring appeals if and only if errors are made at trial, an appeals court can infer that everyone who comes before it ought to obtain a reversal. But I implicitly assumed that appeals courts do not employ this knowledge; rather, they use their usual rules of decision, and they thus fail to reverse with some positive frequency. If appeals courts were to reverse all decisions, on the basis of their inference that all appellants are the victims of error, then disappointed litigants who are not the victims of error clearly would have an incentive to bring appeals, for they could obtain sure reversals. Thus, the separation of disappointed litigants would unravel, and the utility of the appeals process in error correction would be diminished. This suggests that it is not socially desirable for appeals courts to use inferences from the fact that appeals are brought in their decisionmaking. Appeals courts can (and apparently do) refrain from using inferential knowledge by following certain legal procedures, notably, by restricting the evidence considered on appeal to the trial record.

3.4 Functions of the appeals process other than error correction: harmonization of the law; and law-making.   Two purposes of the appeals process apart from error correction that are frequently emphasized are harmonization of the law—reconciliation of conflicting interpretations of the law by different trial courts—and law-making, or amplification of the law through new interpretations. The main observation to be made about these two functions is that, although they in fact are carried out by appeals courts, the appeals process does not seem necessary to accomplish them. A higher level court could readily accomplish harmonization on its own initiative, for conflicts among trial courts are self-evident in nature, meaning that there is no reason to give disappointed litigants the right of appeal in order to have conflicts brought to the attention of a higher court. Similarly, it would seem that the need for amplification of the law is generally fairly clear to higher level courts, so that these courts would not require that litigants bring cases to their attention in order to know where amplification is in the social interest; higher level courts could by themselves choose where to amplify the law and do that in declaratory rulings.

4.   LEGAL ADVICE

4.1 Introduction.   A basic aspect of the legal system is that lawyers provide clients with advice. The advice may be about the nature of legal rules, about the probability and magnitude of sanctions for violations, and about litigation and legal procedure.[25] I have already mentioned some specific aspects of legal advice, concerning the bringing of suit and settle-

---

25. The provision of legal advice is not taken to be coextensive with the provision of legal services in general, however. Some legal services (such as the making of arguments in court) are better regarded as the performance of specialized tasks than as the provision of information to clients.

ment decisions (see section 7 in Chapter 18), and here I consider the topic more generally.[26]

A client may obtain legal advice ex ante—when he is contemplating an action—or he may secure it ex post, after he has acted or someone has been harmed, that is, at the stage of possible or actual litigation. I will consider these two types of advice separately because of their distinctive aspects. A notable difference between these types of advice is that ex ante advice can channel behavior directly in conformity with law, whereas ex post advice comes too late to accomplish that, although, as will be seen, ex post advice has indirect effects on behavior.[27]

Several assumptions will be maintained in most of the discussion in this section: that legal advice is not purposely subversive of the law (for instance, that advice is not intended to enable a person to perpetrate a fraud), that lawyer-client communications and legal work product are confidential, and that lawyers are truthful to clients and endeavor to provide them with good advice. Each of these assumptions, however, will be examined in section 4.4.

4.2 Ex ante advice: advice about contemplated acts. Advice will have private value to a party who is considering taking some action with a possible legal consequence if the advice might lead him to alter his decision. Suppose that a firm is deciding whether to release waste from a holding tank into a river, rather than to spend on transporting the waste to a dump site, but the firm does not know whether a discharge of this particular waste would constitute a violation of law, allowing some class of victims to sue for harm. One possibility is that, without advice, the firm would elect to discharge the waste into the river (suppose the firm thinks discharge probably would not be a violation). In such situations, advice would have private value if it might lead the firm instead to transport the waste to the dump site (the advice might be that a discharge would in fact constitute a viola-

26. Indeed, most of what is written here will apply to the context of public law enforcement as well as civil litigation.

27. Ex ante legal advice was first studied from an economic theoretical perspective in Shavell 1988 and Kaplow and Shavell 1992; ex post legal advice was initially investigated from this standpoint in Kaplow and Shavell 1989, 1990. Legal advice is further studied from an economic viewpoint in Bundy and Elhauge 1991 and Fischel 1998.

tion), because advice would then enable the firm to avoid liability. Also, advice might have value to the firm if, in the absence of advice, the firm would decide to transport the waste to the dump site (suppose the firm believes that a discharge probably would constitute a violation). Here advice would have value to the firm if it might lead the firm instead to discharge the waste into the river (the advice might be that a discharge would not constitute a violation), because advice would then save the firm the transport costs. In general, the private value of legal advice is the expected value of the private gain from possible changes in a party's decisions. This notion of the private value of legal advice is, it may be noted, just an application of the conventional definition of the expected value of information to a decisionmaker.[28]

The social, as opposed to the private, value of ex ante legal advice inheres in the social desirability, or lack thereof, of advice-induced changes in parties' behavior. Suppose that it is socially desirable for the waste not to be discharged, and thus discharging it would constitute a violation (because the harm from a discharge would exceed the cost of transport to the dump site). Then if advice would result in the firm deciding against discharging the waste, the advice would be socially desirable. But if advice would lead the firm to discharge the waste (say, because the firm would learn that the probability of suit is low), the advice would not be socially desirable. The social value of advice is the expected value of the potential social gains and losses produced by the advice.

The comparison between the social and the private values of legal advice depends, among other factors, on the form of liability: whether it is strict or based on the negligence rule. In the consideration of these rules, it will initially be assumed that suit always occurs and that a sanction equal to harm is imposed whenever parties are supposed to be liable for harm.

When parties are strictly liable, the private value of legal advice is the same as its social value. This basic and important conclusion follows essentially because a party's liability burden will equal the harm he causes. If a party learns through advice that taking some precaution will reduce his liability by $10,000, say from $15,000 to $5,000, this also means that the precaution will lower harm by $10,000. Hence, it should not be surprising that the private and social values of advice are equivalent.

28. See, for example, Raiffa 1968.

Under the negligence rule, however, the private value of legal advice tends to exceed its social value. The explanation is suggested by two points. First, if a party avoids negligence because of advice, the party's liability saving will generally be larger than the reduction in expected harm he accomplishes. Suppose that, without advice, the party just mentioned would not take the precaution and would be found negligent and be liable for the harm of $15,000. And suppose that, with advice, the party would take the precaution and thereby avoid liability for negligence. Thus the advice would lead to a reduction in liability for the party of $15,000—an amount exceeding the $10,000 reduction in harm. The reason that the private liability saving from advice is larger than the reduction in harm is that, under the negligence rule, a party escapes having to pay for any harm caused when he acts nonnegligently (the party escapes having to pay for the $5,000 of harm he still generates if he takes the precaution). The second point is similar. If a party would learn from advice that he can relax somewhat his level of precautions and still not be found negligent, his saving will be the full amount of the reduction in precautionary costs. Society will not save as much as the party, however, for when precautions decline, expected harm rises.

It should be emphasized that, whatever may be the difference between the private and the social value of ex ante legal advice, such advice does have positive social value because it can only change private decisions in socially desirable ways, to better conform with the law (or with lawyers' understanding of the law, which is assumed to be superior to clients'). This statement presumes that the law is properly enforced and that decisions that conform with the law are socially desirable. But what if the law is underenforced or is not socially desirable?

When legal rules are underenforced, that is, when the probability of having to pay for harm is less than 100 percent or when the level of damages is less than harm, legal advice might have negative social value because it may lead parties to disobey the law when they otherwise would not. Likewise, when legal rules are incorrectly formulated, legal advice may have negative social value. Suppose, for example, that an environmental authority mistakenly omits a truly harmful waste from its list of substances for which discharge would be considered a negligent act. Then legal advice that gives a party foreknowledge of this error might cause the party to discharge the harmful waste, when it would not otherwise have done so.[29] Thus, the social value of advice may be negative—it would be best for parties not to obtain advice—even though its private value is positive.

4.3 Ex post advice: advice about acts already committed. The private value of ex post legal advice, advice provided after acts have been committed, is analogous to the private value of ex ante legal advice. It resides in the possibility that the advice will lead a party to change his decisions, but is about whether to sue or how to conduct litigation (including settlement negotiation) rather than about the party's earlier, substantive behavior. Ex post legal advice can affect not only what legal arguments to pursue, but also how to develop evidence, what evidence to present and not to present, and how to challenge false arguments. It is virtually inevitable that ex post legal advice will have substantial private value because of the complicated nature of legal procedure and the unlikelihood that potential litigants will know the law in real detail.

(a) *Advice about the bringing of suit.* In considering the social value of ex post advice and comparing it to the private value of ex post advice, let us begin with advice about whether a harmed party should bring suit. The social value of this advice derives principally from the effect of suit on the prior behavior of parties who might be sued, that is, on their precautions and participation in potentially harm-producing activity. This incentive effect of suit could be small or large, and it could be either greater or less than the expected private gain from suit, as was explained in section 2 of Chapter 17. Hence, the private and social value of advice about suit could diverge from each other in either direction.

(b) *Advice about the course of litigation.* Now consider the social value of legal advice that defendant parties obtain during litigation. As noted in the introduction to this section, because such advice is, by its nature, imparted to parties only after they have acted, it cannot have aided them in conforming with the law, in choosing how to act if they were uncertain about the law. (The firm that does not know whether discharging a waste

---

29. The relevance of this case is mainly hypothetical, for if a social authority understands that the law is undesirable, it would make more sense for the authority to alter the law than to seek to influence the giving of legal advice.

into a river will constitute a violation of law cannot be led to behave appropriately by learning what the law is after it decides about discharging the waste.) This simple but fundamental observation means that ex post advice to defendants does not raise social welfare in the direct way that ex ante advice to potential defendants does. Nonetheless, ex post advice certainly may influence prior behavior and social welfare.

One way that ex post advice may affect prior behavior and social welfare is by diluting sanctions and thus deterrence of undesirable conduct. Lawyers may lower expected sanctions by their advantageous use of legal strategy and, importantly, by counseling defendants on the selection of evidence to present and to suppress. Given that individuals anticipate that expected sanctions for causing harm will be reduced due to the subsequent availability of legal advice, fewer individuals will be deterred from engaging in undesirable behavior. Thus, legal advice may have negative social value.[30] (In principle, though, a partial remedy for this problem would be for the state to raise sanctions overall to offset the dilution of deterrence due to legal advice.)

However, ex post advice may also enhance social welfare by raising otherwise inadequate sanctions. Advice may raise expected sanctions because lawyers may help plaintiffs to obtain higher judgments, better reflecting the harms they have sustained, than they would receive if they did not have legal advice.

Additionally, ex post advice may raise social welfare by lowering sanctions for defendants who did not violate the law, or who face higher sanctions than they should. If parties anticipate that if they ever incorrectly face a legal sanction advice will help them to avoid that sanction, they will not be undesirably discouraged from engaging in many useful activities or be led to take expensive and inordinate precautions.

In sum, ex post advice may be either socially desirable or socially undesirable, depending on the context. Moreover, when advice is socially desirable, its social value could be different from its private value.

4.4 Other factors bearing on advice.   Let me now consider several additional issues bearing on the effects and value of legal advice.

(a) *Subversion of the law.* It has been assumed for the most part that

---

30. The point of this paragraph was early emphasized by Bentham 1827.

legal advice is informational in character, conveying knowledge about the law and legal sanctions but not altering expected sanctions. Yet lawyers are sometimes able to subvert the law by effectively lowering sanctions or their probability. As mentioned earlier, lawyers may inappropriately reduce expected sanctions by suppressing or destroying unfavorable evidence, by helping clients to hide assets, and the like. Such legal assistance is to be distinguished from advice that lowers expected sanctions for bona fide reasons, for example, by demonstrating that an asserted harm was not a true harm. Of course, lawyers are not supposed to thwart law enforcement, but they have an economic incentive to do so and can fairly easily avoid punishment for it (lawyers give advice in private and can phrase their advice in hypothetical but readily understood terms). From the social perspective, legal advice that frustrates law enforcement is obviously undesirable.

(b) *Confidentiality of advice.* The legal system protects the confidentiality of communications between lawyers and their clients under wide circumstances, and this protection has been implicitly assumed in the earlier discussion. Confidentiality of legal advice will benefit clients when there is a positive probability that disclosure of advice would lower its value. This would usually be true of advice about the selection of evidence to present in litigation: Such advice generally would be robbed of effectiveness if it were disclosed to the opposing side and the court. Confidentiality is also of obvious importance to those obtaining advice subversive of the law. By contrast, confidentiality often should not matter to parties obtaining ex ante advice about the legality of an act or about the magnitude or likelihood of sanctions, because disclosure of such advice will usually not disadvantage them. For example, disclosure of the ex ante advice that a party obtains about what is considered negligent behavior ordinarily should not matter to the party.

Still, whatever the character of legal advice, maintaining the confidentiality of much information about clients that is revealed to lawyers will frequently be important to the clients. For instance, a firm would usually not want information pertaining to its business plans revealed to others, and an individual would ordinarily not want information of a personal nature disclosed to outsiders.

Because protection of confidentiality can benefit clients (and never is a disadvantage to them), it encourages clients to consult with and reveal information to their lawyers. This in itself is sometimes thought to imply that confidentiality is socially desirable. That reasoning, however, is mistaken: Confidentiality is socially desirable only if the legal advice that confidentiality encourages is socially desirable, and as has been explained above, that may not be the case.

(c) *Protection of legal work product.* The legal system also protects the confidentiality of documents and other records that lawyers generate on behalf of clients in expectation of litigation. The protection of such legal work product is accomplished principally by denying opposing litigants the legal right to discover work product (that is, the right to order the party with work product to produce it). The effect of work product protection is similar to that of protection of confidentiality, so it can be considered very briefly. Protection of work product encourages lawyers to engage in research on and development of their clients' cases, for much of the value of such research and development would be lost if it became immediately known to the other side.[31] Because protection of work product raises the value and quality of legal advice, it inures to clients' benefit. But whether protection of work product is socially desirable is not evident a priori, for it depends on whether or not the advice that the work product supports is socially desirable. A further complication is that, even when the advice is socially desirable, the private value of advice, and thus the amount of work product, may be socially excessive.

(d) *Quality and truthfulness of advice.* To the degree that poor or dishonest advice would be discovered and that lawyers would suffer penalties for having provided such advice, they will have reason not to give bad advice. There are two basic types of penalties that lawyers face for furnishing unsound legal advice: loss of business because of damage to reputation; and legal sanction, in the form of a damage judgment arising from a malpractice action, a fine assessed by a court, or a punishment imposed by a professional association.[32]

31. On this point see, for example, Easterbrook 1981.

32. For a general treatment of these ways of regulating lawyer conduct, see Wilkins 1992.

PART V | PUBLIC LAW ENFORCEMENT AND CRIMINAL LAW

In this part I will first consider the general theory of public law enforcement, by which I mean the use of public law enforcement agents—such as police, tax inspectors, and regulatory personnel—to enforce legal rules. Public law enforcement may be contrasted with private law enforcement, which comes about when private parties assert their legal rights through suit. Why public enforcement should be the method of law enforcement rather than private will be addressed in Part Six.

The major concern of law enforcement is to control harmful, or potentially harmful, behavior. Examples of such behavior include driving through a stop sign, shooting a gun at someone, discharging a pollutant into a lake, or failing to pay taxes owed. In some situations, an act will be virtually certain to cause harm (shooting point-blank at someone), and other times harm will only occur with a probability (driving through a stop sign will usually not result in an accident). I will sometimes call attention to the probabilistic nature of harmful acts, and other times will assume for expositional ease that acts are certain to cause harm.

An act will be said to be socially undesirable if the expected benefit that an actor obtains from it is outweighed by the expected harm caused by it. The reader who is troubled by this definition, because it accords weight to any benefit the actor obtains (such as malicious pleasure from harming someone), should realize that little in what follows depends on the particular definition of an undesirable act. Most of what is analyzed concerns how best to control undesirable behavior, however it is defined.

A number of important dimensions of public law enforcement should be distinguished. One is the choice of the basic rule of liability: whether liability is strict or fault-based, and whether liability is imposed only if harm is done or may be imposed on the basis of acts alone (independently of the occurrence of harm). A second dimension of enforcement is the type of sanction, whether monetary or nonmonetary, notably, imprisonment. A third aspect is the magnitude of sanctions. And a fourth dimension of enforcement is the degree of enforcement effort, which determines the probability of imposition of sanctions.

These dimensions of enforcement will be discussed in the chapters that follow. In Chapter 20, the basic theory of public enforcement employing monetary sanctions is discussed; in Chapter 21, the basic theory of enforcement using nonmonetary sanctions is examined; and in Chapter 22, extensions to the basic theory are considered.

Then, in Chapter 23, functions of sanctions apart from deterrence, namely incapacitation, rehabilitation, and retribution, are discussed. Finally, in Chapter 24, the subject of criminal law is addressed against the background of the theory of public enforcement of law.

20 ||| DETERRENCE WITH MONETARY SANCTIONS

The topic addressed here is the deterrence of undesirable acts through the use, or threatened use, of monetary sanctions by the state.

In the first part of the chapter, I assume for simplicity that monetary sanctions will apply with certainty—that all parties to whom a rule should apply will be brought before social authorities and bear the intended sanctions. Then, in the second part, I assume that sanctions apply only with a probability. There I examine the use of sanctions assuming that the public must incur enforcement expense to locate and/or to convict and ultimately to penalize parties who should bear sanctions. The principal problems for society that are studied are the choice of the level of enforcement effort—which determines the probability of penalizing parties—and the choice of the magnitude of sanctions, so as to maximize social welfare.

For convenience, I focus on the case in which parties are risk neutral, so that parties will commit an act if the benefit to them from so doing exceeds the expected sanction. But I also examine the case in which parties are risk averse. In the risk-neutral case, social welfare is assumed to equal the gains that parties obtain from acts, less the harm done by acts, less the costs of enforcement; in the risk-averse case the measure of social welfare also incorporates the disutility of risk-bearing. By the costs of enforcement, I mean the expenses of apprehending and convicting violators, but I assume that there is no resource cost associated with the actual imposition of monetary sanctions. This assumption is made to capture the important point that the payment of a fine is, in itself, only a transfer of purchasing power, as opposed to an expenditure of real resources.[1] (In contrast, the imposition of the non-monetary sanction of imprisonment involves substantial direct costs. In the next chapter, the significance of this difference will be emphasized.)

1. CERTAIN ENFORCEMENT: BASIC THEORY OF LIABILITY

1.1 Introduction. Here I examine the theory of enforcement assuming that it occurs with certainty. I consider first the two basic forms of harm-based liability: strict liability, and fault-based liability—that is, liability for a harmful act that is judged to be an undesirable act. Then I consider analogous act-based rules. (This discussion will be in substantial respects a restatement of the discussion of strict liability and of negligence rules in Chapter 8.)

1.2 Strict liability for harm. Under this rule, because a party always pays for the harm an act causes, the party's expected sanction equals the expected harm. Hence, he will commit an act if and only if his expected benefit exceeds the expected harm. That is, he will commit an act if and only if the act is socially desirable; the optimal outcome will result.[2] Note

---

1. Of course, in fact the imposition of monetary sanctions does involve social costs, such as those involved in locating a person's assets and collecting a fine; this issue will be discussed in section 3 of Chapter 22.

2. Let g be the gain, h the harm, and q the probability of harm (this notation will also be used in subsequent notes). There are two natural cases to examine: where g is enjoyed only when harm comes about (suppose a person throws a rock at a window and is trying to break it), and where g is enjoyed when the act is committed, regardless of whether harm comes about (suppose that a firm discharges a potentially harmful pollutant into a river in order to save the costs of hauling its waste to a dump site—here it saves the costs for sure, regardless of whether the pollutant causes harm). In either case, liability equal to harm will lead to optimal behavior. In the first case, it is optimal for the act to be committed if and only if $qg > qh$, and because the sanction equals harm, the person will commit the act if and only if that is true. In the second case, it is optimal for the act to be committed if and only if $g > qh$, and again, if the sanction equals harm, the person will commit the act if

that, in general, if the sanction is less than harm, parties will sometimes act in ways that create greater harm than benefits. And if the sanction is greater than harm, there will sometimes be a chilling effect on desirable acts; parties may be discouraged from acts that create greater benefits than harm.

Comments. (a) The only information required by the social authority in order to apply the strict liability rule is the level of harm.

(b) The assets of a party must be sufficient to pay for the harm; otherwise, the party will not generally be induced to act optimally and may engage excessively in harmful acts.

Risk-averse case. If parties are risk averse, they will tend to bear risk because they may find themselves in circumstances where the benefits from a harmful act are high enough to make committing it desirable, meaning that they will bear sanctions. In order to reduce the magnitude of this risk, it may be socially beneficial for the sanction to be less than harm. Moreover, if the sanction is less than harm, overdeterrence, that is, the discouragement of desirable acts, tends to be avoided.[3] (These statements presume that

---

and only if $g > qh$. In the text, I will not usually distinguish these cases for expositional convenience, and it will be clear that the conclusions to be noted hold for both cases, as I will sometimes explicitly note.

3. To be more precise, let me specify the state's problem of maximizing social welfare in a simple model in which parties are risk averse. Suppose that $U(y)$ is the utility function from income y of members of a population of risk-averse individuals with identical initial incomes, and among whom the gain g from committing the act (for concreteness, consider here and in many later notes the case where g is enjoyed with certainty; see note 2) is distributed according to the density $f(g)$. Then, if s is the sanction for harm, an individual will commit the act if and only if $(1 - q)U(y + g) + qU(y + g - s) \geq U(y)$. Thus individuals will commit the act when $g \geq g^*(y, s)$, where the critical g^* can be shown to be decreasing in y and increasing in s. It is presumed that the income y of each individual is income net of taxes, where taxes are set in order to cover the state's expenses. The state collects fine revenue and, for simplicity, is assumed to suffer harms done. Therefore, $y = z - (1 - F(g^*))(qh - qs)$, where z is the initial income of each person and F is the cumulative distribution function of f; for $(1 - F(g^*))$ is the fraction of individuals who commit the act, qh is the expected harm caused by a person who commits the act, and qs is the expected revenue collected from such a person. The social problem is then to choose s to maximize social welfare W, the sum of expected utilities, that is

$$W = F(g^*(y, s))U(y) + \int_{g^*(y,s)}^{\infty} [(1 - q)U(y + g) + qU(y + g - s)]f(g)dg.$$

parties are not insured against sanctions; on such insurance, see section 6 of Chapter 22.)

1.3 Fault-based liability for harm. Under this rule a party who causes harm is liable and bears a sanction equal to harm only if his act was undesirable, that is, only if the social authority finds that the expected harm exceeded his expected benefits. If, for example, the expected harm is $100 and the gain $60, the act would be found undesirable, so there would be liability for harm. A party would, however, not engage in such an undesirable act, for his expected sanction would equal the expected harm and thus exceed his benefit (his expected liability would equal $100 and exceed $60). If an act is desirable, however, a party will clearly commit it, for then he will not bear liability for any harm that comes about as a result.[4]

Note again that if the sanction for an undesirable act is less than harm, then parties may sometimes commit such acts because their gain may exceed their expected sanction. If, however, the sanction for an undesirable act exceeds harm, there will not be an chilling effect on desirable acts, for

---

It can be shown under fairly general conditions that the optimal s is less than h, the intuition being as stated in text. Note that by lowering s from h, there is a gain in social welfare due to a reduction in risk-bearing by those who commit the act and might be sanctioned. This is so as long as the wealth of those who are sanctioned, $y + g - s$, tends to be lower than that of individuals in general (who have to pay higher taxes if s is lowered), for then the marginal utility of those who are sanctioned is higher than average marginal utility.

Finally, it should be observed that the expression for social welfare W reduces in the risk-neutral case to

$$W = z + \int_{qs}^{\infty} gf(g)dg - (1 - F(qs))qh,$$

that is, a constant plus total gains minus total harms. For in the risk-neutral case, we can take $U(y) = y$, so that $g^*(y, s)$ reduces to qs, and substitution in the previous expression for W yields this expression.

4. To amplify, under fault-based liability, a party who commits an act and causes harm will be held liable if and only if the act was undesirable, that is, if and only if $g < qh$; otherwise he will not beheld liable. If the sanction $s = h$, then any party for whom $g < qh$ will face expected liability if he commits the act equal to qh, so will not commit the act; others will face no liability. Hence, if $s = h$, all undesirable acts will be deterred and all desirable acts will be committed.

these acts are not subject to sanctions under fault-based liability; hence, sanctions for undesirable acts that exceed harm will still lead to optimal outcomes.

Comments. (a) The information needed by the social authority to apply the fault-based liability rule is not only the level of harm, but also its likelihood and the benefit from the act, for to determine whether an act is desirable or not, the authority must compare the benefit to the expected harm.

(b) Again, the level of assets must in general be sufficient to pay for the harm, in order that the party be induced not to commit undesirable acts.

Risk-averse case. Parties will bear no risk under fault-based liability if fault is found without error; this is an advantage of the fault-based form of liability over strict liability (again assuming that insurance against sanctions is not sold). Parties will, however, bear some risk of sanctions in the presence of uncertainty concerning findings of fault—generated by errors in the determination of fault or by parties' imperfect ability to control their behavior. Thus, if parties are risk averse, the observations made in the case of strict liability carry over to the present rule, to the extent that the parties bear risk due to uncertainty in findings of fault. Notably, liability exceeding harm may well have a chilling effect on desirable acts.

Sanction equal to wrongdoer's gains. A version of fault-based liability that is of interest is that under which a party who commits a harmful undesirable act bears a sanction equal to his gains.[5] This sanction is sometimes thought to be a natural one for purposes of deterring acts, because it removes a wrongdoer's gains. But although a sanction equal to gains will discourage undesirable behavior, it will, in principle, only barely do so, because parties lose no more than their gains. Consequently, the rule of sanctions equal to gains is peculiarly vulnerable to judicial error in assessment of gains, and for that reason tends to be inferior to fault-based liability with sanctions equal to harm. Specifically, under the rule with sanctions equal to gains, if the gain is underestimated even by a small amount, parties

---

5. I do not consider the analogue to this rule under strict liability, namely, liability equal to gains for desirable acts as well as undesirable acts. Such a rule would obviously be perverse, because it would remove any incentive to engage in desirable acts. Note that under the rule in consideration, if a party obtains his gain g only if he does harm (see note 2), the sanction imposed on the party equals g. But in the case where the party obtains g for sure when he acts, the sanction under the rule in consideration is interpreted to be g/q, so that the expected sanction equals g.

will have an incentive to engage in an act, no matter how much harm it causes. Suppose, for example, that an act creates a gain of $1,000 and harm of $1,000,000. If the gain is estimated to be $950, a party would have an incentive to engage in it, because the sanction would be $950 so that he would profit by $50. In contrast, if liability is equal to harm, parties will be strongly discouraged from committing the act, even if there is substantial judicial error in estimating the harm.[6]

1.4 Act-based liability.   Both strict and fault-based liability for harm have act-based counterparts. The act-based analogue to strict liability for harm is the rule under which a party is liable for the expected harm due to an act, regardless of whether harm actually occurs. Thus, if a party commits an act that will cause harm of $1,000 with probability 10 percent, he will be liable for $100 for having committed the act. It is apparent that under this rule, the party will behave just as under strict liability for harm; he will commit an act if and only if the benefit obtained exceeds the expected harm. Similarly, the act-based analogue to fault-based liability for harm is liability equal to the expected harm for undesirable acts, and it is clear that under this rule, parties will be induced not to commit undesirable acts.

Comments. (a) The social authority needs to know more in order to apply act-based rules than harm-based rules. To apply act-based strict liability, the authority needs to know not only the potential harm—which it does not observe if harm does not come about—but also the probability of harm. By contrast, to apply harm-based strict liability, it needs only to know the harm that has occurred. With regard to act-based fault liability, the social authority also faces the disadvantage that it does not observe harm (but it needs to know the probability of harm and the benefits from the act under either harm-based or act-based fault liability).

(b) The level of assets that a party needs to have in order to be motivated to act appropriately is lower under act-based liability than under harm-based liability. Under act-based liability, to be properly motivated, a party needs assets equal only to the expected harm rather than the actual harm (in the example, assets of $100 rather than $1,000).

---

6. On the advantage under discussion of sanctions equal to harm rather than the wrongdoer's gains, see Polinsky and Shavell 1994.

Risk-averse case. Risk-averse parties bear less risk under act-based liability because sanctions equal the expected harm rather than the realized harm.

1.5 Actual use of rules.   In fact, we often observe use of harm-based sanctions, both on a strict basis and according to fault. Penalties may be imposed by the state for spills of toxic materials, for failure to pay proper taxes, and for many other harmful events. Perhaps more often, however, we see that public law enforcement involves act-based sanctions. This is typically the case with violation of safety, environmental, and many financial regulations, where sanctioned behavior is that which creates a positive expected harm but need not do actual harm.

2.   ENFORCEMENT WITH A PROBABILITY: THE OPTIMAL PROBABILITY AND MAGNITUDE OF SANCTIONS

2.1 Introduction.   Here it will be assumed that it is costly to identify and penalize liable parties, so that society has to choose a level of enforcement effort, which will determine the probability of applying sanctions, as well as the magnitude of sanctions. In determining the social-welfare-maximizing choice of the probability and magnitude of sanctions, I will for simplicity assume that liability is strict and based on harm, for the major points to be made do not depend on the nature of the rule of liability (except as remarked in section 2.6 on fault-based liability).

2.2 Behavior given the probability and magnitude of sanctions. How will a person behave who will face a sanction only with a probability if he commits a harmful act? If the person is risk neutral, he will evaluate the sanction in terms of its expected value. Hence, the person will commit an act if and only if his benefit exceeds the expected sanction.

Risk-averse case. If the individual is risk averse, he will commit a harmful act if and only if his expected utility is raised by so doing, and in general he will not be equally deterred by different combinations of sanction and probability with the same expected value; he will be more deterred the higher the magnitude of the potential sanction in the combination, with the expected sanction held constant. For example, a risk-averse person will be more deterred by a sanction of $1,000 borne with probability 20 percent than by a sanction of $500 borne with probability 40 percent even though their expected values, $200, are equal. The reason is that, for a risk-averse party, the disutility of sanctions rises more than in proportion to their size; when the sanction rises from $500 to $1,000, its disutility more than doubles.[7]

Comments. (a) *Probability versus magnitude of sanction.* It is sometimes asked whether an increase in the probability or an increase in the magnitude of sanctions would make a greater difference in deterrence. But this question is incomplete as stated, for it is not explicit about the degree of change of these two factors. Obviously, if the magnitude of the sanction rises by much more than the probability, an increase in the magnitude would exert a greater effect on deterrence than would an increase in the probability, and conversely.

A natural and well-posed question, however, is how a given percentage increase in the probability of sanctions compares in importance to the same percentage increase in the magnitude of sanctions. If parties are risk neutral, any named percentage increase in the probability of sanctions has an identical effect to an equal percentage increase in the magnitude of sanctions— for a given percentage increase in either the probability or the magnitude of sanction will raise the expected sanction by exactly that percentage. If there is a 20 percent probability of imposition of a sanction of $500 and the probability doubles to 40 percent, the expected sanction will double, from $100 to $200; and likewise if the sanction doubles to $1,000 (and the probability remains at 20 percent), the expected sanction will double to $200. Thus, a risk-neutral party will be affected in the same way by either type of change.

If parties are risk averse, however, they will be more affected by a percentage increase in the magnitude of sanctions than by an equal percentage increase in the probability of sanctions. A risk-averse party will be more

---

7. More generally, if U is the utility of income function of a risk-averse person, y is income, g is the gain from the act, p is the probability of a sanction, and s is the magnitude of the sanction (this notation will be used in many later notes as well), the person's expected utility if he commits the act will be $EU = (1 - p)U(y + g) + pU(y + g - s)$. If p falls to kp, where $k < 1$, and s rises to s/k (so that the expected sanction is still ps), the person's expected utility becomes $(1 - kp)U(y + g) + kpU(y + g - s/k)$. Differentiating the latter expression with respect to k yields $p\{(s/k)U'(y + g - s/k) - [U(y + g) - U(y + g - s/k)]\} > 0$ because U' is decreasing. Hence, the lower is k, the lower is expected utility, and therefore the greater is deterrence.

deterred by the sanction of $1,000 with probability 20 percent than by the sanction of $500 with probability 40 percent. The reason is, as was just noted, that risk-averse parties suffer disutility more than in proportion to increases in the magnitude of sanctions.[8]

Still, one often encounters the notion that the probability of sanctions (or, as it is frequently expressed, the certainty of sanctions) matters more than their magnitude. Although this disagrees with our conclusions for both risk-neutral and risk-averse individuals, it could be the case that probability matters more due to the ineffectiveness of large sanctions, notably, the fact that people may be unable to pay large amounts.

(b) *Perception of the probability of sanctions.* Information that individuals have about the probability of sanctions will often be imperfect. Enforcement authorities generally do not publish data on the likelihood of punishment. Moreover, the probability of sanctions is frequently variable, depending on the circumstances of the violation, so that even if enforcement authorities were forthcoming, there would inevitably be substantial imperfection of knowledge about the probability. In addition, individuals often experience difficulty in assessing and interpreting probabilities, especially small ones, sometimes failing to discriminate among them, sometimes inflating their importance, and sometimes essentially ignoring them. These observations suggest the need for caution in interpreting what would appear to be the effect of the probability of sanctions on behavior.[9]

(c) *Perception of the magnitude of sanctions.* Information about the magnitude of sanctions may also be imperfect. This is most likely to be true when the sanction is decided on by a court or other tribunal that enjoys discretion over sanctions, so that there is no set magnitude of sanctions, but only a distribution of them. In many contexts, however, sanctions are stipulated and well-known in advance.

---

8. Specifically, let us assume as in the previous note that expected utility $EU = (1 - p)U(y + g) + pU(y + g - s)$. We want to show that the (negative of the) elasticity of EU with respect to p is less than that with respect to s. The elasticity of EU with respect to p is $[p/EU][dEU/dp] = p[U(y + g - s) - U(y + g)]/EU$, and the elasticity of EU with respect to s is $[s/EU][dEU/ds] = -psU'(y + g - s)/EU$. We therefore need to show that $sU'(y + g - s) > [U(y + g) - U(y + g - s)]$, but this holds because U' is decreasing.

9. See Bebchuk and Kaplow 1992, Garoupa 1999, and Sah 1991 on perceptions of the likelihood of sanctions and learning about them. For empirical evidence on knowledge of expected sanctions, see, for example, Wilson and Herrnstein 1985.

(d) *Level of wealth of a party.* The level of wealth of a party imposes a ceiling on the maximum sanction. Thus, the lower is the probability of sanctions, the lower is the maximum expected sanction, so that it might be impossible to deter a person from committing an act even if his benefit from it is quite modest if the probability of sanctions is small. For example, consider a risk-neutral individual with wealth of $5,000 who would obtain a benefit of $100 from an act. It would be impossible to deter this person from committing the act if the likelihood of sanctions is 1 percent, for then the highest expected sanction that he could face is 1% × $5,000 = $50.

The level of wealth of a party not only determines the maximum sanction that can be imposed on a party, it also may influence how he reacts to the risk of sanctions generally, for the degree of risk aversion is usually thought to depend on wealth. The more wealthy a party is, the less averse to risk, and thus the less he tends to be deterred by a given probability and magnitude of sanction.[10]

2.3 Optimal sanctions when the probability of their imposition is a given. Let me now address the question about the socially best magnitude of sanction, taking the probability of imposition of sanctions as a given. The assumption that the probability of sanctions is taken as given is relevant in many contexts, because those who decide on the magnitude of sanctions may not have control over enforcement effort. For example, a judge or administrative officer who sets the fine for a regulatory infraction may take the enforcement budget and its allocation as a given. Further, in many areas of enforcement, the probability of sanctions for a particular type of infraction is set by overall policy and is not independently variable (see section 5 of Chapter 22). In any case, the problem of determining the optimal sanction given the probability of sanctions is a subpart in a theoretical sense of the problem of finding the optimal probability and sanction, for to find the optimal probability, one must in general find the optimal sanction for each probability.

If parties are risk neutral, optimal behavior will be induced if the

---

10. I will comment generally on the actual effect of sanctions (both monetary and nonmonetary) on deterrence in section 2.3 of Chapter 21.

expected sanction equals the expected harm, for then a party will compare his benefit to the expected harm. Consequently, the sanction, when imposed, must exceed harm; in particular, the sanction is governed by a fundamental probability-related *multiplier*—the sanction must equal the harm multiplied by the inverse of the probability of its imposition.[11] Thus, if the harm is 100 and the probability of sanctions is 50 percent, the sanction should be multiplied by $1/.5 = 2$, so the sanction should equal 200 (and thus the expected sanction would equal 100); if the probability of sanctions is 25 percent, the sanction should be multiplied by $1/.25 = 4$, so the sanction should equal 400 (again the expected sanction would equal 100); and so forth. In this way, parties will behave optimally; the situation will be as if they faced liability equal to the harm.

Risk-averse case. If parties are risk averse, the optimal sanction tends to be lower than when parties are risk neutral. The reasons are essentially as indicated in section 1.2. First, because parties for whom the act is socially desirable will often commit it, they will bear risk, which is socially undesirable in itself. Second, if the sanction equals its optimal level in the risk-neutral case, risk-averse individuals will tend to be overdeterred. Lowering the sanction ameliorates both of these problems.[12]

Comments. (a) *Practical ability to impose high sanctions reflecting the probability of their imposition.* The theme of this section is that sanctions should be scaled upward to reflect the likelihood of escaping liability. There are several problems, however, that may be faced in actually imposing such sanctions. First, there may be resistance to inflating sanctions on grounds of fairness; the notion that the magnitude of sanctions should be proportional to the gravity of a bad act is a widely held notion of fairness, and this notion does not accord weight to the likelihood of escape from sanctions. For example, the fair punishment for an act such as littering might be thought quite modest (perhaps no more than $10 or $20) because an act of littering is not considered to be seriously harmful, even though the sanction called for by the principles discussed here would

---

11. If harm is h and the probability of proper imposition of the sanction is p, the magnitude of the sanction should be h multiplied by $1/p$, so that the expected sanction is $p(h/p) = h$, resulting in optimal behavior under strict liability (and fault liability).

12. This can be shown along the lines sketched in note 3.

be substantial (such as \$200) if the probability of catching a litterer is small.[13]

A second problem is that there may be significant difficulty in determining the probability of sanctions. For example, if a restaurant violated an ordinance about safety in its kitchen, the sanctioning authority would have to take into account such factors as the probability of inspection of the restaurant, the probability that employees would make reports to authorities themselves, the probability that customers would notice something wrong, and the like. These determinations are often difficult and lend themselves to dispute, although, as with any type of determination, they can be performed more cheaply if demands for accuracy are reduced.

(b) *Effect of wealth.* It should be borne in mind that the wealth of the party may be too low (consider especially individuals with essentially no savings, or thinly capitalized firms) for the party to be induced to act optimally. If the likelihood of being caught is low and the magnitude of the harm high, it may be impossible to induce the party to act optimally, leading to a significant problem of underdeterrence.

2.4 Optimal sanctions when the probability of their imposition is also optimally determined.   One of the basic insights that applies to optimal law enforcement when the state chooses both the probability of imposing sanctions and their magnitude is that a low probability–high magnitude sanction policy is socially advantageous. The reasons are twofold: A social savings in enforcement effort can be achieved by allowing sanctions to be imposed only with a low probability; and sanctions can be raised to avoid dilution of deterrence from the low probability of sanctions.[14] This strategy for conserving enforcement resources without sacrificing deterrence has the apparent implication that enforcement effort and probabilities of sanctions should be very low, but be accompanied by very high sanctions. Such a

---

13. Issues of fairness in sanctions are discussed in Chapter 27. On fairness and the economic theory of law enforcement, see Polinsky and Shavell 2000a and Kaplow and Shavell 2002b, chap. 6.

14. Note that the rise in the sanction does not increase enforcement expenditures; this is an aspect of the maintained assumption of this chapter that the imposition of monetary sanctions does not involve resources costs.

draconian conclusion will shortly be seen to hold if parties are risk neutral. But this strong conclusion does not hold if parties are risk averse (or if any of a variety of other factors are relevant, as will be noted later), even though the conclusion contains an important element of the truth about optimal policy under all circumstances.

Suppose that parties are risk neutral. In this case, it is optimal for the fundamental strategy for saving enforcement resources just mentioned to be employed to the fullest extent, meaning that the sanction should be as high as possible, equal to the entire wealth of an individual. To understand why, suppose that the sanction is less than maximal. Then the sanction can always be raised and the probability lowered proportionally, so that deterrence is not altered; but as the lower probability will mean a savings in enforcement costs, the change must raise social welfare. For example, suppose that the wealth of individuals is $10,000, the likelihood of sanctions is 10 percent, and the sanction is $1,000. Thus, in particular, the expected sanction is $100. Now if the sanction is raised to $2,000 and the probability of sanctions is lowered to 5 percent, the expected sanction and deterrence will be unchanged, and equal $100, but enforcement expenses will be lowered. Indeed, if the sanction is raised to the maximum, $10,000, and the probability of sanctions is reduced to 1 percent, deterrence will be unchanged and more enforcement expenses will be saved. The conclusion, therefore, is that sanctions should be raised until they are maximal.[15]

---

15. To establish this conclusion formally, observe that social welfare in the risk-neutral case, the benefits obtained from committing acts less harm and enforcement costs, is given by

$$W = \int_{ps}^{\infty} (g - h)f(g)\,dg - c(p),$$

where $c(p)$ is the enforcement cost of setting the probability equal to p. (It is assumed here for simplicity that an act causes harm with certainty, rather than only with a probability, and this will also be assumed in subsequent notes.) Clearly, if s is not maximal, s can be raised to the income y of individuals, and p can be lowered to $p(s/y)$, so that the expected sanction $[p(s/y)]y$ remains ps. Hence, the integral in W does not change but $c(p)$ falls, so that W rises, meaning that raising s to y and lowering p increases welfare; thus the optimal sanction must be maximal. Note that this conclusion that the optimal sanction is maximal does not depend on the magnitude of the harm. Becker 1968 first suggested the conclusion (although much of his analysis presumes the sanction is not maximal) and it is noted explicitly in Carr-Hill and Stern 1979 and Polinsky and Shavell 1979.

What is the optimal probability of imposing the sanction? It might at first seem that the best probability is such that the expected sanction equals the harm. In the example under discussion, this would mean that if the harm from the act is $100, the expected sanction should be the same, so that the probability p should satisfy $p \times \$10,000 = \$100$, implying that the best p is 1 percent. But in fact the optimal probability should be lower than 1 percent. In general, the optimal expected sanction is less than the harm. The reason for this conclusion (another basic insight about optimal enforcement when the probability of sanctions is chosen along with the magnitude of sanctions) is essentially that because of the cost of enforcement, it is better to compromise and not achieve perfect behavior, but rather to permit a degree of underdeterrence in order to save enforcement resources.[16] If the cost of enforcement is significant, it may be best to allow substantial underdeterrence to reduce costs of enforcement.

Indeed, because of the costs of enforcement, it is possible that it will be optimal for there not to be any law enforcement, for society to countenance harm in order to save the costs of law enforcement altogether. This can be demonstrated to be true, other things being equal, if the harm from the act is below a certain threshold.

Risk-averse case. In this case, the conclusion differs from that when parties are risk neutral. The main difference is that the optimal sanction is not maximal, in general, and may be much lower than maximal. For instance, in the example discussed above, the optimal sanction might be $300 rather than $10,000, the level of a person's wealth. The reason, roughly, is that the risk aversion of individuals means that their bearing

---

16. To amplify the point that some degree of underenforcement is desirable, suppose in the example that the expected sanction is $99 instead of $100—which would be the case if the probability is .99 percent instead of 1 percent. Then the individuals who would be undesirably led to commit the harmful act would be those obtaining benefits of between $99 and $100 and doing harm of $100. Thus, they would be contributing only slightly to net social harm (harm minus benefit obtained)—for they would cause net social harm of less than $1 each. But the social saving in enforcement expenses from reducing the enforcement probability is proportional to the probability reduction. For this reason, it is always desirable for the probability to be lowered some amount below 1 percent, so that the expected sanction is below $100. Formally, differentiate W in note 15 with respect to p and set this equal to 0, yielding $s(h - ps)f(ps) = c'(p)$. Because the right side is positive, $h < ps$ must hold (whether or not s is optimal, equal to y).

the risk of sanctions constitutes a form of social cost.[17] The optimal level of the sanction will depend, among other things, on the degree of risk aversion of parties; the more risk averse the parties, the lower the optimal sanction will tend to be.[18]

With regard to the optimal probability, two points should be made. First, the optimal probability might be higher than in the risk-neutral case: If the sanction is, in effect, constrained not to be high due to the risk aversion of individuals, say to be in the range of $300, then the only way

17. Another reason that the optimal sanction may not be maximal is that higher sanctions may induce violators to spend additional resources to avoid punishment; see Malik 1990. Further reasons will be given in later chapters.

18. Further insight into the risk-averse case can be gained by considering why, precisely, the argument applying in the risk-neutral case for optimality of maximal sanctions fails when parties are not risk neutral. Consider any situation in which the sanction is less than maximal—consider for instance a sanction of $1,000 and a probability of imposition of sanctions of 10 percent. Now raise the sanction to the wealth of an individual, $10,000. Even though individuals are risk averse, there will be *some* reduction of the probability to a level p that will leave the risk-averse individuals indifferent between bearing the $10,000 sanction with probability p and instead bearing the $1,000 sanction with probability 10 percent. But due to risk aversion, this p will be less than 1 percent, perhaps it will be .1 percent. At the new p and the $10,000 maximal sanction, deterrence will, by construction, be preserved: Parties who commit the harmful act will be just as well-off as they were when they faced the $1,000 sanction with probability 10 percent, and enforcement resources will have been saved (indeed, even more resources will have been saved than in the risk-neutral case, when p falls only to 1 percent). So why will not social welfare necessarily have been raised? The answer is that the state's *revenue* from sanctions will have fallen, because the expected sanction will be lower (such as .1% × $10,000 = $10 for each person who commits the act, instead of $100). This decline in revenue might offset the savings in enforcement costs, and, if so, will result in higher taxes and thus tend to lead to lower welfare.

The formal problem in the risk-averse case is similar to that sketched in note 3, namely, to maximize social welfare

$$W = F(g^*(y, s))U(y) + \int_{g^*(y, s)}^{\infty} [(1 - p)U(y + g) + pU(y + g - s)]f(g)dg$$

over s and p, where $g^*(y, s)$ is defined by $(1 - p)U(y + g) + pU(y + g - s) = U(y)$. Also, $y = z - (1 - F(g^*))(h - ps) - c(p)$, where z is the initial income of each person, so the second term is taxes. Essentially this problem is solved in Polinsky and Shavell 1979. For further analysis, see Kaplow 1992.

to achieve a particular level of deterrence is through use of greater enforcement than would be needed were the sanction maximal. Second, the optimal probability could also be lower than in the risk-neutral case: If the sanction must be fairly low due to risk aversion, the effectiveness of raising the probability is reduced, leading to the possibility that the optimal probability could be lower than in the risk-neutral case, or that it might not be worth controlling the activity at all, even though it would be worth it in the risk-neutral case.

A further point is worth mentioning. The reason that has been discussed why some risk-averse parties bear risk is that it may turn out to be desirable for them to commit harmful acts and they will do so. As we know, however, there are other reasons for risk-bearing—and thus for sanctions to be less than maximal—notably, legal errors that result in the imposition of sanctions on innocent parties.

2.5 Comment on the misleading notion that sanctions are analogous to market prices—that willingness to face sanctions for harmful acts implies that committing such acts is socially correct.   It is sometimes stated that if a party is willing to pay a sanction, or to face an expected sanction, then it is not socially incorrect, indeed it is socially desirable, for him to commit an act, such as to pollute, since his willingness to bear the expected sanction signals that his benefit is higher than the expected sanction. The analogy to paying a price for a good is said to apply, whereby if a party is willing to pay the price of a good, the purchase is inferred to be socially desirable, since his willingness to pay the price implies that the value that the party places on the good must exceed its production cost. This line of thinking is offered both as a criticism of the economic way of thinking by some, and as a point of interest, asserted to be correct, by economists.

This view, however, represents an incorrect interpretation of economic analysis of optimal law enforcement. As has been explained, *optimal law enforcement is characterized by underdeterrence—and perhaps by substantial underdeterrence—due to the costliness of enforcement effort and limits on sanctions.* For example, the probability and magnitude of sanctions against pollution may fall significantly short of discouraging as much pollution as would be ideal—because of the costs of raising the likelihood of enforcement and because of limits on the magnitude of sanctions. Consider a firm that faces a maximum sanction equal to its assets of $100,000, that could take a precaution that costs $10,000 and would prevent pollution harm of $25,000, and that would be sanctioned for pollution only with a probability of 5 percent due to the high cost of detecting the source of the pollution. This firm might well find it in its private interest to pollute—its savings from not taking the precaution of $10,000 is double the maximum possible expected sanction of 5% × $100,000 = $5,000. But the firm's failure to take the precaution would most definitely be socially undesirable— pollution causes harm of $25,000 yet saves prevention costs of only $10,000. It is often the case that when parties choose to commit harmful acts and the likelihood of sanctions is low, it would be socially best that they do not commit the acts; they commit the acts only because the social cost of enforcement effort results in inadequate expected sanctions.

Note, however, that if enforcement is certain, the conclusion may be different. For example, if we imagine pollution taxes to be imposed with certainty in some context (because it is administratively easy to do so), then by setting the tax equal to the harm due to pollution, the privately induced behavior will also be socially desirable.[19] In such a setting, the behavior of the polluter is like that of a person who purchases a good on a market (where, note, the payment for the good is made with certainty).

2.6 Fault-based liability.   The conclusions about the optimal probability and magnitude of sanctions under fault-based liability are similar to those I have discussed for strict liability, but with some differences.

Optimal sanctions given the probability of their imposition. In this case, as under strict liability, it is optimal for the sanction to equal the harm multiplied by the inverse of the probability of its imposition, for that will result in an expected sanction equal to harm, and thus induce individuals not to act with fault.[20] Unlike the outcome under strict liability, however, any higher

19. This will be so provided that the polluters can pay the tax. Polluters are more likely to be able to pay a tax equal to harm than the higher sanction that would be necessary to create an expected sanction equal to harm when sanctions are applied only with a probability. For example, the firm mentioned in the paragraph above would be able to pay a tax equal to the pollution harm of $25,000, because its assets are $100,000, but the firm would not be able to pay $500,000, which is the sanction necessary to create an expected sanction of $25,000 when the probability of sanctions is 5 percent.

20. Under the fault system a person is liable if and only if $g < h$. Thus, if $s = h/p$, then because expected liability for fault is h, no one will act with fault.

sanction will also lead to desirable behavior, assuming that the fault system is error free. Higher sanctions only reinforce the incentive not to act with fault, but do not discourage desirable yet possibly harmful behavior—for such behavior is not sanctioned. Also, unlike the outcome under strict liability, risk aversion does not reduce the optimal sanction, assuming again that the fault system is error free, because parties do not bear risk; parties who do harm will be those whose acts are not faulty and thus will not be sanctioned; others will be discouraged from committing harmful acts.

Yet if the fault system is not error free, the optimal magnitude of sanction could, in general, be different from the harm multiplied by the inverse of the probability; the optimal sanction could be higher or lower depending on circumstances. The presence of error also means that risk aversion becomes relevant under the fault system, and thus lowers the sanction from what would otherwise be its optimal level.

Optimal sanctions and the optimal probability of their imposition. Here, as under strict liability, the optimal policy involves the maximal sanction and a low probability of its imposition if parties are risk neutral, for this policy conserves enforcement resources. If parties are risk averse, there is a lesser need to employ moderate sanctions than under strict liability because many of the parties who do harm are those who act without fault and thus do not bear risk. Yet some risk will tend to be borne by parties if there is error in the fault determination. Also, it will often be the case that some parties will bear risk because of the general optimality of permitting underdeterrence in order to save enforcement costs.

3.   SYPNOSIS

The basic rules of liability and optimal sanctions were first considered here under the assumption of certain enforcement. The main conclusions about liability rules were that both strict liability and the fault rule give rise to correct behavior, but strict liability requires less knowledge on the part of the state (only knowledge of harm). It was also noted that harm-based sanctions require the state to possess less information than act-based sanctions, but that act-based sanctions have the advantage that parties' assets need not be as high for liability rules to function well. The optimal magnitude of sanctions equals harm if parties are risk neutral, and is less than harm if parties are risk averse (and uninsured against sanctions).

Then it was assumed that parties face sanctions only with a probability, but the probability was regarded as fixed (which is sometimes realistic). The main point here was that the magnitude of sanctions should be raised to offset the probability of escaping sanctions. In particular, the optimal sanction equals the harm multiplied by the inverse of the probability of sanctions if parties are risk neutral, and is less than this if parties are risk averse.

Last, it was assumed that parties face sanctions with a probability that is optimally chosen. Here a crucial point was that there is a social advantage associated with a low probability–high sanction enforcement strategy: The low probability means that the state conserves enforcement resources, and the high magnitude of sanctions prevents dilution of desired deterrence. The optimal strategy involves maximal sanctions if parties are risk neutral, but lesser sanctions if parties are risk averse.

A second point to stress about optimal law enforcement is that it will tend to involve underdeterrence, for the costliness of enforcement effort will make it desirable to spend less than what would be needed to achieve perfect deterrence. Therefore, the fact that an individual chooses to commit an act and suffer the consequences does not imply that the act was desirable to commit—the analogy to sanctions as prices that lead to socially desirable choices is misleading.

Note on the literature.   The basic point that sanctions should be inflated to offset the probability of escaping liability, and in particular multiplied by the inverse of the probability of escaping liability, was emphasized by Bentham ([1789] 1973) in his treatment of law enforcement. Becker (1968) first considered the question of the optimal social choice of the probability of enforcement and stressed the advantage of the low probability–high sanction enforcement policy. Polinsky and Shavell (1979) initially considered risk aversion in enforcement policy and showed that it implied that optimal sanctions are not maximal.[21]

21. For surveys of economic literature on enforcement, see Garoupa 1997, Mookherjee 1997, and Polinsky and Shavell 2000a.

21 ||| DETERRENCE WITH NONMONETARY SANCTIONS

In this chapter, I consider the deterrence of undesirable behavior by the state when the form of sanctions is nonmonetary. The important assumption that will be made about nonmonetary sanctions is that they are socially costly to impose, and the primary form of nonmonetary sanction that should be borne in mind is imprisonment. Imprisonment is clearly socially costly to employ: Prisons must be built and operated, production of individuals is forgone during their imprisonment, and individuals suffer disutility during imprisonment.

In the first section, I consider enforcement assuming that nonmonetary sanctions are imposed with certainty, and in the second section, that they are imposed only with a probability determined by the enforcement effort of the state. Then, in sections three and four, I examine the question of when it is socially desirable to employ nonmonetary sanctions, rather than only monetary sanctions. In the last section, I consider types of nonmonetary sanctions apart from imprisonment.

The assumptions about individual behavior and social welfare that I make are similar to those of the last chapter. For simplicity, I focus on the assumption that individuals are risk neutral with respect to sanctions, but I will note other possibilities. Social welfare is assumed to equal the benefits that parties obtain from their acts, less the harm done by the acts, less the costs of enforcement, and less the costs associated with the imposition of sanctions.

1. CERTAIN ENFORCEMENT WITH NONMONETARY SANCTIONS: BASIC THEORY OF LIABILITY

1.1 Introduction. Here I initially consider strict liability and explain why it is generally a disadvantageous form of liability compared to fault-based liability when sanctions are nonmonetary.[1] (This is in fundamental contrast to the conclusions reached when sanctions are monetary, as discussed in Chapter 20.) I then discuss the optimal use of fault liability.

1.2 Strict liability for harm. Suppose that individuals are held strictly liable for causing harm. Then the sanction can generally be chosen so as to induce ideal behavior.[2] If, for instance, an act causes harm of 1,000 and there exists an imprisonment sanction creating disutility equal to 1,000, then individuals will commit the act if and only if they obtain benefits exceeding 1,000, which constitutes ideal behavior under our assumptions.[3]

Although optimal behavior can therefore be induced, this *socially desirable behavior will be accompanied by the imposition of socially costly sanctions on those who commit harmful acts.* If the social cost of imposing the sanction that creates disutility of 1,000 is, for instance, 1,500 (composed of the disutility of 1,000 suffered by a person who is sanctioned and the costs of operating the prisons), then each time a person commits the act (because the person obtains high benefits from so doing), social costs of 1,500 as well as the harm of 1,000 are generated. This makes strict liability a socially expensive way to induce behavior that would be desirable.[4]

---

1. The points made in section 1 are developed in Shavell 1985a, 1987c.

2. The only reason that ideal behavior would not be achievable is that there may not exist a sanction high enough to offset the benefits to an individual. This possibility will be discussed later, but is not important to the argument to be made in this section on strict liability.

3. I will write of nonmonetary sanctions as imprisonment until section 5, where I explicitly consider other forms of nonmonetary sanctions.

4. To amplify, let g be the gain from committing an act that causes certain harm of h, let $f(g)$ be the probability density of g in the population, let s be the sanction, let $d(s)$

Note too that because under strict liability social costs of imposing sanctions are incurred whenever individuals commit harmful acts, the optimal magnitude of the sanction will not be the magnitude that leads to ideal behavior; it will be such as to reduce the social costs of imposing sanctions.[5]

Comment: comparison to the case under monetary sanctions. When sanctions are assumed to be monetary and costless to impose, as in the previous chapter, optimal behavior can be induced at no social cost by setting the sanction equal to the harm. Here, when sanctions are nonmonetary, the situation is altogether different, due to the cost of actually imposing the sanction. For example, consider a harmful act such as polluting. If sanctions are monetary, then strict liability induces optimal behavior at no social cost, for whenever an individual pollutes (because the benefits from doing so are higher than harm), he merely pays for harm, which causes no social cost, because his payment represents merely a transfer of command over resources. But if an individual is jailed for having polluted when the disutil-

---

be the disutility of s to individuals, and let ks be the additional social cost of imposing the sanction s, where $k > 0$. Under strict liability, ideal behavior—commission of the act if and only if g is at least h—can be induced if $s = h$. If so, social welfare equals

$$W = \int_{h}^{m} (g - h - (h + kh)f(g)\,dg,$$

where m is the maximum gain from committing the act. The ideal level of social welfare is not achieved because of the term $-(h + kh)$, which are the total costs associated with imposition of punishment.

5. Using the notation of the previous note, the optimal magnitude of the sanction is the s that maximizes

$$W = \int_{s}^{m} (g - h - (s + ks))f(g)\,dg.$$

Setting the derivative of W with respect to s equal to 0 gives the first-order condition for the optimum, $(h + ks)f(s) = (1 - F(s))(1 + k)$, where F is the cumulative distribution of f. The interpretation of this condition is that the marginal net benefit from deterrence equals the marginal cost. From this condition, it is apparent that the optimal s could be greater than h (reflecting the fact that the harmful act involves social costs of not only h, but also $s + ks$, so exceeding h) or below h (reflecting the fact that social costs of punishment can be reduced by lowering s). The solution to this problem is discussed in Polinsky and Shavell 1984 and Kaplow 1990.

ity of jail equals the harm from pollution, then although his polluting behavior is desirable (by assumption his benefits from so doing are higher than the harm generated), this form of sanction absorbs social resources.

1.3 Fault-based liability for harm.   Under this rule, a person is subject to liability for harm if his act was undesirable, but is not held liable if his act was desirable. Hence, if the sanction for causing harm is sufficiently high, undesirable behavior will be deterred, whereas desirable behavior will not be discouraged because it will not result in punishment. An individual who would obtain a benefit of less than 1,000 from an act that causes harm of 1,000—and thus for whom the act would be socially undesirable—will not commit the act if the sanction is sufficiently high; but an individual who would obtain a benefit exceeding 1,000 from the act—and thus for whom the act would be socially desirable—would commit the act because he would not be held at fault and punished for so doing. Thus, ideal behavior is achieved under fault-based liability without the actual imposition of socially costly punishment.

A corollary point is that the optimal magnitude of the sanction for a socially undesirable act is any sanction sufficient to deter. It does not matter how high the sanction is, for because the threat of sanctions deters, sanctions are never applied, and hence higher sanctions do not result in higher social costs.

An important factor should be added: There is sometimes a possibility that an individual cannot be deterred from committing an undesirable act because his benefit exceeds even the maximal sanction (such as life imprisonment). In this situation, it is optimal not to impose any sanction on the individual even though his act is socially undesirable. For by hypothesis, all that imposing a sanction would create is a social cost; it would not accomplish deterrence of the individual, for that is by hypothesis impossible. For instance, suppose that the highest sanction that can be imposed on a person is 100 (because, say, imprisonment would not create such great disutility for him), and that he would obtain a benefit of 200 from committing the act causing harm of 1,000. Then, although his act is undesirable, it is optimal not to punish him.[6]

---

6. In the previous chapter on monetary sanctions, I did not emphasize the point analogous to the one here—that deterrence of undesirable acts might be impossible because the

The conclusion is that, under optimal fault-based liability, sanctions are never imposed. They are not imposed if individuals act desirably, and their use is threatened when and only when that threat will successfully deter undesirable behavior. In sum, ideal behavior is achieved, except when deterrence is impossible, and it is achieved without the bearing of costs of actually imposing sanctions.[7]

This conclusion about optimally applied fault-based liability will be important to bear in mind in what follows. It should be emphasized that the point that sanctions are never imposed depends on the implicit presumption that the information of the social authority is perfect. In particular, the social authority has to know the benefits that individuals obtain not only to be able to determine which acts are desirable, but also to be able to forecast when imposition of a sanction would deter.

Fundamental advantage of fault-based liability over strict liability. Fault-based liability is different from strict liability because, under fault-based liability, deterrence of undesirable acts is achieved when it can be and without the imposition of sanctions on those who commit socially desirable acts. This feature of fault-based liability constitutes an advantage over strict liability when sanctions are socially costly to impose. As has been noted, however, use of fault-based liability does mean that the social authority

---

assets of a person might be limited. In the case of monetary sanctions, however, there is no advantage of relieving an impossible-to-deter person of liability, for the assumption is that imposing a monetary sanction does not involve a social cost. That is why the situation where individuals cannot be deterred was not a focus of discussion where sanctions are monetary, but it is significant here.

7. Let me be precise about fault-based liability as discussed in this section. Under such liability, any act that is desirable—such that $g \geq h$—is not sanctioned, and hence individuals commit such acts and are not punished. If an act is undesirable—such that $g < h$—then, if there is an s exceeding g for the individual, he will be sanctioned for committing the act with such an s, and thus will be deterred. But if there does not exist an s for the person such that $s > g$, then he cannot be deterred, so that it is optimal to set $s = 0$ for that person (otherwise he will commit the act and the additional social costs will be $h + ks$). In sum, the formula for the optimal sanction under the fault rule is as follows. Let g, h, and m be the gain, harm, and maximal sanction that can be imposed on an individual. Then the optimal sanction $s = s(g,h,m)$ is apparent: if $g \geq h$, then $s = 0$; if $g < h$ and $m < g$, then $s = 0$; if $g < h$ and $m \geq g$, then $s \geq g$. Therefore, all individuals whose acts would be desirable commit them, all those who can be deterred from committing undesirable acts are deterred, and no one actually suffers punishment.

needs greater information than it would to apply strict liability, which requires only information about the harm done.

1.4 Fault-based liability continued: when information of the social authority is imperfect.   Now let us consider the situation in which the social authority's information is imperfect and the authority may err in assessing a person's benefits or how harmful his act was. There are several consequences of such errors.

First, some desirable acts may not be committed. This is because a person might fear that his desirable act would be erroneously seen as undesirable and that he would bear a sanction greater than his benefits. (A lost hiker might not enter an unoccupied cabin to phone for help because of fear that he would be sanctioned for breaking into a property.)

Second, some individuals who could have been deterred from committing undesirable acts will not be deterred. The social authority may believe that for a particular kind of act and person, a sanction of 500 would successfully deter, but in fact it does not, and thus the person commits the act even though a higher sanction would have deterred him.

Third, sanctions will actually be imposed and society will thus incur the costs associated with punishment. Sanctions will be imposed for a variety of reasons: Some who commit desirable acts will erroneously be sanctioned; some who commit undesirable acts and could have been deterred will be sanctioned by too low a sanction, as just discussed; and some who commit undesirable acts and could not have been deterred by any sanction will mistakenly be punished.

The optimal sanction will be chosen taking into account these various consequences of imperfect information. To understand the nature of the optimal sanction, consider an example.

Example 1. There are three types of parties: A's, who obtain a benefit of 500 from committing an act that causes harm of 100; B's, who obtain a benefit of 40 from committing the act; and C's, who obtain a benefit of 70 from committing the act. Assume that the maximum feasible sanction creates disutility of 50. Hence, the situation is that for A's the harmful act is desirable (the benefit exceeds the harm); for B's and C's, the act is undesirable (the harm exceeds the benefit); and B's can be deterred by a sanction of 40 or more, but C's cannot be deterred by any feasible sanction.

If the social authority possesses perfect information, its optimal policy is clear: The authority will not sanction A's, because their act is desirable; it will announce a sanction of at least 40 for B's and thus deter them from acting (so it will not turn out to impose a sanction on them); and it will impose no sanction for C's, because deterring them is impossible. Thus, A's and C's will commit harmful acts, B's will be deterred, and no sanctions will actually be imposed.

Suppose, however, that the social authority has only imperfect information and cannot distinguish between B's and C's. What are optimal sanctions in this case? Clearly, A's will not face a sanction and will commit the act, for A's can be identified by the authority. But because the authority is unable to distinguish B's and C's, they will necessarily face the same sanction.[8] If the sanction for them is 40, B's will just be deterred, but C's will not be deterred and will commit the act and suffer the sanction, resulting in the bearing of social costs. Any sanction above 40 will also deter the B's and will result in the C's bearing a higher sanction, so would be socially inferior to a sanction of 40. Any positive sanction below 40 will not deter either B's or C's, but will be imposed on both, so would be inferior to not imposing any sanction. Hence, what is optimal is either a sanction of 40, the minimum sanction that can deter the B's, or no sanction at all. Which of these two possibilities is best depends on, among other things, the relative numbers of B's and C's. If B's are sufficiently more numerous than C's, the optimal sanction will be 40, because the deterrence of all the B's will be worthwhile even though C's will commit the act and suffer sanctions of 40; whereas if C's are sufficiently numerous, a sanction of 0 will be best, because there are relatively few B's who can be deterred, and to deter them means imposing a sanction of 40 on all the undeterrable C's.

As is demonstrated in this example, because the use of sanctions does result in their actual imposition, the optimal level of sanctions is, in a rough sense, the lowest sanction that will achieve deterrence of the group who can be deterred—if that group is worth deterring given the sanctions that

---

8. If the state announced different sanctions for the two types (such as 40 for B's and 0 for C's), then individuals of the type who would suffer the higher sanction would claim to be of the other type (B's would claim to be C's), so in effect there would be just one sanction for both types, namely, the lesser of the two sanctions.

those who will not be deterred will then suffer.[9] With this in mind, let us examine further the determination of optimal sanctions.

Relationship of optimal sanctions to individual benefits from acts and to the magnitude of harm. What is the relationship between optimal sanctions, the benefits obtained by a person, and the harm? The higher the benefits to a person contemplating a harmful act, the higher should be the sanction, for higher benefits require higher sanctions to deter. The person who would kill in order to obtain a great deal of money may be harder to deter than the person who would kill to obtain a small amount of money or to satisfy a grudge. There is, however, a limit to this relationship: If the benefits become so great that deterrence may not be possible, then the sanction should fall (and to zero if deterrence is impossible for all persons to whom the sanction would apply).

Also, the greater the harm, the higher should be the sanction, for higher harm means that more is gained by deterring, so society should be willing to incur greater costs in actually imposing sanctions in order to achieve greater deterrence. Other things being equal, we should be willing to bear greater costs, associated with imprisoning people, to deter murder than assault, for murder is more harmful.

---

9. This is only an approximate statement of the principle guiding the choice of the optimal sanction, because in reality the choice is more complicated than in the example. Among other things, there will not usually be a single, well-defined group who can be deterred—the B's in the example—and another group—the C's in the example—who cannot be deterred. For instance, suppose in the example that there is another group of D's who obtain a benefit of 45 from committing the harmful act, so that the D's as well as the B's can be deterred. In this instance, it might well be desirable to employ a sanction of 40, and thus to deter the B's but not to deter the D's even though they can be deterred; that would be desirable if the B's were very numerous, the D's very small in number, and the C's modest in number. More generally, there will be a continuum of types of parties, and many different degrees of lack of information that the courts may suffer from.

Nevertheless, the example captures the important compromise that the optimal sanction typically reflects—the tradeoff between greater deterrence of some, and the greater suffering of sanctions by others, and thus the incurring of social costs in respect to them.

Formally, the choice of the optimal sanction under the fault rule is as follows. Given any set of observable characteristics of parties who come before it, the social authority can formulate a probability distribution of gains of parties. Then it can choose an optimal sanction given this probability distribution. The determination of that optimal sanction is essentially as described in note 5.

There is another reason why greater harm may sometimes call for higher sanctions: If the object of an individual is to harm someone, then greater harm will imply higher benefits and deterrence may thus be more difficult.[10]

Comment: comparison of optimal sanctions when sanctions are monetary. In the present setting, the magnitude of sanctions is chosen by balancing deterrence benefits against the costs associated with actually imposing sanctions. Thus, an important theme has been that it is undesirable to impose sanctions that are higher than is likely to be needed to accomplish deterrence, so that those who are not deterred are punished as little as possible. When sanctions are monetary and assumed to be costless to impose (or, more realistically, are costly but significantly less so than imprisonment), the social need to limit the magnitude of sanctions is much lower, and the optimal sanction generally equals the harm. Thus, when sanctions are monetary, there is no need, in principle, to identify the strength of the benefit from an act or the motive for it in order to determine the proper sanction, since only harm need be measured.[11]

Comment: realism of the assumption that the social authority's information is imperfect and that the actual imposition of sanctions is inevitable. It is apparent that the case of imperfect information is the realistic case to consider, for social authorities cannot practically always know which acts are undesirable, and who can be deterred by which sanctions. It is evident as well that deterrence will frequently be impossible to achieve. There will often be individuals who cannot be deterred from committing an act no matter how high the sanction is, especially because, as will be discussed, the probability of the sanction will often be low. Moreover, if we depart momentarily from our model, in which individuals always calculate benefits against expected penalties, we know that individuals may suffer momentary lapses of control

---

10. Additional reasons for sanctions to increase with harm are discussed in sections 2 and 5 of Chapter 22, on marginal deterrence and general enforcement.

11. This point is subject to the qualifications discussed earlier, such as that if parties are risk averse and not insured against sanctions, the proper sanction may be somewhat lower than harm, but the central point emphasized in the text remains true: When sanctions are very cheap to impose socially, the optimal sanction tends to equal the harm, whereas when they are very expensive to impose, as they are when the sanction is imprisonment, the optimal sanction is quite different, and is limited to that necessary to deter those most important to deter.

and not calculate, at least when the sanction will not be immediate and certain, so these individuals in these circumstances will be effectively undeterrable. When the social authority cannot determine who is undeterrable, these individuals will often bear sanctions, creating social costs.

1.5 Act-based liability. The main points just discussed carry over to act-based liability. The strict form of such liability, under which sanctions would be imposed for committing an act, is clearly inferior to fault-based liability, under which sanctions would be imposed less often (and not at all if the social authority has perfect information). The main difference between act-based liability and harm-based liability is that the problem of inability to deter may be greater under harm-based liability. The reason, as was explained in the previous chapter, is that if harm from an act occurs only with a probability, then under harm-based liability, the sanction will be applied only with a probability. (A person who shoots at another will bear a sanction only if he hits his intended target.) As a consequence, the magnitude of the sanction necessary to deter will be larger under harm-based sanctions than under act-based sanctions (under which a person will bear a sanction for shooting, even if he misses). Thus, act-based liability may be superior to harm-based because it achieves deterrence with lower sanctions. Yet the social authority may experience difficulty in assessing the expected harm from an act, whereas under harm-based liability, it at least knows that the act has generated the observed harm.[12]

1.6 Conclusions. When sanctions are nonmonetary, fault-based liability has appeal over strict liability, for under fault liability, deterrence of undesirable acts can be created with less actual imposition of sanctions, and in the ideal—when the courts have perfect information—with no imposition of sanctions. In addition, the theory of the determination of the optimal magnitude of the sanction under fault-based liability can be understood only by recognizing the lack of information of the social authority about parties' benefits from acts, the harmfulness of acts, and the possibility of failure to deter. For only by taking the authority's lack of information into explicit account can it be explained why sanctions are ever imposed (and

---

12. I will return to the issues discussed in this section when criminal attempts are considered in section 4 of Chapter 24.

thus why there is a need to limit their magnitude). These conclusions about the advantage of the fault system and the determination of optimal sanctions derive from the assumption that nonmonetary sanctions are costly to impose.

2. THE OPTIMAL PROBABILITY AND MAGNITUDE OF NONMONETARY SANCTIONS

2.1 Introduction.   The theory here parallels that in the last chapter, so the analysis will be relatively brief.[13] The question under consideration concerns, again, the choice of the probability and the magnitude of sanctions when account is taken of the cost of maintaining the probability of sanctions.

2.2 Behavior given the probability and magnitude of sanctions.   A person may display risk neutrality toward prison sentences and, for instance, be equally deterred by a certain one-year sentence and a 50 percent probability of a two-year sentence. This is the way a person will regard sanctions if the disutility of imprisonment is proportional to its length.[14]

Risk aversion. Individuals may be risk averse with regard to imprisonment, however, and be more deterred by a 50 percent probability of a two-year sentence than by a certain one-year sentence. (In general, risk-averse individuals will be more deterred the greater the uncertainty in the sentence, its expected length held constant.) Individuals will be risk averse if the disutility of imprisonment rises more than in proportion to its length.[15] This could be so because of increasing yearning to join the functioning world or growing distaste for the prison environment as the time spent in prison increases.

Risk preference. Another possibility is that individuals are risk preferrers,

13. The points made in this section are largely developed in Shavell 1985a, 1987c.

14. Let s be the length of the prison sentence and $d(s)$ its disutility. Then the assumption of risk neutrality is that $d(s) = \alpha s$ for some positive α, and for simplicity, I will often assume that $\alpha = 1$.

15. Suppose, for example, that the disutility of the first year of imprisonment is 100 and that of the second is 200. Then the disutility of a certain one-year sentence is 100, and the expected disutility of a 50 percent chance of a two-year sentence is $50\% \times (100 + 200) = 150$, so the individual will be more deterred by the latter. Formally, using the notation of the previous footnote, the assumption of risk aversion is that $d'(s) > d(s)/s$.

and would thus find a certain one-year sentence worse than a 50 percent chance of a two-year sentence. Individuals will prefer risk if the disutility of imprisonment to them rises less than in proportion to its length.[16] That would be so if, over time, imprisonment matters less as a person becomes accustomed to prison life and makes his adjustment, or if he discounts the future disutility of imprisonment. It would also be true if he experiences relatively large disutility from being in jail at all, due to humiliation and the stigmatizing effect of having been in prison for any length of time, or due to brutalization in the beginning of imprisonment.[17]

Probability versus magnitude of sanctions. The analogue of what was stated in Chapter 20 about the importance of the probability versus the magnitude of sanctions is true here. Namely, if a person is risk neutral regarding imprisonment, then a given percentage increase in either the probability or the magnitude of such sanctions will have the same effect on behavior. If a person is risk averse, then a given percentage increase in the magnitude of sanctions will have a greater effect than an equal percentage increase in the probability of sanctions. If a person is risk preferring, however, a given percentage increase in the probability of sanctions will have a greater deterrent effect than the same percentage increase in the magnitude of sanctions.[18] It should also be noted that the general comments made about perceptions of sanctions and their likelihood in the previous

16. Suppose, for instance, that the first year of imprisonment involves disutility of 100 and the second involves disutility of only 50. Then the disutility of a certain one-year sentence is 100, and the expected disutility of a 50 percent chance of a two-year sentence is $50\% \times (100 + 50) = 75$, so the individual will be more deterred by the former. Formally, the assumption of risk preference is that $d'(s) < d(s)/s$.

17. I did not discuss the possibility of risk preference with respect to monetary risks because it does not seem an important possibility, whereas risk preference with respect to imprisonment risks seems often to be descriptively accurate.

18. Let p be the probability of the sanction, so $pd(s)$ is the expected disutility ED. We want to compare the elasticity of ED with respect to p—namely, $(p/ED)(dED/dp)$—with its elasticity with respect to s, namely, $(s/ED)(dED/ds)$. In the risk-neutral case, $ED = pks$, so that $(p/ED)(dED/dp) = (1/ks)(ks) = 1 = (1/kp)(kp) = (s/ED)(dED/ds)$. In the risk-averse case, $(p/ED)(dED/dp) = (1/d(s))(d(s)) = 1$ and $(s/ED)(dED/ds) = (s/pd(s))(pd'(s)) = s(d'(s)/d(s))$. And $s(d'(s)/d(s)) > 1$, for the assumption of risk aversion is that $d'(s) > d(s)/s$. In the case of risk preference, the argument is analogous to that in the risk-averse case.

chapter apply here; it is the perceived rather than the actual sanctions that determine deterrence.[19]

2.3 Comment: actual deterrence based on observed behavior. A multitude of observations from everyday life suggests that individuals are discouraged from all manner of undesirable behavior when the likelihood and magnitude of sanctions is sufficiently high: Drivers slow down and tend to obey traffic rules when they see a police car; students' deportment improves under a teacher's gaze; criminals often refrain from acting when they would be easy to identify as responsible. Various events that result in gross changes in expected penalties have been noted to influence the incidence of violations of law; for example, police strikes have resulted in marked increases in crime, improvements in toxicology have led to declines in the incidence of poisoning, and increases in tax audit rates and sanctions have discouraged tax evasion.[20] In general, there is a great weight of empirical evidence demonstrating that increases in expected sanctions reduce violations.[21] Some studies, however, have questioned the interpretation of these results, and also have found relatively small effects of changes in the probability and magnitude of sanctions on behavior. Such findings may, in part, be due to individuals' inaccurate perceptions of expected sanctions, to the discounting of future imprisonment, and to subtle but important statistical problems.[22]

19. On perceptions of sanctions and their likelihood, see the references cited in note 9 of Chapter 20.

20. On the effects of police strikes and of advancement in toxicology, see Andenaes 1966, 961–962; on the effects of tax auditing and penalties, see Andreoni, Erard, and Feinstein 1998.

21. See, for example, the surveys Cook 1977, Ehrlich 1996, Eide 2000, and Glaeser 1998; see also, for example, Andenaes 1975, Kessler and Levitt 1999, Levitt 1996, 1997, 1998a, 1998b, Viscusi 1986b, Wilson and Herrnstein 1985, chap. 15, and Witte 1980.

22. On weak findings concerning deterrence, and methodological criticisms of studies of deterrence, see Andenaes 1975, Blumstein, Cohen, and Nagin 1978, Cook 1977, Ehrlich 1996, 56–63, and Eide 2000, 364–368. Of the methodological criticisms, two stand out. First, many studies do not take into account that imprisonment reduces crime due both to deterrence and incapacitation (thus, if crime falls due to an increase in imprisonment, the decline cannot be ascribed entirely to deterrence). Second, sanctions may not only influence crime, but also be influenced by it, obscuring statistical findings (jurisdictions with high crime rates might raise levels of punishment to counter their problem; this would result

2.4 Optimal sanctions when the probability of their imposition is a given.
What is the optimal magnitude of sanctions, given their probability? The rough answer is that whatever would be optimal if sanctions were certain should be inflated when sanctions are applied with a probability. If individuals are risk neutral, sanctions should be multiplied by the reciprocal of the probability of sanctions, so that the expected sanction is what it would be in a world with certain sanctions. Thus, where the optimal sanction would be two years of imprisonment with certain sanctions, the optimal sanction would be six years if sanctions are applied with a probability of one-third. If individuals are risk averse, optimal sanctions tend to be lower than otherwise, and if they are risk preferring, higher than otherwise.[23] It must be remembered, however, that the appropriate probability-inflated sanctions may not be feasible to apply (a sentence of one hundred years cannot be imposed), so in general it will not be possible to duplicate the deterrence that would be best to achieve were sanctions certain.

2.5 Optimal sanctions when the probability of their imposition is also optimally determined.
As in the case of monetary sanctions, when the state chooses both the probability of imposing sanctions and their magnitude, a low probability–high sanction policy is often socially advantageous. The reason is again that a social savings can be achieved by conserving enforcement effort, while the magnitude of sanctions can be raised to offset the low probability and thereby to avoid dilution of deterrence.[24] Unlike the case with monetary sanctions, however, raising nonmonetary

---

in a positive correlation between high penalties and crime, but would not imply that high penalties fail to deter).

23. It is possible that optimal sanctions would not change in the stated way, even though one would expect them to. For example, it is possible that risk aversion could increase the optimal sanction. Suppose that if individuals are risk neutral, the optimal sanction is zero, because the six-year sanction needed to deter those who can be deterred would result in excessive social costs from imposition of sanctions on those who cannot be deterred. If individuals are risk averse, however, the optimal sanction might be positive, because only a four-year sanction would be needed to deter those who can be deterred, and the social cost from actual imposition of sanctions on those who cannot be deterred is smaller and worthwhile for society to bear. Thus, the statement in text refers only to a general tendency.

24. This basic point will be qualified when incapacitation is considered, however, for a too-low probability will undesirably lower incapacitation. See Chapter 23, section 1.4(e).

sanctions in itself raises social costs when the sanctions are imposed. Yet because sanctions are imposed less often, the total costs of sanctions may not rise. This suggests what I will now elaborate on, that when individuals are risk neutral, the optimal policy involves low probabilities and maximal sanctions (interpreted, perhaps, as life imprisonment). I will also explain that the conclusion is the same when individuals are risk averse, but when they are risk preferring, less than maximal sanctions are often best.[25]

In the risk-neutral case, suppose that the sanction is less than maximal. For instance, suppose that the sanction is five years of imprisonment, that the maximal sanction is twenty years, and that the probability of sanctions is 40 percent. Now raise the sanction to twenty years and reduce the probability of sanctions to 10 percent. The reduction in the probability from 40 percent to 10 percent will save enforcement costs, a social benefit, and nothing else will change. First, the behavior of individuals will remain the same because the expected sanction will remain equal to two years—40% $\times$ 5 = 10% $\times$ 20. Second, the social costs of imposing sanctions will also be constant, for the expected sanction will remain equal to two years, that is, the number of person-years spent in jail will be unchanged. Although the expense of imposing a sanction on each person who is punished rises by a factor of four (the sentence rises from five years to twenty years), the number of people sanctioned falls by a factor of four (the probability falls from 40 percent to 10 percent).[26]

25. The general problem of choosing the probability p and magnitude of sanctions s optimally is to maximize

$$W(s) = \int_{pd(s)}^{m} [g - h - (pd(s) + pks)]t(g)dg - c(p).$$

Here $t(g)$ is the probability distribution of g conditional on the information that the social authority possesses about the act, under the relevant liability rule. Also, it is assumed that p can be independently chosen for this distribution $t(g)$. Note that the term $(pd(s) + pks)$ corresponds to the costs of imposing sanctions: the expected disutility experienced by a person who commits the harmful act, $pd(s)$, plus the expected public costs due to imprisonment, pks.

26. Referring to note 25, the argument in this paragraph can be restated as follows. Assume s is less than the maximal sanction m, and raise s to m and lower p to p' so that $ps = p'm$. Then the lower limit of integration, $pd(s) = ps$, does not change, nor does the integrand, so that the integral is constant, but $c(p)$ falls to $c(p')$, raising W.

As to what probability is best, the answer to this question reflects two general considerations. First, the higher the probability, the greater are enforcement costs, so that, as emphasized in the previous chapter, it will generally be best for society to tolerate some degree of underenforcement in order to save enforcement resources. Second, the probability should be chosen so that the expected sanction leads to the appropriate tradeoff between actually imposing sanctions and achieving deterrence, as explained in section 1.4.

Risk-averse case. If individuals are risk averse regarding imprisonment sanctions, then the result that optimal sanctions are maximal is reinforced.[27] In the example just discussed, if the imprisonment term is increased to twenty years, the probability of sanctions at which a risk-averse person would be equally deterred as before would be lower than 10 percent, such as 5 percent. This means not only that enforcement cost savings would be greater, but also that there would be a savings in the cost of imposing sanctions, as expected person-years in jail would fall to below two years.[28] (Note that this conclusion that risk aversion reinforces the result that optimal sanctions are maximal is opposite to the case in Chapter 20, in which risk aversion regarding monetary sanctions leads to the optimality of less than maximal sanctions.)[29]

Risk preference. If, however, individuals are risk preferring with regard to imprisonment sanctions, the optimal sanction is not necessarily maximal. For the behavior of risk preferrers to be the same when the magnitude of the sanction is raised from five years to twenty, the probability of sanctions cannot fall to as low as 10 percent; it must be at a higher level, say 15 percent. But this means that enforcement cost savings are less than in the risk-neutral case and also that there is an increase in the cost of imposing sanctions (ex-

27. The conclusions to be stated about risk aversion and risk preference are presented in Polinsky and Shavell 1999.

28. The general argument is as follows. If $s < m$, then raise s to m and lower p to p' such that $pd(s) = p'd(m)$. Because of risk aversion, $p' < p(s/m)$. Now given p' and m, the lower limit of the integral in note 25 is unchanged, and the integrand falls because pks falls to $p'km$ (for $p'km < p(s/m)km = pks$). Moreover, $c(p)$ falls to $c(p')$. Hence W rises.

29. The difference can be explained as due to a difference in the implication that expected sanctions fall when the probability is lowered so as to hold behavior constant: Here the decline in expected sanctions is socially desirable, because it reduces the costs of imposing sanctions, which can be interpreted as lowering taxes; in the previous chapter, the decline in expected sanctions meant that sanction revenue fell and taxes rose.

pected person-years in jail rise from two years to three years). Hence, it is possible that deterrence can be more cheaply achieved with a strategy of use of fairly probable sanctions that are not maximal. Another way to express this point is that raising the sanction from five to twenty years increases the social costs of actually imposing sanctions fourfold for any person who is caught, but it may not enhance deterrence very much because the disutility of sanctions rises less than in proportion to their magnitude. (The person who dislikes imprisonment because of the brutalization and stigma that come from being imprisoned at all will not be four times as deterred by a twenty-year sentence as by a five-year sentence.) Hence, within some range, raising the magnitude of sanctions may be a less economical way of achieving deterrence than raising the likelihood of sanctions.

2.6 Comment on the false notion that willingness to face the sanction for an act implies that committing it is socially correct. In the present context of use of the nonmonetary sanction of imprisonment and fault-based liability, the idea that it is socially desirable for a person to commit a harmful act if he is willing to do so and bear the risk of being sanctioned—if his gain exceeds the expected disutility of the sanction—must be regarded as generally mistaken.

One reason is that emphasized in the previous chapter and noted again here: That because of the expense of catching violators of law, it will be best to save enforcement resources and to countenance underdeterrence relative to ideal deterrence. This factor of the optimality of underdeterrence is of greater significance where the cost of catching violators is high, and that may characterize the typical context of crimes, for which imprisonment sanctions are employed. Hence, to a person who says that he was willing to commit an act, say stealing money, because his gain outweighed the expected sanction, the response could be that the expected sanction was not as high as society would have wished due to the social cost of raising it, especially through raising its likelihood. Thus his decision to steal can hardly be said to have been in the social interest.

A second mistake in the notion that it is socially desirable for a person to commit an act if he is willing to do so concerns the point that we assume fault is the form of liability that applies. Because liability is premised on fault, any liable act that is committed is, prima facie, socially undesirable. Hence, if a person commits an act for which he would be held liable, the most likely explanation for that having occurred, presuming that deterrence was possible, is that the social authority did not gauge properly the magnitude of the sanction needed to deter, not that the act was desirable. If a person who faces a sanction of three years of imprisonment for theft proceeds to steal but could have been deterred by the threat of a six-year sanction, the likely explanation is that the social authority did not realize that discouraging this type of individual from theft required a six-year sanction. (Recall the discussion in section 1.4, which explained why, in the face of imperfect information, the social authority may choose a sanction that is not sufficient to deter some individuals even though they could have been deterred.) Only if the person was found at fault but in fact committed a socially desirable act (as in the case of the lost hiker breaking into a cabin) that the state did not properly evaluate would the proper interpretation of the person's willingness to commit such an act be that it was socially good that he did so. For all the other reasons given here, the usually appropriate interpretation would be that the act was undesirable to commit.

3. WHEN NONMONETARY SANCTIONS ARE OPTIMAL TO EMPLOY

3.1 In general.   It has been supposed that monetary sanctions are socially costless to impose, whereas nonmonetary sanctions are socially costly to employ. Under these assumptions, nonmonetary sanctions are inferior to monetary sanctions and thus should not be used unless monetary sanctions alone cannot adequately deter. When the expected sanctions that can be created with solely monetary sanctions are low relative to the harm that the sanctioned acts generate, however, nonmonetary sanctions may be warranted to create added deterrence.[30]

3.2 Factors bearing on the optimality of use of nonmonetary sanctions.   Several factors are relevant to the desirability of utilizing nonmonetary sanctions. The first three to be mentioned bear on the likelihood

---

30. The point that the nonmonetary sanction of imprisonment is more expensive than monetary sanctions and thus, by implication, should not be employed unless monetary sanctions will not function adequately was made by Bentham [1789] 1973 and emphasized by Becker 1968.

that monetary sanctions will not be sufficient to deter and therefore that use of nonmonetary sanctions may be desirable.[31]

Level of assets. If the assets of parties are low relative to the magnitude of the sanction necessary to deter, then deterrence will tend to be insufficient if only monetary sanctions are employed. If a person's wealth is at most a few hundred dollars, then it would be difficult to deter him from committing acts that yield even modest benefits using solely monetary sanctions.

Probability of escaping sanctions. The greater is the likelihood of escaping sanctions, the greater is the magnitude of the sanction necessary to achieve deterrence, and thus the more likely this sanction is to exceed the assets of a person. Thus, even if a person's assets are not insubstantial, deterrence may become impossible to achieve if the probability of imposing the sanction is sufficiently low.

Level of private benefits obtained from an act. The larger are these benefits, the greater is the sanction needed to deter, and again the more likely it is that the necessary sanction will exceed a person's assets.

The expected harm due to the act committed. The larger the expected harm due to an act—the higher the probability of harm and its potential magnitude—the more important the act is to control, that is, the greater are the consequences of failure to deter it when that is desirable. Hence, other things being equal, the greater the expected harm from an act, the more likely it will be advantageous to use nonmonetary sanctions to deter.

Comment. The factors just mentioned will be considered in Chapter 24 to argue that in the core area of criminal law, monetary sanctions would be grossly inadequate for the purposes of deterrence, and thus that nonmonetary sanctions are justified.

4. JOINT USE OF NONMONETARY AND MONETARY SANCTIONS

4.1 Nonmonetary sanctions should be used only as a supplement to maximal monetary sanctions. It was just explained that nonmonetary sanctions are needed to deter when monetary sanctions would not be adequate for that task. An aspect of this conclusion is that nonmonetary sanc-

---

31. These and related factors are discussed in Shavell 1985a.

tions should not be employed unless monetary sanctions have been imposed to the greatest possible extent, which is to say, unless the monetary sanction equals the entire wealth of a party. Otherwise, the same level of deterrence could be accomplished at lower cost by increasing the monetary sanction. For example, suppose that a person faces a sanction of $20,000 and two years in prison for an act, but has $30,000 in assets. This cannot be optimal because society could construct a sanction that involves equivalent deterrence by increasing the monetary sanction to $30,000 and by decreasing the prison term somewhat; perhaps a $30,000 sanction and a term of one year would be equivalent to the $20,000 sanction and a term of two years. Such a sanction of $30,000 and one year, involving as it does less imprisonment, is cheaper for society. Thus, in general, it cannot be optimal for society to be using imprisonment unless society has already employed the monetary sanction to the utmost.[32]

4.2 Implications of the conclusion that nonmonetary sanctions should only be used as a supplement to maximal monetary sanctions.

There are several implications of the point just explained.[33]

Wealth and optimal sanctions. One implication concerns the specific nature of the relationship between a person's wealth and sanctions. If an

32. See Polinsky and Shavell 1984.

33. In addition to the two points to be discussed, another of note is that when monetary and nonmonetary sanctions are employed together, it is not necessarily optimal to employ maximal nonmonetary sanctions. This can be understood by seeing why the type of argument given in section 2.5 for the optimality of maximal nonmonetary sanctions does not carry forward. For example, suppose that an individual faces a maximal monetary sanction of $10,000 and a prison term of five years, and that this will be imposed with probability 10 percent; thus the expected penalty is $1,000 plus .5 years of imprisonment. Now double his prison sentence to 10 years and reduce the probability so that the expected penalty is the same. The new probability cannot be as low as 5 percent, for if it were 5 percent, the expected penalty would be $500 plus .5 years of imprisonment—the reason being that when the probability falls, the expected monetary component of the penalty falls (because the monetary sanction cannot be raised above $10,000). Hence, the probability that maintains deterrence must be higher than 5 percent, such as 7 percent. But this means that the expected number of person-years in jail will be more than .5 years, so that the social costs of imposition of imprisonment rise. For this reason, it does not follow that optimal imprisonment is maximal (although optimal monetary sanctions are maximal). For details, see Shavell 1991b.

individual's wealth is above the threshold at which deterrence with monetary sanctions will be adequate, the sanction should be entirely monetary. If his wealth is less than this threshold, the sanction should equal the person's entire wealth and should be accompanied by a nonmonetary sanction. Moreover, the lower is the level of a person's wealth below this threshold, the higher should be the nonmonetary sanction, so that the total sanction, reflecting the person's wealth plus the nonmonetary sanction, is maintained at the appropriate magnitude.

Harm and optimal sanctions. Another implication of the conclusion under discussion is that if the harmfulness of an act is below a certain threshold, then monetary sanctions alone will be enough to deter. Once the expected harm surpasses this threshhold, however, it will be desirable for nonmonetary sanctions to accompany the monetary sanction, which will be maximal.

4.3 The conclusion about nonmonetary sanctions and the possibility of costly monetary sanctions.   As noted in the previous chapter, the imposition of monetary sanctions is not in fact socially costless, for assets need to be located and collected and the liable parties may hide assets or resist collection. This reduces the advantage of monetary over nonmonetary sanctions. Yet one presumes that the sanction of imprisonment would still usually be more expensive as a deterrent than money sanctions, in which case the conclusion that monetary sanctions should be imposed to their limit before imprisonment is imposed continues to apply. Nevertheless, that might not always be the case. Having to spend a day or two in jail might serve as a deterrent just as well as a fine of $10,000 for a fairly wealthy person, but be cheaper than collecting $10,000 from such a person.

5.   DIFFERENT TYPES OF NONMONETARY SANCTIONS

5.1 The variety of nonmonetary sanctions.   A variety of nonmonetary sanctions apart from imprisonment may be employed. There are, first of all, a number that involve corporal punishment, notably, whipping, branding, and the death penalty. There are also various sanctions that limit freedom, different from imprisonment, including requirements to live in halfway houses, restriction to one's residence, and other probationary restraints on conduct. Moreover, there are sanctions designed to humiliate and shame, such as publication of the names of individuals who have violated a law (for example, those who have hired prostitutes). Indeed, most nonmonetary sanctions may have a component of humiliation; criminal violations are usually matters of public record, so that the reputations of criminals are forever tainted.

5.2 Cost, disutility, and effectiveness of nonmonetary sanctions.
The various sanctions differ in social cost and in the disutility they create. We might define the *effectiveness* of a sanction to be the disutility it generates per dollar of social cost. By this definition, some sanctions might be significantly more effective than imprisonment for certain people. For example, individuals who especially value their reputations might be significantly deterred by the humiliation of having their names and violations published; and because such humiliation is cheap for society (among other things, it does not remove individuals from the labor force), it might rank high in effectiveness. Similarly, confinement to one's residence might serve as a highly effective deterrent for some, but would not involve use of prisons and thus would be socially inexpensive relative to imprisonment. It should be emphasized that with the advance of technology, possibilities will increase for relatively cheap enforcement of sanctions involving restrictions in behavior through the use of remote electronic monitoring devices.[34]

5.3 Optimal choice among nonmonetary sanctions.   Obviously, it is best for society to employ nonmonetary sanctions in the order of their effectiveness as deterrents. For example, if for a certain type of person humiliation combined with restrictions on freedom of movement would serve as a significantly more effective deterrent than imprisonment, such sanctions should be used before imprisonment is contemplated.[35] Further, if a

34. Not only can devices such as television cameras, or unremovable wrist or ankle bracelets that send signals to a computer, be used to monitor movement; they could also be used to prevent the individuals from violating restrictions. For instance, bracelets could be designed to shock individuals or to inject them with an immobilizing drug by remote command.

35. Consideration of incapacitation, which may favor imprisonment, is omitted here and will be discussed in Chapter 23.

nonmonetary sanction happens to be more effective than monetary sanctions, it should be used first (as was noted in section 4.3).

Note on the literature. The general point that when nonmonetary sanctions are employed, the fault system enjoys a fundamental advantage over strict liability because sanctions are imposed less often, was first emphasized in Shavell (1985a). The theory of the optimal use of nonmonetary sanctions under the fault system is articulated in that article and in Shavell (1987c), but has been adumbrated by Bentham ([1789] 1973) and others.[36] The general point that monetary sanctions enjoy an advantage over costly nonmonetary ones was also noted by Bentham and is emphasized by Becker (1968).[37]

36. Beccaria [1767] 1995, chaps. 2, 6, Montesquieu [1748] 1989, book 6, chaps. 9, 16, and Bentham [1789] 1973, 169–177 (who cites Beccaria and Montesquieu) all suggest that because nonmonetary sanctions are costly to impose, they should be used sparingly under the fault system (they do not consider strict liability) and, generally, only when likely to accomplish deterrence. But they do not take into account the imperfect nature of the court's information. Only by doing so, as the reader knows (especially from sections 1.3 and 1.4), can one answer in an intellectually satisfactory way very basic questions about sanctions, including why sanctions are ever imposed and why extremely high sanctions should not be employed to help guarantee deterrence.

37. The literature on the use of nonmonetary sanctions is discussed in the survey by Polinsky and Shavell 2000a.

22 ||| EXTENSIONS OF THE THEORY OF DETERRENCE

In this chapter, I consider various extensions of the theory of deterrence, most of which apply in their main aspects both when sanctions are monetary and when sanctions are nonmonetary, so that I will usually not distinguish these cases.

1. INDIVIDUAL DETERRENCE

1.1 Definition. In discussions of deterrence, the notion of *individual deterrence* (sometimes called *particular deterrence* or *special deterrence*) is usually mentioned.[1] Individual deterrence is the tendency of a person who has been penalized for committing an illegal act to be more deterred in the future from committing that act than he had been beforehand by the prospect of sanctions. For example, a person who has received a speeding ticket might be thought to be more deterred from speeding in the future by the possibility of sanctions than an otherwise identical person who has not received a speeding ticket. Individual deterrence is contrasted to *general deterrence,* the tendency of people who have not yet been sanctioned to be deterred by the prospect of sanctions for committing an illegal act.

1. See, for example, Andenaes 1983, LaFave 2000, 23, and Packer 1968, 45–48.

1.2 Rationale for individual deterrence. The first point that should be made about individual deterrence is that it should not exist when calculating parties know the probability and the magnitude of sanctions for an illegal act. If a person realizes that he faces a probability of 30 percent of being ticketed for speeding on the highway and that the amount of the penalty is $100, it should not matter to him, when he is contemplating speeding, whether or not he himself has received a ticket in the past: In either case, he will face a 30 percent chance of bearing a $100 penalty if he now speeds.

Hence, for an individual to be more deterred as a consequence of having been penalized in the past—for individual deterrence to exist—it must be that the person does not know the probability or the magnitude of sanctions and, further, that his perception of one or both of them must rise as a consequence of having been penalized.[2]

Will the perceived probability of sanctions increase as a result of having been sanctioned? The answer is yes, provided that a person does not know the precise probability of sanctions. In this situation, when a person is punished, he will rationally increase his estimate of the likelihood of punishment. If, for instance, a person thought the odds of receiving a speeding ticket were in the neighborhood of 30 percent and then actually was caught for speeding, he would rationally raise his estimate of the odds of a ticket, perhaps to 40 percent or 50 percent. That is, whatever his initial beliefs about the probability, being punished will lead a person to increase his estimate of the likelihood of being punished in the future, according to the laws of conditional probability.[3] Moreover, there is reason to believe

---

2. An *actual* increase in the probability or the magnitude of sanctions is, of course, possible as a result of an infraction. After an infraction, an individual could be watched more closely by enforcement authorities than otherwise, or the law could specify that the penalty for a second infraction (such as a second speeding ticket) be higher than that for a first infraction. But an increase in deterrence due to a literal increase in the probability or magnitude of sanctions is not what is meant by individual deterrence; individual deterrence is assumed to come about from the mere fact of having been sanctioned.

3. Suppose that a person believes the probability of being caught and sanctioned is either small, p_s, or high, p_h, where $p_s < p_h$. Further, he believes that the likelihood that p_s is the probability is q and that the likelihood that p_h is the probability is $1 - q$. Then the person's likelihood now of being caught is $qp_s + (1 - q)p_h$. If the person commits the act

that people often adjust their probabilistic beliefs upward as a result of being caught more than is justified by probability theory.[4] Hence, individual deterrence will come about on account of actual punishment influencing the perceived probability of future punishment, and this effect will be greater the more uncertainty parties have about the odds of punishment.

With regard to the perceived magnitude of sanctions, the situation is different. If individuals have imprecise knowledge of the magnitude of sanctions, then there is no systematic reason to believe that they will raise their estimates of the magnitude of future sanctions as a result of being punished. If an individual had underestimated the magnitude of sanctions and learns that they are higher, he will be more deterred in the future; but if he had overestimated the magnitude of sanctions and learns that they are lower, he will be less deterred in the future.[5] Unless individuals underestimate actual sanctions more than they overestimate them, there is no reason to believe that being punished and thereby learning the true sanction would lead those who are punished to be more deterred in the future.

Finally, it may be mentioned that individual deterrence might arise for a reason apart from an increase in the perceived likelihood or magnitude of sanctions. The experience of punishment might trigger feelings of guilt,

---

and is caught, he will revise upward the probability of p_h and downward the probability of p_s. In particular, his probability of p_h conditional on being caught will rise from $1 - q$ to $1 - q' = (1 - q)p_h/[qp_s + (1 - q)p_h]$ (which equals $(1 - q)/[qp_s/p_h + (1 - q)]) > (1 - q)$); and his probability of p_s conditional on being caught will fall from q to $q' = qp_s/[qp_s + (1 - q)p_h]$ (which equals $q/[q + (1 - q)p_h/p_s] < q$). Hence, his probability of being caught will rise to $q'p_s + (1 - q')p_h$.

4. See, for example, Tversky and Kahneman 1974.

5. Suppose that the person does not know the magnitude of the sanction; he believes it is either small, t_s, or large, t_h, where q is the likelihood of t_s and $1 - q$ that of t_h. Suppose for simplicity as well that the probability of sanctions is known and equals p. Then the expected sanction ex ante is $p[qt_s + (1 - q)t_h]$. Suppose also that if a person is punished, he will learn the true sanction, either t_s or t_h. Then, if he is punished and the true sanction is t_s, the expected sanction will be pt_s; and if he learns that the true sanction is t_h, the expected sanction will be pt_h. Hence, the expected sanction after a person is caught is $q(pt_s) + (1 - q)(pt_h)$. But this equals the expected sanction ex ante, $p(qt_s + (1 - q)t_h)$. Thus, there is no individual deterrence due to being sanctioned when there is uncertainty over the magnitude of the sanction.

a realization that one has failed to act responsibly, and thus cause some individuals not to repeat their violations (on such guilt, see sections 2 and 3 of Chapter 26).[6]

1.3 Significance of individual deterrence.   From the foregoing discussion, it appears that individual deterrence is potentially important only when there is substantial uncertainty about the likelihood of sanctions or when, for some reason, parties systematically underestimate the magnitude of sanctions or experience unanticipated feelings of guilt. Otherwise, when actors have reasonably good knowledge of the likelihood of sanctions, individual deterrence does not seem of much relevance. Notably, one suspects that for firms, individual deterrence often does not come about because firms tend to apprise themselves reasonably well of the risk of sanctions for violations of law. In all, it seems that individual deterrence is often of secondary significance.[7]

2.   MARGINAL DETERRENCE

2.1 Definition.   It has so far been assumed that an individual chooses whether or not to commit a single harmful act, so deterrence has been an either-or phenomenon. But an individual might choose which of several harmful acts to commit—for example, whether to release only a small amount of a pollutant into a river or a large amount, or whether only to kidnap a person or also to kill him. In such contexts, the threat of sanctions plays a role in addition to the usual one of deterring individuals from committing harmful acts altogether: For individuals who are not deterred altogether, expected sanctions still influence which harmful acts these individuals choose to commit. These individuals will have a reason to commit less harmful rather

6. To amplify, this explanation rests on the assumption that after being punished, the person will view the act in question differently, and will anticipate that if he commits it again, he will feel more guilty about it than he had anticipated he would beforehand; so an element of his calculus—namely, the internal sanction of guilt for committing the act—will change as a result of punishment.

7. There has been substantial study of individual deterrence from imprisonment, and the general finding is that imprisonment does not have much effect on criminality after release. See, for example, Lab and Whitehead 1988 and Wright 1994, 25–36.

than more harmful acts if expected sanctions rise with harm. Such deterrence of more harmful acts is sometimes referred to as *marginal deterrence.*[8]

2.2 Enforcement policy and marginal deterrence. Other things being equal, it is socially desirable that enforcement policy creates marginal deterrence, so that those who are not deterred from committing harmful acts have a motive to moderate the amount of harm that they cause. This suggests that sanctions should rise with the magnitude of harm (and, therefore, that all but the most harmful acts should be punished with less than maximal sanctions). But fostering marginal deterrence may conflict with achieving deterrence generally: For the schedule of sanctions to rise steeply enough to accomplish marginal deterrence, sanctions for less harmful acts may have to be so low that individuals are not appropriately deterred from committing these acts.[9]

Two additional observations should be made about marginal deterrence. First, marginal deterrence can be promoted by increasing the probability of detection as well as the magnitude of sanctions. For example, kidnappers can be more deterred from killing their victims if greater police resources are devoted to apprehending kidnappers who murder their victims than to apprehending those who do not. (Note, though, that in circumstances in which enforcement is general—see section 5—the probability of detection cannot be independently altered for acts that cause different degrees of harm.)

Second, marginal deterrence is naturally and automatically accomplished if the expected sanction equals harm for all levels of harm; for if a person is paying for harm done, whatever its level, he will have to pay more if he does greater harm. Thus, for instance, if a polluter's expected fine would rise from $100 to $500 if he dumps five gallons instead of one gallon of waste into a lake, where each gallon causes $100 of harm, his marginal incentive not to pollute will be correct.[10]

---

8. The notion of marginal deterrence was remarked upon in some of the earliest writing on enforcement; see Beccaria [1767] 1995, 21, and Bentham [1789] 1973, 171. The term "marginal deterrence" apparently was first used in Stigler 1970.

9. For formal treatments of marginal deterrence, see Friedman and Sjostrom 1993, Mookherjee and Png 1994, Shavell 1992, and Wilde 1992.

10. As emphasized in section 2.4 of Chapter 20, however, it often is desirable for society to tolerate some underdeterrence in order to save enforcement costs, in which case

3. COSTS OF IMPOSING MONETARY SANCTIONS

3.1 Principal conclusion: cost should be added to a sanction.
Although the imposition of monetary sanctions was presumed to be costless in Chapter 20, that is not in fact the case; legal proceedings, locating the assets of a person, and forcing him to disgorge assets all involve expenses.

The main difference that the presence of such costs makes to our conclusions is that the cost of imposing a sanction should be added to the sanction that would otherwise be optimal. The essential reason is that the effective social harm caused by a harmful act is the direct harm *plus* the indirect harm comprised of the expected cost of imposing sanctions. For example, suppose that a person's act causes direct harm of $100, that the person will suffer a sanction with certainty, and that the cost of imposing a sanction is $5. Then the situation is virtually the same as it would be if the person's act caused $105 of direct harm and there were no cost of imposing sanctions, for in either situation society bears $105 of costs. Hence, the optimal penalty for the harmful act that causes $100 of harm and costs $5 to penalize is $105, not $100; society wants the person to refrain from committing the harmful act unless the benefit to him is at least $105, rather than at least $100.

The conclusion that the cost of imposing the sanction should be added to the otherwise-optimal sanction also holds when there is only a probability of catching violators. Suppose that the likelihood of catching individuals who cause harm of $100 is 50 percent. Therefore, as explained in Chapter 20, the optimal sanction would be $200 in the absence of consideration of the cost of imposing sanctions. If, however, it costs $5 to impose the sanction, then the claim here is that the optimal penalty is $205. The reason is that, when a person commits the harmful act, the expected cost of imposing sanctions is 50% × $5 = $2.50, so that the expected sanction should be $102.50. And if the amount paid when the person is caught is $205, the expected sanction will be $102.50. Notice here that although we multiply the harm of $100 by a factor of two to reflect the chance of escaping

---

expected sanctions will be less than harm. Then consideration of marginal deterrence alters the structure of sanctions that would otherwise be best.

sanctions, the basic rule for calculation of the optimal penalty is simply to add the cost of imposing the sanction to its otherwise optimal level.[11]

3.2 Comments.   To the basic rule that the cost of imposing a sanction should be added to the otherwise optimal sanction, a number of qualifications and additions are worth making.

(a) *Marginal versus fixed costs of imposing sanctions.* It was taken for granted earlier that the costs of imposing sanctions are marginal in the sense that they are borne when and only when an additional person is sanctioned, but often there are also fixed costs of imposing sanctions, that is, costs that do not vary with the number of individuals sanctioned. For instance, the expense of a computer system for purposes of enforcement may have to be incurred regardless of the number of individuals sanctioned. Because these costs do not increase if another person is sanctioned, there should be no addition to the sanction on their account. (It would be wrong, for example, to "allocate" these costs, charging each person the average amount.) Such fixed costs might, however, have an effect on the sanctioning policy. The fixed costs might influence the optimal probability of catching individuals (the fixed costs might well rise with the probability of enforcement, even though they are not affected by the number of individuals sanctioned). If large enough, the fixed costs might make it undesirable to sanction parties at all, for then the fixed costs would be avoided. But the point here is that the fixed costs do not affect the optimal magnitude of the sanction given the probability of catching and sanctioning parties.

(b) *Costs increase with the magnitude of sanctions.* The cost of imposing sanctions may increase with the magnitude of the sanction because of greater resistance to sanctions as their amount increases. In this case, it can be shown that the optimal sanction should be the harm plus an amount somewhat lower than the actual cost of imposing sanctions, for this sanctioning policy reduces the incentive of parties to spend on resisting sanctions.

---

11. To be precise, we know from general arguments along the lines of Chapters 8 and 20 that (risk-neutral) parties will be induced to behave socially correctly provided that their expected liability equals the expected social harm due to their acts. If the direct harm due to an act is h, the probability of a monetary sanction is p, and the social cost of imposing the sanction is k, then the expected social harm due to the act is $h + pk$. If the sanction when the person is caught is, as claimed to be optimal, $(h/p) + k$, then the expected sanction is $p((h/p) + k) = h + pk$, so that incentives will indeed be correct.

(c) *Costs borne by sanctioned parties.* Some of the costs of imposing sanctions are borne by the sanctioned parties themselves, in their own time and effort and in hiring legal counsel. Such costs do not affect the optimal sanction, for the parties automatically take them into account as an implicit sanction that they bear.

(d) *The optimal probability.* The appeal of the use of low probabilities of sanctions increases when imposition of sanctions is costly, for then low probabilities mean a savings in costs of imposing sanctions as well as a savings in enforcement expenses.

(e) *The form of liability.* There is an underlying advantage of fault-based liability when there are costs of imposing sanctions. As the reader knows, under a perfectly functioning fault-based rule, all parties will be deterred from acting undesirably and thus no sanctions will ever be imposed, so no costs of imposing sanctions will be borne. Of course, as has also been discussed, various sources of error mean that parties will be found liable under the fault system, and thus the advantage of this form of liability in reducing costs of imposing sanctions is diminished.[12]

4. SELF-REPORTING OF VIOLATIONS

4.1 Definition.   In the consideration of law enforcement, the assumption to this point has been that individuals are sanctioned only if they are detected by an enforcement agent. But in reality parties sometimes disclose their own violations to enforcement authorities. For example, firms often report violations of environmental and safety regulations, individuals frequently notify police of their involvement in traffic accidents, and even criminals sometimes admit their illegal acts and turn themselves in to the police. Such behavior will be called *self-reporting.*

4.2 Inducement of self-reporting and its social desirability.   How, precisely, can individuals be led to report their own violations, and why might it be socially desirable for the structure of enforcement to encourage self-reporting? Self-reporting can be induced by the state's lowering the

---

12. The points made in this section are developed in Polinsky and Shavell 1992, although Becker 1968, 192, recognized that sanctions should reflect enforcement costs.

sanction for individuals who disclose their own infractions. Moreover, the reduction in the sanction for self-reporting can be made small enough that deterrence is only negligibly reduced—thus, self-reporting can be accomplished with only a slight effect on deterrence. To illustrate, consider a situation in which risk-neutral violators of a law face, say, a 50 percent probability of being caught and of having to pay a sanction of $100, so that the expected sanction is $50. If there is no reduction in the sanction for self-reporting, no one will rationally report on himself; for it would not make sense to pay $100 for sure rather than to bear an expected sanction of only $50 if one does not self-report. But suppose that if a person self-reports, he only has to pay a sanction of $49.99. Under this scheme, every violator will in principle decide to come forward since $49.99 is less than the expected sanction of $50 that he would otherwise face.[13] Note as well that because the penalty is $49.99 instead of $50 in expectation, the penalty for a violation has barely fallen, so that deterrence of the violation will be essentially the same under the self-reporting scheme as it would be in the absence of any reduction in the sanction for self-reporting.[14]

Why is self-reporting socially advantageous? One reason is that self-reporting tends to lower enforcement costs because, when it occurs, the enforcement authority does not have to identify and prove who the violator was. For instance, environmental enforcers do not need to spend as much effort trying to detect pollution and establishing its source if firms that pollute report that fact, and police do not have to continue their investigation of a robbery if the robber comes forward and confesses.[15]

13. More realistically, the self-reporting scheme would have to involve greater than a one-cent advantage for violators to be led to report on themselves.

14. To state the argument of this paragraph formally, let p be the probability of being caught for a violation and s the sanction then imposed, so that the expected sanction is ps if the person does not self-report. Let s' be the sanction if a violator self-reports, and set $s' = ps - \varepsilon$, where $\varepsilon > 0$ is arbitrarily small. A violator will therefore want to self-report because s' is less than ps, but the deterrent effect of the sanction will be (approximately) the same as if he did not self-report.

15. In some contexts, however, self-reporting will not save enforcement costs. For example, suppose that a police officer waits by the roadside to spot speeders. Then, were a driver to report that he had sped, this would not reduce policing costs, presuming that the officer still needs to be stationed at the roadside to watch for other speeders. Usually, though, there would be some cost savings as a result of self-reporting (for example, the police officer would not need to chase as many speeders).

Second, self-reporting reduces risk for potential violators, and thus is advantageous if potential violators are risk averse.[16] Drivers bear less risk because they know that if they cause an accident, they will be led to report this to the police and suffer a modest, certain sanction, rather than face the probability of a substantially higher sanction imposed if they are caught for having caused an accident (such as being caught for a hit-and-run driving accident).

Third, self-reporting sometimes allows harm to be mitigated because it may mean that harm is reported without undue delay. Early identification of a toxic leak will facilitate its containment and cleanup, and the reporting of a traffic accident may result in the victim receiving medical attention that otherwise would not have come until later.[17]

5. GENERAL ENFORCEMENT

5.1 Definition.   In many settings, law enforcement may be said to be *general* in the sense that several different types of violations may be detected by an enforcement agent's activity. For example, a police officer waiting at the roadside may notice a driver who litters as well as a driver who goes through a red light or who speeds, or a tax auditor may detect a variety of infractions when he examines a tax return. To investigate such situations, I will suppose for simplicity that a single probability of detection applies to all harmful acts, regardless of the magnitude of the harm.[18] The

16. The argument of note 14 that self-reporting can be induced without lowering deterrence applies with minor modification when individuals are risk averse. Let U be the utility of a person's wealth and y his initial wealth. Then, in the absence of self-reporting, the expected utility of a violator is $(1 - p)U(y) + pU(y - s)$. Let c be such that $U(y - c) = (1 - p)U(y) + pU(y - s)$. (That is, c is the so-called certainty equivalent of the sanction s.) Then any sanction for self-reporting of $c - \varepsilon$, where $\varepsilon > 0$ is small, will lead to self-reporting, with only a negligible effect on deterrence.

17. The basic theory of self-reporting in law enforcement is developed in Kaplow and Shavell 1994b, but see also Malik 1993 and Innes 1999.

18. It will be clear that the main point developed in this section does not depend on the assumption that the same probability of enforcement applies to all acts. The only requirement is that the probabilities for different acts are linked because they are all a function of the same enforcement expenditure.

contrasting assumption, made previously, is that law enforcement is *specific* to the harmful act, meaning that the state selects the probability of sanction independently for each type of harmful act.

5.2 Optimal enforcement policy.   The main point that I want to make is that in contexts in which enforcement is general, the strategy of employing very high sanctions accompanied by very low probabilities of detection, in order to save enforcement costs, is no longer as appealing as had been argued earlier (see especially section 2 of Chapter 20). Further, when enforcement is general, it is optimal to employ maximal sanctions only for the most harmful acts; otherwise, it is best to impose lower sanctions the less harmful the act.

To explain why a high sanction and low probability of enforcement does not always tend to be a desirable enforcement policy, consider the case of risk-neutral parties and deterrence of a relatively small infraction, such as double-parking. Before, it was explained that if the sanction for that infraction was less than maximal, it would typically be beneficial to raise the sanction and lower the probability of apprehension so as to save enforcement expenses while maintaining deterrence of the act. In the context of general enforcement, this scheme is no longer necessarily beneficial, however. If the likelihood of catching double-parking violations is lowered by reducing the number of police, the likelihood of detecting other, perhaps more serious violations, will *also* be lowered due to there being fewer police. And that may be socially undesirable, for it may not be possible to raise the sanctions for these other violations enough to maintain deterrence, because they may already be punished by very high sanctions. Indeed, if a more serious act (say intentionally running someone over with one's car) is already punished by the maximal sanction, deterrence of that act will be reduced if the likelihood of sanctions falls because there are fewer police on duty.

Let me now sketch more of the argument about optimal enforcement policy. Consider the class of very harmful violations. To deter them adequately, society needs a sufficiently high probability of apprehension, meaning a certain number of enforcement agents, even though it can and will impose the greatest sanctions for these serious violations. Now given that society uses the number of enforcement agents that it needs to control adequately the very harmful acts, these enforcement agents will, as a by-product, produce a sufficiently high probability of sanctions for less serious acts that they can be deterred with more moderate sanctions. As a consequence, the optimal sanctions for the less serious acts may well be in proportion to their harmfulness. For example, suppose that the probability of catching violations must be one-third in order to control properly the most serious offenses. Then the optimal sanction for a violation is three times the harm, so that, for the range of harms below one-third of an individual's wealth, the individual will be able to pay the optimal sanction, and in that range the sanction will be higher the higher is the harm.[19]

6. INSURANCE AGAINST SANCTIONS

The possibility of insurance against sanctions has not yet been mentioned, and I have assumed implicitly that parties do not carry such insurance. As a general matter, this is in keeping with reality: Insurers are not permitted to offer coverage against most criminal fines and some civil penalties.[20]

The chief issue of interest to us is whether the observed policy against sanction insurance is socially desirable from a theoretical perspective. The

---

19. The formal argument about optimal enforcement policy of this section may be described roughly as follows in the case of monetary sanctions (the case of nonmonetary sanctions is similar). Let $s(h)$ be the sanction given harm h. Then, for any general probability of detection p, the optimal sanction schedule is $s^*(h) = h/p$, provided that h/p does not exceed the level of wealth of individuals w, which is the maximal feasible sanction; if h/p is not feasible, the optimal sanction is w. In particular, this schedule is obviously optimal given p because it implies that the expected sanction equals harm, thereby inducing ideal behavior, whenever that is possible, and the expected sanction is as high as feasible otherwise. The question remains whether it would be desirable to lower p and raise sanctions to the maximal level for the low-harm acts for which $s^*(h)$ is less than maximal. The answer is that if p is reduced for the relatively low-harm acts (and the sanction raised for them), then p—being general—is also reduced for the high-harm acts for which the sanction is already maximal, resulting in lower deterrence of these acts. The decline in deterrence of high-harm acts may cause a greater social loss than the savings in enforcement costs from lowering p. The optimal lowering of p reflects a compromise between saving enforcement costs and diluting deterrence of relatively high-harm acts. This argument, and the distinction between general and specific deterrence, is introduced in Shavell 1991b; see also Mookherjee and Png 1992 for a closely related analysis.

20. See, for example, Jerry 1996, 471–477, Keeton 1971, 285–305, Keeton, Dobbs, et al. 1984, 586, and McNeely 1941.

relevant issues here are similar to those discussed in relation to the social desirability of liability insurance (see sections 4 and 7 of Chapter 11), so I can be brief. If sanction insurance is available, risk-averse parties who might violate the law will tend to wish to purchase the insurance. Thus, the availability of sanction insurance will reduce the bearing of risk by individuals who violate the law, which is in itself socially desirable. But the ownership of sanction insurance will tend to dilute the deterrent effect of sanctions, for violators will be less afraid of sanctions owing to the insurance. Whether allowing the purchase of liability insurance is socially undesirable or desirable depends on the importance of these two effects.

Some reflection about the context of law enforcement suggests that the social advantage of reducing risk for potential violators is outweighed by the dilution of deterrence factor, making prohibition of sanction insurance socially desirable. First, it seems that, for many acts that society seeks to control through public enforcement of law, the potential violator has a clear ability to commit or not to commit the act giving rise to sanctions. If this is the case, then a person can avoid risk by deciding to obey the law. He does not much need sanction insurance to avoid the risk of penalty for beating someone up, committing fraud, or intentionally cheating on his taxes.[21]

Second, in the context of law enforcement, we have emphasized that it is generally desirable for society to conserve enforcement expenses by maintaining a relatively low probability of sanctions, and to countenance underenforcement as a consequence.[22] The fact that, in reality, there is substantial underdeterrence of many undesirable acts is consistent with this point. Given that there is a problem of underdeterrence because of society's desire to save enforcement expenses, it would only compound the problem of underdeterrence to allow individuals to obtain sanction insurance. To put the point differently, were we to allow individuals to carry sanction insurance, society would have to increase its expenditure on enforcement

21. In contrast, in the typical tort setting, a person may find himself liable through some sort of accident. As discussed in sections 1 and 2 of Chapter 10, individuals may be found negligent by mistake, and may not have complete control over their behavior. Thus, the value of liability insurance in reducing risk in the tort context seems, as a general matter, much greater than in the law enforcement context.

22. See section 2 of Chapter 20.

in order to achieve the level of deterrence that we enjoy when the insurance is forbidden.[23]

The foregoing is not meant to deny the possibility that sanction insurance may be socially desirable in some situations. Suppose that individuals are able to control only probabilistically behavior that may result in sanctions (say they cannot necessarily prevent oil from leaking from a boat into a lake), and there is not a real problem of underdeterrence because the magnitude of harm is not great in relation to individuals' assets and the likelihood of detection is substantial (enforcement agents can easily ascertain when spills occur). Then the value of insurance in reducing risk may be substantial, and the ownership of insurance will not be problematic for incentives (no more so than in the usual tort context). In such circumstances, insurance against sanctions may be desirable.

7. SANCTIONS FOR REPEAT OFFENDERS

In practice, the law often sanctions repeat offenders more severely than first-time offenders. For example, under the U.S. Sentencing Commission's guidelines for punishment of federal crimes, both imprisonment terms and criminal fines are enhanced if a defendant has a prior record; civil monetary penalties also sometimes depend on whether the defendant has a record of prior offenses.[24] I will attempt to explain here why such policies may be socially desirable.

---

23. Again, the contrast with the tort setting is instructive. Society does not face a general problem of underdeterrence in the tort context, at least not one comparable to that in the domain of public enforcement, for harmful events in the area of tort, such as car accidents, will tend to result in suit or settlement if injurers are liable. Hence, if liability insurance reduces somewhat the incentive to take proper care, this does not matter as much in the tort area as it does in the public enforcement area. Moreover, if insurers can observe the level of care, incentives will be appropriate in the usual tort situation. In the context of enforcement, however, that is not necessarily so; if insurers can observe whether individuals violate the law, that will not lead individuals to refrain from violations if the expected sanction is less than the harm.

24. See U.S. Sentencing Commission (1995, sect. 4A1.1, chap. 5 part A, and sect. 5E1.2). Regarding civil penalties, see, for example, 8 *U.S. Code*, sect. 1324a(e)(4)–(5)(1997), imposing minimum fines of $250 for a first offense, $2,000 for a second offense,

Note first that sanctioning repeat offenders more severely cannot be socially advantageous if deterrence always induces ideal behavior. If the sanction for polluting and causing a $1,000 harm is $1,000, then any person who pollutes and pays $1,000 is a person whose gain from polluting (say the savings from not installing pollution control equipment) must have exceeded $1,000. Social welfare therefore is higher as a result of his polluting. If such an individual polluted and was sanctioned in the past, that only means that it was socially desirable for him to have polluted previously. Raising the sanction because of his having a record of sanctions would overdeter him now; it would not be socially desirable to raise sanctions on account of past infractions.

Accordingly, only if deterrence is inadequate is it possibly desirable to make sanctions depend on offense history in order to increase deterrence. Deterrence often will be inadequate because, as I have stressed, it will usually be worthwhile for the state to tolerate some underdeterrence in order to reduce enforcement expenses.

If there is underdeterrence, making sanctions depend on offense history may be beneficial for two reasons. First, the use of offense history may create an additional incentive not to violate the law: When detection of a violation implies not only an immediate sanction, but also a higher sanction for a future violation, an individual will be deterred more from committing a violation presently.[25] Second, making sanctions depend on offense history allows society to take advantage of implicit information about the dangerousness of individuals and the need to deter them. Individuals with offense histories may well be more likely than average to commit future violations,

---

and $3,000 for subsequent offenses concerning hiring, recruiting, and referral behavior under the Immigration Reform and Control Act; and see 29 *U.S. Code*, sect. 666(a)–(c) (1997), stating that the maximum fine is $7,000 for certain violations of the Occupational Safety and Health Act that are not repeated, but that the maximum fine rises to $70,000 if the violations are repeated.

25. There is a subtlety in demonstrating the optimality of punishing repeat offenses more severely. Namely, if there is a problem of underdeterrence, one might wonder why it would not be optimal to raise the sanction for a first offense, rather than to enhance deterrence by punishing repeat offenses more severely. See Polinsky and Shavell 1998a on the possible optimality of making sanctions depend on offense history because of the additional deterrence that such a policy creates.

which might make it desirable for purposes of deterrence to impose higher sanctions on them.[26]

There is also an obvious incapacitation-based reason for making sanctions depend on offense history. Repeat offenders are more likely to have higher propensities to commit violations in the future and thus are more likely to be worth incapacitating by imprisonment.

26. Note that this reason for making sanctions depend on offense history is different from the first reason: This second reason involves the assumption that offenders are different from one another and that the optimal sanction for some offenders is higher than for others; the first reason applies even if individuals are identical. On the second, information-based, reason for making sanctions depend on offense history, see Chu, Hu, and Huang 2000, Polinsky and Rubinfeld 1991, and Rubinstein 1979.

23 ||| INCAPACITATION, REHABILITATION, AND RETRIBUTION

In this chapter, I discuss briefly several functions of sanctions apart from deterrence, namely, incapacitation, rehabilitation, and retribution.

1. INCAPACITATION

1.1 Definition of incapacitation. The most familiar form of incapacitation is imprisonment, which prevents individuals from engaging in undesirable acts in free society by removing them from it. More generally, incapacitation can be defined to be prevention of a class of undesirable acts by barring a party from engaging in an activity that would allow the party to commit the acts. For example, a person could be prevented from causing accidents when driving by voiding his driver's license, or a restaurant could be prevented from causing harm from serving spoiled food by being forced to close.

1.2 Incapacitation distinguished from deterrence. Preventing a party from engaging in an activity in which he could do harm is quite different from deterrence, that is, dissuading the party from committing an undesirable act through the threat to impose sanctions if he commits it. Deterrence works only when the party knows about and considers the possibility of sanctions, and only when the sanctions can actually be applied. (If the person is judgment proof and the sanction is monetary, the sanction cannot be applied; if the person is old or dying of a disease, the imprisonment term cannot be long.) Incapacitation functions independently of these factors.

1.3 Basic model of enforcement and incapacitation.   To focus on incapacitation, let us assume that individuals cannot be deterred and, initially, that each individual has an unchanging propensity to commit harmful acts (measured by the expected harm) per time period.[1] Let us further suppose that society incurs expenses in raising the probability of apprehending individuals who do harm and who will be considered for incapacitation, and that society bears certain costs per period of incapacitation.

Under these assumptions, what is the optimal length of incapacitation of a person who does harm and who has been apprehended? The answer is simply that if the person's propensity to do harm each period exceeds the cost of incapacitation per period, he should be incapacitated each period, that is, forever; otherwise, he should not be incapacitated at all.

The optimal probability of apprehension will reflect the tradeoff between the cost of raising this probability and the benefit in terms of reduced harms through incapacitating more individuals.

1.4 Comments.   (a) *Assumption that propensity to do harm is constant over time.* If the propensity of an individual to do harm diminishes over time, then it becomes optimal to end incapacitation as soon as the propensity to do harm per period falls below the per period cost of incapacitation. This is a significant point, because the evidence is that the propensity to commit many types of crimes declines with age.[2]

---

1. For a formal model of incapacitation, see Shavell 1987b; for theoretically oriented discussions of incapacitation, see, for example, Blumstein 1983 and Packer 1968, 48–53. For extensive and still relevant critical discussion of the literature on incapacitation, see Blumstein, Cohen, and Nagin 1978, and for a recent review and assessment, see Spelman 2000.

2. See, for example, Greenberg 1983, Wilson and Herrnstein 1985, 126–147, and U.S. Department of Justice 2001b, 362–363.

(b) *Optimal sanction unrelated to probability of imposition.* It should be noted that the optimal length of incapacitation depends only on the propensity of individuals to do harm, not on the likelihood with which they are apprehended. In particular, from the standpoint of incapacitation, there is no reason to impose a higher sanction if the probability of detection is low. This contrasts with the situation under deterrence, where, as was emphasized in the previous three chapters, lower probabilities of apprehension call for higher sanctions.

(c) *Relevance of the commission of a harmful act to the imposition of sanctions.* The optimal sanction depends only on the propensity to do harm, that is, the estimated future dangerousness of a person. There is, then, no intrinsic reason to require that a person actually have committed an undesirable act or that he actually have done harm for him to be incapacitated. The commission of a harmful act does often constitute evidence about the propensity to do harm, however, and for that reason a requirement of commission of a harmful act might be socially rational to impose for incapacitation. (In addition, departing from the model, the danger of state abuse of its ability to sanction would be lessened, one supposes, if there is a requirement that a party actually have committed a harmful act for him to be penalized.) According to the theory of deterrence, note, the requirement that there be a harmful act for there to be punishment is fundamental; deterrence can work only if a person knows that he will be punished if, but only if, he commits a harmful act.

(d) *Incapacitation and deterrence.* Suppose that individuals can be deterred as well as incapacitated. Specifically, consider again the model examined in the previous chapters on deterrence, but now assume that sanctions incapacitate as well as deter. Then, having two useful functions, sanctions will be optimal to employ more often than would otherwise be the case. Thus, where imprisonment would not be justified by its ability to deter, imprisonment might be warranted when account is taken also of its value in incapacitation. Similarly, where imprisonment would not be justified by its ability to incapacitate (suppose an embezzler of funds is discovered after he has retired and will have no future opportunity to embezzle), consideration of deterrence might call for imprisonment (potential embezzlers might be discouraged from acting due to the prospect of sanctions).

(e) *Optimal probability of incapacitation and optimal sanctions for deterrence.* To accomplish a desirable degree of incapacitation, the probability of sanctions must not be too low. This in turn may imply that the magnitude of sanctions needed for purposes of deterrence should not be too high. Hence, among other things, the argument (see section 2.5 of Chapter 21) for very low probabilities of apprehension and for maximal sanctions might not apply. For instance, to achieve an appropriate degree of incapacitation of those who rob, it might be necessary to ensure that at least, say, 20 percent of robbers are apprehended. This might mean that the optimal sanction for deterrence purposes should be significantly lower than the maximum possible imprisonment term.

1.5 Actual importance of imprisonment as a form of incapacitation. The number of people who are presently imprisoned in the United States is 1.9 million, representing about 3 percent of the adult population, and the percentage of the population who will be incarcerated at some time during their lives is approximately 5 percent.[3] The annual cost of imprisonment is on the order of $47 billion, or about $24,000 per incarcerated person.[4] The annual incapacitative benefit of imprisonment—its direct effect in reducing crime by keeping those who would otherwise commit crimes imprisoned—has been calculated by some analysts to be in the neighborhood of 20 percent of the present level of crime.[5] The following calculation is also informative. If one estimates that the average prisoner would have committed ten crimes per year were he not incarcerated, then the incapacitative benefit is that in the absence of incarceration, crimes would increase by about 19 million annually, or by about 90 percent.[6] Even

3. See U.S. Department of Justice 2001b, 488, presenting an estimate of 1.933 million individuals for the year 2000. For an estimate of the fraction of the population who will be in prison at some time in their lives, see Bonczar and Beck 1997.

4. Annual expenditures in 1997 were $43.511 billion; see U.S. Department of Justice 2001b, 3. In terms of the consumer price index in 2000, the expenditures equal $46.656 billion; see *Statistical Abstract of the United States, 2001,* 451. Since there were 1.933 million persons imprisoned in 2000, the annual cost per person is $24,137.

5. See Spelman 1994, 227, and the studies cited by Wright 1994, 116–117.

6. The estimate of 10 crimes per year is actually somewhat conservative; see the discussion of literature on incapacitation in Wright 1994, 114–118. See also, for example, DiIulio and Piehl 1991, who find that the average annual number of violations per prisoner would be 141 and that the median would be 12. Using the estimate of 10 crimes per person per year and the fact that there were 1.933 million persons imprisoned in 2000, it follows that had these prisoners been free, they would have committed 19.333 million crimes annually.

if the incapacitative benefit is only 20 percent of the present level of crime, it would save society at least $100 billion, outweighing the $47 billion cost of imprisonment.[7] Accordingly, we can see that incapacitation is a very important and possibly justified function of imprisonment in this country.

2. REHABILITATION

2.1 Definition of rehabilitation. By rehabilitation is meant an induced reduction in a person's propensity to commit undesirable acts. This change may come about through direct effort of the state, notably through educational programs (such as those provided in prison) or as a by-product of imposition of sanctions, when a person reflects on his behavior and decides to behave in a socially more responsible manner in the future.

2.2 Basic model of enforcement and rehabilitation. Assume that the sole function of sanctions is to rehabilitate. Then it is optimal to impose sanctions if and only if the rehabilitative benefit—reduced future harm—exceeds the cost of imposing the rehabilitative sanction. Thus, it is optimal for a person caught for drunk driving to be put in a class on driver responsibility if and only if the benefit, in terms of a reduction in expected accident losses, exceeds the cost of the class. The optimal probability of apprehending individuals who may be subject to sanctions is governed by the rehabilitative benefits that this brings about, assuming optimal imposition of rehabilitative sanctions.

2.3 Comments. (a) *Characteristics of optimal rehabilitative sanctions are similar to those of optimal incapacitative sanctions.* The optimal rehabilitative sanction, like the optimal incapacitative sanction, does not depend on

---

The actual number of crimes committed in 1999 was about 21.84 million; see *Statistical Abstract of the United States, 2001,* 182, so that an increase of 19.333 million crimes would represent an 88.5 percent increase in the overall level of crime.

7. Anderson 1999, 625, estimates the annual cost of crime-related injury and death to be about $574.395 billion, and 20 percent of this amount is over $100 billion. This cost is an incomplete measure of the social cost of crime, for it does not take into account, among other factors, the efforts made to avoid being a victim of crime and the efforts made to undertake crime.

the probability of apprehension. In addition, the actual commission of a harmful act is not intrinsically important to the rehabilitative sanction; in principle it would be desirable to rehabilitate any person who is known to need rehabilitation and can be improved at sufficiently low cost. For instance, someone who is known to get drunk and to be irresponsible, and thus to be likely to drive when drunk, might profit from a class on driver responsibility even if he has not committed any driving infraction. As stated earlier, however, the commission of a harmful act (like drunk driving) as a prerequisite for punishment may serve a valuable informational purpose and make governmental abuse of its authority less likely.

(b) *Rehabilitation and incapacitation.* If sanctions both rehabilitate and incapacitate, then the optimal length of sanction will, of course, reflect these functions. A notable implication is that a person whom society chooses to incapacitate would tend to receive a shorter sanction as a consequence of rehabilitation than incapacitation alone would call for.[8] This is because rehabilitation will hasten the time by which the person becomes sufficiently less dangerous that his release is justified.

(c) *Rehabilitation and deterrence.* To some degree, rehabilitation may dilute deterrence. If a person believes that he will change in positive ways—for instance, that he will learn valuable skills in prison—the sting of the sanction may be lessened. This effect can be counteracted, but at a cost, by increasing the length of the sanction.

2.4 Actual importance of rehabilitation.   Today, there is much skepticism about rehabilitation because there is substantial recidivism and little evidence supporting the notion that, in the United States anyway, those who go to prison are less dangerous when released (except due to the effect of age on criminality).[9] Indeed, it is sometimes asserted that the opposite happens in today's prisons, that people who are in prison learn bad habits and ways of criminal life, so that they will do more harm, rather than less, as a result of

8. There is, in principle, a possibility that rehabilitation would lengthen the stay of a person who would suffer a positive incapacitative sanction. It could be that, although the date at which he would become less dangerous than it costs to incapacitate comes earlier, it would still be beneficial to incarcerate him longer in order to further reduce his harmfulness.

9. See, for example, Andenaes 1975, 339, Cook 1977, 165–166, Packer 1968, 53–58, Schwartz 1983, and Wright 1994, 25–36.

imprisonment. One supposes that the failure of rehabilitation is more a function of present conditions than of intrinsic factors, however, and that rehabilitation might be of substantial importance in the future.

3. RETRIBUTION

3.1 Definition of retribution. The retributive motive is the desire of individuals to see wrongdoers punished. That is, individuals may derive utility from the knowledge that wrongdoers are punished. Such utility may depend on the proportionality of the punishment to the wrongdoing and may be greater the more serious the act of the wrongdoer.[10] Additionally, retributive utility may be more significant for victims of wrongdoing, or for those associated with them, than for the population at large.

3.2 Comments on the retributive desire. (a) *Criticism of the desire.* Some commentators suggest that retributive satisfaction should not be credited in the social calculus because the satisfaction is associated with the suffering of another. This view, that certain types of satisfaction should not be counted in social welfare, is problematic and leads to anomalies, as will be generally discussed later.[11]

(b) *Sociobiological origin.* It has been observed that the desire for retribution serves a helpful sociobiological purpose. The presence of the desire means that those who are attacked will be likely to fight back. This discour-

10. A natural formalization of retributive utility is that it is a function $r(s,w)$ where s is the sanction, w is the degree of wrongdoing, and r is single-peaked in s and maximized at $s(w)$. Here $s(w)$ is the appropriate sanction given w, and $s(w)$ is increasing in w.

11. It is explained in section 5.5 of Chapter 26 that any measure of social welfare that is not based on utilities of individuals sometimes will reduce the well-being of *all* individuals. Therefore, that is true of a measure of social welfare that excludes certain sources of utility. A mundane example of this possibility is that all individuals might sometimes play practical jokes on others, sometimes themselves be the butt of practical jokes, and derive more utility from playing these jokes and enjoying them when others play them than they suffer disutility as victims of the jokes. Therefore, all individuals might prefer a world in which practical jokes are permitted than one in which they are barred. If, however, utility that is derived from the displeasure of others (the victims of jokes) is not credited in the social calculus, practical jokes might be disallowed, making all worse off.

ages attack, which is a good thing because it means that people will not need to devote as much time to protecting what they have nor be as likely to become involved in destructive and wasteful conflict. Hence, one would predict that the retributive urge, at least if not too strong (in which case even slights would trigger conflict), would win out in evolutionary competition (including in animals).[12]

(c) *Effect on the probability of sanctions.* The retributive urge also serves a purpose in present day society, which is to give people a motive to ward off transgression and thus to deter it, as well as to report on transgressors to social authorities so that they can be punished. Pure self-interest would often lead individuals not to respond directly, nor would it usually lead individuals to report transgressors to enforcement agents, because that takes effort and may invite retaliation. Hence, the retributive urge may be a significant factor in maintaining the probability of apprehension at its level; in the absence of the desire for retribution, many more enforcement agents would be needed to maintain the probability of apprehension.[13]

3.3 Basic model of enforcement and retribution.   If the only purpose of punishment were retribution, the optimal magnitude of sanction would be that which maximized the pleasure from satisfying the retributive desire minus the costs of imposing punishment. The optimal probability of apprehension would reflect this retributive gain net of costs as the benefit from capturing a person.

3.4 Comments.   (a) *Retribution and deterrence.* As observed earlier, retribution enhances enforcement by increasing the motive of individuals to report what they know to social authorities, so it generally contributes to enforcement. With regard to the magnitude of sanctions, however, the effect of retribution is unclear. On one hand, the optimal sanction from the perspective of deterrence will often exceed that demanded by the retributive goal: The low probability of sanctions, which is best from the viewpoint of deterrence because it saves enforcement costs, raises the sanction

---

12. On the biological origins of retribution, see, for example, Daly and Wilson 1988, chaps. 10, 11, Frank 1988, chaps. 3, 4, Hirshleifer 1978, 334, Hirshleifer 1987, and Trivers 1971, 49.

13. This point is stressed by Posner 1980.

needed to deter, yet the desire for retribution is not affected by the low probability of sanctions. (From the deterrence perspective, for example, we may want to impose a ten-year prison sentence on a car thief because the odds of finding him are quite low, but the demand for retribution against him may well limit the sentence to a lesser level.) On the other hand, the retributive desire could exceed the proper punishment from the deterrence perspective, as where a person could not have been deterred (suppose a person killed another when in a rage).[14]

(b) *Retribution and incapacitation.* The optimal sanction from the perspective of incapacitation does not seem to be related in a clear way to what is demanded by retribution. The optimal incapacitative sanction would be lower than that needed to satisfy retributive desires if the wrongdoer would be unlikely to do harm in the future (suppose a person murders another in unique circumstances). Conversely, the optimal incapacitative sanction would be higher than that appropriate for retribution if a person did little harm yet would be likely to do great harm in the future.

(c) *Retribution and rehabilitation.* The goal of rehabilitation appears to conflict with that of retribution, supposing that rehabilitation reduces the disutility associated with punishment. As noted earlier, however, this problem can be mitigated at a social cost by increasing the magnitude of the sanction.

14. On enforcement policy in the light of retribution and deterrence, see Polinsky and Shavell 2000b.

24 ||| CRIMINAL LAW

Most legal systems designate an area of law as *criminal,* that is, label certain acts as criminal and punish them in ways that are in some respects unique. This is the subject of the present chapter, which draws on Chapters 20–23.

1. DESCRIPTION OF CRIMINAL LAW

1.1 Domain of criminal law. Although there is no simple, overarching definition of criminal acts, the following categories of criminal acts will help to describe the domain of criminal law.

(a) *Acts that are intended to do substantial harm.* The major category of criminal acts are those in which an individual intends to do significant harm. For example, murder, rape, robbery, counterfeiting, and treason are considered criminal acts. Notice that ordinarily the person carrying out these criminal acts wants harm to occur: The object of the murderer is usually to kill his victim, that of the rapist to rape, and that of the robber to take what is not his.[1] If harm does not actually come about, the act is normally still treated as criminal; thus, if a person attempts murder or rape or robbery but does not succeed, his act is still criminal. If harm is not intended, then even if it comes about as a result of an act, the act is not usually considered criminal. Thus, if a person shoots his gun while hunting and happens to hit another hunter whom he had no reason to notice, his act would not be criminal, or if he takes a suitcase that is someone else's but that he thought was his own, this will not be theft, because he did not intend to take something that was not his. Also, if only a small harm is intended, the act will not usually be considered criminal. Thus, if a person intentionally disturbs another person by, say, speaking loudly, his act will not be criminal even though his purpose may have been to do harm.[2]

(b) *Acts that are concealed, even if substantial harm was not intended.* Another category of act that is often considered criminal is an act that is harmful, or potentially harmful, and for which the actor has attempted to conceal or evade his responsibility. For instance, if a person flees the scene of a car accident, his act will usually be treated as criminal, or if a firm covers up the violation of a safety regulation, its act will often be characterized as criminal. This is a separate category of criminal act from that described in the previous paragraph, because the act that is evaded does not have to be intentional, to have created substantial risk, or to have caused substantial harm for criminal liability to result.

(c) *Certain other acts.* In addition, there are diverse, particular acts that are categorized as criminal, even if substantial harm is not intended and even if concealment or evasion are not necessarily an issue. Falling into this category of criminal acts are, for example, a restaurant serving liquor to minors, and speeding.

---

1. Intent will be more carefully defined later, where the definition will be expanded to include acting in a way that is felt to be extremely likely to cause harm, even if the harm is not itself desired.

2. A minor qualification to this paragraph is that if a person is forced to act in one of several harmful ways, and chooses the least harmful, then he will not be held criminally liable, even though his act is intended to do substantial harm. See section 4.1 for further discussion of this point.

1.2 Criminal sanctions. When an act is criminal, the sanctions that apply may include imprisonment, various other nonmonetary sanctions, fines, and social sanctions associated with being labeled a criminal.

(a) *Imprisonment and other constraints on freedom.* Imprisonment is a sanction that is unique to criminal law, as are certain other constraints on freedom, such as confinement to one's home enforced by electronic monitoring, probation, or required community service.[3] Such sanctions are typically imposed for acts in the central area of crime (a), and sometimes for acts in the second category (b), but usually not for crimes in the third category (c).

(b) *Other nonmonetary punishments.* In addition to constraints on freedom there are such sanctions as whipping, amputation of limbs, banishment, and the death penalty. Today, use of some of these punishments is restricted or nonexistent in many Western countries, but in the past they have been important, and are employed contemporaneously in many areas of the world to one degree or another, mainly for acts in the major area of crime.[4] An additional form of nonmonetary sanction is punishment primarily intended to shame or humiliate; historical examples include the pillory, and today we see such practices as publishing the name of an offender in a newspaper or requiring him to post a sign on his property or a bumper sticker on his automobile.[5]

(c) *Monetary penalties.* Criminal acts may also result in criminal fines. Fines are sometimes imposed for acts in the core area of crime, but are not usually the only sanction for those acts; whereas they may be the only sanction for acts in the second category (b), and they are often the only sanction for acts in the third category (c). Criminal fines differ from civil sanctions, such as tort judgments and civil penalties, in two respects that usually make them more effective. First, parties generally cannot purchase liability insurance against criminal fines, although they can and usually do purchase cov-

---

3. There is, however, the possibility of civil institutionalization of people who are found to be insane. This is similar to imprisonment in that the consequence of certain acts or behavior is a state-enforced restraint on conduct.

4. For example, in certain countries governed by Islamic law, whipping or stoning may occur as punishment for unlawful sexual intercourse, and limbs may be amputated as punishment for theft. See Forte 1983.

5. On the pillory, see Beattie 1986, 464–468, and on humiliations today, see, for example, Hoffman 1997.

erage against civil sanctions.[6] Second, parties cannot deduct criminal fines as business expenses and thereby reduce their income taxes on that account.[7]

(d) *Labeling and reputational penalties.* When an individual is convicted of a criminal offense, he is often said to be labeled as a criminal. Sometimes, however, a convicted criminal may conceal his past, and it may be difficult for others to determine what it was. Efforts to label individuals with criminal records are occasionally made. Historically, labeling was accomplished, among other ways, by branding individuals.[8] The effects of labeling include shame and humiliation as well as an implicit monetary sanction to the extent that labeling compromises a person's earning ability.[9]

2. EXPLANATION FOR CRIMINAL LAW

2.1 Question to be addressed. Having described criminal law, the question arises, why does it exist? That is, why should society want to designate a certain set of acts as falling under a special heading, that of criminal law, and then use imprisonment and other sanctions as punishments for commission of these acts?

2.2 Answer in outline. The answer is at root simple: *Society requires criminal law in order to constrain certain behavior that could not otherwise adequately be controlled.* Specifically, I will suggest that acts in the core area

---

6. See, for example, Jerry 1996, 400–413.

7. Internal Revenue Code, sect. 162(f).

8. See, for example, Baker 2002, 515.

9. It is occasionally observed that the reputational effect of being labeled a criminal becomes diluted as the class of criminal acts broadens to include acts that are not viewed as especially bad. Note that this view rests on the assumption that a person who is labeled a criminal is regarded as having committed some act, perhaps the average act, in the general category of criminal acts. If, by contrast, the specific nature of a criminal's violation becomes known, whether it is rape or income tax evasion, for example, his reputational loss would be determined by what he did, and the breadth of the class of criminal acts would not dull the reputational loss associated with committing this or that criminal act.

of crime—acts intended to do substantial harm, category (a)—cannot be appropriately discouraged by the threat of monetary sanctions alone, so that the additional sanction of imprisonment (and/or other severe punishments) becomes socially desirable as a deterrent, as well as a means of preventing the future commission of undesirable acts by means of incapacitation. I will attempt to explain along similar lines that acts in the other two areas of crime—concealed acts, category (b), and certain additional acts, category (c)—need to be made criminal in order to deter them properly. At the end of this section, I will comment on the relationship of this thesis to the claim that criminal law is intended to punish acts with especially bad moral qualities.

2.3 Acts in the major category of crime would be inadequately deterred by monetary sanctions alone.   The hypothesis under examination is that acts in the major category of crime—namely, rape, murder, theft, robbery, and other acts traditionally punished by imprisonment—would be inadequately deterred if they were punished solely with monetary sanctions. To this end, consider the factors noted in section 3.2 of Chapter 21 that bear on the need for nonmonetary sanctions.

(a) *Level of assets.* Statistics show that individuals who commit crimes tend to have low wealth.[10] This association is not unexpected: Those with little wealth have greater reason to commit economically motivated crimes such as theft than do others, and low wealth is correlated with general characteristics that are linked to criminality, including substandard education, drug and alcohol abuse, and social alienation. To the extent that those who tend to commit crimes have low levels of wealth, the use of monetary sanctions alone would not be likely to provide an effective deterrent against crime because violators would not be able to pay the sanctions needed to accomplish deterrence.

(b) *Probability of escaping sanctions.* The probability of escaping sanctions for crimes is substantial; according to recent data, for example, the rate of incarceration for reported larceny-theft is in the neighborhood of

---

10. Notably, the inmate population is composed of people who have very little income prior to arrest. For example, U.S. Department of Justice 1988, 35, reports that "the average inmate was at the poverty level before entering jail."

just 8 percent, that for reported rape about 25 percent, and even that for murder, only approximately 42 percent.[11] These acts are often planned and executed by individuals in waysthat help them avoid identification or apprehension and thus escapesanctions.[12] To the degree that those who commit crimes can escape punishment, the monetary sanctions necessary to deter are raised, and along with them the likelihood that these sanctions would exceed violators' wealth and not successfully deter them.

(c) *Level of private benefits.* Those who steal significant amounts, who murder, and who rape, are committing acts for which the private benefits are substantial. This factor raises the monetary sanction needed to deter and reduces the ability to deter with monetary sanctions alone.[13]

(d) *Expected harmfulness of acts.* The expected harm caused by acts in the core area of crime appears to be significant. First, the actual magnitude of harm associated with the acts in question tends to be high (certainly this is true when a person is murdered or raped, for example). Second, the likelihood of harm from these acts is generally high.[14] This is both apparent as a matter of observation about the criminal acts (when a person sets out

11. For larceny-theft, the fraction of reported cases leading to arrest and prosecution is about 19 percent, of which about 71 percent result in convictions and about 63 percent result in incarceration, implying that the frequency of incarceration is about 8 percent; see U.S. Department of Justice 2001b, 383, 458, 463. The corresponding statistics for rape are 49 percent, 63 percent, and 79 percent, and for murder 69 percent, 64 percent, and 95 percent; see the same source and pages. Note that because most crimes (other than, probably, murder) are underreported, the true rates of incarceration for larceny-theft and rape must really be lower than the numbers calculated here. For instance, the likelihood that rape is not reported is estimated to be about 48 percent; see U.S. Department of Justice 2001b, 189, 383. On this basis, the likelihood of incarceration for rape would be not 25 percent but roughly 13 percent.

12. In contrast, the typical tort arising from an accident occurs (as the word "accident" suggests) at an unpredictable time and place, and thus only by chance can the responsible party avoid being identified.

13. The situation is different in the context of the typical tort, in which the private benefit that an actor usually obtains from acting improperly is only avoidance of the cost of a precaution, like saving the effort of removing oily rags that could cause a fire. It requires a much smaller penalty to induce a person to give up this sort of gain than it does to induce a person to give up the likely gains from most crimes.

14. Further, acts are sometimes made criminal just because they produce an extremely high likelihood of harm (even though harm is not desired by the actor). Suppose, for instance, that a person knowingly leaves a live wire exposed where children are playing and

to rob or to murder, he is often going to succeed), and it is also something that follows from the frequently intentional character of the criminal acts, that they are such that the person is usually trying to cause harm. If, for these two reasons, the expected harm caused by criminal acts in the core area is high, the acts are more important to deter than others.[15] Thus, society's willingness to bear the cost of employing imprisonment as a sanction in order to enhance deterrence should be greater for acts in the core area of crime than for other acts.

(e) *Illustration: murder.* Consider the crime of murder and ask whether, in view of what has just been said, murder could be controlled tolerably well through the use of money sanctions alone. It appears not. For example, even the median level of wealth of individuals below age thirty-five is less than $9,000,[16] so that the median expected monetary sanction for individuals in this cohort would be about 42% × $9,000 or $3,780—see paragraph (b). Given only this as the penalty, one supposes that the murder rate would mushroom; the number of situations in which the value of murder to a potential murderer would exceed $3,780 is probably great. Because of the substantial social harm due to a much higher murder rate, it thus seems that if society were ever to employ only monetary sanctions to control murder, society would quickly realize that it would be rational to incur the costs of imprisonment in order to reduce the murder rate to a more acceptable level.

2.4 Use of imprisonment for acts in the major category of crime increases deterrence. The use of imprisonment increases deterrence of the major criminal acts from the inadequate level that would result from the threat of monetary sanctions alone. A person whose assets are too low to be deterred from theft, murder, or treason may well be deterred by the

---

a child is electrocuted; this might constitute manslaughter owing to criminal negligence. See, for example, LaFave 2000, 246–257, 721–728.

15. The expected harm associated with negligent acts that result in torts seems to be lower than that caused by criminal acts. The magnitude of the harm caused by negligence may, of course, be as high as that caused by a criminal act—for instance, a tort may result in a person's death. But the likelihood of harm resulting from negligent acts appears to be much less than that from criminal acts (compare the likelihood of death from negligent driving to the likelihood of death from attempted murder by shooting at someone).

16. See *Statistical Abstract of the United States, 2001,* 447, which gives $9,000 as the median net worth of families headed by people younger than age 35.

prospect of imprisonment. This increased deterrence may well justify the use of imprisonment, despite the costs associated with its imposition.

2.5 Although imprisonment sometimes fails to deter acts in the major category of crime, imprisonment incapacitates individuals.   It is often true that even use of imprisonment is not enough to deter people from committing acts in the core area of crime; levels of crime are distinctly positive, and at some times in some places have been quite high.[17] This is not surprising. The likelihood of capture may be small, or at least perceived to be small, making the expected sanction less than the benefit; moreover, people may suffer lapses in their ability to weigh benefits against expected sanctions.

The individuals who commit criminal acts despite the threat of sanctions are individuals whom society may want to incapacitate. This factor adds to the appeal of imprisonment.

2.6 Other types of criminal acts—categories (b) and (c)—would be inadequately deterred if not labeled as criminal.   Criminal acts that are concealed even if substantial harm was not intended, category (b), are by definition relatively hard to deter. A hit-and-run driver is more difficult to deter than a driver who stays at the scene; a firm that pollutes and then tries to evade responsibility by destroying evidence is more difficult to deter than a firm that pollutes and does not conceal its act. Hence, higher sanctions, and possibly imprisonment, are called for when concealment occurs. Further, even if imprisonment is not justified, the labeling of the acts as criminal may be desirable because that augments deterrence due to the associated social sanctions, and the imposition of criminal fines may be useful because that too raises deterrence relative to civil sanctions (see section 1.2).

With regard to the residual category (c) of criminal acts, it seems that,

17. For example, in 2000, the urban robbery rate (all rates in this note are per 100,000 population) was 621 in Washington, D.C., and 224 in New York State, as compared to 52 in Iowa and 27 in Vermont; the urban violent crime rate was 1,508 in Washington, D.C., and 831 in Florida, as compared to 107 in North Dakota and 180 in New Hampshire; see Morgan and Morgan 2002, 407, 425. For another example, in 1997, the homicide rate was 57 in Washington, D.C., and 43 in Pretoria, South Africa, as compared to about 2 each in Oslo, Lisbon, and London; see *International Comparisons of Criminal Justice Statistics, 1999* (May 2001), *www.homeoffice.gov.uk/rds/pdfs/hosb601.pdf,* table 1.2.

as with category (b), the likelihood of sanctions is often low. Consider the crime of serving liquor to minors. The likelihood of sanctions for this act may be low, not necessarily due to active concealment by violators, but rather because of difficulty in determining when a violation has occurred (an establishment may serve liquor to a minor and not know this). Acts in the residual category (c) frequently seem to have the characteristic that the chance of imposing sanctions is significantly less than 100 percent, and/ or that the acts are either harmful in themselves or are likely to lead to harm. Whether solely monetary sanctions or nonmonetary sanctions as well will be called for will depend on other factors, as discussed generally earlier.

2.7 A different explanation for criminal law—based on the moral quality of acts—versus the present, functional explanation. Perhaps the major alternative explanation for criminal law is that it allows society to demarcate and to punish in a special way those acts that are deemed particularly morally offensive. I will not attempt to define here the moral quality of an act, but will rely on the reader's intuition as a guide. I will briefly suggest that the moral character of acts is unsatisfactory as a unitary explanation of criminal law, and is inferior to the functional explanation advanced here (although the true explanation of criminal law is undoubtedly not unitary).

(a) *Moral theory of criminal law is unable to explain why some criminal acts are less bad morally than some noncriminal acts.* Compare the crime of the theft of $100 worth of food from a supermarket by a hungry person, or the crime of a bartender unintentionally serving liquor to a minor, to a tort such as the calculated omission by a corporate officer of a warning about a product hazard that results in multiple deaths. Such comparisons are problematic for the moral-theoretical explanation of criminal law. Yet these comparisons are resolved by the functional theory, in that the sanctions of criminal law are needed to control theft and the serving of liquor to minors, but are not generally needed to control corporate torts such as failure to warn of product hazards (because corporations ordinarily have the assets to be deterred tolerably well by solely monetary, civil sanctions).

(b) *Moral theory fails to explain important characteristics of criminal law.* The moral theory does not explain certain significant features of criminal law, whereas the functional theory does. Consider first that under criminal law, an attempt, such as shooting at someone but missing, is punished. It is incumbent on the moral theorist to say why such attempts should be sanctioned even though they do not result in harm, whereas under tort law, a very dangerous wrongful act, such as negligently leaving a live wire exposed at a playground, will not be sanctioned if it does not result in harm. As I will explain in section 4.2, there is a functional explanation for this difference between criminal and tort law (based on the need to enhance deterrence in the criminal context, but not in the tort context, by means of punishing dangerous acts that do not result in harm). Second, consider that a basic feature of criminal law is that a victim and an offender are not allowed to settle their differences privately, whereas in civil disputes private settlement is permitted (indeed, encouraged). Why this difference should exist is not clear on moral grounds, whereas a straightforward functional explanation is offered for it in section 4.12 (based on the dilution of deterrence that settlement would engender in the criminal context).

(c) *Moral theory does not address the fact that many present-day crimes were punished primarily by fines or equivalents in the past—that tort and criminal law were not distinct.* Historically, tort and criminal law were not separate. Rather, penalties denominated in terms of wealth (in money or goods), paid to victims, often according to a schedule, were employed for undesirable acts, including those that today would be considered criminal, such as murder and rape; prisons were not used.[18] That for a long time societies did not formally distinguish crime from torts requires explanation. The moral theory does not offer obvious possibilities, assuming, as I do, that basic attitudes about what acts are especially bad were similar in the past to what they are today. The functional theory, however, does provide possible explanations for why a system based on wealth sanctions could have worked reasonably well in the past to prevent what we today call crimes. One conjecture is that the likelihood of escaping punishment for bad acts was much less in the past than in our modern, anonymous society, so that the magnitude of wealth penalties necessary to deter may have been smaller. Another hypothesis is that because wealth penalties were often imposed on kinship groups that had the capacity to pay (and which could

18. See, for example, Berman 1983, 53–56, and Pollock and Maitland 1911, 2:449–462. The payments were apparently often enforced by subjecting a violator who refused to pay to blood-feud, or by declaring him an outlaw; see, for instance, the section cited in Pollock and Maitland 1911.

exert pressure on the particular offender), the problem of the judgment-proof offender, which I have emphasized as the major explanation of the need for criminal law now, may not have been severe then. In addition, one supposes that informal social sanctions operated with greater effect than in present-day society, lessening the need for criminal sanctions. Moreover, the institution of prisons may have been excessively costly for societies in the past, because they were generally much less wealthy; building and operating prisons, and taking people out of the labor force, might have been close to an unthinkable economic burden for most societies over the course of history. In sum, the lesser social need to develop a separate criminal law and the relatively high cost of establishing a system of imprisonment may have been such that it was socially rational not to distinguish in a formal and self-conscious way tort law from criminal law as we know it.[19] Although frankly speculative, this line of reasoning illustrates the ability of the functional theory to explain why criminal law and tort law were not separate in the past.

(d) *Conclusion.* The moral-theoretical explanation for criminal law seems inferior to the functional explanation. This is hardly to deny, however, that there is a general congruence between criminal acts and morally offensive acts, or to ignore that there exist important relationships between criminal law and our system of morality (on which see Chapters 26 and 27).

3. OPTIMAL USE OF IMPRISONMENT REVIEWED

Having attempted to explain why criminal law exists and why the domain of criminal acts is what it is, I want to review here the nature of the theoretically desirable use of the sanction of imprisonment from the point of view

19. To be clear, I am not claiming that, for example, an accidental killing would have been viewed in the same way as murder in former times; I suppose that the two acts would have been seen as quite different. (For example, as Pollock and Maitland 1911, 2:450–452, suggest, whether a slayer would have the option to pay for the death, rather than be subject to blood-feud or outlawry if the victim's kin wanted that, may at times have depended on the nature of the killing.) What I am asserting is that there was no need comparable to ours for a distinctly different legal treatment of torts and crimes. The institution of criminal law is a product of our times, not an intrinsic feature of the legal system.

of both deterrence and incapacitation. This will be referred to in the next section, where I examine important doctrines of criminal law.

3.1 Optimal deterrence and imprisonment. The point developed in Chapter 21 was that imprisonment, being costly to impose, should be employed so that it accomplishes deterrence at a low cost. This implies that the socially desirable sanction for an act is that which would be just sufficient to deter most of those who would tend to commit the act; thus, the sanction should be such that the expected sanction should just outweigh the expected benefit that most potential offenders would obtain from the act. (A higher sanction would not, by hypothesis, be needed to deter most in the group, but some in the group could not or would not be deterred, and would commit the act; for them, imposing a greater sanction would mean that society would bear a larger cost.) Further implications about the optimal use of imprisonment to deter socially undesirable acts are as follows:

(a) The sanction should be higher the greater the probability or the magnitude of harm due to the act, for the greater the expected harm, the more socially worthwhile it will be to increase deterrence despite the higher social cost of using sanctions.

(b) The sanction should be higher the greater is the private benefit the actor obtains, as long as the benefit appears to be within the range that allows for the possibility of deterrence. This follows because the sanction should be just high enough to deter.

(c) The sanction should be zero, or small, if the actor appears to be impossible to deter.

(d) The sanction should be higher the lower is the probability of apprehending the actor, provided that there is a possibility of deterrence. This follows because, in order to create an expected sanction necessary to deter, the actual sanction must rise if the probability of its imposition falls.

3.2 Optimal incapacitation and imprisonment. The point emphasized about incapacitation in Chapter 23 was that a person who is apprehended should be imprisoned and thereby incapacitated as long as the expected harm he would do per period if free exceeds the cost per period of imprisonment. This implies that the character of the act a person committed is relevant insofar as it provides information about a person's future propensity to do harm. If the harmfulness of acts that a person committed is predictive of the person's future harmfulness, then if the committed act exceeds a threshold in seriousness, he should be imprisoned.

Note that from the perspective of incapacitation, the probability of apprehension is irrelevant to the optimal sanction. Also, the ability to deter the actor is irrelevant; if someone could not have been deterred, the person should still be imprisoned if his future dangerousness is sufficiently high.

4. PRINCIPLES OF CRIMINAL LAW

In this part, I canvass important principles and doctrines of criminal law, and examine them briefly in light of the theory concerning optimal deterrence and optimal incapacitation. The major principles and doctrines of concern will be intent, attempt, causation, and a variety of defenses to criminal liability.

4.1 Intent. A central feature of the criminal law is the emphasis it places on intent. To analyze intent, it is best to begin by making several definitions. Let us say that a party "desires" a result if it would either directly or indirectly raise his utility.[20] Let us also say that a party "intends" a result if he (a) desires the result and (b) acts in a way that he believes will raise the probability of the result.[21] This definition of intent seems to comport with its ordinary meaning.[22] According to the definition, we would say that X intended that Y die if he desired Y's death and shot at Y and killed him. If, however, X shot at Y but instead struck Z whose death he did not desire, we would not say that he intended that Z die. Also, we would not say that X intended that Y die if X desired Y's death, played golf with Q, and Y

20. In the language of utility theory, a result is desired (a) if the result is an argument in the individual's utility function and thus would raise his utility in a direct manner, or (b) if the result would lead to an increase in his expected utility because it is correlated or associated with a change in an argument in his utility function.

21. The significance of erroneous beliefs is discussed below. For now, I assume that the party's beliefs about the probability are correct.

22. The traditional definition of intent in the criminal law is broader: A party "intends" a result even where he does not desire it if he acts in a way that makes it highly probable (rather than only more probable).

happened to be killed in an automobile accident (since the round of golf with Q did not increase the probability of Y's death).

In criminal law, the role of intent, as I have defined the term, may be summarized by several statements.[23] First, intent to do harm is ordinarily a principal factor in determining liability and the severity of punishment. Second, the effect of intent on liability and punishment is generally the same whether an intended harmful result is directly desired or indirectly desired. Whether X shot Y because Y was his enemy or only because Y stood in the way of an inheritance will not ordinarily affect the punishment of X under the law. Third, whether a harmful result different from the desired result occurs does not usually influence a party's legal treatment. When X aims at Y but shoots Z instead, it is murder just as if X had aimed at Z.

These features describing the role of intent in criminal law are roughly consistent with the purposes of deterrence, for intent appears to be linked to the factors that, according to theory, call for, or increase, the level of sanctions.[24] Intent is, first of all, positively related to the probability of harm, for when a party intends to do harm, he acts so as to raise the probability of harm. This factor is particularly significant when the courts' direct evidence about the probability of harm is limited, because courts can often make inferences about the probability of harm from knowledge of a party's desires. For instance, when a court has little evidence about X's shooting of Y but knows that X had the purpose of killing Y, the court might infer that X carefully drew a bead on Y.[25] Second, intent may be correlated with

23. See, for example, LaFave 2000, 229– 241.

24. Oliver Wendell Holmes, Jr., was one of the first writers to try to establish a connection between intent and factors that ought to increase the sanction appropriate for deterrence. His discussion focused on the relationship between intent and the probability of doing harm. See Holmes [1881] 1963, 52–62.

25. It is worth developing this example in more detail. Suppose that X and Y were hunting together when X shot Y. But X claims that he fired at a deer running between him and Y and unfortunately did not see Y. A witness who was standing at some distance away confirms that there was a deer running between X and Y, but he is not able to say whether X noticed Y or aimed at him rather than at the deer. With only this very imperfect knowledge of X's act, a court could highly value information about X's intent (for example, evidence that he would profit from Y's death and planned to kill Y at a good opportunity) or lack thereof (for example, evidence that X had nothing to gain from Y's death). Thus, knowledge of X's intent may alter a court's assessment of the probability of harm due to

the likely magnitude of harm, because a party who desires a harmful result is prone to do greater damage than one who does not. Party X will be more likely to shoot Y in a vital spot than in an arm or a leg if X desires to harm Y. Intent is also closely associated with the private benefits that parties expect to derive from their acts. By definition, the utility of parties who intend harm is raised by the occurrence of harm, and as just indicated, both the probability and magnitude of such desired harm tend to be higher when there is intent. Thus, parties who intend to do harm will be more difficult to deter.[26] Finally, intent may be linked to the probability that a party will escape a sanction, since a party who intends to commit a harmful act is more likely to choose a particular place and time to commit the act so as to avoid identification and arrest, or to take steps thereafter to do so.[27]

These arguments suggest why intent, though mainly a mental factor, ought to influence liability and punishment according to deterrence theory. Moreover, it should be noted that the arguments do not depend on whether the intended harm is directly or indirectly desired. In either case the probability and magnitude of harm, the expected private benefits, and the likelihood of escaping sanctions are likely to be higher than for unintentional conduct. Further, the arguments are largely unaffected by whether the actual result was the same as the desired result. It therefore makes sense that such distinctions usually do not affect a party's punishment.

From the standpoint of optimal incapacitation, intent is significant insofar as it provides information about the future dangerousness of a person. Is a person who commits an act in which he intends harm going to be

---

X's act. If, however, the court's direct knowledge of X's act were complete (for example, suppose the court possessed a close-up video recording of his behavior), it would not need to know anything about intent in order to assess the probability of harm. But, as will be seen, the court might well find knowledge of intent valuable for other reasons.

26. If X intends to kill Y, it will be difficult to deter him, because he wants Y dead and because shooting at Y makes this result likely. By contrast, if X is a true friend of Y, to deter a negligent or reckless shot will not require a substantial sanction (if it requires any sanction at all).

27. In some cases, however, the factor of intent could increase the probability of sanctions because a person's motives might be discoverable and lead police to investigate him. The importance of this consideration depends on the type of crime and the particular case. It might be significant in some cases of murder, for instance, but would probably not be in most cases of theft and robbery.

dangerous in the future? As a general matter, the answer seems to be in the affirmative; we infer something about the character of a person when we learn that he intended to cause harm, and this leads us to increase our estimate of the probability that the person will do harm in the future. But the importance of this factor depends on the particulars of the case. On one hand, if husband X murders his wife in order to be free to marry his lover, and the circumstances leading to this act are unlikely to repeat themselves, then his intent per se would not seem to signify much about future dangerousness. On the other hand, if Y, who has never had a full-time job, intends to and does carry out a robbery, we would surmise that his intentional behavior does suggest future danger, because the circumstances that gave rise to his actions are likely to apply again; he is likely to want more money in the future and to be able to steal to obtain it. In each case, intent tells us something about the character of the individual that is relevant to predicting future behavior, but what it tells us is only partial. Thus, we may conclude that intent has relevance for the need to incapacitate, but it does not seem that we can explain the importance given to intent mainly through appeal to incapacitation.

Consideration of situations in which a party is not liable despite his intent to do harm sheds further light on intent with respect both to deterrence and to incapacitation.[28] A party may intend to do harm but escape liability because circumstances make his act socially desirable. For example, a party forced to choose between two harmful acts may invoke the defense of necessity if he chooses the less harmful act. In addition, a party may act under duress and escape liability; here deterrence is difficult or impossible and there is no reason to incapacitate, so imposing sanctions would not be socially worthwhile.

Conversely, parties are sometimes punished despite their lack of intent to do harm. When a party does not desire a harmful result but acts in such a way that serious harm becomes very likely (suppose that a drunk person drives at ninety miles per hour through a school zone and runs over a child), he may be punished under criminal law. Imposition of sanctions here may be justified because the expected harm is high; the fact that the party does not desire the harm does not make his behavior less dangerous. Similarly,

---

28. That there should be such situations is not surprising a priori, for intent was only claimed to be linked with factors leading to the optimality of liability.

when a party does not desire harm but commits a strict liability crime, his punishment may be justified in principle if the courts find it very difficult to differentiate between desirable and undesirable acts.

4.2 Attempt. The criminal law punishes attempts to do harm. If a person shoots at another but misses, if he picks a pocket that turns out to be empty, if he is found with a forged check but has not yet cashed it, he is guilty of a crime of attempt even though he has not done harm.[29]

The punishment of attempts enhances deterrence, because it effectively raises the probability of sanctions for potentially harmful acts: A person who commits a potentially harmful act faces the prospect of sanctions not only if his act turns out to cause harm, but also if it does not and constitutes only an attempt.[30] Moreover, the punishment of attempts is a socially inexpensive means of increasing the probability of sanctions, for opportunities to punish attempts often arise as a by-product of society's investment to apprehend parties who actually do cause harm.[31] Hence, it can be argued that punishment of attempts is socially desirable from the standpoint of the theory of deterrence.[32]

---

29. See, for example, LaFave 2000, 535–567. As mentioned in section 2.7, this is in contrast to the situation in tort law, where there is no liability unless harm is done. See Keeton, Dobbs, et. al. 1984, section 30.

30. In the tort context, punishing the analogue of attempts—negligent acts that do not result in harm—would also raise the probability of sanctions and enhance deterrence. But in the tort context, the need to enhance deterrence is much less than that in the criminal context, for in the tort context parties typically do not escape suit with high probability. Hence, in the tort context, making parties pay damages only when they actually do harm, and in an amount equal to the harm, should tend to create adequate incentives to reduce harm, as is emphasized in Chapter 8.

31. Given that the police stand ready to apprehend those who do harm (by giving chase, investigating suspicious behavior, and the like), apprehending individuals who commit unsuccessful attempts may not involve substantial marginal cost. At least the added cost of raising the probability of sanctions by apprehending those who commit unsuccessful attempts should be much less than the added cost of raising comparably the probability of sanctions by apprehending only more of those parties who succeed in causing harm.

32. This thesis, and the arguments sketched later, are developed in Shavell 1990. Among other things, that article explains why raising the probability of sanctions by punishing attempts is advantageous, given the apparent alternative strategy of imposing a higher level of sanctions but imposing them only when harm is done. The essence of the explanation is that raising the magnitude of sanctions may have various disadvantageous effects

The force of this argument for sanctioning attempts clearly increases with the likelihood that a party will be apprehended for an attempt. When an act takes a long time to execute (especially when it requires preparations) or when it has a substantial chance of not succeeding (for example, shooting from a distance), the probability of being caught for an attempt will be higher than otherwise. Therefore, the deterrent value of punishing attempts will also be higher.

With regard to the theory of incapacitation, it is evident that, to the degree that attempts signify future dangerousness, attempts call for punishment.

The possible desirability of punishing attempts according to the theory of deterrence or of incapacitation does not imply in any obvious way that there is an advantage in punishing attempts in the manner that criminal law does, namely, less severely than acts that actually result in harm. In discussing this feature of criminal law, it is useful to consider separately two types of attempts that do not cause harm: interrupted attempts—acts discovered before they could have succeeded—and completed attempts that might have succeeded.

With respect to interrupted attempts and deterrence, the following argument is sometimes made.[33] If the sanction for an attempt is lower than that for doing harm, a party who begins an attempt might be induced to reevaluate and abandon it, since he then will be punished less. If, however, the sanction for the attempt is the same as for doing harm, he may as well continue. As stated, this argument fails to recognize the possibility of treating the abandoned attempt leniently, while imposing a full sanction on attempts that are not abandoned but only interrupted by others. Suppose, for instance, that no sanctions are imposed for abandoned attempts and that the sanction for an interrupted attempt is the same as the sanction for an act that causes harm. Then the party who sets out to commit a harmful act will certainly have reason to abandon it; not only will he escape sanctions, but he will also otherwise face a sanction for any later interrupted attempt equal to the sanction for doing harm.[34]

(such as distorting marginal deterrence) and may not be workable because of the upper limit on sanctions.

33. See, notably, Beccaria [1767] 1995, 95.

34. This argument presumes that courts are able to distinguish between abandoned and interrupted attempts.

Nevertheless, punishing interrupted attempts less severely than acts that result in harm may be advantageous under both deterrence and incapacitation theory. Because interrupted attempts may later be abandoned or fail, there is less evidence of the dangerousness of interrupted attempts and thus less reason for sanctioning them than acts that do result in harm.[35] The significance of this argument plainly depends on the character of the attempt and the point at which it is interrupted. If an attempt is nearly complete and is likely to succeed, the argument does not carry much weight. That would be so, for instance, where a person had already dropped a lethal dose of poison into his intended victim's drink. An attempt interrupted further from completion might properly be sanctioned less severely, however. Indeed, an attempt might reasonably escape a sanction altogether if it is interrupted so early that there is great doubt whether and in what manner it would have been continued. Thus, if a person was apprehended merely when leaving a drugstore with poison, it might be unclear whether he would have used the poison, and unclear too whether his behavior would satisfy the definition of attempt in criminal law.

Two arguments analogous to those just discussed are often advanced to justify imposition of lower sanctions for unsuccessful completed attempts than for acts that succeed in causing harm. First, it is asserted that if the sanction for an unsuccessful completed attempt is equal to the sanction for a successful attempt, a party whose initial attempt fails will have nothing to lose by trying again. This argument overlooks the point that the sanction for an initial unsuccessful attempt may equal the sanction for an initial successful attempt, and yet the party will have something to lose by trying a second time as long as the sanction for a second successful attempt is higher. For example, if the sanction for an initial attempt is a sentence of five years whether or not it succeeds, but the sanction for causing harm on a second attempt is ten years, a party who at first fails will clearly have reason not to try a second time.[36]

The other argument for punishing unsuccessful completed attempts

---

35. This the reader will recognize as a version of the general argument advanced earlier that the actual harm done might influence the sanction because of the court's incomplete information about the dangerousness of an act.

36. The argument in this paragraph presumes that courts can determine if a party repeats an attempt.

less severely than those resulting in harm is that the failure of an attempt may constitute evidence that it was a less dangerous act. As with interrupted attempts, the strength of this evidentiary rationale depends on the nature of the attempt. And while one can think of situations in which the rationale would be important, in many that come to mind, it does not seem so.[37]

Finally, it is interesting to consider attempts that cannot possibly succeed.[38] There are two types of such attempts. The first, for which it is often said liability should not be imposed, is exemplified by the case of a person who sticks pins in a voodoo doll, intending to kill his enemy.[39] Here an objective observer might say that the type of act committed never causes harm, so that there is no reason to deter the act or to incapacitate the actor.[40] The second kind of attempt, for which there would be liability, is illustrated by the case of a person who shoots a bullet into a dummy that he thinks is his enemy. In this instance, an objective observer would say that the type of act committed creates positive expected harm, for shooting things that appear to be human beings will usually result in harm. Hence, according to both deterrence and incapacitation theory, the act should be punished.

4.3 Causation.   When a party's act is followed by harm, two causal issues may arise.[41] The first concerns the question of whether the act was the "necessary" cause of the harm, that is, whether the harm would not have

37. For instance, if a person puts poison in his intended victim's drink but the victim fails to succumb, it is true that the act was less dangerous than one that would have caused a death—perhaps because the dosage of poison was too low. But this might not constitute enough evidence to lower the sanction significantly. In any event, there is less reason to lower the sanction than if the person had been interrupted before he completed the attempt, for then there would have been doubt about whether the attempt would have been completed, as well as whether it would have been successful if completed.

38. See, for example, LaFave 2000, 552–560.

39. Note that because this person believes he is raising the probability of his enemy's death, we would say he intends his death under the definition of intent used in this chapter.

40. This presumes that the person who failed with the voodoo doll would not have tried other ways of killing his enemy, such as shooting at him. If there is evidence that the person would have turned to other methods, then his act would appropriately be defined as "trying to kill an enemy by some means" rather than "trying to kill an enemy using a voodoo doll," and there would be a reason to punish him.

41. See, for example, LaFave 2000, 292–320.

occurred but for the act. Thus, if X poisons Y's drink and Y then dies, yet an autopsy reveals that Y coincidentally died of a heart attack before he could have succumbed to the poison, X's act would not be the necessary cause of Y's death. The criminal law ordinarily treats an act that was not the necessary cause of harm as if it were an attempt: The party is punished for the act, but less so than if the act were the necessary cause of the harm.[42]

This outcome makes sense—though only partial sense—according to deterrence theory. It makes sense that acts that are not the necessary causes of harm are punished, for this enhances deterrence in the same way that punishment of attempts does, namely, by increasing the probability of sanctions.[43] The reason for the imposition of lesser sanctions, however, is not apparent. That acts sufficient to cause harm turn out not to be the necessary causes of harm is happenstance; it does not mean that the expected harmfulness of the acts was any lower. Therefore, the sanctions for such acts ought not to be diminished, according to deterrence theory.[44]

If a party's act was the necessary cause of harm, the legal issue arises of whether his act was the "proximate cause" of harm. Generally, acts said to be the proximate cause of harm can be recognized as those that substantially increased the probability or magnitude of the type of harm that occurred. To illustrate, if X severely beats Y and Y later dies in the hospital from internal injuries, it would probably be said that X's actions were the proximate cause of Y's death. If, however, Y dies in an automobile accident while being taken to the hospital after the beating, it would probably not be said that X's actions were the proximate cause of Y's death.[45] In determining

42. This situation is different under tort law, where a party usually escapes liability if his act was not the necessary cause of harm. See Keeton, Dobbs, et al. 1984, 265.

43. In the usual model of torts, there is no reason to enhance deterrence by use of sanctions when a party's act is not the necessary cause of harm. The threat of liability only when their acts are necessary causes of harm is enough to induce parties to take adequate care, assuming that suit will be brought when parties are liable. See Shavell 1987a, chap. 5.

44. The fact that Y died of a heart attack does not cast doubt on the potency of the poison. Note that this is in contrast to a failed or interrupted attempt to murder Y by poisoning.

45. The probability of dying in an automobile accident on a single trip (even if by ambulance) is small, and is therefore not much increased by X's beating of Y. Indeed, Y might have been going somewhere else by automobile if he had not been going to the hospital, in which case Y's chance of dying in an automobile accident would not have been raised by X's beating him.

punishment, the criminal law usually takes into account whether or not the harm was proximately caused. X might be held liable for murder if Y dies from his internal injuries, but not if Y dies in the automobile accident.

Punishing a party for harm that he proximately caused—and not just for the act he committed, as the act is otherwise understood by the court—might sometimes be justified in view of the evidentiary value of the actual harm done for the assessment of the act by the court. Y's death from internal injuries would be indicative of the severity of the beating he received, whereas his death in an automobile accident would not convey such information.[46]

The implications of incapacitation theory are similar to those just discussed. Namely, an act that turns out not to be the necessary cause of harm should be punished as much as a similar act that does cause harm. For when X poisons Y's drink and Y happens to die of a heart attack, we generally have as much information about the dangerousness of the act and the actor as we would have if Y had not died of a heart attack. But to the degree that proximate causation implicitly supplies us with information about the expected harmfulness of the act, such causation is relevant to proper punishment for purposes of incapacitation.

4.4 Responsibility. Under criminal law, the imposition of sanctions depends on whether a person who commits a harmful act is deemed "responsible," in whole or in part, for his behavior. Major reasons why a person may not be held responsible are insanity, automatism, involuntary intoxication, or youth. If these reasons apply, the person's liability may be diminished or eliminated.

This aspect of criminal law has an obvious potential justification according to deterrence theory, because the conditions that reduce or relieve one's responsibility for otherwise criminal acts make it unlikely that the use of sanctions would accomplish significant deterrence.[47] An insane or

---

46. That the logic of this paragraph applies generally and is not a feature of my example can be appreciated from the characterization of proximately caused harms as those whose probability or severity was increased in a substantial way by a party's act. It is exactly when this is true that the occurrence of the outcome may convey useful information about how much the party's act increased the expected harm.

47. This point is stressed by Bentham [1789] 1973, 164.

involuntarily intoxicated person, for example, cannot be deterred from committing certain acts by the threat of punishment, so that the elimination of punishment might be appropriate. Two general reasons for restricting such escape from liability suggest themselves, however. First, individuals may often be able to feign successfully the conditions that limit their responsibility. This possibility may be significant with respect to some of the conditions (for example, insanity), but not for all (youth is difficult or impossible to pretend). Second, individuals may sometimes choose to act in ways that make their (true) conditions especially dangerous. An epileptic might drive an automobile, or a person subject to insane rages might decide to purchase a gun. The imposition of liability could induce these individuals to act differently and thereby to reduce dangers over which they later would have no control.

With regard to incapacitation theory, it is apparent that in many cases where a person is not legally responsible for his act, he will be no less dangerous to society than if he were responsible. A person who has an uncontrollable urge to set fires, or who is subject to insane, violent rages, is dangerous to society even though he cannot help himself. Therefore, his lack of responsibility does not diminish the need to incapacitate him. Hence, contrary to the implication of deterrence theory, sanctions are called for from the point of view of incapacitation. (Of course, the form of incapacitation need not be incarceration in a prison; it could be confinement to a facility for the criminally insane.)

In some cases, lack of responsibility might not imply future dangerousness, or at least not dangerousness sufficient to warrant punishment. If youth is the reason for lack of responsibility, it might be felt that with time and maturation, the person would be unlikely to commit a similar act. Certainly with involuntary intoxication that would be the case.

4.5 Ignorance of the law. If a person claims that he was unaware that his act was unlawful, he will ordinarily be found liable anyway.[48] He may sometimes escape liability, however, if he had little opportunity to learn about the law (as with an unpublished or little-known ordinance) or

---

48. In this and the next several sections, I will discuss various justifications and excuses for committing harmful acts that lead to escape from criminal liability. They are considered separately from responsibility, and from each other, since they present different issues.

if he was acting in reliance on a mistaken interpretation of the law made by a court or an appropriate government officer.[49]

Such an approach is consonant with the theory of deterrence.[50] If a person is held liable for violating well-appreciated laws or laws that can be learned through reasonable effort, he will have an incentive to learn the laws and adhere to them. If, however, a reasonable effort is insufficient to learn a legal rule, it is best to permit parties to escape liability, since a party can be deterred by possible sanctions only if he knows which acts will lead to the application of sanctions.

4.6 Mistake. A person may commit an act that he believes to be innocent although it is actually harmful. In a classic case, a person takes an umbrella from a restaurant assuming that it is his, when it really belongs to someone else. There is no criminal liability in such instances.[51] This feature of criminal law makes sense, for people cannot be deterred from committing acts that they are unaware are harmful. Moreover, assuming that acts believed to be harmless usually are harmless, the expected harm associated with the acts is too low to warrant the use of sanctions.[52]

A related type of mistake arises when a party knowingly commits an undesirable act but believes it to be either more or less harmful than it actually is. For example, an individual might steal a valuable piece of jewelry, thinking it a mere bauble, or he might shoot to kill a "person" who turns out to be a dummy (as I mentioned in the section on attempt). The legal principles employed in these situations are not uniform; although sanctions are frequently based on what a party did in fact, many times they are affected by what he thought he was doing.

There are two reasons why the harmfulness of the act the party thought he was committing should influence the sanction under deterrence theory.

49. See, for example, LaFave 2000, 432–434, 440–449.

50. See Bentham [1789] 1973, 164.

51. See, for example, LaFave 2000, 432–437.

52. Note that the situation under discussion in this paragraph, of not knowing that an act is harmful because of lack of knowledge of some circumstance (who owns the umbrella), is analytically indistinguishable from that of the previous section, of lack of knowledge of the law. In this vein, it should be noted that a person who could easily have determined that his act was not innocent (say the umbrella he took was obviously not his—it had another person's monogram on it) might not be able to escape liability.

First, the benefits an individual expects to derive from committing an act, and thus the ability to deter him, depend on what he thinks he is doing, not on what he is in fact doing.[53] Second, the expected harm associated with an act may be more closely related to what the party thinks it is than to what it turns out to be in the particular instance. The act of taking what one thinks is a bauble might usually mean that only a bauble is missing; the act of shooting at what one thinks is a person will usually be very harmful. This second reason is also applicable according to incapacitation theory; if the future dangerousness of a person is more closely associated with the act the party thought he was committing (shooting at what he thought was a person), then that should guide the sanction, and not the harm actually done.

Nevertheless, one important factor suggests that the actual harm should influence the sanction. Individuals may be able to convince the courts that they thought they were doing little harm when in truth they knew they were doing greater harm. If so, and if the sanction is based on the courts' erroneous assessment of parties' beliefs, sanctions will be too low and diminished deterrence will result.[54] Hence, there is some reason to raise the sanction when the actual harm exceeds what the wrongdoer claims to have thought it would be. But note that there is no corresponding argument for lowering the sanction when the actual harm turns out to be less than what the individual thought it would be, since he will have no incentive to exaggerate the harm he thought he was doing.

4.7 Entrapment. A person may raise the defense of entrapment if a law enforcement official induces him to commit a criminal act that he would not ordinarily commit.[55] When, for instance, a game warden induces a hunter to shoot at bald eagles and the hunter would not otherwise have done this, the hunter can assert the defense of entrapment.

The argument for this defense on grounds of deterrence theory is that if persons would not ordinarily commit criminal acts, there is no behavior

---

53. The individual who thinks he is stealing a bauble, and thus not obtaining much of value, might be easier to deter than the individual who thinks he is stealing valuable jewelry.

54. Individuals may not be properly deterred from stealing valuable jewelry if they know they can convince the courts that they thought the jewelry was only a bauble.

55. See, for example, LaFave 2000, 449–466.

that needs to be deterred. Similarly, according to incapacitation theory, if individuals do not have a general tendency to cause harm, but act intending to cause it only in the restricted and unusual circumstances of entrapment, they do not represent a future danger to society. Thus, under either theory, punishment of the individuals, and effort devoted to their entrapment, must be considered a social waste;[56] moreover, their entrapment might also result in the actual doing of harm.[57] Hence, it is best not to punish the parties who were entrapped, and to discourage entrapment activity. The former is directly accomplished by allowing the entrapment defense; and the latter is indirectly accomplished by allowing the defense, since enforcement officials will not then derive the benefit of securing additional criminal convictions.

The defense of entrapment may not be justifiable, however, when individuals would often commit by themselves the criminal acts that they are led to commit by an enforcement agent. In such cases, it is by hypothesis desirable to deter the individuals or to incapacitate them. Therefore, it may be useful to employ certain law enforcement activity, including deception and subterfuge leading to the inducement of criminal acts, in order to raise adequately the probability of sanctioning the individuals.

4.8 Duress.   A person will not be held liable for a harmful act if he committed the act only because of duress—a threat of serious injury or death. To invoke the defense of duress, the threat to a person must have been both imminent and credible, and the person must not have killed someone (although the sanction may still be mitigated in that case). Whether or not the defense is available, the threatening party will be liable for the act he induced.[58]

The defense of duress is obviously desirable if the threatened party truly cannot be deterred by the prospect of a legal sanction for committing the

---

56. To clarify this point, consider a situation in which a person would never commit a criminal act if not entrapped. Here, plainly, punishing the person and devoting effort to entrap him is wasteful, since otherwise the person would never cause harm. (It is irrelevant under deterrence theory that the person might be thought bad because he could be induced to commit a criminal act in certain contrived circumstances.)

57. For example, the game warden might not be able to take the hunter into custody before he shoots a bald eagle.

58. See, for example, LaFave 2000, 467–476.

act.[59] Hence, the law's insistence on the imminence and credibility of the threat, and on its being one of serious injury or of death, seems understandable. But its refusal to allow the defense when the threatened party has killed someone does not seem rational according to deterrence theory, because it is quite possible that the threatened party could not have been deterred from killing; after all, he will often be comparing an immediate threat to a sanction that will not be immediate, if it is imposed at all.

According to incapacitation theory, the defense of duress is also warranted, for the party who is forced by a threat to commit a harmful act probably does not represent a future threat to society.

Moreover, it is desirable that an individual who makes a threat be held liable for crimes committed as a result of that threat, for this will be necessary to deter and/or incapacitate such individuals.

4.9 Necessity. The defense of necessity may be asserted when an individual, forced by circumstances to choose between two harmful acts, chooses the less harmful act.[60] This makes clear sense according to deterrence theory, because it is socially desirable for a party to minimize harm. Furthermore, the defense is rational according to incapacitation theory for similar reasons: The individual who would choose to do the lesser of two harms does not pose a danger to society; quite the opposite.

4.10 Defense of self, of another, or of property. The law regarding self-defense and protection of others and of property is, roughly, that one may use the amount of force apparently necessary to ward off an aggressor whose threat one believes is unlawful and immediate, and who cannot be stopped by police intervention.[61] Plainly, allowing the use of protective force will enhance deterrence of aggression. Limiting the justified use of such force makes sense under the presumption that the courts are better able than threatened parties to decide on sanctions.

4.11 Consent. A person may sometimes escape criminal liability if the individual affected by his act had consented to its commission. The defense of consent, however, is not available when serious bodily injury is

---

59. This is pointed out by Bentham [1789] 1973, 165.
60. See, for example, LaFave 2000, 476–486.
61. See, for example, ibid., 491–508.

done.[62] The justification for the defense, under deterrence or incapacitation theory, centers on the concept of harm: If consent is taken to mean that there is no harm, then there is no reason to deter acts to which someone has consented.[63] According to this reasoning, a person's consent even to serious bodily injury apparently ought to be allowed as a defense. Yet consideration must be given to the counterarguments that the person who consents may not properly evaluate his situation, that his family and friends may be affected by the contemplated act, and that the injuring party may deceive the courts about the victim's consent.

4.12 Condonation and settlement. The fact that a person who has suffered harm may later condone, or settle with, the individual who is responsible for the harm[64] may not be used as a defense against criminal liability.[65] If a person is robbed, for example, and he then discovers the robber and forgives him, the robber will still be subject to punishment.[66] According to deterrence and incapacitation theory, the major reason for not allowing condonation as a defense to criminal liability is that deterrence would be diluted and incapacitation negated. Were the defense allowed, the "sanctions" imposed by victims—usually some form of apology, the return of property, or a payment, but never imprisonment, would be less than the sanctions the courts would otherwise impose.[67] Moreover, victims might many times wish to condone injuring parties, for there is no reason to believe that a victim's personal interest in punishing an injuring party would generally correspond to the social interest in deterrence or in incapacitation. (This point is closely related to that about the divergence between the private and social incentives to litigate discussed in Chapter 17.) Finally,

62. See, for example, ibid., 516–519.

63. See Bentham [1789] 1973, 163.

64. Condonation is distinct from giving the party prior consent; it occurs after the harm is done.

65. See, for example, LaFave 2000, 521–523.

66. As a practical matter, however, prosecution may be difficult if the victim is reluctant to provide testimony about the crime.

67. It should be observed that in tort law, where of course settlement is allowed, payments made in settlement would often approximate the expected court-determined monetary sanctions, since otherwise victims would tend not to want to settle.

were the defense allowed, there might be a real danger that victims would be coerced into "condoning" injuring parties.[68]

Note on the literature.   Economic analysis of the criminal law began with Beccaria ([1767] 1995) and, especially, Bentham ([1789] 1973), who succinctly made general, major points about restricting use of sanctions to situations where they would accomplish deterrence. Holmes ([1881] 1963) contains a chapter on criminal law with insightful remarks about deterrence and, especially, attempt and intent. Posner (1985a) and Shavell (1985a) contain brief examinations of the doctrines of criminal law from an economic perspective.[69]

---

68. The argument of this paragraph, that allowing settlements between injurers and victims would compromise public law enforcement, did not clearly apply before the development of effective mechanisms of public law enforcement. For an interesting illustration of this point, see Klerman 2001, who emphasizes that in thirteenth-century England, when private prosecutions of crime were usually necessary to bring wrongdoers to justice, it was found that when courts frowned on settlements, private prosecutions declined, and many wrongdoers undesirably escaped sanction; thus courts were led to respect settlements between injurers and victims for a period.

69. See also, for example, Ben-Shahar 1998 and Shavell 1990 on attempt, and Cohen 1989, Fischel and Sykes 1996, Khanna 1996, and Lott 2000 on corporate crime.

PART VI | GENERAL STRUCTURE OF THE LAW

In this part, consisting of only one chapter, I consider basic structural features of the legal system, including whether the law directly constrains behavior or channels it by the threat of sanctions, and whether the law is brought into play by private legal action or involves public enforcement. I investigate the conditions under which one or another structure of law will be socially desirable, and I then discuss tort, contract, criminal law, and several other areas of law in light of the analysis of the optimal structure of the law.

25 | THE GENERAL STRUCTURE OF THE LAW AND ITS OPTIMALITY

In this chapter, I will consider the general structure of the law, answering such questions as the following: Should the law directly constrain behavior, or should the law employ the threat of imposition of sanctions to channel behavior? If sanctions are utilized, should they be applied whenever behavior is judged undesirable or only when behavior results in harm? And should the law be initiated by the legal actions of private parties or should it involve public enforcement?

These questions are implicitly answered in one way by the law that we observe. Under tort and contract law, for example, the legal system is triggered only by the occurrence of harm, namely, by a tort or a breach of contract, whereas under criminal law, legal sanctions may be imposed even if harm is not done, notably, when individuals commit attempts; and under property law the legal system may intrude before harm is done, such as when dangerous behavior is enjoined. Enforcement of tort and contract law is essentially private in nature, whereas criminal law is publicly enforced. And so on.

Such differences in the structure of our major subject areas of law lead us to ask what the socially advantageous structure of law might be, as well as in what respects the structure that we see follows or deviates from the ideal. I will now examine a relatively simple theory of the determinants of the answers to these questions, and will consider briefly tort and contract law, safety regulation, the injunction, and criminal law in light of the analysis of optimal general structure of the law.[1]

1. FUNDAMENTAL DIMENSIONS OF LEGAL INTERVENTION

Here I discuss three primary dimensions of legal methods of controlling behavior and then describe major areas of law in terms of these basic dimensions.

1.1 Timing of intervention: before acts, after acts, after harm. The time at which legal intervention takes place is a primary dimension of any means of controlling behavior. Intervention may occur before an act is committed, usually through outright prevention of the act. Examples include fencing a reservoir to prevent people from polluting it, denying a company authority to operate a nuclear power plant in order to prevent harm from use of the plant, exercising force to stop a person from shooting another, and imprisoning an individual to prevent him from committing bad acts.

A second time of legal intervention is after an act has been committed but before harm occurs (or independently of whether it occurs). Such intervention involves the use of sanctions triggered by the commission of acts. If society punishes someone for shooting at another person regardless of whether he hits him, it is imposing a sanction based on the commission of the act of shooting. Likewise, if society employs a safety regulation requiring that sprinklers be installed in a hotel and the hotel operates without them and is fined (regardless of whether a fire occurs), society is imposing a sanction based on an act. In neither case, note, is society preventing undesirable acts directly; rather, society is attempting to deter the acts by the threat of sanctions for committing them.

The third time of legal intervention is after harm has occurred, by means of harm-based sanctions. This is the method of tort law, or of fines based on harm done. Also, in criminal law, harm-based sanctions are often

---

1. This chapter follows the general outline of Shavell 1993a.

imposed (if a person murders someone, he will be punished more severely than if he only attempted murder).

Comment. The model that I have in mind in making the distinctions above involves a party choosing whether to commit a single act, like shooting a gun at someone. A more detailed model would allow for parties to commit multiple acts, such as first brandishing a gun and then shooting it. In such a model, the description of legal intervention would be more refined; for example, what I call prevention in the simple model might correspond to prevention of one type of act (shooting a gun) based on a party committing another type of act (brandishing a gun). But the basic thrust of the analysis of such more complex models would not be different from that of the simple model.

1.2 Form of intervention: prevention or imposition of a sanction (and its type). The second dimension of legal intervention is its form. The form of legal intervention may involve a method of preventing an act from occurring, typically through use of force (as when a police officer takes a gun away from a person or when a regulatory authority locks the doors of a power plant) or physical barriers (as when a reservoir is fenced to prevent intrusions). Another major form of intervention is the imposition of sanctions, notably, monetary sanctions or imprisonment.[2]

1.3 Privately versus publicly initiated intervention. The third dimension of legal intervention concerns its initiation. The use of the legal system may be instigated when a private party asks for that to occur, such as when a person brings a tort suit or seeks an injunction; this constitutes private enforcement of law. The legal system may also be brought to bear when the state's enforcement agents determine that it is appropriate, such as when police officers or tax collection agents find violations of law and sanction them. (In such a case, the state's agents may obtain information from private parties who volunteer it, but I shall for the most part ignore that point for present purposes.)

---

2. A reward can be interpreted as a negative sanction, so is implicitly included as a possible sanction.

Table 25.1 Methods and dimensions of legal intervention

Method of legal intervention	Fundamental dimensions of legal intervention		
	Time of intervention	Form of intervention	Private vs. public
Tort law	After harm	Monetary sanctions	Private
Safety regulation	Before and after acts	Various	Public
Injunction	Before and after acts	Various	Private
Contract law	After harm	Monetary sanctions; other	Private
Criminal law	Before and after acts; after harm	Various	Public

1.4 Methods of legal intervention described in terms of the three fundamental dimensions.   It may be helpful to consider a matrix describing certain areas of law and commonly employed legal methods of control (the matrix is obviously not intended to be exhaustive) in terms of the three dimensions of legal intervention just mentioned (see Table 25.1).

The entry on tort law is self-explanatory. I describe safety regulation as applying both before and after acts occur because sometimes safety regulation functions through preventing certain acts from being committed—as when a restaurant is not allowed to open its doors unless it has passed a safety inspection—and at other times, regulation works through imposition of sanctions in response to a person's violation of regulation, as when a restaurant is penalized for failing to clearly mark exits or a person is given a ticket for going through a stop sign. I also describe the form of intervention under regulation as various because, as just mentioned, acts can be prevented, and they can also result in sanctions, including nonmonetary ones.

The injunction is similar to safety regulation in that it can be employed to prevent a dangerous act (usually after some prior behavior suggesting danger) or it can be a consequence of a potentially or actually dangerous act (as when a person who has ferocious dogs as pets is enjoined from keeping them). The main difference between the injunction and safety regulation is that the injunction is brought by private parties.

Contract law, like tort law, is a method of legal intervention that generally applies only after harm is done, when there is a breach of a contractual obligation, and it is private in that private actions must be brought for relief. The form of intervention is usually damages for breach, but may also involve specific performance, which is to say, use of methods, possibly including the police powers of the state, to enforce contractual obligations, such as the conveyance of land.

Criminal law, as indicated earlier, is employed before certain acts occur in order to prevent them, as well as after they occur and after harm is done. The form of intervention not only involves prevention, but also includes monetary and nonmonetary sanctions. Enforcement of criminal law is public.

2. OPTIMAL STRUCTURE OF LEGAL INTERVENTION

The state has to choose methods of legal intervention to control behavior, and in order to analyze the optimal means of intervention, I will first define the social welfare criterion and then discuss the optimal choice of each of the three primary dimensions of the means of intervention. This will allow us to organize our thinking about the determinants of the optimal structure of legal intervention.

2.1 Social welfare criterion.   The measure of social welfare will for simplicity be taken to be the benefits that individuals obtain from acts minus the harms done and the costs of enforcement of law.[3] These costs include the costs of identifying parties to whom sanctions ought to apply, the costs of applying the law, and also the costs of imposing sanctions. When the sanctions are monetary, I will generally assume that there is little expense associated with their actual imposition. This is motivated by the point that the imposition of monetary sanctions amounts to a transfer of purchasing power, not a use of resources (see the discussion in Chapters 20 and 21). When the sanction is imprisonment, I will assume that there is substantial social cost associated with its imposition, for imprisonment absorbs social resources.

2.2 Determinants of the optimal timing of intervention.   Several factors bear on the socially optimal time of legal intervention.

Information about the character of acts possessed by the state versus infor-

---

3. The significance of various omissions from the social welfare criterion will be briefly noted at the end of the chapter.

mation possessed by private parties. As a general matter, it appears that the worse is the knowledge possessed by the state about the dangerousness of parties' acts relative to the knowledge of the parties themselves, the more attractive will be legal intervention that occurs at later stages. If the state knows relatively little about the harmfulness of an act, then sanctions based on the occurrence of harm and its magnitude will be appealing, for harm constitutes evidence of dangerousness, whereas appropriate sanctions based on acts alone will be difficult for the state to determine. If the state does not know how dangerous it is to leave a live wire exposed (because the state does not know the likelihood that someone would step on it), a sanction based on harm resulting from that act will be more attractive than a sanction based only on commission of the act. Likewise, if the state does not know the particular nature of the act a person is likely to commit, only its general character, a sanction based on the commission of specific acts will be more attractive than prevention of a whole class of acts. If the state does not know whether a person will draw his gun and threaten another, it may be best not to prevent the category of acts, carrying guns, but only to sanction those persons who commit the act of brandishing their weapons in a menacing way.

If, rather than private parties possessing superior information to the state, it is the state that enjoys superior information, then the conclusions just discussed are reversed: Earlier legal intervention will become more attractive than later. If the state, but not a person, knows that a certain insecticide is carcinogenic, then the state might prefer to prevent its use through regulation, because the threat of sanctions based on expected danger from its use or on harm caused would tend to be ineffective. Note, though, that an alternative for the state would be for it to inform individuals of danger, in which case there would be no reason for early legal intervention. In some circumstances, however, communication is not possible or is costly.

Effectiveness and feasibility of sanctions. The effectiveness of sanctions depends on the likelihood that they will be applied and on their feasible magnitude. If sanctions will not be applied with high likelihood because individuals who commit undesirable acts or cause harm cannot easily be identified, sanctions will not be very effective. And if feasible sanctions will not be high, as would be the case if they are monetary but a person has little wealth, they would again be limited in effectiveness.

As a general matter, sanctions are disfavored, and prevention of acts is attractive, when sanctions are sufficiently lacking in effectiveness. If it would be difficult to catch a person who pollutes a reservoir, the best method for controlling this undesirable behavior may be to prevent it by fencing the reservoir. Similarly, use of an injunction may be the best method to control the behavior of a firm that could cause large harm by its activities and that possesses little in assets, because it would not be deterred much by the threat of a monetary penalty.

When sanctions increase in effectiveness, act-based and harm-based sanctions may become useful. In this regard, note that act-based sanctions do not require that sanctions be as high as harm-based sanctions, if the harm due to an act is probabilistic. To illustrate, consider monetary sanctions and the possibility that a person may not be able to pay for harm done, so that he would not be adequately deterred by fear of such sanctions from doing great harm. Yet sanctioning him for his act may still be effective, for the sanction necessary to deter him may be much lower. Suppose that a person's act would cause harm of 1,000 with probability 10 percent, that is, expected harm of 100, and would yield him a benefit of only 50, so that his act is undesirable. If society relies on an ex post sanction, imposed only if harm occurs, the person will not be deterred unless his assets are at least 500, for 10% × 500 is 50. But if society imposes a certain sanction for his act of only 100—the expected harm caused by it—the individual will be deterred as long as he has assets of at least 50. A party needs to have much higher assets to be deterred by the threat of sanctions for doing harm than by the threat of sanctions for committing an act, if the act causes harm only with a low probability.

In summary, then, ineffectiveness of sanctions may lead to the desirability of prevention over act-based or harm-based sanctions, and also to the appeal of act-based over harm-based sanctions.

Administrative cost. There may be substantial variations in the cost society bears for different methods of intervention. For example, it may be that prevention of some types of act is relatively cheap, compared to policing the acts or the harm due to them. To stop people from entering a reservoir, all that is needed is a fence; this may be much less expensive than stationing police around the reservoir to catch polluters and then imposing sanctions. When prevention can be accomplished by use of a physical barrier, whereas sanctioning would require monitoring to see when an act or harm is done, prevention may be economical. In other circumstances, prevention may be more expensive than the use of sanctions. To ensure that people behave correctly when driving, society could place a police officer next to the driver inside each car and have the officer stop the driver from making improper turns, speeding, and the like. But this prevention of bad driving would be absurdly expensive. As a far cheaper alternative, society uses sanctions to penalize bad driving and the harm it causes.

With regard to act-based versus harm-based sanctions, administrative costs are also relevant. Harm-based sanctions have an advantage in that they are applied only a certain percentage of the time, because acts often do not result in harm. This makes harm-based sanctions cheaper, other things being equal, although act-based sanctions are sometimes more easily imposed.

2.3 Determinants of the optimal form of intervention. With regard to the choice between forms of sanctions, what was discussed in Chapter 21 applies—namely, that sanctions should tend to be employed in the order of their cost. This means that monetary sanctions should be employed first, and then imprisonment only after monetary sanctions cannot be used because a person's wealth has been exhausted. (This point was subject to some qualifications, such as that monetary sanctions will not achieve incapacitation, but these qualifications need not detain us here.) With regard to the use of sanctions to discourage acts versus the prevention of acts, the cost element also comes into play, as just mentioned in section 2.2, for sanctions may be cheaper than prevention, or the converse.

2.4 Determinants of the optimality of private versus public enforcement. Whether it is advantageous for legal intervention to come about through legal actions brought by private parties or through efforts of public enforcement agents depends on which method most economically results in the identification and, if necessary, the apprehension, of the parties to whom the law should apply. In answering this question, it is useful to consider whether or not private parties naturally hold information about the identity of violators, that is, those to whom the law should apply.

Private parties naturally possess information about the identity of violators. Suppose that victims or potential victims of harm from dangerous acts, or perhaps other parties, can identify the violators with little or no effort. Then a private role in law enforcement is apparently desirable, for it is advantageous for society to harness this information that private parties have rather than to spend resources on public enforcement to uncover violations.

To avail itself of victims' information, society must provide them with an incentive to report their information to social authorities. One way to furnish victims an incentive to report is to give them a monetary reward for doing so. Notably, if victims can sue injurers for harm that they sustain, as they do under tort and contract law, they will have a motive to report harm that they suffer. Another possibility is that victims can be paid rewards by the state, rather than by those who injured them. Victims may also be motivated to report violators in order to obtain retributive satisfaction, presuming the violators will be sanctioned. Additionally, potential victims may be led to report violators in order to avoid future harm, as when a person brings an injunction to stop a dangerous activity that could cause him to suffer losses. Through these various means, society can induce victims and potential victims to report violations when the victims know the identity of the violators.

In some contexts, private parties other than victims will have information about violators, for they will witness violators' actions, such as when a person observes a hit-and-run automobile accident or knows that someone has violated the tax laws. When such parties have information about violations, financial incentives to report can be provided, usually rewards of some type. These parties' motives to collect, however, are often less strong than those of victims who have suffered loss. Also, these parties are less likely to obtain retributive satisfaction from reporting violations than would victims. Additionally, these parties do not usually benefit personally from halting an ongoing dangerous activity, unlike victims and potential victims. Consequently, the task of providing incentives to report is, in an approximate sense, more difficult when it is parties other than victims and potential victims who possess information about violations.

A possible difficulty connected with payment of money to private parties for reporting violations is that of false assertions of violations, as where a person sues for losses that he did not sustain, or an individual illegitimately claims that he observed another person speeding on the highway. To combat this problem, the state needs to be able to verify the validity of reported violations, and the ability to do this will vary. If a person sues for losses that he did not really sustain, it may be fairly easy to determine whether the losses were suffered because there will normally be evidence of loss; but if a person is reported to have sped, it is not clear that that can be verified. Where the problem of verification is serious, the use of financial incentives to obtain reports of infractions will be compromised.[4]

Effort must be expended to identify or to apprehend violators. When the identification or apprehension of violators is difficult and requires effort, enforcement by public agents may be required. If private parties are unlikely naturally to be able to spot and identify violators, such as those who discharge pollutants into a lake or those who speed on the highway, then a public enforcement effort may be needed to identify them. Even if a private party knows the identity of a violator, such as who it was that stole something, it might not be easy to locate that person, again possibly calling for public effort.

It is true that private parties might be provided with a motive to identify and apprehend violators by being paid bounties for so doing. This method, however, raises a number of difficulties. One is that payment of bounties may engender false accusations (similar to the problem just mentioned of false accusations if victims are rewarded for reporting violations). Another difficulty is that the incentive of private parties to find violators might be excessive for reasons analogous to those that explain why fishing effort is excessive (when one person devotes effort to finding a violator, he does not take into account that he lowers the likelihood that others will find him— see section 1.3 of Chapter 4). A more general issue is that there are many respects in which efficient effort to identify and apprehend violators requires coordination and, sometimes, investment in information systems (such as fingerprint records). A different problem with payment of bounties is that the social interest might not be served by maximizing bounty income, for the reduction in the number of violations is society's ultimate interest, yet this would reduce bounty income. The import of these various problems associated with payment of bounties is that public enforcement may hold out advantages over private. Another possible implication is that,

---

4. Of course, public enforcement involves similar problems: A public enforcement agent might frame a person to collect a reward for turning him in, or in order to extort money from him in exchange for not turning him in. But the methods available to control this problem are different from those available to control false reports by private parties (for instance, a police officer who observes speeding can be required to turn in an electronic record of a radar gun that clocked speed; his bank accounts can be monitored for extra income, and the like).

if private enforcement is desirable, it would probably have to be accomplished by large enterprises, and perhaps by regulated monopolies that would be rewarded not only by bounties but also for reducing the number of harmful acts. In any case, what is important for us is not so much whether enforcement by a public agency is best, but that the enforcement activity must be undertaken by a large organization that has the basic characteristics of public enforcement organizations: It must have a hired corps of enforcement agents who work in a coordinated way on a large scale to apprehend violators, and its interest must be not only penalizing violators but also deterrence. For simplicity, I will refer to this organization of enforcement as public enforcement.

Conclusion. This discussion suggests that when private parties themselves, and especially victims, can naturally identify violators, it will often be desirable to make use of their socially valuable information through a privately initiated means of law enforcement. But when effort is required to identify or apprehend violators, it will usually be advantageous to employ public enforcement agents to enforce the law.

3. OPTIMAL STRUCTURE OF LEGAL INTERVENTION ILLUSTRATED

I will now illustrate the analysis of the optimal structure of the law by considering important areas of legal intervention, and suggest that the characteristics of the legal regime that we observe are rational in an approximate sense. I will also examine the possibility of beneficial changes in the overall design of the legal system in the light of the foregoing theory about its optimal structure. I should note at the outset that much of the discussion of this section is conjectural and is motivated mainly by a desire to demonstrate the value of analyzing the gross structure of the law from an economic perspective.

3.1 Tort law. Consider the usual type of tort, such as an automobile accident, or an injury caused when an object falls from a crane at an urban construction site and injures a person walking by.[5] The question to be addressed is why is it socially advantageous for the behavior giving rise to

---

5. I restrict attention in this section to unintentional torts.

such harms to be controlled by means of a method of legal intervention with the characteristics of the tort system, namely, a system that imposes monetary sanctions when harm is done and when private parties sue to collect?

A speculation is as follows. First, the use of monetary sanctions alone for harm done leads to reasonably good incentives to reduce risk in the domain of tort, because the identity of the responsible party is known to the victim—this would tend to be true in an automobile accident, or if an object is dropped by a crane—and the responsible party often has assets or liability insurance coverage sufficient to pay for the harm. This is hardly to deny that incentives may be diluted by victims' inability to determine the authors of harm and by the judgment-proof problem. But these problems do not seem to be great enough in the general domain of tort to make resort to imprisonment advantageous as a sanction. If society were to imprison individuals for causing automobile accidents of the usual tortious nature, for harms caused when objects are released by cranes, and for the whole range of torts that we experience, the costs of this much more expensive form of sanction would be enormous and essentially unbearable.

To continue, if society were not usually to limit sanctions in the area of tort to occasions when harm occurs, but instead were to penalize potentially harmful acts or were to attempt to prevent them, it would encounter serious informational problems and incur staggering administrative costs. Society would have to identify which behavior was really dangerous enough to warrant sanctions. Given the great mass of behavior that could result in tortious harms (including the millions of daily instances of bad driving, failure to clear sidewalks of ice, and so on), the task of sorting out which behavior is dangerous enough to be punished could not be performed well. The courts would not know enough to be able to do that; making such determinations is more difficult than evaluating behavior that has resulted in harm. Moreover, the volume of cases that would have to be considered would be plausibly at least a hundred times larger than the volume of torts cases, for the simple reason that most dangerous behavior does not actually result in harm. Society saves greatly under the tort system because it engages the legal apparatus only in those instances in which harm eventuates.

It remains to be explained why it makes sense for private parties to have the role that they do under the tort system, that is, for sanctions to be imposed only when private parties sue and for the parties to collect the sanctions. The explanation is that in the circumstances of the usual tort, the victim knows or can readily ascertain the identity of the injurer. When a person is injured in an automobile accident or by an object that falls from a crane, as mentioned earlier, the victim will usually know or be able to learn easily who the injurer was. (Indeed, if this is not the case because the injurer attempts to conceal his identity, as in a hit-and-run accident, the injurer's act may be treated as a crime, and thus public enforcement will be employed to raise the likelihood of identifying him.) If the victims generally know or can learn the identity of their injurers, then they can be and will be led to initiate legal intervention by being allowed to collect the monetary sanction. Granting victims the right to sue and collect damages leads to the identification of injurers, and importantly, to the supply of information about their behavior that society would otherwise not be able to obtain or would have to spend to determine. If the state had to monitor the number of automobile accidents and impose fines for harm done, but victims would not collect as a consequence, how often would victims report the accidents, testify, and otherwise provide information about their harm and about the behavior of injurers? The private nature of the tort system, with the reward of damages paid to victims, allows society to enjoy the benefit of the knowledge that victims naturally acquire about the identity and behavior of injurers.

3.2 Safety regulation. Consider now types of behavior that classically are regulated: use of materials and devices influencing fire risks, elevator maintenance, the making and preparation of foods and drugs, the building and operation of nuclear reactors, and so forth. Here the question at issue is why we should control such behavior by means of regulation—that is, why should we employ in these cases prevention and act-based sanctions using public enforcement?[6]

With regard to our intervening before harm occurs, I surmise that reliance on harm-based sanctions would not be adequate to control much of the behavior under discussion. Where safety regulation is employed, it seems that the magnitude of possible harms is often large in relation to the

---

6. This behavior is also controlled by tort law, in that if it results in harm, tort cases may usually be brought; see section 3.6.

assets of actors. A fire at a movie theater could kill many people, substantially exceeding the assets of the theater owner; a nuclear power plant accident could cause vast harm, injury to tens of thousands of individuals, greatly exceeding the assets of its owner; and likewise with contaminated food and its producer or preparer. Moreover, in some cases, there would be difficulty in identifying the party who caused harm; the long-term harm generated by a nuclear leak might be hard to ascribe to the accident, due to the multiplicity of possible causes of certain cancers; food poisoning might be hard to trace to its origin.

If harm-based sanctions are inadequate to control harm, and prevention and act-based sanctions become appealing, society confronts the general problem that it needs to determine which behavior is really dangerous. In the areas of safety regulation, it appears that we have attempted to meet this problem by limiting the scope of regulation to those behaviors that we can say with fair confidence are undesirable. When regulating fire safety, we concern ourselves with such actions as the marking of fire exits and the installation of sprinkler systems, where it is not difficult for society to make a judgment about benefits and costs. Normally, society does not regulate safety where at issue are details of behavior, such as how much wood is stored in the basement of a hotel, because it is harder for a regulator to make a sound judgment about something like this than about whether there ought to be a sprinkler system in the hotel.

Society also tends to conserve the administrative costs of act-based intervention and prevention by such techniques as focusing on installation of devices that are easy to check (such as sprinkler systems) rather than on modifiable behavior (whether barbecue grills are used in a safe way), because that would often entail expensive, continuous monitoring; and when behavior is regulated, administrative cost savings are sometimes obtained by use of random monitoring.

Additionally, society sometimes uses methods of prevention of undesirable behavior when that is inexpensive. Consider the example mentioned of fencing a reservoir. Or consider the use of a tollgate at the entrance to a tunnel to prevent oversize vehicles or ones carrying hazardous materials from entering. In such instances, prevention is cheap, and by its nature does not rely on incentives to stop undesirable behavior.

The form of sanction employed in safety regulation, when methods of prevention are not employed, is often monetary because, as mentioned in section 2.2, act-based sanctions may not need to be very high to induce desired behavior. To induce a firm to install fire extinguishers costing $1,000, all society need do is impose a certain fine exceeding $1,000; the firm will then be led to install the extinguishers as long as its assets are at least $1,000. But if society relied on harm-based sanctions to induce the firm to install the extinguishers, the firm might not do that because of the judgment-proof problem. When monetary sanctions are not adequate to enforce regulations, however, we would expect, and we see, regulations enforced through the threat of criminal sanctions.

Finally, why is regulated activity publicly enforced? The answer seems mainly to be that individuals are often unable to identify dangerous behavior of the types at issue, for several reasons. One reason is that a person may not have the expertise necessary to evaluate risk; to evaluate the risk of the design and operation of a nuclear power plant, of methods of food preparation, of the likelihood that a type of drapery would burn and give off toxic fumes in a fire, and so forth, requires knowledge beyond that of the typical individual. A second, independent reason is that individuals may not be able to observe the behavior in question; they would not ordinarily be admitted into a nuclear power plant, a drug manufacturing facility, or a restaurant's kitchen. Hence, it seems that effort is needed to obtain information about dangerous behavior. Thus, for the general reasons furnished in section 2.4, public enforcement appears to be more desirable than reliance on private enforcement actions.

3.3 Injunctions.   Individuals bring injunctions for nuisances and clear, continuing threats to health or safety. We have to say why, for such behavior, it makes sense for society to make use of injunctions, that is, of prevention and act-based intervention that is privately initiated. As with the behaviors controlled by safety regulation, a partial answer may lie in the inadequacy of harm-based sanctions. A firm that fails to properly maintain a holding pool containing toxic waste might not be able to pay for harm done, so that sanctions for harm might not lead it to take ameliorative action, making an injunction a socially desirable method of controlling its behavior. One can imagine, however, many circumstances in which parties bring injunctions but where the judgment-proof problem is not clearly at issue, such as injunctions against the making of noise.[7] In any case, it appears that the areas of application of injunctions are such that the information the courts come to possess gives them confidence that enjoined activity is undesirable. Indeed, substantial information is provided to the courts by the fact that enjoined activity is often of a continuing character, and that it is sometimes activity that has produced harm in the past, as when a person has a history of making noise or of generating noxious odors.

That the behaviors at issue should be controlled through privately initiated legal action, rather than through public enforcement effort, is explained by the fact that the types of behavior that are usually enjoined are a subset of behaviors that can be observed and recognized as dangerous by individuals. There are many types of dangerous activities that individuals naturally recognize, such as the presence of vicious dogs, noxious odors, and so forth; virtually by definition, nuisances are activities of which we are aware, for they bother us. Individuals become aware of these acts because of where they occur, because little or no technical knowledge is needed to understand the danger they present, and for other reasons. For such acts, society benefits by allowing the individuals to bring injunctions to prevent harm; it would be a social waste to have public enforcement agents expending effort to find the nuisances and other dangerous conditions that individuals naturally recognize themselves.

3.4 Contract law.   Under contract law, private parties can bring suit for relief only when there is a breach, only when harm is done. Why does it make sense to govern behavior in contracts by means of harm-based legal intervention? The answer, in part, is that this will generally be enough to guarantee socially desirable behavior. Usually the use of ex post sanctions will be sufficient to accomplish the purposes of contract law. Indeed, as argued in the chapters on contract law, the payment of expectation damages (or whatever the measure is that the parties specify) will accomplish the purposes of the parties. The judgment-proof problem will be substantially mitigated by the fact that the parties tend to know about each other;

---

7. Here, though, it is possible that tort damages for noise are too low, for doctrinal reasons, effectively rendering harm-based sanctions inadequate, in which case it might be said (taking the inadequacy of damages as a constraint) that the injunction is desirable to control behavior.

if one contracting party believes that the other could not pay damages and would not have another reason to perform (such as a desire to maintain his reputation), the first party might choose not to contract or to take other steps to protect himself (perhaps not rely very much on performance).

To continue, let me suggest why a system under which the state intervenes in contractual relations earlier than when a breach occurs would be unworkable. The primary reason is that the state does not have enough information to know when a party is likely to commit a breach, and breach is often an event that occurs suddenly, for instance when a supplier decides to sell to another party, or does not deliver something on time because he neglects to ship it on the planned date. Indeed, it requires a real mental effort even to conceive of a world in which there is significant legal intervention before breaches of contract actually occur.

Regarding the form of remedy, several points should be made. As noted earlier, the use of monetary damages for breach is generally beneficial for the parties. This is not only because the system of monetary damages tends to induce performance, but also because it allows those with an obligation to commit breach when performance is very expensive or when highly favorable alternative opportunities present themselves. Note that if the form of sanction for breach were imprisonment (or another costly nonmonetary sanction), the costs of the sanction would be borne to the detriment of both the parties. (The victim of the breach would not only receive no compensation; he would also have to pay in the form of a higher price for the anticipated losses the party in breach would suffer.) Thus, monetary damages rather than imprisonment are the best form of sanction for breach. It remains to account, though, for the use of specific performance as a remedy for breach. As the reader will recall from Chapters 15 and 16, specific performance is desirable for the parties only in situations in which an escape hatch like breach with monetary payment is not mutually advantageous for the parties (typically, for contracts to transfer property that already exists, like land). Thus there is no conflict between what was just written about the undesirability of costly nonmonetary sanctions for breach when an escape hatch is mutually desirable and the use of specific performance in certain contractual contexts.

Finally, that it is rational for legal intervention for breach to be privately initiated by the victims of breach is virtually self-evident. When individuals make contracts, they know each others' identity, and when one of the parties defaults on his obligation, the other automatically knows it. Hence, society ensures that this information about breach is reported by allowing the victim of a breach to collect or to obtain specific performance. It would be a wasteful folly to have public enforcement agents attempt to identify those who made contracts and whether they were living up to them in a world where victims of breach were not given redress and would not be motivated to report breach (except out of irritation or anger).

3.5 Criminal law.   I now want to explain why the category of acts that we treat as crimes—murder, robbery, theft, and so forth—are controlled with the nonmonetary sanction of imprisonment, whether or not harm is done, and through the use of public enforcement. This discussion will be relatively brief given the consideration of aspects of this question in section 4 of Chapter 24. As emphasized there, the use of monetary sanctions alone would be grossly inadequate to control the acts in the core area of crime. The types of individuals who commit crimes often have little or no assets and are often unlikely to be identified, or at least apprehended, by private parties for having done harm. Car thieves, for example, tend to have little personal wealth and most instances of car theft do not result in sanctions. If car theft and most other acts in the core area of crime were to be punished solely by monetary sanctions, deterrence of these acts would be terribly inadequate.

The problems of achieving deterrence for criminal acts are sufficiently great that society cannot rely merely on sanctions for the doing of harm, and will find it desirable to impose sanctions when acts are committed that are potentially very harmful even though they do not result in harm, or in much harm, in a given instance. This is why it is rational for society to punish the whole class of attempts, and also why society punishes acts like carrying certain types of concealed weapons. These acts are very harmful in an expected sense, so it may well be rational for society to punish them. To restrict sanctions only to acts where a person succeeds in doing harm would be undesirable because of the inadequacy of that policy as a deterrent. Society does, however, tend not to punish acts that are not associated with a sufficiently large expected harm. Thus, if a person is discovered only at a very early stage of a murder attempt, or, say, if he is found to have only a concealed pocketknife, he might well not face sanctions. In such a

fashion, society addresses the problem of lack of information about dangerousness, at the same time that it augments deterrence by penalizing acts
before harm is done if the expected harm is large enough.

That society employs public enforcement agents in the area of criminal
behavior is chiefly due to the fact that it takes effort to identify and capture
those who commit criminal acts. Hence, for the general reasons advanced
earlier, it makes sense to use public enforcement agents to discover and apprehend criminals. In addition, those who commit criminal acts would often
retaliate against those who seek to sanction them; this could be problematic
for a system that depended on private enforcement (and is in practice a difficulty for public enforcement when the cooperation of witnesses is needed).

3.6 Joint use of methods of legal intervention.   Much behavior is
controlled by several methods of legal intervention. For example, many
harms are controlled both by tort law and safety regulation, and crimes
resulting in harm are usually also torts. At the most general level of explanation, joint use of methods of legal intervention seems socially desirable, for
we would expect that gaps in the effectiveness of one method of intervention would often usefully be filled by other methods of intervention. Let
us consider more specifically, although very briefly, the benefits of joint
use of safety regulation and tort law, and of criminal law and tort law, to
demonstrate the value of analyzing joint use of methods of control from
the perspective of this chapter.

Safety regulation and tort law. One observes that many harms are controlled both by safety regulation and by tort law. For example, harms due
to fire are controlled both by regulation dealing with such conduct as installation of sprinkler systems and fire exit signs, and harms due to fires are
also affected by the possibility of suits. What we need to explain is why
neither safety regulation alone nor tort liability alone is sufficient to control
harm due to fire (let me focus on this example here).

The answer as to why it is not advantageous to use the liability system
alone essentially matches the reason for use of safety regulation in the first
place: that liability may fail to deter where parties are judgment-proof or
would not be identified as the authors of harm. Some parties will thus not
be deterred by the threat of liability for causing harm (consider a restaurant
with meager assets), implying that it will be useful to have safety regulation
to induce or to force these parties at least to install sprinkler systems and

fire extinguishers to reduce fire risks. Safety regulation, in other words, operates as a kind of backstop to the liability system, when that system fails adequately to deter.

With regard to the converse question, why safety regulation alone is not used to control fire risks, the kernel of the explanation concerns the drawback of safety regulation that was emphasized earlier, that desirable regulation requires the government to obtain information that it is unlikely to possess for many acts affecting risk. The government may be able to determine that certain risk-reducing steps, such as installing sprinkler systems, are worth taking, and may be able to monitor them relatively cheaply, but there is much behavior that the government cannot assess with respect to its social desirability or that it cannot easily regulate. Consider whether restaurants keep flammable materials away from stoves, whether oily rags that could catch on fire are left in storage closets, and the like. The use of the liability system gives the many actors who do have assets sufficient incentive to take such precautions as removing oily rags and keeping flammables in safe places. This is why it is rational for the liability system to be used to complement safety regulation, and why compliance with safety regulation is not a general defense to liability in a tort action.

Criminal law and tort law. Most crimes that cause harm are also torts, for which victims can collect against injurers. Why should this be so? The primary answer involves the point that monetary sanctions are less expensive than imprisonment. If society determines that a person has committed a crime, then deterrence of this type of act can be increased inexpensively, from society's point of view, by imposing monetary sanctions.[8] Giving victims a right to sue in tort is one way of augmenting imprisonment with monetary sanctions. It might be asked, however, why that should be done using the tort system rather than solely by imposition of fines. Possible answers are that when victims can collect, rather than the state, their incentives to supply information to the state and to cooperate in prosecution are enhanced, and that this affords them with compensation if uninsured. In any case, the state also has the option to impose fines, and sometimes does so.

8. Recall from sections 3 and 4 of Chapter 21 that it is optimal to impose monetary sanctions equal to wealth before imposing imprisonment sanctions.

3.7 Possibly beneficial changes in the structure of legal intervention.   Although I have suggested that important aspects of the gross structure of our system of legal intervention may be seen as rational, there are significant beneficial changes that could be pursued. For example, greater use of financial rewards for those who report on infractions of law seems promising; it seems that public enforcement could be aided significantly by paying private actors for information. A basis for this belief is that private actors, especially those working within organizations, often possess information about violations of law; and to offer this information, they need to receive significant rewards (so-called whistle-blower rewards). Another general avenue for improvement would be to reduce the amount of regulation, given that it requires regulators to have more information than they can be expected to possess, and to substitute for regulation publicly imposed sanctions based on harm: namely, fines for harm (or fines inflated by the probability of discovery of harm), and corrective taxes for expected harm. Although fines are in fact employed, of course, that is done mainly to enforce regulatory requirements rather than to impose a bill on injurers equal to harm; and corrective taxes for expected harm are rarely used. These methods of intervention offer great advantages over regulation because they do not require the state to determine optimal behavior.

4.   REMARKS: INCOMPLETENESS OF ANALYSIS

There are several important respects in which the discussion here is incomplete. First, although I discussed the structure of legal intervention, I did not address the closely related issue of the overall scope of legal intervention: that is, which behaviors and conduct are desirable to control legally and which are not. The answer to this question depends in part on the social costs associated with legal intervention and on extralegal mechanisms of social control, notably, extralegal social sanctions associated with loss of reputation, and also the internally felt sanctions associated with breach of norms of morality. The stronger are these social sanctions and the force of morality, the lesser is the need for legal sanctions. These issues will be discussed in part in Chapter 27.

A second aspect of incompleteness of the treatment here is that some significant forms of legal intervention in our affairs were not noted or barely so. For example, I did not analyze corrective taxation, and I did not discuss declaratory actions.

A third element that I did not consider is the protection of risk-averse individuals against risk as a social goal. This was a simplification that I think is sensible to make because, as mentioned several times in this book, insurance is widely available on markets, and the state can always provide public insurance coverage against a risk if for some reason individuals do not purchase it and it is deemed socially desirable. Hence, it does not seem that satisfying insurance needs should be an important consideration in the choice of methods of legal intervention.

A final omission was the issue of income distributional equity as a social goal. As with omission of insurance needs, I believe this simplification was reasonable to make. The reason, which has been mentioned earlier and will be amplified in Chapter 28, is that income distributional equity can be pursued directly through the use of the income tax and public welfare systems. Thus, altering the design of the legal system to achieve distributional equity might needlessly compromise achievement of other social goals.

Note on the literature.   A number of articles analyze particular issues concerning the optimal structure of law from an economic perspective. See in particular Calabresi and Melamed (1972) and Kaplow and Shavell (1996b), emphasizing tort law and liability rules versus property rules and injunctions; Posner (1985a) and Shavell (1985a) on criminal law and tort law; Shavell (1984b, 1984c) on tort law and liability rules versus regulation; and Becker and Stigler (1974), Landes and Posner (1975), and Polinsky (1980a) on public versus private enforcement of law. Also, as noted, my article Shavell (1993a) sketches optimal legal design along the lines of this chapter. In all, however, the analysis of the structure of law is at an early stage of development.[9]

---

9. See also Polinsky 1980b on tort law and liability rules versus property rules and injunctions; Kolstad, Ulen, and Johnson 1990 and Wittman 1977 on liability rules versus regulation; Baumol and Oates 1988, Kaplow and Shavell 2002c, and Weitzman 1974 on corrective taxation versus regulation.

PART VII

WELFARE ECONOMICS, MORALITY, AND THE LAW

In this last substantive part of the book, I begin in Chapter 26 with a discussion of the normative foundations of economic analysis, namely, the subject of welfare economics. I also describe notions of morality and fairness, which play an important, if not dominant, role in most normative discourse about law, and I discuss the relationship between the two. A theme of this discussion is that notions of morality have functional aspects, and that, for a complex of reasons, they take on importance in their own right to individuals.

Then in Chapter 27, I consider the observed relationship between law and morality, and comment on it in respect to what might be thought to be the optimal relationship of law and morality.

In Chapter 28, I discuss somewhat separate issues concerning income distributional equity and the law, including the question whether distributional effects of legal rules should influence their selection. The answer to this question will be a qualified no, given that society has an income tax system to rely upon to redistribute income, or to correct problems with distribution that arise due to the effect of legal rules.

26 ||| WELFARE ECONOMICS AND MORALITY

In this chapter, I first discuss the framework of welfare economics that, as sketched in Chapter 1, has been used throughout the book in undertaking normative analysis of law. Then I define and describe the role of notions of morality and, at the end of the chapter, relate these notions to welfare economics.[1] This will enable us, in the succeeding chapter, to discuss the relationship between law and morality and to understand the connections between normative evaluation of legal rules that is based on welfare economics and that relying, at least in part, on ideas of what is right and just.

1. WELFARE ECONOMICS

1.1 General framework. The term *welfare economics* refers to a general framework for normative analysis, that is, for evaluating different choices that society may make. Under the framework, the social evaluation

---

1. I am, of course, well aware that in dealing with the general subject of morality, which has been intensively and continuously debated for more than two thousand years, no position that a writer advances is likely to be viewed as free from difficulty. A writer can, however, endeavor to be clear, especially about separating the description of moral notions from the prescription of behavior and social decisions on the basis of their agreement or disagreement with moral notions.

of a situation consists of two elements: first, determination of the utility of each individual in the situation, and second, amalgamation of individuals' utilities in some way. I will now discuss each of these elements.

1.2 Individual utility.   The *utility* of a person is an indicator of his well-being, whatever might constitute that well-being.[2] Thus, not only do food, shelter, and all the material and hedonistic pleasures and pains affect utility, but so also does the satisfaction, or lack thereof, of a person's aesthetic sensibilities, his altruistic and sympathetic feelings for others, his sense of what constitutes fair treatment for himself and for others (a point that will be of particular importance here), and so forth. It is important to note too that if there is uncertainty about the future and thus about the utility that individuals will turn out to experience, individuals will have a prospective evaluation of their well-being, which can be expressed as their expected utility, that is, as probability-discounted utility.[3] As the reader knows, this implies that the existence of insurance may benefit individuals because insurance raises their expected utility.

It is apparent, then, that the idea of utility is of encompassing generality; by definition, utility is advanced by anything that raises a person's well-being.

2. More precisely, a utility indicator or utility function attaches a number to each situation in which a person could find himself, and in such a way that higher numbers are associated with higher well-being. Thus, if situation x is preferred to situation y by a person, the utility associated with x must be higher than that associated with y. For instance, 2 might be the utility of x and 1 that of y, or 20 that of x and 12 that of y. Many different possible utility functions can *represent* the same ordering of possible situations by an individual according to his well-being. For concreteness, however, the reader might sometimes find it convenient to imagine (whether or not it is true) that there is a measurable level of a chemical, or of electrical activity in a region of the brain, that is higher the higher the person's reported well-being is, and that this particular quantity serves as utility.

3. A person must have *some* way of evaluating situations involving uncertainty, because the supposition is that he can always state his well-being and state a preference for one situation over another, and some situations involve uncertainty. Thus, the statement in the text that a person has a prospective evaluation is merely an observation about his having well-formed preferences, not a distinct claim about their nature. That a person's prospective evaluation of an uncertain situation can be expressed as a probability-discounted sum of utilities—as an expected utility—is a distinct claim about preferences, and it can be proved under very weak assumptions (see in particular Savage 1972), but these assumptions need not detain us here.

1.3 Amalgamation of utilities through the social welfare function.

According to the welfare economic framework, the social evaluation of situations is assumed to be based on individual well-being. In particular, it is presumed that the social evaluation, labeled *social welfare,* depends positively on each and every individual's utility—social welfare is raised when any individual's utility increases—and does not depend on factors apart from their utilities.[4]

There is a vast multitude of ways of aggregating individual utilities into a measure of social welfare, and no single way is endorsed under welfare economics. One possible measure of social welfare is that of classical utilitarianism, the sum of individuals' utilities. Under other measures, not just the sum (or something like it) but also the distribution of utilities generally matters, and more equal distributions of utility may be superior to less equal distributions.[5] Under welfare economics, the assumption is not that the evaluation of social states is guided by one particular view about the proper way of amalgamating individuals' utilities (within the general class of ways of so doing), but only that there is some way of doing this.

Comments. (a) *Distribution of income.* Considerations about equity in

---

4. To express the framework formally, suppose that there are n individuals, and let the utility of the first individual be denoted U_1, that of the second U_2, and so forth. Also, let x stand for an exhaustive description of a situation. Then social welfare, $W(x)$, can be written as $W(x) = F(U_1(x), U_2(x), \ldots, U_n(x))$. Here, $W(x) > W(x')$ is interpreted to mean that situation x is socially preferred to situation x'. As noted, it is assumed that $W(x)$ increases as each person's utility (U_1, U_2, etc.) increases. It should be noticed that social welfare, $W(x)$, is influenced by x *only* insofar as x affects the utilities of individuals; it is solely the utilities of individuals that determine social welfare. It should also be observed that the mathematical form of the social welfare function W depends on the utility functions U_i that are chosen to represent the well-being of individuals; if, for instance, for person i we altered the utility function U_i by doubling it to $U_i^*(x) = 2U_i(x)$, then W would be modified such that half of U_i^* would play the role of U_i in W.

5. For example, suppose that W equals the sum of square roots of utilities, and consider a situation where there are two individuals, and each has the same utility, 100. Then social welfare is 20, namely, $\sqrt{100} + \sqrt{100} = 10 + 10$. This equal distribution of utility is superior to the unequal distribution where one person has utility of 50 and the other 150, in which case social welfare is 19.32 (for $\sqrt{50} + \sqrt{150} = 7.07 + 12.25$), and this distribution is superior to the extreme distribution in which one person has all the utility of 200, in which case social welfare is 14.14 (for $\sqrt{200} = 14.14$).

the distribution of income can be expressed in the measure of social welfare. Notably, the distribution of income affects the distribution of utilities, and this distribution, as just stated, may influence social welfare in any way. For further discussion of why the distribution of income affects social welfare, see section 1 of Chapter 28.

(b) *Exclusion of factors unrelated to individuals' utilities.* The assumption that social welfare does not depend on factors apart from the utilities of individuals can be formally defined in the following way: Suppose that in two different social situations, say x and y, every single individual says, "I am just as happy in situation x as I am in situation y." Then situations x and y must be accorded the same level of social welfare.[6] (If this x and this y were said to possess different levels of social welfare, it would have to be that something apart from the profile of utilities across the population matters to the evaluation of the social situations.) I will sometimes call this kind of measure of social welfare, the kind that is studied under welfare economics, a *utility-based* measure of social welfare in order to differentiate it from a measure of social welfare that depends on something else as well.[7]

(c) *Exclusion of "objective" notions of well-being as the basis of social welfare.* Consider an objective notion of well-being, for example, the notion that any enjoyment derived from the unhappiness of others ought not count as objective utility. Such an objective notion of utility cannot be employed as the basis of social welfare under welfare economics, given the assumption that social welfare is a function solely of individuals' (subjective) utilities.

2.   NOTIONS OF MORALITY DESCRIBED

2.1 Definition of a notion of morality.   There are numerous conceptions of what actions are said to be correct, right, fair, just, or moral (I will use these words interchangeably, for convenience). These conceptions

---

6. Formally, the assumption is as follows. Suppose in two situations x and y, for each individual i, $U_i(x) = U_i(y)$. Then $W(x) = W(y)$. This assumption may easily be verified to be equivalent to the assumption (see note 4) that social welfare $W(x)$ may be expressed in the form $W(x) = F(U_1(x), U_2(x), \ldots , U_n(x))$.

7. In economics, what I am calling a utility-based measure of social welfare is usually called *individualistic,* or sometimes *welfaristic.*

are, at least implicitly, ways of evaluating situations; the correct, right, fair, or moral behavior or action is ranked above the incorrect, wrong, unfair, or immoral behavior or action.

Some conceptions of fairness concern equity in the distribution of things. Thus if there is a cake to be divided between two individuals, it might be said that it is generally right for each to be allocated an equal share. Many such ideas of fair distribution may be viewed as methods of evaluation based on the distribution of utilities of individuals. (In the cake example, the idea of fair division of the cake corresponds to a distribution of the cake such that each individual derives the same utility from his portion of the cake.) Any idea of *distributional fairness* can be expressed as a utility-based social welfare function and is thus comprehended under the framework of welfare economics.

Other conceptions of fairness and morality involve factors distinct from, or in addition to, the distribution of utility among individuals. For example, it is said that if a person makes a promise, it is correct for him to keep it; that if one person wrongly injures another, fairness requires that he compensate the victim for his losses (the classic notion of corrective justice); or that if a person commits a bad act, it is right that he be punished in proportion to the gravity of the act. On reflection, the reader can verify that these examples of nondistributional moral notions share a basic feature: They are all means of evaluating behavior, and thus social situations, that *do not depend at all, or at least do not depend exclusively, on the utilities of individuals*—they depend on something else. Promises are supposed be kept not because, or not only because, this raises the well-being of those who make and benefit from promises (even though that may generally happen); compensation is supposed to be paid for harm wrongly done not because, or not only because, this will insure victims, discourage future harmful behavior, and keep the peace (even though these things will tend to occur); punishment is supposed to be imposed in proportion to the seriousness of the bad acts not because, or not only because, this will lead to reasonable deterrence of bad acts and raise potential victims' utility (even though that may generally happen). Rather, promise-keeping, compensation for wrongs, and correct punishment are important, as moral notions, because they are intrinsically good, or for some underlying reason (such as that they are in accord with a system of natural justice), but in any case not solely, if at all, because of their effects on the well-being of individuals.[8] I will henceforth focus on these *nondistributional* ideas of fairness and, for expositional ease, will mean by fairness or morality, and the like, a nondistributional conception.[9]

Now to say that a moral notion is a means of evaluating behavior that does not depend exclusively on the utilities of individuals is not enough to define what is usually meant by a moral notion. Consider a rule of behavior such as "Do not wear a hat when butterflies can be seen." This principle of behavior does not depend on individuals' utilities, but the principle is not one that we would call moral. The reason is that what is said to be a moral notion is one that is accompanied by particular types of sentiments on our part.[10] I now turn to a description of these sentiments, that is, of the psychological aspects of moral notions.

2.2 Definition continued: psychological attributes associated with notions of morality. One psychological attribute associated with what we tend to call a notion of morality is a feeling of *virtue*, of pleasure of a type, that a person experiences when he obeys a notion; and an opposite psychological attribute is a feeling of *guilt* or remorse, of displeasure, that

---

8. Formally, a notion of morality that does not depend exclusively on the utilities of individuals is associated with a social welfare function $W(x)$ that is not individualistic, and cannot be written in the form $F(U_1(x), U_2(x), \ldots, U_n(x))$. That is, given W, there must exist situations x and y such that for each individual i, $U_i(x) = U_i(y)$, yet $W(x)$ does not equal $W(y)$.

9. Although I am calling notions of fairness that do not depend exclusively on utilities nondistributional, some writers occasionally use the term "distribution" in connection with these notions. For example, corrective justice requires that a wrongdoer compensate his victim, and a writer might say that the compensation paid is a matter of just distribution. I am reserving the term distribution to refer to the allocation of utilities across the population and hope that the reader will not be confused by my usage.

10. One observation about moral notions (but this is not part of the definition in the text) is that they apply primarily where the well-being of more than one person is at issue. Promise-keeping involves a promisor and a promisee; punishment involves a wrongdoer and a victim; and so forth. A principle that affects only one individual (such as "go on a diet") would not tend to fit with our use of the term "moral." (There are some exceptions, having to do with ideas of prudence, temperance, and self-control, but the reasons for these principles having the attributes of the other moral principles are, it can be argued, similar to those that will be adduced for other moral principles.)

a person suffers when he disobeys a notion. Thus, when a person keeps a promise, he may feel virtue, and if he breaks a promise, he may feel guilt.

Moreover, it is not just the individual who acts morally or who fails to act morally who may experience an increase or a decrease in utility, as the case may be; it is also *other parties,* including onlookers, who know about the event, who may experience an increase or a decrease in well-being. For example, if we learn that a person has committed a wrong but has been properly punished, we may feel good about the punishment; and if we learn that he has not been punished at all, or has been punished too severely given the gravity of his act, we may feel worse for that reason.

It is also true that onlookers will sometimes derive utility from taking certain actions in the light of behavior that obeys moral notions—onlookers may praise and otherwise reward good behavior, and obtain utility from so doing (otherwise they would not do it)—and in the light of actions that violate moral notions, onlookers may disapprove and otherwise punish bad behavior.[11]

To summarize, then, I am *defining* a (nondistributional) notion of morality to be a principle for the evaluation of situations that (a) does not depend exclusively on the utilities of individuals, and (b) is associated with the distinctive psychological attributes leading, as described, to virtue and guilt, praise and disapproval.[12]

2.3 Tastes for notions of morality and individual utility. It is apparent from the foregoing section that individuals possess, in connection with a notion of morality, a set of tastes that affect their utility. A person will feel happier, his utility will be higher, if he feels virtue because he kept a promise, or if he learns that punishment of a wrongdoer was correct; and a person will feel worse if he experiences guilt because he broke a promise, or if he learns that punishment of a wrongdoer was harsh. That such sources of utility and disutility are different in their character from conventional

11. The connection between morality and feelings of virtue and guilt, the moral sentiments, has been developed over the years by, among others, Hutcheson [1725–1755] 1994, Hume [1751] 1998, Smith [1790] 1976, Mill [1861] 1998, and Sidgwick [1907] 1981.

12. It should be remarked that purely distributional notions of fairness and morality (such as "act so as to ensure that the utilities of individuals are equal") are also often associated with guilt and virtue, praise and disapproval.

springs of utility and disutility (such as satisfying one's hunger and skinning one's knee) is of no moment from the perspective of welfare economics. I will address later the implications of the point that individuals' utility is affected by the satisfaction or failure to satisfy moral notions; here my object is just to make that observation.[13]

2.4 Comment: The existence of tastes for satisfying notions of morality is different from their possible deontological significance. When philosophers discuss moral notions and urge that they be adhered to, they do not generally give as the reason that individuals will be made happy by so doing. Philosophers do not say that individuals should be punished in proportion to the badness of their acts because this will make victims and onlookers happy in a direct sense. They recommend moral actions on other bases, which may be broadly described as deontological. Indeed, they often are explicit in saying that the justification for a conception of morality is not dependent on the tastes, the sources of happiness, of individuals in the population, but instead derives from independent factors. Otherwise, the answer to the question whether an action is recommended as right by philosophers would depend on the contingency of what the inclinations, the preferences, of the population happen to be.[14] Similarly, when individuals themselves (as opposed to philosophers) explain why a moral notion should be respected, they usually will not say that it is only because that will make them happy; rather, part of their rationale ordinarily is that obeying the notion is correct per se.

2.5 Analysis is descriptive. The reader should bear in mind that what I have written to this point is entirely descriptive; it is what a social scientist would report about notions of morality. I have not stated what role moral notions ought to have in the evaluation of social situations, and in particular in the choice of legal policy. Rather, I have attempted to describe a certain class of evaluative principles, the moral ones, and have pointed out that they are associated with a particular set of tastes (those producing feelings of virtue, guilt, and so forth).

13. This point was, to my knowledge, first made by Mill [1861] 1998, 82–84.
14. See, for example, Kant [1785] 1998, 21–22.

3. FUNCTIONALITY OF NOTIONS OF MORALITY

3.1 Notions of morality tend to advance our well-being.   It has been long observed, and has been articulated in considerable detail, that the satisfaction of our broadly held notions of morality tends to advance our well-being. The keeping of promises allows people to plan and leads to cooperative ventures that raise our well-being; punishment according to the gravity of acts deters bad behavior in an effective way and thus raises our well-being; and so forth.[15]

3.2 Comment: Fostering our well-being is different from the deontological basis for notions of morality.   That obeying notions of morality fosters our well-being is not the justification for such notions, according to deontologists. They may admit, and think it good, that obeying promises promotes our welfare, but that is not the warrant for obeying promises in their eyes; they would want promises obeyed even if that did not advance our well-being.[16]

3.3 One reason why obeying moral notions tends to advance our well-being: socially undesirable self-interest is curbed.   One general reason why obeying moral notions promotes our well-being is that this means that individuals will not behave in self-interested, opportunistic ways when doing so would be socially undesirable. If I adhere to the principle of keeping promises, then I will not break my promise whenever that becomes advantageous to me, whereas if I were to break promises for any personal gain, the value of promises would be diluted and the social benefits associated with promises would diminish. If I follow the principle of punishing in proportion to the gravity of the bad act, I will be less likely to shy away from punishing a person because of fear of retaliation or because of squeamishness, nor will I allow anger to result in excessive punishment; were I to act otherwise, the purposes of deterrence might not be well served.

15. See especially Hume [1751] 1998 and Sidgwick [1907] 1981, and see also Mill [1861] 1998.
16. See, for example, Kant [1785] 1998 and Ross 1930.

3.4 Another reason why obeying moral notions tends to advance our well-being: myopic decisions are prevented.   A second way in which following moral notions may advance our well-being is by serving as guides for behavior in situations where it may be difficult to perceive what would maximize our own utility. For example, breaking a promise may be tempting, but keeping promises tends to be in our self-interest in the long run, because doing so means that those with whom we interact now and in the future will come to trust us, and this trust will benefit us in manifold ways (promises will be made and kept with us, we will be honored and admired, and so forth). Or it may be that punishing in proportion to the badness of an act will serve our self-interest because we will be dealing with the punished person repeatedly in the future (suppose the punished person is our child). By following a set of relatively simple moral principles, individuals may, to a degree, promote their self-interest without having to think carefully about how they should act to do that.

3.5 Why we tend to obey moral notions: internal and external incentives associated with the psychological attributes of moral notions.   For individuals to obey moral notions, they must *want* to do so.[17] Otherwise, they would follow their self-interest, or their apparent, myopic, self-interest.

There are two fundamental reasons why individuals will often want to obey moral notions, connected with their associated psychological attributes described in section 2.2. One is that individuals have *internal incentives* to do so, namely, they will feel virtuous if they adhere to them, and experience guilt if they do not. Second, individuals have *external incentives* to obey moral notions in that they will be praised by others for that behavior and admonished, scolded, or otherwise punished for immoral behavior.

3.6 Moral notions themselves must also be of a particular nature to be functional; in strict logic they could be perverse.   The argument that our well-being is advanced by our adhering to moral notions depends, of course, on the assumption that the particular moral notions to which we subscribe are beneficial. If, for instance, there was a moral notion that we should break promises rather than keep them, then adhering to this moral notion would lower our welfare. In that case, if we curbed our self-

---

17. This basic point was early stressed by Hume [1751] 1998.

interest when self-interest would lead us to keep promises, and instead broke promises in order to adhere to the moral notion, the moral notion would tend to reduce our well-being. The question arises, therefore, why, if the class of moral notions that exists tends to advance our well-being, that it is this class, and not a perverse set of moral notions, that we observe. A suggested answer to that question is given next.

4. ORIGINS OF NOTIONS OF MORALITY

4.1 Inculcation. It appears that many notions of what is right are taught to us, especially as children, by our parents, teachers, religious figures, and other authoritative individuals, as well as by our peers (notably, in play, when we are children). To a degree, the teaching occurs through example, or sometimes through pronouncement and command, or sometimes through reasoning that refers to the functionality of moral rules—for instance, a parent might explain to a child, "Think of where the world would be if no one kept his promises." The process of teaching, and of reinforcing, notions of morality continues beyond childhood as well. The claim that moral notions are to an important degree taught is clear, not only because we know from common experience that teaching does occur, but also from the fact that there is, within a society, substantial homogeneity of moral notions, and that among different societies there is significant heterogeneity in moral beliefs (compare the norms of the orthodox Muslims of Saudi Arabia to those of present-day Americans, or those of either to the norms of the Aztecs). It is hard to explain why moral notions within a given society are similar, and why those among different societies may display real variation, if moral notions are not to an important extent instilled.

4.2 Evolutionary advantage. Some notions of what is correct may have an evolutionary basis, at least in part.[18] A possible example is the principle that punishment should be imposed, and in proportion to the seriousness of the transgression, for this principle has an evolutionary advan-

18. On the general theme of this section, see Darwin [1874] 1998, chaps. 4, 5, and, for example, Frank 1988, Hirshleifer 1977, and Wilson 1980.

tage. In particular, if a person is harmed, say if food is taken from him, this will reduce his chances of survival. Thus, a behavior that reduces the incidence of harm like theft of food will be favored in an evolutionary sense; the genes leading to behavior that prevents theft of food will tend to predominate in the population over time. But the pattern of behavior of punishing, of retaliating, when harm has been done is often against the narrow, momentary self-interest of a person, because after a harm is done, it may be too late to undo it, and retaliation may also absorb effort and subject the retaliating person to risk. Thus, a person is likely to retaliate and punish only if he has a *desire* to punish per se. Therefore, we would expect the desire to punish those who have caused harm to be selected as a trait in an evolutionary sense. Further arguments along these lines can be offered for why the desire to punish should be calibrated to the level of harm done. Evidence for the claim that this desire has an evolutionary basis is not only theoretical; behavior that suggests that animals are motivated to retaliate in proportion to harm done has also been widely observed.[19]

Other moral notions that arguably have an evolutionary basis include altruism (certainly for family members; broader forms of altruism may also have an evolutionary basis, or may be a sublimated form of that for relatives).[20]

Of course, only a subset of our moral notions can have an evolutionary basis, or they can only have a rough basis, for otherwise they could not be malleable, as they are, and could not be learned.

It may well be, however, that our *generalized capacity* to learn and to obey moral notions has an evolutionary basis. People who are capable of learning and of desiring to adhere to a set of moral beliefs are likely to survive better than those who are not. In the mists of time, such individuals could have learned a set of behaviors that would, given their circumstances, lead them to survive better, cooperate in ways that were good in their environment, and the like. Thus, a certain blank-slate character of the capacity to learn moral notions must be valuable, because it allows the notions to develop in a way that is beneficial for persons in a given environment. This capacity to learn a somewhat flexible set of moral notions, in combination

19. On the biological origins of retribution, see for example, Daly and Wilson 1988, chaps. 10, 11, and Trivers 1971, 49; on the retributive urge in animals, see, for example, Waal 1982, 205–207.

20. On altruism, see Trivers 1971 and Wilson 1980.

with the inherited, genetic predisposition to want to adhere to the learned notions (to feel virtuous if they are obeyed, to feel guilty if not), whatever they are, is highly functional and should have been favored in an evolutionary sense. (If so, then the fact that we appear to have an ability to inculcate moral notions, as just described in section 4.1, is explained.)

4.3 Comments.   Several additional remarks about notions of morality are worth making.

(a) *Simple character of moral notions.* From what has been written, it seems to follow that moral notions must be the way that they are observed to be, namely, relatively simple in character. In particular, for moral notions to be taught, especially to children at an early age, they have to be fairly basic. If moral notions were too nuanced, they could not be readily absorbed by children nor by the mass of individuals whose ability to ratiocinate is not high. In addition, if we consider the ways in which moral notions raise our welfare, it is apparent that the notions cannot be too complicated. To be practically useful, moral notions have to be capable of being applied quickly, without great deliberation, for many decisions in which they are needed have to be made rapidly. In addition, to serve to curb opportunism, it is advantageous for moral notions to be of a relatively unqualified nature, for otherwise they would be vulnerable to manipulation by individuals who could find reasoning supporting their self-interest. For example, if the moral notion about promise-keeping includes the qualification that promises can be broken for a substantial range of excuses, a person would be able, and perhaps likely, to fashion excuses for breaking his promise when that would not be socially desirable.[21]

(b) *Imperfect functional nature of moral notions.* The simplicity of moral notions implies that they will only imperfectly serve to advance social welfare. Because they are simple, they will inevitably fail to induce socially desirable behavior in some circumstances.[22] For example, in some situations, it will be desirable for a promise to be broken, because the cost of

21. The general view that moral notions must be of a fairly simple character is developed by Austin [1832] 1995, lecture 2, and is emphasized, among others, by Sidgwick [1907] 1981 and Hare 1981.

22. This point is stressed by the authors cited in the previous note, and by Baron 1993, 1994, among many others.

satisfying it exceeds the benefit it brings about (as I explained at length in Chapters 13 and 15), yet this will not agree with the simple moral notion, which requires that the promise be kept. Another reason, apart from simplicity, that moral notions will not perfectly advance social welfare (whatever that measure may be) is that the notions are learned. This implies that they will have a certain inertia about them, possibly lasting generations, even though they may lose their functionality as circumstances change. Likewise, to the extent that moral notions are inherited due to the evolutionary pressures of the eons, reflecting factors that may no longer exist, they may not be functional, or not perfectly so. The desire to retaliate when we have been wronged may be an example in point, for although there are still benefits associated with this desire, it may be too strong for our purposes, so that if we could mold it, we would reduce its power.

5. WELFARE ECONOMICS AND NOTIONS OF MORALITY

5.1 In general.   In this section, I want to sketch the relationship between welfare economics and notions of morality in light of what has just been discussed. The main points are, first, that because of the functionality of notions of morality, they should be inculcated and fostered—this raises social welfare overall.[23] Second, because individuals have a taste for the satisfaction of the notions of morality (whether inculcated or inherited), there is a direct sense in which the notions have importance in the social welfare calculus; their satisfaction matters apart from the benefits they bring us through effects on our behavior. But third, the notions should not be given importance in social welfare evaluation beyond that associated with their functionality and with our taste for their satisfaction—no deontological importance should be accorded them—for doing so would conflict with social welfare and lead to its reduction.

5.2 The functionality of notions of morality implies that society should invest in their inculcation.   The arguments given in sections 2 and 3 explaining how notions of morality advance social welfare imply that

23. Kaplow and Shavell 2002b investigates the optimal inculcation of moral notions, and the optimal use of guilt and virtue to enforce the notions, in a formal model of social welfare maximization.

it is worthwhile for social resources to be devoted to instill and reinforce these notions. Social resources are in fact directed toward teaching moral notions through the efforts of parents and other authority figures, religious institutions, and the like, as described in section 4.1, and possibly through the law as well, as will be discussed in the next chapter. Altogether, the investment of social resources in inculcation of morality is substantial, and may well be justified by the social benefits thereby derived; indeed, greater investment may be warranted. In any case, the point of emphasis here is that, from the perspective of welfare economics, investment in fostering the learning of notions of morality is investment in a valuable form of social capital.

5.3 Notions of morality as tastes affect social welfare. Given that individuals attach importance to notions of morality as tastes, the notions of morality exert a direct effect on social welfare. For example, if I keep a promise and feel virtuous as a result, this feeling, which augments my utility, thereby raises social welfare. Other things being equal, that in turn means that to maximize social welfare, promises should be kept somewhat more often than would be optimal if the measure of social welfare did not reflect this utility that individuals experience from keeping promises. In other words, satisfying notions of morality is itself a component of social welfare, even though it happens to be the case, under the view advanced here, that the reason for the existence of these notions is also to advance social welfare. To put the point differently, the notions of morality have, and must have, importance to individuals in order to induce them to act against their narrow self-interest to advance social welfare. But once this is true, it happens, as a kind of by-product of their ultimate purpose, that the notions affect social welfare themselves, in their own right.[24] (I will sometimes use the term *conventional* social welfare to refer to the measure of social welfare in which tastes for morality are not included, and will use the term *morally inclusive* social welfare to refer to the measure of social welfare in which the tastes are reflected.)

5.4 Ascribing independent importance to notions of morality reduces social welfare. The point that satisfying notions of morality influences social welfare by affecting individuals' utilities should be sharply distinguished from the assumption that the notions have independent im-

---

24. As noted earlier, essentially this view was advanced by Mill [1861] 1998, 82–84.

portance, regardless of the degree to which they raise the utility of individuals. The view that a moral notion, such as the duty of promise-keeping, matters in itself to the evaluation of social welfare is (see section 2.4) the deontological view that is shared, at least in part, by virtually all philosophers. Such views conflict with a fundamental assumption of welfare economics, which is that social welfare depends exclusively on the utilities of individuals.

If a notion of morality is given independent significance in the evaluation of social welfare, a utility-based measure of social welfare will tend to be reduced, for that measure will be compromised to some extent in order to adhere to the notion of morality. For example, if promise-keeping is granted independent significance, more promises will be kept than would be best if the goal were to keep promises only to advance individuals' utilities, and whatever utility-based measure of social welfare one endorses will likely be lower than it could be.

5.5 Pareto Conflict Theorem. That according weight to a notion of morality per se tends to lower social welfare is reflected in the following conclusion: *If independent weight is given to a notion of morality under a measure of social welfare, then in some situations the utility of every individual will be lowered as a result of advancing that measure of social welfare.*[25] That this claim should be true is not surprising, for if the notion of morality has independent weight, this weight will exceed the importance of individuals' utilities between two possible social states if the utility differences between the two social states are sufficiently small. Suppose, for instance, that independent weight is given to promise-keeping, and that all individuals very slightly prefer that promisors be able to break promises when a certain type

---

25. The conclusion can be more precisely expressed. Let W be a social welfare function that is not individualistic. Then the assertion is that it is possible to find two social situations x and y such that $U_i(x) > U_i(y)$ for each individual i (that is, x is Pareto preferred to y), yet $W(y) > W(x)$. The proof of this requires only very weak assumptions, essentially that there is some good, such as a consumption good, that all individuals like to possess and that W is continuous in the amounts that individuals have of this good (a much weaker assumption than that W is continuous in many, or all, components of social situations). The conclusion is informally discussed in Kaplow and Shavell 1999 and formally demonstrated in Kaplow and Shavell 2001a.

of difficulty arises.[26] Now if the preference of each individual for being able to break promises when this difficulty arises is small enough, the fact that promise-keeping has independent weight implies that social welfare will be promoted by insisting on promise-keeping when the difficulty arises. Thus, all individuals will be made worse off—their utilities will be reduced—as a result of the independent weight placed on promise-keeping. Such situations in which all individuals are made worse off can be shown definitely to arise; whatever is the notion of morality, and whatever is the strength and character of its independent significance, there will *always* exist situations in which maximizing the measure of social welfare reflecting this notion will reduce the utility of *all* individuals. Let me call this conclusion the Pareto conflict theorem, because it states that giving weight to a notion of morality leads to conflict with the Pareto principle—that if all individuals prefer one situation to a second, the first should be socially preferred.

Several comments should be made about the Pareto conflict result. First, the result implies that any person who believes that a measure of social welfare should rise whenever the utilities of all individuals rise— the Pareto principle—must abandon any view that ascribes independent importance to a notion of morality, that is, any deontological view. This implication is forced on the person by the requirements of logical consistency. If a theory about the social good conflicts with a principle that one endorses in any situation, the theory must be rejected for that reason.

Second, a response that I have sometimes encountered to the Pareto conflict result is that, in actual fact, one social choice will rarely, if ever, be preferred by all individuals to another, so that what would be true were there unanimity of preference can be ignored. This response suffers from a nonsequitur. The premise that, in reality, one social choice will rarely, or never, be preferred by all to another may well hold. But it does not follow from this premise that what would be true in that situation is irrelevant. For if what would happen under a deontological principle would contradict

26. The reason that all individuals—promisors and promisees—might prefer that promisors be able to break promises if a difficulty arises is that this may raise the value of contracts to both parties. As explained in Chapter 15, if the cost of performance in the difficulty exceeds the value of performance, allowing nonperformance will raise the value of the contract to the promisor and to the promisee; the latter will gain because the promisor will be willing to lower the price by more than the decline in value to the promisee due to the increased likelihood of nonperformance.

unanimous preferences in a hypothetical situation, such a principle must be abandoned provided that we endorse the Pareto principle. A hypothetical situation that never arises can be quite relevant, because it can reveal a property of a view that leads us to abandon the view; that the situation never really arises hardly means that we cannot draw implications from what would occur in that situation. If we know that a theory of addition implies that, were we on the planet Pluto, two plus two would equal five, we must abandon that theory even if we know we will never be on Pluto.

Note on the literature. The views presented in this chapter are synthetic, and are based, as indicated in the notes, on sometimes long scholarly traditions. The general conception that moral notions are associated with feelings of virtue, a form of utility, if one obeys them, and are associated with guilt and other emotions creating disutility if one disobeys them, is developed especially by Hume ([1751] 1998), Mill ([1861] 1998), Sidgwick ([1907] 1981), and Smith ([1790] 1976). The fundamental idea that moral notions serve functional purposes is also advanced by these authors, among many others. The observation that moral notions are to a degree inculcated is discussed, for example, by Austin ([1832] 1995) and Mill, and by Hare (1981); and the point that the notions are in some ways produced by evolutionary forces is stressed by Darwin ([1874] 1998) and in much modern-day sociobiological literature, for instance, by Trivers (1971) and Wilson (1980). The point that, although moral notions advance social welfare, they do so only imperfectly, due in part to their relative simplicity, is emphasized by Austin and Sidgwick, and see also Baron (1993) and Hare. Regarding the implications of the moral notions for social welfare, the point that it is socially worthwhile to invest in fostering them is consistent with the view of all who see functionality in the notions. The point that moral notions do enjoy importance because individuals derive utility from their satisfaction, and thus for that reason constitute a part of the social welfare calculus, is made by Mill. The conflict between utility-based social welfare and deontological views of morality has in a general sense been the stuff of debates about utilitarianism and related issues in philosophy; the point that all deontological views necessarily conflict with the Pareto principle, and thus are in deep tension with individual well-being, is demonstrated in Kaplow and Shavell (2001a).

27 ||| IMPLICATIONS FOR THE ANALYSIS OF LAW

Having discussed welfare economics and morality in general, let me now examine some implications for the legal system. In particular, I here consider the observed relationship between law and morality; the optimal domain and design of the law, taking morality as a regulator of conduct into account; and the nature of normative discourse concerning law and morality.

1. OBSERVED RELATIONSHIP BETWEEN LAW AND MORALITY

1.1 Rough congruence exists. Most legal systems appear to reflect, in a broad and approximate manner, the moral notions of the societies in which the legal systems apply. In our own country, we see that many acts that the law penalizes are considered wrong, violative of shared ideas of what is moral. Consider murder, rape, robbery, and most crimes; much negligent, tortious behavior; opportunistic breaches of contract; or the creation of nuisances.

Moreover, not only do the acts about which the law is concerned often seem to be wrongful, the legal sanctions that are imposed in response appear to be in rough accord with basic moral remedial principles. In the area of civil law, the general character of the legal remedy is that the wrongdoer pays the victim for harm sustained; notably, tort damages are supposed to indemnify victims for losses and contract damages to make the victim of a breach whole. This central tendency of the civil law is interpretable as that of classical corrective justice, that wrongdoers compensate their victims for harm suffered. In the area of criminal law, penalties rise in some fashion with the gravity of the bad act; roughing someone up in a brawl is penalized less than stalking him and beating him severely, and this less so than his murder. That is to say, criminal punishment tends to bear a proportion to the degree of wrongdoing, which is the underlying principle of retributive justice.

Additional evidence for the claim that the law reflects morality is that legal systems vary over time and among countries in a way that comports with differences in notions of morality. For example, laws concerning the permissibility of types of sexual relations (out of marriage, homosexual) have changed in character over the years in our country, and are much unlike those of conservative Islamic countries, such as Saudi Arabia.

1.2 But substantial differences between law and morality are apparent.

Yet there are important respects in which legal systems do not reflect the notions of morality that a society holds. First, many acts considered to be wrong are not sanctioned by the law. Lying is generally considered immoral, but it often is not legally punishable (a vast range of false statements that are made in social settings, at the workplace, and in commerce are not actionable). Changing one's plans for modest personal advantage, but to the greater detriment of others, is also often considered wrong but does not give rise to legal sanctions (suppose that I say that I will teach a much needed course, but then bow out because I would slightly prefer to teach something else). Also, acting in a grossly negligent way (such as leaving a live wire exposed where children are playing) is wrong, but will probably not result in a legal action unless somebody actually comes to harm. It is evident, therefore, that there is a substantial domain of behavior that is wrong but is not addressed by our formal legal system.

Second, many acts that are penalized under the law are not considered wrong, or only in a very attenuated way. Where liability is strict, parties face sanctions even if they take all reasonable precautions and thus even if their behavior is not wrongful.[1] Another general example is provided by legal rules that most would describe as technical, especially those concerned with finance and business—consider the requirements for registration of securities with the Securities and Exchange Commission and fine points of the doctrines governing the permissibility of mergers under the antitrust laws. These rules cannot easily be linked to our notions of morality. It is possible, though, that because individuals understand such technical rules to have been designed to promote the common good in some way, however indirect and ramified (registration of securities promotes trade in securities, which allows firms to raise capital and individuals to invest, which leads to more economic activity and ultimately to greater welfare), there does exist a refined sense in which individuals feel a duty to obey the technical rules. Nevertheless, I believe the reader will agree that these technical areas of the law do not have a clear moral basis.[2]

Third, the magnitude and character of legal sanctions sometimes depart significantly from what our moral sense would require. Tort damages are often different from what would seem to be an actor's just deserts. A firm that knowingly acts negligently and in such a way as is likely to cause great harm (including many deaths) but that turns out to cause only modest harm may be required to pay just for that harm, whereas we might well believe that the firm deserves to be punished severely and that responsible individuals within it should bear strong penalties. A party who decides to break a contract because a more advantageous opportunity has arisen may only have to pay modest damages, whereas the moral duty to keep promises

---

1. Sometimes, however, it is asserted that our sense of morality would lead to liability for harms arising from engaging in the activities for which strict liability applies (such as transporting wastes across a lake). If this were so, then I would say that the sense of the moral obligation is a weak one, but the reader can judge that issue for himself.

2. It is no answer to say that individuals feel a moral obligation to obey all our laws, whether technical or not. This may be true (in which case, any rule whatever would be considered to have a moral basis). The question under consideration here is whether legal rules have an independent moral basis—a basis such that, were they *not* part of our legal system, there would be a moral reason to adhere to them (virtue would be felt if they were obeyed, guilt if not; see section 2 of Chapter 26).

might seem to call for more serious legal sanctions. Fines and other criminal penalties also often deviate from retributive principles of proportionality. For example, fines for parking violations may be many multiples of harm done (consider a $25 fine for parking too long at a metered space), whereas the punishment for murder may be less than the harm done (a few years in jail arguably translates into less than the loss of a life).

1.3 Explanation of the foregoing.   The descriptions of the preceding sections make basic sense from the point of view of economic analysis and what has been written in Chapter 26 about notions of morality. Specifically, we would expect to observe substantial, if rough, congruence between law and morality for two reasons. The first is simply that individuals want moral notions to be obeyed; as discussed in section 2 of the previous chapter, individuals attach importance to the moral notions themselves and desire that they be satisfied. Because the law is designed by individuals, it is not surprising that the law should be influenced by the value that individuals place on adherence to the moral notions. Thus, for instance, because we believe that promise-keeping is desirable, we wish contract law to promote the keeping of contracts, and because we desire punishment to be in proportion to the seriousness of bad acts, we want criminal sanctions to be fashioned in that way.

The second reason that an observer would expect there to be a degree of resemblance between morality and law is different. If morality and law have the same underlying objective, to promote social welfare, we would predict that these two systems of rules would display similarities. For example, we would expect both morality and our legal system to foster the keeping of promises because that promotes social welfare through inducing cooperative efforts, trade, and production. In other words, it is not just that the law fosters the keeping of contracts because of the moral value people place on promise-keeping. Rather, the law has also evolved to foster the keeping of contracts because of the functional value of so doing, and the moral notion of promise-keeping has evolved because of the same functional value.

We would also expect there to be substantial differences between our system of morals and law. The first difference that I mentioned, that there are many immoral acts (like lying) that the law does not sanction, is understandable from the economic perspective. As will be discussed in section

2, it is impractically costly for society to attempt to govern a significant domain of undesirable human behavior through the legal system, whereas it is relatively inexpensive and generally sufficient to control much such behavior through our notions of morality alone. Additionally, some immoral behavior is not socially undesirable, so that we would not want to control it through use of the legal system; because our notions of morality are, and must be, relatively simple in character (as was discussed in section 4 of Chapter 26), certain acts that are socially desirable will be seen as immoral, and it would be unwise policy to make them illegal.

The second difference that I noted was that there are many acts that are punished under the law (like improper mergers of businesses) but which are not immoral, or not obviously so. The main explanation for this is that there is much behavior that is worthwhile controlling in order to raise social welfare, and which the law therefore does control. At the same time, some of this behavior is not offensive to our system of morality, because again, our notions of morality are relatively simple. This point will be amplified in section 2.

Similarly, the third difference that I noted, concerning deviations between legal punishment and what seems meet from a moral perspective, can be explained by the fact that the law is fairly flexibly designed to promote social welfare, whereas our system of morality has a relatively unrefined character. For a variety of reasons, sanctions that advance our welfare will not necessarily be set in proportion to the gravity of bad acts. Notably, the optimal magnitude of sanctions from a social welfare standpoint will reflect the likelihood of their imposition and the costs of their imposition (as was spelled out in Chapters 20 and 21), but these factors are largely independent of the moral quality of acts. This too will be discussed later, in section 3.

1.4 Effect of law on morality. To this point in my consideration of the relationship between law and morality, I have not mentioned the possibility of an effect of the law on our notions of morality and its force,[3]

---

3. What has been noted so far is the influence of morality on law—in that we design the law to reflect our moral tastes—and an influence on both law and morality of the underlying goal of advancing social welfare.

but it is probable that this effect exists and I mention here two possible ways in which it may come about.

First, it is plausible that the law influences the moral beliefs that individuals hold. As mentioned in section 4 of Chapter 26, our moral views seem to a significant extent to be inculcated and learned. Thus, the law might influence our moral beliefs if it plays a role in instilling and teaching individuals moral values, and one can see that this may be so. For example, a parent or a minister, in trying to impress on a child the lesson that theft is wrong or that discrimination based on skin color is wrong, could mention to the child that the law holds that theft and discrimination are illegal and result in sanctions. This statement about the law could lend authority to the message and make it more likely that the child would learn the lessons and ultimately adopt them as moral values. There is also a possibility that legal rules would exert a similar effect on adults and help to alter their moral beliefs. (But to me this seems a less important factor, given what I perceive to be the small degree to which adults change their fundamental moral beliefs.)

Second, the law can enhance the effectiveness of our moral beliefs by changing our willingness to impose social sanctions on those who have violated notions of morality; this in turn will enhance deterrence of immoral behavior. Consider whether a person who believes that discrimination is wrong will be inclined to chastise those who engage in it and otherwise impose on them social sanctions. It seems plausible that such a person would be more likely to impose these social sanctions if there exists a law penalizing discrimination. The person might infer from the existence of the law that the view that discrimination is wrong is more widely held in the population than he otherwise believed, and thus that more individuals would join him in condemning this behavior, or would give silent approval, or at least would not resist his condemnation. The existence of the law might also reduce the chance of retaliation against the person contemplating admonishing the discriminator, for the latter could be threatened with legal sanctions. In other words, the rational calculus of a person who holds moral beliefs against a type of behavior, and who contemplates imposing social sanctions on those who engage in the bad behavior, changes in favor of so doing when there is a law against the behavior. In this way, without altering intrinsic moral beliefs, the law can influence their effectiveness because the law increases the likelihood of social sanctions for immoral behavior.

2. OPTIMAL DOMAIN OF LAW AND OF MORALITY

I now consider the question of the optimal domain of morality and of the legal system.[4] That is, which behaviors are socially advantageous to control solely through use of our notions of morality, which behaviors are best to control jointly through morality and law, and which ones are desirable to control through law alone? In examining these issues, I will assume that our notions of morality are as described generally in section 2 of Chapter 26, and that the social goal is to employ morality and law so as to maximize social welfare, taking into account the costs and effectiveness of morality and of law as social regulators of conduct.[5]

2.1 General comparison of law and morality as regulators of conduct. As I discussed in section 3 of Chapter 26, notions of morality can serve to govern behavior so as to further social welfare by means of internal incentives—the reward of the feeling of virtue, the penalty of guilt—and also by means of external incentives—the reward of praise, the penalty of chastisement. The legal system of course governs behavior through use of external incentives, principally monetary sanctions and imprisonment. Let me now compare morality and law as methods of social control of behavior. After doing so, I will make use of the comparison in an examination of the optimal domains of law and morality.

Establishment of rules. The establishment of legal rules ordinarily is not a very expensive process, requiring only that a law be passed by a legislative body or that a judge make a decision that helps to articulate a rule, and that the rule be properly communicated. But the establishment of moral rules is evidently very expensive from a social perspective, assuming that

---

4. This section is based largely on Shavell 2002.

5. To amplify, in this section the object is to maximize social welfare where, for convenience, I focus on the effectiveness and the costs of the law and of morality, without taking into explicit account that our notions of morality themselves enter into individual utility and thus into social welfare. This simplification will not affect the qualitative nature of the conclusions reached. For example, were I to take into account how adherence to moral notions itself raises utility and thus is a source of welfare, the conclusion that it is socially desirable sometimes to regulate conduct solely through moral notions, because they are cheapest, would not change (only the boundaries of the domain of behavior over which the sole use of morality would be optimal would change).

this occurs through socialization and inculcation. To instill the moral rules that one should not litter, or lie, or cheat, and the like, requires constant effort over the years of childhood (and reinforcement thereafter). If we regard the duties of parents, schools, and religious institutions as comprised importantly of the teaching of children in the moral dimension, then we can appreciate that society's investment in imbuing moral rules is substantial. Yet one should also note that where moral notions are inborn, or virtually so, establishment of the notions is essentially free from a social perspective.

Specificity and flexibility of rules; degree to which rules reflect socially desirable conduct. Legal rules can be as specific as we please because they are consciously and deliberately fashioned by us. Hence, legal rules can in principle be tailored to promote socially desirable conduct and to discourage undesirable conduct at a highly detailed level. Legal rules are also flexible in the sense that they can be changed essentially at will, as circumstances require. Hence, if what is socially desirable or undesirable changes, so can legal rules change.

By contrast, it seems that moral rules cannot be highly detailed and finely nuanced in character. As discussed in section 4.3 of Chapter 26, these rules need to be inculcated in children, be easy to apply in everyday life, and not be vulnerable to self-interested manipulation. Also, to the degree that moral rules have an evolutionary basis, they will often tend to be simple, because very specific rules are generally not ones that have functional value over the long periods of time during which the forces of natural selection operate. Additionally, moral rules are not very flexible. Rules that are inculcated are not subject to alteration in the short run, and when the moral rules have a biological basis, they obviously cannot be changed.

The implication of the lack of specificity and flexibility of moral rules relative to legal rules is that moral rules will more often lead to errors in conduct than legal rules. For instance, a person may decide to honor a contract due to the moral obligation to keep the promise it represents, even though breaching the contract would be socially preferable under the circumstances (perhaps the expense of performance greatly outweighs its value to the promisee) and the law would allow breach. Or a person might refrain from reporting the bad behavior of a friend out of a moral duty of fidelity, even though it would be socially desirable for the friend to be reported (perhaps his bad behavior would otherwise continue), and the law might allow or require reporting.

Magnitude of sanctions. Legal rules can be enforced by monetary sanctions and by imprisonment, with no limit in principle save for the wealth of an individual and his remaining lifetime. As such, the potential magnitude of legal sanctions is great.

What is the magnitude of the moral sanctions? I will assume here that the moral sanctions are, over most of their range and for most individuals, weaker, and perhaps much weaker, than high legal sanctions. This is based on the judgment that, at least for the great mass of individuals in modern industrialized nations, the disutility due to losing one's entire wealth or going to jail for life outweighs, and probably by a significant amount, the sting of guilt and of disapproval (or rather, that plus the utility from virtue and praise).[6] This is not to deny that for some individuals, the moral sanctions might have greater weight than the legal (a person might fear burning in hell forever, or find the disapproval of the public to be almost intolerable), nor is it to deny the possibility that in some future world, moral socialization could be such that doing the right thing mattered much more than it now does. But in the type of society in which we find ourselves, where internal moral sanctions appear limited and external ones are diluted by, among other things, the ability of individuals to move away from those who might reproach them, the assumption that moral sanctions are weaker seems to be the correct one. Another point that should be made is that moral sanctions are unable to prevent bad conduct through incapacitation of individuals, which is accomplished by the legal sanction of imprisonment. Thus, an important tool for reducing bad conduct that is available under the law is absent from the moral arsenal.

Probability of sanctions. The probability of legal sanctions depends on circumstances; the imposition of sanctions for violations is not automatic. For a legal sanction to be imposed, the violation of law needs to be observed by someone, and then it has to be reported. Even where it is observed by

6. The true incentive to act in a moral way is the difference between one's position when one acts morally and when one does not; it is thus the sum of the utility of the reward for acting morally (the utility from virtue and praise) and the disutility from doing otherwise (the disutility from guilt and disapprobation).

the victim and he can bring suit, such as might be the case with a tortious harm and would usually be the case with a breach of contract, the victim might not find legal action worthwhile given its cost. Also, for many violations for which enforcement is public, the likelihood of sanctions is notoriously low.

In contrast, the probability of imposition of the internal moral sanctions is 100 percent, as previously noted (self-deception aside). A person who believes that it is immoral to cheat on his taxes will definitely feel guilty for so doing, and will definitely feel virtuous for paying the proper amount, because he will know whether he honestly paid his taxes.

The probability of imposition of the external moral sanctions, of disapprobation and praise, is a different matter, and may or may not be higher than that of imposition of legal sanctions, depending on the context. For instance, the likelihood that a person would be seen cutting into a line and would suffer the external moral sanction of sour looks is presumably high (for others in the line would notice), but the likelihood of being found out and of experiencing disapproval for cheating on one's taxes might be lower than that of being caught in a tax audit, for tax cheaters are unlikely to be caught by their fellow citizens.

Availability of information for the application of rules. In the application of legal rules, certain information is needed. But information can be difficult to acquire or verify, such as that concerning whether a person committed a crime and, if so, what exactly the circumstances were. The difficulty associated with substantiation of information has two disadvantageous implications. One is that errors may be made, such as when a person is found guilty of murder when he really acted in self-defense, or when he is found to have acted in self-defense when he in truth did not. The other is that legal rules are sometimes designed in a less refined manner than would be desirable if more information were available. For example, bartenders might be held strictly liable for serving liquor to minors because information about bartenders' true opportunities to determine the age of customers is generally hard to obtain.

These disadvantages due to difficulties in obtaining information do not apply in regard to the enforcement of moral rules with internal sanctions, because a person will naturally know what he did and why. If a person kills someone, he will know whether he acted in self-defense; if he serves liquor to a customer, he will know whether he suspected that the customer was underage. The virtually perfect quality of the information that a person has about himself means that the internal moral sanctions will not be erroneously applied and that the moral rules need not exclude any potentially relevant information.[7]

The conclusion is somewhat different, however, with respect to enforcement of moral rules with external sanctions. Here there may be informational difficulties, for the observer of conduct may not have all the relevant information or may make errors. Nevertheless, these problems are often less serious than those faced by the legal system. When a person's conduct is observed by another person, such as when one person catches another in a lie, the observing party who chides or reprimands the wrongdoer does not have to establish what he knows to the satisfaction of a tribunal. Additionally, there is a peculiar self-correcting mechanism at work in respect to the imposition of external sanctions: If a person is mistaken in his criticism of another, the reproval may be dulled in its effect, for it seems to be a psychological fact that disapproval will not register as much if it is not deserved.

A further point about external moral sanctions, but working in favor of legal sanctions, is that parties who observe the conduct of others may sometimes not possess certain relevant information that could be acquired in a legal setting. For instance, if one person observes that another breaks a promise to him and is given an excuse as the rationale, the victim of the broken promise might not be able to determine whether the excuse is the truth. In a legal setting, however, an excuse offered for breaking a contract could be investigated; witnesses could be forced to come forward and to testify under oath.

Costs of enforcement. The costs of enforcement of legal rules have to do with the expenses of identifying violators and of adjudication, which can be substantial, especially when public enforcement agents are involved. By contrast, the costs of enforcement of moral rules are nonexistent in regard to internal sanctions. In regard to external sanctions, costs of enforcement

7. The point of this paragraph may be compared to the point made earlier that moral rules may lead to socially worse outcomes than legal rules because of the limited complexity of moral rules. Here, the point is that moral rules may lead to socially superior outcomes than legal rules do, because of the greater information that may be available for application of the moral rules.

are probably lower on average than those of legal rules, even though there might be some adjudication in the form of gossip and discussion of the propriety of acts.

Costs of imposition of sanctions. Legal rules involve sanctioning costs, and these depend on whether the sanctions are monetary or are terms of imprisonment. As has been discussed in Chapters 20 and 21, monetary sanctions are sometimes said to be socially free, or at least much less expensive than imprisonment.

Regarding moral sanctions, consider first guilt. Because guilt does not involve administrative expense, it appears to be a socially cheaper form of sanction than imprisonment. Disapproval is much like guilt as a sanction, except that the consequences of its use for those who express it need to be incorporated into the social calculus, and what should be assumed about this matter is not entirely obvious. Virtue and praise obviously differ from guilt and disapproval in that they are sanctions that create utility, rather than lower it.[8]

The conclusions about the costs of imposing sanctions may be summarized as follows: The legal sanction of imprisonment appears to be the most costly, monetary sanctions may or may not be more costly than guilt and disapprobation, and virtue and praise actually increase social welfare when employed as incentives.

Amoral individuals. To this point, I have been considering general factors bearing on legal versus moral rules, but a particular factor of potential significance bears mention. Namely, there may be individuals in the population for whom moral incentives are not very important. Indeed, this group may not be small in size, especially in societies, like that of the present-day United States, where families and other social institutions that provide stable environments for the socialization of children are often weak. The existence of a relatively amoral subgroup of the population implies that, for them, moral sanctions will fail to prevent much immoral behavior. Members of this subgroup will, by assumption, not be significantly affected by the internal moral incentives of virtue and guilt, and will probably also not care as much as others about the external incentives of disapproval and

8. For an economically oriented analysis of the moral sanctions of guilt and virtue, taking into account that guilt is costly and that virtue creates utility, see Kaplow and Shavell 2001b.

praise. Moreover, these individuals will be unlikely themselves to impose the external moral sanctions called for by the misconduct of others, exacerbating the breakdown of the power of moral incentives. The presence of amoral individuals is thus a factor that favors legal rules over moral rules.

Firms (and other organizations). Another special factor worthy of note is that the power of moral incentives may be diluted within firms (and other organizations). Consider first the internal moral incentives, and let me note initially the familiar point that, because a firm is not in fact a person, but rather a collective comprised of different individuals, we cannot speak in a literal sense of internal moral incentives in respect to a firm. Individuals within a firm, however, can feel guilt or virtue in regard to their own behavior. A reason for thinking that the internal moral incentives may be less effective in the setting of the firm than outside that setting is that decisions within firms are often made jointly by groups, or influenced by orders from above, or acted on and influenced by subsequent decisions made below; this serves to attenuate the sense of personal responsibility for one's acts. Another factor is that firms often attempt to establish their own norms of loyalty (consider the corporate ethos at companies like IBM), which may tend to offset the usual moral incentives when such incentives come into conflict with the objectives of the firm.

Second, the external moral incentives have unclear force in relation to employees of firms. One reason is that, as just remarked, responsibility within a firm is often diffused, so that there often will not be specific individuals within firms whom outsiders will be able to identify and punish for wrongful behavior. Another reason is that a firm may have an incentive to conceal the identity of responsible individuals within it, just so they can escape external social sanctions. But outsiders may impose external sanctions on a firm even though they have not identified a responsible individual within it. For example, they might refuse to make purchases from a firm that acted in a grossly negligent manner.

Summary. Law and morality each has advantages over the other in certain respects. Law may enjoy advantages over morality due to the ease with which legal rules can be established, their flexible character, and the plausibly greater magnitude of legal sanctions over moral sanctions. Also, the presence of amoral individuals favors reliance on law, as does the presence of firms, for whom moral forces are likely to be relatively weak. Moral sanctions, however, are often applied with higher likelihood than legal ones (notably, internal moral sanctions apply with certainty), may reflect superior and more accurate information about conduct, and may involve lower costs of enforcement and imposition.

2.2 Domain in which morality alone is optimal.   It will be best to control behavior solely through use of morality when three conditions hold: first, that morality functions reasonably well by itself; second, that morality is not worthwhile supplementing with law, given the social benefits that would flow from that and the added costs; third, that law alone is not as desirable to employ as morality alone.

These conditions will tend to apply when two things are true: The expected private gain from undesirable conduct is not too great, and the expected harm due to such conduct is also not too great. For if the expected private gain from bad conduct is not too great, then the moral sanctions, even though not as strong as legal sanctions, will very often be sufficient to discourage the conduct. And if the expected harm from bad conduct is not too great, then on those occasions when moral sanctions fail to prevent the conduct, the social effects will not be so serious, and thus would not warrant the added expense of the legal system as a supplement to morality. The question remains, however, whether it might be more desirable to employ law alone than morality alone. The points just made imply that the social value of law over morality will not be great, so that use of morality alone will be superior to use of law alone when the added expense of the law exceeds its modest marginal social value.

Let us now examine the domain in which behavior is in fact controlled primarily by morality. This area of behavior is, as indicated earlier, comprised of a great multitude of acts that we undertake in everyday life. Consider the keeping of promises about social engagements, acting so as to refrain from creating minor nuisances, or lending a helping hand when it is easy to do so. I suggest that this domain of behavior where mainly morality applies is broadly consistent with the theory just advanced. In particular, the expected private gains from bad conduct are in fact typically small or modest. If a person breaks a lunch date, cuts into a line, or fails to keep quiet in a movie theater, the benefits that he obtains are not usually large. This being so, the moral sanctions will often be enough to deter bad conduct; the automatic functioning of the internal moral sanction of guilt, combined with the external sanctions, will frequently be sufficient to dissuade individuals from acting incorrectly. Further, when that is not so and individuals do engage in bad conduct, the harms they cause appear on average to be minor. Again, if a person breaks a lunch date, cuts into a line, or talks in a movie theater, the social detriment will usually not be significant. Hence, the claim is that it would not be socially worthwhile to append the legal system to the moral system in order to help prevent this residuum of bad acts from occurring. That is, it would not be advantageous to subsidize civil suit to bring about legal actions for such harms as broken lunch dates, or to employ public enforcement authorities to hand out tickets for cutting in line or talking in movie theaters, because the cost of doing so would outweigh the benefit from the not-too-great additional harms that would be prevented.

Moreover, it is also likely that many mistakes would be made under the legal system relative to that under the moral one. When an individual breaks a lunch date or cuts into a line, he will know about this and, as noted earlier, will not make errors in judging the correctness of his own behavior. Also, the assessments of those around him will tend to be reasonably accurate, at least by comparison to those that would be made under the legal system. The legal system could not hope to sort out, in the way we do ourselves, broken lunch dates due to valid excuses (suppose that a truly good friend appeared unannounced from out of town) from those that are not. The mistakes that would inevitably be made under the legal system, especially punishment that is not merited, constitute a separate cost that reinforces the argument against use of the law in the domain of everyday conduct.

It remains to consider whether it might be desirable to employ the law alone instead of morality alone for such behaviors. In order to assess how law alone would function, we must imagine a world in which people are unlike people as we know them—we must envision individuals who are devoid of compunctions about breaking promises, lying, and the like, who essentially do not care about each other, who are sociopathic. And we must ask in this notional world how well law would control the behavior and about the expense of control. A strong surmise is that it would be enormously expensive to control the behavior at issue because of its variousness and extent, that society might be bankrupted by a serious attempt to do so, and, as mentioned in the previous paragraph, that many mistakes would be made. The conclusion is that use of law alone would be clearly inferior to use of morality alone in the domain where morality is observed to be relied on.

2.3 Domain in which morality and law are optimal. It will be best to use law to supplement morality where the cost of so doing is justified by the extra social benefit. This will tend to be true when two conditions hold: The expected private gains from undesirable conduct are often large, and the expected harms due to such conduct are also often large. For if the expected gains from bad conduct are great, then the moral sanctions may not be enough to prevent it. And if the expected harms from bad conduct are substantial, then failure to prevent bad conduct will be socially serious, and thus make worthwhile the additional expense of the legal system as a supplement to morality.

Let us now consider the range of behavior that is regulated both by morality and by law. This area covers most acts that are criminal; murder, rape, robbery, fraud, and the like are not only crimes, but also generally are said to be immoral. Additionally, many torts, including most acts of negligence, many breaches of contract, and many violations of regulations not only are legally sanctionable but also are considered not to be moral.

It appears that this domain of behavior is characterized by the condition that the private gains from bad conduct are often large. The utility obtained by those who commit criminal acts tends to be significant; the murderer, the rapist, and the thief generally have strong motivations to act. Also, the private benefits obtained by those who commit many torts or breaches of contract are substantial, especially because large amounts of money are frequently at stake. Hence, the internal moral sanctions alone will often not be enough to prevent the bad conduct.

Another reason for failure of moral incentives to control conduct in the domain is that the external moral incentives are often unlikely to apply, because the bad actor will not be noticed or, if noticed, will not be reprimanded. This is obviously so of many criminal acts. Similarly, behavior that can give rise to torts often goes unspotted, or at least does not result in disapproval. For example, consider improper driving behavior, such as speeding or going through a red light. If a driver does these things, he often will not be noticed, and if he is, how can other drivers scold him? The external sanction of disapprobation is unlikely to be brought to bear in many other situations in which accidents might occur, and in which tort law and safety regulation are in fact brought to bear. This point should not be overstated, however. There are important situations, such as breaches of contract, in which problematic conduct will be noticed and there will be ample opportunity for observers to express their disapproval of it.

The condition concerning the harm from bad conduct also applies in the domain in question. The social consequences of failure to control crimes and torts, which often result in injury and death, as well as breaches of contract and many of the other acts to which our legal system applies, are manifestly great (especially in comparison to the consequences of broken lunch dates, cutting in line, and other quotidian misbehavior). Hence, the benefits from preventing these harms through use of the law, when they are not prevented by morality, are significant, and these benefits outweigh the costs of employing the legal system.

Additionally, the problem of amoral individuals is of obvious relevance to the issue at hand. Because the magnitude of harm from the undesirable conduct that we are considering is great, the existence of amoral subgroups is of special significance. Even if small, such subgroups, if unchecked, can wreak great social harm, especially through repeated crimes, but also through extremely negligent behavior, failure to obey contracts, and other bad acts.

The presence of firms further supports the thesis that law is needed as a supplement to morality in the realm of behavior under discussion. As suggested earlier, the force of moral sanctions, both internal and external, is diluted in respect to the behavior of firms. Firms, though, are often in a position to do large harm by virtue of their size and importance in modern economies; they mediate most production and exchange and can cause much physical and economic injury from misconduct. Hence, if society attempted to control the behavior of firms only by resort to moral sanctions, substantial harm would result. Legal rules, however, do alter the behavior of firms for the good, either directly, by fiat, or by threat of monetary sanctions.

Thus, altogether, my conclusion is that for most of the acts that society has chosen to control through the law and through morality, the use of moral incentives alone would not function well due to some combination of the following factors: substantial private benefits from committing bad acts, inadequacy of internal and external moral sanctions to counter the private benefits, the presence of amoral subgroups, and the activity of firms.

The imperfect performance of our moral system as a regulator of conduct, together with very high social costs of failure to control conduct, warrants the use of our costly legal system.

A different reason why law may be socially useful in controlling conduct where morality also applies is, in a sense, the opposite of what has been discussed so far in this section. Namely, it may happen that a notion of morality is socially counterproductive, and legal rules are needed to channel behavior in a different, and socially desirable, direction (rather than that legal rules are needed to steer behavior in the direction that morality already points).[9] For example, I mentioned the possibility that a person might refrain from reporting a friend's bad conduct because of a feeling of loyalty, even though reporting the conduct might be socially desirable, or that a person might not want to breach a contract, even though breaching might be socially desirable given the high cost of performance. If so, legal intervention, requiring the reporting of the friend or permitting breach, might be socially desirable. Although these situations in which law may be needed to offset the effect of morality are not typical, neither are they rare, and this should not be considered surprising. As stressed above, moral notions cannot be too complex for various reasons, and thus we would predict that they would come into conflict with socially desirable behavior in some circumstances.

Having considered why it is beneficial to supplement morality with law to control the behavior under discussion, let me address the question of why it would not make sense for society to rely solely on the law to control the behavior—that is, why it is beneficial to supplement law with morality. For example, why should society not rely solely on criminal law to combat murder? A primary answer must be that law will only imperfectly deter murder, and given the seriousness of that act, society will find it advantageous to employ morality also as an instrument of control. There will be many occasions in which a person would be unlikely to be caught for a murder that would advantage him, but if he thinks murder is a moral evil, he might not even contemplate that act, much less commit it. As a general matter, legal rules do not always apply, and even when they do apply with high likelihood, the sanctions may not be strong enough to deter bad behavior. For this reason, and because the harm from the acts

9. This is a theme of E. Posner 1996.

in question tends to be large, society will find it worthwhile to buttress legal rules with moral ones, presuming that the cost of so doing is not too large. (And as I will explain, the cost of these supporting moral rules may often be quite low, possibly zero.)

A second rationale for supplementing law with morality is that legal rules may not reflect certain information that is relevant to achieving socially desirable outcomes, whereas moral rules can reflect such information. For example, the law might award low damages for breach of a contract to photograph an important event, since proving its significance to a court might be difficult. The photographer, however, might well realize from personal observation that the event is important, and thus if he feels it is his moral duty to keep promises, he will not breach the contract even though he can do so by law and it may be in his self-interest to do so. This is an example of what was discussed in part in section 2.1, that the information that is available to apply moral rules may be superior to that available to apply legal rules. On reflection, there are many cases in which the law does not take into account factors of relevance, due to difficulty of proof, but the involved parties know of these factors and, spurred by moral considerations, might act in a socially desirable way even though the law would not lead them to do this.

A third consideration is that moral rules may often be inexpensive supplements to legal ones. Let us consider the moral rule against murder as an example. The act of murder falls into a general category of conduct—that of intentionally harming others—that it is socially desirable to treat as wrongful. It is desirable to treat this general category of conduct as immoral because the acts in it tend to be socially undesirable and because much of the category is not controlled by law: There are innumerable ways in which individuals may intentionally harm each other in everyday life that we do not want to occur and that the broad moral rule at issue discourages, but which the law does not affect. Moreover, a refined moral rule under which murder would not be viewed as immoral would probably be unnatural and psychologically jarring, because of the evident underlying similarity between murder and many of the other acts that involve intentional harm and that are classified as immoral. Additionally, for the various reasons given earlier, moral rules cannot be too nuanced and thus could not accommodate such distinctions. In sum, then, the argument concerning the moral rule against murder is this: Given that society finds it advantageous to have a *general* moral rule against intentionally harming individuals, society enjoys, as a by-product, the application of the general moral rule to murder, as a supplement to criminal law. Similar arguments can be given for many other acts that are in the domain controlled by both law and morality; these acts fit under the heading of some general moral rule that society has good reason to establish.

2.4 Domain in which law alone is optimal.   It will be best to control behavior solely through use of law when, among other things, morality does not function well alone and law is needed to control behavior. These two conditions will tend to hold when the expected private gains from undesirable conduct are large and the expected harms due to such conduct are also large. For, as has been discussed, if the expected private gains from bad conduct are large, then the moral sanctions may not be enough to prevent it; and if the expected harms from bad conduct are substantial, then failure to prevent bad conduct will be socially serious, and thus will justify use of the legal system. A third condition that must hold in order for law alone to be optimal is that law is not worth supplementing with moral rules in view of the cost of so doing.

Before considering the relevance of the foregoing to what is observed, let us ask whether there does exist a domain of behavior in which primarily the law applies, in which morality is only weakly or not at all relevant. It was suggested earlier that many of our technical, often fairly detailed, legal rules have this character, such as a rule requiring that a company have at least a stipulated amount of capital to be allowed to sell securities on an equity market. Another example is a rule mandating the use of a particular accounting convention for valuation of inventories (such as last-in-first-out), or a rule proscribing the planting of an apparently innocuous species of tree in an area. What I am claiming is that it would not strike a person as intrinsically immoral—as immoral in the absence of a law bearing on the matter—for a company to sell securities when the company possesses less than the stipulated amount of capital, or for a company to use some other accounting practice for valuing inventories, or for a person to plant the species of tree that is mentioned as prohibited. (Although I do not think that people would view such conduct as intrinsically immoral, that is, as immoral were the conduct legal, individuals would be likely to think this conduct immoral just because it is illegal; there is a general moral duty to do what the law asks. I am, however, excluding this particular moral rule from consideration, for otherwise the question that I think it natural to examine here would be moot.)

Now let us consider whether the two conditions about gains and harm that I mentioned hold in the domain at issue. Regarding the first, it is fairly clear that the private gains from undesirable conduct are frequently large enough that legal sanctions, as opposed to merely moral sanctions, are needed to obtain a tolerably good level of compliance with rules. Consider the often substantial gains that can be obtained from improper sale of securities, or from a self-serving choice of method for the valuation of inventories. Moreover, the actors whose conduct needs to be controlled are often firms, which, as noted, dilute the force of moral sanctions. It seems doubtful on the whole that many of the regulations now enforced through use of the legal system, many times through public enforcement effort and the threat of criminal sanctions, could be reasonably well enforced by moral sanctions alone.

The second condition that we want to verify is that substantial harm would follow from failure to comply with the rules in question. This becomes evident from reflection on the purposes of the rules. Consider the minimum capital requirements for the registration of securities. If these are not met, there may ultimately be nontrivial consequences for the functioning of securities markets (for instance, erosion of investor confidence in the quality of securities). Because the securities markets contribute greatly to the health and productivity of our economy, it is very valuable for the rules about the registration of securities to be satisfied. Likewise, if there are not uniform accounting rules for the valuation of inventories, investors and lenders will have to spend more time than they now do unraveling the meaning of financial statements, which would impede the functioning of our capital and credit markets. The general claim, in other words, is that our somewhat detailed technical rules are often like these examples; on examination, one finds that they have real and significant rationales, and that substantial social harm will result if they are violated. Thus, when one considers the two conditions in the domain in question, it does indeed seem that legal rules are needed as a mechanism of control.

The question remains, however, why morality is not desirable to employ as a supplement to the law in the domain we are discussing. For morality to function in this way, one approach that could be taken would be to teach as individual moral rules the various legal rules at issue. Thus, we could teach children that it would be immoral for a firm to sell securities unless the firm's capital is higher than X, that it is immoral to plant species Y of tree, and so forth. But it is manifestly impractical to accomplish this task, and it would be nonsensical to think that we could, or would, try to instill rules like this in our children. The sheer number and the changing nature of the rules would bar our teaching them to children, and in any case the specific nature of the rules would often render them difficult for children to absorb (what does a child know about the sale of securities, particular species of trees, and so forth?).

Another approach might be to instill in children some overarching moral principle that, in its application by adults, would yield the many particular rules under consideration as subsidiary, implied moral rules. Arguably, the only overarching principle that could rationalize all these diverse rules is that of a general utilitarianism, of social welfare maximization. It does seem true that a form of this principle not only could be, but in fact is, imbued in us: the general obligation to do good, to do whatever it is that helps society. But the force of this moral rule is attenuated when it is not clear how it applies, and this tends to be the case with regard to the legal rules under consideration; identifying them as being in the social interest involves a fairly complicated train of thinking. Recall the argument given earlier for why a firm ought to have at least X in assets before it can sell securities; the logic behind the social desirability of this rule is not transparent (it is far more complex than that behind the typical moral rule, such as that one ought not hit someone, or one ought not lie). In other words, I am suggesting that the only overarching moral rule that could resolve itself into the body of technical legal rules in question is the general moral rule to maximize social welfare, and while we do have this general rule instilled in us, it is rendered weak in the domain in question because it is too difficult to apply, owing to our inability to recognize easily which of the technical rules are or are not in the social interest.[10] Thus, we must rely primarily on the law to induce compliance with such rules.

10. In fact, society is able to harness the general moral rule to do social good by making an act illegal. For then the rule is marked as likely to advance the social good. For example, an individual need not understand *why* selling securities without having capital of X is against the social interest; the fact that doing so is illegal conveys this to the individual.

3. OPTIMAL DESIGN OF THE LAW TAKING MORALITY INTO ACCOUNT

Having discussed in general terms the optimal domains of law and of morality, I now want to focus on the area of behavior in which both law and morality apply, and to examine the more specific question of how the law should be designed in the light of morality. For instance, how should tort liability be determined given our ideas of wrongful behavior? I will also briefly consider, in section 3.5, the question of how law should be designed if it can influence morality.

3.1 In general. In fashioning legal rules to maximize social welfare, the moral system must be taken into direct account to the extent that individuals have a taste for satisfaction of moral notions. That is, legal rules should be designed to maximize morally inclusive social welfare. As I emphasized in section 5 of Chapter 26, however, moral notions should not be given weight per se, independently of the importance individuals place on them as tastes, for that would lower social welfare. To appreciate the significance of these distinctions, it will be helpful to reconsider briefly several of the major subject areas of law examined in this book and to comment on how taking morality into account would, or would not, affect the previous analysis of them, which was based on conventional, not morally inclusive, social welfare.

3.2 Torts. The main notion of morality that bears on tort law appears to be that of classical corrective justice—the wrongdoer must make his victim whole—and it will serve my purposes to focus on this principle even though there are others, mainly subsidiary, that could be considered as well. The most natural interpretation of corrective justice is that the negligence rule should govern liability, for negligence connotes wrongful behavior. Conversely, strict liability would seem to be inconsistent with corrective justice, for it results in liability independently of whether a person has acted wrongly.[11]

---

11. There are other interpretations of corrective justice that might be advanced, under which, although negligence is usually the best rule, strict liability is said to be appropriate when activities impose unusual risks on others. But the qualitative nature of the arguments

How moral notions ought to be taken into account. Under the assumption just made about corrective justice, the negligence rule will be the optimal legal rule more often than I found it to be best under conventional measures of social welfare. In particular, where I suggested that the negligence rule was inferior to strict liability, due to excessive activity levels under the negligence rule (see Chapter 8), the negligence rule might now be optimal because of the taste individuals have for it. Or individuals' taste for the negligence rule might imply that that rule is best where, under conventional social welfare analysis, no liability would be desirable owing to the administrative costs of the liability system or its small effect on incentives.

Individuals' taste for corrective justice might also affect the conclusions about the magnitude of damages, for corrective justice implies that damages should make the victim whole, but this was not always the result found earlier. For example, I wrote that damages received should usually be limited to monetary losses, and not compensate for nonmonetary losses (essentially because receipt of more money by the victim is not as beneficial as receipt of fine revenue by the state).[12] In such situations, the factor of corrective justice would lead to the desirability of raising damages paid to victims. There were other cases that I investigated in which the influence of corrective justice on optimal damages would be similar.[13]

The degree to which the conclusions reached under conventional social welfare maximization should be altered depends on the strength of individuals' tastes for corrective justice. In making a conjecture about that taste, the reader should bear in mind the point that in order to determine the importance of it, a person must be able to separate the functional value of corrective justice in reducing harm and in compensating victims from its other value. The mental experiment that this requires is not easy to perform. One would have to answer questions such as the following: "Suppose that, under the negligence rule, society experiences the same number of accidents as it would under a no-fault system and that compensation of victims is

---

I will make would not be altered were I to consider such an interpretation of corrective justice.

12. See section 6 of Chapter 11.

13. For instance, I wrote that if administrative costs are high, it may be best not to estimate losses, and on certain further assumptions not to include certain components of loss in damages; see sections 7 and 8 of Chapter 10.

also the same. How much would you be willing to pay each year to have the negligence rule govern, even though it has no effect on outcomes?" It is not obvious to me how most people would answer such questions.

Another problem in assessing the importance of corrective justice in the tort context concerns insurance. One needs to know how a person's taste for satisfaction of corrective justice is influenced by the fact that judgments are usually paid by liability insurers rather than by wrongdoers, and by the fact that victims may well be compensated by their own first-party insurers, or that they would be in the absence of receipt of damage payments.

How moral notions are actually taken into account. What the analyst should not do is ascribe importance to moral notions apart from their importance as tastes. This, however, seems widely to be done. It is typical for commentators (and others in general) to give intrinsic significance to the negligence rule, or to whatever their preferred tort rule is. Commentators' statements are not represented as reflecting solely the functional values of tort rules and the tastes of the population for the rules. To be sure, the functionality of rules is usually mentioned by commentators, but it is only one part of the argument that they advance.

Has social decisionmaking been harmed in a substantial way because of the view of commentators? I think so. To illustrate, it seems to me possible that the general scope of tort liability is too great because of commentators' orientation. For instance, in substantial domains that I noted earlier, such as automobile accidents and product harms to consumers, liability may be too broadly used: First, tort liability may provide little deterrence (in the automobile case, because people worry about harm to themselves in the first place; in the product context, because reputational concerns of firms may lead them to take precautions in the absence of liability, and government could provide consumer information). Second, tort liability is very expensive as a means of compensation compared to the insurance system. Third, the true taste for tort liability may not be strong, and greatly compromised by the presence of insurance. In the face of this, why do we not have a more restricted set of circumstances in which liability is imposed? An answer is that the tort system we observe is the product of invocations of corrective justice by commentators, judges, and others of influence, rather than of an objective assessment of its importance as a taste, set off against conventional social welfare considerations. Whether or not I am right that tort liability is used excessively is not really important. What is important is that I *could* be right: Because there is little real consideration given by commentators of the true instrumental benefits of liability, and no real attempt to assess the taste for corrective justice, errors in evaluation can be made.

3.3 Contracts. The notion of morality that is most relevant in the context of contract law is that of promise-keeping: that it is right to keep promises and wrong to break them. The translation of this moral norm into contract law is that one is supposed to honor a contract and not breach it, and if one does breach it, that one should suffer a sanction. What this sanction should be, according to the promise-keeping norm, is not entirely clear, and some ancillary principle has to be used to determine it.

How moral notions ought to be taken into account. The way that this moral notion ought to be taken into consideration is that, whatever weight conventional analysis would lead one to accord to keeping contractual promises, extra weight should be given to keeping such promises owing to the taste for promise-keeping. Second, whatever level of damages for breach of contract is best according to conventional analysis would be altered in the direction of the level of damages for which there is a taste.

What do these general observations imply? The answer depends on what the understanding of breaking a contract is to individuals. Consider the example of a contract that reads something like, "I will produce a machine for you." One understanding of breaking a contract, the standard one, is that if the machine is not delivered, then the contract is breached. Under this understanding of breach, the promise-keeping norm says that breach is wrong, and consequently should not come about. The implication of this view is that whatever level of damages I said was desirable is too low, for I said that breach of this type of contract is often desirable, and damages should be chosen so as to allow an escape hatch that will lead to breach whenever the cost of performance exceeds the value of performance; see Chapters 13 and 15. This is why, in the paradigm case, I said that expectation damages are desirable; they lead to breach whenever the cost of performance exceeds its value to the promisor. Thus, the promise-keeping norm would lead us to say that damages should be higher than expectation damages, so as to lead to more frequent performance.

The importance of this argument for raising damages above expectation damages depends on the true taste individuals have for keeping promises, and remarks analogous to those made earlier about the importance of corrective justice apply here. Namely, it is not clear that individuals have thought carefully about how important they believe promise-keeping is; indeed, their statements probably do not reflect a true parsing of the instrumental from the intrinsic importance of promise-keeping. I should observe also that, when individuals name liquidated damages for breach, such damages are often fairly low, and very often equal expectation damages, suggesting that individuals do not strongly want to induce promise-keeping, but rather to allow breach when the cost of performance would be excessive.

Finally, let me comment that this discussion has been premised on the standard interpretation of breach, that not honoring the words of the contract is a breach. It is possible, however, that a deeper view of a contractual arrangement is held by some individuals, under which the contract is interpreted in the way that I did in Chapter 13. Namely, the contract is regarded as an incomplete promise, and it reads as it does only because of the inconvenience of writing a highly specified contractual promise. Under this view, the breach of the incomplete contract, such as "I will produce a machine for you," is not a true breach. A true breach would be not honoring the completely specified contract that would have been written had the parties included all relevant contingencies. Under this completely specified contract, the obligation to produce the machine would hold only when production cost is less than the value of performance; otherwise there would be no obligation to produce it. Hence, the promise-keeping norm would turn out to imply that one should obey contracts and perform only if the cost of performance is below the value of performance, and thus would be consistent with the economic analysis of contracts. But this view of contracts and promises is not the one that is in fact held by very many individuals in my experience (even though I think it is the view that ought to be held).

How moral notions are actually taken into account. In fact, the way that moral notions are taken into account in contract law has distinct aspects. First, the language of commentators suggests that breaking the agreements that are written, such as that I will produce a machine for you, is viewed as bad.[14] Thus, we see criticism of the idea that it is permissible to break

14. See, for example, Barnett 1986 and Fried 1981; and see the views about promise-keeping of such philosophers as Kant [1785] 1998, 15, 32, 38, and Ross 1930, chap. 2.

a contract as long as one pays damages. If, consistent with this view and the strength with which it is often expressed, damages for breach were really high, or if specific performance were widely employed as a remedy, then contract law would be very different from what it is; contracts would be performed much more often, and breach would be much less common than it is.

This leads to the second point about moral notions and contract law. Namely, when it comes to damages, the commentators seem usually to endorse the view that damages should equal the expectation measure (or sometimes the reliance measure), not that damages should be so high as to induce performance.[15] Thus, there is tension between the commentators' view that damages should be moderate but that contractual promises ought to be kept.

In any case, because of the opinion that damages should be moderate, there does not seem to be a general, socially disadvantageous effect on contract law flowing from the application of morality to it. Although there are many particular instances of socially undesirable aspects of contract law that are probably influenced by notions of morality, I will not discuss them here.[16]

3.4 Public law enforcement and criminal law.   The notion of morality that is most important in regard to public law enforcement and crime is retributivist, that wrongdoing merits punishment and the punishment should be in proportion to the gravity of the bad act. The proportion could be one to one, as under the biblical principle of an eye for an eye, or different, typically higher. Of significance is that the level of punishment depends on the degree of wrongfulness of the act and not on other factors, notably, not on the likelihood of punishment or on the cost of imposing it.

15. For example, Fried 1981 endorses the expectation measure.

16. One important example is the notion that damages should not be altered from their fair level for reasons having to do with incentives. Thus, suppose that expectation damages are felt to be correct, but it turns out that breach (such as improper quality of service of the promisor) would often go undetected. In such a situation, the two parties might want to specify a multiple of expectation damages as liquidated damages in order to provide proper incentives to perform. This, though, might be seen as unfair and not honored as the measure of damages.

How moral notions ought to be taken into account. Whatever was the optimal level of sanctions from the point of view of our previous analysis should be modified somewhat to reflect the taste for retributive justice. This might mean that the sanction should be lowered from what I suggested was optimal. This would be the case, importantly, where a low likelihood of catching violators and imposing sanctions on them leads to the desirability of sanctions substantially exceeding harm. Recall from Chapters 20 and 21 that we concluded that it is desirable for sanctions to equal the harm multiplied by the reciprocal of the probability of punishment (or something reflecting that in the case of nonmonetary sanctions), so that, for example, if the chance of being caught is one-third, the sanction should equal three times the harm. This can easily lead to a level of sanctions exceeding that given by the proportionality criterion of retributive justice. For instance, the optimal sanction for tax cheating might be many times the understatement of the tax due, and the optimal sanction for stealing a car might be a significant number of years in jail. Taking account of the proportionality principle would reduce these conventionally optimal sanctions.

Note, however, that if sanctions should be smaller than the conventionally optimal magnitude, due to our taste for retributively correct punishment, achieving more deterrence would require investing more resources in enforcement to catch violators of law. If we can only impose a sentence of one year on a car thief even though a three-year sentence would be more appropriate for purposes of preventing such theft given the present probability of apprehension, we had best increase the likelihood of apprehension of car thieves even though that involves extra expense. This general implication of retributive tastes is of special note because, as I emphasized in earlier chapters, the nature of the conventionally optimal enforcement policy involves low likelihoods of catching violators to save enforcement resources, and accompanying high penalties to maintain deterrence. Retributivist tastes moderate the use of this strategy because these tastes increase the effective cost of raising penalties above a fair level.

An opposite possibility, that retributive tastes might lead to higher sanctions than called for under the conventional social welfare calculus, arises in several circumstances. One is where individuals are certain to be caught and the correct proportion of punishment under retributivist principles exceeds 100 percent. For instance, suppose a firm knowingly pollutes a lake, causing $1,000,000 of harm. Here the economically optimal fine is $1,000,000, but the retributively best punishment is by hypothesis higher, such as $2,000,000. A closely related reason why the retributive punishment might exceed the economically appropriate one has to do not with the proportionality factor, but rather with the assessment of the gravity of the act. Although the harm caused by the pollution might be $1,000,000 and the proportionality factor might be one, the retributively best punishment might be $2,000,000 because the assessment of the gravity of the firm's act might be high if the firm's behavior had an outrageous aspect, for instance, if its employee was drunk. Another reason that the retributively appropriate punishment might exceed the economically optimal one is that the costs of imposing punishment might be too high to make any punishment, or much punishment, worthwhile, whereas retributivist principles are not influenced by the cost of punishment.

How much the conventionally optimal punishments should be modified depends on our taste for retributive justice, and it is hard to know what this is because of our ignorance of the degree to which individuals separate their desire for appropriate punishment from that for the consequences that punishment brings about, principally in terms of deterrence and incapacitation.

How moral notions are actually taken into account. It appears to me that our notions of correct punishment have considerable effect on our punishment policy. Certainly this is clear from the rhetoric surrounding punishment. Many punishments are much lower than they ought to be according to conventional economic thinking. The penalties for tax cheating are a good example; these are quite small, even though the chance of being found out for that misbehavior is slight. Likewise for many criminal acts, for car theft for example, sanctions may be inadequate given the likelihood of capture. Because the probability of catching many types of violations is so low, the needed sanctions for deterrence are often very high, but come into conflict with our notions of fair punishment.

If sanctions are inappropriately constrained by retributivist thinking—more than is merited by our true tastes for retributivist principles—then society suffers from a number of disadvantages. First, deterrence and incapacitation are too low, relative to what they ought to be. Second, expenditures on enforcement are greater than needed, because we are unwilling to raise sanctions in many areas, which would allow us to lower enforcement expenditures. Consider the enforcement of parking violations. If we were willing to double the magnitude of tickets for parking too long at a metered space from their usual level of about $20 to about $40, we could halve enforcement effort, which is substantial in our country, and use these freed resources in other areas, or save taxpayer money, without altering deterrence. While mundane, this example illustrates one way in which society is paying for its desire to employ proportionate sanctions.

When the sanctions that are felt to be fair exceed those that make economic sense (rather than fall below the economically optimal sanctions), society also suffers a cost. Perhaps the best example is that of firms that cause harm and suffer large penalties, such as punitive damages, making their financial burden exceed harm done. What this produces is excessive precautions, high product prices, and withdrawal of firms from socially valuable lines of business.

These costs to society in terms of social welfare, conventionally measured, are the price we pay for proportionality of punishment. I have suggested that the costs are substantial, and that they are not warranted by the actual taste we have for proportionality. To know whether the conjecture is correct, we would have to assess the strength of that taste, something that, as with the other moral notions, has not been done to my knowledge.

3.5 Influence of law on moral beliefs and their effectiveness. I noted earlier that, to some degree, the law can influence moral beliefs and that it can also alter their effectiveness by leading individuals to act on their beliefs to impose social sanctions on those who deviate from moral behavior. This has obvious implications for the design of the law, for it constitutes an effect of a legal rule that must be reckoned in the calculus of its design, along with other consequences. For example, in assessing the desirability of passage of civil rights laws, one would take into account not only their direct effects on behavior, such as changes in the hiring practices of businesses to avoid liability, but also that the laws may alter basic beliefs about race and individual rights, as well as the willingness of individuals to admonish those who discriminate.[17] One suspects that in most instances, how-

---

17. Of course, a necessary part of this calculus is evaluation of the social value of the changed moral beliefs themselves. In essence, such evaluation involves taking into account the direct effect on utility of the moral beliefs (consisting of the experience of virtue for doing right, here of not discriminating, or of guilt for doing wrong, and of associated feelings

ever, unlike in that of the civil rights laws, the influence of a legal rule on moral beliefs is a minor, if not nonexistent, factor.

4. THE NATURE OF NORMATIVE DISCOURSE ABOUT LAW AND MORALITY

What has been suggested to be the proper approach to understanding the relationship between law and morality, and especially how best to design the law, is quite different from the approach to these issues that is commonly found, whether in the classroom, scholarly journals, legal opinions, or other forums. Here I want to characterize briefly salient aspects of the normative discourse about law and morality that we encounter, contrast it with the welfare economic view, and attempt to explain why the nature of actual normative discourse is what it is. This will help to reconcile the differences that exist between the usual normative views and the welfare economic view, and I hope will lead the reader in the direction of endorsing the welfare economic view.

4.1 Characteristics of observed discourse. Normative discourse about law and morality appears to have three general characteristics. The first is that independent weight is given to moral factors. For example, when crime is discussed, the blameworthiness of criminals and the proportionality of punishment are typically accorded independent importance, or when the subject of torts is addressed, corrective justice and compensation of victims are accorded significance of their own. The second characteristic is that the moral factors typically are not adequately distinguished from the instrumental ones. For instance, when a person says that punishment for car theft ought to be a five-year sentence, it will be unclear to what extent this reflects the person's view of just punishment and to what extent it is based on his judgment about conventional economic factors, notably deterrence, incapacitation, and enforcement costs. The third characteristic of observed normative discourse is that it is generally not neutral in tone. When individuals debate issues of legal policy, their interchanges frequently

---

with respect to giving praise or admonishing others), and taking into account the indirect effects due to behavioral changes induced by the moral beliefs.

include elements of moral suasion. I am certain that the reader has seen that when a person advances a right as a reason for this or that legal policy, the person typically evinces feelings of virtue on his own part—in his tone of voice, in his rhetorical and expressive style. Likewise, if a contrary view is advanced by another person, that person is subjected to attack, and certain types of social sanctions are imposed that are not entirely dissimilar to those experienced by individuals who have acted immorally in reality. In other words, the person advancing a legal policy felt to be morally incorrect is subjected to a translated form of the social sanction that he would suffer if he had actually acted immorally.

4.2 Chief difference between observed normative discourse and the proper normative view.   Perhaps the principal difference between the observed normative discourse about law and morality and the views that I have been expressing is that the psychological aspects of morality and the instrumental role of moral notions are generally ignored in the observed discourse. In this discourse, there is usually no acknowledgment that individuals have tastes for the satisfaction of notions of morality and that these notions may serve to promote social welfare.

4.3 Explanation for the difference.   It is not mysterious that there should be this difference. Since we care about adherence to moral notions, at least if we are well-socialized individuals, it is natural for us to import our feelings about them into the realm of analytical discussion. Suppose that we believe that there should be no punishment without fault and that punishment should be in proportion to the gravity of bad acts. Then if one of us becomes a legal academic, or an editorialist for a newspaper, it might be expected that we would carry our views into our writing concerning legal policy. This simple observation also helps to explain the nonneutral character of observed discourse about normative legal issues.

By contrast, the view of morality that I have been advancing is not a natural one for most individuals to hold. For it requires us to reflect on our own psychology and to examine why we ascribe the importance that we do to moral notions. Because this is a difficult exercise, it is not entirely surprising that it is so infrequently done. Yet it is somewhat strange that academics have paid so little attention to the view advanced here, for it is in many respects well known. Famous philosophers have developed important elements of this view—I refer especially to Hume ([1751] 1998), Smith ([1790] 1976), and Mill ([1861] 1998), and more recently to such writers as Hare (1981).

4.4 Conclusion. Welfare economics, as described in the previous chapter and this one, seems to provide an intellectually attractive and generally satisfactory lens for understanding and analyzing morality and law. In part, this is so because welfare economics (and other disciplines) allow one to see through the veil of morality and to appreciate its functions and origins. Although I realize that this view is in tension with the great weight of legal writing and thinking, it is the only one that I can comfortably endorse, and I hope that the reader, even if unable to accept it, will appreciate its value.

28 ||| INCOME DISTRIBUTIONAL EQUITY AND THE LAW

Let me now turn to the topic of the distribution of income and the legal system. Here the question to be addressed is how the effects of legal rules on the distribution of income should influence the choice of legal rules. I will first review how the distribution of income enters into the determination of social welfare, and how the income tax and transfer system can be utilized to achieve income distributional objectives. Then I will discuss the effects of legal rules on the distribution of income and whether the choice of legal rules should be a function of their distributional effects. The main point will be that income distributional objectives are best pursued through the use of the income tax and transfer system, implying that legal rules should be selected on the basis of nondistributional objectives.[1]

---

1. The questions discussed in this chapter fall under the heading of conventional welfare economics, and do not involve issues of morality in the sense in which I have used this term in the two previous chapters. Nevertheless, because the distribution of income is usually described using words such as "equity" and "fairness," it seems natural to treat the relation between law and income distribution in this part of the book.

1. THE DISTRIBUTION OF INCOME AND SOCIAL WELFARE

Most concerns about the overall distribution of income can be accommodated by, and are embodied in, the measures of social welfare of conventional welfare economics, as was mentioned in section 1 of Chapter 26. In particular, there are three channels through which the distribution of income may influence social welfare.

First, the distribution of income may matter to social welfare because the poor may value a dollar more than the rich—the marginal utility of a dollar to a poor person is likely to exceed the marginal utility of a dollar to a rich person. If so, social welfare will tend to be increased by redistributing income from the rich to the poor.[2]

Second, the distribution of income may matter to social welfare because the distribution of income affects the distribution of *utility,* and under the welfare economic approach social welfare may depend directly on how equally utility is distributed among individuals. Thus, even if the rich and the poor obtain the same marginal utility from a dollar, it may be desirable to redistribute from rich to poor because the rich enjoy greater overall utility.[3]

Third, the distribution of income may matter to social welfare because

---

2. For example, consider the classical utilitarian social welfare function, the sum of utilities. Under it, redistributing a dollar from a rich individual with a low marginal utility of income to a poor individual with a high marginal utility of income will raise social welfare, for the utility of the rich individual will fall by less than the utility of the poor individual will rise, meaning that total utility will be greater.

3. Suppose that social welfare equals the sum of the square roots of utility (this is a social welfare function under which more equal distributions of utility are desirable; see note 5 of Chapter 26). Suppose also that the utility of a person equals simply his level of wealth (so that the marginal utility of a dollar is 1, regardless of whether a person is rich or poor). Now consider two individuals, one who has wealth of $100 and the other wealth of $1,000, and suppose that $100 is transferred from the wealthy person to the poor person, so that the former is left with $900 and the latter possesses $200. The $100 gain by the poor person raises his utility by 100, which is exactly the loss in utility for the rich person, so the redistribution does not lead to any change in the sum of utilities. Yet, because the redistribution makes the distribution of utilities more equal, it raises social welfare: social welfare is originally $\sqrt{100} + \sqrt{1,000} = 10 + 31.62 = 41.62$, and rises after the redistribution to $\sqrt{200} + \sqrt{900} = 14.14 + 30 = 44.14$.

an individual's utility may depend on the distribution of income in the population at large, owing to generalized feelings of altruism or of sympathy. Thus, even if the rich and the poor obtain the same direct marginal utility from a dollar, and even if social welfare equals the sum of utilities and thus does not depend in an intrinsic way on the distribution of utility, it may still be true that social welfare may rise if the distribution of income is more equal.[4]

In what follows, it will not be important to refer to the particular source of importance of the distribution of income to social welfare; I will simply assume that the distribution of income enters into the determination of social welfare.

2. THE INCOME TAX SYSTEM, INCOME DISTRIBUTION, AND SOCIAL WELFARE

2.1 The income tax system. By the income tax and transfer system is meant the combined effect of the various taxes (federal, state, and local) on income, together with programs (such as Medicare, food stamps) that transfer money to individuals based on their income. For brevity, I will speak of these taxes and transfers simply as the income tax system.

---

4. For example, suppose that the utility of each person equals the sum of two components: his own wealth (which he spends on personal consumption), and the sum of the square roots of the utilities of all individuals (that is, the measure of social welfare discussed in the previous note). Notice, therefore, that the direct marginal utility of a dollar for a person is 1, regardless of his wealth, for the first component of utility is equal to his wealth; but the utility of a person also depends on the distribution of utilities in the population through the second component of his utility. Suppose too that social welfare is utilitarian, the sum of utilities, so that, as stated in the text, social welfare is insensitive in a direct sense to the distribution of utilities. Then, as also stated in the text, social welfare rises if wealth is more equally distributed because that tends to raise individuals' utilities, and thus the sum of utilities, for the individuals' utilities (as opposed to social welfare) depend on the distribution of utilities and thus on the distribution of wealth. For instance, suppose that, initially, one person has wealth of 0 and the other 1,000. The utility of the first person is $0 + \sqrt{1,000} = 31.62$, and that of the second is $1,000 + \sqrt{1000} = 1,031.62$, so, considering these two people, social welfare is 1,063.24. If wealth is redistributed so each person has 500, the utility of each is $500 + 2\sqrt{500} = 500 + 2(22.36) = 544.72$, so social welfare is 1,089.44, which is higher.

There are two chief purposes of the income tax system: to raise revenues for the purposes of the state, and to redistribute income.[5] The second purpose may not seem important to some readers, perhaps because few individuals receive outright transfers and because there is relatively little frank discussion in public forums of the tax system as a means of redistribution. A moment's reflection, however, makes one realize that the tax system does in fact possess substantial redistributive effects—the relative situations of many individuals, especially of the poor and of the rich, are changed significantly by the existence of the tax system.

2.2 The income tax system and optimal redistribution.   To see how the income tax system can be employed to redistribute income, let us suppose for simplicity that redistribution is its sole purpose (that is, let us ignore the government's need to raise revenue) and consider the following problem: Design the income tax system to maximize social welfare, assuming that the measure of social welfare is one that favors equality of income; thus, if a fixed amount of income exists to be divided, the best way to divide it would be equally.[6]

To solve this problem, suppose first that the amount of income that each individual earns is fixed. Then, the total income of all individuals is obviously fixed, implying that the optimal income tax would be designed so as to give all individuals an equal income, namely, the average income. If, for instance, the average income were $20,000, then any person earning over $20,000 would pay in taxes the excess earned over $20,000, so that he would be left with $20,000, and any person earning less than $20,000 would receive enough to bring him up to $20,000. Thus, the income tax would be employed to achieve the ideal distribution of income, and associated with it, the ideal level of social welfare.

There are, however, two important reasons why the income tax system cannot achieve the ideal level of social welfare. One concerns the administrative costs of taxation. Suppose that transferring a dollar among individuals via the tax system involves an administrative cost (because individuals have to fill out tax forms, incomes must be verified to combat evasion, and

5. When I say redistribute income, I mean to include wealth as well as income.

6. One measure of social welfare under which this would be so is, as mentioned, the sum of the square roots of utilities; see note 3.

so forth). Then it is clear that the social welfare–maximizing income tax system will not result in an equal distribution of income, for that would involve too great a loss due to administrative costs. In general, the optimal income tax system will strike an implicit balance between the social benefits of redistribution and the administrative costs of redistribution; therefore, the level of redistribution and social welfare achieved will fall short of the ideal. This point may be helpfully described in terms of the metaphor of a leaky bucket: When transferring income in buckets for the purpose of redistribution, some income leaks from the buckets and is wasted, so it is not desirable to carry as much in buckets as society otherwise would want. Another metaphor is that the size of the pie to be divided among the population, that is, the sum of incomes, shrinks when the pie is divided.

The second reason why the income tax system cannot be employed to achieve the ideal level of social welfare through redistribution concerns distortion of work incentives. Although it was assumed in the previous paragraphs that the earnings of each individual were fixed, this is unrealistic. Let us now assume that a person's earnings depend on how hard he works and on his ability. In this situation, the income tax may alter work incentives and thus earnings. Notably, a person who has to pay a substantial percentage of earnings in taxes, such as 50 percent, may well work less hard, and earn less, than if he paid no income taxes; and a person who will receive a payment if his earnings fall below some threshold might have diluted incentives to work relative to what they would be if he would not receive this payment. Hence, the use of the income tax to redistribute may lead to a reduction in work effort and earnings, and through this route, reduce the total amount of income available to redistribute. Therefore, when one takes into account how the income tax influences work incentives in solving for the optimal income tax, it turns out that the level of redistribution and social welfare falls short of the ideal.[7] In a rough sense, the reason is similar to that due

7. This problem was first formally studied by Mirrlees 1971 and emphasized by Vickrey 1947; it has been developed in a vast "optimal income tax literature." In this literature, the standard model is as follows: Each individual has an unobservable-to-the-government ability to work, a. His earnings y equal aw, where w is work effort (thus, the higher his ability, the more he earns), where w is also unobservable. Work effort involves an effort cost to him of $c(w)$. He pays an income tax $t(y)$, which could be negative (corresponding to receipt of money). Thus, an individual will choose work effort w to maximize his net utility: $y - t(y) - c(w) = aw - t(aw) - c(w)$. Clearly, the individual's choice of w will depend

to administrative costs; the distortion of incentives is in effect another source of leakage from the buckets used to redistribute.

A comment about the work incentive factor should be made. Economists sometimes emphasize the point that this problem can be viewed as due to inability of the tax authorities to determine the innate ability to earn of individuals. The reason is that if a person's ability to earn could be observed, the tax could be based on this ability and not on actual income earned. For instance, a person who has the ability to earn $100,000 a year and who would earn this amount in an ideal world, and for whom in that world the ideal tax would be, say, $50,000, would face an unconditional flat tax of $50,000, not a tax based on income earned. Hence, he would not have a disincentive to earn, because he would face the $50,000 tax based on his ability and could not escape the tax by working less hard. In reality, however, government cannot observe innate ability and earning capacity, and it must largely base taxes on earned income.[8]

In summary, then, we can assert that the optimal use of the income tax to redistribute income does not lead to an ideal distribution of income because of two costs associated with redistribution: administrative costs and the implicit costs of the dulling of work incentives.

3.   EFFECT OF LEGAL RULES ON THE DISTRIBUTION OF INCOME

3.1 In general.   It is clear that legal rules generally affect the distribution of income. If we trace the consequences of any legal rule for each income class, we can determine its effects. Consider, for example, a rule

---

on the tax schedule $t(y)$, and it will also generally depend on his ability, a. Denote this net utility of a person of ability a who chooses his work effort given the tax schedule t by $u(a,t)$, and denote the person's choice of work effort by $w(a,t)$. The problem of the government is to choose the income tax schedule, that is the *function* $t(y)$, so as to maximize social welfare, subject to the constraint that taxes collected sum to zero (that is, what is collected equals what is given out). Social welfare can be expressed as $\int u(a,t)f(a)da$, where $f(a)$ is the probability density of individuals of ability a. The condition that taxes net to zero is $\int t(aw(a,t))f(a)da = 0$.

8. Society can and sometimes does base income taxes on certain observable indicators of earning capacity. For example, the blind have a lower earning capacity than those with sight, so we do not tax them as heavily (and perhaps there are other reasons why that makes

that makes owners of large recreational boats liable for harms they negligently cause. This rule leaves the large recreational boat owners less well-off both because they will be led to spend on safety equipment and to take precautions that they would not otherwise have taken, and because they will have to pay for any negligently caused accidents that still result; and it will benefit possible victims, including small boat owners and swimmers, because they will suffer from accidents less often and, if involved in accidents, will sometimes be able to collect. Because the large recreational boat owners will tend to be a wealthy class, and their potential victims will not, the rule will redistribute from rich to poor; a refined understanding of this effect could be ascertained from data on who purchases large recreational boats and from data on victims of accidents. In such a manner, the influence of any legal rule on the income distribution can be determined.

3.2 Comments.   Several remarks about the assessment of the distributional effects of legal rules are worth bearing in mind.

Diffused effects. Although in the example concerning recreational boats the distributional effects of the legal rule might be fairly clear, because the injurers and the victims might be expected to comprise reasonably distinct income groups, that is not always so. Consider, for example, the effects of using the negligence rule for accidents involving automobiles and pedestrians. This rule of liability imposes costs on drivers and it benefits pedestrians, but drivers constitute an extremely diverse group by income, and so do pedestrians. Moreover, drivers and pedestrians are not even distinct groups—most drivers sometimes walk and most pedestrians sometimes drive. Thus, the distributional effects of the legal rule concerning drivers and pedestrians might be quite diffuse.

Attenuated effects in contractual contexts. Another general observation about distributional effects is that if legal rules affect parties who are in a contractual arrangement with each other, the effects may be muted or even eliminated by changes in contract prices. Suppose that a legal rule that

---

sense as well). But society does not make use of all observable indicators of earnings capacity, such as educational attainment. Using that factor might be undesirable; for instance, it would discourage educational attainment, and such an accomplishment has benefits to individuals apart from how it raises earning power. In any event, I will abstract from such considerations in the text.

increases liability of manufacturers of a product for harms to buyers raises their liability-related unit costs by $100, and benefits buyers by this amount because they collect the $100 in expected liability payments. If the price of the product did not rise, buyers would be better off and a redistribution would have resulted. But, of course, prices will tend to rise, and in a competitive market they would rise fully by $100, negating the redistributive effect. It is true that price changes do not always offset the influence of legal rules on prices, but the point here is that there is a significant difference in the distributional effects of legal rules in contractual contexts from the effects in noncontractual settings.

Interrelated nature of, and totality of, effects of different legal rules. Two further comments should be made. First, the change brought about by a legal rule will often depend on other legal rules. For example, the effect of holding drivers liable for negligently caused accidents to pedestrians will depend on speed limits and other traffic laws (the more rigorous they are, the less the influence of the negligence rule) and on legal regulation of vehicle manufacturers (for instance, requiring sideview mirrors on automobiles, or devices that make beeping sounds when trucks are put into reverse). Second, the income distribution is determined by the totality of effects of different legal rules, many of which work counter to one another. Thus, although automobile owners may suffer because an antipollution statute requires expensive pollution control devices in automobiles and raises their prices, automobile owners may benefit from reduced pollution, and also from other legal rules, such as antitrust rules. In strict logic, the distribution of income is the resultant of the whole legal system—not only of the legal rules that we might think of as variable because they are in flux or are under consideration for modification, but also of the whole background of legal rules of property, contract law, criminal law, and so forth that we view as stable and that order our society.

4. SHOULD INCOME DISTRIBUTIONAL EFFECTS OF LEGAL RULES INFLUENCE THEIR SELECTION?

4.1 Given the availability of the income tax system for achieving distributional goals, legal rules should generally not be chosen on the basis of their distributional effects. Because society possesses the income tax system for attaining income distributional goals, legal rules do not need to be chosen with these goals in mind. In particular, if there is a reason to effect further redistribution from the rich to the poor, society can do this with an appropriate adjustment to the income tax, rather than through adoption of this or that legal rule. Moreover, if a legal rule happens to have an undesirable redistributive effect, harming the poor and benefiting the rich, that can be counterbalanced by a suitable change in the income tax system, helping the poor and harming the rich. Thus, there is no evident need to take distributional considerations into account in selecting legal rules.

Further, if distributional considerations were taken into account in choosing legal rules, society would be led to compromise the social benefits that the rules generate, such as lowering the total costs of accidents. Hence, it is not only that distributional effects of the choice of legal rules do not need to be taken into account; it is also that social welfare would be *lowered* by taking those effects into account in the selection of legal rules. Indeed, it can be demonstrated that if distributional effects do influence the choice of a legal rule, it would be possible to make *all* individuals better off by altering the choice of rule to the otherwise optimal rule and by making an appropriate change in the income tax system.[9]

9. To illustrate with a simple version of the argument: Consider a world with two equally numerous income classes, rich and poor; a conventionally optimal rule of tort liability that lowers expected accident losses net of costs of precautions by $20 per person, which is as much as possible, and that otherwise leaves incomes unaffected; and a second liability rule that lowers net accident losses by only $10 per person but reduces the wealth of each rich person by $50 and raises the wealth of each poor person by $50. Suppose that the second rule is selected because its distributional effects are preferred. The claim is that all individuals can be made better off if, instead, the optimal rule is chosen. In particular, suppose that, in place of the second rule, the first is chosen and income taxes are raised by $50 on the rich and lowered by $50 on the poor. Then each poor person is better off under the optimal rule than under the other rule, for the reduction by $50 in income taxes compensates for the loss of the $50 benefit from the rule, and his accident losses fall by $20 instead of only by $10. Likewise, each rich person is better off under the optimal rule, for the increase by $50 in income taxes is offset by the $50 benefit from the optimal rule, and his accident losses fall by $20 instead of only by $10. This argument is easily shown to hold generally where incomes of individuals are fixed, rather than a function of work effort, but it carries over to the latter setting as well; see section 4.6.

In view of the importance of this argument against choosing legal rules on the basis of their distributional effects, it is worth considering, in the following sections, various complicating factors.

4.2 Speed of adjustment of the income tax system. Although undesirable distributive aspects of legal rules can be offset by adjustments in the income tax system, it might take time for the tax system to adjust, and in the period before adjustment, social welfare would suffer. This speed-of-adjustment factor, then, could in principle lead one to take distributive effects of legal rules into account. Yet it is not obvious why we should expect the income tax system to be slow to adjust, and in fact, it seems to be under more or less constant modification.

4.3 Adjustment of the income tax system to specific legal rules. A closely related consideration that is sometimes mentioned is that the tax system cannot practically be adjusted to offset the undesired distributional effects of specific legal rules. Hence, it is asserted, there is some reason for the distributional effects of the choice of a legal rule to be taken into account in its selection. This line of thinking, however, is insufficiently articulated to be well understood, and when one attempts to amplify it, one is left wondering about its meaning. For example, an important reason why it would be impractical to alter the tax system in response to each and every choice of legal rule is that some administrative cost is involved in so doing; another reason is that different legal rules often have counterbalancing effects, so that it may be desirable to wait for some period to see their cumulated effect before adjusting the tax system. But both of these reasons would also apply to a court or a legislature in designing legal rules. They would face administrative costs in determining the distributional effects of legal rules, and they would need to assess the cumulated effect of different rules, not just an isolated rule at a moment in time.

4.4 Administrative costs. Administrative cost considerations may bear on the comparison of legal rules and the income tax system for the purpose of altering the distribution of income. If legal rules allowed income to be redistributed more cheaply than the income tax system does, then the conclusion that legal rules should not be chosen on the basis of their redistributive effects would not necessarily hold. Conversely, if legal rules involved greater administrative costs in connection with redistribution than the income tax system, the conclusion that legal rules should not be selected on the basis of distributional effects would be reinforced.

The question at issue, therefore, is how the administrative costs of legal rules and of the income tax system compare. Several remarks are worth making about this. First, the administrative costs of the income tax system (as distinct from distortions in work effort that it causes) are not negligible, probably more than 5 percent of dollars collected.[10] Second, the administrative costs of redistribution through use of legal rules should be divided into two components. One is the administrative cost of redistribution through litigation and settlement, and, as discussed in Chapter 12, this is very high, on the order of 100 percent. But the other way that legal rules redistribute is through effects on behavior, for instance, by inducing injurers to take precautions. This would not usually seem to involve such substantial administrative costs. The administrative costs of redistribution through use of legal rules are thus some combination of high and low, and depend on the rule in question.

4.5 Multiplicity of legal rules. Supporting the general argument against use of legal rules to redistribute income is the sheer number of legal rules, for this complicates the task of assessing their distributive effects. If legal rules were chosen individually, on the basis of their particular effects on income distribution, needless social losses would result, especially because of failure to take into account the offsetting effects of different rules.[11] Because legal rules are affected by different legislative bodies and are also

10. See Slemrod and Bakija 2000, 134–138, for estimates of the costs to government and to taxpayers of the tax collection process.

11. For example, suppose that initially the distribution of income is thought to be desirable and at time 1, there is a choice between two rules, A1 and B1, where A1 is superior on nondistributional grounds but would favor the rich. Hence, the rule B1 might be chosen if distribution is taken into account, so that the rich do not become richer. Suppose too that at time 2, there is a choice between two rules, A2 and B2, where A2 is superior on nondistributional grounds and favors the poor. At this time, we could imagine that B2 might be chosen, to prevent the previously corrected income distribution from being again upset. Thus, we could imagine two inferior choices of rule, favoring B1 and B2, even though the superior rules, A1 and A2, have opposite distributional effects that could be exactly offsetting.

shaped by courts, one does not have confidence that the choice of legal rules to accomplish distributional objectives is, or would be, done in an integrated way that reflects the summed influence of different rules.

4.6 Distortion of work effort under the income tax and consequent less-than-ideal income distribution. As explained in section 2.2, the income tax distorts work effort, and as a result, the distribution of income that results under the optimal income tax system involves inequality; although an equal distribution of income may be possible to achieve, it is generally not optimal because it would dilute work incentives too much. This raises the question of whether legal rules should be selected in part so as to bridge the gap between the distribution under the income tax and what is socially ideal. Somewhat surprisingly, perhaps, the answer is no; it remains true that legal rules should not be selected on the basis of distributional effects.

The kernel of the explanation is that if legal rules are chosen to redistribute, this too will distort work effort. If, for instance, those who earn an extra $1,000 know that they will pay $500 more due to legal rules (say they will pay more in tort damages if they are held liable), then this will reduce their incentive to earn the $1,000 just as much as if they had to pay $500 more in income taxes. Whether it is the income tax arm of government or the judicial arm that takes the $500 is of no consequence to a person; it is the fact that earning $1,000 more will result in $500 of that amount being taken that reduces the person's incentive to work. Using legal rules to redistribute income distorts work incentives just as much as the income tax does. But using legal rules to redistribute *also* tends to interfere with achievement of the beneficial purposes of the legal rules, notably in channeling behavior. Hence, it is best to use legal rules to achieve the beneficial purposes for which they are directly intended, and not to select them on the basis of their distributional effects.

I should add for clarity that this point has been formally established in a version of the standard model of the income tax and distortion of work effort. In that model, the following conclusion (an extension of the conclusion mentioned in section 4.1) holds: Suppose that there is an income tax system in place and that a legal rule that is not conventionally optimal has been selected. If that rule is replaced by the conventionally optimal legal rule and the income tax system is suitably modified, *all* individuals will be made better off. This conclusion is stronger than what was discussed in the previous paragraphs of this section in that it states that all individuals can be made better off if legal rules are not selected on the basis of distributional considerations.[12]

4.7 The political process that determines the income tax is not socially desirable.

One occasionally encounters the argument that the income tax is set by an imperfect political process and that, as a consequence, the income tax schedule does not lead to optimal redistribution. Therefore, the argument continues, legal rules should be chosen at least in part on the basis of their distributive aspects, so as to correct for the problem with the political process. This argument, however, overlooks the ability of those with political power to neutralize attempts by those controlling legal rules to redistribute income. If legal rules were used in an attempt to take more from the rich and give to the poor, one presumes that those who control the income tax could offset this effect by reducing tax rates on the rich to compensate them for the extra burden they suffer under the legal system. Thus, in the end, those who would choose inefficient legal rules in order to redistribute income would only cause a loss in social welfare

12. This result is first shown in Shavell 1981 and is amplified and discussed in Kaplow and Shavell 1994c; it builds on a result in the optimal income tax literature proved in Hyllund and Zeckhauser 1979. The model used in Shavell and in Kaplow and Shavell is that of the optimal tax literature, as described in note 7, but in which there is included as well an activity controlled by a legal rule. Specifically, individuals choose a variable x called care that reduces harm to others $h(x)$ but that involves disutility $d(x)$ to them. The legal rule imposes a liability cost $l(x)$ on them. Let l^* be the "efficient" legal rule—that which results in minimization of $h(x) + d(x)$ summed across the population. And let t be any income tax schedule. Now let l' be any alternative legal rule that is not efficient—such as one chosen because of its distributional characteristics. Then there exists a modified tax schedule t' such that, under t' and the efficient legal rule l^*, *all* individuals are better off than they are under t and the inefficient rule l'. As we discuss in Kaplow and Shavell 1994c, this conclusion does depend on a separability assumption about the disutility of work effort and of the functions determining accidents. That assumption seems the natural one to consider as a benchmark for thinking. In any case, were the assumption relaxed, although the optimal legal rule would not in general be the efficient one, there is no reason for the optimal rule to be such that it would redistribute toward the poor. On the latter issues, see Sanchirico 2000 and Kaplow and Shavell 2000.

and not accomplish additional redistribution. If, however, one assumes that the political process is imperfect not only in failing to achieve society's redistributive goals, but also in failing to offset attempts to redistribute through the choice of legal rules, the argument just stated would not apply.

4.8 Conclusion. The initial point made here that legal rules should not be selected on the basis of their income distributional effects is somewhat qualified, and is in certain respects reinforced, by consideration of a number of factors that bear on it. In particular, we found that where the administrative costs of the income tax system exceed those of legal rules as a means of transferring income, then legal rules might be selected on the basis of their distributional effects; and that if the speed of adjustment of the tax system were slow, the same might occur. The reader may judge the relevance of these two points. We also found that the multiplicity of legal rules and the need to coordinate responses to them argues against selecting rules on the basis of their distributional effects; that the distortion of work effort under the income tax is also a disadvantage of redistribution through legal rules, and so does not alter our initial conclusion; and finally, that asserted defects in the political process also do not alter our basic conclusion that legal rules should not be selected on distributional grounds.

29 ||| CONCLUDING OBSERVATIONS

Let me close this book with a brief discussion of a number of issues that are often raised about economic analysis of law.

1. DESCRIPTIVE ANALYSIS: CONCERNING THE EFFECTS OF LEGAL RULES

What is the basis for the general assumption that individuals' behavior is explained by the calculated pursuit of self-interest? The basis for this assumption is, I think, largely self-evident. If we wish to describe the behavior of individuals, then we will succeed to a substantial extent if we identify their goals and ask what they would do to foster the goals if they are consciously acting to do so. For example, if we wish to know whether individuals will take due care under the negligence rule (Chapter 8), then we will learn a great deal by asking what they will do if they compare the advantages of taking due care, in terms of avoiding liability, against the costs of exercising due care.

This is not to say that analysts believe that the assumption of the calculated pursuit of goals is correct in a literal sense. Most analysts recognize that, in reality, an individual may not be following a completely fixed goal; his mood and other psychological factors may alter his goals unpredictably. They recognize that an individual may not be pursuing his goal perfectly at all moments; he may err due to perceptual biases or limitations of time and of powers of ratiocination. Indeed, in the examination of behavior under the negligence rule, I investigated the possibility that individuals do not constantly maximize their well-being because of lapses of concentration and the like (section 1 of Chapter 10); one of the purposes there was to explain why negligent behavior is observed. Similarly, in discussing criminal law, I discussed the possibility that individuals might lose control of themselves and commit bad acts (section 4 of Chapter 24); there one of the purposes was to suggest a circumstance in which punishment might not accomplish deterrence. Thus, although the predominant assumption in the analysis of this book has been calculated maximization of a goal, and it would have cluttered the statement of conclusions to qualify them too frequently, there have been occasions where the usual suppositions have been relaxed.

Why is it generally assumed in theoretical models that only a fairly narrow set of considerations govern behavior? The main reason that fairly simple, stylized models of reality are employed to predict behavior in theoretical inquiries is to clarify understanding; because the description of behavior becomes very complex as the number of factors influencing it grows, it is generally best to begin one's analysis by investigating the effects of a small number of important factors. Consider again the example of behavior under the negligence rule. When I first addressed this rule (Chapter 8), I asked whether or not it would discourage negligent behavior presuming that the actor is risk neutral, would definitely be sued for negligently caused harm, has the assets to pay a judgment, does not possess liability insurance, and would be tried by a court that operates free from error. Once I deduced the actor's behavior under all of these simplifying assumptions—and recall that the actor's behavior was not entirely trivial to describe—I was able to proceed (Chapter 10) to further our understanding in various ways: by allowing for parties to escape suit with some probability, for their assets to be less than harm, for them to own liability insurance, and for legal error to occur. It would not have been easy to come to an understanding of how the negligence rule affects behavior if we had begun with a model that included all of these factors, because it would have been difficult to untangle their separate effects. It is the general nature of the theoretical, scientific method to first avoid complications in order to focus on the influence of the subset of central factors on outcomes, and then to build from this knowledge.

Prediction in theoretical models versus empirical prediction. It is important to separate prediction of behavior in theoretical models, which is what I have been addressing, from prediction in an empirical sense, by which I mean prediction of actual outcomes. In theoretical models, we seek to predict behavior in constructed worlds, and we do this largely to achieve intellectual insight into the broad, qualitative characteristics of behavior in the actual world. When we investigate the theoretical models, we do so with a conscious understanding that they are artificial renderings of the real world, and we appreciate that one would not usually employ the models in a direct way to forecast actual behavior. To make such a forecast, one would typically make use of more complete models, and one would gather data and employ statistical techniques to estimate the parameters of these models. Thus, if we were to try to predict the actual incidence of negligent behavior among drivers, one might use a statistical regression model with explanatory variables that include the social and economic characteristics of drivers, geographic factors, characteristics of roads, characteristics of traffic law enforcement, and so forth. In this empirical predictive work, the theoretical models of behavior would typically be helpful, in telling us which variables to include (income would be relevant, as the judgment-proof problem becomes important and tends to reduce deterrence) and how to interpret results (liability insurance would tend to reduce, not increase, accident risks when insurers can monitor insured care); but the theoretical models would not tell us how much negligent driving there is in an immediate sense. I believe that many of the questions and criticisms of descriptive economic analysis as being simplistic result from confusion about the different goals of theoretical and of empirical prediction.

2. NORMATIVE ANALYSIS: CONCERNING THE SOCIAL DESIRABILITY OF LEGAL RULES

Why is the measure of social desirability often taken to be a simple aggregate— that does not reflect many factors that in reality matter to social welfare, notably, compensation of victims, the distribution of income, and satisfaction of principles of fairness? In this book, as in most economically oriented normative analysis of legal rules, the criterion of social welfare that is usually analyzed concerns a standard aggregate. For example, the goal might be to maximize the sum of the benefits derived from an activity minus the harms it causes and minus the administrative costs of the legal system, or it might be to minimize total social costs, that is, the sum of prevention costs plus harm plus administrative costs.

The main reasons that such goals are considered are twofold. First, we are naturally interested in determining the extent to which legal rules foster production and beneficial activity and also reduce prevention expenses and harm; for production and beneficial activity generally raise our well-being, and the bearing of prevention expenses and of harm generally reduce our well-being. This means that a natural focus for analytical attention is a measure of social welfare that rises with benefits and falls with expenses and with harms. And an aggregate, such as the mathematical sum of benefits minus all prevention expenses and harms, has this characteristic.

But second, the question arises: Why not study a broader measure of social welfare than a simple aggregate, when we know that other factors matter to individuals' well-being and thus to social welfare? A partial answer is that restricting attention to an aggregate like the one mentioned allows us to clarify our understanding of the virtues of legal rules, because it allows us to isolate the importance of a legal rule to promotion of production and reduction of expenses and harm. If we were to employ a broader measure of social welfare, we would not know why a legal rule that turns out to be best is best. For instance, suppose that we consider a social welfare criterion that includes not only the factors in the usual aggregate, but also compensation of victims, and suppose that we conclude from analysis that the rule of strict liability is superior to negligence under the broader criterion. We would not know whether that superiority rests on some quality of strict liability in providing incentives to reduce accident risks, or instead derives from the fact that, by its definition, strict liability provides compensation more often than the negligence rule; thus, we would not be able to interpret the meaning of the superiority of strict liability with respect to the broader measure of social welfare.

In other words, the motivation for use of a restricted-in-breadth aggregate measure of social welfare is that it allows us to achieve a better understanding of certain desirable features of legal rules, having to do with provision of incentives to promote benefits and to reduce expenses and harms.

The reader should bear this motivation in mind, and appreciate the meaning of "socially desirable" in many contexts against this background, not as socially desirable in an expansive sense.

These comments about analytical convenience and the desire for a particular type of understanding as the reasons for use of basic, aggregate measures of social welfare lead us to ask what is sacrificed, or what would change, if we were to include other factors that do affect social welfare, especially compensation, the distribution of income, and notions of fairness. Let me now address these factors.

What difference for the evaluation of legal rules would it make to include in the measure of social welfare a factor reflecting compensation of victims, or more generally, the allocation of financial risk? The allocation of risk, and thus the social desirability of assuring that risk-averse individuals are compensated for losses they suffer, can be taken into account in the measure of social welfare. (As a formal matter, all we need do is consider the expected utility of risk-averse individuals as arguments in social welfare; thus, social welfare will depend on the allocation of risk, for the allocation of risk will affect the expected utilities of risk-averse individuals.) But as I emphasized in various parts of the book, taking the allocation of risk and protection of the risk averse into account would not alter materially the conclusions reached about the desirability of legal rules for a simple and important reason: Protection against risk is accomplished by private insurance and, if need be, can be provided by social insurance, whereas legal rules are a more expensive, and thus inferior, means of compensation. Therefore, as I wrote in sections 4 and 5 of Chapter 11, tort rules should not be evaluated on the basis of how well they compensate victims—first-party insurance does, or can, serve this function; likewise, I mentioned in section 2 of Chapter 6 that the legal rule that requires the government to compensate for takings should not be considered desirable because of its insurance function rather than its other virtues (such as mitigating abuse of the government's power to take)—a form of "takings" insurance would emerge in the absence of the compensation requirement; and so forth. This is not to say that compensation and risk-bearing would not ever be relevant to the choice of legal rules; imperfections in insurance markets might in some circumstances make it relevant, but in the main, our conclusions about the choice of legal rules would not be altered were we to deal explicitly with issues of risk allocation.

What difference for the evaluation of legal rules would it make to include in the measure of social welfare a factor reflecting distributional equity? As I explained at length in Chapter 28, formal inclusion of distributional equity in the measure of social welfare would not have altered the thrust of the conclusions about the comparison of legal rules, however important a determinant of social welfare distributional equity actually is. The essential reason is that the income tax and transfer system can be employed to pursue income distributional objectives, and utilizing legal rules to accomplish distributional objectives leads to social harm because it can only compromise other social purposes that legal rules can serve (section 4 of Chapter 28). For example, suppose that it is felt that the rich are becoming richer, and the poor are increasingly suffering, such that something needs to be done about the state of affairs. Does that imply, for instance, that the high prices that drug companies with patents are able to charge for products, especially those used predominantly by the poor, should be capped, or that the scope of intellectual property protection given to the drug companies should be limited (so as to permit similar, generic drugs to be sold more often)? The answer is no; the income tax and transfer system can be adjusted to remedy the problem of the rich being richer and poor less well-off; adjustment of the tax and transfer system is a socially superior way to cure distributional inequity than is weakening an otherwise socially desirable system of intellectual property rights that is designed to spur the development of new drugs. In other words, the law regarding intellectual property rights would not be influenced by income distributional considerations if we took them into account, owing to the existence of the income tax and transfer system; so analysis of the law is made easier simply by omitting income distributional considerations in the first place.

What difference for the evaluation of legal rules would it make to include in the measure of social welfare notions of morality, fairness, and justice? As I discussed in Chapters 26 and 27, conceptions of morality and cognate notions could have been included in the measure of social welfare and in the analysis of legal rules. I stressed that there are several ways in which principles of morality enter into normative analysis of law under the framework of welfare economics.

The first is that individuals may have a taste for satisfaction of a moral notion, such as that promises ought to be kept or that punishment ought to be in proportion to the gravity of the offense. To the extent that individuals have such tastes, their satisfaction will raise social welfare just as does the satisfaction of any other taste. It follows that the choice of legal rules may be affected by consideration of notions of morality. As an example, I noted that the magnitude of socially desirable punishment might be lower than our theory would otherwise require in circumstances where the likelihood of punishment is low. Whether and when there would be much change in our conclusions were tastes for satisfaction of moral principles taken into account is a complex question, for a variety of reasons that I considered.

The second way that morality enters into welfare economic analysis of law concerns the observation that the existence of tastes for notions of morality tends to promote our well-being in the conventional sense—because of the effects that such tastes have on our behavior. For instance, the desire to keep promises will lead to trust and the maintaining of promises where external enforcement of promises is lacking. Hence, the inculcation and promotion of tastes for principles of morality becomes socially desirable. In principle, this bears on the choice of legal rules, because that choice can itself play a role in the shaping of our tastes for moral notions. Yet one might be somewhat skeptical about the empirical importance of the influence of law on morality.

What can be said about the social goal known as "wealth maximization"? I have just discussed the answers to normative questions about economic analysis of law, assuming that the criterion of social welfare is a measure of the general form employed in welfare economics, namely, that it is a function of the utilities of individuals. What, however, can be said of the notion of "wealth maximization," a social goal advanced by many scholars who have analyzed legal rules in an economically oriented manner?[1] As I will now explain, (a) the goal of wealth maximization is not one employed in welfare economics—indeed, it is not a well-defined goal, that is, it is theoretically incoherent—even though the impression in legal academic circles is that wealth maximization is the general normative goal endorsed by economists; (b) the goal of wealth maximization has been criticized by legal academics for reasons that are, ironically, largely consistent with

---

1. Richard Posner defended wealth maximization early in his career; see, for example, Posner 1979. But he has since adopted instead other social goals (which he labels pragmatic); see, for example, Posner 1999.

welfare economics; and (c) nevertheless, the value of the actual analysis of legal rules undertaken under the rubric of wealth maximization is largely unaffected by the problematic character of that goal. Let me amplify on this curious situation.

The notion of wealth maximization is that the value of wealth in society should be maximized. This goal certainly seems economic; after all, economists are interested in money and enrichment, speak of the gross national product, and so on. As I discussed in section 1 of Chapter 26, however, the standard normative criterion studied in welfare economics is a social welfare function: a function of the *utilities* of individuals in the population. Total wealth is not a function of the utilities of individuals, so is not, on its face, a social welfare function. Moreover, I stated that wealth maximization is not even well defined. In particular, wealth cannot be computed unless one has set out a system of prices—how do we know the value of a house, a car, a person's labor, unless we know the price of the home and of the car, and unless we know the person's wages? But there is no natural system of prices to use as a benchmark for computing wealth, so in fact we do not know what wealth is.[2] The relevance to the evaluation of legal rules of this ambiguity in the definition of wealth may not usually be evident to the reader, but the ambiguity is always latent. Consider, for instance, the question of whether it is socially desirable for a firm to have a duty to buy a sprinkler system to reduce the risk of a fire that might spread and burn down homes in the neighborhood. The answer to this question about the socially best legal rule will depend on the cost of the sprinkler system and the value of the homes, but what should they be taken to be? Is there a natural, correct, price of a sprinkler system, of homes in the neighborhood? Without a theory explaining what the correct prices are, the notion of wealth, and thus the proposed basis for the choice of legal rules, is left undefined.[3]

2. A mundane question illustrating this point is this: Which represents more wealth, one apple or one banana? Obviously, there is no way to know the answer unless we know the prices of both apples and bananas.

3. Also, to my knowledge, no advocate of wealth maximization has proposed a natural system of prices to be used in computing wealth, nor even addressed this as a problem. Some writers seem to assume that the existing system of prices should be used to compute wealth. Although this would be *a* system of prices that could be employed to compute wealth, it is unclear what its appeal would be over another system of prices. Moreover, the

Notwithstanding these points, critics of wealth maximization in legal academia have attacked it as endorsed by economics and as an ethically improper goal.[4] The gist of their argument is that the criterion of wealth is an aggregate one, and thus does not reflect the value of ensuring that those who suffer losses are compensated, nor does it reflect the distribution of wealth in society, whereas both the compensation of those who suffer losses and the overall distribution of wealth in society matter. The gravamen of these criticisms is of a piece with welfare economics; as has been discussed, compensation matters to measures of social welfare once risk aversion is taken into account, and the distribution of wealth and utility matter to social welfare for a variety of reasons (see section 1 of Chapter 26, and section 1 of Chapter 28). Thus the situation is that legal academics who do not understand the basic elements of welfare economics attack what they incorrectly perceive to be the conventional normative economic framework, and employ arguments that are intrinsically those of welfare economics. At the same time, many of the advocates of the "economic" position appear themselves to be ignorant of the fundamental definitions and concepts of welfare economics.

Still, as I indicated, when one actually examines the analysis of legal rules by scholars who have cast their normative conclusions in terms of wealth maximization, one sees that there is a sense in which their conclusions are sound. On one hand, their conclusions have mostly to do with the identification of useful incentive properties of legal rules. On the other hand, their implicit exclusion of considerations of risk-bearing and of distributional equity turn out not to matter, for the reasons I have mentioned in response to the preceding italicized questions noted in this section. Hence, the thrust of the conclusions about legal rules made by those who endorse wealth maximization seem sensible, even though the goal of wealth maximization is incoherent as a general matter and, were it well defined,

present system of prices depends (as does any such system) on a vast body of legal rules—those of property law, of labor law, of the income tax system, and so forth—whereas the object of the normative analysis is to choose legal rules. Thus, adopting the existing system of prices as the benchmark for computing wealth, and using this to choose among legal rules, involves a circularity: Legal rules are to be selected on the basis of a criterion that itself depends on a set of legal rules.

4. See, for example, Dworkin 1980, Kronman 1980, and Symposium on Efficiency as a Legal Concern 1980.

would not accord with what most of us think is the appropriate notion of the social good.

How consistent are observed legal rules with socially desirable legal rules, in the sense that they maximize the type of measure of social welfare studied in this book? It seems that legal rules do serve to promote, in at least an approximate and gross manner, the basic elements of social welfare considered in this book: The rules of tort law generally foster reduction of harm when that is not too expensive to bring about; the rules of contract law lead to the making of contracts and their performance, when that is not overly burdensome; the rules of property law spur work effort, the maintenance of property, and trade in property; and the rules of criminal law tend to prevent crime. It is also apparent that legal rules enhance social welfare as I have defined it in a variety of more particular senses as well. Consider, for example, the functionality of the defense of contributory negligence in tort law (section 2 of Chapter 8), or of punishment for attempted crimes in criminal law (section 4 of Chapter 24).

Many times, however, I suggested that the law might deviate from what seems socially desirable. In the area of tort, for instance, I observed that the payments made for nonmonetary harms, notably for causing death, might be systematically low, and that an improvement could be obtained through the use of a combined system of fines and damages (section 6 of Chapter 11); I also discussed the point that when victims are the customers of firms, the entire basis of tort liability is called into question (section 2 of Chapter 9). In contract law, I noted the possible desirability for the parties of damages that exceed what appears to be the harm to the victim of the breach, yet the courts are disinclined to allow such damages (section 2 of Chapter 15). In the area of law enforcement, I mentioned society's reluctance to make use of high penalties even though this can be coupled with less enforcement and a savings in enforcement costs (section 3 of Chapter 27). I also stressed that social and private incentives to use the legal system are fundamentally divergent, and that in some domains we might well do better to curtail or even bar use of the legal system (section 1 of Chapter 17).

Thus, the picture appears to be one in which our theory of what is socially desirable, with respect to the fairly simple measures of social welfare that we considered, sometimes is consistent with our legal system and other times conflicts with it.

What is the interpretation of any observed consistency between legal rules and their optimality with respect to the measures of social welfare studied here? In a gross, overall sense, consistency of the law with promotion of social welfare as characterized here is to be expected, for how could it be the case that the law would not be generally designed to prevent harm, to promote work and trade, and to achieve other social benefits? (One could hardly imagine the opposite, that the legal system would reward people for causing accidents, for appropriating the property of others, and the like.)

There are, though, many aspects of the law that promote social welfare in ways that are not entirely obvious. To take an example that I mentioned earlier, consider the functionality of punishing attempts in criminal law (in contrast to the lack of functionality of punishing negligent acts that do not cause harm in the tort context). Or consider the point that the payment of only moderate damages, such as the expectation measure, for breach of contract is beneficial for both parties to contracts (section 2 of Chapter 15). Here economic analysis provides a type of explanation of observed law that is of some interest and novelty. I also note that the consistency between a legal rule and promotion of social welfare may not be due to direct appreciation of the instrumental virtues of the rule by those who shape the law or by the population; rather, they may be moved more by the appeal of the rule on grounds of fairness (punishment of attempted crimes may just seem right).[5] Thus the explanation of some elements of consistency between the law and the predictions of economic theory may be rooted importantly in the functional origin of the notions of morality (section 4 of Chapter 26).

What is the interpretation of suboptimality of the legal system with respect to the measures of social welfare studied here? There are two basic interpretations of such suboptimality. One is that the law is not really socially undesirable; rather, the deviation between what is observed and what appears optimal is explained by the narrowness of the measure of social welfare under review. It is possible, for instance, that our failure to employ higher sanctions for crimes when the likelihood of capture is low is due to our attachment to the principle that punishment be in proportion to the gravity of bad acts, as I indicated, and if we were to take this taste into account,

---

5. If attempted crimes were not punished, however, and the incidence of crime increased, it is likely that people would realize that deterrence was weakened, and argue for punishment of attempts on explicit instrumental grounds as well as on moral ones.

our use of punishment would not be seen as suboptimal or would be taken to be considerably less so.

The other interpretation of suboptimality is, of course, that the law is not in fact serving our social purposes. According to this view, our failure to use higher criminal penalties when the likelihood of their imposition is low; our reluctance to use fines for nonmonetary harms in combination with tort damages; our unwillingness to limit access to the legal system, or to subsidize it, according to a cost-benefit calculus about access; and so forth, lower true social welfare. It seems clear, at least to me, that this view has substantial credence, especially because of the general failure of legal academics and of others who are called on to provide expertise about the legal system to consider systematically the instrumental benefits and disadvantages of the system. Social scientific examination, and especially empirical investigation, still play a relatively small role in the formation of recommendations and advice about the legal system. In any event, when theoretically oriented study suggests that an improvement in the law is possible, one hopes that helpful inquiry will sometimes be stimulated.

REFERENCES

AUTHOR INDEX

SUBJECT INDEX

REFERENCES

Abel, Andrew B. 1985. Precautionary Saving and Accidental Bequests. *American Economic Review* 75:777–791.

ACLI Life Insurance Fact Book. 1999. Washington, D.C.: American Council of Life Insurance.

Aghion, Philippe, and Patrick Bolton. 1987. Contracts as a Barrier to Entry. *American Economic Review* 77:388–401.

Aghion, Philippe, and Benjamin Hermalin. 1990. Legal Restrictions on Private Contracts Can Enhance Efficiency. *Journal of Law, Economics, and Organization* 6:381–409.

Aghion, Philippe, Mathias Dewatripont, and Patrick Rey. 1994. Renegotiation Design with Unverifiable Information. *Econometrica* 62:257–282.

Alces, Peter A., and Harold F. See. 1994. *The Commercial Law of Intellectual Property.* Boston: Little, Brown.

Alston, Lee J., Gary D. Libecap, and Robert Schneider. 1996. The Determinants and Impact of Property Rights: Land Titles on the Brazilian Frontier. *Journal of Law, Economics and Organization* 12:25–61.

Altonji, Joseph G., Fumio Hayashi, and Laurence J. Kotlikoff. 1997. Parental Altruism and Inter Vivos Transfers: Theory and Evidence. *Journal of Political Economy* 105:1121–1166.

Andenaes, Johannes. 1966. The General Preventive Effects of Punishment. *University of Pennsylvania Law Review* 114:949–983.

———— 1975. General Prevention Revisited: Research and Policy Implications. *Journal of Criminal Law and Criminology* 66:338–365.

———— 1983. Deterrence. In *Encyclopedia of Crime and Justice,* edited by Sanford H. Kadish, 2:591–597. New York: Free Press.

Anderson, David A. 1999. The Aggregate Burden of Crime. *Journal of Law and Economics* 42:611–642.

Anderson, Terry L., and Peter J. Hill. 1990. The Race for Property Rights. *Journal of Law and Economics* 33:177–197.

Andreoni, James. 1990. Impure Altruism and Donations to Public Goods: A Theory of Warm-Glow Giving. *Economic Journal* 100:464–477.

Andreoni, James, Brian Erard, and Jonathan Feinstein. 1998. Tax Compliance. *Journal of Economic Literature* 36:818–860.

Andrews, Edmund L. 1995. Winners of Wireless Auction to Pay $7 Billion. *New York Times,* Mar. 14, 1995, p. D1.

Arlen, Jennifer, Matthew Spitzer, and Eric Talley. 2002. Endowment Effects within Corporate Agency Relationships. *Journal of Legal Studies* 31:1–37.

Arrow, Kenneth J. 1969. The Organization of Economic Activity: Issues Pertinent to the Choice of Market versus Nonmarket Allocation. In *The Analysis and Evaluation of Public Expenditures: The PPB System.* Joint Economic Committee, 91st Congress, 1st Session, 1:47–64. Washington, D.C.: Government Printing Office.

———— 1971. *Essays in the Theory of Risk-Bearing.* Chicago: Markham Publishing.

———— 1974. Optimal Insurance and Generalized Deductibles. *Scandinavian Actuarial Journal* 1974:1–42.

Ashenfelter, Orley. 1998. Arbitration. In *The New Palgrave Dictionary of Economics and the Law,* edited by Peter Newman, 1:88–93. London: Macmillan.

Ashenfelter, Orley, and David E. Bloom. 1984. Models of Arbitrator Behavior: Theory and Evidence. *American Economic Review* 74:111–124.

Atkinson, Anthony B., and Joseph E. Stiglitz. 1980. *Lectures on Public Economics.* New York: McGraw-Hill.

August, Ray. 1993. Cowboys v. Rancheros: The Origins of Western American Livestock Law. *Southwestern Historical Quarterly* 96:457–488.

Austin, John. [1832] 1995. *The Province of Jurisprudence Determined.* Edited by Wilfrid E. Rumble. Cambridge: Cambridge University Press.

Ayres, B. Drummond, Jr. 1996. A Toll Road in California Offers a High-Tech Answer to Traffic. *New York Times,* Jan. 2, 1996, p. A1.

Ayres, Ian, and Robert Gertner. 1989. Filling Gaps in Incomplete Contracts: An Economic Theory of Default Rules. *Yale Law Journal* 99: 87–130.

Bailey, Martin J. 1998. Property Rights in Aboriginal Societies. In *The New Palgrave Dictionary of Economics and the Law,* edited by Peter Newman, 3:155–157. London: Macmillan.

Baird, Douglas, and Thomas Jackson. 1984. Information, Uncertainty, and the Transfer of Property. *Journal of Legal Studies* 13:299–320.

Baker, John. H. 2002. *An Introduction to English Legal History.* Fourth edition. London: Butterworths.

Ballantine, Henry W. 1918. Title by Adverse Possession. *Harvard Law Review* 32: 135–159.

Barnett, Randy E. 1986. A Consent Theory of Contract. *Columbia Law Review* 86:269–321.

Baron, Jonathan. 1993. *Morality and Rational Choice.* Boston: Kluwer Academic Publishers.

——— 1994. Nonconsequentialist Decisions (with Commentary and Reply). *Behavioral and Brain Sciences* 17:1–42.

Barton, John H. 1972. The Economic Basis of Damages for Breach of Contract. *Journal of Legal Studies* 1:277–304.

Bassano, Joseph, Laura Dietz, Edward Esping, Tammy Hinshaw, Theresa Leming, Anne Payne, Jeanne Philbin, Kimberly Simmons, Susan Thomas, Lisa Zakolski, and Anne Melley. 1997. Automobiles and Highway Traffic. In *American Jurisprudence,* second edition, 7A:477–914, 8:1–870. Saint Paul, Minn.: West Group.

Baumol, William J., and Wallace E. Oates. 1988. *The Theory of Environmental Policy.* New York: Cambridge University Press.

Baxter, William F., and Lillian R. Altree. 1972. Legal Aspects of Airport Noise. *Journal of Law and Economics* 15:1–113.

Bean, Michael J. 1983. *The Evolution of National Wildlife Law.* Revised edition. New York: Praeger, Environmental Defense Fund.

Beattie, J. M. 1986. *Crime and the Courts in England, 1660–1800.* Princeton, N.J.: Princeton University Press.

Bebchuk, Lucian A. 1984. Litigation and Settlement under Imperfect Information. *RAND Journal of Economics* 15:404–415.

——— 1988. Suing Solely to Extract a Settlement Offer. *Journal of Legal Studies* 17:437–450.

——— 1996. A New Theory Concerning the Credibility and Success of Threats to Sue. *Journal of Legal Studies* 25:1–25.

——— 1998. Suits with Negative Expected Value. In *The New Palgrave Dictionary of Economics and the Law,* edited by Peter Newman, 3:551–554. London: Macmillan.

Bebchuk, Lucian A., and Omri Ben-Shahar. 2001. Precontractual Reliance. *Journal of Legal Studies* 30:423–457.

Bebchuk, Lucian A., and Howard Chang. 1999. The Effect of Offer-of-Settlement Rules on the Terms of Settlement. *Journal of Legal Studies* 28:489–513.

Bebchuk, Lucian A., and Louis Kaplow. 1992. Optimal Sanctions When Individuals Are Imperfectly Informed about the Probability of Apprehension. *Journal of Legal Studies* 21:365–370.

Bebchuk, Lucian A., and Ivan P. L. Png. 1999. Damage Measures for Inadvertant Breach of Contract. *International Review of Law and Economics* 19:319–331.

Bebchuk, Lucian A., and Steven Shavell. 1991. Information and the Scope of Liability for Breach of Contract: The Rule of *Hadley v. Baxendale. Journal of Law, Economics, and Organization* 7:284–312.

Beccaria, Cesare. [1767] 1995. *On Crimes and Punishments, and Other Writings.* Edited by Richard Bellamy, translated by Richard Davies, with Virginia Cox and Richard Bellamy. New York: Cambridge University Press.

Becker, Gary S. 1968. Crime and Punishment: An Economic Approach. *Journal of Political Economy* 76:169–217.

Becker, Gary S., and George J. Stigler. 1974. Law Enforcement, Malfeasance, and Compensation of Enforcers. *Journal of Legal Studies* 3:1–18.

Beltramo, Mario. 1995. Italy. In *International Civil Procedures,* edited by Christian T. Campbell, 419–494. London; Lloyd's of London Press.

Ben-Shahar, Omri. 1998. Criminal Attempts. In *The New Palgrave Dictionary of Economics and the Law,* edited by Peter Newman, 1:546–550. London: Macmillan.

Benson, Bruce L. 2000. Arbitration. In *Encyclopedia of Law and Economics,* edited by Boudewijn Bouckaert and Gerrit De Geest, 5:159–193. Cheltenham, Eng.: Edward Elgar.

Bentham, Jeremy. [1789] 1973. *An Introduction to the Principles of Morals and Legislation.* In *The Utilitarians.* Reprint of 1823 edition. Garden City, N.Y.: Anchor Books.

——— [1802] 1987. *The Theory of Legislation.* Translated by Richard Hildreth, edited by C. K. Ogden. Littleton, Colo.: Fred B. Rothman & Co.

——— 1827. *Rationale of Judicial Evidence.* Vol. 5. London: Hunt and Clarke.

Berger, Lawrence. 1974. A Policy Analysis of the Taking Problem. *New York University Law Review* 49:165–226.

Berman, Harold J. 1983. *Law and Revolution: The Formation of the Western Legal Tradition.* Cambridge, Mass.: Harvard University Press.

Berndt, Ernst R., Iain M. Cockburn, and Zvi Griliches. 1996. Pharmaceutical Innovations and Market Dynamics: Tracking Effects on Price Indexes for Antidepressant Drugs. *Brookings Papers on Economic Activity: Microeconomics* 1996:133–188.

Bernheim, B. Douglas. 1991. How Strong Are Bequest Motives? Evidence Based on Estimates of the Demand for Life Insurance and Annuities. *Journal of Political Economy* 99:899–927.

Bernheim, B. Douglas, Andrei Shleifer, and Laurence Summers. 1985. The Strategic Bequest Motive. *Journal of Political Economy* 93:1045–1076.

Bernstein, Lisa. 1992. Opting Out of the Legal System: Extralegal Contractual Relations in the Diamond Industry. *Journal of Legal Studies* 21:115–157.

———— 1998. Private Commercial Law. In *The New Palgrave Dictionary of Economics and the Law,* edited by Peter Newman, 3:108–114. London: Macmillan.

———— 2001. Private Commercial Law in the Cotton Industry: Creating Cooperation through Rules, Norms, and Institutions. *Michigan Law Review* 99:1724–1790.

Besen, Stanley M. 1998. Intellectual Property. In *The New Palgrave Dictionary of Economics and the Law,* edited by Peter Newman, 2:348–352. London: Macmillan.

Besen, Stanley M., and Leo J. Raskind. 1991. An Introduction to the Law and Economics of Intellectual Property. *Journal of Economic Perspectives* 5, no. 1: 3–27.

Besley, Timothy. 1995. Property Rights and Investment Incentives: Theory and Evidence from Ghana. *Journal of Political Economy* 103:903–937.

———— 1998. Investment Incentives and Property Rights. In *The New Palgrave Dictionary of Economics and the Law,* edited by Peter Newman, 2:359–365. London: Macmillan.

Biblowit, Charles. 1991. International Law and the Allocation of Property Rights in Common Resources. *New York International Law Review* 4:77–85.

Biggar, Darryl. 1995. A Model of Punitive Damages in Tort. *International Review of Law and Economics* 15:1–24.

Birmingham, Robert L. 1970. Breach of Contract, Damage Measures, and Economic Efficiency. *Rutgers Law Review* 24:273–292.

Bishop, William. 1985. The Choice of Remedy for Breach of Contract. *Journal of Legal Studies* 14:299–320.

Blackstone, William. [1765–1769] 1992. *Commentaries on the Laws of England.* Reprint of the first edition. Buffalo: William S. Hein & Co.

Blume, Lawrence, and Daniel L. Rubinfeld. 1984. Compensation for Takings: An Economic Analysis. *California Law Review* 72:569–628.

Blume, Lawrence, Daniel L. Rubinfeld, and Perry Shapiro. 1984. The Taking of Land: When Should Compensation Be Paid? *Quarterly Journal of Economics* 99:71–92.

Blumstein, Alfred. 1983. Incapacitation. In *Encyclopedia of Crime and Justice,* edited by Sanford H. Kadish, 3:873–880. New York: Free Press.

Blumstein, Alfred, Jacqueline Cohen, and Daniel S. Nagin, editors. 1978. *Deterrence and Incapacitation: Estimating the Effects of Criminal Sanctions on Crime Rates.* Washington, D.C.: National Academy of Sciences.

Bonczar, Thomas P., and Allen J. Beck. 1997. Lifetime Likelihood of Going to State or Federal Prison. Bureau of Justice Statistics Special Report, Mar. 1997, NCJ-160092. Washington D.C.: U.S. Department of Justice.

Bosselman, Fred P., David L. Callies, and John Banta. 1973. *The Taking Issue: A Study of the Constitutional Limits of Governmental Authority.* Washington, D.C.: U.S. Council on Environmental Quality.

Bouckaert, Boudewijn, and Ben W. F. Depoorter. 2000. Adverse Possession—Title Systems. In *Encyclopedia of Law and Economics,* edited by Boudewijn Bouckaert and Gerrit De Geest, 2:18–31. Cheltenham, Eng.: Edward Elgar.

Bovenberg, A. Lans, and Lawrence H. Goulder. 2002. Environmental Taxation and Regulation. In *Handbook of Public Economics,* edited by Alan J. Auerbach and Martin Feldstein, 3:1471–1545. Amsterdam: Elsevier.

Braeutigam, Ronald, Bruce Owen, and John Panzar. 1984. An Economic Analysis of Alternative Fee Shifting Systems. *Law and Contemporary Problems* 47:173–185.

Breyer, Stephen. 1970. The Uneasy Case for Copyright: A Study of Copyright in Books, Photocopies, and Computer Programs. *Harvard Law Review* 84:281–351.

——— 1982. *Regulation and Its Reform.* Cambridge, Mass.: Harvard University Press.

Brickman, Lester, Michael Horowitz, and Jeffrey O'Connell. 1994. *Rethinking Contingency Fees.* New York: Manhattan Institute.

Brown, John P. 1973. Toward an Economic Theory of Liability. *Journal of Legal Studies* 2:323–349.

Brown, Ray Andrews. 1975. *The Law of Personal Property* Third edition. Edited by Walter B. Raushenbush. Chicago: Callaghan.

Buchanan, James M., and Wm. Craig Stubblebine. 1962. Externality. *Economica* 29:371–384.

Bundy, Stephen McG., and Einer R. Elhauge. 1991. Do Lawyers Improve the Adversary System? A General Theory of Litigation Advice and Its Regulation. *California Law Review* 79:313–420.

Burgunder, Lee B. 1985. An Economic Approach to Trademark Genericism. *American Business Law Journal* 23:391–416.

Byrd, Robert W., and Marion Barbier. 1992. France. In *Civil Appeal Procedures Worldwide,* edited by Charles Platto, 158–168. London: Graham and Trotman.

Cahoon, Colin. 1990. Low Altitude Airspace: A Property Rights No-Man's Land. *Journal of Air Law and Commerce* 56:157–198.

Calabresi, Guido. 1961. Some Thoughts on Risk Distribution and the Law of Torts. *Yale Law Journal* 70:499–553.

——— 1965. The Decision for Accidents: An Approach to Nonfault Allocation of Costs. *Harvard Law Review* 78:713–745.

———— 1968. Transaction Costs, Resource Allocation and Liability Rules—A Comment. *Journal of Law and Economics* 11:67–73.

———— 1970. *The Costs of Accidents: A Legal and Economic Analysis.* New Haven: Yale University Press.

———— 1975. Concerning Cause and the Law of Torts. *University of Chicago Law Review* 43:69–108.

Calabresi, Guido, and A. Douglas Melamed. 1972. Property Rules, Liability Rules, and Inalienability: One View of the Cathedral. *Harvard Law Review* 85:1089–1128.

Calamari, John D., and Joseph M. Perillo. 1998. *The Law of Contracts.* Fourth edition. St. Paul, Minn.: West Group.

Calandrillo, Steve P. 1998. An Economic Analysis of Property Rights in Information: Justifications and Problems of Exclusive Rights, Incentives to Generate Information, and the Alternative of a Government-Run Reward System. *Fordham Intellectual Property, Media and Entertainment Law Journal* 9:301–360.

Calfee, John, and Richard Craswell. 1984. Some Effects of Uncertainty on Compliance with Legal Standards. *Virginia Law Review* 70:965–1003.

Cane, Peter. 1999. *Atiyah's Accidents, Compensation, and the Law.* Sixth edition. London: Butterworths.

Carlton, Dennis W., and Glenn C. Loury. 1980. The Limitations of Pigouvian Taxes as a Long-Run Remedy for Externalities. *Quarterly Journal of Economics* 95:559–566.

Carr-Hill, Roy A., and Nicholas H. Stern. 1979. *Crime, the Police, and Criminal Statistics: An Analysis of Official Statistics for England and Wales Using Econometric Methods.* London: Academic Press.

Carroll, Stephen J., James S. Kakalik, Nicholas M. Pace, and John L. Adams. 1991. *No-Fault Approaches to Compensating People Injured in Automobile Accidents.* Santa Monica, Calif.: RAND Institute for Civil Justice.

Chang, Howard F. 1995. Patent Scope, Antitrust Policy, and Cumulative Innovation. *RAND Journal of Economics* 26:34–57.

Charny, David. 1990. Nonlegal Sanctions in Commercial Relationships. *Harvard Law Review* 104:373–467.

Che, Yeon-Koo, and Tai-Yeong Chung. 1999. Contract Damages and Cooperative Investments. *RAND Journal of Economics* 30:84–105.

Che, Yeon-Koo, and Donald B. Hausch. 1999. Cooperative Investments and the Value of Contracting. *American Economic Review* 89:125–147.

Che, Yeon-Koo, and Jong Goo Yi. 1993. The Role of Precedents in Repeated Litigation. *Journal of Law, Economics, and Organization* 9:399–424.

Cheung, Steven N. S. 1973. The Fable of the Bees: An Economic Investigation. *Journal of Law and Economics* 16:11–33.

————— 1982. Property Rights in Trade Secrets. *Economic Inquiry* 20:40–53.

Chisum, Donald S. 1996. *Chisum on Patents: A Treatise on the Law of Patentability, Validity, and Infringement.* New York: LEXIS Publishing.

Chisum, Donald S., Craig Allen Nard, Herbert F. Schwartz, Pauline Newman, and F. Scott Kieff. 2001. *Principles of Patent Law.* Second edition. New York: Foundation Press.

Chu, C. Y. Cyrus, Sheng-cheng Hu, and Ting-yuan Huang. 2000. Punishing Repeat Offenders More Severely. *International Review of Law and Economics* 20: 127–140.

Chung, Tai-Yeong. 1991. Incomplete Contracts, Specific Investments, and Risk Sharing. *Review of Economic Studies* 58:1031–1042.

————— 1992. On the Social Optimality of Liquidated Damage Clauses: An Economic Analysis. *Journal of Law, Economics, and Organization* 8:280–305.

Clark, Barkley, and Barbara Clark. 2001. *The Law of Secured Transactions under the Uniform Commercial Code.* Revised edition. Vol. 1. Arlington, Va.: A.S. Pratt & Sons, Thomson Financial.

Clarkson, Kenneth W., Roger Leroy Miller, and Timothy J. Muris. 1978. Liquidated Damages v. Penalties: Sense or Nonsense? *Wisconsin Law Review* 1978: 351–390.

Coase, Ronald H. 1959. The Federal Communications Commission. *Journal of Law and Economics* 2:1–40.

————— 1960. The Problem of Social Cost. *Journal of Law and Economics* 3:1–44.

————— 1974. The Lighthouse in Economics. *Journal of Law and Economics* 17: 357–376.

————— 1988. *The Firm, the Market, and the Law.* Chicago: University of Chicago Press.

Cohen, George M. 2000. Implied Terms and Interpretation in Contract Law. In *Encyclopedia of Law and Economics,* edited by Boudewijn Bouckaert and Gerrit De Geest, 3:78–99. Cheltenham, Eng.: Edward Elgar.

Cohen, Jerry, and Alan S. Gutterman. 1998. *Trade Secrets Protection and Exploitation.* Washington, D.C.: Bureau of National Affairs.

Cohen, Mark A. 1989. Corporate Crime and Punishment: A Study of Social Harm and Sentencing Practice in the Federal Courts, 1984–1987. *American Criminal Law Review* 26:605–660.

Cook, Philip J. 1977. Punishment and Crime: A Critique of Current Findings Concerning the Preventive Effects of Punishment. *Law and Contemporary Problems* 41:164–204.

Cook, Philip J., and Daniel A. Graham. 1977. The Demand for Insurance and Protection: The Case of Irreplaceable Commodities. *Quarterly Journal of Economics* 91:143–156.

Cooley, John W., and Steven Lubet. 1997. *Arbitration Advocacy.* South Bend, Ind.: National Institute for Trial Advocacy.

Cooper, Russel, and Thomas W. Ross. 1985. Product Warranties and Double Moral Hazard. *RAND Journal of Economics* 16:103–113.

Cooter, Robert D. 1982. Economic Analysis of Punitive Damages. *Southern California Law Review* 56:79–101.

――― 1985. Unity in Tort, Contract, and Property: The Model of Precaution. *California Law Review* 73:1–51.

――― 1989. Punitive Damages for Deterrence: When and How Much? *Alabama Law Review* 40:1143–1196.

Cooter, Robert D., and Daniel L. Rubinfeld. 1989. Economic Analysis of Legal Disputes and Their Resolution. *Journal of Economic Literature* 27:1067–1097.

――― 1994. An Economic Model of Legal Discovery. *Journal of Legal Studies* 23:435–463.

Cooter, Robert, and Thomas Ulen. 2000. *Law and Economics.* Third edition. Reading, Mass.: Addison-Wesley.

Corpus Juris Secundum. 1961. St. Paul, Minn.: West Publishing.

Couture, Tony. 1999. State. In *The Philosophy of Law,* edited by Christopher Berry Gray, 2:834–837. New York: Garland Publishing.

Cox, Donald. 1987. Motives for Private Income Transfers. *Journal of Political Economy* 95:508–546.

Craswell, Richard. 1988. Contract Remedies, Renegotiation, and the Theory of Efficient Breach. *Southern California Law Review* 61:629–670.

――― 1996. Offer, Acceptance, and Efficient Reliance. *Stanford Law Review* 48: 481–553.

Craswell, Richard, and John E. Calfee. 1986. Deterrence and Uncertain Legal Standards. *Journal of Law, Economics, and Organization* 2:279–303.

Croley, Steven P., and Jon D. Hanson. 1993. Rescuing the Revolution: The Revived Case for Enterprise Liability. *Michigan Law Review* 91:683–797.

Cropper, Maureen L., and Wallace E. Oates. 1992. Environmental Economics: A Survey. *Journal of Economic Literature* 30:675–740.

Croson, Rachel, and Jason S. Johnston. 2000. Experimental Results on Bargaining under Alternative Property Rights Regimes. *Journal of Law, Economics, and Organization* 16:50–73.

Cummins, J. David, Richard D. Phillips, and Mary A. Weiss. 2001. The Incentive Effects of No-Fault Automobile Insurance. *Journal of Law and Economics* 44: 427–464.

Dales, J. H. 1968. *Pollution, Property, and Prices.* Toronto: University of Toronto Press.

Daly, Martin, and Margo Wilson. 1988. *Homicide.* New York: A. de Gruyter.

Dam, Kenneth W. 1994. The Economic Underpinnings of Patent Law. *Journal of Legal Studies* 23:247–271.

Dana, James D., Jr., and Kathryn E. Spier. 1993. Expertise and Contingent Fees: The Role of Asymmetric Information in Attorney Compensation. *Journal of Law, Economics, and Organization* 9:349–367.

Danzon, Patricia M. 1983. Contingent Fees for Personal Injury Litigation. *Bell Journal of Economics* 14:213–224.

——— 1984. Tort Reform and the Role of Government in Private Insurance Markets. *Journal of Legal Studies* 13:517–549.

——— 1985. *Medical Malpractice: Theory, Evidence, and Public Policy.* Cambridge, Mass.: Harvard University Press.

Darwin, Charles. [1874] 1998. *The Descent of Man.* Reprint of second edition. Amherst, N.Y.: Prometheus Books.

Daughety, Andrew F. 2000. Settlement. In *Encyclopedia of Law and Economics,* edited by Boudewijn Bouckaert and Gerrit De Geest, 5:95–158. Cheltenham, Eng.: Edward Elgar.

Daughety, Andrew F., and Jennifer F. Reinganum. 1993. Endogenous Sequencing in Models of Settlement and Litigation. *Journal of Law, Economics, and Organization* 9:314–348.

——— 2000. Appealing Judgments. *RAND Journal of Economics* 31:502–525.

Davenport, Neil. 1993. *United Kingdom Copyright and Design Protection: A Brief History.* Emsworth, Eng.: K. Mason Publications.

Davies, James B. 1981. Uncertain Lifetime, Consumption, and Dissaving in Retirement. *Journal of Political Economy* 89:561–577.

Davis, Otto A., and Andrew Whinston. 1962. Externalities, Welfare, and the Theory of Games. *Journal of Political Economy* 70:241–262.

De Geest, Gerrit, and Filip Wuyts. 2000. Penalty Clauses and Liquidated Damages. In *Encyclopedia of Law and Economics,* edited by Boudewijn Bouckaert and Gerrit De Geest, 3:141–161. Cheltenham, Eng.: Edward Elgar.

De Meza, David. 1998. Coase Theorem. In *The New Palgrave Dictionary of Economics and the Law,* edited by Peter Newman, 1:270–282. London: Macmillan.

Demsetz, Harold. 1967. Toward a Theory of Property Rights. *American Economic Review: Papers and Proceedings* 57, no. 2:347–359.

Derfner, Mary Francis, and Arthur D. Wolf. 1995. *Court Awarded Attorney Fees.* New York: Matthew Bender.

De Vany, Arthur S., Ross D. Eckert, Charles J. Meyers, Donald J. O'Hara, and Richard C. Scott. 1969. A Property System for Market Allocation of the Electromagnetic Spectrum: A Legal-Economic-Engineering Study. *Stanford Law Review* 21:1499–1561.

Devlin, Rose Ann. 1990. Some Implications of No-Fault Automobile Insurance. *International Review of Law and Economics* 10:193–205.

Dewees, Don, David Duff, and Michael Trebilcock. 1996. *Exploring the Domain of Accident Law: Taking the Facts Seriously.* New York: Oxford University Press.

Diamond, Peter A. 1974a. Accident Law and Resource Allocation. *Bell Journal of Economics* 5:366–405.

————1974b. Single Activity Accidents. *Journal of Legal Studies* 3:107–164.

Diamond, Peter A., and Eric Maskin. 1979. An Equilibrium Analysis of Search and Breach of Contract: Steady States. *Bell Journal of Economics* 10:282–316.

Dietz, Laura H. 2000. Salvage. In *American Jurisprudence,* second edition, 68:211–289. St. Paul, Minn.: West Group.

DiIulio, John J., Jr., and Anne Morrison Piehl. 1991. Does Prison Pay? *Brookings Review* 9, no. 4:28–35.

Dinwoodie, Graeme B., William O. Hennessey, and Shira Perlmutter. 2001. *International Intellectual Property Law and Policy.* Newark: LexisNexis.

Dobbs, Dan B. 2000. *The Law of Torts.* St. Paul, Minn.: West Group.

Donohue, John D, III. 1989. The Law and Economics of Tort Law: The Profound Revolution. Review of *The Economic Structure of Tort Law,* by William M. Landes and Richard A. Posner, and *Economic Analysis of Accident Law,* by Steven Shavell. *Harvard Law Review* 102:1047–1073.

Dukeminier, Jesse, and James E. Krier. 1998. *Property.* Fourth edition. New York: Aspen Law and Business.

Dworkin, Ronald M. 1980. Is Wealth a Value? *Journal of Legal Studies* 9:191–226.

Easterbrook, Frank H. 1981. Insider Trading, Secret Agents, Evidentiary Privileges, and the Production of Information. *Supreme Court Review* 1981:309–365.

Eckert, Ross D. 1979. *The Enclosure of Ocean Resources: Economics and the Law of the Sea.* Stanford, Calif.: Hoover Institution Press.

Economides, Nicholas S. 1988. The Economics of Trademarks. *Trademark Reporter* 78:523–539.

———— 1998. Trademarks. In *The New Palgrave Dictionary of Economics and the Law,* edited by Peter Newman, 3:601–603. London: Macmillan.

Edlin, Aaron S. 1998. Breach Remedies. In *The New Palgrave Dictionary of Economics and the Law,* edited by Peter Newman, 1:174–179. London: Macmillan.

Edlin, Aaron S., and Stefan Reichelstein. 1996. Holdups, Standard Breach Remedies, and Optimal Investment. *American Economic Review* 86:478–501.

Ehrlich, Issac. 1996. Crime, Punishment, and the Market for Offenses. *Journal of Economic Perspectives* 10, no. 1:43–67.

Eide, Erling. 2000. Economics of Criminal Behavior. In *Encyclopedia of Law and Economics,* edited by Boudewijn Bouckaert and Gerrit De Geest, 5:345–389. Cheltenham, Eng.: Edward Elgar.

Eisenberg, Melvin A. 1979. Donative Promises. *University of Chicago Law Review* 47:1–33.

Eisenberg, Theodore. 1990. Testing the Selection Effect: A New Theoretical Framework with Empirical Tests. *Journal of Legal Studies* 19:337–358.

Eisenberg, Theodore, and Henry S. Farber. 1997. The Litigious Plaintiff Hypothesis: Case Selection and Resolution. *RAND Journal of Economics* 28:S92–S112.

Eisenberg, Theodore, John Goerdt, Brian Ostrom, David Rottman, and Martin T. Wells. 1997. The Predictability of Punitive Damages. *Journal of Legal Studies* 26:623–661.

Eisner, Robert, and Robert H. Strotz. 1961. Flight Insurance and the Theory of Choice. *Journal of Political Economy* 69:355–368.

Ellickson, Robert C. 1973. Alternatives to Zoning: Covenants, Nuisance Rules, and Fines as Land Use Controls. *University of Chicago Law Review* 40:681–781.

——— 1986. Adverse Possession and Perpetuities Law: Two Dents in the Libertarian Model of Property Rights. *Washington University Law Quarterly* 64:723–737.

——— 1991. *Order without Law: How Neighbors Settle Disputes.* Cambridge, Mass.: Harvard University Press.

——— 1993. Property in Land. *Yale Law Journal* 102:1315–1400.

Ely, Northcutt. 1938. The Conservation of Oil. *Harvard Law Review* 51:1209–1244.

Emons, Winand. 1990. Efficient Liability Rules for an Economy with Non-Identical Individuals. *Journal of Public Economics* 42:89–104.

——— 2000. Expertise, Contingent Fees, and Insufficient Attorney Effort. *International Review of Law and Economics* 20:21–33.

Emons, Winand, and Joel Sobel. 1991. On the Effectiveness of Liability Rules When Agents Are Not Identical. *Review of Economic Studies* 58:375–390.

Eörsi, Gyula. 1983. Private and Governmental Liability for the Torts of Employees and Organs. In *International Encyclopedia of Comparative Law,* edited by André Tunc, vol. 11, ch. 4. Tübingen, Ger.: J. C. B. Mohr.

Epple, Dennis, and Artur Raviv. 1978. Product Safety: Liability Rules, Market Structure, and Imperfect Information. *American Economic Review* 68:80–95.

Epstein, Richard A. 1980. *Modern Products Liability Law: A Legal Revolution.* Westport, Conn.: Quorum Books.

——— 1985. *Takings: Private Property and the Power of Eminent Domain.* Cambridge, Mass.: Harvard University Press.

Evans, Robert. 1987. The Early History of Fire Insurance. *Journal of Legal History* 8:88–91.

Eyre, Frank, and E. C. R. Hadfield. 1945. *The Fire Service Today.* London: Oxford University Press.

Fact Book, 2001. 2001. New York: Insurance Information Institute.

Farber, Daniel A. 1992. Economic Analysis and Just Compensation. *International Review of Law and Economics* 12:125–138.

Farber, Henry S., and Michelle J. White. 1991. Medical Malpractice: An Empirical Examination of the Litigation Process. *RAND Journal of Economics* 22:199–217.

Farmer, Amy, and Paul Pecorino. 1996. Issues of Informational Asymmetry in Legal Bargaining. In *Dispute Resolution: Bridging the Settlement Gap,* edited by David A. Anderson, 79–105. Greenwich, Conn.: JAI Press.

Farnsworth, E. Allan. 1999. *Contracts.* Third edition. New York: Aspen Law and Business.

Farnsworth, Ward. 1999. Do Parties to Nuisance Cases Bargain after Judgment? A Glimpse inside the Cathedral. *University of Chicago Law Review* 66:373–436.

Faure, Michael G. 2000. Environmental Regulation. In *Encyclopedia of Law and Economics,* edited by Boudewijn Bouckaert and Gerrit De Geest, 2:433–520. Cheltenham, Eng.: Edward Elgar.

Feder, Gershon, and David Feeny. 1991. Land Tenure and Property Rights: Theory and Implications for Development Policy. *World Bank Economic Review* 5:135–153.

Federal Procedure. 2000. Lawyers Edition. St. Paul, Minn.: West Group.

Feldman, Allan M. 1987. Welfare Economics. In *The New Palgrave: A Dictionary of Economics,* edited by John Eatwell, Murray Milgate, and Peter Newman, 4:889–896. London: Macmillan.

Fischel, Daniel R. 1998. Lawyers and Confidentiality. *University of Chicago Law Review* 65:1–33.

Fischel, Daniel R., and Alan O. Sykes. 1996. Corporate Crime. *Journal of Legal Studies* 25:319–349.

Fischel, William A. 1995. *Regulatory Takings: Law, Economics, and Politics.* Cambridge, Mass.: Harvard University Press.

Fisher, William W., III. 1988. Reconstructing the Fair Use Doctrine. *Harvard Law Review* 101:1659–1795.

Fishman, Michael J., and Kathleen M. Hagerty. 1990. The Optimal Amount of Discretion to Allow in Disclosure. *Quarterly Journal of Economics* 105:427–444.

Fleming, John G. 1998. *The Law of Torts.* Ninth edition. Syndey: LBC Information Services.

Flinn, Patrick J. 2001. *Handbook of Intellectual Property Claims and Remedies.* New York: Aspen Law and Business.

Forte, David F. 1983. Comparative Criminal Law and Enforcement: Islam. In *Encyclopedia of Crime and Justice,* edited by Sanford H. Kadish, 1:193–200. New York: Free Press.

Foster, Seena. 2000. Validity, Construction, and Application of Abandoned Shipwreck Act of 1987. *American Law Reports, Federal Cases and Annotations* 163: 421–444.

Frank, Robert H. 1988. *Passions within Reason: The Strategic Role of the Emotions.* New York: W. W. Norton.

Frech, H. E., III. 1973. Pricing of Pollution: The Coase Theorem in the Long Run. *Bell Journal of Economics and Management Science* 4:316–319.

Fried, Charles. 1981. *Contract as Promise: A Theory of Contractual Obligation.* Cambridge, Mass.: Harvard University Press.

Friedman, Alan E. 1969. An Analysis of Settlement. *Stanford Law Review* 22:67–100.

Friedman, David, and William Sjostrom. 1993. Hanged for a Sheep—The Economics of Marginal Deterrence. *Journal of Legal Studies* 22:345–366.

Friedman, David D., William M. Landes, and Richard A. Posner. 1991. Some Economics of Trade Secret Law. *Journal of Economic Perspectives* 5, no. 1:61–72.

Fudenberg, Drew, and Jean Tirole. 1990. Moral Hazard and Renegotiation in Agency Contracts. *Econometrica* 58:1279–1319.

Fuller, Lon L., and William R. Perdue, Jr. 1936. The Reliance Interest in Contract Damages, Part 1. *Yale Law Journal* 46:52–96.

Gabel, George F., Jr. 1994. Abandoned, Lost, and Unclaimed Property. In *American Jurisprudence,* second edition, 1:1–54. Rochester, N.Y.: Lawyers Cooperative Publishing.

Gale, William G., and John Karl Scholz. 1994. Intergenerational Transfers and the Accumulation of Wealth. *Journal of Economic Perspectives* 8, no. 4:145–160.

Gallini, Nancy. 2002. The Economics of Patents: Lessons from Recent U.S. Patent Reform. *Journal of Economic Perspectives* 16, no. 2:131–154.

Garner, J. F., editor. 1975. *Compensation for Compulsory Purchase: A Comparative Study.* London: United Kingdom National Committee of Comparative Law.

Garoupa, Nuno. 1997. The Theory of Optimal Law Enforcement. *Journal of Economic Surveys* 11:267–295.

———— 1999. Optimal Law Enforcement with Dissemination of Information. *European Journal of Law and Economics* 7:183–196.

Geistfeld, Mark. 2000. Products Liability. In *Encyclopedia of Law and Economics,* edited by Boudewijn Bouckaert and Gerrit De Geest, 3:347–395. Chelten-ham, Eng.: Edward Elgar.

Gertner, Robert H. 1998. Disclosure and Unravelling. In *The New Palgrave Dictionary of Economics and the Law,* edited by Peter Newman, 1:605–608. London: Macmillan.

Gilbert, Richard, and Carl Shapiro. 1990. Optimal Patent Length and Breadth. *RAND Journal of Economics* 21:106–112.

Ginsburg, Douglas H., and Paul Shechtman. 1993. Blackmail: An Economic Analysis of the Law. *University of Pennsylvania Law Review* 141:1849–1876.

Glaeser, Edward L. 1998. Economic Approach to Crime and Punishment. In *The New Palgrave Dictionary of Economics and the Law,* edited by Peter Newman, 2:1–6. London: Macmillan.

Glendon, Mary Ann. 1989. *The Transformation of Family Law: State, Law, and Family in the United States and Western Europe.* Chicago: University of Chicago Press.

Goetz, Charles J., and Robert E. Scott. 1977. Liquidated Damages, Penalties and the Just Compensation Principle: Some Notes on an Enforcement Model and a Theory of Efficient Breach. *Columbia Law Review* 77:554–594.

———— 1980. Enforcing Promises: An Examination of the Basis of Contract. *Yale Law Journal* 89:1261–1322.

Goldberg, Stephen B., Frank E. A. Sander, and Nancy H. Rogers. 1999. *Dispute Resolution: Negotiation, Mediation, and Other Processes.* Third edition. Gaithersburg, Md.: Aspen Law and Business.

Goldberg, Victor P. 1974. The Economics of Product Safety and Imperfect Information. *Bell Journal of Economics and Management Science* 5:683–688.

Goldstein, Paul. 2001a. *Copyright.* Second edition. New York: Aspen Law.

———— 2001b. *International Copyright: Principles, Law, and Practice.* New York: Oxford University Press.

Gordon, Wendy J. 1982. Fair Use as Market Failure: A Structural and Economic Analysis of the *Betamax* Case and Its Predecessors. *Columbia Law Review* 82:1600–1657.

Gordon, Wendy J., and Robert G. Bone. 2000. Copyright. In *Encyclopedia of Law and Economics,* edited by Boudewijn Bouckaert and Gerrit De Geest, 2:189–215. Cheltenham, Eng.: Edward Elgar.

Gould, John P. 1973. The Economics of Legal Conflicts. *Journal of Legal Studies* 2:279–300.

Grabowski, Henry G., and John M. Vernon. 1992. Brand Loyalty, Entry, and Price Competition in Pharmaceuticals after the 1984 Drug Act. *Journal of Law and Economics* 35:331–350.

Grady, Mark F. 1983. A New Positive Economic Theory of Negligence. *Yale Law Journal* 92:799–829.

Graetz, Michael J. 1985. Retroactivity Revisited. *Harvard Law Review* 98:1820–1841.

Gravelle, H. S. E. 1993. The Efficiency Implications of Cost-Shifting Rules. *International Review of Law and Economics* 13:3–18.

Green, Jerry. 1976. On the Optimal Structure of Liability Laws. *Bell Journal of Economics* 7:553–574.

Green, Jerry R., and Suzanne Scotchmer. 1995. On the Division of Profit in Sequential Innovation. *RAND Journal of Economics* 26:20–33.

Greenberg, David F. 1983. Age and Crime. In *Encyclopedia of Crime and Justice,* edited by Sanford H. Kadish, 1:30–35. New York: Free Press.

Greif, Avner. 1998. Informal Contract Enforcement: Lessons from Medieval Trade. In *The New Palgrave Dictionary of Economics and the Law,* edited by Peter Newman, 2:287–295. London: Macmillan.

Grossman, Sanford J. 1981. The Informational Role of Warranties and Private Disclosure about Product Quality. *Journal of Law and Economics* 24:461–483.

Grout, Paul A. 1984. Investment and Wages in the Absence of Binding Contracts: A Nash Bargaining Approach. *Econometrica* 52:449–460.

Haddock, David D., Fred S. McChesney, and Menahem Spiegel. 1990. An Ordinary Economic Rationale for Extraordinary Legal Sanctions. *California Law Review* 78:1–51.

Hadfield, Gillian K. 1994. Judicial Competence and the Interpretation of Incomplete Contracts. *Journal of Legal Studies* 23:159–184.

Hahn, Robert W. 1990. Regulation: Past, Present, and Future. *Harvard Journal of Law and Public Policy* 13:167–228.

Hahn, Robert W., and Robert N. Stavins. 1991. Incentive-Based Environmental Regulation: A New Era from an Old Idea? *Ecology Law Quarterly* 18:1–42.

Halpern, Paul. 1998. Limited and Extended Liability Regimes. In *The New Palgrave Dictionary of Economics and the Law,* edited by Peter Newman, 2:581–591. London: Macmillan.

Hamada, Koichi. 1976. Liability Rules and Income Distribution in Product Liability. *American Economic Review* 66:228–234.

Hamilton, Jonathan H., Eytan Sheshinski, and Steven M. Slutsky. 1989. Production Externalities and Long-Run Equilibria: Bargaining and Pigovian Taxation. *Economic Inquiry* 27:453–471.

Hannesson, Rögnvaldur. 1991. From Common Fish to Rights Based Fishing. *European Economic Review* 35:397–407.

Hansmann, Henry, and Reinier Kraakman. 1991. Toward Unlimited Shareholder Liability for Corporate Torts. *Yale Law Journal* 100:1879–1934.

———— 2002. Property, Contract, and Verifications: The *Numerus Clausus* Problem and the Divisibility of Rights. Harvard John M. Olin Discussion Paper Series, no. 388. Cambridge, Mass.: Harvard Law School.

Hare, Richard M. 1981. *Moral Thinking: Its Levels, Method, and Point.* Oxford: Oxford University Press.

Harsanyi, John C. 1977. *Rational Behavior and Bargaining Equilibrium in Games and Social Situations.* Cambridge: Cambridge University Press.

Hart, H. L. A., and Tony Honoré. 1985. *Causation in the Law.* Second edition. Oxford: Clarendon Press.

Hart, Oliver D. 1987. Incomplete Contracts. In *The New Palgrave Dictionary of Economics,* edited by John Eatwell, Murray Milgate, and Peter Newman, 2: 752–759. London: Macmillan.

Hart, Oliver D., and Bengt Holmström. 1987. The Theory of Contracts. In *Advances in Economic Theory,* Fifth World Congress, edited by Truman Bewley, 71–155. New York: Cambridge University Press.

Hart, Oliver D., and John Moore. 1988. Incomplete Contracts and Renegotiation. *Econometrica* 56:755–785.

Hatzis, Aristedes N. 2002. Having the Cake and Eating It Too: Efficient Penalty Clauses in Common and Civil Contract Law. *International Review of Law and Economics* 22:381–406.

Hau, Timothy D. 1990. Electronic Road Pricing: Developments in Hong Kong, 1983–1989. *Journal of Transport Economics and Policy* 24:203–214.

Hause, John C. 1989. Indemnity, Settlement, and Litigation, or I'll Be Suing You. *Journal of Legal Studies* 18:157–179.

Hausman, Jerry A., editor. 1993. *Contingent Valuation: A Critical Assessment.* Amsterdam: North Holland.

Hawes, James E. 1997. *Trademark Registration Practice.* Second edition. St. Paul, Minn.: West Group.

Hay, Bruce L. 1994. Civil Discovery: Its Effects and Optimal Scope. *Journal of Legal Studies* 23:481–515.

———— 1995. Effort, Information, Settlement, Trial. *Journal of Legal Studies* 24: 29–62.

———— 1996. Contingent Fees and Agency Costs. *Journal of Legal Studies* 25: 503–533.

Hay, Bruce L., and Kathryn E. Spier. 1998. Settlement of Litigation. In *The New Palgrave Dictionary of Economics and the Law,* edited by Peter Newman, 3: 442–451. London: Macmillan.

Heilbroner, Robert L. 1962. *The Making of Economic Society.* Englewood Cliffs, N.J.: Prentice-Hall.

———— 1987. Capitalism. In *The New Palgrave Dictionary of Economics,* edited by John Eatwell, Murray Milgate, and Peter Newman, 1:347–353. London: Macmillan.

Heller, Michael A. 1999. The Boundaries of Private Property. *Yale Law Journal* 108:1163–1223.

Heller, Michael A., and Rebecca S. Eisenberg. 1998. Can Patents Deter Innovation? The Anticommons in Biomedical Research. *Science* 280:698–701.

Henry, David J. 1977. Multi-National Practice in Determining Provisions in Compulsory Patent Licenses. *Journal of International Law and Economics* 11: 325–351.

Hensler, Deborah R., Mary E. Vaiana, James S. Kakalik, and Mark A. Peterson. 1987. *Trends in Tort Litigation.* R-3583-ICJ. Santa Monica, Calif.: RAND Institute for Civil Justice.

Hermalin, Benjamin E. 1995. An Economic Analysis of Takings. *Journal of Law, Economics, and Organization* 11:64–86.

Herzog, Peter E., and Delmar Karlen. 1982. Attacks on Judicial Decisions. Chapter 8 in volume 16, *Civil Procedure,* edited by Mauro Cappelletti. *International Encyclopedia of Comparative Law.* Tübingen, Ger.: J. C. B. Mohr.

Hesse, Carla. 1989. Economic Upheavals in Publishing. In *Revolution in Print,* edited by Robert Darnton and Daniel Roche, 69–97. Berkeley: University of California Press.

Higgins, Richard S. 1978. Producers' Liability and Product-Related Accidents. *Journal of Legal Studies* 7:299–321.

Hirshleifer, Jack. 1971. The Private and Social Value of Information and the Reward to Inventive Activity. *American Economic Review* 61:561–574.

——— 1977. Economics from a Biological Viewpoint. *Journal of Law and Economics* 20:1–52.

——— 1978. Natural Economy versus Political Economy. *Journal of Social and Biological Structures* 1:319–337.

——— 1987. On the Emotions as Guarantors of Threats and Promises. In *The Latest on the Best: Essays on Evolution and Optimality,* edited by John Dupré, 307–326. Cambridge, Mass.: MIT Press.

Hobbes, Thomas. [1651] 1958. *Leviathan, Parts I and II.* Introduction by Herbert W. Schneider. Indianapolis: Library of Liberal Arts, Bobbs-Merrill.

Hoffman, Elizabeth, and Matthew L. Spitzer. 1982. The Coase Theorem: Some Experimental Tests. *Journal of Law and Economics* 25:73–98.

Hoffman, Jan. 1997. Crime and Punishment: Shame Gains Popularity. *New York Times,* Jan. 16, 1997, p. A1.

Holmes, Oliver Wendell, Jr. [1881] 1963. *The Common Law.* Mark DeWolfe Howe, editor. Boston: Little, Brown.

Honoré, Anthony. 1983. Causation and Remoteness of Damage. Chapter 7 of volume 11, *Torts,* in *International Encyclopedia of Comparative Law.* Tübingen, Ger.: J. C. B. Mohr.

Huber, Peter W. 1988. *Liability: The Legal Revolution and Its Consequences.* New York: Basic Books.

Huberman, Gur, David Mayers, and Clifford W. Smith, Jr. 1983. Optimal Insurance Policy Indemnity Schedules. *Bell Journal of Economics* 14:415–426.

Hughes, James W., and Edward A. Snyder. 1995. Litigation and Settlement under the English and American Rules: Theory and Evidence. *Journal of Law and Economics* 38:225–250.

———— 1998. Allocation of Litigation Costs: American and English Rules. In *The New Palgrave Dictionary of Economics and the Law,* edited by Peter Newman, 1:51–56. London: Macmillan.

Hume, David. [1739] 1992. *Treatise of Human Nature.* Buffalo, N.Y.: Prometheus Books.

———— [1751] 1998. *An Enquiry Concerning the Principles of Morals.* Edited by Tom L. Beauchamp. Oxford: Oxford University Press.

Hurd, Michael D. 1989. Mortality Risk and Bequests. *Econometrica* 57:779–813.

Hurt, Robert M., and Robert M. Schuchman. 1966. The Economic Rationale of Copyright. *American Economic Review: Papers and Proceedings* 56:421–432.

Hutcheson, Francis. [1725–1755] 1994. *Philosophical Writings.* Edited by R. S. Downie. London: Everyman Library.

Hyllund, Aanund, and Richard Zeckhauser. 1979. Distributional Objectives Should Affect Taxes but Not Program Choice or Design. *Scandinavian Journal of Economics* 81:264–284.

Hylton, Keith N. 1993. Asymmetric Information and the Selection of Disputes for Litigation. *Journal of Legal Studies* 22:187–210.

Innes, Robert. 1999. Remediation and Self-Reporting in Optimal Law Enforcement. *Journal of Public Economics* 72:379–393.

Izuel, Leeanna. 1991. Property Owners' Constructive Possession of Treasure Trove: Rethinking the Finders Keepers Rule. *UCLA Law Review* 38:1659–1702.

Jacobs, Alan J. 1987. *Trademarks throughout the World.* Fourth edition. New York: Trade Activities.

Jacobs, Allan B. 1993. *Great Streets.* Cambridge, Mass.: MIT Press.

Jaffe, Adam B. 2000. The U.S. Patent System in Transition: Policy Innovation and the Innovation Process. *Research Policy* 29:531–557.

Jerry, Robert H. 1996. *Understanding Insurance Law.* Second edition. New York: Matthew Bender.

Johnson, Ronald N., and Gary D. Libecap. 1982. Contracting Problems and Regulation: The Case of the Fishery. *American Economic Review* 72:1005–1022.

Johnston, Jason S. 1990. Strategic Bargaining and the Economic Theory of Contract Default Rules. *Yale Law Journal* 100:615–664.

Jolls, Christine. 1997. Contracts as Bilateral Commitments: A New Perspective on Contract Modification. *Journal of Legal Studies* 26:203–237.

Jolls, Christine, Cass R. Sunstein, and Richard Thaler. 1998. A Behavioral Approach to Law and Economics. *Stanford Law Review* 50:1471–1550.

Jones, G. Kevin. 1984. The Development of Outer Continental Shelf Energy Resources. *Public Land and Resources Law Digest* 21:36–111.

Jones, William K. 1995. Confiscation: A Rationale of the Law of Takings. *Hofstra Law Review* 24:1–88.

Joost, Robert H. 1992. *Automobile Insurance and No-Fault Law.* Second edition. Deerfield, Ill.: Clark Boardman Callaghan.

Joskow, Paul L. 1977. Commercial Impossibility, the Uranium Market and the Westinghouse Case. *Journal of Legal Studies* 6:119–176.

Jost, Peter-J. 1996. Limited Liability and the Requirement to Purchase Insurance. *International Review of Law and Economics* 16:259–276.

Kahan, Marcel. 1989. Causation and Incentives to Take Care under the Negligence Rule. *Journal of Legal Studies* 18:427–447.

Kahn, Alfred E. 1988. *The Economics of Regulation: Principles and Institutions.* Second edition. Cambridge, Mass.: MIT Press.

Kahneman, Daniel, Jack L. Knetsch, and Richard L. Thaler. 1990. Experimental Tests of the Endowment Effect and the Coase Theorem. *Journal of Political Economy* 98:1325–1348.

Kahneman, Daniel, Paul Slovic, and Amos Tversky, editors. 1982. *Judgment under Uncertainty: Heuristics and Biases.* New York: Cambridge University Press.

Kakalik, James S., and Nicholas M. Pace. 1986. *Costs and Compensation Paid in Tort Litigation.* Report R-3391-ICJ. Santa Monica, Calif.: RAND Institute for Civil Justice.

Kakalik, James, Patricia Ebener, William Felstiner, and Michael Shanley. 1983. *Costs of Asbestos Litigation.* Report R-3042-ICJ. Santa Monica, Calif.: RAND Institute for Civil Justice.

Kane, Siegrun D. 2001. *Trademark Law: A Practitioner's Guide.* Third edition (1997, updated 2001). New York: Practising Law Institute.

Kant, Immanuel. [1785] 1998. *Groundwork of the Metaphysics of Morals.* Translated and edited by Mary Gregor. Cambridge: Cambridge University Press.

Kaplow, Louis. 1984. The Patent-Antitrust Intersection: A Reappraisal. *Harvard Law Review* 97:1813–1892.

———— 1986a. An Economic Analysis of Legal Transitions. *Harvard Law Review* 99:509–617.

———— 1986b. Private versus Social Costs in Bringing Suit. *Journal of Legal Studies* 15:371–385.

———— 1990. A Note on the Optimal Use of Nonmonetary Sanctions. *Journal of Public Economics* 42:245–247.

———— 1992. The Optimal Probability and Magnitude of Fines for Acts That Definitely Are Undesirable. *International Review of Law and Economics* 12:3–11.

———— 1994. The Value of Accuracy in Adjudication: An Economic Analysis. *Journal of Legal Studies* 23:307–401.

———— 1995. A Note on Subsidizing Gifts. *Journal of Public Economics* 58:469–477.

———— 1996. The Optimal Supply of Public Goods and the Distortionary Cost of Taxation. *National Tax Journal* 49:513–533.

Kaplow, Louis, and Steven Shavell. 1989. Legal Advice about Information to Present in Litigation: Its Effects and Social Desirability. *Harvard Law Review* 102:565–615.

———— 1990. Legal Advice about Acts Already Committed. *International Review of Law and Economics* 10:149–159.

———— 1992. Private versus Socially Optimal Provision of Ex Ante Legal Advice. *Journal of Law, Economics, and Organization* 8:306–320.

———— 1994a. Accuracy in the Determination of Liability. *Journal of Law and Economics* 37:1–15.

———— 1994b. Optimal Law Enforcement with Self-Reporting of Behavior. *Journal of Political Economy* 102:583–606.

———— 1994c. Why the Legal System Is Less Efficient Than the Income Tax in Redistributing Income. *Journal of Legal Studies* 23:667–681.

———— 1996a. Accuracy in the Assessment of Damages. *Journal of Law and Economics* 39:191–210.

———— 1996b. Property Rules versus Liability Rules: An Economic Analysis. *Harvard Law Review* 109:713–790.

———— 1999. The Conflict between Notions of Fairness and the Pareto Principle. *American Law and Economics Review* 1:63–77.

———— 2000. Should Legal Rules Favor the Poor? Clarifying the Role of Legal Rules and the Income Tax in Redistributing Income. *Journal of Legal Studies* 29:821–835.

———— 2001a. Any Non-Welfarist Method of Policy Assessment Violates the Pareto Principle. *Journal of Political Economy* 109:281–286.

———— 2001b. Moral Rules and the Moral Sentiments: Toward a Theory of an

Optimal Moral System. Harvard John M. Olin Discussion Paper Series, no. 342. Cambridge, Mass.: Harvard Law School.

———— 2002a. Economic Analysis of Law. In *Handbook of Public Economics,* edited by Alan J. Auerbach and Martin Feldstein, 3:1661–1784. Amsterdam: Elsevier.

————2002b. *Fairness versus Welfare.* Cambridge, Mass.: Harvard University Press. (Also published in *Harvard Law Review* 114:961–1388.)

———— 2002c. On the Superiority of Corrective Taxes to Quantity Regulation. *American Law and Economics Review* 4:1–17.

Karpoff, Jonathan M., and John R. Lott, Jr. 1999. On the Determinants and Importance of Punitive Damage Awards. *Journal of Law and Economics* 42: 527–573.

Katz, Avery. 1987. Measuring the Demand for Litigation: Is the English Rule Really Cheaper? *Journal of Law, Economics, and Organization* 3:143–176.

———— 1988. Judicial Decisionmaking and Litigation Expenditure. *International Review of Law and Economics* 8:127–143.

———— 1990a. The Effect of Frivolous Lawsuits on the Settlement of Litigation. *International Review of Law and Economics* 10:3–27.

———— 1990b. The Strategic Structure of Offer and Acceptance: Game Theory and the Law of Contract Formation. *Michigan Law Review* 89:215–295.

————1990c. Your Terms or Mine? The Duty to Read the Fine Print in Contracts. *RAND Journal of Economics* 21:518–537.

————1993. Transaction Costs and the Legal Mechanics of Exchange: When Should Silence in the Face of an Offer Be Construed as Acceptance? *Journal of Law, Economics, and Organization* 9:77–97.

————1996. When Should an Offer Stick? The Economics of Promissory Estoppel in Preliminary Negotiations. *Yale Law Journal* 105:1249–1309.

————1998. Contract Formation and Interpretation. In *The New Palgrave Dictionary of Economics and the Law,* edited by Peter Newman, 1:425–432. London: Macmillan.

Keeton, Robert E. 1963. *Legal Cause in the Law of Torts.* Columbus: Ohio State University Press.

———— 1971. *Basic Text on Insurance Law.* St. Paul, Minn.: West Publishing.

Keeton, W. Page, Dan Dobbs, Robert Keeton, and David Owen. 1984. *Prosser and Keeton on the Law of Torts.* Fifth edition. St. Paul, Minn.: West Publishing.

Keeton, W. Page, Robert Keeton, Lewis Sargentich, and Henry Steiner. 1983. *Cases and Materials on Tort and Accident Law.* St. Paul, Minn.: West Publishing.

Keeton, William R., and Evan Kwerel. 1984. Externalities in Automobile Insurance and the Underinsured Driver Problem. *Journal of Law and Economics* 27:149–179.

Kennan, John, and Robert Wilson. 1993. Bargaining with Private Information. *Journal of Economic Literature* 31:45–104.

Kessler, Daniel, and Steven D. Levitt. 1999. Using Sentence Enhancements to Distinguish between Deterrence and Incapacitation. *Journal of Law and Economics* 42:343–363.

Kessler, Daniel, and Mark McClellan. 1996. Do Doctors Practice Defensive Medicine? *Quarterly Journal of Economics* 111:353–390.

Khanna, Vikramaditya S. 1996. Corporate Criminal Liability: What Purpose Does It Serve? *Harvard Law Review* 109:1477–1534.

Kitch, Edmund W. 1977. The Nature and Function of the Patent System. *Journal of Law and Economics* 20:265–290.

———— 1998. Patents. In *The New Palgrave Dictionary of Economics and the Law,* edited by Peter Newman, 3:13–17. London: Macmillan.

Klein, Benjamin, and Keith B. Leffler. 1981. The Role of Market Forces in Assuring Contractual Performance. *Journal of Political Economy* 89:615–641.

Klein, Benjamin, Robert G. Crawford, and Armen A. Alchian. 1978. Vertical Integration, Appropriable Rents, and the Competitive Contracting Process. *Journal of Law and Economics* 21:297–326.

Klemperer, Paul. 1990. How Broad Should the Scope of Patent Protection Be? *RAND Journal of Economics* 21:113–130.

Klerman, Daniel. 2001. Settlement and the Decline of Private Prosecution in Thirteenth-Century England. *Law and History Review* 19:1–65.

Knetsch, Jack L., and Thomas E. Borcherding. 1979. Expropriation of Private Property and the Basis for Compensation. *University of Toronto Law Journal* 39:237–252.

Kolstad, Charles D., Thomas S. Ulen, and Gary V. Johnson. 1990. *Ex Post* Liability for Harm vs. *Ex Ante* Safety Regulation: Substitutes or Complements? *American Economic Review* 80:888–901.

Kornhauser, Lewis A. 1982. An Economic Analysis of the Choice between Enterprise and Personal Liability for Accidents. *California Law Review* 70:1345–1392.

Kornhauser, Lewis A., and Richard L. Revesz. 1998. Regulation of Hazardous Wastes. In *The New Palgrave Dictionary of Economics and the Law,* edited by Peter Newman, 3:238–242. London: Macmillan.

Korobkin, Russell. 1994. Policymaking and the Offer/Asking Price Gap: Toward a Theory of Efficient Entitlement Allocation. *Stanford Law Review* 46:663–708.

Kosmo, Fred. 1988. The Commercialization of Space: A Regulatory Scheme That Promotes Commercial Ventures and International Responsibility. *Southern California Law Review* 61:1055–1089.

Kotlikoff, Laurence J. 1988. Intergenerational Transfers and Savings. *Journal of Economic Perspectives* 2, no. 2:41–58.

——— 2001. *Essays on Saving, Bequests, Altruism, and Life-Cycle Planning.* Cambridge, Mass.: MIT Press.

Kotlikoff, Laurence J., and Avia Spivak. 1981. The Family as an Incomplete Annuities Market. *Journal of Political Economy* 89:372–391.

Kowalik, Tadeusz. 1987. Central Planning. In *The New Palgrave Dictionary of Economics,* edited by John Eatwell, Murray Milgate, and Peter Newman, 1: 389–392. London: Macmillan.

Kraakman, Reinier H. 1986. Gatekeepers: The Anatomy of a Third-Party Enforcement Strategy. *Journal of Law, Economics, and Organization* 2:53–104.

Kremer, Michael. 1998. Patent Buyouts: A Mechanism for Encouraging Innovation. *Quarterly Journal of Economics* 113:1137–1167.

Kritzer, Herbert M. 1984. Fee Arrangements and Fee Shifting: Lessons from the Experience in Ontario. *Law and Contemporary Problems* 47:125–138.

Kronman, Anthony T. 1978a. Mistake, Disclosure, Information, and the Law of Contracts. *Journal of Legal Studies* 7:1–34.

——— 1978b. Specific Performance. *University of Chicago Law Review* 45:351–382.

——— 1980. Wealth Maximization as a Normative Principle. *Journal of Legal Studies* 9:227–242.

Krutilla, John V. 1967. Conservation Reconsidered. *American Economic Review* 57:777–786.

Kull, Andrew. 1998. Gratuitous Promises. In *The New Palgrave Dictionary of Economics and the Law,* edited by Peter Newman, 2:203–207. London: Macmillan.

Lab, Steven P., and John T. Whitehead. 1988. An Analysis of Juvenile Correctional Treatment. *Crime and Delinquency* 34:60–83.

Ladas, Stephen P. 1964. Legal Protection of Know-How. *Trademark Reporter* 54: 160–183.

LaFave, Wayne R. 2000. *Criminal Law.* Third edition. St. Paul, Minn.: West Group.

Laffont, Jean-Jacques. 1987a. Externalities. In *The New Palgrave Dictionary of Economics,* edited by John Eatwell, Murray Milgate, and Peter Newman, 2:263–265. London: Macmillan.

——— 1987b. Incentives and the Allocation of Public Goods. Chapter 10 in *Handbook of Public Economics,* edited by Alan J. Auerbach and Martin Feldstein, 2:537–569. Amsterdam: North-Holland.

Landes, Elisabeth M. 1982. Insurance, Liability, and Accidents: A Theoretical and Empirical Investigation of the Effect of No-Fault Accidents. *Journal of Law and Economics* 25:49–65.

Landes, William M. 1971. An Economic Analysis of the Courts. *Journal of Law and Economics* 14:61–107.

Landes, William M., and Richard A. Posner. 1975. The Private Enforcement of Law. *Journal of Legal Studies* 4:1–46.

———— 1978. Salvors, Finders, Good Samaritans, and Other Rescuers: An Economic Study of Law and Altruism. *Journal of Legal Studies* 7:83–128.

———— 1981a. An Economic Theory of Intentional Torts. *International Review of Law and Economics* 1:127–154.

———— 1981b. The Positive Economic Theory of Tort Law. *Georgia Law Review* 15:851–924.

———— 1983. Causation in Tort Law: An Economic Approach. *Journal of Legal Studies* 12:109–134.

———— 1987a. *The Economic Structure of Tort Law.* Cambridge, Mass.: Harvard University Press.

———— 1987b. Trademark Law: An Economic Perspective. *Journal of Law and Economics* 30:265–309.

———— 1989. An Economic Analysis of Copyright Law. *Journal of Legal Studies* 18:325–363.

———— 2003. *The Economic Structure of Intellectual Property Law.* Cambridge, Mass.: Harvard University Press.

Langbein, John H., and Lawrence W. Waggoner. 1987. Redesigning the Spouse's Forced Share. *Real Property, Probate and Trust Journal* 22:303–328.

Lanjouw, Jean O., and Josh Lerner. 1998. The Enforcement of Intellectual Property Rights: A Survey of the Empirical Literature. *Annales d'Economie et de Statistique* 49/50:223–246.

Larson, Arthur. 1994. *Larson's Worker's Compensation Law.* New York: Matthew Bender.

Lee, Rex E. 1985. The American Courts as Public Goods: Who Should Pay the Costs of Litigation? *Catholic University Law Review* 34:267–276.

Lee, Sabing H. 1997. Protecting the Private Inventor under the Peacetime Provisions of the Invention Secrecy Act. *Berkeley Technology Law Journal* 12:345–411.

Le Gall, Jean-Pierre. 1983. Liability for Persons under Supervision. Chapter 3 of volume 11, *Torts,* in *International Encyclopedia of Comparative Law.* Tübingen, Ger.: J. C. B. Mohr.

Lemley, Mark A. 1997. The Economics of Improvement in Intellectual Property Law. *Texas Law Review* 75:989–1084.

———— 1999. The Modern Lanham Act and the Death of Common Sense. *Yale Law Journal* 108:1687–1715.

Levitt, Steven D. 1996. The Effect of Prison Population Size on Crime Rates: Evidence from Prison Overcrowding Litigation. *Quarterly Journal of Economics* 111:319–351.

———— 1997. Using Electoral Cycles in Police Hiring to Estimate the Effect of Police on Crime. *American Economic Review* 87:270–290.

———— 1998a. Juvenile Crime and Punishment. *Journal of Political Economy* 106: 1156–1185.

———— 1998b. Why Do Increased Arrest Rates Appear to Reduce Crime: Deterrence, Incapacitation, or Measurement Error? *Economic Inquiry* 36:353–372.

Levmore, Saul. 1987. Variety and Uniformity in the Treatment of the Good-Faith Purchaser. *Journal of Legal Studies* 16:43–65.

———— 1993. The Case for Retroactive Taxation. *Journal of Legal Studies* 22:265–307.

Libecap, Gary D. 1986. Property Rights in Economic History: Implications for Research. *Explorations in Economic History* 23:227–252.

———— 1989. *Contracting for Property Rights.* Cambridge: Cambridge University Press.

Lichtman, Douglas Gary. 1997. Pricing Prozac: Why the Government Should Subsidize the Purchase of Patented Pharmaceuticals. *Harvard Journal of Law and Technology* 11:123–139.

———— 2003. Copyright as a Rule of Evidence. *Duke Law Journal* 52:683–743.

Limpens, Jean, Robert Kruithof, and Anne Meinertzhagen-Limpens. 1983. Liability for One's Own Act. Chapter 2 of volume 11, *Torts,* in *International Encyclopedia of Comparative Law.* Tübingen, Ger.: J. C. B. Mohr.

Lindgren, James. 1984. Unraveling the Paradox of Blackmail. *Columbia Law Review* 84:670–717.

Litan, Robert E. 1991. The Safety and Innovation Effects of U.S. Liability Law: The Evidence. *American Economic Review: Papers and Proceedings* 81:59–64.

Locke, John. [1689] 1988. *Two Treatises of Government,* edited by Peter Laslett. Cambridge: Cambridge University Press.

Loewenstein, George, Samuel Issacharoff, Colin Camerer, and Linda Babcock. 1993. Self-Serving Assessments of Fairness and Pretrial Bargaining. *Journal of Legal Studies* 22:135–159.

Lott, John R., Jr. 2000. Corporate Criminal Liability. In *Encyclopedia of Law and Economics,* edited by Boudewijn Bouckaert and Gerrit De Geest, 5:492–501. Cheltenham, Eng.: Edward Elgar.

Lueck, Dean. 1998. First Possession. In *The New Palgrave Dictionary of Economics and the Law,* edited by Peter Newman, 2:132–144. London: Macmillan.

Lund, Thomas A. 1980. *American Wildlife Law.* Berkeley: University of California Press.

Machlup, Fritz. 1958. *An Economic Review of the Patent System.* Study of the Subcommittee on Patents, Trademarks, and Copyrights, Committee on the Judiciary, U.S. Senate, Study no. 15. Washington D.C.: Government Printing Office.

Machlup, Fritz, and Edith Penrose. 1950. The Patent Controversy in the Nineteenth Century. *Journal of Economic History* 10:1–29.

Mahoney, Paul G. 2000. Contract Remedies: General. In *Encyclopedia of Law and Economics,* edited by Boudewijn Bouckaert and Gerrit De Geest, 3:117–140. Cheltenham, Eng.: Edward Elgar.

Malik, Arun S. 1990. Avoidance, Screening, and Optimum Enforcement. *RAND Journal of Economics* 21:341–353.

———— 1993. Self-Reporting and the Design of Policies for Regulating Stochastic Pollution. *Journal of Environmental Economics and Management* 24:241–257.

Mankiw, N. Gregory. 2001. *Principles of Economics.* Second edition. Fort Worth, Tex.: Harcourt College Publishers.

Markesinis, B. S. 1994. *A Comparative Introduction to the German Law of Tort.* Third edition. Oxford: Clarendon Press.

Mathios, Alan D. 2000. The Impact of Mandatory Disclosure Laws on Product Choices: An Analysis of the Salad Dressing Market. *Journal of Law and Economics* 43:651–677.

McAfee, R. Preston, and John McMillan. 1996. Analyzing the Airwaves Auction. *Journal of Economic Perspectives* 10, no. 1:159–175.

McCarthy, J. Thomas. 1996 (updated through 2002). *McCarthy on Trademarks and Unfair Competition.* Fourth edition. Deerfield, Ill.: Clark Boardman Callaghan.

McCarthy, Patrick S., and Richard Tay. 1993. Pricing Road Congestion: Recent Evidence from Singapore. *Policy Studies Journal* 21:296–308.

McChesney, Fred S. 1986. Government Prohibitions on Volunteer Firefighting in Nineteenth-Century America: A Property Rights Perspective. *Journal of Legal Studies* 15:69–92.

McClure, Daniel M. 1979. Trademarks and Unfair Competition: A Critical History of Legal Thought. *Trademark Reporter* 69:305–356.

McCormack, John L. 1992. Torrens and Recording: Land Title Assurance in the Computer Age. *William Mitchell Law Review* 18:61–129.

McCormick, Charles T. 1935. *Handbook on the Law of Damages.* St. Paul, Minn.: West Publishing Co.

McGregor, Harvey. 1983. Personal Injury and Death. Chapter 9 of volume 11, *Torts,* in *International Encyclopedia of Comparative Law.* Tübingen, Ger.: J. C. B. Mohr.

McMillan, John. 1994. Selling Spectrum Rights. *Journal of Economic Perspectives* 8, no. 3:145–162.

McNeely, Mary C. 1941. Illegality as a Factor in Liability Insurance. *Columbia Law Review* 41:26–60.

Menell, Peter S. 1983. A Note on the Private versus Social Incentives to Sue in a Costly Legal System. *Journal of Legal Studies* 12:41–52.

———— 1998. Regulation of Toxic Substances. In *The New Palgrave Dictionary of Economics and the Law,* edited by Peter Newman, 3:255–263. London: Macmillan.

———— 2000. Intellectual Property: General Theories. In *Encyclopedia of Law and Economics,* edited by Boudewijn Bouckaert and Gerrit De Geest, 2:129–188. Cheltenham, Eng.: Edward Elgar.

Menell, Peter S., and Richard B. Stewart. 1994. *Environmental Law and Policy.* Boston: Little, Brown.

Merges, Robert P., and Richard R. Nelson. 1990. On the Complex Economics of Patent Scope. *Columbia Law Review* 90:839–916.

Merrill, Thomas W. 1986. The Economics of Public Use. *Cornell Law Review* 72: 61–116.

Merrill, Thomas W., and Henry E. Smith. 2000. Optimal Standardization in the Law of Property: The *Numerus Clausus* Principle. *Yale Law Journal* 110:1–70.

Metaxas-Maranghidis, George, editor. 1995. *Intellectual Property Laws of Europe.* Chichester, Eng.: John Wiley & Sons.

Meurer, Michael J. 1992. The Gains from Faith in an Unfaithful Agent: Settlement Conflicts between Defendants and Liability Insurers. *Journal of Law, Economics, and Organization* 8:502–522.

Meyer, Keith G. 1990. UCC Issues. *Journal of Agricultural Taxation and Law* 12: 179–187.

Miceli, Thomas J. 1998. Land Title Systems. In *The New Palgrave Dictionary of Economics and the Law,* edited by Peter Newman, 2:433–437. London: Macmillan.

Miceli, Thomas J., and Kathleen Segerson. 1996. *Compensation for Regulatory Takings: An Economic Analysis with Applications.* Greenwich, Conn.: JAI Press.

———— 1998. Compensation for Regulatory Takings. In *The New Palgrave Dictionary of Economics and the Law,* edited by Peter Newman, 1:360–364. London: Macmillan.

———— 2000. Takings. In *Encyclopedia of Law and Economics,* edited by Boudewijn Bouckaert and Gerrit De Geest, 4:328–357. Cheltenham, Eng.: Edward Elgar.

Miceli, Thomas J., and C. F. Sirmans. 1995. An Economic Theory of Adverse Possession. *International Review of Law and Economics* 15:161–173.

Michelman, Frank. 1967. Property, Utility, and Fairness: Comments on the Ethical Foundations of "Just Compensation" Law. *Harvard Law Review* 80: 1165–1258.

Milgrim, Roger M. 1995. *Milgrim on Trade Secrets.* New York: Matthew Bender.

Milgrom, Paul R. 1981. Good News and Bad News: Representation Theorems and Applications. *Bell Journal of Economics* 12:380–391.

———— 1993. Is Sympathy an Economic Value? Philosophy, Economics, and the Contingent Valuation Method. Chapter 11 in *Contingent Valuation: A Critical Assessment,* edited by Jerry A. Hausman. Amsterdam: North-Holland.

Mill, John Stuart. [1848] 1872. *Principles of Political Economy.* Boston: Lee and Shephard.

————[1861] 1998. *Utilitarianism.* Edited by Roger Crisp. Oxford: Oxford University Press.

Miller, Arthur R., and Michael H. Davis. 2000. *Intellectual Property: Patents, Trademarks, and Copyright in a Nutshell.* Third edition. St Paul, Minn.: West Group.

Miller, Geoffrey P. 1986. An Economic Analysis of Rule 68. *Journal of Legal Studies* 15:93–125.

———— 1987. Some Agency Problems in Settlement. *Journal of Legal Studies* 16: 189–215.

Mims, Peter E. 1984. Promotional Goods and the Functionality Doctrine: An Economic Model of Trademarks. *Texas Law Review* 63:639–669.

Mirrlees, James A. 1971. An Exploration in the Theory of Optimum Income Taxation. *Review of Economic Studies* 38:175–208.

Mitchell, Robert C., and Richard T. Carson. 1989. *Using Surveys to Value Public Goods.* Washington, D.C.: Resources for the Future.

Mnookin, Robert H. 1993. Why Negotiations Fail: An Exploration of Barriers to the Resolution of Conflict. *Ohio State Journal on Dispute Resolution* 8:235–249.

Mnookin, Robert, and Robert Wilson. 1998. A Model of Efficient Discovery. *Games and Economic Behavior* 25:219–250.

Montesquieu, Charles-Louis de Secondat, baron. [1748] 1989. *The Spirit of the Laws.* Translated and edited by Anne M. Cohler, Basia Carolyn Miller, and Harold Samuel Stone. Cambridge: Cambridge University Press.

Mookherjee, Dilip. 1997. The Economics of Enforcement. In *Issues in Economic Theory and Public Policy: Essays in Honour of Professor Tapas Majumdar,* edited by Amitava Bose, Mihir Rakshit, and Anup Sinha, 202–249. Oxford: Oxford University Press.

Mookherjee, Dilip, and Ivan P. L. Png. 1992. Monitoring vis-à-vis Investigation in Enforcement of Law. *American Economic Review* 82:556–565.

———— 1994. Marginal Deterrence in Enforcement of Law. *Journal of Political Economy* 102:1039–1066.

Moore, Michael J., and W. Kip Viscusi. 1990. *Compensation Mechanisms for Job Risks: Wages, Workers' Compensation, and Product Liability.* Princeton, N.J.: Princeton University Press.

Morgan, Kathleen O'Leary, and Scott Morgan, editors. 2002. *Crime State Rankings, 2002.* Lawrence, Kans.: Morgan Quitno Press.

Munch, Patricia. 1976. An Economic Analysis of Eminent Domain. *Journal of Political Economy* 84:473–497.

Musgrave, Richard A. 1985. A Brief History of Fiscal Doctrine. Chapter 1 in *Handbook of Public Economics,* edited by Alan J. Auerbach and Martin Feldstein, 1:1–59. Amsterdam: North-Holland.

Netter, Jeffry M. 1998. Adverse Possession. In *The New Palgrave Dictionary of Economics and the Law,* edited by Peter Newman, 1:18–21. London: Macmillan.

Nicholas, Barry. 1962. *An Introduction to Roman Law.* Oxford: Clarendon Press.

Niedercorn, John H., and Edward F. R. Hearle. 1964. Recent Land-Use Trends in Forty-Eight Large American Cities. *Land Economics* 40:105–110.

Nimmer, Melville B., and David Nimmer. 1995. *Nimmer on Copyright.* Second revised edition. New York: Matthew Bender.

Nöldeke, Georg, and Klaus M. Schmidt. 1995. Option Contracts and Renegotiation: A Solution to the Hold-up Problem. *RAND Journal of Economics* 26: 163–179.

Nordhaus, William D. 1969. *Invention, Growth, and Welfare: A Theoretical Treatment of Technological Change.* Cambridge, Mass.: MIT Press.

Nowak, John E., and Ronald D. Rotunda. 2000. *Constitutional Law.* Sixth edition. St. Paul, Minn.: West Group.

Oakland, William H. 1987. Theory of Public Goods. Chapter 9 in *Handbook of Public Economics,* edited by Alan J. Auerbach and Martin Feldstein, 2:485–535. Amsterdam: North-Holland.

O'Connell, Jeffrey, Phillip A. Bock, and Stewart Petoe. 1994. Blending Reform of Tort Liability and Health Insurance: A Necessary Mix. *Cornell Law Review* 79:1303–1338.

Oi, Walter Y. 1973. The Economics of Product Safety. *Bell Journal of Economics and Management Science* 4:3–28.

Okuno-Fujiwara, Masahiro, Andrew Postlewaite, and Kotaro Suzumura. 1990. Strategic Information Revelation. *Review of Economic Studies* 57:25–47.

Opoku, Kwame. 1972. Delictual Liability in German Law. *International and Comparative Law Quarterly* 21:230–269.

Ordover, Janusz A. 1978. Costly Litigation in the Model of Single Activity Accidents. *Journal of Legal Studies* 7:243–261.

Osborne, Evan. 1999. Who Should Be Worried about Asymmetric Information in Litigation? *International Review of Law and Economics* 19:399–409.

Ostrom, Brian J., Neil B. Kauder, and Robert C. LaFountain. 2001a. *Examining the Work of State Courts, 1999–2000.* Williamsburg, Va.: National Center for State Courts.

——— 2001b. *Examining the Work of State Courts, 2001.* Williamsburg, Va.: National Center for State Courts.

Ostrom, Elinor. 1990. *Governing the Commons: The Evolution of Institutions for Collective Action.* New York: Cambridge University Press.

——— 2000. Private and Common Property Rights. In *Encyclopedia of Law and Economics,* edited by Boudewijn Bouckaert and Gerrit De Geest, 2:332–379. Cheltenham, Eng.: Edward Elgar.

Packer, Herbert L. 1968. *The Limits of the Criminal Sanction.* Stanford, Calif.: Stanford University Press.

Palladino, Vincent N. 2000. Genericism Rationalized: Another View. *Trademark Reporter* 90:469–488.

Palmer, Geoffrey. 1994. New Zealand's Accident Compensation Scheme: Twenty Years On. *University of Toronto Law Journal* 44:223–273.

Patry, William F. 1994. *Copyright Law and Practice.* Washington, D.C.: Bureau of National Affairs.

——— 1995. *The Fair Use Privilege in Copyright Law.* Second edition. Washington, D.C.: Bureau of National Affairs.

Patterson, Lyman Ray. 1968. *Copyright in Historical Perspective.* Nashville: Vanderbilt University Press.

Payne, Anne M. 1996. Energy and Power Sources. In *American Jurisprudence,* second edition, 27A:1–355. Rochester, N.Y.: Lawyers Cooperative Publishing.

Pendergrast, Mark. 1993. *For God, Country, and Coca-Cola: The Unauthorized History of the Great American Soft Drink and the Company That Makes It.* New York: Macmillan.

Philbin, Jeanne. 1997. Aviation. In *American Jurisprudence,* second edition, 8A:1–247. West Group.

Phillips, Jerry J. 1998. *Products Liability in a Nutshell.* Fifth edition. St. Paul, Minn: West Group.

Pigou, A. C. 1912. *Wealth and Welfare.* London: Macmillan.

——— 1932. *The Economics of Welfare.* Fourth edition. London: Macmillan.

Pinner, H. L. 1978. *Pinner's World Unfair Competition Law: An Encyclopedia.* Second edition, edited by Heinz David. Alphen aan de Rijn, Netherlands: Sijthoff & Noordhoff.

Pitchford, Rohan. 1995. How Liable Should a Lender Be? The Case of Judgment-Proof Firms and Environmental Risk. *American Economic Review* 85:1171–1186.

———. 1998. Judgment-Proofness. In *The New Palgrave Dictionary of Economics and the Law,* edited by Peter Newman, 2:380–383. London: Macmillan.

Platto, Charles, editor. 1992. *Civil Appeal Procedures Worldwide.* London: Graham and Trotman.

Png, Ivan P. L. 1986. Optimal Subsidies and Damages in the Presence of Judicial Error. *International Review of Law and Economics* 6:101–105.

Polanvyi, Michael. 1944. Patent Reform. *Review of Economic Studies* 11:61–76.

Polborn, Mattias K. 1998. Mandatory Insurance and the Judgment-Proof Problem. *International Review of Law and Economics* 18:141–146.

Polinsky, A. Mitchell. 1980a. Private versus Public Enforcement of Fines. *Journal of Legal Studies* 9:105–127.

——— 1980b. Resolving Nuisance Disputes: The Simple Economics of Injunctive and Damage Remedies. *Stanford Law Review* 32:1075–1112.

——— 1980c. Strict Liability vs. Negligence in a Market Setting. *American Economic Review: Papers and Proceedings* 70:363–367.

——— 1983. Risk Sharing through Breach of Contract Remedies. *Journal of Legal Studies* 12:427–444.

Polinsky, A. Mitchell, and William P. Rogerson. 1983. Products Liability, Consumer Misperceptions, and Market Power. *Bell Journal of Economics* 14:581–589.

Polinsky, A. Mitchell, and Daniel L. Rubinfeld. 1988. The Deterrent Effects of Settlements and Trials. *International Review of Law and Economics* 8:109–116.

——— 1991. A Model of Optimal Fines for Repeat Offenders. *Journal of Public Economics* 46:291–306.

——— 1993. Sanctioning Frivolous Suits: An Economic Analysis. *Georgetown Law Journal* 82:397–435.

——— 1996. Optimal Awards and Penalties When the Probability of Prevailing Varies among Plaintiffs. *RAND Journal of Economics* 27:269–280.

Polinsky, A. Mitchell, and Steven Shavell. 1979. The Optimal Tradeoff between the Probability and Magnitude of Fines. *American Economic Review* 69:880–891.

——— 1984. The Optimal Use of Fines and Imprisonment. *Journal of Public Economics* 24:89–99.

——— 1992. Enforcement Costs and the Optimal Magnitude and Probability of Fines. *Journal of Law and Economics* 35:133–148.

——— 1994. Should Liability Be Based on the Harm to the Victim or the Gain to the Injurer? *Journal of Law, Economics, and Organization* 10:427–437.

——— 1998a. On Offense History and the Theory of Deterrence. *International Review of Law and Economics* 18:305–324.

——— 1998b. Punitive Damages: An Economic Analysis. *Harvard Law Review* 111:869–962.

——— 1999. On the Disutility and Discounting of Imprisonment and the Theory of Deterrence. *Journal of Legal Studies* 28:1–16.

——— 2000a. The Economic Theory of Public Enforcement of Law. *Journal of Economic Literature* 38:45–76.

———— 2000b. The Fairness of Sanctions: Some Implications for Optimal Enforcement Policy. *American Law and Economics Review* 2:223–237.

Pollock, Frederick, and Frederic William Maitland. 1911. *The History of English Law before the Time of Edward I.* Second edition. Cambridge: Cambridge University Press.

Pooley, James. 2001. *Trade Secrets.* (Update of 1997 edition.) New York: Law Journal Seminars Press.

Posner, Eric A. 1996. Law, Economics, and Inefficient Norms. *University of Pennsylvania Law Review* 144:1697–1744.

————1997. Altruism, Status, and Trust in the Law of Gifts and Gratuitous Promises. *Wisconsin Law Review* 1997:567–609.

Posner, Richard A. 1972a. *Economic Analysis of Law.* Boston: Little, Brown.

———— 1972b. A Theory of Negligence. *Journal of Legal Studies* 1:29–96.

———— 1973. Strict Liability: A Comment. *Journal of Legal Studies* 2:205–221.

———— 1977. Gratuitous Promises in Economics and Law. *Journal of Legal Studies* 6:411–426.

———— 1979. Utilitarianism, Economics, and Legal Theory. *Journal of Legal Studies* 8:103–140.

———— 1980. Retribution and Related Concepts of Punishment. *Journal of Legal Studies* 9:71–92.

———— 1985a. An Economic Theory of the Criminal Law. *Columbia Law Review* 85:1193–1231.

———— 1985b. *The Federal Courts: Crisis and Reform.* Cambridge, Mass.: Harvard University Press.

———— 1993. Blackmail, Privacy, and Freedom of Contract. *University of Pennsylvania Law Review* 141:1817–1844.

———— 1998. *Economic Analysis of Law.* Fifth edition. New York: Aspen Law & Business.

———— 1999. *The Problematics of Moral and Legal Theory.* Cambridge, Mass.: Belknap Press of Harvard University Press.

Posner, Richard A., and Andrew M. Rosenfield. 1977. Impossibility and Related Doctrines in Contract Law: An Economic Analysis. *Journal of Legal Studies* 6:83–118.

Postan, M. M., and Edward Miller, editors. 1987. *Cambridge Economic History of Europe,* vol. 2: *Trade and Industry in the Middle Ages.* Second edition. Cambridge: Cambridge University Press.

Pound, Roscoe. 1959. *An Introduction to the Philosophy of Law.* Revised edition. New Haven: Yale University Press.

Priest, George L. 1981. A Theory of the Consumer Warranty. *Yale Law Journal* 90:1297–1352.

———— 1988. Products Liability Law and the Accident Rate. In *Liability: Perspectives and Policy,* edited by Robert Litan and Clifford Winston, 184–222. Washington, D.C.: Brookings Institution.

———— 1991. The Modern Expansion of Tort Liability: Its Sources, Its Effects, and Its Reform. *Journal of Economic Perspectives* 5, no. 3:31–50.

Priest, George L., and Benjamin Klein. 1984. The Selection of Disputes for Litigation. *Journal of Legal Studies* 13:1–55.

Prott, Lyndel V., and P. J. O'Keefe. 1995. *Law and the Cultural Heritage,* vol. 4: *Movement.* New York: Lexis Publishing.

Quinn, John, and Michael J. Trebilcock. 1982. Compensation, Transition Costs, and Regulatory Change. *University of Toronto Law Journal* 32:117–175.

Raiffa, Howard. 1968. *Decision Analysis: Introductory Lectures on Choices under Uncertainty.* Reading, Mass.: Addison-Wesley.

Ramseyer, J. Mark, and Minoru Nakazato. 1989. The Rational Litigant: Settlement Amounts and Verdict Rates in Japan. *Journal of Legal Studies* 18:263–290.

Rasmusen, Eric, and Ian Ayres. 1993. Mutual and Unilateral Mistake in Contract Law. *Journal of Legal Studies* 22:309–343.

Rea, Samuel A., Jr. 1998. Penalty Doctrine in Contract Law. In *The New Palgrave Dictionary of Economics and the Law,* edited by Peter Newman, 3:23–27. London: Macmillan.

Reinganum, Jennifer F. 1989. The Timing of Innovation: Research, Development, and Diffusion. In *Handbook of Industrial Organization,* edited by Richard Schmalensee and Robert D. Willig, 1:849–918. Amsterdam: North-Holland.

Reinganum, Jennifer F., and Louis L. Wilde. 1986. Settlement, Litigation, and the Allocation of Litigation Costs. *RAND Journal of Economics* 17:557–566.

Restatement of the Law Second: Torts. 1965. St. Paul, Minn.: American Law Institute.

Riesenfeld, Stefan A. 1958. Patent Protection and Atomic Energy Legislation. *California Law Review* 46:40–68.

Ringleb, Al H., and Steven N. Wiggins. 1990. Liability and Large-Scale, Long-Term Hazards. *Journal of Political Economy* 98:574–595.

Roberts, Lawrence D. 2000. A Lost Connection: Geostationary Satellite Networks and the International Telecommunication Union. *Berkeley Technology Law Journal* 15:1095–1144.

Rogerson, William P. 1984. Efficient Reliance and Damage Measures for Breach of Contract. *RAND Journal of Economics* 15:39–53.

———— 1992. Contractual Solutions to the Hold-Up Problem. *Review of Economic Studies* 59:777–794.

Rose, Carol M. 1998. Evolution of Property Rights. In *The New Palgrave Dictionary of Economics and the Law,* edited by Peter Newman, 1:93–98. London: Macmillan.

Rose, Mark. 1993. *Authors and Owners: The Invention of Copyright.* Cambridge, Mass.: Harvard University Press.

Rose-Ackerman, Susan. 1985. Inalienability and the Theory of Property Rights. *Columbia Law Review* 85:931–969.

Rose-Ackerman, Susan, and Mark Geistfeld. 1987. The Divergence between Social and Private Incentives to Sue: A Comment on Shavell, Menell, and Kaplow. *Journal of Legal Studies* 16:483–491.

Rosenberg, David. 1984. The Causal Connection in Mass Exposure Cases: A "Public Law" Vision of the Tort System. *Harvard Law Review* 97:849–929.

Rosenberg, David, and Steven Shavell. 1985. A Model in Which Suits Are Brought for Their Nuisance Value. *International Review of Law and Economics* 5:3–13.

Ross, W. D. 1930. *The Right and the Good.* Oxford: Clarendon Press.

Rowe, Thomas D., Jr. 1982. The Legal Theory of Attorney Fee Shifting: A Critical Overview. *Duke Law Journal* 1982:651–680.

Rubin, Paul H. 1993. *Tort Reform by Contract.* Washington, D.C.: AEI Press.

Rubinfeld, Daniel L. 1998. Discovery. In *The New Palgrave Dictionary of Economics and the Law,* edited by Peter Newman, 1:609–615. London: Macmillan.

Rubinfeld, Daniel L., and Suzanne Scotchmer. 1993. Contingent Fees for Attorneys: An Economic Analysis. *RAND Journal of Economics* 24:343–356.

——— 1998. Contingent Fees. In *The New Palgrave Dictionary of Economics and the Law,* edited by Peter Newman, 1:415–420. London: Macmillan.

Rubinstein, Ariel. 1979. An Optimal Conviction Policy for Offenses That May Have Been Committed by Accident. In *Applied Game Theory,* edited by Stephen J. Brams, Andrew Schotter, and G. Schwodiauer, 406–413. Wurzburg: Physica-Verlag.

Rudden, Bernard. 1966. *Soviet Insurance Law.* Law in Eastern Europe Monograph no. 12. Leiden, Netherlands: A. W. Sijthoff.

——— 1987. Economic Theory v. Property Law: The *Numerus Clausus* Problem. In *Oxford Essays in Jurisprudence,* edited by John Eekelaar and John Bell. Oxford: Clarendon Press.

Rüster, Bernd, editor. 1991. *World Intellectual Property Guidebook: Federal Republic of Germany, Austria, Switzerland.* New York: Matthew Bender.

Sackman, Julius L. 2000. *Nichols on Eminent Domain.* Revised third edition (updated). New York: Matthew Bender.

Sah, Raaj K. 1991. Social Osmosis and Patterns of Crime. *Journal of Political Economy* 99:1272–1295.

Samuelson, Paul A. 1954. The Pure Theory of Public Expenditure. *Review of Economics and Statistics* 36:387–389.

——— 1958. Aspects of Public Expenditure Theories. *Review of Economics and Statistics* 40:332–338.

Sanchirico, Chris William. 2000. Taxes versus Legal Rules as Instruments for Equity: A More Equitable View. *Journal of Legal Studies* 29:797–820.

Savage, Leonard J. 1972. *The Foundations of Statistics.* Second edition. New York: Dover Publications.

Sax, Joseph L. 1971. Takings, Private Property and Public Rights. *Yale Law Journal* 81:149–186.

Schäfer, Hans-Bernd. 2000. Tort Law: General. In *Encyclopedia of Law and Economics,* edited by Boudewijn Bouckaert and Gerrit De Geest, 2:569–596. Cheltenham, Eng.: Edward Elgar.

Schechter, Frank I. 1925. *The Historical Foundations of the Law Relating to Trademarks.* New York: Columbia University Press.

Scherer, F. M. 1972. Nordhaus' Theory of Optimal Patent Life: A Geometric Representation. *American Economic Review* 62:422–427.

——— 1980. *Industrial Market Structure and Economic Performance.* Second edition. Boston: Houghton Mifflin.

Scherer, F. M., and David Ross. 1990. *Industrial Market Structure and Economic Performance.* Third edition. Boston: Houghton Mifflin.

Schlatter, Richard. 1951. *Private Property: The History of an Idea.* London: Allen & Unwin.

Schlicher, John W. 2001. *Patent Law: Legal and Economic Principles.* Deerfield, Ill.: Clark Boardman Callaghan.

Schoenbaum, Thomas J. 2001. *Admiralty and Maritime Law.* Third edition. St. Paul, Minn.: West Group.

Schrag, Joel L. 1999. Managerial Judges: An Economic Analysis of the Judicial Management of Legal Discovery. *RAND Journal of Economics* 30:305–323.

Schwartz, Alan. 1979. The Case for Specific Performance. *Yale Law Journal* 89:271–306.

——— 1992. Relational Contracts in the Courts: An Analysis of Incomplete Agreements and Judicial Strategies. *Journal of Legal Studies* 21:271–318.

——— 1998. Incomplete Contracts. In *The New Palgrave Dictionary of Economics and the Law,* edited by Peter Newman, 2:277–283. London: Macmillan.

Schwartz, Gary T. 1992. The Beginning and the Possible End of the Rise of Modern American Tort Law. *Georgia Law Review* 26:601–702.

Schwartz, Richard D. 1983. Rehabilitation. In *Encyclopedia of Crime and Justice,* edited by Sanford H. Kadish, 4:1364–1374. New York: Free Press.

Schweizer, Urs. 1989. Litigation and Settlement under Two-Sided Incomplete Information. *Review of Economic Studies* 56:163–177.

Scotchmer, Suzanne. 1991. Standing on the Shoulders of Giants: Cumulative

Research and the Patent Law. *Journal of Economic Perspectives* 5, no. 1: 29–41.

———— 1998. Incentives to Innovate. In *The New Palgrave Dictionary of Economics and the Law,* edited by Peter Newman, 2:273–277. London: Macmillan.

———— 1999. On the Optimality of the Patent Renewal System. *RAND Journal of Economics* 30:181–196.

Scott, Anthony. 1988. Development of Property in the Fishery. *Marine Resource Economics* 5:289–311.

Searle, John R. 1964. How to Derive "Ought" from "Is." *Philosophical Review* 73: 43–58.

Settanni, Andrea M. 1994. Competitive Bidding for the Airwaves: Meeting the Budget and Maintaining Policy Goals in a Wireless World. *CommLaw Conspectus* 2:117–132.

Shapo, Marshall S. 1994. *The Law of Products Liability.* Third edition. Salem, N.H.: Butterworth Legal Publishers.

Shavell, Steven. 1980a. An Analysis of Causation and the Scope of Liability in the Law of Torts. *Journal of Legal Studies* 9:463–516.

———— 1980b. Damage Measures for Breach of Contract. *Bell Journal of Economics* 11:466–490.

———— 1980c. Strict Liability versus Negligence. *Journal of Legal Studies* 9: 1–25.

———— 1981. A Note on Efficiency vs. Distributional Equity in Legal Rulemaking: Should Distributional Equity Matter Given Optimal Income Taxation? *American Economic Review: Papers and Proceedings* 71:414–418.

———— 1982a. On Liability and Insurance. *Bell Journal of Economics* 13:120–132.

———— 1982b. The Social versus the Private Incentive to Bring Suit in a Costly Legal System. *Journal of Legal Studies* 11:333–339.

———— 1982c. Suit, Settlement, and Trial: A Theoretical Analysis under Alternative Methods for the Allocation of Legal Costs. *Journal of Legal Studies* 11:55–81.

———— 1984a. The Design of Contracts and Remedies for Breach. *Quarterly Journal of Economics* 99:121–148.

———— 1984b. Liability for Harm versus Regulation of Safety. *Journal of Legal Studies* 13:357–374.

———— 1984c. A Model of the Optimal Use of Liability and Safety Regulation. *RAND Journal of Economics* 15:271–280.

———— 1985a. Criminal Law and the Optimal Use of Nonmonetary Sanctions as a Deterrent. *Columbia Law Review* 85:1232–1262.

———— 1985b. Uncertainty over Causation and the Determination of Civil Liability. *Journal of Law and Economics* 28:587–609.

———— 1986. The Judgment Proof Problem. *International Review of Law and Economics* 6:45–58.

———— 1987a. *Economic Analysis of Accident Law*. Cambridge, Mass.: Harvard University Press.

———— 1987b. A Model of Optimal Incapacitation. *American Economic Review: Papers and Proceedings* 77:107–110.

———— 1987c. The Optimal Use of Nonmonetary Sanctions as a Deterrent. *American Economic Review* 77:584–592.

———— 1988. Legal Advice about Contemplated Acts: The Decision to Obtain Advice, Its Social Desirability, and Protection of Confidentiality. *Journal of Legal Studies* 17:123–150.

———— 1989. Sharing of Information Prior to Settlement or Litigation. *RAND Journal of Economics* 20:183–195.

———— 1990. Deterrence and the Punishment of Attempts. *Journal of Legal Studies* 19:435–466.

———— 1991a. An Economic Analysis of Altruism and Deferred Gifts. *Journal of Legal Studies* 20:401–421.

———— 1991b. Specific versus General Enforcement of Law. *Journal of Political Economy* 99:1088–1108.

———— 1992. A Note on Marginal Deterrence. *International Review of Law and Economics* 12:345–355.

———— 1993a. The Optimal Structure of Law Enforcement. *Journal of Law and Economics* 36:255–287.

———— 1993b. An Economic Analysis of Threats and Their Illegality: Blackmail, Extortion, and Robbery. *University of Pennsylvania Law Review* 141:1877–1903.

———— 1994. Acquisition and Disclosure of Information Prior to Sale. *RAND Journal of Economics* 25:20–36.

———— 1995a. Alternative Dispute Resolution: An Economic Analysis. *Journal of Legal Studies* 24:1–28.

———— 1995b. The Appeals Process as a Means of Error Correction. *Journal of Legal Studies* 24:379–426.

———— 1996. Any Frequency of Plaintiff Victory at Trial Is Possible. *Journal of Legal Studies* 25:493–501.

———— 1997. The Fundamental Divergence between the Private and the Social Motive to Use the Legal System. *Journal of Legal Studies* 26:575–612.

———— 1998. Contracts. In *The New Palgrave Dictionary of Economics and the Law,* edited by Peter Newman, 1:436–445. London: Macmillan.

———— 1999. The Level of Litigation: Private versus Social Optimality of Suit and of Settlement. *International Review of Law and Economics* 19:99–115.

———— 2000. On the Social Function and the Regulation of Liability Insurance. *Geneva Papers on Risk and Insurance: Issues and Practice* 25:166–179.

———— 2002. Law versus Morality as Regulators of Conduct. *American Law and Economics Review* 4:227–257.

Shavell, Steven, and Tanguy van Ypersele. 2001. Rewards versus Intellectual Property Rights. *Journal of Law and Economics* 44:525–547.

Shepherd, George B. 1999. An Empirical Study of the Economics of Pretrial Discovery. *International Review of Law and Economics* 19:245–263.

Shleifer, Andrei. 1998. State versus Private Ownership. *Journal of Economic Perspectives* 12, no. 4:133–150.

Sidgwick, Henry. 1901. *The Principles of Political Economy.* Third edition. London: Macmillan.

———— [1907] 1981. *The Methods of Ethics.* Reprint of seventh edition. Indianapolis: Hackett Publishing.

Sieg, Holger. 2000. Estimating a Bargaining Model with Asymmetric Information: Evidence from Medical Malpractice Disputes. *Journal of Political Economy* 108:1006–1021.

Simes, Lewis M. 1955. *Public Policy and the Dead Hand.* Ann Arbor: University of Michigan Law School.

Simes, Lewis M., and Allan F. Smith. 1956. *The Law of Future Interests.* Second edition, volume 3. St. Paul, Minn.: West Publishing.

Singer, Charles, E. J. Holmyard, A. R. Hall, and Trevor I. Williams. 1958. *A History of Technology,* vol. 4: *The Industrial Revolution.* Oxford: Clarendon Press.

Sinnot, John P. 1988. *World Patent Law and Practice.* Vol. 2M. New York: Matthew Bender.

Skogh, Göran. 2000. Mandatory Insurance: Transaction Costs Analysis of Insurance. In *Encyclopedia of Law and Economics,* edited by Boudewijn Bouckaert and Gerrit De Geest, 2:521–537. Cheltenham, Eng.: Edward Elgar.

Slemrod, Joel, and Jon Bakija. 2000. *Taxing Ourselves: A Citizen's Guide to the Great Debate over Tax Reform.* Second edition. Cambridge, Mass.: MIT Press.

Sloan, Frank A. 1998. Automobile Accidents, Insurance, and Tort Liability. In *The New Palgrave Dictionary of Economics and the Law,* edited by Peter Newman, 1:140–144. London: Macmillan.

Sloan, Frank A., Bridget A. Reilly, and Christoph M. Schenzler. 1994. Tort Liability versus Other Approaches for Deterring Careless Driving. *International Review of Law and Economics* 14:53–71.

Smith, Adam. [1790] 1976. *The Theory of Moral Sentiments.* Reprint of sixth edition. Edited by D. D. Raphael and A. L. Macfie. Oxford: Clarendon Press.

Smith, Janet Kiholm, and Richard L. Smith. 1990. Contract Law, Mutual Mistake, and Incentives to Produce and Disclose Information. *Journal of Legal Studies* 19:467–488.

Snyder, Edward A., and James M. Hughes. 1990. The English Rule for Allocating Legal Costs: Evidence Confronts Theory. *Journal of Law, Economics and Organization* 6:345–380.

Sobel, Joel. 1989. An Analysis of Discovery Rules. *Law and Contemporary Problems* 52, no. 1:133–159.

Spelman, William. 1994. *Criminal Incapacitation.* New York: Plenum Press.

———— 2000. The Limited Importance of Prison Expansion. In *The Crime Drop in America,* edited by Alfred Blumstein and Joel Wallman, 97–129. Cambridge: Cambridge University Press.

Spence, Michael. 1977. Consumer Misperceptions, Product Failure, and Producer Liability. *Review of Economic Studies* 44:561–572.

Spier, Kathryn E. 1992a. The Dynamics of Pretrial Negotiation. *Review of Economic Studies* 59:93–108.

———— 1992b. Incomplete Contracts and Signalling. *RAND Journal of Economics* 23:432–443.

———— 1994a. Pretrial Bargaining and the Design of Fee-Shifting Rules. *RAND Journal of Economics* 25:197–214.

———— 1994b. Settlement Bargaining and the Design of Damage Awards. *Journal of Law, Economics and Organization* 10:84–95.

———— 1997. A Note on the Divergence between the Private and the Social Motive to Settle under a Negligence Rule. *Journal of Legal Studies* 26:613–621.

Spier, Kathryn E., and Michael D. Whinston. 1995. On the Efficiency of Privately Stipulated Damages for Breach of Contract: Entry Barriers, Reliance, and Renegotiation. *RAND Journal of Economics* 26:180–202.

Spitzer, Matthew, and Eric Talley. 2000. Judicial Auditing. *Journal of Legal Studies* 29:649–683.

St. Julian, Andrea R. 1995. Animals. In *American Jurisprudence,* second edition, 4:337–512. Rochester, N.Y.: Lawyers Cooperative Publishing.

Stake, Jeffrey Evans. 2000. Decomposition of Property Rights. In *Encyclopedia of Law and Economics,* edited by Boudewijn Bouckaert and Gerrit De Geest, 2: 32–61. Cheltenham, Eng.: Edward Elgar.

Staple, Gregory C. 1986. The New World Satellite Order: A Report from Geneva. *American Journal of International Law* 80:699–720.

Starrett, David A. 1972. Fundamental Nonconvexities in the Theory of Externalities. *Journal of Economic Theory* 4:180–199.

Statistical Abstract of the United States, 2001. 2001. Economics and Statistics Administration, U.S. Census Bureau. Washington, D.C.: U.S. Department of Commerce.

Stepanov, S. 1958. Increasing the Role of Innovators and Inventors in Improving Socialist Production. *Problems of Economics* 1:75–78.

Stevens, Timothy T. 1992. The Abandoned Shipwreck Act of 1987: Finding the Proper Ballast for the States. *Villanova Law Review* 37:573–617.

Stigler, George J. 1970. The Optimum Enforcement of Laws. *Journal of Political Economy* 78:526–536.

Stiglitz, Joseph E. 1986. *Economics of the Public Sector.* New York: W. W. Norton.

Stoebuck, William B., and Dale A. Whitman. 2000. *The Law of Property.* Third edition. St. Paul, Minn.: West Group.

Stole, Lars A. 1992. The Economics of Liquidated Damage Clauses in Contractual Environments with Private Information. *Journal of Law, Economics, and Organization* 8:582–606.

Stoll, Hans. 1983. Consequences of Liability: Remedies. Chapter 8 of volume 11, *Torts,* in *International Encyclopedia of Comparative Law,* edited by André Tunc. Tübingen, Ger.: J. C. B. Mohr.

Stone, Ferdinand F. 1983. Liability for Damage Caused by Things. Chapter 5 of volume 11, *Torts,* in *International Encyclopedia of Comparative Law,* edited by André Tunc. Tübingen, Ger.: J. C. B. Mohr.

Sugarman, Stephen D. 1985. Doing Away with Tort Law. *California Law Review* 73:555–664.

Swann, Jerre B. 1999. Genericism Rationalized. *The Trademark Reporter* 89:639–656.

Sweeney, Richard James, Robert D. Tollison, and Thomas D. Willett. 1974. Market Failure, the Common-Pool Problem, and Ocean Resource Exploitation. *Journal of Law and Economics* 17:179–192.

Sykes, Alan O. 1984. The Economics of Vicarious Liability. *Yale Law Journal* 93:1231–1280.

——— 1990. The Doctrine of Commercial Impracticability in a Second-Best World. *Journal of Legal Studies* 19:43–94.

——— 1994. "Bad Faith" Refusal to Settle by Liability Insurers: Some Implications of the Judgment-Proof Problem. *Journal of Legal Studies* 23:77–110.

Symposium on Efficiency as a Legal Concern. 1980. *Hofstra Law Review* 8:485–770.

Thomas, David A. 1994. *Thompson on Real Property.* Thomas edition. Charlottesville, Va.: Michie Company.

Tietenberg, Thomas H. 1996. *Environmental and Natural Resource Economics.* Fourth edition. New York: Harper Collins.

Tillinghast-Towers Perrin. 1995. *Tort Cost Trends: An International Perspective.* Chicago: Tillinghast-Towers Perrin.

——— 2002. *U.S. Tort Costs, 2000: Trends and Findings on the Costs of the U.S. Tort System.* February 2002. Chicago: Tillinghast-Towers Perrin.

Tirole, Jean. 1988. *The Theory of Industrial Organization.* Cambridge, Mass.: MIT Press.

Trebilcock, Michael J. 1993. *The Limits of Freedom of Contract.* Cambridge, Mass.: Harvard University Press.

Treitel, G. H. 1988. *Remedies for Breach of Contract: A Comparative Account.* Oxford: Clarendon Press.

Triantis, George C. 2000. Unforeseen Contingencies: Risk Allocation in Contracts. In *Encyclopedia of Law and Economics,* edited by Boudewijn Bouckaert and Gerrit De Geest, 3:100–116. Cheltenham, Eng.: Edward Elgar.

Tribe, Laurence H. 1971. Trial by Mathematics: Precision and Ritual in the Legal Process. *Harvard Law Review* 84:1329–1393.

Tritton, Guy, Richard Davis, Michael Edenborough, James Graham, Simon Malynicz, and Ashley Roughton. 2002. *Intellectual Property in Europe.* Second edition. London: Sweet and Maxwell.

Trivers, Robert L. 1971. The Evolution of Reciprocal Altruism. *Quarterly Review of Biology* 46:35–57.

Tullock, Gordon. 1971. Inheritance Justified. *Journal of Law and Economics* 14: 465–474.

Tunc, André. 1983. Introduction. Chapter 1 of volume 11, *Torts,* in *International Encyclopedia of Comparative Law.* Tübingen, Ger.: J. C. B. Mohr.

Tversky, Amos, and Daniel Kahneman. 1974. Judgment under Uncertainty: Heuristics and Biases. *Science* 185:1124–1131.

The 2001 Survey of Law Firm Economics. 2001. Newtown Square, Pa.: Altman Weil Publications.

Tyerman, Barry W. 1971. The Economic Rationale for Copyright Protection for Published Books: A Reply to Professor Breyer. *UCLA Law Review* 18:1100–1125.

Ulen, Thomas S. 1984. The Efficiency of Specific Performance: Toward a Unified Theory of Contract Remedies. *Michigan Law Review* 83:341–403.

Umbeck, John R. 1981. *A Theory of Property Rights with Application to the California Gold Rush.* Ames: Iowa State University Press.

U.N. Convention on the Law of the Sea. 1982. *United Nations Treaty Series* (1998), 1833:397–581.

U.S. Census Bureau. 2001. *Health Insurance Coverage: 2000.* Current Population Reports, P60–215, September 2001. Washington D.C.: U.S. Census Bureau.

U.S. Department of Justice. 1988. *Report to the Nation on Crime and Justice, Technical Appendix.* Bureau of Justice Statistics, second edition, NCJ-112011. Washington, D.C.: U.S. Department of Justice.

——— 2001a. *Judicial Business of the United States Courts, 2001 Report of the*

Director. Administrative Office of the U.S. Courts, Statistics Division. Washington, D.C.: U.S. Department of Justice.

———— 2001b. *Sourcebook of Criminal Justice Statistics, 2000.* Bureau of Justice Statistics, NCJ-190251. Washington D.C.: U.S. Department of Justice.

U.S. Department of Labor. December 19, 2001. Employee Benefits in Private Industry, 1999. USDL 01–473. *www.bls.gov/ncs/ebs/sp/ebnr0006.txt.*

U.S. Sentencing Commission. 1995. *Federal Sentencing Guidelines Manual.* 1995 edition. St. Paul, Minn.: West Group.

U.S. Social Security Administration. 2000. *Annual Statistical Supplement, 2000, to the Social Security Bulletin.* Washington, D.C.: Social Security Administration.

Van der Walt, A. J. 1999. *Constitutional Property Clauses: A Comparative Analysis.* Cambridge, Mass.: Kluwer Law International.

Van Zandt, David E. 1993. The Lessons of the Lighthouse: "Government" or "Private" Provision of Goods. *Journal of Legal Studies* 22:47–72.

Vickrey, William S. 1947. *Agenda for Progressive Taxation.* New York: Ronald Press Company.

Viscusi, W. Kip. 1983. *Risk by Choice: Regulating Health and Safety in the Workplace.* Cambridge, Mass.: Harvard University Press.

———— 1986a. The Determinants of the Disposition of Product Liability Claims and Compensation for Bodily Injury. *Journal of Legal Studies* 15:321–346.

———— 1986b. The Risks and Rewards of Criminal Activity: A Comprehensive Test of Criminal Deterrence. *Journal of Labor Economics* 4:317–340.

———— 1991. *Reforming Products Liability.* Cambridge, Mass.: Harvard University Press.

———— 1992. *Fatal Tradeoffs: Public and Private Responsibilities for Risk.* New York: Oxford University Press.

———— 1998. *Rational Risk Policy.* New York: Oxford University Press.

Viscusi, W. Kip, and William N. Evans. 1990. Utility Functions That Depend on Health Status: Estimates and Economic Implications. *American Economic Review* 80:353–374.

Viscusi, W. Kip, John M. Vernon, and Joseph E. Harrington, Jr. 2000. *Economics of Regulation and Antitrust.* Third edition. Cambridge, Mass.: MIT Press.

Von Bar, Christian. 1998. *The Common European Law of Torts.* Oxford: Clarendon Press.

Von Mehren, Arthur T., and James R. Gordley. 1977. *The Civil Law System: An Introduction to the Comparative Study of Law.* Second edition. Boston: Little, Brown.

Waal, Frans de. 1982. *Chimpanzee Politics: Power and Sex among Apes.* New York: Harper and Row.

Waggoner, Lawrence W., Richard V. Wellman, Gregory S. Alexander, and Mary Louise Fellows. 1991. *Family Property Law.* Westbury, N.Y.: Foundation Press.

Waldfogel, Joel. 1995. The Selection Hypothesis and the Relationship between Trial and Plaintiff Victory. *Journal of Political Economy* 103:229–260.

———— 1998. Selection of Cases for Trial. In *The New Palgrave Dictionary of Economics and the Law,* edited by Peter Newman, 3:419–424. London: Macmillan.

Ware, Stephen J. 2001. *Alternative Dispute Resolution.* St. Paul, Minn.: West Group.

Wehrt, Klaus. 2000. Warranties. In *Encyclopedia of Law and Economics,* edited by Boudewijn Bouckaert and Gerrit De Geest, 3:179–199. Cheltenham, Eng.: Edward Elgar.

Weinberg, Harold R. 1980. Sales Law, Economics, and the Negotiability of Goods. *Journal of Legal Studies* 9:569–592.

Weitzman, Martin L. 1974. Prices vs. Quantities. *Review of Economic Studies* 41: 477–491.

White, C. Michael. 1956. Why a Seventeen Year Patent? *Journal of the Patent Office Society* 38:839–860.

Wilde, Louis L. 1992. Criminal Choice, Nonmonetary Sanctions, and Marginal Deterrence: A Normative Analysis. *International Review of Law and Economics* 12:333–344.

Wilkins, David B. 1992. Who Should Regulate Lawyers? *Harvard Law Review* 105:799–887.

Williams, Howard R., and Charles J. Meyers. 2001. *Oil and Gas Law.* Volume 6, release no. 36. New York: Matthew Bender.

Williamson, Oliver E. 1975. *Markets and Hierarchies: Analysis and Antitrust Implications.* New York: Free Press.

Wils, Wouter P. J. 1993. Who Should Bear the Costs of Failed Negotiations? A Functional Inquiry into Precontractual Liability. *Journal des Economistes et des Etudes Humaines* 4:93–134.

Wilson, Edward O. 1980. *Sociobiology.* Abridged edition. Cambridge, Mass.: Belknap Press of Harvard University Press.

Wilson, James Q., and Richard J. Herrnstein. 1985. *Crime and Human Nature.* New York: Simon & Schuster.

Wineburg, Arthur, editor. 1999. *Intellectual Property Protection in Asia.* Second edition (updated). Charlottesville, Va.: LexisNexis.

Witte, Ann Dryden. 1980. Estimating the Economic Model of Crime with Individual Data. *Quarterly Journal of Economics* 94:57–84.

Wittman, Donald. 1977. Prior Regulation versus Post Liability: The Choice between Input and Output Monitoring. *Journal of Legal Studies* 6:193–211.

———— 1981. Optimal Pricing of Sequential Inputs: Last Clear Chance, Mitigation of Damages, and Related Doctrines in the Law. *Journal of Legal Studies* 10:65–91.

———— 1985. Is the Selection of Cases for Trial Biased? *Journal of Legal Studies* 14:185–214.

Wiygul, Robert B. 1992. The Structure of Environmental Regulation on the Outer Continental Shelf: Sources, Problems, and the Opportunity for Change. *Journal of Energy, Natural Resources and Environmental Law* 12:75–180.

Wolfram, Charles W. 1986. *Modern Legal Ethics.* St. Paul, Minn.: West Publishing.

Wright, Brian D. 1983. The Economics of Invention Incentives: Patents, Prizes, and Research Contracts. *American Economic Review* 73:691–707.

Wright, Richard A. 1994. *In Defense of Prisons.* Contributions in Criminology and Penology, no. 43. Westport, Conn.: Greenwood Press.

Yaari, Menahem E. 1965. Uncertain Lifetime, Life Insurance, and the Theory of the Consumer. *Review of Economic Studies* 32:137–150.

Zakolski, Lisa A. 1997. Boats and Boating. In *American Jurisprudence,* second edition, 12:273–364. Rochester, N.Y.: Lawyers Cooperative Publishing.

Zeckhauser, Richard J. 1973. Coverage for Catastrophic Illness. *Public Policy* 21:149–172.

Zweigert, Konrad, and Hein Kötz. 1998. *An Introduction to Comparative Law.* Third edition. Oxford: Clarendon Press.

AUTHOR INDEX

SUBJECT INDEX

abandoned property, 43

accidents: bilateral, 182–193, 199–206; unilateral, 178–182, 193–199. *See also* insurance; liability; liability insurance

accuracy: damages and, 240–241, 453; litigation and, 450–456; negligence determination and, 224–229

acquisition and transfer of property: absence of registration system, 52–55; adverse possession, 72–76; bequests, 59–66; constraints on sale of property, 55–57; dead hand, 67–72; gifts, 58–59; loss and recovery of property, 38–45; original acquisition, 33–38; registration systems, 46–51; sale of property, 45–46; unowned property, 33–38

activity level, 193–206, 209–211, 231, 233

administrative costs: insurance and, 281–282; liability and, 280–282; optimal use of liability and, 283–285; private

versus socially desirable use of liability, and, 285–287, 391–401, 411–415, 416–417; strict liability versus negligence, and, 282–283

adverse possession, 72–76

advice, legal, 463–470

alternative dispute resolution, 445–450

annuities, 61–62

appeals, 456–463

bargaining: contracts and, 314–320; externalities and, 83–92, 101–109; litigation and, 407–410

bequests, 59–66

bonafide purchase rule, 52–53, 54, 55

breach of contract. *See* contracts; damages: for breach of contract; specific performance

care: dimensions of, 181–182, 189; due care, 180–181, 184–187, 190–192; momentary level of, 227; uncertainty in determination of, 224–228